Guide to Networking Essentials

Seventh Edition

Greg Tomsho

CENGAGE
Learning

Australia • Brazil • Mexico • Singapore • United Kingdom • United States

CENGAGE
Learning®

**Guide to Networking Essentials,
Seventh Edition**
Greg Tomsho

SVP, GM Skills & Global Product
Management: Dawn Gerrain

Product Director: Kathleen McMahon

Product Team Manager: Kristin McNary

Senior Director, Development: Marah
Bellegarde

Product Development Manager:
Leigh Hefferon

Senior Content Developer: Michelle Ruelos
Cannistraci

Development Editor: Lisa M. Lord

Senior Product Assistant: Abigail Pufpaff

Marketing Director: Michele McTighe

Senior Production Director: Wendy Troeger

Production Director: Patty Stephan

Senior Content Project Manager: Brooke
Greenhouse

Managing Art Director: Jack Pendleton

Manufacturing Planner: Ron Montgomery

Quality Assurance Testers: Serge Palladino
and John Freitas

Cover Image(s): © Mega Pixel/Shutterstock

For product information and technology assistance, contact us at
Cengage Learning Customer & Sales Support, 1-800-354-9706

For permission to use material from this text or product,
submit all requests online at **www.cengage.com/permissions.**
Further permissions questions can be e-mailed to
permissionrequest@cengage.com.

Library of Congress Control Number: 2015949720

ISBN: 978-1-305-10543-0

Cengage Learning
20 Channel Center Street
Boston, MA 02210
USA

Cengage Learning is a leading provider of customized learning solutions
with employees residing in nearly 40 different countries and sales in
more than 125 countries around the world. Find your local representative
at **www.cengage.com.**

Cengage Learning products are represented in Canada by
Nelson Education, Ltd.

To learn more about Cengage Learning, visit **www.cengage.com.**

Purchase any of our products at your local college store or at our preferred
online store **www.cengagebrain.com.**

Notice to the Reader

Printed in the United States of America
Print Number: 01   Print Year: 2015

Brief Table of Contents

Table of Contents

CHAPTER 3

Network Topologies and Technologies **93**

CHAPTER 6
IP Addressing 237

CHAPTER 7
Network Reference Models and Standards **291**

CHAPTER 13

Troubleshooting and Support **581**

Introduction

Guide to Networking Essentials, Seventh Edition, serves the needs of students, instructors, aspiring information technology professionals, and others who are interested in learning more about networking technologies but who might have little or no background in this subject matter. This book's extensive and broad coverage of computer networking technologies and network operating systems gives you a solid networking background to pursue a number of certifications, including Network+, CCNA, MCSA, and Security+. In fact, although it's not intended as a certification study book, many instructors use it for Network+ and CCENT test preparation. With the extensive use of tables that compare important properties of networking technologies, this book also makes an excellent reference.

The seventh edition builds on the strengths of the sixth edition, giving you easy-to-understand explanations of often difficult concepts and a solid grounding in topics such as routing, switching, IP addressing, and virtualization. Many students are learning computer concepts at the same time they're learning about networking, so the first chapter includes a refresher on computer components and terminology. This new edition covers the latest networking technologies and operating systems, including new Ethernet standards, cloud computing, Windows 10, Windows Server 2016, and recent Linux distributions. In keeping with the latest trends in networking, this edition has updated and expanded coverage on IPv6 operation and addressing, network security, the 802.11 wireless standards, network switches, and routing. A new section on cloud computing explains that many networks are using the "as a" technologies, such as infrastructure as a service and platform as a service.

All new hands-on projects interspersed throughout the chapter text allow you to apply the concepts you learn in the chapter. A new feature of this book, the "Critical Thinking" section, offers challenge labs and case projects at the end of each chapter. Challenge labs give you an opportunity to apply what you have learned from the chapter material and hands-on projects in a format that might require additional research and skills. For case projects, you use your knowledge and critical thinking skills to devise solutions to networking problems.

The simulations in the previous three editions of *Guide to Networking Essentials* are now available on the Cengage Learning Web site at *www.cengagebrain.com*; you can search there by author, title, or ISBN to find the simulations. These simulations with audio narrations give you an innovative tool to help you grasp difficult networking concepts. They cover topics ranging from basic LAN communication to Network Address Translation (NAT) and Internet e-mail operation. Drag-and-drop exercises reinforce concepts of the OSI model and network frame formats. You can find more simulations and visual troubleshooting on the author's Web site at *http://books.tomsho.com*.

Intended Audience

Guide to Networking Essentials, Seventh Edition, is intended for people who are getting started in computer networking and want to gain a solid understanding of a broad range of networking technologies. This book is ideal for would-be information technology professionals who want to pursue certifications in a variety of computer networking fields as well as those in a managerial role who want a firm grasp of networking technology concepts. To understand the material in this book, you should have a background in basic computer concepts and have worked with the Windows operating system. This book is ideal for use in a classroom or an instructor-led training environment and is also an effective learning tool for individual self-paced training.

Coping with Change on the Web

Sooner or later, all the specifics on Web-based resources mentioned in this book will become outdated or be replaced by newer information. In some cases, the URLs listed in this book might lead to their replacements; in other cases, they'll lead nowhere, resulting in the dreaded error message "Server not found."

When that happens, please don't give up! There's always a way to find what you want on the Web, if you're willing to invest some time and energy. Most large or complex Web sites offer a search engine. As long as you can get to the site itself, you can use this tool to help you find what you need. In addition, try using general search tools, such as *www.google.com* or *www.bing.com*, to find related information. The bottom line is if you can't find something where the book says it should be, start looking around. It's likely to be somewhere!

Chapter Descriptions

Here's a summary of the topics covered in each chapter of this book:

- **Chapter 1**, "Introduction to Computer Networks," introduces many of the computer and networking terms and technologies discussed in detail in later chapters.

- In **Chapter 2**, "Network Hardware Essentials," you learn about the basic operation of hubs, switches, access points, network interface cards, and routers.

- **Chapter 3**, "Network Topologies and Technologies," discusses logical and physical topologies and the LAN technologies that use them.

- **Chapter 4**, "Network Media," covers the cables and connectors required to connect network devices, including structured cabling techniques, and describes wireless networking.

- In **Chapter 5**, "Network Protocols," you learn about the purpose and operation of network protocols, focusing on the TCP/IP protocol suite. Special emphasis is given to the TCP/IP layered model and the protocols that work at each layer.

- In **Chapter 6**, "IP Addressing," you learn about IPv4 addressing, including address classes, public and private addresses, subnetting, and Network Address Translation. New expanded coverage on IPv6 addressing and operation has been added to reflect the growing importance of this protocol.

- **Chapter 7**, "Network Reference Models and Standards," discusses the OSI model's seven-layer architecture and gives you an overview of the IEEE 802 networking standards.

- **Chapter 8**, "Network Hardware in Depth," delves into the hardware components of networks discussed in Chapter 2, giving you more in-depth coverage of each type of device.

- In **Chapter 9**, "Introduction to Network Security," you learn about network security policies, securing access to equipment and data, network security devices (such as firewalls and intrusion detection systems), and malware.

- In **Chapter 10**, "Wide Area Networking and Cloud Computing," you learn how to use WAN technologies, such as frame relay and SONET, to create networks that can extend across your town or across the country. In addition, you're introduced to remote access protocols and cloud computing concepts, such as IaaS and PaaS.

- In **Chapter 11**, "Network Operating System Fundamentals," you learn about network operating system features and the most common types of services provided by server OSs. This chapter also covers virtualization and using virtual machines in data centers and on the desktop. Finally, you learn how to plan for an OS installation and perform postinstallation tasks.

- **Chapter 12**, "Network Management and Administration," discusses everyday tasks that network and server administrators perform, including working with user and group accounts, creating and managing file shares, monitoring system performance and reliability, and using fault-tolerance and backup solutions.

- **Chapter 13**, "Troubleshooting and Support," discusses what you can do to prevent network downtime, data loss, and system failures. In addition, you learn about the problem-solving process, several different approaches to solving network problems, the tools for troubleshooting networks, and disaster recovery procedures.

- **Appendix A**, "Network Troubleshooting Guide," summarizes advice on how to recognize, isolate, and diagnose trouble on a network, whether it's related to media, hardware, or software.

Features

To help you understand networking concepts thoroughly, this book incorporates many features designed to enhance your learning experience:

- *Chapter objectives*—Each chapter begins with a detailed list of the concepts to be mastered. This list is a quick reference to the chapter's contents and a useful study aid.

- *A requirements table*—At the beginning of each chapter is a table listing the hands-on projects along with their requirements and estimated time of completion.

- *Hands-on projects*—Although understanding the theory behind networking technology is important, nothing can improve on real-world experience. Projects are interspersed throughout each chapter to give you hands-on experience.

- *Screen captures, illustrations, and tables*—Numerous screen captures and illustrations of concepts help you visualize network setups, theories, and architectures and see how to use tools. In addition, tables summarize details in an at-a-glance format and give you comparisons of both practical and theoretical information; they can be used for a quick review. Because most school labs use Windows OSs, these products have been used for most screenshots and hands-on projects.

- *Simulations*—In many chapters, you'll see references to simulations, which are available online at *www.cengagebrain.com*; you can search by the book's author, title, or ISBN. These simulations demonstrate concepts such as basic LAN communication, Ethernet switches, routing, Network Address Translation, Internet e-mail operation, and more.

- *Chapter summary*—Each chapter ends with a summary of the concepts introduced in the chapter. These summaries are a helpful way to recap the material covered in the chapter.

- *Key terms*—All terms in the chapter introduced with bold text are gathered together in the Key Terms list at the end of the chapter. This list gives you an easy way to check your understanding of important terms and is a useful reference.

- *Review questions*—The end-of-chapter assessment begins with review questions that reinforce the concepts and techniques covered in each chapter. Answering these questions helps ensure that you have mastered important topics.

- *Critical Thinking sections*—The end-of-chapter Critical Thinking section gives you more opportunities for hands-on practice with challenge labs, which enable you to use the knowledge you've gained from reading the chapter and performing hands-on projects to solve more complex problems without step-by-step instructions. This section also includes case projects that ask you to evaluate a hypothetical situation and decide on a course of action to propose a solution. These valuable tools help you sharpen decision-making, critical thinking, and troubleshooting skills—all important aspects of network administration.

Text and Graphics Conventions

Additional information and exercises have been added to this book to help you better understand what's being discussed in the chapter. Icons throughout the book alert you to these additional materials:

Tips offer extra information on resources, how to solve problems, and time-saving shortcuts.

Notes present additional helpful material related to the subject being discussed.

The Caution icon identifies important information about potential mistakes or hazards.

Each hands-on project in this book is preceded by this icon.

Simulation icons refer you to simulations that reinforce the concepts being discussed.

This icon marks end-of-chapter labs that challenge you to apply what you've learned without step-by-step instructions.

Case Project icons mark the end-of-chapter case projects, which are scenario-based assignments that ask you to apply what you have learned in the chapter.

Instructor Companion Site

Everything you need for your course in one place! This collection of book-specific lecture and class tools is available online via *www.cengage.com/login*. Access and download PowerPoint presentations, images, the Instructor's Manual, and more. In addition, the author maintains a Web site at *http://books.tomsho.com* with lab notes, errata, additional exercises, the latest lab setup guide, and hints and tips for teaching with this book.

- *Electronic Instructor's Manual*—The Instructor's Manual that accompanies this book includes additional instructional material to assist in class preparation, including suggestions for classroom activities, discussion topics, and additional quiz questions.

- *Solutions Manual*—The instructor's resources include solutions to all end-of-chapter material, including review questions and case projects.
- *Cengage Learning Testing Powered by Cognero*—This flexible, online system allows you to do the following:
  - Author, edit, and manage test bank content from multiple Cengage Learning solutions.
  - Create multiple test versions in an instant.
  - Deliver tests from your LMS, your classroom, or wherever you want.
- *PowerPoint presentations*—This book comes with Microsoft PowerPoint slides for each chapter. They're included as a teaching aid for classroom presentation, to make available to students on the network for chapter review, or to be printed for classroom distribution. Instructors, please feel free to add your own slides for additional topics you introduce to the class.
- *Figure files*—All the figures and tables in the book are reproduced in bitmap format. Similar to the PowerPoint presentations, they're included as a teaching aid for classroom presentation, to make available to students for review, or to be printed for classroom distribution.

Contact the Author

I would like to hear from you. Please e-mail me at *NetEss@tomsho.com* with any problems, questions, suggestions, or corrections. I even accept compliments! This book has staying power, so I wouldn't be surprised to see an eighth edition in the future. Your comments and suggestions are invaluable for shaping the next edition's content. In addition, please visit my Web site at *http://books.tomsho.com*, where you can find lab notes, errata, and other information related to this book and my other titles. You can also submit comments and suggestions.

Acknowledgments

I would like to thank the team at Cengage Learning for this opportunity to improve and expand on the fifth edition of this book. This team includes Kristin McNary, Product Team Manager; Michelle Ruelos Cannistraci, Senior Content Developer; Brooke Greenhouse, Senior Content Project Manager; and Serge Palladino and John Freitas, Manuscript Quality Assurance, for testing projects and labs for accuracy. Thanks especially to my development editor, Lisa Lord, for her excellent guidance in creating a polished product. Additional praise and special thanks goes to my beautiful wife, Julie; our daughters, Camille and Sophia; and our son, Michael. They all deserve medals for their patience and support while going husbandless and fatherless during the development of this book.

Before You Begin

The importance of a solid lab environment can't be overstated. This books contains hands-on projects that require a variety of network equipment and software. Most of the hands-on projects use a PC with Windows 10 installed. However, other versions of Windows (such as Windows 7 and Windows 8.1) can be used with modifications to the steps. Using virtualization can simplify the lab environment. For example, you can use VMware Player, VMware Workstation, VirtualBox, and other products to install Windows and Linux in a virtual machine, regardless of the OS running on your physical computer. The following section lists the requirements and gives you ideas for how to best configure your lab environment.

Lab Setup Guide

Both the hands-on projects and challenge labs have setup requirements. Some labs require two or three computers, called "lab computers," that you connect to hubs and routers to create small test networks. Lab computers use Windows 10 (but earlier versions can be substituted) and should be physical computers that have easy access to power, a NIC, and other ports. Many other labs simply require a computer that's connected to a network in a classroom setting, with access to the Internet. Students must have administrator access to these computers, and the use of virtual machines is recommended. An instructor computer is also required for some labs. The instructor computer can also be set up as a virtual machine and must be accessible to student computers on the network.

Student Computers (Net-*XX*)

- Use of virtual machines recommended
- Windows 10 Enterprise or Education Edition
- Computer name: Net-*XX* (replacing *XX* with a student number, such as 01, 02, and so forth)
- Administrator account: NetAdmin with the password Password01 set to never expire
- Workgroup name: NetEss
- Memory: 1 GB required, 2 GB or more recommended
- Hard disk 1: 60 GB or more (Windows installed on this drive); a second NTFS-formatted partition assigned drive letter D is preferable but not required.
- Hard disk 2: Unallocated 60 GB or more
- IP address via DHCP server or static if required on your network
- Wireshark installed (a free protocol analyzer from *www.wireshark.org*)
- Internet access

Instructor Computer (Net-Instr)

- Same requirements as Net-*XX* except for the following:
  - Computer name: Net-Instr
  - No second hard disk required
- Create a shared folder named NetDocs, giving the NetAdmin user Read and Change sharing permissions and Modify NTFS permissions. You access this share by using \\net-instr\netdocs in Chapter 1.

Lab Computers (Three Computers Minimum)

- Windows 10 Enterprise or Education Edition (or other versions, including Windows 7 and Windows 8.1; however step-by-step instructions are written for Windows 10)
- Computer names: Computer1, Computer2, Computer3
- Administrator account: NetAdmin with the password Password01 set to never expire
- Workgroup name: NetEss
- Memory: 1 GB required, 2 GB or more recommended
- Hard disk 1: 60 GB or more (Windows installed on this drive)
- IP address: Set to use DHCP, but no DHCP server should be present, so APIPA addresses are assigned.
- Wireshark installed (a free protocol analyzer from *www.wireshark.org*)
- No Internet access

Network Equipment for Lab Computers (for Each Group of Three Computers)

- Two 10/100 hubs
- Two 10/100 switches
- One WPA 802.11 b/g/n SSID NetEss; open security
- 802.11 b/g/n NICs (USB Wi-Fi NICs are ideal)
- Five patch cables and one crossover cable

Additional Supplies and Tools

- RJ-45 crimping tool
- Punchdown tool
- Cable stripper
- Cat 5e or higher cable
- Cat 5e or higher patch panel
- RJ-45 plugs (at least four per student)
- A Cisco switch with Cisco IOS for configuring VLANs (for Challenge Lab 8-3)
- A Cisco router with CISCO IOS (for Challenge Lab 8-4)
- Network diagram software, such as Visio, or online diagramming software, such as *www.gliffy.com*
- A Fedora Linux Live DVD or ISO file or an Ubuntu Linux DVD or ISO file
- Windows Server 2012 R2 ISO file (downloaded from the Microsoft evaluation center) for Hands-On Project 11-9
- A shared printer (optional)
- NetInfo and Simple Server Monitor (downloaded and installed by students or the instructor)
- VMware Player (downloaded and installed by students or the instructor)

You can find additional lab setup instructions and videos on the author's Web site at *http://books.tomsho.com*. Click the menu item Networking Essentials 7th Edition. You can also find videos by the author on YouTube at *https://www.youtube.com/user/gtomshobooks*. More information is available on the author's Amazon page at *https://www.amazon.com/author/gregtomsho*, Facebook page at *www.facebook.com/gtomshobooks*, and Twitter (@gtomshobooks).

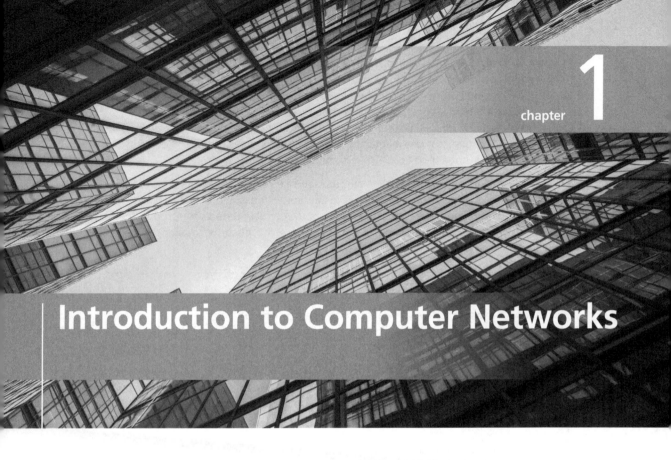

chapter 1

Introduction to Computer Networks

After reading this chapter and completing the exercises, you will be able to:

- Describe basic computer components and operations
- Explain the fundamentals of network communication
- Define common networking terms
- Compare different network models

In only a few decades, computer networks have evolved from being a complex technology accessible to only the most tech-savvy users to being part of most people's everyday lives. Computer networks can be found in almost every business, school, and home. Their use is available to anyone with a computer and a network connection, but installation and upkeep of all but the smallest networks still require considerable know-how. This chapter starts you on the path toward acquiring the skills to manage a large corporate network or simply configure a home network with a wireless router.

This chapter begins by discussing the computer and its role in a network to give you a foundation for the topics in this book. Next, you examine the components of a network and the fundamentals of communication between computers. Many new terms are introduced and defined, and the varied types of networks and network servers you might encounter are described.

An Overview of Computer Concepts

The hands-on projects in this book require setting up your lab environment so that it's ready to go, so make sure you read and follow the step-by-step instructions in the "Before You Begin" section of the Introduction, which help you set up your lab for all projects in this book.

The hands-on projects in this book contain information about how networks work that's best understood by hands-on experience. If you can't do some of the projects, you should at least read through each one to make sure you don't miss important information. Table 1-1 summarizes what you need for the hands-on projects in this chapter.

Table 1-1 Hands-on project requirements

Hands-on project	Requirements	Time required	Notes
Hands-On Project 1-1: Examining a Computer's Boot Procedure	Net-*XX*	10 minutes	A Windows 10 computer configured as described in "Before You Begin" Must be able to access the BIOS setup screen
Hands-On Project 1-2: Upgrading a Stand-alone Computer to a Networked Computer	Net-*XX*, a NIC, a patch cable, and a hub or switch	30 minutes	A lab computer set up as described in "Before You Begin"
Hands-On Project 1-3: Viewing Network Software Layers	Net-*XX*	10 minutes	
Hands-On Project 1-4: Using ipconfig, ping, and arp	Net-*XX*	15 minutes	
Hands-On Project 1-5: Exploring Peer-to-Peer Networking	Net-*XX*	15 minutes	
Hands-On Project 1-6: Creating a Shared Folder	Net-*XX*	15 minutes	
Hands-On Project 1-7: Transferring a Document to Another Computer	Net-*XX*	15 minutes	A share named NetDocs on the instructor's computer (Net-Instr)
Hands-On Project 1-8: Looking Up Computer and Networking Acronyms	Net-*XX*	20 minutes	Internet access

At the heart of a computer network is the computer. Networks were created to facilitate communication between computing devices, which ultimately facilitates communication between people. So to better understand networks, how they work, and how to support them, you must have a solid understanding of computer operations. In fact, most of the devices you encounter when working with a network involve a computer. The most obvious are network servers and workstations that run operating systems, such as Windows, Linux, UNIX, and Mac OS X. Not as obvious are devices such as routers and switches, which move network data from computer to computer and network to network. These complex devices are also computers, although they're specialized computers for performing specific tasks. The next sections discuss the basic functions of a computer and its associated components, along with computer hardware, the boot procedure, and the basic functions of an operating system (OS). Networking is the focus of this book, but your grasp of the fundamentals of computer components and operations helps you understand networking components and operations.

Basic Functions of a Computer

A computer's functions and features can be grouped into the three basic tasks all computers perform: input, processing, and output. Information is input to a computer from a device such as a keyboard or from a storage device such as a hard drive; the central processing unit (CPU) processes the information, and then output is usually created. The following example illustrates this process:

- *Input*—A user running a word-processing program types the letter A on the keyboard, which results in sending a code representing the letter A to the computer.
- *Processing*—The computer's CPU determines what letter was typed by looking up the keyboard code in a table.
- *Output*—The CPU sends instructions to the graphics card to display the letter A, which is then sent to the computer monitor.

Some components of computers are designed to perform only one of these three functions; others are designed to perform two or all three functions. For example, a standard keyboard and mouse perform input functions, and storage devices, such as hard drives, perform both input (when files are read from the drive) and output (when files are written to the drive). Network cards can perform all three functions. A network card is an output device when data is sent from the computer to the network and an input device when data comes from the network to the computer. In addition, many network cards have rudimentary processors that perform actions on incoming and outgoing data to help supplement the computer's main CPU.

Input Components   Before a computer can do any processing, it requires input, commonly from user-controlled devices, such as keyboards, microphones, Webcams, and scanners. External interfaces, such as serial, FireWire, and USB ports, can also be used to get input from external devices.

Input is also generated by storage devices, such as hard disks and CDs/DVDs that store programs and data files containing computer instructions and data. For example, a spreadsheet program, such as Microsoft Excel, might contain instructions for the CPU to calculate formulas for adding the values of two columns of data and a spreadsheet file called `MyBudget.xls` containing the numbers and formulas the spreadsheet program should use. Both the program (Microsoft Excel) and the data file (`MyBudget.xls`) are used as input to the CPU, which then processes the program instructions and data.

A spreadsheet program normally starts when a user double-clicks the spreadsheet program icon or the icon representing the spreadsheet data file. These actions are instigated by user input. Sometimes, however, your computer seems to start performing actions without user input. For example, you might have noticed that your hard drive sometimes shows activity without any obvious action from you to initiate it. However, inputs to a computer can include timers that cause programs to run periodically and data arriving from network cards, for example, that cause a program or process to run. So although it sometimes seems as though your computer has a mind of its own, computers don't actually do anything without first getting input to jolt them into action.

Processing Components   A computer's main processing component is the CPU, which executes instructions from computer programs, such as word-processing programs and Web browsers. It also runs the instructions making up the OS, which provides a user interface and the environment in which applications run. Aside from the CPU, computers usually include ancillary processors associated with input/output (I/O) devices, such as graphics cards. These processors are often referred to as "onboard processors." The processor on a graphics card, called a "graphics processing unit (GPU)," takes a high-level graphics instruction, such as "draw a circle," and performs the calculations needed to draw the circle on a display device. With an onboard GPU, the main CPU doesn't have to handle many of the complex calculations graphical applications require, thereby improving overall system performance. Other devices, such as network interface cards and disk controller cards, might also include onboard processors.

CPUs are usually composed of two or more processors, called **cores**, in one package. A **multicore CPU** is like a person with two brains. With only one brain, you could add four numbers, but you would probably do it in three sequential summing operations: Add the first number to the second number, take the first sum and add it to the third number, and add that sum to the fourth number to arrive at the final sum. If you had two brains, you'd still need three summing operations, but two could be done simultaneously: The first brain adds the first two numbers while the second brain is adding the third and fourth numbers; then the second brain gives its results to the first brain, and the first brain sums the results of the first two summing operations. So multicore CPUs enable computers to carry out multiple instructions simultaneously, which results in better overall performance when running demanding applications.

Output Components   Output components include monitors and printers, but they also include storage devices, network cards, and speakers, to name a few. The external interfaces mentioned previously as input components can be used as output components, too. For example, a disk drive connected to a USB port allows reading files from the disk (input) and writing files to the disk (output).

Storage Components

Storage components are a major part of a computer's configuration. Generally speaking, the more storage a computer has, the better the performance is. As you saw in the previous section, most storage components are both input and output devices, allowing data to be saved (output) and then accessed again later (input). When most people think of storage, they think of disk drives, CD/DVD drives, and USB or flash drives. However, there are two main categories of storage: short-term storage and long-term storage.

RAM: Short-Term Storage   Short-term storage is the random access memory (RAM) on a computer. RAM is short-term storage because when power to the computer is turned off, RAM's contents are gone, just as though you erased a whiteboard. When power is restored, RAM has no data stored until the CPU begins to write data to it.

The amount of RAM, or memory, in a computer is crucial to the computer's capability to operate efficiently. RAM is also referred to as "working storage." Everything the CPU is currently processing must be available in RAM, including program instructions and the data the current application requires. So to run a spreadsheet program, there must be enough RAM to load both the spreadsheet program and the data in the spreadsheet. If there's not enough available memory, the spreadsheet program won't run, or the computer uses the disk drive to supplement RAM temporarily.

Neither option is desirable. The reason temporary use of the disk drive isn't optimal is because RAM is thousands of times faster than the fastest disk drives. The time required to access data in RAM is measured in nanoseconds (billionths of a second), but access to data on a disk drive is measured in milliseconds (thousandths of a second). So if the disk drive must be used to supplement RAM while running an application, that application, and indeed the entire computer, slows down precipitously.

On current computers, the amount of RAM installed is usually 1 GB or more. More is generally better, but the amount of RAM that a system can use effectively depends on the OS installed. The 32-bit version of an OS can usually access a maximum of 4 GB of RAM, whereas the 64-bit version can access many thousands of gigabytes. The amount of RAM you actually need depends on how you use your computer. If you usually have only one or two typical business applications open at once, 1 GB or even less is probably enough. However, if you run complex graphics applications or games or have several applications open simultaneously, you'll likely benefit from having more RAM.

Long-Term Storage Long-term storage maintains its data even when there's no power. Examples include hard disks, CDs/DVDs, and USB flash drives as well as other types of removable media. Long-term storage is used to store document and multimedia files as well as the files that make up applications and the OS. The amount of storage a computer needs depends on the type and quantity of files to be stored. In general, office documents, such as word-processing files, spreadsheets, and presentations, require comparatively little space. Multimedia files—pictures, music files, and videos—require much more space. Long-term storage is plentiful and extremely inexpensive. Hard drive specifications are in hundreds of gigabytes, with terabyte (1000 GB) drives quite commonplace. More details about hard disks are discussed later in "Personal Computer Hardware."

Data Is Stored in Bits Whether storage is long term or short term, data on a computer is stored and processed as binary digits ("bits," for short). A bit holds a 1 or 0 value, which makes representing bits with electrical pulses easy. For example, a pulse of 5 volts of electricity can represent a 1 bit, and a pulse of 0 volts (or the absence of a pulse) can represent a 0 bit. Bits can also be stored as pulses of light, as with fiber-optic cable: A 1 bit is represented by the presence of light and a 0 bit as the absence of light.

Data in a computer, such as the letters in a word-processing document or the music played from an MP3 music file, is represented by collections of 8 bits, called a byte. You can look at each byte as a printable character in a document. For example, a single byte from an MP3 file plays about 1/17 thousandth of a second of music. To put it another way, one second of MP3 music takes more than 17,000 bytes.

Personal Computer Hardware

Most people are familiar with personal computer (PC) hardware. Other types of computers, such as minicomputers and mainframes, are usually locked away in a heavily air-conditioned room and privy only to the eyes of IT staff. Besides, the basic hardware used to build a PC or a mainframe differs only in the details. This section describes four major PC components housed in a computer case:

- Motherboard
- Hard drive
- RAM
- BIOS/CMOS

The Motherboard and Its Components   The motherboard is the nerve center of a computer, much like the spinal cord is the nerve center of the human body. It's a network of wires and controlling circuits that connects all computer components, including the CPU, RAM, disk drives, and I/O devices, such as network interface cards. Some key components of a motherboard are labeled in Figure 1-1 and explained in Table 1-2.

Figure 1-1   A PC motherboard

Table 1-2 Key components of a motherboard

Component	Description
CPU socket	The CPU is installed in this socket.
PCI bus expansion slots	Used to add functionality to a PC by adding expansion cards that have a Peripheral Component Interconnect (PCI) connector.
PCI-Express expansion slots	PCI-Express supersedes PCI and supports faster data transfer speeds. The larger slots are suitable for high-performance expansion cards, such as graphics cards and disk controllers. The smaller slots are best suited to sound cards and network interface cards.
RAM slots	Slots for installing RAM on the motherboard.
Chipset with heat sinks	The chipset consists of two chips referred to as the Northbridge and the Southbridge. These chips control data transfers between memory, expansion slots, I/O devices, and the CPU. The heat sink sits on top of the chipset to prevent it from overheating.
SATA connectors	Used for connecting hard drives and CD/DVD drives that use the Serial AT Attachment (SATA) specification.
IDE connector	Used for connecting Integrated Drive Electronics (IDE) hard drives and CD/DVD-ROM drives. Most systems now use SATA for hard drives and IDE for CD/DVD-ROM drives.
Main power connector	This connector is where the motherboard receives power from the system power supply.

All data that goes into or comes out of a computer goes through the motherboard because all storage and I/O devices are connected to the motherboard, as is the CPU, which processes data going in and coming out of a computer.

Computer Bus Fundamentals Table 1-2 mentions PCI bus expansion slots as a component of a motherboard. A **bus** is a collection of wires carrying data from one place to another on the computer. There are many bus designs and formats, each for a particular purpose. Although bus types come and go, it's safe to say that replacements for an older bus design will almost certainly be faster than their predecessor.

In a computer, there are buses between the CPU and RAM, between the CPU and disk drives, and between the CPU and expansion slots, among others. For the purposes of this book, you're most interested in the bus connecting expansion slots to the motherboard because you usually connect a network interface card (NIC) into one of these slots. NIC installation and expansion slot bus types are discussed in Chapter 2. What you need to know now is that not all motherboards come with all types of expansion slots, and the faster and busier your computer is, the faster its bus type needs to be.

Hard Drive Fundamentals The hard drive is the primary long-term storage component on your computer. Hard drives consist of magnetic disks, called "platters," that store data in the form of magnetic pulses. These magnetic pulses are maintained even when power is turned off. Each pulse represents a single bit of data.

The platters spin at extremely fast speeds, with some faster disks having rotational speeds of 15,000 revolutions per minute (rpm). A read/write head is attached to an actuator arm that moves across the spinning platters in response to commands from the computer to read or write a file (see Figure 1-2). Generally, the faster the rotational speed, the better the hard drive performance is. When a file is requested to be written or read, its location is determined, and then the read/write heads are moved over the corresponding spot on the platter. After the platter spins to the file's starting location, the read/write heads are activated to read or write the data. The average amount of time platters take to spin into position is called the "rotational delay" or "latency." The amount of time required to move read/write heads to the correct place is the seek time, and the time it takes to read or write data is the transfer time. The average amount of time between the request to read or write data and the time the action is performed is the access time.

Actuator arm

Magnetic platters

Read/write heads

Courtesy of 2010 Western Digital Technologies, Inc.

Figure 1-2 Inside a hard drive

The terms used to measure hard drive performance aren't universal among manufacturers, but the terms used in the preceding paragraph represent most specifications.

Hard disks store the documents you use with your computer as well as the applications that open these documents. In addition, the hard disk stores the OS your computer loads when it boots. As mentioned, the hard disk acts as an input device when files are read. When the computer boots, the OS files are read from the disk, and instructions in these files are processed by the CPU. However, the files don't go directly from the hard disk to the CPU; first, they're transferred to short-term storage (RAM).

Solid State Drives Solid state drives (SSDs) are used in place of hard drives in many systems because of their speed and reliability. An SSD uses a type of storage called "flash memory" that contains no moving parts and has faster access times than a mechanical hard drive. SSDs are more expensive than hard drives when you compare the price per gigabyte of storage, but their price continues to fall. SSDs are most often used in mobile devices (such as laptops, smartphones, and tablets) but are also found on high-performance desktops and servers, often supplementing, rather than replacing, hard drive storage.

RAM Fundamentals RAM, the main short-term storage component on a computer, consists of capacitors to store data and transistors to control access to data. Capacitors require power to maintain the bits they store. Because RAM requires continuous power to store data, it's referred to as "volatile memory."

RAM has no moving parts, so as mentioned, accessing data in RAM is much faster than accessing data on a hard drive—there's no seek time or rotational delay. Because RAM is so much faster than a hard drive, any information the CPU processes should be in RAM. If data the CPU requires is located on the hard drive, it's loaded into RAM first, which takes considerable time. Therefore, the more RAM your system has, the more likely it is that all the data needed by running programs can be stored in RAM, making the system perform much faster.

BIOS/CMOS Fundamentals A key component of every computer is its basic input/output system (BIOS), which is a set of instructions located in a chip on the motherboard. A main function of the BIOS is to tell the CPU to perform certain tasks when power is first applied to the computer, including initializing motherboard hardware, performing a power-on self-test (POST), and beginning the boot procedure.

Because of the complexity of motherboards, configuring some hardware components and tuning performance parameters are often necessary. When a computer begins to boot, the BIOS program offers the user an opportunity to run the Setup utility to perform this configuration. The configuration data the user enters is stored in complementary metal oxide semiconductor (CMOS) memory. It holds information such as devices the CPU should check for an OS to boot, the status of hardware devices, and even a system password, if needed. CMOS is a type of low-power memory that requires only a small battery to maintain its data. It's also referred to as "nonvolatile memory" because it doesn't require power from the computer's main power supply.

Computer Boot Procedure

To take a computer from a powered-off state to running an OS, such as Windows or Linux, the following steps must take place:

1. Power is applied to the motherboard.
2. The CPU starts.

3. The CPU carries out the BIOS startup routines, including the POST.

4. Boot devices, as specified in the BIOS configuration, are searched for an OS.

5. The OS is loaded into RAM.

6. OS services are started.

These steps apply to almost every type of computer, including very small computing devices, such as smartphones and tablets. Probably the biggest difference between computers is what occurs in the last step. OS services are programs that are part of the OS rather than applications a user starts. The services an OS starts can vary greatly, depending on which OS is loaded and how it's configured. The number and type of services started on a system are what, at least in part, account for the time it takes a system to boot completely. Examples of common OS services include the user interface, the file system, and, of course, networking services.

 The projects in this book involving a Windows client OS use Windows 10 Enterprise Edition. Other editions of Windows 10 can be used, and Windows 8.1 and Windows 7 can also be used with some changes to the steps.

Hands-On Project 1-1: Examining a Computer's Boot Procedure

Time Required: 10 minutes

Objective: Examine the computer boot procedure and BIOS Setup utility.

Required Tools and Equipment: Net-XX (a Windows computer configured as described in "Before You Begin")

Description: In this project, you examine the computer boot procedure from beginning to end, using a Windows computer. You also examine the BIOS Setup utility and view the configuration that specifies which devices the BIOS should search for an OS. Because the BIOS varies among computers, your instructor might have to assist with the keystrokes you enter to run the BIOS Setup utility and view the boot order menu. This project uses a virtual machine and the BIOS Setup utility in VMware Workstation. If you aren't using virtual machines for the projects in this book, the BIOS on most computers is similar.

 Your computer must be turned off before you begin this project. Read the first step carefully before turning on the computer, as you need to act quickly to enter the BIOS Setup utility.

1. Turn on your computer. Watch the screen carefully for a message telling you what key to press to activate the BIOS Setup utility. On many systems, this key is F1, F2, or Delete. If you don't press the key in time, the OS boots normally. If this happens, shut down the computer and try again.

2. When you have entered the BIOS Setup utility, your screen might look similar to Figure 1-3, but many BIOS setup screens look different. Before continuing, write down the steps of the boot procedure, listed earlier under "Computer Boot Procedure," that have taken place to this point:

_____

_____

_____

```
                    PhoenixBIOS Setup Utility
  Main     Advanced    Security    Boot     Exit

 ┌─────────────────────────────────────────────┬──────────────────────────┐
 │                                              │   Item Specific Help     │
 │  System Time:          [11:08:57]            ├──────────────────────────┤
 │  System Date:          [04/17/2010]          │                          │
 │                                              │  <Tab>, <Shift-Tab>, or  │
 │  Legacy Diskette A:    [1.44/1.25 MB  3½"]   │  <Enter> selects field.  │
 │  Legacy Diskette B:    [Disabled]            │                          │
 │                                              │                          │
 │ ▶ Primary Master       [None]                │                          │
 │ ▶ Primary Slave        [None]                │                          │
 │ ▶ Secondary Master     [VMware Virtual ID]   │                          │
 │ ▶ Secondary Slave      [None]                │                          │
 │                                              │                          │
 │ ▶ Keyboard Features                          │                          │
 │                                              │                          │
 │  System Memory:        640 KB                │                          │
 │  Extended Memory:      1047552 KB            │                          │
 │  Boot-time Diagnostic Screen:  [Disabled]    │                          │
 │                                              │                          │
 └─────────────────────────────────────────────┴──────────────────────────┘
  F1   Help    ↑↓  Select Item    -/+    Change Values      F9   Setup Defaults
  Esc  Exit    ↔   Select Menu    Enter  Select ▶ Sub-Menu  F10  Save and Exit
```

Figure 1-3 The BIOS Setup utility

Source: **Phoenix Technologies, Ltd.**

3. Navigate the BIOS Setup utility until you find the boot order menu (see Figure 1-4). You can change the order in which the BIOS looks for boot devices or exclude a device from the boot order. The BIOS boots from the first device in which it finds an OS. You might need to change the boot order if, for example, you have an OS installed on the hard drive but want to boot from an installation CD/DVD to install a new OS. In this case, you move the CD/DVD device to the first entry in the boot order.

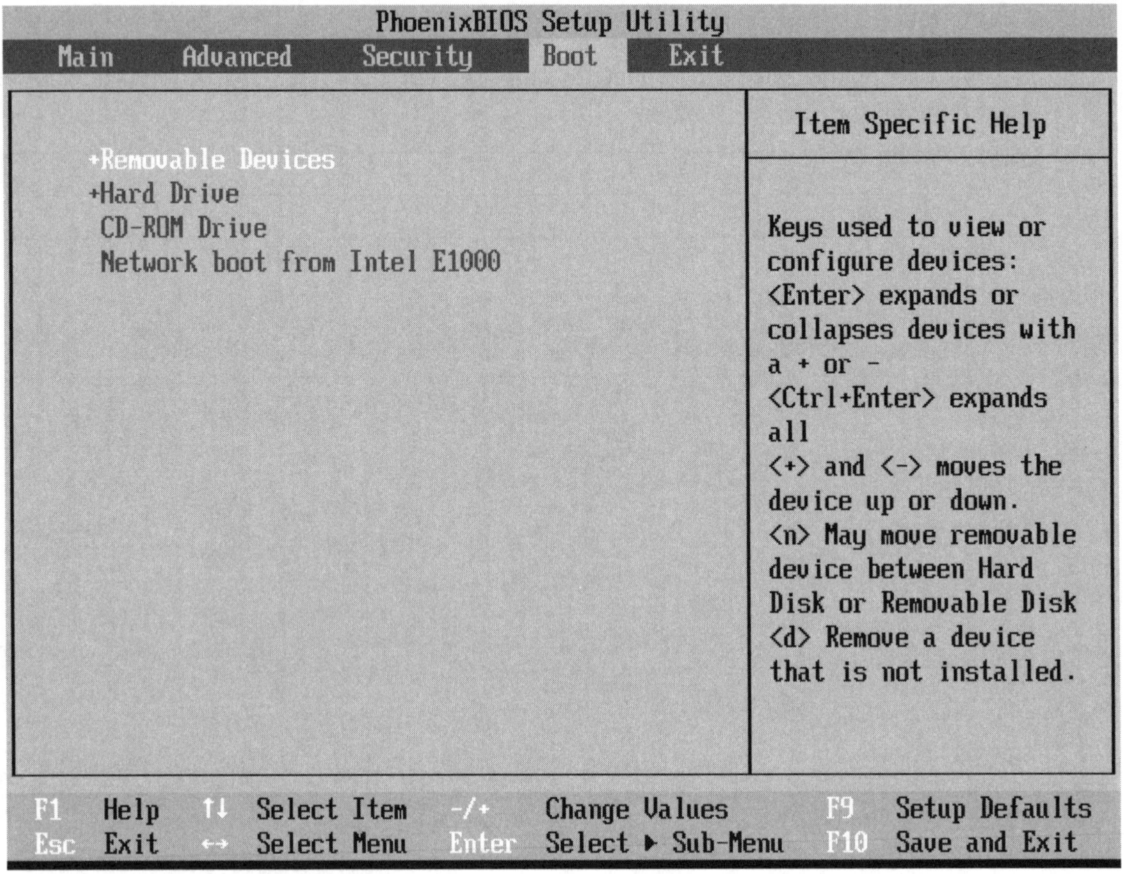

```
                    PhoenixBIOS Setup Utility
   Main    Advanced    Security    Boot    Exit
┌─────────────────────────────────────────────┬──────────────────────────┐
│                                              │   Item Specific Help     │
│     +Removable Devices                       ├──────────────────────────┤
│     +Hard Drive                              │                          │
│      CD-ROM Drive                            │  Keys used to view or    │
│      Network boot from Intel E1000           │  configure devices:      │
│                                              │  <Enter> expands or      │
│                                              │  collapses devices with  │
│                                              │  a + or -                │
│                                              │  <Ctrl+Enter> expands    │
│                                              │  all                     │
│                                              │  <+> and <-> moves the   │
│                                              │  device up or down.      │
│                                              │  <n> May move removable  │
│                                              │  device between Hard     │
│                                              │  Disk or Removable Disk  │
│                                              │  <d> Remove a device     │
│                                              │  that is not installed.  │
│                                              │                          │
├─────────────────────────────────────────────┴──────────────────────────┤
│  F1   Help    ↑↓  Select Item   -/+   Change Values    F9   Setup Defaults │
│  Esc  Exit    ↔   Select Menu   Enter Select ▶ Sub-Menu F10  Save and Exit │
└──────────────────────────────────────────────────────────────────────────┘
```

Figure 1-4 The BIOS boot order menu

Source: Phoenix Technologies, Ltd.

4. For now, you can leave the boot order unchanged. To quit the Setup utility, press the correct key (usually specified at the bottom of the screen). For example, press Esc to exit without saving changes or F10 to save the changes before exiting. In either case, when you exit, the computer restarts. Press the key for exiting without saving changes.

5. Write the final steps of the boot procedure that occurred as Windows started:

   _____

   _____

   _____

6. Shut down the computer for the next project.

The Fundamentals of Network Communication

A computer **network** consists of two or more computers connected by some kind of transmission medium, such as a cable or air waves. After they're connected, correctly configured computers can communicate with one another. The primary motivation for networking was the need for people to share resources, such as printers and hard drives, and information, such as word-processing files, and to communicate by using applications such as e-mail. These motivations remain, especially for businesses, but another motivating factor for both businesses and homes is to "get online"—to access the Internet. The Internet, with its wealth of information, disinformation, fun, and games, has had a tremendous impact on how and why networks are used. Indeed, many of the networking technologies used now that you learn about in this book were developed as a result of the Internet explosion.

You might know how to use a network already; in particular, you probably know how to use programs that access the Internet, such as Web browsers and e-mail programs. To understand *how* networks work, however, you need to learn about the underlying technologies and processes used when you open a Web browser or an e-mail program. A good place to start is with the components that make a stand-alone computer a networked computer.

Network Components

Imagine a computer with no networking components—no networking hardware or software. It's hard to imagine in this age of seemingly everything being connected. However, not too long ago, when you bought a computer, its main purpose was to run applications such as word-processing and spreadsheet programs, not Web browsers and e-mail. In fact, a computer had neither the hardware nor software needed to run these programs. These computers were called **stand-alone computers**. If you wanted to network this type of computer, you had to add these required components:

- *Network interface card*—A NIC is an add-on card that's plugged into a motherboard expansion slot and provides a connection between the computer and the network. Most computers have a NIC built into the motherboard, so no additional card is necessary. NICs are discussed in more detail in Chapter 2.

- *Network medium*—A cable that plugs into the NIC and makes the connection between a computer and the rest of the network. In networks with just two computers, the other end of the cable can plug into the second computer's NIC. More likely, the other end of the cable plugs into an interconnecting device that accommodates several computer connections. Network media can also be the air waves, as in wireless networks. In this case, the connection is between the antenna on the NIC and the antenna on another NIC or interconnecting device. Network media are discussed in more detail in Chapter 4.

- *Interconnecting device*—Although this component isn't always necessary because two computers can be connected directly with a cable and small wireless networks can be configured without an interconnecting device, most networks include these components. They allow computers to communicate on a network without having to be connected directly to one another. They include switches, hubs, routers, and wireless access points, discussed in Chapters 2 and 8. A small network connected to a switch is shown in Figure 1-5.

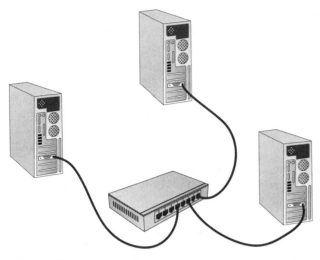

Figure 1-5 A network of computers connected to a switch

Hands-On Project 1-2: Upgrading a Stand-alone Computer to a Networked Computer

Time Required: 30 minutes

Objective: Upgrade a stand-alone computer to a networked computer.

Required Tools and Equipment: Lab computer (as specified in the book's lab setup instructions), a NIC, a patch cable, and a hub or switch

Description: In this project, you install a NIC and connect it to an interconnecting device with a cable. This project can be done in groups or as an instructor demonstration. It's intended only to familiarize you with the hardware components needed to make a stand-alone computer a networked computer.

1. Install the NIC, following the steps your instructor provides. This process might involve opening the computer case or simply plugging a USB NIC into a USB slot.

2. Turn on the computer. If necessary, insert a disk containing the NIC driver and follow the instructions for installing it.

3. Using the supplied cable, plug one end into the NIC and the other end into the interconnecting device, which should be a hub or a switch.

4. Examine the indicator lights on the NIC and the hub or switch. There might be one or two lights on each port of the device, depending on its features. There's at least one indicator on the NIC and on each port of the hub or switch that's usually referred to as a "link light." The link light glows when a data connection has been made between the NIC and the hub or switch. Your instructor can supply more details about the indicator lights available on your hub or switch. List the status of indicators on the NIC and the hub or switch port into which the NIC is plugged:

5. Shut down the computer and unplug and put away the cables.

The previous list of components satisfies the hardware components needed to make a stand-alone computer a networked computer. The computer must also have the necessary software to interact with network hardware and communicate with other computers on the network. Network software transforms a stand-alone OS into a network OS. It's the software that allows a word-processing program to open a document on a server or knows how to request a Web page or send an e-mail. It's also the software that communicates between the OS and network hardware. Network software can be divided into the following categories:

• *Network clients and servers*—**Network client software** requests information that's stored on another network computer or device. **Network server software** allows a computer to share its resources by fielding resource requests generated by network clients. Network client software can be an integral part of well-known applications, such as Web browsers and e-mail programs. A Web browser, for example, sends a request for a Web page to a Web server. Network client software can also run in the background, usually installed as a networking service. In this case, it enables programs without built-in client software to access shared network resources on other computers. For example, Client for Microsoft Networks, which is installed automatically in Windows, allows a word-processing program to open a file that's shared on another Windows computer or print to a printer attached to another Windows computer. In this setup, the server software called File and Printer Sharing for Microsoft Networks receives the request from the client and provides access to the shared file or printer.

• *Protocols*—When clients and servers need to send information on the network, they must pass it to **network protocols,** which define the rules and formats a computer must use when sending information across the network. A network protocol can be likened to a human language. Just as two people who want to communicate must speak the same language, two computers that want to communicate must use the same protocol. An example of a network protocol is TCP/IP. Network protocols do all the behind-the-scenes tasks required to make networking work and handle most of the complexity in networking; they're discussed in depth in Chapter 5.

The term "NIC device driver" is often shortened to simply "NIC driver," which is the term used throughout this book.

• *NIC driver*—After a network protocol has formatted a message correctly, it hands the data off to the NIC driver for transmission onto the network. NIC drivers receive data from protocols and then forward this data to the physical NIC, which transmits data onto the medium. The reverse is also true. When data arrives at the NIC from the medium, the NIC hands it off to the NIC driver, which then hands it off to network protocols. Every NIC card installed in a computer must have an associated device driver installed in the OS. The device driver software manages the details of communicating with the NIC hardware to send and receive data to and from network media.

Each of these software components plays a role in the steps of network communication, described in the next section.

Steps of Network Communication

Most network communication starts by a user needing to access a resource on another computer, such as a Web server or file server. A user's attempt to access network resources is summarized in these basic steps:

1. An application tries to access a network resource by attempting to send a message to it.

2. Network client software detects the attempt to access the network. Client software formats the message generated by the application and passes the message on to the network protocol.

3. The protocol packages the message in a format suitable for the network and sends it to the NIC driver.

4. The NIC driver sends the data in the request to the NIC card, which converts it into the necessary signals to be transmitted across the network medium.

Remember that there are two sides to a communication session, and most of them involve a client trying to access network resources and a server providing those resources. The steps taken on the server side are essentially the reverse of those on the client side:

1. The NIC card on the server receives signals from the network medium and converts them into message data, which is read by the NIC driver.

2. The NIC driver passes the message to the network protocol.

3. The network protocol determines which server software the message is targeting and passes the message to this designated software. Remember that a computer can have many clients and many servers running at the same time. For example, a computer running Windows Server 2012 might be acting as a mail server and a file server. Each server function requires different server software.

4. The server software receives the message and responds by sending the requested data to the client computer, using the four steps outlined previously.

Layers of the Network Communication Process

Each step of a client accessing network resources is often referred to as a "layer" in the network communication process. Each layer has a specific function to accomplish, and all the layers work together. Figure 1-6 illustrates this process, and Simulation 1 shows an animation of this process. (Refer to this book's introduction for information on accessing simulations.) Keep in mind that the steps outlined previously simplified the communication process, which is one reason the layered approach is so effective: Complex concepts can be described in simple steps. Chapter 7 discusses the layered approach to networking in more detail, and Chapter 5 explains the role of protocols in network communication.

Simulation 1: Layers of the network communication process

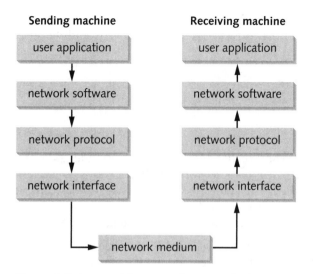

Figure 1-6 Layers of the network communication process

As you see in Chapter 7 when the OSI model of networking is discussed, the layers are given different names and divided into additional pieces. What's important now is grasping the idea of a layered approach, in which a complex process is broken into manageable steps, each with a specific role to play. Table 1-3 maps the resource access steps listed previously to the four layers in Figure 1-6.

Table 1-3 Layers of the network communication process

Step	Description	Layer
1	An application tries to access a network resource.	User application
2	Client software detects the attempt to access the network and passes the message on to the network protocol.	Network client or server software
3	The protocol packages the message in a format suitable for the network and sends it to the NIC driver.	Network protocol
4	The NIC driver sends the data in the request to the NIC, which converts it into the necessary signals to be transmitted across the network medium.	Network interface

How Two Computers Communicate on a LAN: Some Details

The layers of the network communication process give an overview of how network communication works. However, there are few details on what each layer accomplishes. This discussion focuses on computer addresses and how they're used during network communication.

In a network using a protocol such as TCP/IP (the most common network protocol), computers have two addresses: a logical address and a physical address. The logical address is the IP address, and the physical address is called the Media Access Control (MAC) address. You can look at these two addresses much like the addresses used to send mail through the postal system. When a letter is mailed in the United States, it requires a street address and a zip code. The zip code gets the letter to the correct region of the country, and the street address gets the letter to the correct home or business.

The MAC address is stored as part of the physical NIC, which is why the MAC address is referred to as the "physical address."

You can liken the zip code to the logical or IP address and the street address to the physical or MAC address. When a message is sent on a network, the IP address is used to get the message to the correct network, and the MAC address gets the message to the correct computer on this network. If the sender and receiver are on the same network, the IP address in the message is used mainly as a means to ascertain the destination computer's MAC address.

For example, Figure 1-7 shows two computers connected to a switch. Computer A wants to communicate with Computer B. One of the simplest forms of communication is a ping. The `ping` command sends a message from one computer to another, essentially asking the other computer whether it's listening on the network. If a computer receives a ping, it replies so that the sending computer knows the message was received. It's like the cell phone commercial with a person asking "Can you hear me now?" Here are the steps of this communication process:

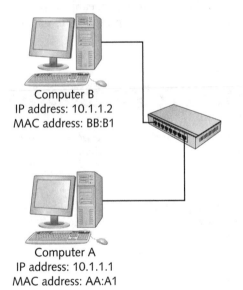

Computer B
IP address: 10.1.1.2
MAC address: BB:B1

Computer A
IP address: 10.1.1.1
MAC address: AA:A1

Figure 1-7 Communication between two computers

1. A user at Computer A types `ping 10.1.1.2` (the IP address of ComputerB) at a command prompt.
2. The network software creates a ping message.
3. The network protocol packages the message by adding IP addresses of the sending and destination computers and acquires the destination computer's MAC address.

4. The network interface software adds MAC addresses of the sending and destination computers and sends the message to the network medium as bits.

5. Computer B receives the message, verifies that the addresses are correct, and then sends a reply to Computer A, using Steps 2 through 4.

Simulation 2 shows this communication process in action.

Simulation 2: Communication between two computers

Users don't usually initiate network communication by using a computer's IP address; instead, they use the computer name. However, just as you can't mail a letter with only the recipient's name, you can't communicate over a network with only the computer's name. You certainly know the name of the person you're writing to, but you might have to look up his or her address in your address book before you can address the envelope. Similarly, computers use an address book of sorts, called a **name server**, to get a computer's IP address, given its name. TCP/IP provides name server functions through its Domain Name System (DNS, discussed in more detail in Chapter 5). With this information in mind, the preceding steps can be expanded as follows:

1. A user at Computer A types `ping Computer B` at a command prompt.

2. A name lookup is done to retrieve Computer B's IP address.

3. The network software creates a ping message.

4. The network protocol packages the message by adding IP addresses of the sending and destination computer and acquires the destination computer's MAC address.

5. The network interface software adds MAC addresses of the sending and destination computers and sends the message to the network medium as bits.

6. Computer B receives the message, verifies that the addresses are correct, and then sends a reply to Computer A, using Steps 3 through 5.

Quite a few details in these steps have been left out for now, but they're expanded on in the TCP/IP discussion in Chapter 5. Next, take a look at an example of using a network to save a word-processing document to a Windows server and see how the layers of the network communication process are used. Several components are involved in this task, as you see in Hands-On Project 1-3. In this example, shown in Table 1-4, a user at ClientA is running a word-processing program, such as Microsoft Word, and wants to save the file to a shared folder on another Windows computer named ServerX.

In Table 1-4, there's no "User application" step on the server. When a server is involved, typically the last step is handled by network software, such as File and Printer Sharing for Microsoft Networks, a Web server, or other server software.

Table 1-4 Saving a file with the network communication process

Step	Description	Layer
1	The user on ClientA clicks Save in the word-processing program and chooses a shared folder on ServerX to save the file.	User application
2	Client for Microsoft Networks detects the attempt to access the network, formats the message, and passes the message to the network protocol.	Network software
3	The network protocol (in this case, TCP/IPv4) packages the message in a format suitable for the network interface and sends it to the NIC driver.	Network protocol
4	The NIC driver sends the data in the request to the NIC (in this case, Ethernet0), which converts it into signals to be transmitted across the network medium.	Network interface
5	ServerX's NIC receives the message from the network medium, processes it, and sends the data to TCP/IPv4.	Network interface
6	TCP/IPv4 on ServerX receives the message from the NIC, processes it, and sends the data to the network software (in this case, File and Printer Sharing for Microsoft Networks).	Network protocol
7	File and Printer Sharing for Microsoft Networks formats the message and requests that the OS save the file to the disk.	Network software

HANDS-ON PROJECTS

Hands-On Project 1-3: Viewing Network Software Layers

Time Required: 10 minutes

Objective: View the properties of your computer's network connection and identify the layers of the network communication process.

Required Tools and Equipment: Net-XX

Description: In this project, you view the properties of your computer's local area connection and identify the layers of the network communication process. Each network connection in Windows contains the software responsible for the steps of the network communication process.

1. Start your computer, and log on as **NetAdmin**.

2. Open the Network Connections dialog box by right-clicking **Start** and clicking **Network Connections**.

3. Right-click **Ethernet0** and click **Properties** to open the Ethernet0 Properties dialog box (see Figure 1-8).

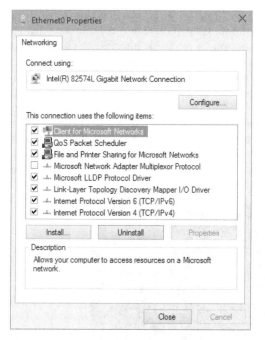

Figure 1-8   The Ethernet0 Properties dialog box

4. The "Connect using" text box displays the NIC. In the list box under it, you see several items. Client for Microsoft Networks, File and Printer Sharing for Microsoft Networks, and Internet Protocol Version 4 are the items you're most interested in right now, as they're the most necessary software components to make network communication work.

5. Assume a user is running a word-processing program and saves a file to a Windows server. Use the information you learned in this chapter to write which of the four layers of the network communication process each component corresponds to. Note that some layers can be used more than once.

   • Word-processing program: _____

   • NIC displayed in the "Connect using" text box: _____

   • Client for Microsoft Networks: _____

   • File and Printer Sharing for Microsoft Networks: _____

   • Internet Protocol Version 4 (TCP/IPv4): _____

6. Close all open windows, but leave your computer running for the next project.

Hands-On Project 1-4: Using `ipconfig`, `ping`, and `arp`

Time Required: 15 minutes

Objective: Use `ipconfig`, `ping`, and `arp` to view and test network addresses and connectivity.

Required Tools and Equipment: Net-*XX*

Description: In this project, you use command-line tools to view your network configuration and test your computer's capability to communicate with other computers. The `ipconfig` command displays the IP address configuration of network interfaces. The `ping` command sends a message to a computer to verify the capability to communicate with it, and `arp` displays the MAC (physical) addresses your computer has discovered.

1. Start your computer, and log on as **NetAdmin**, if necessary.

2. Right-click **Start** and click **Command Prompt** to open a command prompt window. At the command prompt, type **ipconfig** and press **Enter**. You should see a screen similar to Figure 1-9, although the numbers you see will vary. The `ipconfig` command lists the IP address configuration for network interfaces as well as other network settings.

```
C:\Users\NetAdmin>ipconfig

Windows IP Configuration

Ethernet adapter Ethernet0:

   Connection-specific DNS Suffix  . : yc-cnt.edu
   Link-local IPv6 Address . . . . . : fe80::90e7:d59d:958:4de3%3
   IPv4 Address. . . . . . . . . . . : 172.31.1.11
   Subnet Mask . . . . . . . . . . . : 255.255.0.0
   Default Gateway . . . . . . . . . : 172.31.1.250

Tunnel adapter isatap.yc-cnt.edu:

   Media State . . . . . . . . . . . : Media disconnected
   Connection-specific DNS Suffix  . : yc-cnt.edu

C:\Users\NetAdmin>
```

Figure 1-9   The `ipconfig` command output

3. To see more details about your network configuration, type **ipconfig /all** and press **Enter**. You can scroll up the command prompt window to see all the output. Under the heading "Ethernet adapter Ethernet0," find the row labeled Physical Address (see Figure 1-10). The number you see in this row is the MAC address, a 12-digit

```
Ethernet adapter Ethernet0:

   Connection-specific DNS Suffix  . : yc-cnt.edu
   Description . . . . . . . . . . . : Intel(R) 82574L Gigabit Network Connection
   Physical Address. . . . . . . . . : 00-0C-29-F4-62-18
   DHCP Enabled. . . . . . . . . . . : Yes
   Autoconfiguration Enabled . . . . : Yes
   Link-local IPv6 Address . . . . . : fe80::90e7:d59d:958:4de3%3(Preferred)
   IPv4 Address. . . . . . . . . . . : 172.31.1.11(Preferred)
   Subnet Mask . . . . . . . . . . . : 255.255.0.0
   Lease Obtained. . . . . . . . . . : Thursday, January 29, 2015 11:21:51 AM
   Lease Expires . . . . . . . . . . : Friday, January 30, 2015 11:21:51 AM
   Default Gateway . . . . . . . . . : 172.31.1.250
   DHCP Server . . . . . . . . . . . : 172.31.1.205
   DHCPv6 IAID . . . . . . . . . . . : 50334761
   DHCPv6 Client DUID. . . . . . . . : 00-01-00-01-1C-5A-EF-95-00-0C-29-F4-62-18
   DNS Servers . . . . . . . . . . . : 172.31.1.205
                                       172.31.1.206
   NetBIOS over Tcpip. . . . . . . . : Enabled

Tunnel adapter isatap.yc-cnt.edu:

   Media State . . . . . . . . . . . : Media disconnected
   Connection-specific DNS Suffix  . : yc-cnt.edu
   Description . . . . . . . . . . . : Microsoft ISATAP Adapter #2
   Physical Address. . . . . . . . . : 00-00-00-00-00-00-00-E0
   DHCP Enabled. . . . . . . . . . . : No
   Autoconfiguration Enabled . . . . : Yes

C:\Users\NetAdmin>
```

Figure 1-10   Using `ipconfig /all` to list physical (MAC) and IP addresses

hexadecimal value. Also, find the IP address in the IPv4 Address row. Write down these two addresses:

_____

_____

4. Tell your partner what your IP address is and make a note of your partner's IP address. At the command prompt, type **ping *IPaddress*** and press **Enter** (replacing *IPaddress* with your partner's IP address). You should see output similar to Figure 1-11.

```
C:\Users\NetAdmin>ping 172.31.1.205

Pinging 172.31.1.205 with 32 bytes of data:
Reply from 172.31.1.205: bytes=32 time=1ms TTL=128
Reply from 172.31.1.205: bytes=32 time<1ms TTL=128
Reply from 172.31.1.205: bytes=32 time<1ms TTL=128
Reply from 172.31.1.205: bytes=32 time<1ms TTL=128

Ping statistics for 172.31.1.205:
    Packets: Sent = 4, Received = 4, Lost = 0 (0% loss),
Approximate round trip times in milli-seconds:
    Minimum = 0ms, Maximum = 1ms, Average = 0ms

C:\Users\NetAdmin>
```

Figure 1-11 Results of the `ping` command

5. Remember that your computer needs both the destination IP address and MAC address to communicate with another computer. You supplied the IP address by typing it at the command prompt. Your computer discovered the MAC address of your partner's computer by using Address Resolution Protocol (ARP). To see this address, type **arp-a** and press **Enter**. The output should be similar to Figure 1-12. You might see more lines of output, depending on what other devices your computer has been communicating with. ARP is discussed in more detail in Chapter 5, but for now, just know that it works automatically without user intervention.

```
C:\Users\NetAdmin>arp -a

Interface: 172.31.1.11 --- 0x3
  Internet Address        Physical Address      Type
  172.31.1.205            00-15-5d-01-01-1b     dynamic
  224.0.0.22              01-00-5e-00-00-16     static

C:\Users\NetAdmin>
```

Figure 1-12 The `arp -a` command displays MAC addresses

6. Use the **ping** command to communicate with other computers and devices on your network, and use **ipconfig /all** to find the addresses of your default gateway (a router in your network) and your DNS servers. Write the MAC addresses of your default gateway and DNS servers:

• Default gateway: _____

• DNS servers: _____

7. Close all open windows, but leave your computer running for the next project.

Now that you have a solid idea of how network communication takes place and how networks are depicted in drawings, you can learn some common terms for describing networks and network components in the next section. Along the way, you see more figures of different types of networks.

Network Terms Explained

Every profession has its own language with its own unique terms and acronyms. Learning this language is half the battle of becoming proficient in a profession, and it's no different in computer and networking technology. The following sections explain some common terms used in discussing computer networks. Because some of these terms are associated with network diagrams, a number of figures are included in the following sections to show different ways of depicting networks.

LANs, Internetworks, WANs, and MANs

A small network, limited to a single collection of machines and connected by one or more interconnecting devices in a small geographic area, is called a **local area network (LAN)**. LANs also form the building blocks for constructing larger networks called "internetworks." In Figure 1-13, the computers in a LAN are interconnected by a switch, and Figure 1-14 shows a wireless LAN.

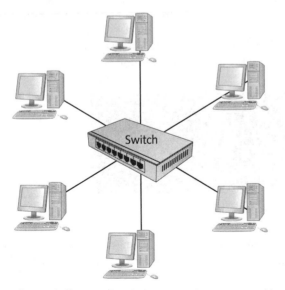

Figure 1-13 A LAN with computers interconnected by a switch

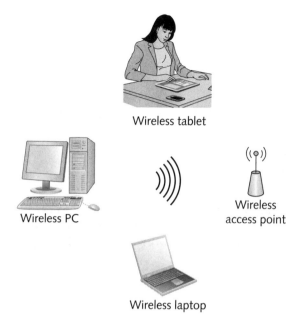

Figure 1-14   A wireless LAN

LANs are represented in other ways, as in Figure 1-15; note the different symbols for a hub and a switch. Figure 1-16 shows a logical depiction of the same network; a logical depiction leaves out details such as interconnecting devices, showing only the computers making up the network.

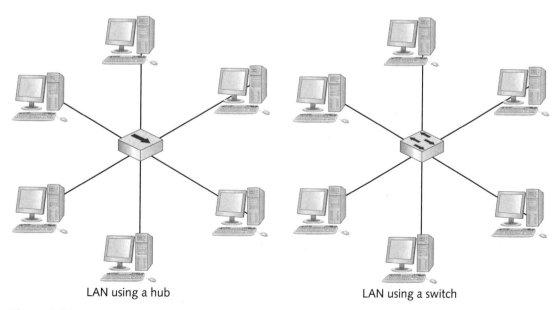

LAN using a hub   LAN using a switch

Figure 1-15   A LAN with a symbolic hub (left) and a symbolic switch (right)

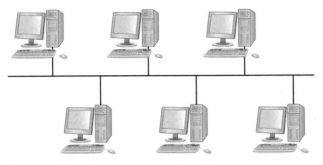

Figure 1-16   A logical depiction of a LAN

An **internetwork** is a networked collection of LANs tied together by devices such as routers, discussed in Chapters 2 and 8. Figure 1-17 shows two LANS interconnected by a router (represented by the standard symbol). Internetworks are usually created for these reasons:

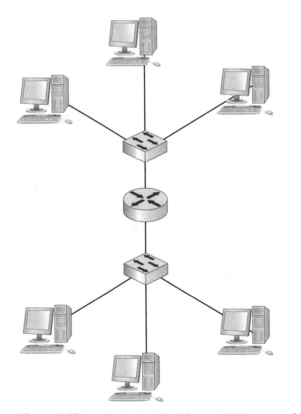

Figure 1-17   An internetwork with two LANS connected by a router

- Two or more groups of users and their computers should be logically separated on the network yet still allow the groups to communicate. For example, in a school, you might want to logically separate the LAN containing student computers from the LAN containing faculty computers. Routers provide this logical separation but still allow communication between groups, as you see in Chapter 2.

- The number of computers in a single LAN has grown to the point that network communication is no longer efficient. The nature of certain network protocols and devices make network communication increasingly less efficient as the number of computers on a LAN grows. Routers can be used to separate the computers into two or more smaller LANs, thereby increasing communication efficiency.

- The distance between two groups of computers exceeds the capabilities of most LAN devices, such as hubs and switches. This problem can happen, for example, when a company has multiple buildings or multiple floors in a building. Routers are often used to communicate between groups of computers that are separated geographically.

You might not realize it, but the computer you have at home is probably part of an internetwork. Every time you go online to browse the Web or check your e-mail, your computer (or LAN, if you have a home network) becomes part of the largest internetwork in the world: the Internet.

As a network's scope expands to encompass LANs in geographically dispersed locations, internetworks become classified as **wide area networks (WANs)**. A WAN spans distances measured in miles and links separate LANs. WANs use the services of third-party communication providers, such as phone companies, to carry network traffic from one location to another. So although both internetworks and WANs connect LANs, the difference lies mainly in the LANs' proximity to each other and the technologies used to communicate between LANs. Therefore, the Internet is both an internetwork and, because it spans the globe, a very large WAN.

Occasionally, you might encounter a network type called a **metropolitan area network (MAN)**. MANs use WAN technologies to interconnect LANs in a specific geographic region, such as a county or city. It's not uncommon to find large, complex networks involving all four network types: LANs and internetworks for purely local access, MANs for regional or citywide access, and WANs for access to remote sites elsewhere in the country or around the world. Take, for example, a nationwide bank. The main branch in a large city has a building with multiple floors and hundreds of computers. Each floor constitutes a LAN, and these LANs are connected to form an internetwork. The internetwork at the main branch is then connected to other branches throughout the city to form a MAN. In addition, the main branch is connected to other branches in other cities and states to form a WAN.

In network drawings, WANs are often shown with a jagged or thunderbolt-shaped line representing the connection between two devices, usually routers, and the Internet is usually represented as a cloud. A cloud is used to obscure the details of a large network, as if to say "There's some collection of networks and network devices, but the details aren't important." Figure 1-18 shows a WAN connection between two routers with a connection to the Internet. A grouping of three computers is often used to represent multiple computers on a LAN when the exact number doesn't matter.

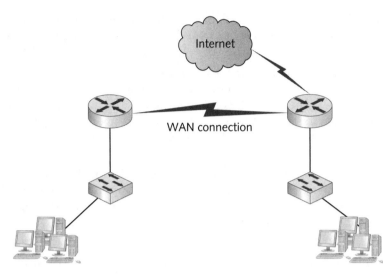

Figure 1-18   A WAN with a connection to the Internet

Internet, Intranet, and Extranet

The **Internet** is a worldwide public internetwork that uses standard protocols, such as TCP/IP, DNS, HTTP, and others, to transfer and view information. It's a public network because the devices such as routers and Web servers that make up much of the network are accessible directly through an IP address. An **intranet**, on the other hand, is a private network, such as a school or company network, in which the devices and servers are available only to users connected to the internal network. Many of the same protocols and technologies used on the Internet are used to access information on an intranet. An **extranet** sits somewhere between the Internet and an intranet. It allows limited and controlled access to internal network resources by outside users. It's used when two organizations need to share resources, so controls are put in place to allow these organizations to access resources without making resources available to the wider Internet.

Packets and Frames

When computers transfer information across a network, they do so in short bursts of about 1500 bytes of data. Each burst, or chunk, of data has the same basic structure; specifically, each chunk of data contains the MAC addresses and IP addresses of both the sending (source) and receiving (destination) computers. So to transfer a small word-processing file, only one burst of data transfer might be needed, but large photo or music files are first divided into several hundred or even thousands of chunks before they're transferred. After each chunk of data is sent, the computer pauses momentarily. Data is transferred in this way for a number of reasons:

- The pause between bursts might be necessary to allow other computers to transfer data during pauses.
- The pause allows the receiving computer to process received data, such as writing it to disk.
- The pause allows the receiving computer to receive data from other computers at the same time.

- The pause gives the sending computer an opportunity to receive data from other computers and perform other processing tasks.

- If an error occurs during transmission of a large file, only the chunks of data involved in the error have to be sent again, not the entire file.

To use another analogy, you can look at chunks of data as sentences people use when speaking. Pauses in conversation give listeners an opportunity to register what has been said and possibly get a word in themselves.

To get an idea of how many chunks of data are involved in transferring a typical file, a 3-minute music file is about 3 million bytes (3 MB) of data, which takes about 2000 chunks of data.

Packets The chunks of data sent across the network are usually called "packets" or "frames." **Packet**, the more well-known term, is often used generically to mean a chunk of data sent over the network. However, this term does have a particular meaning: It's a chunk of data with source and destination IP addresses (as well as other IP protocol information) added to it. Figure 1-19 shows a representation of the original data to be transferred, and Figure 1-20 shows the packets created after the data has been broken into chunks and IP addresses added.

Lorem ipsum dolor sit amet, consectetuer adipiscing elit. Maecenas porttitor congue massa. Fusce posuere, magna sed pulvinar ultricies, purus lectus malesuada libero, sit amet commodo magna eros quis urna.

Nunc viverra imperdiet enim. Fusce est. Vivamus a tellus.

Pellentesque habitant morbi tristique senectus et netus et malesuada fames ac turpis egestas. Proin pharetra nonummy pede. Mauris et orci.

Lorem ipsum dolor sit amet, consectetuer adipiscing elit. Maecenas porttitor congue massa. Fusce posuere, magna sed pulvinar ultricies, purus lectus malesuada libero, sit amet commodo magna eros quis urna.

Nunc viverra imperdiet enim. Fusce est. Vivamus a tellus.

Pellentesque habitant morbi tristique senectus et netus et malesuada fames ac turpis egestas. Proin pharetra nonummy pede. Mauris et orci.

Lorem ipsum dolor sit amet, consectetuer adipiscing elit. Maecenas porttitor congue massa. Fusce posuere, magna sed pulvinar ultricies, purus lectus malesuada libero, sit amet commodo magna eros quis urna.

Nunc viverra imperdiet enim. Fusce est. Vivamus a tellus.

Pellentesque habitant morbi tristique senectus et netus et malesuada fames ac turpis egestas. Proin pharetra nonummy pede. Mauris et orci.

Figure 1-19 Original data

Dest: IP: 172.16.1.2, Source IP: 172.16.1.1	Lorem ipsum dolor sit amet, consectetuer adipiscing elit. Maecenas porttitor congue massa. Fusce posuere, magna sed pulvinar ultricies.
Dest: IP: 172.16.1.2, Source IP: 172.16.1.1	purus lectus malesuada libero, sit amet commodo magna eros quis urna. Nunc viverra imperdiet enim. Fusce est. Vivamus a tellus.
Dest: IP: 172.16.1.2, Source IP: 172.16.1.1	Pellentesque habitant morbi tristique senectus et netus et malesuada fames ac turpis egestas. Proin pharetra nonummy pede. Mauris et orci
Dest: IP: 172.16.1.2, Source IP: 172.16.1.1	Lorem ipsum dolor sit amet, consectetuer adipiscing elit. Maecenas porttitor congue massa. Fusce posuere, magna sed pulvinar ultricies
Dest: IP: 172.16.1.2, Source IP: 172.16.1.1	Pellentesque habitant tristique senectus et netus et malesuada fames ac turpis egestas. Proin pharetra nonummy pede. Mauris et orci.

Figure 1-20 Data divided into several packets

Using the U.S. mail analogy, you can look at a packet as an envelope with the zip code added but not the street address. In relation to the layers of the network communication process, packets are generated by and processed by the network protocol. You learn more details about this process in Chapters 5 and 6.

Frames A **frame** is a packet with the source and destination MAC addresses added to it. In addition, frames have an error-checking code added to the back end of the packet, so the packet is "framed" by MAC addresses (and other network interface information) on one end and an error-checking code on the other. A frame is like a letter that's been addressed and stamped and is ready to deliver.

Frames are essentially the final state of data before it's placed on the network medium as bits. The network interface is the layer of the network communication process that works with frames. Figure 1-21 shows what the packets from Figure 1-20 look like after the frame information is added.

est MAC, Source MAC	Dest IP, Source IP	Lorem ipsum dolor sit amet, consectetuer adipiscing elit. Maecenas porttitor congue massa. Fusce posuere, magna sed pulvinar ultricies,	Error check
Dest MAC, Source MAC	Dest IP, Source IP	purus lectus malesuada libero, sit amet commodo magna eros quis urna. Nunc viverra imperdiet enim. Fusce est. Vivamus a tellus.	Error check
Dest MAC, Source MAC	Dest IP, Source IP	Pellentesque habitant morbi tristique senectus et netus et malesuada fames ac turpis egestas. Proin pharetra nonummy pede. Mauris et orci	Error check
Dest MAC, Source MAC	Dest IP, Source IP	Lorem ipsum dolor sit amet, consectetuer adipiscing elit. Maecenas porttitor congue massa. Fusce posuere, magna sed pulvinar ultricies	Error check
Dest MAC, Source MAC	Dest IP, Source IP	Pellentesque habitant tristique senectus et netus et malesuada fames ac turpis egestas. Proin pharetra nonummy pede. Mauris et orci.	Error check

Figure 1-21 The packets are now frames and ready for delivery

The process of adding IP addresses and then MAC addresses to chunks of data is called **encapsulation**. Information added at the front of data is called a **header**, and information added at the end of data is called a **trailer**. Data is encapsulated several times as it works its way down from the sending application until it makes it to the network interface as a frame. When the destination computer receives the frame, the process is reversed as the network interface deencapsulates (has the header and trailer removed) the frame so that it becomes a packet again. This process continues until the packet arrives at the receiving application or service as the original data. This process is all part of the layered approach to networking.

Clients and Servers

You've already learned about the role of client network software and server network software. Unfortunately, the world of networking sometimes uses the same terms to discuss two different things. The following sections clarify what these terms mean and how their meanings can differ depending on how they're used.

Client A **client**, in networking terms, can be a workstation running a client OS, such as Windows 10, or the network software on a computer that requests network resources from a server. In addition, you can refer to a physical computer as a client computer. What the term "client" means, therefore, depends on the context in which it's used. To clarify, it's usually used in these three contexts:

- *Client operating system*—The OS installed on a computer is designed mainly to access network resources, even though it might be capable of sharing its own resources. Windows 10, Windows 8.1, and Mac OS X fit this description, for example, as do certain distributions of Linux. A client OS is also often referred to as a "desktop OS."

- *Client computer*—This computer's primary role in a network is to run user applications and access network resources. Most computers in a network fit this description.

- *Client software*—It's the software that requests network resources from server software running on another computer. For example, a Web browser, an e-mail client (such as Microsoft Outlook), and Client for Microsoft Networks fit into this category.

Server When most people hear the word "server," they conjure up visions of a large tower computer with lots of hard drives and memory. This image is merely a computer hardware configuration that may or may not be used as a server, however. In short, a computer becomes a **server** when software is installed on it that provides a network service to client computers. In other words, you can install certain software on an inexpensive laptop computer and make it act as a server. By the same token, a huge tower computer with six hard drives and 64 GB of RAM can be used as a workstation for a single user. So although some hardware configurations are packaged to function as servers, and others are packaged as client or desktop computers, what makes a computer a server is the software installed on it. Just as there are three contexts in which the term "client" is used, so it is with the term "server":

- *Server operating system*—This term is used when the OS installed on a computer is designed mainly to share network resources and provide other network services (some discussed later in "Network Servers"). A server OS is tuned to be able to share files efficiently and perform network operations in response to client requests, even though the OS might also be able to run user applications and client software. Windows Server 2012, Mac OS X Server, UNIX, and many Linux distributions fit this description.

- *Server computer*—This term is used when a computer's primary role in the network is to give client computers access to network resources and services. The computers that most often fit this description are usually in the IT room or locked away in a closet.

- *Server software*—It's the software that responds to requests for network resources from client software running on another computer. A Web server (such as Internet Information Services), an e-mail server (such as Microsoft Exchange), and File and Printer Sharing for Microsoft Networks fit into this category.

 Microsoft refers to server software components as "services." Other OSs use other terms; for example, in Linux/UNIX, server software components are referred to as "daemons."

As you can see, the lines between a client computer and a server computer are often blurred because OSs are designed as network operating systems, and most can take on the roles of both server and client. As you're learning, however, the language of networking is often imprecise, and you must pay attention to the context in which networking terms are used to grasp their meaning. As you get more comfortable with all the terms and better understand how networks work, the nuances of the terminology will fall into place.

Network Models

A **network model** defines how and where resources are shared and how access to these resources is regulated. Network models fall into two major types: peer-to-peer and server-based (also called client/server). This discussion of network models addresses the role that computers play on the network and how these roles interact. Server-based networks are the most common in business settings, but understanding both types is essential, especially as they compare with one another.

 Peer-to-peer networks running Windows OSs are referred to as "workgroup networks," and server-based networks running Windows Server are called "domain-based networks."

In a **peer-to-peer network**, most computers function as clients or servers, as circumstances dictate. For example, a computer can act as a server by sharing a printer it's connected to and simultaneously act as a client by accessing a file shared by another computer on the network. In this type of network, there's no centralized control over who has access to network resources; each user maintains control over his or her own shared resources. The computers in peer-to-peer networks usually run desktop or client OSs.

In a **server-based network**, certain computers take on specialized roles and function mainly as servers, and ordinary users' machines tend to function mainly as clients. Windows Server 2012, RedHat Enterprise Linux, and UNIX are OSs designed primarily for server use. In these networks, servers have centralized authority over who has access to network resources.

Peer-to-Peer/Workgroup Model

As you have learned, computers on a peer-to-peer network can take both client and server roles. Because all computers on this type of network are peers, these networks impose no centralized control or security over shared resources. Any user can share resources on his or her computer with any other user's computer, and each user can determine what level of access other users have to his or her shared resources. Physically, a peer-to-peer network looks just like a server-based network; mainly, location and control over resources differentiate the two.

In a peer-to-peer network, every user must act as the administrator of his or her computer's resources. Users can give everyone else unlimited access to their resources or grant restricted (or no) access to other users on the network. To grant this access, users must create user accounts and passwords for each user who will access shared resources on their computers. The username and password for accessing a computer are called **credentials**. If you have five computers in a peer-to-peer network, each user might have to remember as many as five different sets of credentials. Because of the lack of centralized authority over resources, controlled chaos is the norm for all but the smallest peer-to-peer networks, and security can be a major concern because not all users might be educated in creating secure passwords.

On a Windows-based peer-to-peer network, computers are members of a workgroup, but a workgroup is simply an identifier and doesn't constitute a network security boundary. In other words, users on computers in Workgroup A can access resources on computers in Workgroup B as long as they have the correct credentials.

Although this system can work on small networks, as the number of users and computers grows, these networks can become unworkable—not because they don't operate correctly, but because users can't cope with having to remember multiple sets of credentials to access resources spread out over several computers. This limitation is in contrast to a server-based network, in which security of all resources is administered centrally.

Most peer-to-peer networks consist of collections of desktop PCs linked by a common network medium and connectivity device, such as a switch. The machines and the OS installed on them aren't tuned to provide network services as efficiently as dedicated network servers configured with server OSs. They can bog down easily under increasing loads, as more users try to access resources from a particular machine. The user whose machine is being accessed across the network also has to endure a performance reduction while his or her machine is busy handling network information requests. For example, if a user's machine has a network-accessible printer attached, the machine slows down every time someone sends a job to that printer. In addition, if a user restarts the machine not knowing that someone is accessing a resource on it, the network user's access fails or, even worse, data loss can occur.

Another issue that affects peer-to-peer networks is data organization. If every machine can be a server, how can users keep track of what information is stored on which machine? If five users are responsible for a collection of documents, any of those users might have to search through files on all five machines to find a document. The decentralized nature of peer-to-peer networks makes locating resources more difficult as the number of peers increases. Likewise, decentralization makes backup much trickier: Instead of backing up a single server that holds the shared documents, each machine must be backed up to protect shared data.

Given these issues and complexities, peer-to-peer networks might not seem worth using. However, they offer some advantages, particularly for small organizations. Peer-to-peer networks are the easiest and most inexpensive to install. Most require only a client OS on desktop computers along with cabling and connectivity devices. After computers are connected and configured correctly, users can begin sharing information immediately. Desktop computers and client OSs cost considerably less than their server counterparts.

Peer-to-peer networks are also well suited to small organizations, which tend to have small networks and small operating budgets. They're easy to use and don't require extensive staff training or a dedicated network administrator. With no centralized control, the loss of a machine means only the loss of access to the resources on it; otherwise, a peer-to-peer network continues to function when one computer fails. However, because managing resources and their security is difficult on a peer-to-peer network, even small networks of a few computers sometimes opt to use the server or domain network model.

Server/Domain-Based Model

Server-based networks allow centralized control over network resources, mainly by providing an environment in which users log on to the network with a single set of credentials maintained by one or more servers running a server OS. Server OSs are designed to handle many simultaneous user logons and requests for shared resources efficiently. In most cases, servers are dedicated to running network services and shouldn't be used to run user applications. You want to reserve servers' CPU power, memory, and network performance for user access to network services.

When you're using Windows server OSs in a server-based network with centralized logons, you're running a Windows domain. A **domain** is a collection of users and computers whose accounts are managed by Windows servers called **domain controllers**. Users and computers in a domain are subject to network access and security policies defined by a network administrator and enforced by domain controllers. The software managing centralized access and security is a **directory service**. On Windows servers, the directory service software is **Active Directory**, and it's what makes a Windows server a domain controller.

The Windows domain model came about with Windows NT in the early 1990s. However, the Active Directory implementation of the domain model was first used in Windows 2000.

The Linux OS supports a centralized logon service called Network Information Service (NIS), but more often Linux administrators use a service compatible with Active Directory called Lightweight Directory Access Protocol (LDAP) if they want to use a directory service. A directory service is one of several network services usually found only on server OSs running in a server-based network. Others include the following:

- *Naming services*—Translate computer names to their addresses.
- *E-mail services*—Manage incoming and outgoing e-mail from client e-mail programs.
- *Application services*—Grant client computers access to complex applications that run on the server.
- *Communication services*—Give remote users access to an organization's network.
- *Web services*—Provide comprehensive Web-based application services.

Unlike peer-to-peer networks, server-based networks are easier to expand. Peer-to-peer networks should be limited to 10 or fewer users, but server-based networks can handle anywhere from a handful to thousands of users. In addition, multiple servers can be configured to work together, which enables administrators to add more servers to share the load when an application's performance wanes or to provide fault tolerance if a server's hardware malfunctions.

Like peer-to-peer networks, server-based networks have some disadvantages. The most obvious is the additional overhead of operating a server-based network. Server-based networks require one or more dedicated computers to run the server OS. Computers sold as servers usually have features that improve reliability and performance and cost more than desktop computers. In addition, these networks usually require at least part-time support from a person skilled in managing server OSs. Acquiring the skills to manage a server-based network or hiring a trained network administrator adds quite a bit to operating costs.

Housing all your network resources and services on a single server makes administration of resources easier in the long run, but it also creates a single point of failure. Fortunately, most server OSs now have redundancy features that allow taking a single server offline while other machines assume that server's duties. Naturally, having redundant hardware is costly. You must carefully weigh the costs of lost productivity if a server fails against the additional hardware and software costs of redundancy features.

Table 1-5 summarizes the strengths and weaknesses of peer-to-peer/workgroup and server/domain-based networks.

Table 1-5 Peer-to-peer versus server-based networks

Network attribute	Peer-to-peer network	Server-based network
Resource access	Distributed among many desktop/client computers; makes access to resources more complex	Centralized on one or more servers; streamlines access to resources
Security	Users control their own shared resources and might have several sets of credentials to access resources; not ideal when tight security is essential	Security is managed centrally, and users have a single set of credentials for all shared resources; best when a secure environment is necessary
Performance	Desktop OS not tuned for resource sharing; access to shared resources can be hindered by users running applications	Server OS tuned for resource sharing; servers are usually dedicated to providing network services
Cost	No dedicated hardware or server OS required, making initial costs lower; lost productivity caused by increasing complexity can raise costs in the long run	Higher upfront costs because of dedicated hardware and server OSs; additional ongoing costs for administrative support

Both peer-to-peer networks and server-based networks have advantages. For this reason, using a combination of the two models isn't uncommon. For example, a user might want to share a printer with a group of users in close proximity or a document folder with a department colleague. With this arrangement, a user is in control of a shared resource yet can still assign permissions to this resource by using accounts from the central user database on the server. Although sharing the resource is decentralized, the logon credentials to access the resource are still centralized.

Hands-On Project 1-5: Exploring Peer-to-Peer Networking

Time Required: 15 minutes

Objective: View other computers and shared resources on a peer-to-peer network.

Required Tools and Equipment: Net-*XX*

Description: In this project, you view other computers and shared resources in a peer-to-peer network. Your instructor should have a computer named Net-Instr available on the network with a share named NetDocs. You also view and, if necessary, change the type of network (public or private) you're connected to.

All students should use the same username and password.

1. Start your computer, and log on as **NetAdmin**, if necessary.

2. Right-click **Start** and click **System** to open the System control panel. In the "Computer name, domain, and workgroup settings" section, examine the current settings. Does your computer belong to a workgroup or a domain? Is this computer operating in a peer-to-peer or server-based environment? Write your answers on the following lines:

   _____

   _____

3. Your computer name should be NET-*XX* (with *XX* representing your student number) and your workgroup should be NETESS. Verify with your instructor whether they're the right settings for your environment. If the settings are incorrect, click **Change settings**; otherwise, close the System control panel and skip to Step 4. In the System Properties dialog box, click **Change**. Type **NET-*XX*** in the "Computer name" text box (replacing *XX* with your student number), type **NETESS** in the Workgroup text box, and click **OK**. Click **OK** in the message box welcoming you to the NETESS workgroup, and then click **OK** in the message box stating that you must restart your computer. Click **Close**, and then click **Restart Now** to restart your computer. When the computer restarts, log on.

4. To see other computers on the network and share files, you need to verify that certain network settings are correct. Open the Network and Sharing Center by right-clicking **Start** and clicking **Control Panel**, and under Network and Internet, click **View network status and tasks**. In the "View your active networks" section, verify that the network is listed as "Private network."

5. Click **Change advanced sharing settings** to open the Advanced sharing settings dialog box (see Figure 1-22).

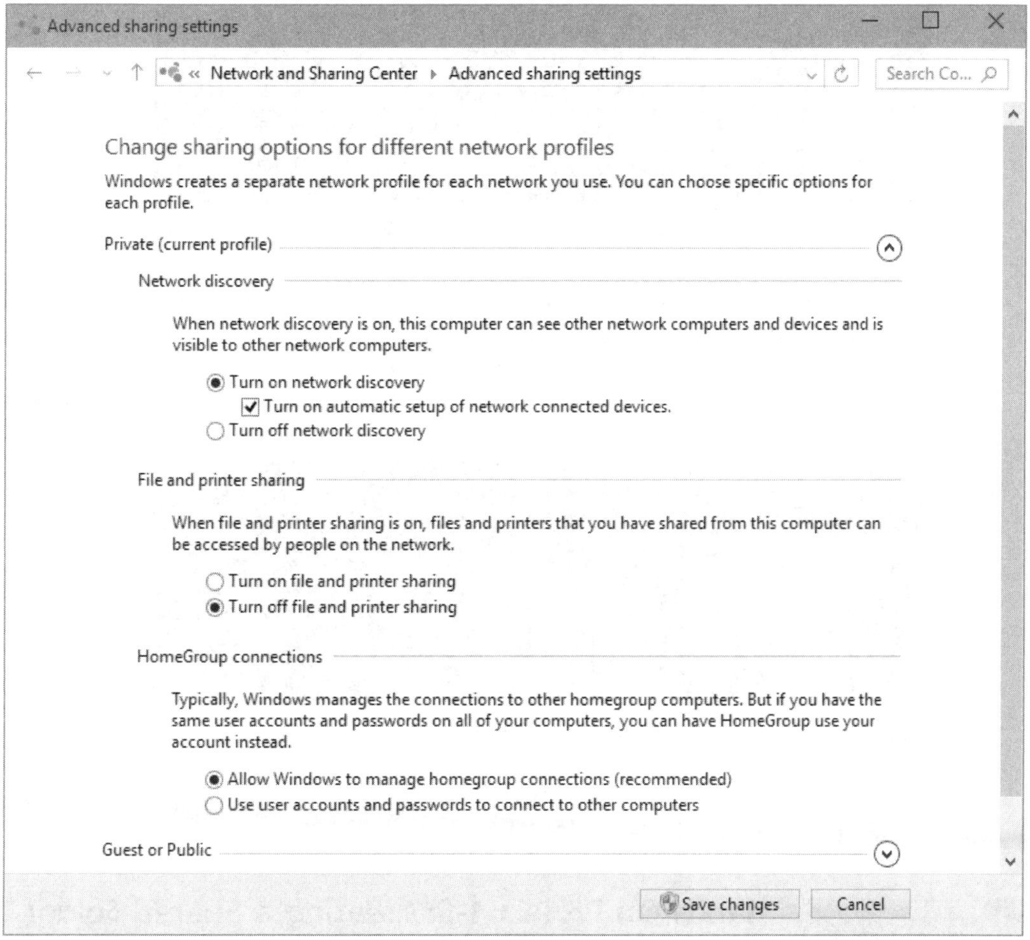

Change sharing options for different network profiles

Windows creates a separate network profile for each network you use. You can choose specific options for each profile.

Private (current profile) .... ⌃

   Network discovery

When network discovery is on, this computer can see other network computers and devices and is visible to other network computers.

    ● Turn on network discovery
      ☑ Turn on automatic setup of network connected devices.
    ○ Turn off network discovery

   File and printer sharing

When file and printer sharing is on, files and printers that you have shared from this computer can be accessed by people on the network.

    ○ Turn on file and printer sharing
    ● Turn off file and printer sharing

   HomeGroup connections

Typically, Windows manages the connections to other homegroup computers. But if you have the same user accounts and passwords on all of your computers, you can have HomeGroup use your account instead.

    ● Allow Windows to manage homegroup connections (recommended)
    ○ Use user accounts and passwords to connect to other computers

Guest or Public .... ⌄

[Save changes]   [Cancel]

Figure 1-22 The Advanced sharing settings dialog box

6. Under Network discovery, click the **Turn on network discovery** option button, if necessary. Under File and printer sharing, click the **Turn on file and printer sharing** option button, if necessary. If you had to make any changes, click the **Save changes** button; otherwise, click **Cancel**. Close all open windows.

7. Right-click **Start** and click **Command Prompt** to open a command prompt window.

8. At the command prompt, type **net view** and press **Enter**. You should see a list of computers in your workgroup, similar to Figure 1-23.

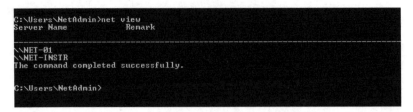

Figure 1-23 Using the `net view` command to list computers in a workgroup

9. To view shared resources on a computer, you use the `net view` *computername* command. For example, to see whether there are any shared folders or printers on the instructor's computer, type **net view net-instr** and press **Enter**. You should see a screen similar to Figure 1-24, in which the share name is listed as NetDocs and the type is listed as Disk.

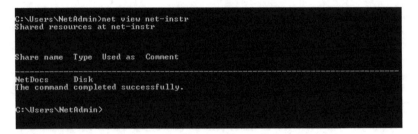

Figure 1-24 Viewing shared resources with the `net view` command

10. Close the command prompt window, but leave your computer running for the next project.

Hands-On Project 1-6: Creating a Shared Folder

Time Required: 15 minutes

Objective: Create a folder on your computer and share it with the rest of the network.

Required Tools and Equipment: Net-*XX*

Description: In this project, you create a folder and then share it so that other users can add files to the folder via the network. Your instructor might assign you a partner.

1. Start your computer, and log on as **NetAdmin**, if necessary.

2. Right-click **Start** and click **File Explorer**. Double-click the **D** drive (or another drive specified by your instructor). Right-click in the right-pane, point to **New**, and click **Folder**. Type **MyData**, and press **Enter** to name the folder.

3. Right-click **MyData** and click **Properties**. In the Properties dialog box, click the **Sharing** tab.

4. Click **Share**. In the File Sharing dialog box, click the list arrow and click **Everyone**. Click **Add**. Notice that the default permission level is Read. Click the **Read** list arrow, and then click the **Read/Write** permission level. Notice that the account you used to

create the share has the permission level Owner, which grants the user full access to the share, including the ability to change its permissions.

5. Click **Share** to finish sharing the folder. In the confirmation dialog box shown in Figure 1-25, notice the notation under the share name: \\NET-*XX*\MyData. It's the network path to the share that users on other computers can use to access the shared folder. This notation is the Universal Naming Convention (UNC) path, which you learn more about in Chapter 11. Click **Done**, and then click **Close**.

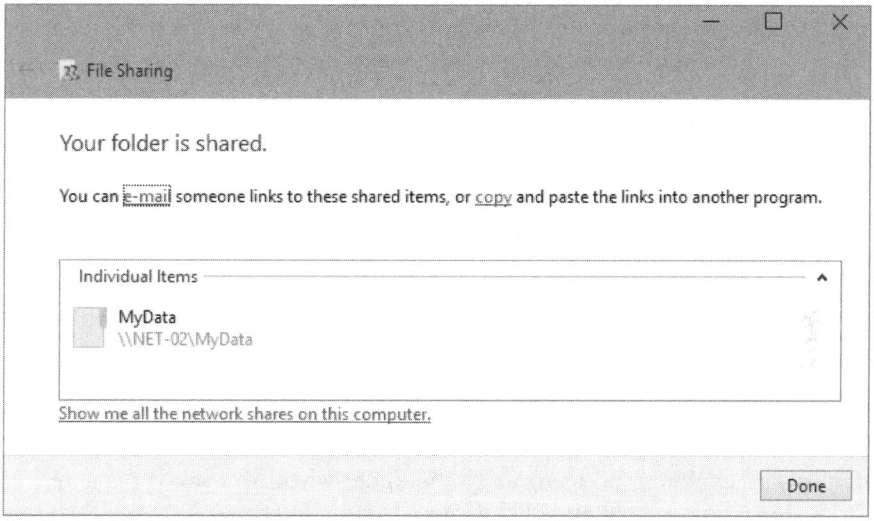

Figure 1-25 The confirmation dialog box displayed after creating a share

6. Try opening another student's shared folder by right-clicking **Start,** clicking **Run,** typing **\\NET-*XX*\MyData** (substituting your partner's student number for *XX*), and pressing **Enter.** A File Explorer window should open. To create a new file, right-click the File Explorer window, point to **New,** and click **Text Document.** Type your initials and press **Enter** to name the file.

7. To verify that your partner created a folder in your MyData share, open File Explorer, and then double-click the **D** drive and the **MyData** folder. If your partner finished Step 6, a new file should be there.

8. Close all open windows. You just performed some basic tasks associated with maintaining a network: creating shared folders and assigning permissions. You assigned Read/Write permissions to the Everyone group, which is a special group in Windows. All user accounts created on your computer belong to the Everyone group automatically, and you can't change this setting. You were able to access your partner's shared folder because you were both logged on to your computers with the same username and password, so you had the correct credentials.

9. Write down which network model was used in this activity:

_____

10. Close all open windows, but leave your computer running for the next project.

Hands-On Project 1-7: Transferring a Document to Another Computer

Time Required: 15 minutes

Objective: Create a document and copy it to your instructor's computer.

Required Tools and Equipment: Net-*XX*

Description: This project requires some setup by your instructor, so verify that the setup has been finished before continuing. In this project, you write a memo to your instructor containing the information specified in the following steps. Then you copy the file you created to a file share on your instructor's computer (or some other computer your instructor designates).

1. Start your computer, and log on as **NetAdmin**, if necessary.
2. Start Microsoft Word or another word-processing program; even a simple text editor, such as Notepad, will do. Write a letter to your instructor that includes the following:
   - The reason you're taking this class:
   - What you hope to get out of this class:
   - How much time you expect to put into this class each week outside classroom hours:
   - Whether you expect to take more computer and networking classes:
3. Save the document in your **Documents** folder (or a folder your instructor designates), naming it *yourname*. For example, if your name is Bill Smith, name the document **billsmith**.
4. Start File Explorer and navigate to the folder where you saved the letter. Right-click the document you created and click **Copy**.
5. To paste the document to the instructor's shared folder, use the UNC path of your instructor's computer, which should be \\Net-Instr\NetDocs, unless your instructor specifies otherwise. Click **Start**, type **\\Net-Instr\NetDocs**, and press **Enter**.
6. You should see a File Explorer window open. (The folder might contain documents if some of your classmates have already completed the activity.) Right-click a blank space on the right and click **Paste**. Your document should now be available on your instructor's computer.
7. Close all open windows, but leave your computer running for the next project.

Hands-On Project 1-8: Looking Up Computer and Networking Acronyms

Time Required: 20 minutes

Objective: Do online research to learn the meaning of common computer and networking acronyms.

Required Tools and Equipment: Net-*XX* and Internet access

Description: This project requires access to the Internet. Half the battle of learning any new field or technology is learning the language used by professionals in the field. Computer and networking technologies are well known for their heavy use of acronyms. In this project, you use the Acronym Finder Web site to look up acronyms.

1. Start your Web browser, and go to **www.acronymfinder.com**. Figure 1-26 shows the Acronym Finder home page.

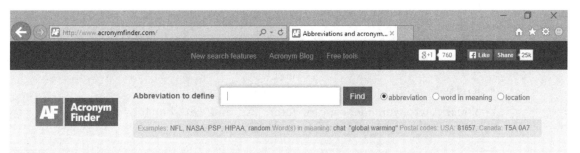

Find out what any acronym, abbreviation, or initialism stands for

With more than 1,000,000 human-edited definitions, Acronym Finder is the world's largest and most comprehensive dictionary of acronyms, abbreviations, and initialisms. Combined with the **Acronym Attic**, Acronym Finder contains more than 5 million acronyms and abbreviations. You can also **search** for more than 850,000 US and Canadian postal codes.

THE WALL STREET JOURNAL.
WSJ   "An exponentially expanding dictionary consulted by bureaucrats, translators, doctors, weapons designers and anyone else who needs help decrypting the wide world's daily output of acronyms"

 USA TODAY   "Get an astounding array of explanations for things like HRT and NASP. And if you're really bored, make up an acronym and see what it means"

The Washington Post   "What a fabulous find!"   More press coverage

You can search or filter terms from the following categories:

Information Technology (IT)
Information technology, Internet/Web, telecommunications, computing & computer science, hardware, software, etc. (over 86,000 definitions)
Examples: AJAX, CMM, DHCP, FTP, HTTP, PDA, RSS, SDK, TCP, WWW

Science & Medicine
Popular science, hard science, medicine, nature, engineering, physics, space, astronomy, geology, chemistry, etc. (over 145,000 definitions)
Examples: ACL, DNA, HEPA, LASER, MRI, PTFE, SSRI, TIA, TENS, VOC

Figure 1-26 The Acronym Finder home page

Source: *www.acronymfinder.com*

Web locations and Web pages change constantly. Don't worry if the Acronym Finder home page looks a little different from the example—you should still be able to navigate it in much the same way.

2. You can look up acronyms by typing them in the "Abbreviation to define" text box at the top and clicking the **Find** button. If there's more than one common definition for an acronym, Acronym Finder lists them by popularity ranking. Look up the following acronyms; you'll need some of them later:

- TCP/IP
- Wi-Fi
- SSID

- WEP
- OSI
- Ping
- UTP
- Cat6
- EMI
- RJ-45

3. Bookmark Acronymfinder.com for future use, and exit your browser. Shut down your computer, unless you're continuing to the case projects.

Chapter Summary

- All computers perform three basic tasks: input, processing, and output. Some components of computers are designed to perform only one of these three functions; others are designed to perform two or all three functions.

- Storage is a major part of a computer's configuration. Storage types include short-term storage (RAM) and long-term storage (disk drives and USB or flash drives).

- PC hardware consists of four major components: motherboard, hard drive, RAM, and BIOS/CMOS. The motherboard is the nerve center of the computer and contains the CPU, expansion slots, and RAM slots.

- The components needed to make a stand-alone computer a networked computer include a NIC, a network medium, and usually an interconnecting device. In addition, network software consisting of client and server software, protocols, and the NIC driver are needed to enable a computer to communicate on a network.

- The layers of the network communication process can be summarized as user application, network software, network protocol, and network interface.

- The terms for describing networks of different scopes are LAN, internetwork, WAN, and MAN. A LAN is a single collection of devices operating in a small geographic area. An internetwork is a collection of LANs tied together by routers, and a WAN and MAN are geographically dispersed internetworks.

- Packets and frames are the units of data handled by different network components. Packets, which are processed by the network protocol, are units of data with the source and destination IP addresses added. Frames, which are processed by the network interface, have MAC addresses and an error-checking code added to the packet.

- A client is the computer or network software that requests network data, and a server is the computer or network software that makes network data available to requesting clients.

- A peer-to-peer network model has no centralized authority over resources; a server-based network usually uses a directory service for centralized logon, security settings, and resource management.

Key Terms

Active Directory   The directory service used by Windows servers.

bus   A collection of wires that carry data from one place to another on a computer's motherboard.

client   The term used to describe an OS designed mainly to access network resources, a computer's primary role in a network (running user applications and accessing network resources), and software that requests network resources from servers.

core   An instance of a processor inside a single CPU chip. *See also* multicore CPU.

credentials   A username and password or another form of identity used to access a computer.

directory service   The software that manages centralized access and security in a server-based network.

domain   A collection of users and computers in a server-based network whose accounts are managed by Windows servers called "domain controllers." *See also* domain controller.

domain controller   A computer running Windows Server with Active Directory installed; maintains a database of user and computer accounts as well as network access policies in a Windows domain. *See also* directory service.

encapsulation   The process of adding header and trailer information to chunks of data.

extranet   A private network that allows limited and controlled access to internal network resources by outside users, usually in a business-to-business situation.

frame   A packet with source and destination MAC addresses added and an error-checking code added to the back end. Frames are generated by and processed by the network interface. *See also* packet.

header   Information added to the front end of a chunk of data so that the data can be correctly interpreted and processed by network protocols.

Internet   A worldwide public internetwork that uses standard protocols, such as TCP/IP, DNS, and HTTP, to transfer and view information.

internetwork   A networked collection of LANs tied together by devices such as routers. *See also* local area network (LAN).

intranet   A private network in which devices and servers are available only to users connected to the internal network.

local area network (LAN)   A small network, limited to a single collection of machines and linked by interconnecting devices in a small geographic area.

metropolitan area network (MAN)   An internetwork confined to a geographic region, such as a city or county; uses third-party communication providers to provide connectivity between locations. *See also* internetwork.

multicore CPU   A CPU containing two or more processing cores. *See also* core.

name server A computer that stores names and addresses of computers on a network, allowing other computers to use computer names rather than addresses to communicate with one another.

network Two or more computers connected by a transmission medium that allows them to communicate.

network client software The application or OS service that can request information stored on another computer.

network model A model defining how and where resources are shared and how access to these resources is regulated.

network protocols The software defining the rules and formats a computer must use when sending information across the network.

network server software The software that allows a computer to share its resources by fielding requests generated by network clients.

packet A chunk of data with source and destination IP addresses (as well as other IP information) added to it. Packets are generated by and processed by network protocols.

peer-to-peer network A network model in which all computers can function as clients or servers as needed, and there's no centralized control over network resources.

server The term used to describe an OS designed mainly to share network resources, a computer with the main role of giving client computers access to network resources, and the software that responds to requests for network resources from client computers.

server-based network A network model in which servers take on specialized roles to provide client computers with network services and to maintain centralized control over network resources.

stand-alone computer A computer that doesn't have the necessary hardware or software to communicate on a network.

trailer Information added to the back end of a chunk of data so that the data can be correctly interpreted and processed by network protocols.

wide area networks (WANs) Internetworks that are geographically dispersed and use third-party communication providers to provide connectivity between locations. *See also* internetwork.

Review Questions

1. Which of the following is a basic function a computer performs? (Choose all that apply.)

    a. Processing

    b. Internet access

    c. Input

    d. Graphics

    e. Output

    f. E-mail

2. The _____ executes instructions provided by computer programs.

   a. CPU

   b. NIC

   c. hard drive

   d. USB

3. When a CPU has two or more processors, each one is referred to as a(n) _____.

   a. I/O

   b. core

   c. OS

   d. flash

4. Which of the following is considered long-term storage? (Choose all that apply.)

   a. USB or flash drive

   b. RAM

   c. Working storage

   d. Hard drive

5. Which motherboard component controls data transfers between memory, expansion slots, I/O devices, and the CPU?

   a. RAM slots

   b. IDE connectors

   c. Chipset

   d. PCI-Express

6. You want to purchase a high-performance graphics card for your computer. Which type of connector should it have?

   a. PCI

   b. SATA

   c. IDE

   d. PCI-Express

7. The time it takes for read/write heads to move to the correct spot on the platter is called which of the following?

   a. Rotational delay

   b. Seek time

   c. Transfer time

   d. Access time

8. Which of the following is a task usually performed by the BIOS? (Choose all that apply.)

   a. Perform a POST.

   b. Create an interrupt.

   c. Store the operating system.

   d. Begin the boot procedure.

9. Place the following steps of the boot procedure in order.

   a. The OS is loaded into RAM.

   b. CPU starts.

   c. OS services are started.

   d. Power is applied.

   e. The POST is executed.

   f. Boot devices are searched.

10. You have just installed a new NIC in your PC to replace the old one that had started malfunctioning. What additional software must be installed to allow the OS to communicate with the new NIC?

    a. Network application

    b. Device driver

    c. BIOS

    d. Protocol

11. Which of the following requests information stored on another computer?

    a. NIC

    b. Network client

    c. Network server

    d. Network protocol

    e. Device driver

12. Choose the correct order for the process of a user attempting to access network resources:

    1. Network protocol

    2. Application

    3. Network client

    4. NIC driver

       a. 4, 2, 1, 3

       b. 3, 2, 1, 4

       c. 1, 4, 2, 3

       d. 2, 3, 1, 4

       e. 3, 1, 2, 4

13. TCP/IP is an example of which of the following?

    a. NIC

    b. Network client

    c. Network server

    d. Network protocol

    e. Device driver

14. In network communication, the _____ address is used to deliver a frame to the correct computer on the network. (Choose all that apply.)

    a. MAC

    b. logical

    c. IP

    d. physical

15. A(n) _____ message is used to determine whether a computer is listening on the network.

    a. MAC

    b. ping

    c. IP

    d. TCP

16. TCP/IP uses _____ to look up a computer's IP address, given its name.

    a. DNS

    b. ping

    c. MAC

    d. TCP

17. The unit of information containing MAC addresses and an error-checking code that's processed by the network interface layer is called a _____.

    a. packet

    b. ping

    c. frame

    d. chunk

18. Data is processed from the time an application creates it to the time it reaches the network medium. This process includes adding information such as addresses and is called which of the following?

    a. Packetization

    b. Encapsulation

    c. Deencapsulation

    d. Layering

19. You're the network administrator for a company that has just expanded from one floor to two floors of a large building, and the number of workstations you need has doubled from 50 to 100. You're concerned that network performance will suffer if you add computers to the existing LAN. In addition, new users will be working in a separate business unit, and there are reasons to logically separate the two groups of computers. What type of network should you configure?

    a. WAN

    b. MAN

    c. Internetwork

    d. Extended LAN

20. Which of the following best describes a client?

    a. A computer's primary role in the network is to give other computers access to network resources and services.

    b. A computer's primary role in the network is to run user applications and access network resources.

    c. It's the software that responds to requests for network resources.

    d. The OS installed on a computer is designed mainly to share network resources.

21. You work for a small company with four users who need to share information on their computers. The budget is tight, so the network must be as inexpensive as possible. What type of network should you install?

    a. Server-based network

    b. Peer-to-peer network

    c. Wide area network

    d. Storage area network

22. Which of the following characteristics is associated with a peer-to-peer network? (Choose all that apply.)

    a. Decentralized data storage

    b. Inexpensive

    c. User-managed resources

    d. Centralized control

    e. Uses a directory service

23. A device interconnects five computers and a printer in a single office so that users can share the printer. This configuration is an example of which of the following?

    a. LAN

    b. MAN

    c. WAN

    d. Internetwork

24. A company has just made an agreement with another organization to share their two networks' resources by using TCP/IP protocols. What best describes this arrangement?

    a. MAN

    b. LAN

    c. Intranet

    d. Extranet

25. You have installed Windows Server 2012 on a new server and want to centralize user logons and security policies. What type of software should you install and configure on this server?

    a. Naming services

    b. Application services

    c. Communication services

    d. Directory services

26. Peer-to-peer networks aren't suitable in which of the following situations?

    a. Tight security is required.

    b. Five or fewer users need network access.

    c. Budget is the primary consideration.

    d. No one uses the network heavily.

Critical Thinking

The following activities give you critical thinking challenges. Challenge labs (which start in Chapter 2) give you an opportunity to use the skills you have learned to perform a task without step-by-step instructions. Case projects offer a practical networking setup for which you supply a written solution.

Case Project 1-1

Networking Gadgets, Inc., currently employs 8 people but plans to hire 10 more in the next four months. Users will work on multiple projects, and only users assigned to a project should have access to the project files. You're instructed to set up the network to make it easy to manage and back up yet still provide centralized storage for project files. Would you choose a peer-to-peer network, a server-based network, or a combination? Why?

Case Project 1-2

CNT Books hired you as a productivity consultant. Currently, it employs six people who will be moving into new office space. You are to configure a network that allows them to share files and printers. Employees must also be able to control resources on their own machines. The company wants the most inexpensive solution and only minimal training for employees. Would you choose a peer-to-peer network or a server-based network? Write a list of supplies you might need to purchase to perform this task. What computer configuration tasks might you need to perform?

Case Project 1-3

CNT Books has expanded considerably since you got the network up and running three years ago. It now occupies an entire floor in the building, and its LAN has grown to include several servers and more than 60 workstations. CNT Books has recently purchased another book company and needs more space and computers. Expansion plans include leasing another floor four stories above the current offices in the same building and adding 35 workstations and at least one more server immediately, with additional equipment purchases expected. What type of network is called for—LAN, WAN, MAN, or internetwork? What additional devices might be needed to ensure efficient network communication?

Case Project 1-4

Chapter 2 discusses network hardware. To prepare for this topic, search for the following terms online. Read at least one article about each term and be prepared to discuss these terms in class:

- Network interface card
- Hub
- Switch
- Router

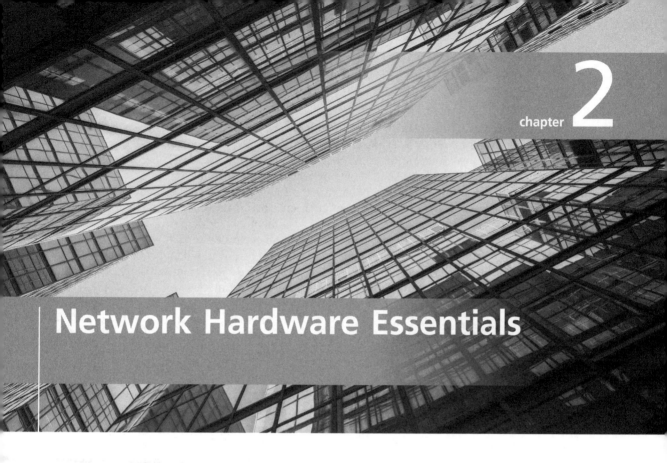

Network Hardware Essentials

After reading this chapter and completing the exercises, you will be able to:

- Describe the basic operation of network repeaters and hubs
- Explain the purpose of network switches
- Summarize the operation of wireless access points
- Describe the basic operation of network interface cards
- Explain the function of routers

LANs, WANs, MANs, and internetworks are built with a variety of network hardware. Your understanding of how the most common network hardware works is crucial to your success in building reliable, high-performance networks.

This chapter begins by discussing the simplest of network devices: the hub, a device that's nearly obsolete but is still found in older installations. Switches have largely supplanted hubs in networks large and small and are the main network building block today. Wireless networking can be found everywhere from small home networks to coffee shops and bookstores to large corporate networks. Wireless access points are the foundation of wireless networks, and you learn about their operation and basic configuration later in this chapter. Network interface cards have become such an essential component of computers that they're now built into most motherboards. Whether they're built in or installed as an expansion card, however, your understanding of NIC configuration options and properties will help you build a better network. The last section of this chapter covers the most complex network devices: routers, the gateway to the Internet that make it possible for large companies to build vast internetworks and WANs.

 Because Ethernet is the dominant network technology used in LANs today, the network hardware components discussed in this chapter are Ethernet devices, unless otherwise stated.

Network hardware devices can be complex. This chapter serves as an introduction to the most common devices so that you have a basic understanding of their function when they're discussed with other topics in later chapters. The function of these devices is intertwined with network topologies and technologies (discussed in Chapter 3) and network protocols (discussed in Chapter 5). Chapter 8 includes a more thorough examination of the devices described in this chapter and discusses some specialized devices as well.

Network Repeaters and Hubs

Table 2-1 summarizes what you need for the hands-on projects in this chapter.

Table 2-1 Hands-on project requirements

Hands-on project	Requirements	Time required	Notes
Hands-On Project 2-1: Using Wireshark with a Hub	Three computers, three patch cables, hub	20 minutes	
Hands-On Project 2-2: Using Wireshark with a Switch	Three computers, three patch cables, switch	20 minutes	
Hands-On Project 2-3: Examining Hub and Switch Indicator Lights and Uplink Ports	Three computers, four patch cables, two hubs, switch	30 minutes	
Hands-On Project 2-4: Connecting to a Wireless Access Point	Two computers with wireless NICs, wireless AP or router	15 minutes	
Hands-On Project 2-5: Communicating over a Router	Three computers, two switches, router, five patch cables	20 minutes	
Hands-On Project 2-6: Using Trace Route to See How Packets Travel Through the Internet	Net-XX	15 minutes	Internet access

Early networks didn't use interconnecting devices. Computers were connected in daisy-chain fashion by lengths of cable (see Figure 2-1). The problem with this arrangement was that you were limited in the total length of the cabling and the number of computers that could be connected.

Figure 2-1 Older networks didn't use interconnecting devices

Some problems associated with the type of network shown in Figure 2-1 were solved with a device called a "repeater." A **repeater** has the rather straightforward job of receiving bit signals generated by NICs and other devices, strengthening them, and then sending them along or repeating them to other parts of the network. Think of a repeater as a microphone for network signals. When people speak, their voices carry only so far until people in the back of the room can no longer hear what's being said. Network signals, too, carry only so far on their medium before receiving computers can no longer interpret them correctly. A repeater enables you to connect computers whose distance from one another would otherwise make communication impossible.

 Repeaters don't strengthen signals in the sense that the original signal is amplified; instead, a repeater takes a weakened signal and repeats it at its original strength.

A traditional repeater has two ports or connections that you can use to extend the distance your network can cover, as shown in Figure 2-2. Assuming the two groups of computers in

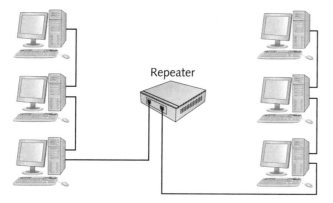

Repeater

Figure 2-2 A repeater extends the distance a network can cover

this figure are separated by several hundred feet, the repeater is needed to allow them to communicate with one another.

Multiport Repeaters and Hubs

A multiport repeater is just a repeater with several ports you can connect cabling to. Most multiport repeaters have at least four ports, and some have 24 or more. A multiport repeater is commonly called a **hub**, and although it performs the same function as a traditional repeater, it's used as a central connecting device for computers instead of merely a way to extend the network. So instead of daisy-chaining computers together, all computers are connected to the central hub (see Figure 2-3), as you saw in Chapter 1. Because "hub" is the more common term and is much easier to write and say, a multiport repeater is often referred to as a "hub" in this book.

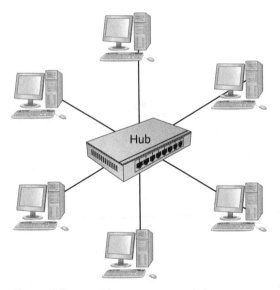

Figure 2-3   A multiport repeater or hub

A hub performs the same function as a repeater but with more outgoing ports to which bit signals are repeated, so its function is as follows:

- Receives bit signals generated from a connected computer on one of its ports (with all ports capable of receiving signals)
- Cleans the signal by filtering out electrical noise
- Regenerates the signal to full strength
- Transmits the regenerated signal to all other ports a computer (or other network device) is connected to

Like repeaters, hubs require power to operate, so they're sometimes referred to as "active hubs." However, this term isn't common because unpowered devices known as "passive hubs" aren't used for the same purposes.

Simulation 3 shows basic hub operation.

Simulation 3: Basic operation of a hub

Hubs and Network Bandwidth Network **bandwidth** is the amount of data that can be transferred on a network during a specific interval. It's usually measured in bits per second, and networks operate at speeds from 10 million bits per second (10 Mbps) up to 10 gigabits per second (Gbps). This bandwidth is determined by how fast network devices can send bits of data to the medium. A 10 Mbps hub, for example, transmits bits at the rate of 10 million per second. To put this rate into perspective, two computers connected to a 10 Mbps hub can copy one minute of MP3 music to each other in about 1.25 seconds, but a 100 Mbps hub can transfer the same amount of information in about one eighth of a second.

One drawback of using hubs as the central connecting device on a network is that only one computer can transmit data at a time. On a busy network with dozens of computers transferring large files and accessing network applications and databases, this limitation is serious. This setup is called **bandwidth sharing** because all computers connected to the hub must share the amount of bandwidth the hub provides. For example, a network has 10 computers connected to a 10 Mbps hub, and all 10 computers are trying to send and receive files frequently. Because the computers must share the bandwidth, the average effective bandwidth for each computer is only 1 Mbps. Transferring that one minute of MP3 music in this example takes more than 12 seconds.

In the early days of networking, bandwidth sharing wasn't a big problem because the number and frequency of data transfers in a typical LAN were low and files tended to be small, making the actual effective bandwidth in the preceding example much higher than 1 Mbps. However, large multimedia data files are transferred often in LANs now, so the need for additional dedicated bandwidth is paramount. In fact, this need has become so critical that network administrators stopped including hubs in their network designs, and finding a hub to buy from major computer parts retailers is difficult now.

There are more details involved in the concept of bandwidth sharing and how computers transmit data to the medium. The details vary for different network technologies, such as Ethernet, token ring, and Wi-Fi, and are hammered out in Chapter 3.

Hub Indicator Lights Most hubs have indicator lights for power, link status, network activity, and collisions. Each port has a link status indicator (link light) that glows (usually green) when a cable has been plugged in and a valid network connection, or link, has been made to a device on the other end of the cable. Some hubs have a separate indicator, or the indicator might vary in color for different connection speeds. For example, the link light might glow green for a 100 Mbps connection and amber for a 10 Mbps connection.

Another indicator light you're likely to find on a hub is for network activity. When the hub receives bit signals on any of its ports, this indicator flashes. Some hubs combine the link status indicator with the network activity indicator so that when the light is on solidly, a valid link is detected, and when the light is blinking, a valid link and network activity are detected.

A third type of indicator is for collisions. A collision occurs on a hub when two stations try to transmit at the same time, which isn't allowed on a hub-based network. When a collision occurs, the stations that were transmitting must retransmit their data. Collisions are discussed in more detail in Chapter 3.

Figure 2-4 shows a typical hub with indicator lights. This hub also has a series of indicator lights showing the utilization percentage for the network. In addition, the rightmost port has a button next to it for changing the port's configuration, depending on whether it's connected to a computer's NIC or another hub or switch. This port is referred to as the **uplink port**. The term "uplink" is used when multiple hubs or switches are connected. When this button is pressed in, you can connect the hub to another hub or switch with a standard cable rather than a crossover cable. Cable types are discussed more in Chapter 4.

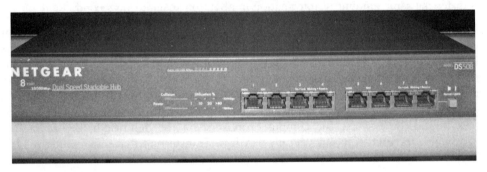

Figure 2-4 A typical hub with indicator lights

Network hubs were the mainstay for connecting computers in a LAN for several years, but although you can still find hubs in the workplace, they're becoming obsolete. Because of their disadvantages, mainly bandwidth sharing, they're being replaced with switches, discussed in the next section.

Network Switches

A network **switch**, like a hub, is used to interconnect multiple computers so that they can communicate with one another. A switch looks just like a hub, with several ports for plugging in network cables. However, instead of simply regenerating incoming bit signals and repeating them to all other ports, a switch actually reads data in the message, determines which port the destination device is connected to, and forwards the message to only that port. So the first important difference between hubs and switches is that hubs work only with electrical signals and the bits these signals represent, whereas switches work with the actual information these bits combine to make frames.

Basic Switch Operation

Data is sent to the medium one frame at a time, and the beginning of each frame contains the destination computer's MAC address and the source computer's MAC address. When the frame reaches a switch, the switch reads both addresses. By reading the source MAC address, the switch keeps a record of which port the sending computer is on. This function is referred to as "learning" because the switch is learning to which port each MAC address in the network corresponds. By reading the destination MAC address, the switch can forward the frame to the port the destination computer is on. A switch maintains a **switching table** (see Figure 2-5) of MAC addresses that have been learned and their associated port numbers.

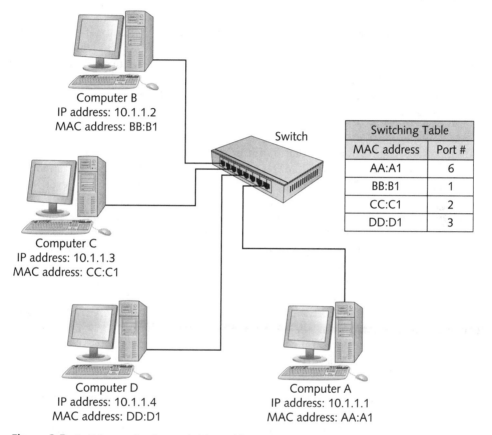

Switching Table	
MAC address	Port #
AA:A1	6
BB:B1	1
CC:C1	2
DD:D1	3

Figure 2-5 Switches maintain a switching table

MAC addresses are 12 hexadecimal digits. Figure 2-5 uses shorter addresses only as an example.

A switch's operation can be summarized in these steps:

1. The switch receives a frame.
2. The switch reads the source and destination MAC addresses.
3. The switch looks up the destination MAC address in its switching table.
4. The switch forwards the frame to the port where the computer owning the MAC address is found.
5. The switching table is updated with the source MAC address and port information.

Simulation 4 shows basic switch operation.

Simulation 4: Basic operation of a switch

These steps raise some questions. For example, what happens if the switch doesn't find the destination MAC address in its switching table? In this case, the switch does the most reasonable thing: It forwards the frame to all ports. You can think of a switch as acting like a switchboard operator. When a call comes in for a person the operator knows, the operator can forward the call to the correct phone extension. If the call is for a person the operator doesn't know, the person can be paged via an intercom system.

You might also be wondering what happens if the source address is already in the switching table and how long each MAC address stays in the switching table. The answers to these questions are related. MAC addresses can't stay in the switching table forever because computers might be shut down or moved to other locations, and their MAC addresses can change. Leaving MAC addresses in the switching table for a long time is akin to having an out-of-date employee phone directory that still lists people who have left the company and others who have changed locations. To ensure that the switching table doesn't become out of date, a timestamp is included in each entry, and each entry can stay in the table for only a certain amount of time unless the timestamp is updated. So when a switch first sees a source MAC address, it creates the switching table entry that includes the MAC address, the port from which the frame arrived, and a timestamp. If the same MAC address is seen again coming from the same port, the timestamp is updated. If the entry remains in the table beyond the maximum allowed time (which varies between switches but is often about 5 minutes) without being updated, it's deleted.

Switches and Network Bandwidth Because a switch is capable of forwarding frames to only a single port instead of all ports, as a hub does, it can handle several computer conversations at one time, thereby allowing each device the full network bandwidth, or **dedicated bandwidth**, instead of requiring bandwidth sharing. In other words, if the switch in Figure 2-5 is a 10 Mbps switch, Computer A could communicate with Computer C at an uninterrupted 10 Mbps rate, and Computer B could communicate with Computer D at 10 Mbps simultaneously. Furthermore, each computer can receive data at 10 Mbps at the same time it's sending data at 10 Mbps, making each conversation between computers effectively 20 Mbps (10 Mbps in both directions). When a device can send data and receive data simultaneously, it's called **full-duplex mode**. When a device can send or receive, but not both at the same time, it's called **half-duplex mode**. Hubs operate only in half-duplex mode, but switches can operate in both half-duplex and full-duplex modes. To use another form of communication as an example, full-duplex mode is like talking on a telephone and half-duplex mode is like talking on a walkie-talkie. Chapter 3 describes these modes of communication in more detail.

The performance advantage of switches has made them the device of choice in networks of all sizes. In addition, although they used to cost more than hubs because of their higher complexity, this is no longer the case. As mentioned, you can still find hubs in the workplace, but new installations rarely specify them, and the tables have been turned—hubs are now usually more expensive than switches because manufacturers simply aren't making them in large quantities.

Switch Indicator Lights Like hubs, switches have indicator lights so that you can see the basic operating status of the ports with a quick glance. Aside from the requisite power indicator, switches have link status indicators and activity indicators. They might also have indicators to show whether a port is operating in full-duplex or half-duplex mode. Switches, like hubs, can be connected to one another so that your LAN can grow beyond the limitations of the number of ports on a single switch. Some switches also have a dedicated port for uplinking to another switch. **Uplinking** is making a connection between devices such as two switches, usually for the purpose of expanding a network. Switches are complex devices, and this section just introduces their basic operation. You can find a more detailed examination of switches in Chapter 8.

Hands-On Project 2-1: Using Wireshark with a Hub

Time Required: 20 minutes

Objective: Use the Wireshark protocol analyzer on a computer connected to other computers via a hub to see that all data is repeated to all stations.

Required Tools and Equipment: Three lab computers, three patch cables, and a hub. Review the lab setup instructions in "Before You Begin" for more information on lab equipment.

Description: In this project, you run Wireshark on a group of computers connected via a hub. This project shows that a hub repeats all data to all stations so that Wireshark can capture packets generated by all stations. In the next project, you compare this behavior with a switch.

This project requires at least three computers connected to a hub, with at least one computer running Wireshark. It's probably best done in groups. The steps in this project assume three computers are connected to the hub and labeled Computer1, Computer2, and Computer3. Wireshark must be installed on Computer1, but it can be installed on all computers. It's preferable that the computers aren't attached to the classroom network and don't have access to the Internet.

1. Connect three lab computers to a hub with patch cables. Make sure the device is a hub, not a switch.

2. Turn on the computers and log on as **NetAdmin**. Open a command prompt window on each computer. (In Windows 10, right-click **Start** and click **Command Prompt**.) On each computer, type **ipconfig** and press **Enter** to display its IP address configuration. Write down these IPv4 addresses so that you know each computer's address:

   - Computer1: _____
   - Computer2: _____
   - Computer3: _____

3. To verify connectivity, type **ping *IPaddress*** from each computer and press **Enter** (replacing *IPaddress* with another computer's IP address). Repeat this step until you have successfully pinged each computer from the other computers.

If the pings aren't successful, you might need to turn off Windows Firewall. To do so, right-click Start and click Control Panel, and under Network and Internet, click "View network status and tasks." In the Network and Sharing Center, click Windows Firewall at the lower left, and then click Turn Windows Firewall on or off. Under Public network location settings, click Turn off Windows Firewall, and then click OK. Close the Windows Firewall window, and repeat Step 3.

4. On Computer1, start Wireshark. (If Wireshark isn't on your desktop, right-click **Start**, click **Run**, type **Wireshark** in the text box, and press **Enter**.)

5. By default, Wireshark captures all the packets your NIC sees. You want to limit the packets to only those created by the ping command, so click **Capture Options** on the left (see Figure 2-6). In the Capture Filter text box, type **icmp**. You must use lowercase letters. (Internet Control Message Protocol [ICMP] packets are created by the ping command.) Click **Start**.

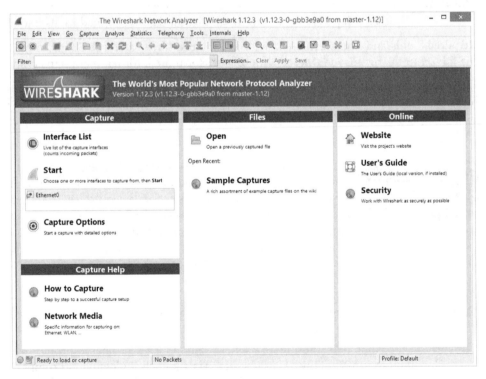

Figure 2-6   The Wireshark main window

Source: Wireshark Foundation, *www.wireshark.org*

6. First, you ping from Computer2 to Computer1. On Computer2, type **ping *IPaddress*** at the command prompt and press **Enter** (replacing *IPaddress* with the IP address of Computer1).

7. On Computer1, click the **Stop the running live capture** toolbar icon to stop the capture. You should see a window similar to Figure 2-7.

Stop the running
live capture

Figure 2-7 Ping packets captured on Computer1

Source: Wireshark Foundation, *www.wireshark.org*

8. On Computer1, click **Capture, Start** from the Wireshark menu. Click **Continue without Saving**.

9. Next, you ping from Computer2 to Computer3. On Computer2, type `ping IPaddress` at the command prompt and press **Enter** (replacing *IPaddress* with the IP address of Computer3). Wireshark running on Computer1 should have captured the ping packets. Stop the capture and exit Wireshark. Why are the packets sent between Computer2 and Computer3 captured by Computer1?

_____

_____

10. Close the command prompt window, and shut down all computers.

Hands-On Project 2-2: Using Wireshark with a Switch

Time Required: 20 minutes

Objective: Use Wireshark on a computer connected to other computers via a switch to see that all data isn't repeated to all stations.

Required Tools and Equipment: The same requirements as Hands-On Project 2-1, replacing the hub with a switch

Description: In this project, you run Wireshark on a group of computers connected via a switch. This project shows that a switch only forwards data to the station to which the frame is addressed. In Hands-On Project 2-1, you configured Wireshark to capture only ICMP packets. In this project, you configure Wireshark to also capture Address Resolution Protocol (ARP) broadcast packets to show that switches forward broadcasts to all stations.

1. Connect the computers you used in Hands-On Project 2-1 to a switch instead of a hub, using the same patch cables you used previously.

2. Turn on the computers, and log on as **NetAdmin**. Open an elevated command prompt window on each computer by right-clicking **Start** and clicking **Command Prompt (Admin)**. Click **Yes** in the User Account Control (UAC) message box. If the computers were shut down or restarted, their IP addresses might have changed. Type `ipconfig` and press **Enter** on each computer. Write down each computer's IP address again:

   - Computer1: _____
   - Computer2: _____
   - Computer3: _____

3. To make sure you have connectivity with the switch, at each computer, type `ping IPaddress` and press **Enter** (replacing `IPaddress` with the IP address of another computer). Repeat this step until you have successfully pinged each computer from all other computers. Leave the command prompt window open.

4. At each computer, type `arp -d` and press **Enter**. As mentioned in Chapter 1, ARP manages the MAC addresses your computer has learned. This command deletes the entries created from the pings in Step 3 so that the computers have to learn the MAC addresses of other computers again. Leave the command prompt window open.

5. On Computer1, start Wireshark, and click **Capture Options**. In the Capture Filter text box, type **icmp or arp.** (You must use lowercase letters.) This capture filter tells Wireshark to capture only ICMP or ARP packets. Click **Start**.

6. On Computer2 at the command prompt, type `ping IPaddress` and press **Enter** (replacing `IPaddress` with the IP address of Computer1).

7. On Computer1, click the **Stop the running live capture** toolbar icon. You should see a window similar to Figure 2-8. Notice that the first ARP packet you see has the destination address "Broadcast." Click this packet, and the middle pane displays the MAC address ff:ff::ff:ff:ff:ff.

8. On Computer1, click **Capture**, **Start** from the Wireshark menu, and then click **Continue without Saving**.

9. On Computer2 at the command prompt, type `ping IPaddress` and press **Enter** (replacing `IPaddress` with the IP address of Computer3). Wireshark running on Computer1 should have captured only the ARP broadcast packet, not the actual ping ICMP packets, which are unicast packets (explained later in "NIC Basics"). Because the switch doesn't forward unicast packets except to the intended destination, Computer1 never received the ping packets between Computer2 and Computer3. Stop the capture in Wireshark. Why did Computer1 capture the ARP packets from Computer2 and Computer3 but not the ICMP packets?

```
◢                    *Ethernet0 (icmp or arp)  [Wireshark 1.12.3  (v1.12.3-0-gbb3e9a0 from master-1.12)]        – ☐ ✕
File  Edit  View  Go  Capture  Analyze  Statistics  Telephony  Tools  Internals  Help
◎ ◉ ◢ ■ ◢ | ▣ 🖺 ✕ ⟳ | 🔍 ← → ⇗ 🐦 🔽 🔼 | ▤ ▥ | 🔍 🔍 🔍 ▣ | ▥ ☑ ▦ ✕ | 🗔
Filter:                                        ∨  Expression... Clear  Apply  Save
No.    Time        Source            Destination        Protocol  Length  Info
     1 0.00000000  Vmware_ba:c7:4b   Broadcast          ARP       60  who has 192.168.106.128?  Tell 192.168.106.129
     2 0.00002900  Vmware_92:0d:f1   Vmware_ba:c7:4b    ARP       42  192.168.106.128 is at 00:0c:29:92:0d:f1
     3 0.00022500  192.168.106.129   192.168.106.128    ICMP      74  Echo (ping) request  id=0x0001, seq=24/6144, ttl=128
     4 0.00030500  192.168.106.128   192.168.106.129    ICMP      74  Echo (ping) reply    id=0x0001, seq=24/6144, ttl=128
     5 1.00755100  192.168.106.129   192.168.106.128    ICMP      74  Echo (ping) request  id=0x0001, seq=25/6400, ttl=128
     6 1.00763600  192.168.106.128   192.168.106.129    ICMP      74  Echo (ping) reply    id=0x0001, seq=25/6400, ttl=128
     7 2.02270400  192.168.106.129   192.168.106.128    ICMP      74  Echo (ping) request  id=0x0001, seq=26/6656, ttl=128
     8 2.02279800  192.168.106.128   192.168.106.129    ICMP      74  Echo (ping) reply    id=0x0001, seq=26/6656, ttl=128
     9 3.03875500  192.168.106.129   192.168.106.128    ICMP      74  Echo (ping) request  id=0x0001, seq=27/6912, ttl=128
    10 3.03883700  192.168.106.128   192.168.106.129    ICMP      74  Echo (ping) reply    id=0x0001, seq=27/6912, ttl=128

⊞ Frame 1: 60 bytes on wire (480 bits), 60 bytes captured (480 bits) on interface 0
⊞ Ethernet II, Src: Vmware_ba:c7:4b (00:0c:29:ba:c7:4b), Dst: Broadcast (ff:ff:ff:ff:ff:ff)
⊟ Address Resolution Protocol (request)
     Hardware type: Ethernet (1)
     Protocol type: IP (0x0800)
     Hardware size: 6
     Protocol size: 4
     Opcode: request (1)
     Sender MAC address: Vmware_ba:c7:4b (00:0c:29:ba:c7:4b)
     Sender IP address: 192.168.106.129 (192.168.106.129)
     Target MAC address: 00:00:00_00:00:00 (00:00:00:00:00:00)

0000  ff ff ff ff ff ff 00 0c  29 ba c7 4b 08 00 06 01  ........)..K..
0010  08 00 06 04 00 01 00 0c  29 ba c7 4b c0 a8 6a 81  ........)..K..j.
0020  00 00 00 00 00 00 c0 a8  6a 80 00 00 00 00 00 00  ........j.......
0030  00 00 00 00 00 00 00 00  00 00 00 00

○ 📄 Frame (frame), 60 bytes          Packets: 10 · Displayed: 10 (100.0%) · Dropped: 0 (0.0%)        Profile: Default
```

Figure 2-8 Ping and ARP packets

Source: Wireshark Foundation, *www.wireshark.org*

10. What do you think the purpose of the ARP protocol is?

_____

_____

11. Close all open windows, and shut down the computers.

Hands-On Project 2-3: Examining Hub and Switch Indicator Lights and Uplink Ports

Time Required: 30 minutes

Objective: Examine the indicator lights of a hub or switch and understand the purpose of the uplink port.

Required Tools and Equipment: Three lab computers, four patch cables, one crossover cable, two hubs, and a switch

Description: In this project, you view the indicator lights of hubs and switches. Ideally, your hub has indicators for link status, activity, and collisions. In addition, if your hub has an uplink port, you test its function. Like the previous two projects, this project can be done in groups or as a class demonstration.

1. The computers should be shut down and one hub should be plugged in and turned on, if necessary. Connect all three computers to the hub with patch cables, but don't use the uplink port on the hub. Turn on the computers.

2. Examine the hub's indicator lights. A link status light should be glowing for each port a computer is connected to. Next, examine the indicator lights on the NIC, if they're

accessible. They should also be glowing to indicate a good connection. See whether the hub's indicator lights vary for different connection speeds. Write the link status light's color and the connection speed, if available, in the following chart:

Computer	Link status light's color	Connection speed
Computer1		
Computer2		
Computer3		

3. Generate some traffic by using `ping` commands on each computer. At each computer, open a command prompt window and ping another computer (Computer1 ping Computer2, Computer2 ping Computer3, and Computer3 ping Computer1, for example) by typing **ping -n 20 *IPaddress*** and pressing **Enter**. Examine the activity indicator lights, which should blink as data is received. (On hubs combining the activity indicator with the link status, network activity just causes the link status indicator to blink.) The -n 20 option in the `ping` command specifies sending 20 ICMP packets instead of just 4.

4. Next, if your hub has collision indicators, try to get them to glow. Note that the pings must be sent from each computer at the same time for a collision to occur. At each computer, type **ping -n 20 -l 60000 *IPaddress*** and press **Enter**. The -l 60000 (lowercase "L") option makes each ping packet 60,000 bytes in length. Even with these large amounts of data being transferred, you might not see a collision. Remember that a collision occurs when two or more computers send data simultaneously, which isn't permitted when using a hub. However, if your hub and NICs are operating at 100 Mbps, data is transferred so quickly that producing a collision might be difficult.

5. Leave the first hub powered on, and power on the second hub. With a regular patch cable, connect the first hub to the second hub, but don't use the uplink port. In most cases, you won't see the link lights glow at the ports where the two devices are connected. To fix this problem, plug one end of the patch cable into the uplink port on one hub (not on both hubs) and set the switch to the uplink position. You should now have connectivity between the hubs, and the link lights should be on.

6. If your hubs don't have an uplink port, you can connect two hubs with a crossover cable. To do this, disconnect the two hubs, and using a crossover cable from your instructor, connect each end of it to regular (not uplink) ports on the two hubs. The link lights should glow. (You learn more about patch and crossover cables in Chapter 4.)

7. List any other indicator lights you find on the hub and what these lights tell you:

_____

_____

8. Disconnect the computers from the hubs and put the hubs away. Connect the computers to the switch, and then power on the switch.

9. Along with link status lights, most switches have lights on each port to indicate whether the port is operating in full-duplex or half-duplex mode. If your switch has these indicators, find them and try to determine in which mode your NIC and switch are

communicating. Most NICs and switches support full-duplex communication, and this mode is chosen automatically.

10. List any other indicator lights you find on the switch, and explain what these lights tell you:

_____

_____

11. Close all open windows, and shut down the computers.

Wireless Access Points

As you probably know, not all networks require a cable tethering the computer to a switch or hub. Wireless networks have become ubiquitous in college and corporate campuses and in many public locations, such as airports and libraries. At the heart of a wireless LAN is the wireless **access point (AP)**. An AP is a lot like a hub, in that all computers send signals through it to communicate with other computers. The obvious difference is that signals don't travel through a physical medium; they travel through the airwaves as radio signals.

Most small business and home networks with wireless networks use a device typically called a wireless router that combines the functions of an AP, a switch, and a router (see Figure 2-9). Wireless routers can usually be identified by the two or more antennae on the device. These devices are usually used with a cable or DSL modem to provide wireless access to the Internet. Large businesses use dedicated APs to give users wireless access to the corporate network as well as the Internet.

Figure 2-9 A wireless router combines an access point, a switch, and a router

Source: Cisco Systems, Inc.

Wireless networks rarely stand by themselves. They're almost always connected to a wired network at some point. APs typically have one or more connectors for connecting to a wired Ethernet network.

Basic AP Operation

An AP is much like a wired hub, in that all stations hear all network data transmitted by all other wireless devices in the network. All communication goes to the AP, which then retransmits or repeats the transmission to the destination station. However, unlike hubs, communication between two stations requires an extra step. The destination device sends an acknowledgement back to the sending device to indicate that the frame was received. When the sending device receives the acknowledgement, it knows that no error or collision has occurred.

Some wireless configurations require additional handshaking between two communicating devices. Before a computer can transmit data to the AP, it must first send a short **request to send (RTS)** message to let the AP know it intends to transmit data. If no other stations are trying to send data, the AP responds with a **clear to send (CTS)** message letting the requesting station (and all other stations on the network) know that it can send data. The RTS and CTS messages are sent in addition to the acknowledgement the receiving computer sends. Imagine if you had to communicate in this fashion while speaking. Before each sentence you wanted to speak, you would have to ask a moderator whether you could speak, and the moderator would have to answer affirmatively. Then after each sentence, the moderator would have to acknowledge that you were heard before you could speak the next sentence. Conveying any real information would take much longer because so much time would be wasted on the overhead required by the communication rules. Fortunately, most wireless networks don't use the RTS/CTS configuration, but it's available as an option on some higher-end APs and wireless NICs.

Wireless APs and Network Bandwidth

Wireless APs and Network Bandwidth All the extra chatter required to send data in a wireless network slows communication quite a bit. In fact, the effective bandwidth (that is, the bandwidth used for actual data transmission) is about half the physical bandwidth. Keep in mind, too, that wireless network bandwidth is shared, as with a hub.

Most APs operate at anywhere from 11 Mbps to several hundred Mbps. So a wireless AP operating at 11 Mbps shares this 11 Mbps with all computers in the wireless network. Therefore, if 11 stations are connected to an 11 Mbps wireless network, each station has 1 Mbps of effective bandwidth; with all the extra network traffic (acknowledgements and possible RTS/CTS messages), however, you must halve this amount, leaving only about 500 Kbps of effective bandwidth. That's why developers are constantly striving to get more bandwidth out of wireless networks. In recent years, the performance of basic 11 Mbps wireless networks has increased to more than 100 Mbps, and APs that can operate at speeds of 300 Mbps and higher are becoming common, with speeds over 600 Mbps on the horizon.

Wireless networking is a big subject to tackle, and you learn more about wireless networking standards and technologies in Chapter 3.

Network Interface Cards

As a networking professional, you must understand what a network interface card does and how it works as well as what's involved in configuring a NIC for special network situations in which the default configuration is inadequate. Although most NICs are built into a computer's motherboard, they occasionally fail or additional NICs are needed for your application, so you should know how to install a new NIC, too. The following sections discuss the basic operation of a NIC along with its device driver, its most common features, and some configuration options.

NIC Basics

Attaching a computer to a network requires a **network interface card** (**NIC**) to create and mediate the connection between the computer and the networking medium. The networking medium might be copper wire, fiber-optic cable, or the airwaves, but in all cases, data is represented as bit signals that the NIC transmits or receives.

For incoming data, the NIC must be able to interpret the signals used for the network medium, which are electrical for copper wire, light for fiber-optic cable, or radio waves for wireless networks. These signals are then converted to bits and assembled into frames. For outgoing data, the NIC converts frame data into bits and transmits these bits to the medium in the correct signal format. The following list summarizes the tasks a NIC and its driver perform:

- Provide a connection from the computer to the network medium.
- For incoming messages, receive bit signals and assemble them into frames, verify the frame's destination address, remove the frame header and trailer, and transfer the packet to the network protocol.
- For outgoing messages, receive packets from the network protocol and create frames by adding source and destination MAC addresses and error-checking data.
- Convert the frame data into bit signals in a format suitable for the network medium and transmit the signals.

Figure 2-10 shows a NIC handling incoming data, and Figure 2-11 shows a NIC handling outgoing data.

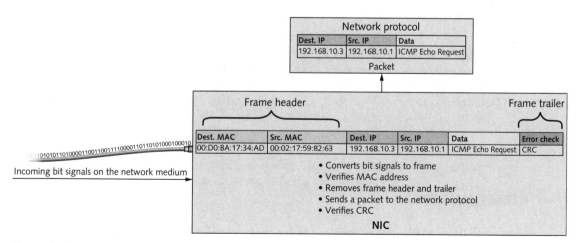

Figure 2-10 A NIC handles incoming data from the network medium

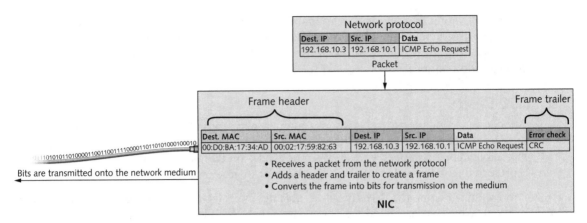

Figure 2-11 A NIC handles outgoing data to be sent to the network medium

Simulation 5 shows an animated version of these figures.

Simulation 5: How a NIC works

NICs and MAC Addresses Aside from the tasks described previously, a NIC has the important function of giving a computer a MAC address, an integral part of each NIC. NIC manufacturers ensure that every NIC has a unique address because networks don't function correctly if duplicate MAC addresses exist. The MAC address is stored in read-only memory (ROM) on the NIC. Because the address is said to be burned into memory, it's sometimes referred to as the "burned-in address" (BIA). The MAC address is composed of two 24-bit numbers:

- A 24-bit manufacturer ID called an organizationally unique identifier (OUI)
- A 24-bit serial number assigned by the manufacturer

The 48-bit MAC address is expressed in hexadecimal notation, usually as six two-digit alphanumeric characters separated by dashes or colons, such as 04-40-31-5B-1A-C4. The first three two-digit groups represent the OUI, and the last three are the unique serial number. A hexadecimal number is based on powers of 16. There are 16 symbols to represent each hexadecimal number: 0 to 9, A, B, C, D, E, and F. The symbol A represents the decimal value 10, and F represents the decimal value 15.

You can find a NIC's manufacturer by its MAC address. Go to *http://standards.ieee.org/regauth/oui/index.shtml* and enter the first three numbers (six digits) of a MAC address, separated by dashes.

The NIC as Gatekeeper When a frame arrives at a NIC, the NIC doesn't simply read the frame and send a packet to the network protocol. It examines incoming network frames and checks the frame's destination MAC address to see whether it matches its built-in MAC address. The NIC acts as a gatekeeper and permits inbound communications to pass through the interface only if the destination MAC address meets these criteria:

- The destination MAC address in the frame matches the NIC's built-in MAC address.
- The destination MAC address in the frame is the broadcast address.
- The NIC is operating in promiscuous mode.

A frame with a destination MAC address composed of all binary 1s or FF-FF-FF-FF-FF-FF in hexadecimal is a **broadcast frame**. Broadcast frames are intended to be processed by all computers on the network. Destination MAC addresses intended for a single computer are called **unicast frames**. Most NICs can operate in what's called **promiscuous mode**—essentially, this mode turns off the gatekeeper functions and enables the NIC to process all frames it sees. This mode is used by software called a protocol analyzer or packet sniffer (such as the Wireshark program you used in Hands-On Project 2-2) that captures frames and displays their contents for the purposes of troubleshooting and learning.

A third type of MAC address, called a "multicast address," is intended to be processed by a group of computers running a particular application or service. These MAC addresses are identified by a value of 1 in the rightmost bit of the first two digits, such as 01-22-33-44-55-66.

NIC Indicator Lights Like hubs and switches, NICs have indicator lights to show status information. Although the details vary across NIC models, NICs usually have a link status indicator and an activity indicator. The link status light is usually green when the NIC has a valid connection between the network medium and another device, such as a hub or switch. NICs usually also have an indicator light that flashes when the NIC detects network activity. As with hubs and switches, the link light and activity indicators are sometimes combined.

Some NICs supporting multiple speeds, such as 100 Mbps and 1000 Mbps, have a separate link light for each speed so that you can determine at what speed the NIC is connected to the hub or switch. In other cases, the link light indicates the connection speed by using a different color, such as amber for 100 Mbps and green for 1000 Mbps. There's no standard for NIC indicator lights, so you should consult the NIC's documentation to determine their purposes.

Selecting a NIC

The average user might never have to install a NIC because most NICs are built into the motherboard. However, onboard interfaces can fail or prove inadequate for how the computer is to be used. For example, the built-in NIC might operate at only 100 Mbps, and you want the interface to operate at 1000 Mbps, or there might be only one built-in NIC, and you want two or more NICs for a server. In these cases, you need to select a NIC with the correct bus interface to connect to your computer.

The connection the NIC makes to the motherboard is the bus connection, and when a NIC receives data, the data must be transferred to the bus and then to the CPU so that it can be processed. The bus speed determines how fast data can be transferred between components. When data is to be transmitted to the network, it goes from the CPU through the bus and to the NIC before being sent to the network medium.

Several bus types are in common use on PC motherboards. Chapter 8 delves into specifics of the bus architectures commonly used for NICs, but for now, you just need to know that PCI Express (PCIe) is the one you're most likely to encounter when installing an internal NIC. To make installation easier, you might want to choose a NIC that connects to your computer via an external USB connector.

What's most important in selecting a NIC to install is that you choose one your system supports, both in bus type and availability of device drivers for your computer's OS. The NIC's specifications tell you the bus type, and the packaging or manufacturer's Web site lists the OSs for which device drivers are available.

A close second in importance is selecting a NIC that's suitable for the role your computer will play in the network. If the computer is a typical desktop system, a standard $10 PCI NIC that operates at speeds of 10/100/1000 Mbps is probably enough. For servers or high-performance workstations, consider a NIC that has onboard memory and multiple ports and connects with the faster PCIe bus.

NIC Drivers

Installing a driver for a NIC is usually easy. Most OSs ship with drivers for a wide range of NIC manufacturers and models. Also, most NICs include drivers for the most common OSs, including current Windows and Linux versions. In most cases, you simply need to shut down your computer, install the NIC, and restart the computer. If the OS has a suitable driver available, it's installed automatically. If not, you're usually prompted to insert a CD/DVD containing the driver files.

After the drivers are installed, the NIC is usually ready to function without further configuration. In Windows 8.1 and later, you can verify that the NIC is installed in the Network Connections window, which you access by right-clicking Start and clicking Network Connections. The Network Connections window in Windows 10 (see Figure 2-12) is nearly identical to the one in earlier versions of Windows.

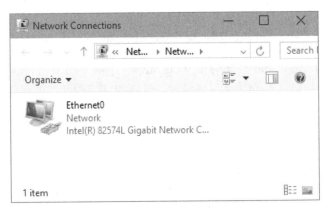

Figure 2-12 The Network Connections window in Windows 10

In Windows, each NIC is assigned a connection name. The first NIC in the system is assigned the name Ethernet0. If you have a second NIC, it's assigned Ethernet1, and so forth, but you can change the name to be more descriptive. To view a connection's settings, right-click the connection and click Properties to open the dialog box shown in Figure 2-13. The "Connect using" text box shows the type of NIC that's installed. To change the NIC's settings and its driver, click the Configure button. Common NIC configuration options are discussed in Chapter 8.

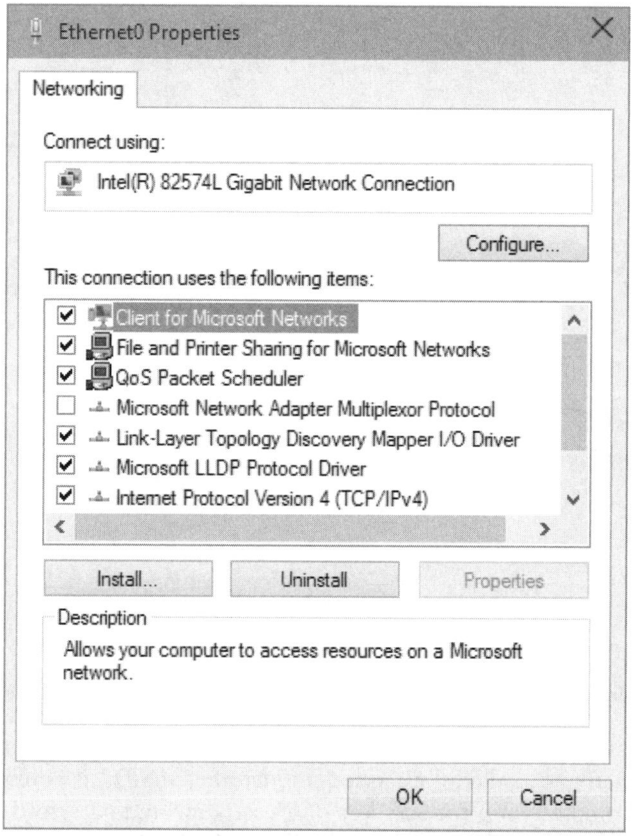

Figure 2-13   The Ethernet0 Properties dialog box

Wireless NICs

The selection process for a wireless NIC differs somewhat from selecting a wired NIC. Wireless NICs are most often built into laptops and other portable computers, but you still might want to install one on a desktop computer, particularly in a small business that uses wireless networking exclusively.

Wireless NICs must be chosen according to the type of wireless AP you have installed. Most are described in terms such as Wireless-n or 802.11ac or perhaps 802.11a/b/g/n. The letters a, b, g, n, and ac refer to the wireless networking standard the device supports. These standards support increasing speeds and features in this order from slowest to fastest: b, g, a, n, and ac. Wireless-b, or 802.11b, is among the earliest wireless standards and supports up to 11 Mbps transfer rates. 802.11a and 802.11g came next and support up to 54 Mbps transfer rates. 802.11n supports speeds from 54 Mbps to more than 600 Mbps. The newest standard, 802.11ac, supports speeds faster than 1 Gbps and will eventually support almost 7 Gbps. Chapter 3 covers these standards in more detail.

Unlike a wired NIC, a wireless NIC often requires a few more steps before a successful connection can be made. Figure 2-14 shows the Network & Internet control panel in Windows 10, which lists all wireless APs in the range of your wireless NIC. You can click the network ID and then click the Connect button to connect to a wireless network. You also have

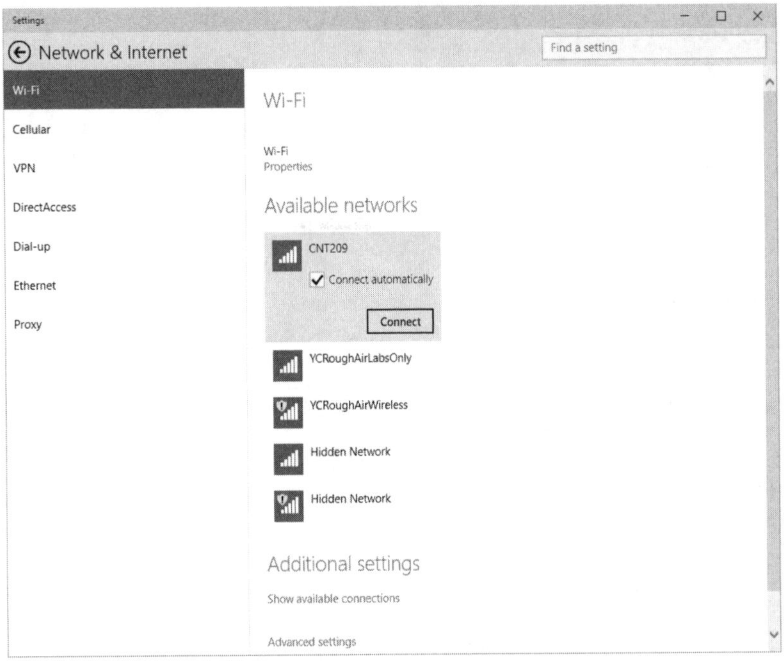

Figure 2-14 Connecting to a wireless network

the option to connect automatically whenever the network is in range of your computer. The name assigned to a wireless network, called the **service set identifier (SSID)**, is configured on the AP. You might also be prompted for a security key or a username and password, depending on the network's security configuration. When security is enabled on a wireless LAN (WLAN), communication is encrypted so that unauthorized parties can't connect or easily interpret the data traveling through airwaves. The security key serves as a decryption key, allowing a client to access the wireless network. You learn more about wireless networks and how to configure them in Chapter 3.

Hands-On Project 2-4: Connecting to a Wireless Access Point

Time Required: 15 minutes

Objective: Install a wireless NIC and connect to an access point.

Required Tools and Equipment: Two lab computers with 802.11 wireless NICs installed. USB wireless NICs work well, as they don't require opening the computer case. Laptops with built-in wireless NICs will also do. One wireless AP or wireless router configured with the SSID "NetEss." The 802.11 standard supported doesn't matter as long as the AP is compatible with the NICs. The computers shouldn't be connected to a hub or switch.

Description: In this project, you connect to a wireless AP and test the connection by pinging another computer connected to the same AP.

1. Start your computer and log on as an administrator. If the wireless NIC isn't installed yet, install it according to your instructor's instructions.

2. After the wireless NIC has been installed, click the network connection icon in the notification area to display a list of available wireless networks (shown previously in Figure 2-14).

3. Click the **NetEss** wireless network. A message is displayed, stating that information sent over the network might be visible to others because it's not secured with encryption. You secure the network later, so click the **Connect** button.

4. After a short time, you should see the Set Network Location window. The network location can be Home, Work, or Public and is used to set up firewall rules for the connection. Click the **Work** network, and then click **Close**.

5. You're now connected to the NetEss wireless network. To test the connection, get the IP address of another computer connected to the wireless network and ping the address. Alternatively, you can ping the router, which should be at the address 192.168.1.1. Ask your instructor for the correct address if pinging 192.168.1.1 doesn't work.

6. Close all open windows, and shut down all computers.

Routers

Routers are the most complex devices discussed in this chapter. Hubs and switches connect computers to the LAN; routers connect LANs to one another. Routers typically have two or more network ports to which switches or hubs are connected to form an internetwork. Figure 2-15 is a diagram of an internetwork, with two LANs connected via a router. Each LAN in this example uses switches to connect workstations and a router port to the LAN. LAN 2 has two switches that are connected.

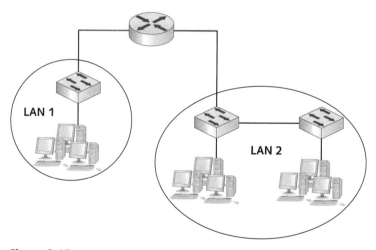

Figure 2-15 Two LANs connected by a router to make an internetwork

Routers enable multiple LANs to communicate with one another by forwarding packets from one LAN to another. They also forward packets from one router to another when LANs are separated by multiple routers. The Internet is built on a vast collection of LANs, all interconnected via routers. Figure 2-16 shows a small business network connected to its Internet service provider (ISP), followed by connections to several other Internet routers and ultimately to a Web server on the Cengage.com network.

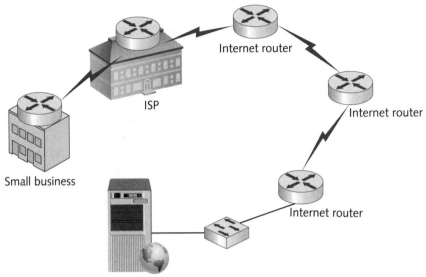

Figure 2-16   Routers interconnect LANs to form the Internet

 Recall from Chapter 1 that the Internet and its complex arrangement of routers is usually shown as a cloud in network diagrams to hide the complex web of routers and devices that make up the Internet.

On the surface, it might seem as though switches and routers perform a similar function, but in reality, they have very different jobs to do and how they work with network data differs substantially. The following points summarize the key properties and features of a router versus a switch:

- Routers connect LANs, and switches connect computers.
- Routers work with logical (IP) addresses rather than physical (MAC) addresses, as switches do.
- Routers work with packets rather than the frames that switches work with.
- Routers don't forward broadcast packets, but switches do.
- Routers use routing tables, and switches use switching tables.

The following sections discuss how and why routers are used to connect LANs and how routers use routing tables. Simulation 6 shows basic router operation.

 **Simulation 6: Router operation in a simple internetwork**

Routers Connect LANs

Switches are the device of choice to connect computers to create a LAN. However, if you look at a LAN as a group of people with similar interests getting together to converse and share information, there's a point at which the group can become too large for effective communication. For example, in most group discussions, several conversations often occur at once, but periodically, someone wants to speak to the entire group. For small groups with tightly coupled interests, this method works well, but as the group gets larger, the frequency of group announcements can affect the flow of communication adversely. This is particularly true when only a small subset of the group is interested in the announcement, yet the whole group must stop to listen. In this case, communication can be enhanced by dividing the large group into smaller groups of similar interests in different locations. By doing so, announcements to the entire group are contained in the small group and need not interrupt other groups' conversations. You can look at these announcements as network broadcast frames that switches (and hubs) are obliged to forward to all connected stations.

Breaking a large group into smaller groups works well until a member of one group must communicate with a member of another group. A messenger could be used to get a message from one group to another and would normally forward only messages directed to a person in another group, not announcements to the entire group. This messenger is analogous to a router in an internetwork, and like the messenger, the router doesn't forward announcements (broadcasts); it forwards only messages destined for a particular address.

Examine Figure 2-17, which shows a large LAN with all workstations and servers connected via switches. All these switches are connected through the switch the servers are on. This arrangement works fine if the number of workstations on each switch doesn't exceed about 20. However, if each group of computers represents as many as 25 computers (making 150 total workstations), announcement messages (broadcasts) will probably start affecting communication efficiency. Remember that each time a computer sends a broadcast frame, the switch forwards it out all connected ports so that all computers eventually receive the broadcast. One deleterious effect of broadcast frames is that when a computer receives a broadcast,

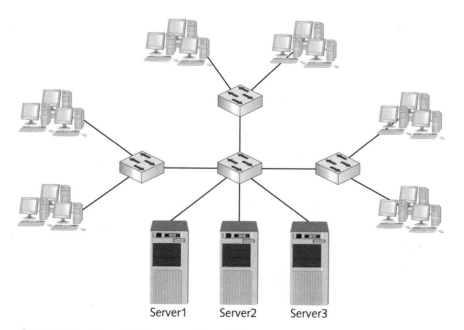

Server1   Server2   Server3

Figure 2-17 A large LAN connected by switches

a CPU interrupt occurs, causing the computer to stop what it's doing to service the interrupt. If enough interrupts occur in a short period because of many broadcast frames, the computer's overall performance can suffer as a result of the CPU having to service the interrupt and process the broadcast.

Now look at Figure 2-18, in which the network has been redesigned for efficiency. Workstations have been organized so that each department's users are grouped together, and servers have been configured so that each department's frequently accessed documents and applications reside on the departmental server. In this arrangement, the switches for each LAN allow all computers in the LAN to communicate with one another and forward important broadcast frames so that all computers receive the announcement, but broadcasts aren't forwarded to other LANs because the router doesn't forward broadcast frames. However, the router does allow communication between LANs so that if a management computer needs to access data on the marketing server, it can do so.

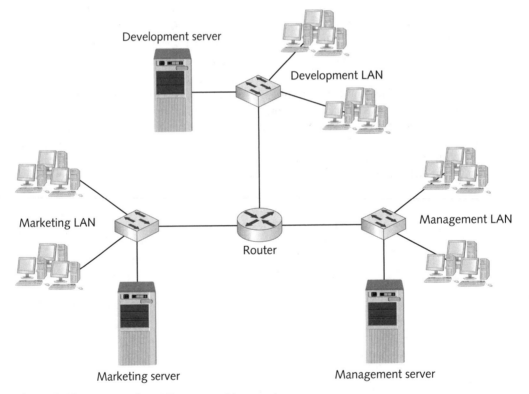

Figure 2-18   Three smaller LANs connected by a router

Routers Create Broadcast Domains

The scope of devices to which broadcast frames are forwarded is called a **broadcast domain**. Because routers don't forward broadcasts, router interfaces are the delimiter for broadcast domains. In other words, each router interface in a network creates another broadcast domain. Figure 2-19 shows the same network as Figure 2-18, with circles around each broadcast domain. (Note that Figure 2-17, with no routers at all, is a single broadcast domain.) Chapter 8 describes broadcast domains and how to create them with advanced switch features.

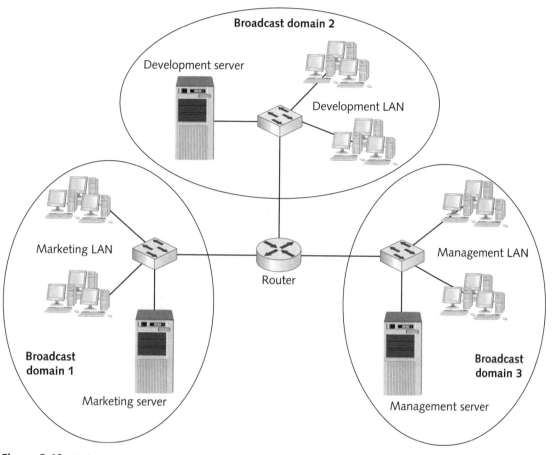

Figure 2-19   Each router interface creates a broadcast domain

Routers Work with IP Addresses and Routing Tables

Switches, as you know, maintain a switching table of MAC address and switch port pairs to determine where to forward frames in a LAN. Routers maintain routing tables composed of IP network addresses and interface pairs to determine where to forward packets in an internetwork.

Routers have two or more interfaces, with each interface connected to a different network. When a router receives a packet on one interface, it looks at the destination IP address in the packet to determine which network the packet is addressed to. Then it forwards the packet out of the interface that its routing table indicates is the best way to get the packet to its destination. Figure 2-20 shows the same internetwork as Figure 2-19, with each LAN assigned a network number, and an example of what the routing table might look like. The router's three interfaces are labeled EthA, EthB, and EthC.

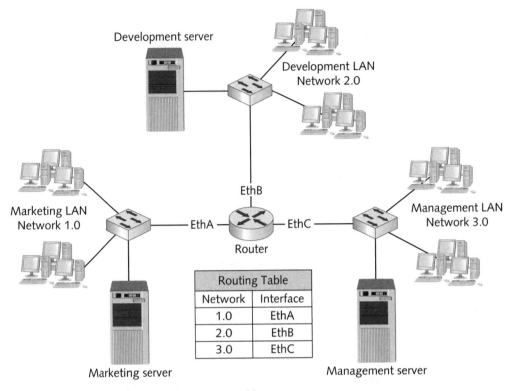

Figure 2-20 An internetwork with a routing table

When the router receives a packet from a computer in Network 1.0 that has a destination address of a computer in Network 3.0, the router looks in its routing table and discovers that Network 3.0 can be found via the EthC interface. The router then forwards the packet out its EthC interface to reach the intended computer.

This routing table has been simplified for demonstration purposes; routing tables have more information than simply the network number and interface name. In addition, network numbers are derived from IP addresses and contain more numbers than shown. Chapter 7 has additional details about how routers work, and Chapter 5 discusses IP addresses and network addresses in more depth.

You might wonder what happens when a router isn't connected to the network the packet is addressed to. Figure 2-21 illustrates this situation and shows what the routing table would look like on each router between the source and destination networks. In this example, if a computer on Network 1.0 sends a packet to a computer on Network 5.0, router R1 receives the packet and looks up Network 5.0 in its routing table. According to its routing table, it forwards the packet out its WAN A interface. Router R2 receives the packet and forwards it out its WAN B interface, as specified by its routing table, and finally, router R3 receives the packet and forwards it out its EthA interface to the destination computer.

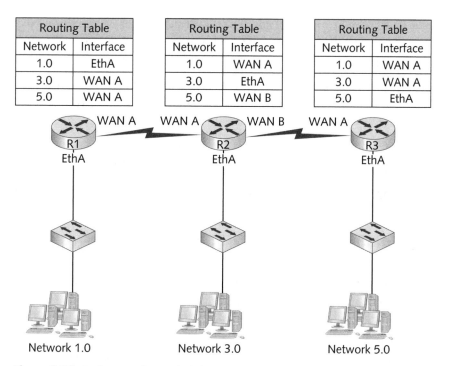

Figure 2-21 Packets are forwarded through multiple routers

Default Routes Routers on a corporate network might have a routing table entry for every network in the organization, but what about routers connected to the Internet? The Internet is composed of hundreds of thousands of networks, and routers on the Internet are responsible for getting packets from any network to any other network. Although it might be technically possible for routers to have a record of every network in the Internet, having such large routing tables isn't practical. To solve this dilemma, routers can have a special routing table entry called a **default route**, which tells a router where to send a packet with a destination network that can't be found in the routing table. The default route usually leads to another router with the network address in its table or results in the packet being sent to another default route and so on, until it reaches a router that has the network address in its routing table.

Network Unreachable Most routers are configured with a default route, but not always. If a router receives a packet with a destination network address that isn't in its routing table and no default route is configured, the router simply discards the packet. The router may also send a message to the sending station informing it that the network is unreachable. By doing so, the sender is made aware that the destination network doesn't exist or the routers must be configured differently to access the destination network.

Default Gateway Just as a router must know where to forward a packet it receives, a workstation must know when to send a packet to the router instead of simply addressing the packet and sending it to the local LAN. When a workstation has a packet ready to send, it compares its own IP address with the destination IP address in the packet. If the two addresses are on the same network, the workstation gets the destination computer's MAC address and sends the frame to the local LAN to be delivered to the destination. If the two addresses are on separate networks, the workstation must instead get the router's MAC address and send the frame to the router, which then tries to get the packet to the destination network. In this case, the workstation must know the address of a router. The **default gateway** in a computer's IP address settings must be set to the address of a router to which the computer can send all packets destined for other networks. If the default gateway doesn't have a valid address of a router, the computer can communicate only with computers on the same LAN. In Chapter 5, you learn more about how a computer determines its network address.

This chapter has explained the basic operation of the most common network hardware components. There's more to learn about all these components, but before you delve deeper into network hardware, examining other aspects of networking is helpful. The next several chapters discuss network topologies and technologies, network media, protocols, and networking standards, among other topics.

Hands-On Project 2-5: Communicating over a Router

Time Required: 20 minutes

Objective: Configure workstations to communicate with one another through a router.

Required Tools and Equipment: Three lab computers, two switches, a router, and five patch cables

Description: This project requires some setup by your instructor. You should verify with your instructor that it's complete before starting this project. In this project, you configure workstations to communicate with each other through a router. The router is configured to support two networks: 192.168.1.0 and 192.168.2.0. Computer1 and Computer2 are configured to operate in the 192.168.1.0 network, and Computer3 is configured to work in the 192.168.2.0 network. Figure 2-22 shows the network setup, in which all three computers are connected to the same switch. Cable the network as shown. The router should already be configured.

Network 192.168.1.0

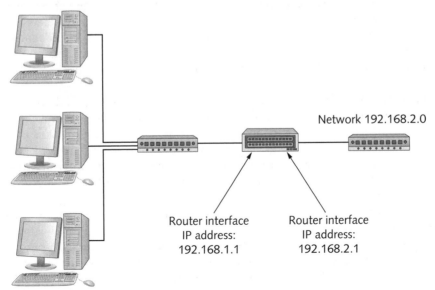

Figure 2-22 Network setup for Hands-On Project 2-5

1. Start all three computers. To configure the IP address of each computer, right-click **Start** and click **Network Connections**. Right-click **Ethernet0** and click **Properties**. Double-click **Internet Protocol Version 4 (TCP/IPv4)**, and then click **Use the following IP address**. For now, just set the IP address and subnet mask, using the following values:

   • Computer1: IP address **192.168.1.11**, subnet mask **255.255.255.0**

   • Computer2: IP address **192.168.1.12**, subnet mask **255.255.255.0**

   • Computer3: IP address **192.168.2.21**, subnet mask **255.255.255.0**

2. After you have entered these values, click **OK** twice and close all windows.

3. To test your configuration, open a command prompt window on Computer1 and Computer2, and ping each other's IP address. The ping should be successful. If it's not, verify that the IP address settings are correct by typing `ipconfig` and pressing **Enter** and comparing the values with the ones listed in Step 1. From both computers, type `ping 192.168.1.1` and press **Enter** to verify that they can communicate with the router.

4. On Computer1, ping Computer3 by typing `ping 192.168.2.21` and pressing **Enter**. You should get a message that the ping failed or timed out. The reason is that the two computers are configured to be on different networks. In this case, Computer1 is configured to be on network 192.168.1.0, and Computer2 is configured to be on network 192.168.2.0. When two computers are configured to be on separate networks, their connection to each other must be separated by a router. Move Computer3 to the other network by plugging the cable from Computer3 into the other switch so that your network configuration now looks like Figure 2-23.

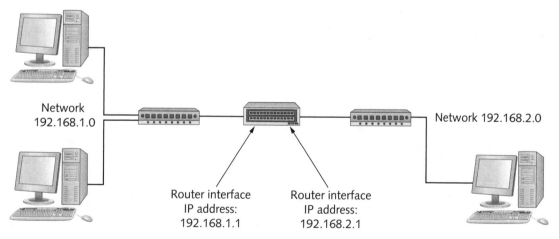

Figure 2-23   Corrected network setup

5. Try the ping again from Computer1 to Computer3. Again, you get an error because one piece of the IP address configuration has been omitted. When a computer needs to send a packet to a device on another network, it must know the address of the router to which to send the packet. This address is called the "default gateway." To set the default gateway for

all three computers, follow the instructions in Step 1 to get to the IP settings. In the "Default gateway" text box, enter the following values:

- Computer1: **192.168.1.1**
- Computer2: **192.168.1.1**
- Computer3: **192.168.2.1**

6. After you have finished configuring the default gateway for all three computers, you should be able to ping from Computer1 to Computer3 and from Computer2 to Computer3 and vice versa. Try it now, and write down your results:

_____

_____

7. Next, try another command that shows the route your packet travels to get to the other computer. From Computer1 and Computer2, type **tracert 192.168.2.21** and press **Enter**. From Computer3, type **tracert 192.168.1.11** and press **Enter**. You'll see a few lines of output showing that the packet had to travel through the router to get to its destination. This command is used again in the next project.

8. Close all open windows on all three computers.

Hands-On Project 2-6: Using Trace Route to See How Packets Travel Through the Internet

Time Required: 10 minutes

Objective: Use the Trace Route program to see the routers packets must travel through to get from your computer to a destination on the Internet.

Required Tools and Equipment: Net-*XX* and Internet access

Description: The importance of routers is clear when you need to access servers on the Internet. The Trace Route program (tracert.exe) lists each router your packets must travel through between your computer and an Internet server.

1. Log on to your computer as **NetAdmin**, if necessary, and open a command prompt window.

2. Type **tracert www.yahoo.com** and press **Enter**. You should see output that's similar to Figure 2-24, but the details will vary, depending on your location. In this output, there are five columns of information. The first column is just a count of how many routers the packet traversed. The second, third, and fourth columns show the amount of time in milliseconds (ms) the router took to respond. Three packets are sent, so three times are listed. The last column is the router's IP address or name and IP address.

3. You can garner some information about the geography of the path your packet took by looking at the router's name. For example, in Figure 2-24, the domain name of the first router is yc-cnt.edu, which is a router at Yavapai College in Prescott, Arizona, where this book has been written. Other routers have the domain name qwest.net, which tells you that the router is on Qwest's network. You get the idea. However, looking up router names can sometimes make the trace run slowly. To do the same trace without looking up names, type **tracert -d www.yahoo.com** and press **Enter**. This time, you should see only the IP address of each router.

```
C:\Users\NetAdmin>tracert www.yahoo.com

Tracing route to fd-fp3.wg1.b.yahoo.com [206.190.36.45]
over a maximum of 30 hops:

  1    <1 ms    <1 ms    <1 ms  cntrouter.yc-cnt.edu [172.31.1.250]
  2     1 ms     1 ms    <1 ms  172.16.0.1
  3    <1 ms    <1 ms    <1 ms  domain.not.configured [198.60.126.30]
  4     1 ms    <1 ms    <1 ms  198.60.121.20
  5     5 ms     5 ms     4 ms  63-158-78-209.dia.static.qwest.net [63.158.78.209]
  6     *       15 ms    15 ms  los-brdr-01.inet.qwest.net [67.14.102.30]
  7    15 ms    16 ms    15 ms  63.146.27.222
  8    50 ms    50 ms    50 ms  po3-20g.ar7.sea1.gblx.net [67.16.153.206]
  9    50 ms    49 ms    50 ms  64.211.195.66
 10    55 ms    55 ms    55 ms  ae-7.pat1.gqb.yahoo.com [216.115.96.45]
 11    55 ms    55 ms    55 ms  ae-0.msr1.gq1.yahoo.com [66.196.67.1]
 12    55 ms    55 ms    55 ms  xe-1-2-1.clr1-a-gdc.gq1.yahoo.com [67.195.1.165]
 13    55 ms    56 ms    55 ms  et-18-1.fab4-1-gdc.gq1.yahoo.com [67.195.1.85]
 14    65 ms    56 ms    56 ms  po-12.bas2-7-prd.gq1.yahoo.com [206.190.32.35]
 15    56 ms    59 ms    57 ms  ir1.fp.vip.gq1.yahoo.com [206.190.36.45]

Trace complete.

C:\Users\NetAdmin>_
```

Figure 2-24 Output of the `tracert` command

4. Try using Trace Route to determine the path packets take to other destinations. Try **books.tomsho.com,** and for a destination on the East Coast, try **www.cengage.com**. For a destination in Germany, try **www.kontron.de**. If the trace repeatedly times out (indicated by an asterisk, *, in the output), press **Ctrl+C** to stop the trace.

5. Close the command prompt window.

6. You can also find tools that show you the route on a map. Start your Web browser, and go to **www.yougetsignal.com/tools/visual-tracert**. In the Remote Address text box, type any of the destinations in Step 4 or any other address you like. This online tool attempts to map out the path your packets take to get to their destination.

7. Exit your Web browser, and shut down your computer, unless you're continuing to the critical thinking activities at the end of the chapter.

Chapter Summary

- Network repeaters and hubs take incoming bit signals and repeat them at their original strength out all connected ports. A hub is just a multiport repeater. Hubs are a central connecting device for multiple computers, but because hubs allow only one device to communicate at a time, the bandwidth of each port must be shared between all connected computers.

- Network switches interconnect multiple computers, just as hubs do. However, instead of simply regenerating incoming bit signals and repeating them to all other ports, a switch reads the destination MAC address in the frame to determine which port the destination device is connected to and forwards the frame to only that port.

- Switches use switching tables to determine which MAC address can be found on which port. Switches can operate in full-duplex mode, allowing connected devices to both transmit and receive data simultaneously. Hubs operate only in half-duplex mode.

- Access points are a central device in a wireless network and perform a similar function to hubs. An AP requires devices to use an RTS signal when they want to transmit data, and the AP responds with a CTS signal when it's okay to transmit. This extra network traffic reduces the effective bandwidth of wireless networks.

- Network interface cards create and mediate the connection between the computer and network medium. A computer's MAC address is defined on the NIC as a burned-in address. The NIC reads each frame arriving on the network medium and determines whether the frame's destination address matches its MAC address. If it matches or is a broadcast frame, the NIC processes the frame; otherwise, it's discarded.

- Wireless NICs perform the same function as wired NICs. Wireless NICs must be selected to match the wireless standard supported on the AP. When a wireless client connects to an AP, it uses the SSID to identify the wireless network's name.

- Routers connect LANs to one another and forward packets from one LAN to another, according to the destination IP address specified in the packet. Routers use routing tables to determine where to forward packets.

- Unlike hubs and switches, routers don't forward broadcast frames. Each interface on a router is the delimiter for a broadcast domain. When a router receives a unicast frame, it reads the destination IP address and compares it with the list of networks in its routing table. If a match is found, the router forwards the packet to the destination network or to another router that gets the packet to its destination. If no match is found, the router discards the frame. If a router has a default route defined, it forwards any packets that don't match networks in its routing table to the default route.

Key Terms

access point (AP)   A wireless device that serves as the central connection point of a wireless LAN and mediates communication between wireless computers.

bandwidth sharing   A network design in which interconnecting devices allow only one connected device to transmit data at a time, thus requiring devices to share available bandwidth.

broadcast domain   The scope of devices to which broadcast frames are forwarded. Router interfaces delimit broadcast domains because they don't forward broadcasts, whereas switches and hubs do.

broadcast frame   A network message intended to be processed by all devices on a LAN; has the destination address FF:FF:FF:FF:FF:FF.

clear to send (CTS)   A signal an AP generates in response to a request-to-send signal. A CTS signal indicates that the computer that sent an RTS can transmit data. *See also* access point (AP) *and* request to send (RTS).

dedicated bandwidth   A property of switches in which each port's bandwidth is dedicated to the devices connected to the port; on a hub, each port's bandwidth is shared between all devices connected to the hub.

default gateway   The address configured in a computer's IP address settings specifying the address of a router to which the computer can send all packets destined for other networks.

default route   A routing table entry that tells a router where to send a packet with a destination network address that can't be found in the routing table.

full-duplex mode   A communication mode in which a device can simultaneously transmit and receive data on the same cable connection. Switches can operate in full-duplex mode, but hubs can't.

half-duplex mode   A communication mode in which a device can send or receive data but can't do both simultaneously. Hubs operate only in half-duplex mode; switches can operate in both half-duplex and full-duplex modes.

hub   A network device that performs the same function as a repeater but has several ports to connect a number of devices; sometimes called a multiport repeater. *See also* repeater.

network bandwidth   The amount of data that can be transferred on a network during a specific interval; usually measured in bits per second.

network interface card (NIC)   A device that creates and mediates the connection between a computer and the network medium.

promiscuous mode   An operational mode of a NIC in which all frames are read and processed rather than only broadcast and unicast frames addressed to the NIC. Protocol analyzer software sets a NIC to promiscuous mode so that all network frames can be read and analyzed.

repeater   A network device that takes incoming signals and regenerates, or repeats them to other parts of the network.

request to send (RTS)   A signal used in wireless networks indicating that a computer has data ready to send on the network. *See also* access point *and* clear to send (CTS).

routers   Devices that enable LANs to communicate with one another by forwarding packets from one LAN to another. Routers also forward packets from one router to another when LANs are separated by multiple routers; they have multiple interfaces, and each interface communicates with a LAN.

service set identifier (SSID)   The name assigned to a wireless network so that wireless clients can distinguish between them when more than one is detected.

switch   A network device that reads the destination MAC addresses of incoming frames to determine which ports should forward the frames.

switching table   A table containing MAC address and port pairs that a switch uses to determine which port to forward frames it receives.

unicast frame   A network message addressed to only one computer on the LAN.

uplinking   Making a connection between devices such as two switches, usually for the purpose of expanding a network.

uplink port   A designated port on a hub or switch used to connect to another hub or switch without using a crossover cable.

Review Questions

1. Which of the following is a limitation of early networks that used a daisy-chain method of connecting computers? (Choose all that apply.)

   a. Total number of computers that could be connected

   b. The processing speed of the computers connected

   c. Cable length

   d. No Internet access

2. Which of the following is true of a repeater?

   a. Receives frames and forwards them

   b. Determines which network to send a packet

   c. Receives bit signals and strengthens them

   d. Has a burned-in MAC address for each port

3. Which of the following is true of a hub? (Choose all that apply.)

   a. Usually has just two ports

   b. Transmits regenerated signals to all connected ports

   c. Usually has four or more ports

   d. Works with MAC addresses

4. Which of the following is the unit of measurement by which a hub's bandwidth is usually specified?

   a. Bytes per second

   b. Bits per second

   c. Packets per second

   d. Bytes per minute

5. Which of the following describes how devices connected to a hub use the speed at which the hub can transmit data?

   a. Bandwidth optimization

   b. Bandwidth dedication

   c. Bandwidth sharing

   d. Bandwidth multiplier

6. Which of the following is a likely indicator light on a hub? (Choose all that apply.)

   a. CRC error

   b. Link status

   c. Connection speed

   d. Activity

   e. Signal strength

7. Which of the following describes how devices connected to a switch use the speed at which the switch can transmit data?

   a. Dedicated bandwidth

   b. Half-duplex bandwidth

   c. Half-scale bandwidth

   d. Shared bandwidth

8. What does a switch use to create its switching table?

   a. Source IP addresses

   b. Destination logical addresses

   c. Destination physical addresses

   d. Source MAC addresses

9. What purpose does the timestamp serve in a switching table?

   a. Tells the switch when to forward a frame

   b. Tells the switch how long to wait for a response

   c. Tells the switch when to delete an entry

   d. Tells the switch how long it has been running

10. What feature of a switch allows devices to effectively communicate at 200 Mbps on a 100 Mbps switch?

    a. Uplink port

    b. Full-duplex mode

    c. Shared bandwidth

    d. Bit strengthening

    e. Frame doubling

    f. Signal regeneration

11. To which device is a wireless access point most similar in how it operates?

    a. Hub

    b. Switch

    c. NIC

    d. Router

12. What's the purpose of an RTS signal in wireless networking?

    a. It allows the AP to request which device is the transmitting station.

    b. It allows the AP to tell all stations that it's ready to transmit data.

    c. It allows a client to notify the AP that it's ready to send data.

    d. It allows a client to request data from the AP.

13. Which of the following is a common operational speed of a wireless network?

    a. 10 Kbps

    b. 110 Gbps

    c. 600 Kbps

    d. 11 Mbps

14. Which of the following is a task performed by a NIC and its driver? (Choose all that apply.)

    a. Provides a connection to the network medium

    b. Converts bit signals into frames for transmission on the medium

    c. Receives packets from the network protocol and creates frames

    d. Adds a header before sending a frame to the network protocol

    e. Adds error-checking data to the frame

15. Which of the following best describes a MAC address?

    a. A 24-bit number expressed as 12 decimal digits

    b. Two 24-bit numbers, in which one is the OUI

    c. A 48-bit number composed of 12 octal digits

    d. A dotted decimal number burned into the NIC

16. Under which circumstances does a NIC allow inbound communications to pass through the interface? (Choose all that apply.)

    a. The source MAC address is the broadcast address.

    b. The destination MAC address matches the built-in MAC address.

    c. The destination MAC address is all binary 1s.

    d. The NIC is operating in exclusive mode.

17. How does a protocol analyzer capture all frames?

    a. It configures the NIC to capture only unicast frames.

    b. It sets all incoming destination addresses to be broadcasts.

    c. It configures the NIC to operate in promiscuous mode.

    d. It sets the exclusive mode option on the NIC.

    e. It captures only multicast frames.

18. In Windows 10, which of the following displays information about currently installed NICs?

    a. Network Connections

    b. NICs and Drivers

    c. Local Area Networks

    d. Computers and Devices

19. Which of the following is the purpose of an SSID?

    a. Assigns an address to a wireless NIC

    b. Acts as a unique name for a local area connection

    c. Acts as a security key for securing a network

    d. Identifies a wireless network

20. Which of the following describe the function of routers? (Choose all that apply.)

    a. Forward frames from one network to another

    b. Connect LANS

    c. Attach computers to the internetwork

    d. Work with packets and IP addresses

21. What information is found in a routing table?

    a. Computer names and IP addresses

    b. Network addresses and interfaces

    c. MAC addresses and ports

    d. IP addresses and MAC addresses

22. You currently have 15 switches with an average of 20 stations connected to each switch. The switches are connected to one another so that all 300 computers can communicate with each other in a single LAN. You have been detecting a high percentage of broadcast frames on this LAN. You think the number of broadcasts might be having an impact on network performance. What should you do?

    a. Connect the switches in groups of five, and connect each group of switches to a central hub.

    b. Upgrade the switches to a faster speed.

    c. Reorganize the network into smaller groups and connect each group to a router.

    d. Disable broadcast forwarding on the switches.

23. Review the routing table in Figure 2-25. Based on this figure, where does the router send a packet with the source network number 1.0 and the destination network number 3.0?

    a. EthA

    b. WAN A

    c. WAN B

    d. None of the above

Routing Table	
Network	Interface
1.0	EthA
2.0	WAN A
3.0	WAN B

Figure 2-25 Routing table

24. If a router receives a packet with a destination network address unknown to the router, what does the router do?

    a. Send the packet out all interfaces.

    b. Discard the packet.

    c. Add the destination network to its routing table.

    d. Query the network for the destination network.

25. Which of the following is true about routers? (Choose all that apply.)

    a. Forward broadcasts

    b. Use default routes for unknown network addresses

    c. Forward unicasts

    d. Used primarily to connect workstations

Critical Thinking

The following activities give you critical thinking challenges. Challenge labs give you an opportunity to use the skills you have learned to perform a task without step-by-step instructions. Case projects offer a practical networking setup for which you supply a written solution.

Challenge Lab 2-1: Determining Whether Your Computer Is Connected to a Hub or Switch

Time Required: 15 minutes

Objective: Use packet information captured with Wireshark to determine whether your computer is attached to the rest of the classroom with a hub or switch.

Required Tools and Equipment: Net-XX

Description: You saw the difference between hubs and switches in earlier projects. Specifically, you saw which packets Wireshark captured when your computer was connected to a hub versus a switch. In this challenge lab, set up a test, working with your classmates, to determine whether classroom computers are connected to a hub or switch. Write a short memo to your instructor with the following information:

*   What filter options (if any) did you configure in Wireshark?

*   What commands did you use to generate packets on the network?

*   What IP addresses did you attempt to communicate with?

*   What was your result? Is your computer attached to a hub or switch? Why did you come to this conclusion?

Challenge Lab 2-2: Capturing Trace Route Packets

Time Required: 15 minutes

Objective: Use Wireshark to capture Trace Route packets.

Required Tools and Equipment: Net-*XX*

Description: In this challenge lab, you capture packets generated by the Trace Route program. You need to determine what types of packets are generated so that you know which types of packets to capture and inspect. Run Trace Route (using any Web sites you like) and capture the packets your computer generates and the router responses. After you have finished this lab, write a short memo discussing the following points:

- What type of packets does Trace Route use?
- What's the response each router sends back to your computer?
- How does your computer get a response from each router between your computer and the destination?

You can look up information on Trace Route at *www.ehow.com/how-does_5164102_traceroute-work.html* or do a Google search for it.

Case Project 2-1

You have been hired to upgrade a network of 50 computers currently connected to 10 Mbps hubs. This long-overdue upgrade is necessary because of poor network response time caused by a lot of collisions occurring during long file transfers between clients and servers. How do you recommend upgrading this network? What interconnecting devices will you use, and what benefit will you get from using these devices? Write a short memo describing the upgrade and, if possible, include a drawing of the new network.

Case Project 2-2

Two hundred workstations and four servers on a single LAN are connected by a number of switches. You're seeing an excessive number of broadcast packets throughout the LAN and want to decrease the effect this broadcast traffic has on your network. What steps must you take to achieve this goal?

Case Project 2-3

In Chapter 3, you learn about network topologies and technologies. As preparation, do Internet research on the following topics:

- Physical versus logical topology
- Bus topology
- Star topology
- Ring topology
- Ethernet and CSMA/CD

Write a short explanation (two to three sentences) of each concept and be prepared to discuss it with the class.

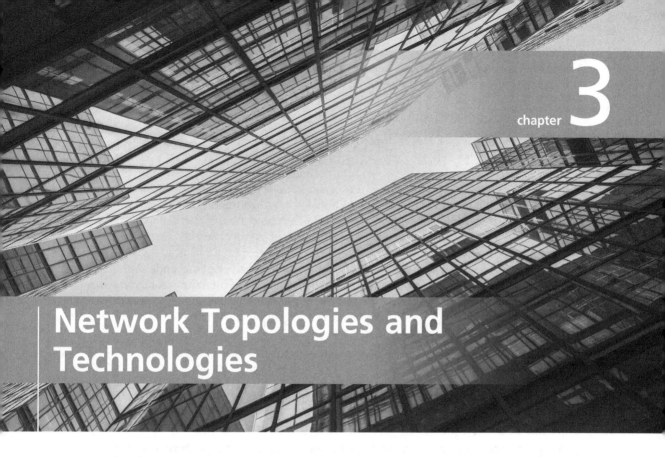

chapter 3

Network Topologies and Technologies

After reading this chapter and completing the exercises, you will be able to:

- Describe the primary physical networking topologies in common use
- Describe the primary logical networking topologies in common use
- Describe major LAN networking technologies
- Compare Wi-Fi standards

Not so long ago, there was a real choice to be made between available network topologies and technologies when designing and building a new internetwork. Thankfully, this area of networking has gotten simpler rather than more complex, mainly because the choices have narrowed, with inferior or costly solutions becoming obsolete.

This chapter discusses network topologies, which describe both the physical arrangement of cabling or pathways between network devices and the logical manner in which data is transferred from device to device. Next, you learn about network technologies or architectures that describe the methods computers use to transmit data to the networking medium in an orderly fashion. As you'll see, the topology and technology are often tightly coupled, as certain technologies can be used only with certain topologies. The choices have been limited because only a few technologies and topologies remain viable choices. As is often the case, however, it helps to know where networking started to get an idea of where it might be heading. So even though some information covered in this chapter is obsolete or nearly so, your understanding of these older technologies will help you better understand current and future technologies. Finally, you learn about 802.11 Wi-Fi standards and methods. Wi-Fi is developing as rapidly as wired Ethernet and is replacing wired LANs as the connection of choice in some environments.

Physical Topologies

Table 3-1 summarizes what you need for the hands-on projects in this chapter.

Table 3-1   **Hands-on project requirements**

Hands-on project	Requirements	Time required	Notes
Hands-On Project 3-1: Building a Physical Star Topology Network	Three lab computers, hub, three patch cables	20 minutes	
Hands-On Project 3-2: Determining and Changing Your Ethernet Standard	Two lab computers, switch, two patch cables	15 minutes	
Hands-On Project 3-3: Viewing an Ethernet Frame	Two lab computers, switch, two patch cables	20 minutes	

The word "topology," for most people, describes the lay of the land. A topographic map, for example, shows the hills and valleys in a region, whereas a street map shows only the roads. A network topology describes how a network is physically laid out and how signals travel from one device to another. However, because the physical layout of devices and cables doesn't necessarily describe how signals travel from one device to another, network topologies are categorized as physical and logical.

The arrangement of cabling and how cables connect one device to another in a network are considered the network's **physical topology**, and the path data travels between computers on a network is considered the network's **logical topology**. You can look at the physical topology as a topographic map that shows just the lay of the land along with towns, with only simple lines showing which towns have pathways to one another. The logical topology can be seen as a street map that shows how people actually have to travel from one place to another. As you'll see, a network can be wired with one physical topology but pass data from machine to machine by using a different logical topology.

All network designs are based on these basic physical topologies: bus, star, ring, and point-to-point. A bus consists of a series of computers connected along a single cable segment. Computers connected via a central device, such as a hub or switch, are arranged in a star topology. Devices connected to form a loop create a ring. Two devices connected directly to one another make a point-to-point topology. Keep in mind that these topologies describe the physical arrangement of cables. How the data travels along these cables might represent a different logical topology. The dominant logical topologies in LANs include switching, bus, and ring, all of which are usually implemented as a physical star (discussed later in "Logical Topologies").

Physical Bus Topology

The **physical bus topology**, shown in Figure 3-1, is by far the simplest and at one time was the most common method for connecting computers. It's a continuous length of cable connecting one computer to another in daisy-chain fashion. One of this topology's strengths is that you can add a new computer to the network simply by stringing a new length of cable from the last computer in the bus to the new machine. However, this strength is countered by some weaknesses:

- There's a limit of 30 computers per cable segment.
- The maximum total length of cabling is 185 meters.
- Both ends of the bus must be terminated.
- Any break in the bus brings down the entire network.
- Adding or removing a machine brings down the entire network temporarily.
- Technologies using this topology are limited to 10 Mbps half-duplex communication because they use coaxial cabling, discussed in Chapter 4.

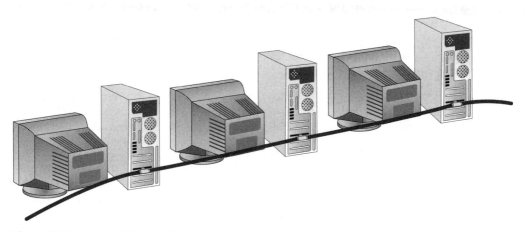

Figure 3-1 A physical bus topology network

Because of the preceding limitations, a physical bus topology is no longer a practical choice, and technology has moved past this obsolete method of connecting computers. However, the original Ethernet technology was based on this topology, and the basis of current LAN technology has its roots in the physical bus. So your understanding of bus communication aids your general understanding of how computers communicate with each other across a network.

How Data Travels in a Physical Bus Two properties inherent in a physical bus are signal propagation and signal bounce. In any network topology, computers communicate with each other by sending information across the media as a series of signals. When copper wire is the medium, as in a typical physical bus, these signals are sent as a series of electrical pulses that travel along the cable's length in all directions. The signals continue traveling along the cable and through any connecting devices until they weaken enough that they can't be detected or until they encounter a device that absorbs them. This traveling across the medium is called **signal propagation**. However, even if a signal encounters the end of a cable, it bounces back and travels in the other direction until it weakens or is otherwise impeded.

When a signal hits the end of a cable and bounces back up the cable's length, it interferes with signals following it, much like an echo. Imagine if you were trying to communicate in an empty room with hard walls that caused your voice to echo continuously. The echo from the first words out of your mouth would garble the sound of words that followed, and your message would be unintelligible. The term used when electricity bounces off the end of a cable and back in the other direction is called **signal bounce** (or "reflection"). To keep signal bounce from occurring, you do what you would to keep excessive echo from occurring; you install some type of material at both ends of the medium to absorb the signal. In a physical bus, you install a **terminator**, which is an electrical component called a "resistor" that absorbs the signal instead of allowing it to bounce back up the wire.

Physical Bus Limitations Now that you know more about how a physical bus works, the previous list of weaknesses needs some additional explanation. The limitation of 30 stations per cable segment means only 30 computers can be daisy-chained together before the signal becomes too weak to be passed along to another computer. As an electrical signal encounters each connected workstation, some of its strength is absorbed by both the cabling and the connectors until the signal is finally too weak for a computer's NIC to interpret. For the same reason, the total length of cabling is limited to 185 meters, whether there's 1 connected station or 30 connected stations. The network can be extended in cable length and number of workstations by adding a repeater to the network, which, as you know, regenerates the signal before sending it out.

At all times, both ends of the bus must be terminated. An unterminated bus results in signal bounce and data corruption. When a computer is added or removed from the network, both ends are no longer terminated, resulting in an interruption to network communication.

For a small network of only a few computers, you might think a bus topology is fine, until you consider the last weakness: maximum bandwidth of 10 Mbps half-duplex communication. A physical bus uses coaxial cable (a cabling type discussed in Chapter 4, similar to what's used in cable TV connections), which is limited to a top speed of 10 Mbps and communication in only half-duplex mode. Most networks now use twisted-pair cabling, which can operate at 1000 Mbps or faster and run in full-duplex mode, so communication between devices is much faster. For all these reasons, the physical bus topology has long since fallen out of favor and been replaced largely by the star topology, discussed next.

Physical Star Topology

The **physical star topology** uses a central device, such as a hub or switch, to interconnect computers in a LAN (see Figure 3-2). Each computer has a single length of cable going from its NIC to the central device.

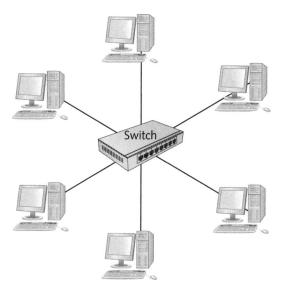

Figure 3-2 A physical star topology network

Some advantages of a physical star topology are the following:

- Much faster technologies are used than in a bus topology.
- Centralized monitoring and management of network traffic are possible.
- Network upgrades are easier.

A physical star is the topology of choice for these reasons and more. With a central device, communication options are available that simply aren't possible with a physical bus. For example, the central device can be a 1000 Mbps switch, which increases a physical bus's top speed 100 times and works in full-duplex mode, further increasing overall bandwidth.

As a budding network administrator, being able to monitor and manage your network with a central device is a big advantage over what was possible with a physical bus topology. Today's switches can include software that collects statistics about your network traffic patterns and even alerts you when excessive errors or unusually high traffic rates are occurring on your network. You don't get these features in a $19.99 switch, but enterprise-level devices can be equipped with several network management tools.

As long as your current cabling and installed NICs support it, your network can be upgraded quickly and easily from a ponderous 10 Mbps hub-based LAN to a blazing fast 1000 Mbps switched network simply by replacing the central device. In addition, if your NICs must also be upgraded, you can upgrade in steps because most devices support multiple speeds. So if you want to upgrade from 100 Mbps to 1000 Mbps, you can replace the central device with a switch that supports both speeds, and then upgrade NICs as time and money allow. The switch transmits and receives on each port at the speed supported by the NIC connected to that port.

What happens if the number of workstations you need to connect exceed the number of ports on the central device? In this case, you can connect switches together, as you learned in Chapter 2. When several switches must be connected, usually one device is used as the central connecting point, forming an extended star.

Extended Star The **extended star topology**, shown in Figure 3-3, is the most widely used in networks containing more than just a few computers. As the name implies, this topology is a star of stars. A central device, usually a switch, sits in the middle. Instead of attached computers forming the star's arms, other switches are connected to the central switch's ports. Computers and peripherals are then attached to these switches, forming additional stars. The extended star is sometimes referred to as a "hierarchical star" because there are two or more layers of stars, all connecting back to the central star.

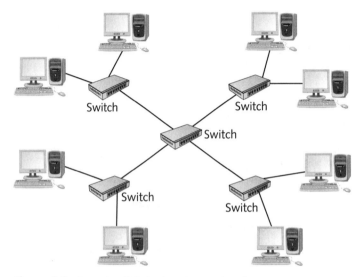

Figure 3-3 An extended star topology network

The extended star can be used to connect many computers, with the central device running at a very fast speed to shuttle data between the LAN's outer stars. This topology is most effective when the center of the star is running at a much faster speed than other devices; for example, the central device can run at 1000 Mbps while other devices run at 100 Mbps.

How Data Travels in a Physical Star The details of how data travels from computer to computer in a physical star depend on the type of central device. Data transmission starts at a device at the end of one of the central device's arms. From there, it travels along the network medium's length until it arrives at the central device. As you know from learning how hubs and switches work, the transmission path differs, depending on the device. Other devices, such as multistation access units (MAUs) used in token ring networks, move data differently. The type of central device, therefore, determines the logical topology, discussed later in "Logical Topologies."

Physical Star Disadvantages With all the clear advantages of a physical star, you might wonder whether there are any disadvantages. None outweigh the advantages, but it's worth mentioning that the central device represents a single point of failure. In other words, if the switch fails or someone kicks the power cord out of the outlet, down goes the entire network. Thankfully, these devices tend to be reliable and are usually placed out of the way of everyday foot traffic. That being said, they do fail from time to time, and having a spare on hand is a good idea.

When a physical bus was still the norm and the physical star was just coming on the networking scene in the late 1980s, it was often argued that because each computer must be cabled directly to the central device, instead of a bus's daisy-chain arrangement, more cable was required to connect computers. This point is indeed true, and at the time, the amount of cabling needed was a factor in designing a network with a bus or star arrangement. By the time the star network's advantages were fully realized in the mid-1990s, however, the cabling cost difference had diminished substantially, and the advantages clearly outweighed the minor cost disadvantage.

Physical Ring Topology

A **physical ring topology** is like a bus, in that devices are daisy-chained one to another, but instead of terminating each end, the cabling is brought around from the last device back to the first device to form a ring. This topology had little to no following in LANs as a way to connect computers. It was used, however, to connect LANs with a technology called Fiber Distributed Data Interface (FDDI). FDDI was most often used as a reliable and fast **network backbone**, which is cabling used to communicate between LANs or between switches. In Figure 3-4, the devices used to connect buildings form a ring, but computers on each LAN are connected with a physical star topology.

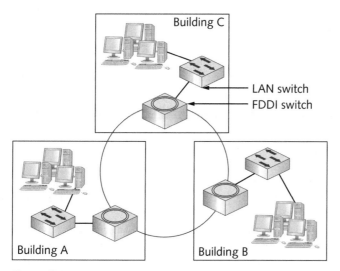

Figure 3-4 A physical ring topology is usually used to connect LANs

The physical ring also had reliability issues because data had to be forwarded from one station to the next. Unlike a bus, in which data travels in all directions and is terminated at both ends, a ring doesn't have any beginning or end. So each station must reproduce data and pass it along to the next station until it reaches the destination or the originator of the data. In other words, data always travels in one direction. If any station in the ring fails, data can no longer be passed along, and the ring is broken.

Technologies such as FDDI overcome some problems with a physical ring network by creating a dual ring, in which data can travel in both directions so that a single device failure doesn't break the entire ring. However, this technology is costly, and it has mostly been supplanted by extended star Ethernet installations.

Point-to-Point Topology

As its name implies, a **point-to-point topology** is a direct link between two devices. It's most often used in WANs, in which a device on a business's network has a dedicated link to a telecommunication provider, such as the local phone company. The connection then hooks into the phone company's network to provide Internet access or a WAN or MAN link to a branch office. The advantage of this topology is that data travels on a dedicated link, and its bandwidth isn't shared with other networks. The disadvantage is that it tends to be quite expensive, particularly when used as a WAN link to a distant branch office.

Point-to-point topologies are also used with wireless networks in what's called a **wireless bridge**. This setup can be used to connect two buildings without using a wired network (see Figure 3-5) or to extend an existing wireless network.

Figure 3-5   A point-to-point wireless topology

A rudimentary LAN can also be set up with a point-to-point topology by connecting a cable between the NICs on two computers. Of course, this method allows only two computers on the network, but it can be used effectively for transferring files from one computer to another in the absence of a switch.

So as you can see, point-to-point topologies are used for specialized purposes. They aren't commonly used in LANs; they're used more often in WANs and large internetworks.

Point-to-Multipoint Topology

A **point-to-multipoint (PMP) topology** is an arrangement in which a central device communicates with two or more other devices, and all communication goes through the central device. It's often used in WANs where a main office has connections to several branch offices via a router. Instead of the router having a separate connection to each branch office, a single connection is made from the router to a switching device, which then directs traffic to the correct branch office. In drawings of PMP networks, the switching device is often shown as a cloud, as in Figure 3-6. A PMP topology is also used in wireless network arrangements consisting of a single base station that communicates with multiple subscriber stations. Each subscriber station can communicate with the others, but all communication goes through the base station.

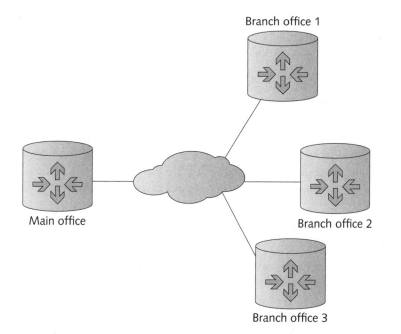

Figure 3-6 A point-to-multipoint topology

Mesh Topology A **mesh topology** connects each device to every other device in a network. You can look at a mesh topology as multiple point-to-point connections for the purposes of redundancy and fault tolerance. Figure 3-7 shows a full mesh topology between four locations, with the switch in each location providing connectivity to multiple computers. Each switch is connected to every other switch, which is called a "full mesh." If each switch were

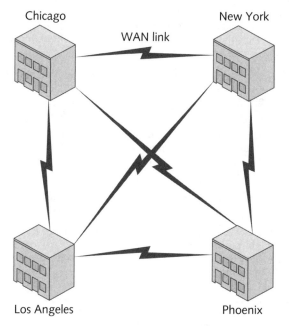

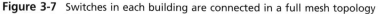

Figure 3-7 Switches in each building are connected in a full mesh topology

connected to only two other switches, it would be called a "partial mesh." In either case, the purpose of creating a mesh topology is to ensure that if one or more connections fail, there's another path for reaching all devices on the network. For example, in this figure, two connections could fail, but all devices could still communicate with one another. This topology is used most commonly in large internetworks and WANs, where routers or switches in multiple buildings or towns are connected in a partial or full mesh. Parts of the Internet are also designed with a partial mesh topology, in which major ISPs are connected so that even if one ISP's network fails, data can bypass this part of the network to get to its destination.

Mesh topologies, although reliable, are also expensive because of the additional cabling and ports required. In most cases, the ports used to connect devices are the highest speed available, such as 1 Gbps or 10 Gbps, and they often use expensive fiber-optic cabling for connecting buildings.

Logical Topologies

As mentioned, a network's logical topology describes how data travels from computer to computer. In some cases, as with a physical bus and physical ring, the logical topology mimics the physical arrangement of cables. In other cases, as with a physical star, the electronics in the central device determine the logical topology. A network's logical topology reflects the underlying network technology (covered later in "Network Technologies") used to transfer frames from one device to one another. Table 3-2 summarizes the main logical topologies, the technologies using them, and the physical topologies for implementing them.

Table 3-2 Logical topologies and associated network technologies and physical topologies

Logical topology	Network technology	Physical topology	Description
Bus	Ethernet	Bus or star	A logical bus topology can be implemented as a physical bus (although this topology is now obsolete). When a logical bus is implemented as a physical star using wired Ethernet, the center of the star is an Ethernet hub. Whatever the physical topology is, data transmitted from a computer is received by all other computers.
	Wireless LANs	Star	Wireless LANs use a physical star topology because they connect through a central access point. However, only one device can transmit at a time and all devices hear the transmission, so a wireless LAN can be considered a logical bus topology.
Ring	Token ring	Star	Token ring networks use a central device called a multistation access unit (MAU or MSAU). Its electronics form a logical ring, so data is passed from computer to computer in order, until it reaches the destination device.
	FDDI	Ring	As discussed, FDDI devices are connected in a physical ring, and data passes from device to device until it reaches the destination.
Switched	Ethernet	Star	A switched logical topology using a physical star topology running Ethernet is by far the most common topology/technology combination now and likely will be well into the future. A switched topology creates dynamic connections or circuits between two devices whenever data is sent. This topology is sometimes considered a switched point-to-point topology because a circuit is established between two points as needed to transfer data (like turning on a switch), and then the circuit is broken when it's no longer needed (like turning off a switch).

You have seen what a logical bus looks like when implemented as a physical bus. All computers are daisy-chained to one another, and network signals travel along the cable's length in all directions, much like water flowing through interconnected pipes. When a logical bus is set up as a physical star, the same process occurs, but the pathways are hidden inside the central hub. Figure 3-8 shows what a logical bus might look like when implemented with a hub.

A logical bus is sometimes called a "shared media topology" because all stations must share the bandwidth the media provides.

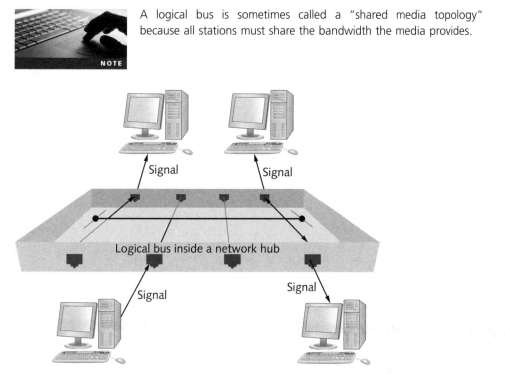

Figure 3-8 A logical bus implemented as a physical star

A logical ring using a physical star implements the ring inside the central device's electronics, which is an MAU in the token ring technology. Data is passed from one node or computer to another until it reaches the destination device (see Figure 3-9). When a port has no device connected to it, it's simply bypassed, and data is sent out the next connected port.

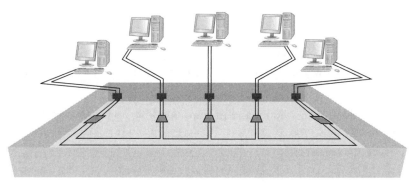

Figure 3-9 A logical ring implemented as a physical star

A switched topology works something like what's shown in Figure 3-10. Although there's always an electrical connection between the computer and switch, when no data is being transferred, there's no logical connection or circuit between devices. However, when the switch receives a frame, a logical circuit is made between the source and destination devices until the frame is transferred.

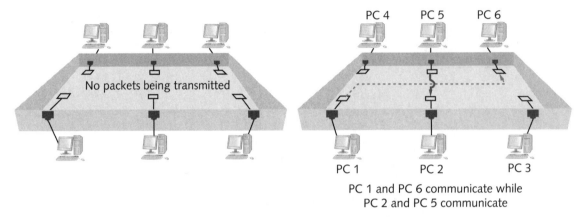

Figure 3-10 and nearby labels:
No packets being transmitted

PC 4   PC 5   PC 6

PC 1   PC 2   PC 3

PC 1 and PC 6 communicate while
PC 2 and PC 5 communicate

Figure 3-10 The logical functioning of a switch

To better understand how these logical topologies work, it helps to know the network technology that drives each topology (discussed later in "Network Technologies").

Enter ⏎
HANDS-ON PROJECTS

Hands-On Project 3-1: Building a Physical Star Topology Network

Time Required: 20 minutes

Objective: Build a physical star topology network.

Required Tools and Equipment: Three lab computers named Computer1, Computer2, and Computer3; a hub; and three patch cables

Description: In this project, you build a small physical star topology. After each station is connected to the hub, you ping another station to verify connectivity. Next, you use Wireshark to capture ping packets so that you can determine the network's logical topology.

1. Power on the hub.

2. Connect each workstation to the hub with the supplied cables.

3. Inspect the hub and the workstation NIC to verify that you have a good connection with the hub. Write down how you determined whether the connection with the hub is good:

_____

4. On each workstation, open a command prompt window, and then type **ipconfig** and press **Enter** to determine your IP address. Write down the IP address of each computer:

- IP address of Computer1: _____
- IP address of Computer2: _____
- IP address of Computer3: _____

5. Ping each computer to verify that you can communicate with it. If the pings aren't successful, check that the IP addresses you wrote down are correct and the connection with the hub is good, and then try again.

6. Make sure you coordinate the rest of the project, starting with this step, with students at the other computers. Start Wireshark, and start a capture session by clicking the interface name listed in the Interface List section.

7. At the command prompt, ping the next computer. For example, if you're at Computer1, ping Computer2; if you're at Computer2, ping Computer3; and if you're at Computer3, ping Computer1. Based on which packets Wireshark captured, what's your logical topology?

_____

8. Exit Wireshark, close all open windows, and leave the computers running if you're continuing to the next project.

Network Technologies

A network technology, as the phrase is used here, can best be described as the method a network interface uses to access the medium and send data frames and the structure of these frames. Other terms include network interface layer technologies, network architectures, and Data Link layer technologies. What it comes down to is whether your network uses Ethernet, 802.11 wireless (Wi-Fi), or some combination of these and other technologies to move data from device to device in your network. Most LANs are now based on a combination of Ethernet and 802.11 wireless. WANs use technologies designed to carry data over longer distances, such as frame relay, SONET, Asynchronous Transfer Mode (ATM), and others.

The network technology sometimes, but not always, defines frame format and which media types can be used to transfer frames. For example, different Ethernet speeds specify a minimum grade of copper or fiber-optic cabling that must be used as well as the connectors attached to the ends of cables. FDDI requires fiber-optic cabling, but other technologies, such as frame relay, can run on a variety of media types.

This book focuses on LAN technologies with particular emphasis on Ethernet and 802.11 wireless because they're the most commonly used. Some WAN technologies are described briefly in this chapter and in more detail in Chapter 10.

Network Technologies and Media

Because some of the network technologies discussed in this chapter specify the types of media they require to operate, the following sections summarize the most common media types. However, you can find more details on network media in Chapter 4.

Unshielded Twisted Pair
Unshielded twisted pair (UTP) is the most common media type in LANs. It consists of four pairs of copper wire, with each pair tightly twisted together and contained in a plastic sheath or jacket (see Figure 3-11).

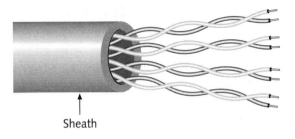

Figure 3-11   UTP cabling

UTP comes in numbered categories, up to Category 8 as of this writing. The higher the category, the higher the cable's bandwidth potential. Category 5 Enhanced (Cat 5E) and Category 6 (Cat 6) are the most common in wired LANs, allowing speeds up to 10 Gbps. UTP cabling is used in physical star networks, and the maximum cable length from NIC to switch is 100 meters in LAN applications. UTP cabling is susceptible to electrical interference, which can cause data corruption, so it shouldn't be used in electrically noisy environments.

Fiber-Optic Cabling Fiber-optic cabling uses extremely thin strands of glass to carry pulses of light long distances and at high data rates. It's usually used in large internetworks to connect switches and routers and sometimes to connect high-speed servers to the network. Because of its capability to carry data over long distances (several hundred to several thousand meters), it's also used in WAN applications frequently. Fiber-optic cabling isn't susceptible to electrical interference, so unlike UTP, it can be used in electrically noisy environments. It requires two strands of fiber to make a network connection: one for transmitting and one for receiving.

Coaxial Cable Best known for its use in cable TV, coaxial cable is obsolete as a LAN medium, but it's used as the network medium for Internet access via cable modem. Coaxial cable was the original medium used by Ethernet in physical bus topologies, but its limitation of 10 Mbps half-duplex communication made it obsolete for LAN applications after star topologies and 100 Mbps Ethernet became the dominant standard. Coaxial cable in LANs can be around 200 meters long.

Baseband and Broadband Signaling Network technologies can use media to transmit signals in two main ways: baseband and broadband. The **baseband** transmission method sends digital signals in which each bit of data is represented by a pulse of electricity (on copper media) or light (on fiber-optic media). These signals are sent at a single fixed frequency, using the medium's entire bandwidth. In other words, when a frame is sent to the medium, it occupies the cable's entire bandwidth, and no other frames can be sent along with it—much like having cable TV that carries only a single channel. LAN technologies, such as Ethernet and token ring, use baseband transmission. If cable TV used baseband signaling, you would need one cable for each channel!

Thankfully, cable TV and cable modem Internet access use broadband transmission. Instead of digital pulses, **broadband** systems use analog techniques to encode binary 1s and 0s across a continuous range of values. Broadband signals move across the medium in the form of continuous electromagnetic or optical waves rather than discrete pulses. On broadband systems, signals flow at a particular frequency, and each frequency represents a channel of data. That's why broadband systems, such as cable TV and Internet, can carry dozens or hundreds of TV channels plus Internet access on a single cable wire: Each channel operates at a different frequency. In addition, incoming and outgoing Internet data use separate channels operating at different frequencies from TV channels.

Ethernet Networks

Ethernet, the most popular LAN technology, has many advantages, including ease of installation, scalability, media support, and low cost. It supports a broad range of transmission speeds, from 10 Mbps to 10 Gbps. As discussed, it can operate in a bus or star physical topology and a bus or switched logical topology. It has been in use since the mid-1970s but didn't mature as a technology until the early to mid-1980s. Ethernet being around for almost 40 years is a testament to the original designers, whose forethought enabled Ethernet to scale from a 3 Mbps technology in its early years to a 100 Gbps technology today.

Although there are many variations of Ethernet, all forms are similar in their basic operation and frame formatting. What differs in the variations are the cabling, speed of transmission, and method by which bits are encoded on the medium. Because the frame formatting is the same, however, Ethernet variations are compatible with one another. That's why you often see NICs and Ethernet switches described as 10/100 or 10/100/1000 devices. These devices can support multiple Ethernet speeds because the underlying technology remains the same, regardless of speed.

Ethernet Addressing Every Ethernet station must have a physical or MAC address. As you learned in Chapter 2, a MAC address is an integral part of network interface electronics and consists of 48 bits expressed as 12 hexadecimal digits. When a frame is sent to the network medium, it must contain both source and destination MAC addresses. When a network interface detects a frame on the media, the NIC reads the frame's destination address and compares it with its own MAC address. If they match or if the destination address is the broadcast MAC address (all binary 1s or FF:FF:FF:FF:FF:FF in hexadecimal), the NIC reads the frame and sends it to the network protocol for further processing.

Ethernet Frames A frame is the unit of network information NICs and switches work with. It's the NIC's responsibility to transmit and receive frames and a switch's responsibility to forward frames out the correct switch port to get the frame to its destination.

Ethernet networks can accommodate frames between 64 bytes and 1518 bytes. Shorter or longer frames are usually considered errors. Each frame is composed of the following (see Figure 3-12):

- A 14-byte frame header composed of these three fields:
  - A 6-byte Destination MAC Address field
  - A 6-byte Source MAC Address field
  - A 2-byte Type field
- A Data field from 46 to 1500 bytes
- A frame trailer (frame check sequence [FCS]) of 4 bytes

Destination MAC Address (6 bytes)	Source MAC Address (6 bytes)	Type (2 bytes)	Data (46–1500 bytes)	FCS (4 bytes)
Frame header			Data (frame payload)	Frame trailer

Figure 3-12 Ethernet frame format

You've already learned the purpose and format of destination and source MAC addresses. The Type field in the frame header indicates the network protocol in the data portion. For example, this field might indicate that the Data field contains an IP, IPv6, or ARP packet, to name just a few possibilities. The data portion, often referred to as the "frame payload," contains network protocol header information as well as the actual data an application is transferring. The FCS in the frame trailer is an error-checking code (discussed later in "Ethernet Error Handling").

There are exceptions to the 1518-byte maximum frame size. For example, a function of some switches requires an additional 4-byte field in the Ethernet frame, bringing the maximum size to 1522 bytes. In addition, Jumbo frames of up to 9000 bytes are supported by some NICs and switches but aren't officially supported in the current Ethernet standards. To use Jumbo frames, the feature must be enabled on every device on the LAN and be implemented the same way by these devices. Some storage area network (SAN) devices also use Jumbo frames.

Ethernet Media Access Before a NIC can transmit data to the network medium, it must adhere to some rules governing how and when the medium can be accessed for transmission. The rules ensure that data is transmitted and received in an orderly fashion and all stations have an opportunity to communicate. The set of rules for each networking technology is referred to as its **media access method** (or "media access control").

The acronym for "media access control" is MAC, which is where the term "MAC address" comes from.

The media access method Ethernet uses in half-duplex mode is **Carrier Sense Multiple Access with Collision Detection (CSMA/CD)**. To understand this method better, break this term down into parts. "Carrier sense" means to listen. The rules for half-duplex Ethernet state that a device can send or receive data but can't do both simultaneously. So before a device can send, it must listen to see whether the medium is already busy, much like a group of people having a conversation. Each person listens for a pause in the conversation before speaking up. "Multiple access" simply means that multiple computers can be listening and waiting to transmit at the same time, which brings you to "collision detection." A **collision** occurs if two or more devices on the same medium transmit simultaneously. For example, if two people are waiting to chime in on a group conversation, they both hear a lull in the conversation at the same time and speak up simultaneously, causing a "collision" in the conversation. Ethernet's collision detection method is much like a person's; Ethernet detects, or "hears," the other station transmit, so it knows a collision has occurred. The NIC then waits for a random period before attempting to transmit again. Ethernet repeats the "listen before transmitting" process until it transmits the frame without a collision. Simulation 7 shows the CSMA/CD process.

Simulation 7: Ethernet operation using CSMA/CD

As you determined in Hands-On Project 2-3, when you attempted to create enough traffic to generate a collision, the CSMA/CD access method is efficient. It takes quite a bit of traffic to generate collisions, especially on a 100 Mbps or 1 Gbps network. However, the more devices on a logical bus topology and the more data they transmit, the greater the chance of a collision. So although CSMA/CD works well, today's multimedia-heavy networks have somewhat outgrown it, and Ethernet has adapted to this development.

CSMA/CD is considered a contention-based access method, which means computers are allowed to send whenever they have data ready to send. CSMA/CD modifies this rule somewhat by stipulating that the computer must listen first to ensure that no other station is in the process of transmitting.

Collisions and Collision Domains Remember that collisions can occur only in an Ethernet shared-media environment, which means a logical bus topology is in use. In this environment, all devices interconnected by one or more hubs hear all signals generated by all other devices. The signals are propagated from hub to hub until there are no more devices or until a device is encountered that doesn't use a logical bus topology, such as a switch or a router. The extent to which signals in an Ethernet bus topology network are propagated is called a **collision domain**. Figure 3-13 shows a network diagram with two collision domains enclosed in circles. All devices in a collision domain are subject to the possibility that whenever a device sends a frame, a collision might occur with another device sending a frame at the same time. This fact has serious implications for the number of computers that can reasonably be installed in a single collision domain. The more computers, the more likely it is that collisions occur. The more collisions, the slower network performance is.

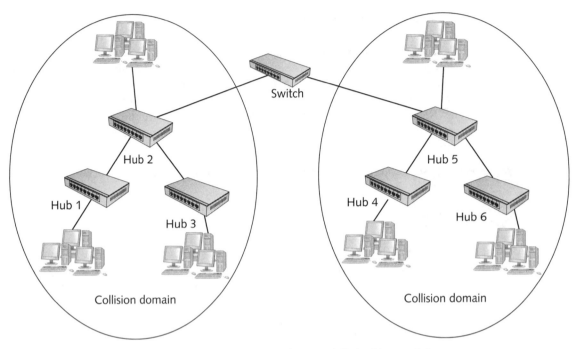

Figure 3-13 A network diagram showing two collision domains delimited by a switch

Notice in this figure that all computers connected to Hubs 1 to 3 are in the same collision domain, and computers connected to Hubs 4 to 6 are in a different collision domain. This is because a switch port delimits the collision domain, which means collisions occurring in one collision domain don't propagate through the switch.

Although collisions in an Ethernet network are usually associated with hubs, technically it's possible for a collision to occur with a computer connected to a switch, but it can happen only if the NIC connected to the switch port is operating in half-duplex mode. In addition, the collision domain is limited to only the devices connected to a single switch port. The same is true of routers. However, given that an Ethernet frame of maximum size is transmitted on a 10 Mbps switch in just over a millisecond and on a 100 Mbps switch in just over a microsecond, the likelihood of a collision with a switch is low.

If a hub is connected to a switch port in an extended star topology, collisions can occur between devices connected to the hub and the switch port. To avoid collisions altogether, use only switches in your network design with computers that have NICs operating in full-duplex mode.

Ethernet Error Handling One reason for Ethernet's low cost and scalability is its simplicity. It's considered a best-effort delivery system, meaning that when a frame is sent, there's no acknowledgement or verification that the frame arrived at its intended destination. Ethernet relies on network protocols, such as TCP/IP, to ensure reliable delivery of data. It's similar to the package delivery guy at a company. His job is to take what he's given to its intended destination; it's the package receiver's job to verify its contents and let the sender know it was received.

Ethernet can also detect whether a frame has been damaged in transit. The error-checking code in an Ethernet frame's trailer is called a **Cyclic Redundancy Check (CRC)**, which is the result of a mathematical algorithm computed on the frame data. The CRC is calculated and placed in the frame trailer before the frame is transmitted. When the frame is received, the calculation is repeated. If the results of this calculation don't match the CRC in the frame, it indicates that the data was altered in some way, possibly from electrical interference. If a frame is detected as damaged, Ethernet simply discards the frame but doesn't inform the sending station that an error occurred (because it's a best-effort delivery system). Again, it's the network protocol's job to ensure that all expected data was actually received. The network protocol or, in some cases, the application sending the data is responsible for resending damaged or missing data, not Ethernet.

A collision is the exception to Ethernet's lack of action when an error occurs. When frames are involved in a collision, Ethernet resends them automatically because all stations detect that a collision has occurred.

Half-Duplex Versus Full-Duplex Communication As discussed in Chapter 2, half-duplex communication means a station can transmit and receive data but not at the same time, much like a two-way radio. When Ethernet is implemented as a logical bus topology (using hubs), NICs can operate only in half-duplex mode and must use the CSMA/CD access method. However, a network switch allows half-duplex or full-duplex communication. If a NIC is operating in half-duplex mode while connected to a switch, it must use CSMA/CD. However, the only time a collision can occur in this circumstance is if the switch happens to transmit a frame to the NIC at the same time the NIC is attempting to transmit.

Full-duplex mode, by definition, means a NIC can transmit and receive simultaneously. Therefore, when an Ethernet NIC is operating in full-duplex mode connected to a switch, CSMA/CD isn't used because a collision can't occur in full-duplex mode. Because full-duplex mode eliminates the delays caused by CSMA/CD and allows double the network bandwidth, most Ethernet LANs now operate in this mode using switches.

Ethernet Standards

Ethernet can operate at different speeds over different types of media, and each variation is associated with an IEEE standard. The following sections discuss many of these standards, some of which are obsolete or had limited use.

Standards Terminology Ethernet standards are generally expressed in one of two ways. One way is using the IEEE document number defining the standard. For example, IEEE 802.3 is the parent document specification for 10 Mbps Ethernet using thick coaxial cable, which was ratified in 1983. All other variations and speeds of Ethernet are subdocuments of the original 802.3 specification.

The second way of expressing an Ethernet standard is to use the XBaseY terminology. Most IEEE 802.3 documents describe the transmission speed, type of transmission, and length or type of cabling and are designated with terms such as 100BaseT. In 100BaseT, for example, the "100" designates the speed of transmission (100 Mbps), the "Base" indicates a baseband signaling method, and the "T" specifies twisted-pair cabling. All the BaseT Ethernet standards use a physical star topology. The following sections discuss the major standards and their designations.

10BaseT Ethernet 10BaseT Ethernet, defined by IEEE 802.3i, has been the mainstay of Ethernet networks since the early 1990s. It runs over Category 3 or higher UTP cabling and uses two of the four wire pairs. Because of its slower transmission speed, 10BaseT networks using a logical bus topology (with hubs) are more susceptible to collisions than faster 100BaseT networks are. In addition, the amount of data sent and received by a typical user makes 10BaseT seem slow in typical media-heavy environments compared with the more common 100BaseT and 1000BaseT standards.

If you work for an organization still using hubs, you need to know that there are limits to how many hubs you can string together to connect all computers. The rule for expanding a 10BaseT network with hubs is that no more than four hubs can be placed between two communicating workstations. This rule ensures that all stations on the network can detect a collision. Because of the limited time for signals to propagate through a network, if more than four hubs exist between end stations, a collision on one end of the network might not be detected by stations on the other side of the network in time for them to react properly. If switches rather than hubs are used, there's no such limitation because a collision on a switch can take place only between the switch and a single workstation.

A business network still using 10BaseT should upgrade to 100 or 1000BaseT to take full advantage of current technology. A home or small-office network that uses the network mainly for sharing Internet access and transferring documents can still use 10BaseT effectively if its Internet connection is considerably slower than 10 Mbps. However, 10BaseT is essentially an obsolete technology, and networks using it should upgrade as soon as circumstances permit.

100BaseTX Ethernet 100BaseTX (often called simply "100BaseT"), defined by IEEE 802.3u, is still the most common Ethernet variety. It runs over Category 5 or higher UTP cable and uses two of the four wire pairs: one to transmit data and the other to receive data. There are other varieties of 100BaseT Ethernet (discussed later in this section), but 100BaseTX is the standard that's usually in mind when discussing 100 Mbps Ethernet. It's also sometimes called "Fast Ethernet."

An important consideration when designing a 100BaseTX network with hubs is the total number of hubs allowed between end stations. There are two types of 100BaseTX hubs: class I and class II. Class I hubs can have only one hub between communicating devices; class II hubs can have a maximum of two hubs between devices. This limitation is designed to ensure that when a collision occurs on a hub-based network, all stations in the collision domain have enough time to hear the collision and respond appropriately. If a 100BaseTX network uses mainly hubs to connect computers, a switch is often used in the center of an extended star to interconnect multiple hubs, as shown in Figure 3-14, to avoid this

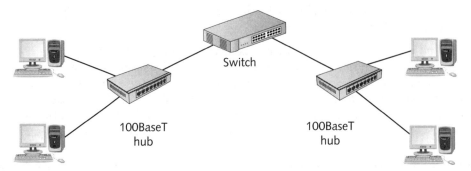

Switch

100BaseT
hub

100BaseT
hub

Figure 3-14 Using a switch to interconnect 100BaseTX hubs

limitation. If you're using only switches in your network, this limitation doesn't apply. You'll probably see hubs of any type only in older network installations; all new designs and upgrades use switches of at least 100 Mbps.

100BaseFX Ethernet In environments that aren't conducive to using copper wiring to carry network data (such as electrically noisy settings) or where the cable run length exceeds the reach of twisted-pair wiring, the only real choice in a wired network is fiber optics. **100BaseFX** (with the F indicating "fiber optic"), which uses two strands of fiber-optic cable, is often the best choice of network technology in these settings. Fiber-optic cable installation is still far more expensive than twisted-pair cable, but its advantages of being impervious to electrical noise and supporting longer cable segment lengths are worth the cost if the network requires these properties. 100BaseFX is rarely used as a complete replacement for 100BaseTX; instead, it's typically used as backbone cabling between hubs or switches and to connect wiring closets between floors or buildings. It's also used to connect client or server computers to the network when immunity to noise and eavesdropping is required.

1000BaseT Ethernet 1000BaseT Ethernet, released as the IEEE 802.3ab standard, supports 1000 Mbps Ethernet (usually called "Gigabit Ethernet") over Category 5 or higher UTP cable. The 1 Gbps data rate results from sending and receiving data simultaneously (in full-duplex mode) at 250 Mbps in both directions over each of the four wire pairs in Category 5e cable. Therefore, each wire pair can send and receive data at the same time at 250 Mbps, which results in a bandwidth of 1000 Mbps (or 1 Gbps) in each direction in full-duplex mode. To support full-duplex transmission over a single pair of wires, 1000BaseT uses hybrid and canceller equipment, which combines multiple signals and cancels interference. So if the link operates in half-duplex mode, the channel speed is 1000 Mbps (250 Mbps times four wire pairs). When operating in full-duplex mode, 1000BaseT actually delivers 2 Gbps total bandwidth. In most cases, it runs in full-duplex mode connected to switches.

Unlike 10BaseT and 100BaseT Ethernet, 1000BaseT Ethernet doesn't dedicate a wire pair to transmitting or receiving. Each wire pair is capable of transmitting and receiving data simultaneously, thereby making the 1000 Mbps data rate possible in both half-duplex and full-duplex modes. Similarly to 100BaseT, 1000BaseT allows only one hub or repeater between end stations when using half-duplex communication. Most installations use switches that detect the speed of the connected device automatically, whether it's 10 Mbps, 100 Mbps, or 1000 Mbps. In addition, you'll be hard-pressed to find a 1000BaseT hub to purchase, making the one-repeater limitation an unlikely problem in new network designs.

10GBaseT Ethernet The 2006 IEEE 802.3an standard defines 10 Gigabit Ethernet as running over four pairs of Category 6A or Category 7 UTP cabling. Unlike the other BaseT Ethernet standards, **10GBaseT** operates only in full-duplex mode, so you won't find any 10 Gbps hubs—only switches. 10GBaseT NICs are pricey compared with NICs supporting 1 Gbps and less, but prices continue to drop. As of this writing, you can purchase a 10GBaseT NIC for under $200; a few years ago, the price was more than $1000. Although this cost might still be a lot for a desktop computer, you might need to equip network servers with 10 Gigabit Ethernet NICs so that they can keep up with desktop systems that commonly operate at 1 Gbps.

Additional Ethernet Standards

Although the standards discussed previously constitute the majority of Ethernet LANs, quite a few other standards exist; some are common, and others are uncommon or obsolete. The following sections describe these other standards and their use in current networks briefly.

100BaseT4 As the name implies, 100BaseT4 Ethernet uses all four pairs of wires bundled in a UTP cable. The one advantage that 100BaseT4 has over 100BaseTX is the capability to run over Category 3 cable. When 100 Mbps speeds became available, many companies wanted to take advantage of the higher bandwidth. However, if the cable plant consisted of only Category 3 cable, there were just two choices: Replace the cabling with higher-grade Category 5 cabling so that 100BaseTX could be used, or use 100BaseT4 Ethernet. One of the biggest expenses of building a network is cable installation, so many organizations chose to get higher speeds with the existing cable plant by using 100BaseT4. Although these differences from 100BaseTX might seem like a good idea, 100BaseT4 never caught on and is essentially obsolete.

1000BaseLX 1000BaseLX uses fiber-optic media; the "L" stands for "long wavelength," the kind of laser used to send signals across the medium. These lasers operate at wavelengths between 1270 to 1355 nanometers and work with single-mode fiber (SMF) and multimode fiber (MMF). Long-wavelength lasers cost more than short-wavelength lasers but can transmit their signals over longer lengths of cable.

Although the 1000BaseLX standard specifies a maximum cable segment length of 5000 meters, some manufacturers have extended it by using specialized and proprietary optical transceivers. Cisco Systems, for example, offers 1000BaseLH ("LH" stands for "long haul"), which provides a maximum cable segment length of 10,000 meters over SMF cable. For extremely long-distance Gigabit Ethernet communication, 1000BaseZX, another Cisco product, is capable of distances up to 100,000 meters over SMF cable.

1000BaseSX 1000BaseSX uses fiber-optic media; the "S" stands for "short wavelength." These lasers operate at wavelengths between 770 to 860 nanometers and work only with MMF cable. Short-wavelength lasers can't cover as much distance as long-wavelength lasers, but they are less expensive (and use cheaper MMF cable).

1000BaseCX 1000BaseCX uses specially shielded, balanced, copper jumper cables; the "C" stands for "copper," the kind of electrical signaling used. Jumper cables are normally used for interconnections between devices or to link virtual LANs (VLANs) on a switch; these jumper cables might also be called "twinax" (short for "twin-axial") or "short-haul" copper cables. Segment lengths for 1000BaseCX cables top out at 25 meters, which means they're used mostly in wiring closets or equipment racks.

10 Gigabit Ethernet IEEE 802.3ae Standards The 802.3ae standard governing several varieties of 10 Gigabit Ethernet before 10GBaseT was adopted in June 2002. This Ethernet version is much like the others in frame formats and media access method. However, it does have some important technical differences. It's defined to run only on fiber-optic cabling, but the 10 Gigabit Ethernet standard specifies a maximum distance of 40 kilometers, compared with just 5 kilometers for the 1000BaseLX Gigabit Ethernet. This distance has important implications for WANs and MANs because although most WAN and MAN technologies can be measured in megabits, 10 Gigabit Ethernet provides bandwidth that can transform how WAN speeds are considered. Like 10GBaseT Ethernet, 802.3ae 10 Gigabit Ethernet technologies run in full-duplex mode only, so the CSMA/CD access method isn't necessary.

The primary use of 10 Gigabit Ethernet technologies is as the network backbone, interconnecting servers and network segments running 100 Mbps and 1000 Mbps Ethernet technologies. However, they also have their place in storage area networks (SANs) and, along with 10GBaseT, can be used as the interface for enterprise-level servers.

As this technology matured, a number of implementations were developed that are divided into two basic groups: 10GBaseR for LAN applications and 10GBaseW for WAN applications. The W group of standards uses SONET framing over OC-192 links. (SONET and OC standards are explained in Chapter 10.) Both groups have (S)hort range, (L)ong range, and (E)xtended range versions. The short-range versions use MMF fiber-optic cabling, and the long-range and extended-range versions run over SMF fiber-optic cabling. (These fiber-optic types are discussed in Chapter 4.) The following list summarizes the 802.3ae technologies:

- *10GBaseSR*—Runs over short lengths (between 26 and 82 meters) on MMF cabling. Applications are likely to include connections to high-speed servers, interconnecting switches, and SANs.
- *10GBaseLR*—Runs up to 10 km on SMF cabling and is used for campus backbones and MANs.
- *10GBaseER*—Runs up to 40 km on SMF cabling; used primarily for MANs.
- *10GBaseSW*—Uses MMF cabling for distances up to 300 meters; used for SONET campus network applications.
- *10GBaseLW*—Uses SMF cabling for distances up to 10 km; used for SONET WAN applications.
- *10GBaseEW*—Uses SMF cabling for distances up to 40 km; used for SONET WAN applications.

40 Gigabit and 100 Gigabit Ethernet IEEE 802.3ba was ratified on June 17, 2010, and it paves the way for extremely fast communication channels. Pricing on 40 Gbps and 100 Gbps products is still prohibitive, and adoption of these standards has been slow. Fiber-optic cabling is the primary medium for supporting these speeds, although there are provisions to use special copper assemblies over short distances. Related standards that support 100 Gbps include 802.3bj and 802.3bm.

Although the 802.3ba task force has completed its work, you can read more about this standard at *www.ieee802.org/3/ba/index.html*.

As you can see, Ethernet has come a long way since Xerox transmitted at 3 Mbps over coaxial cable, and the journey from 3 Mbps to 10 Gbps isn't over yet. Table 3-3 summarizes many features and properties of the Ethernet standards discussed in this section.

Table 3-3 Ethernet standards and properties

Ethernet standard	IEEE document #	Transmission speed	Cable type	Minimum cable grade	Maximum distance	Design notes
10Base-T	802.3i	10 Mbps	UTP	Cat 3	100 meters	Maximum four hubs between stations
100BaseT/TX	802.3u	100 Mbps	UTP	Cat 5	100 meters	Maximum two hubs between stations
100BaseFX	802.3u	100 Mbps	MMF or SMF	N/A	2 km over MMF, 10 km over SMF	
1000BaseT	802.3ab	1000 Mbps	UTP	Cat 5 (Cat 5e or 6 preferred)	100 meters	Maximum one hub between stations
10GBaseT	802.3an	10 Gbps	UTP	Cat 6A	100 meters	Full-duplex only; no hubs
100BaseT4	802.3u	100 Mbps	UTP	Cat 3	100 meters	Obsolete; saw little use
1000BaseLX	802.3z	1000 Mbps	MMF or SMF	N/A	550 meters over MMF, 5 km over SMF	
1000BaseSX	802.3z	1000 Mbps	MMF	N/A	550 meters	
1000BaseCX	802.3z	1000 Mbps	Twinax	N/A	25 meters	Succeeded by 1000BaseT
10GBaseSR 10GBaseLR 10GBaseER 10GBaseSW 10GBaseLW 10GBaseEW	802.3ae	10 Gbps	MMF or SMF	N/A	Varies from 82 meters up to 40 km	Choice of technology depends on application
40 Gigabit Ethernet and 100 Gigabit Ethernet	802.3ba	40 and 100 Gbps	MMF, SMF, and copper assembly	N/A	40 km over SMF, 7 meters over copper	Standard ratified June 2010

What's Next for Ethernet? Estimations are that Ethernet speeds will continue to increase, with Terabit Ethernet (1000 Gbps) as part of the discussion. In March 2013, a study group began work on a 400 Gbps standard that could be available by 2017. This kind of mind-boggling speed will allow networks to transfer data across a city faster than some CPUs can transfer data to memory. When Internet providers begin using this level of bandwidth to connect to the Internet backbone, and when homes and businesses can tap into it, too, extraordinary amounts of information will be at your fingertips. This speed has major implications for the entertainment industry and many other fields.

Hands-On Project 3-2: Determining and Changing Your Ethernet Standard

Time Required: 15 minutes

Objective: Determine your Ethernet standard and change your connection speed to use a different standard.

Required Tools and Equipment: Two lab computers, a switch, and two patch cables. The switch and NICs must be capable of connecting at multiple speeds. For example, if you're using a 10/100 Mbps switch, and your NICs are capable of 10/100 Mbps, you change the connection speed to the slower rate. Work in pairs.

Description: In this project, you view your network connection properties to see at what speed your NIC is operating. Then you send a large ping message to a partner and note how long the reply takes. Next, you change the speed, if your NIC driver allows, and perform the same ping to see whether you can detect a time difference.

This project works best with physical computers rather than virtual machines. Even if you change the connection speed on the virtual machine, it transmits bits at the host computer's connection speed.

1. Log on to your computer as **NetAdmin**.

2. Open a command prompt window, and then type **ipconfig** and press **Enter**. Exchange your IP address with your partner and write down your partner's IP address on the following line. Leave the command prompt window open for later.

3. Right-click **Start** and click **Network Connections**. Right-click **Ethernet0** and click **Status** (see Figure 3-15).

Figure 3-15 The Ethernet0 Status dialog box

4. In the Connection section, find the line labeled "Speed." Write down this information and, based on the speed listed, the Ethernet variety your computer is running:

- Connection speed: _____

- Ethernet variety: _____

5. At the command prompt, ping your partner by typing **ping -1 60000 *IPaddress*** and pressing **Enter**. The -1 60000 option in the command specifies that the ping message should be 60000 bytes instead of the typical length of 32 bytes. Note the time values in the ping replies and write them down. For example, yours might say "time<1ms," meaning the reply took less than 1 millisecond. Not all times might be the same. Sometimes the first time is slower than the rest. Try pinging a few times to get an idea of the average time. Write the ping reply times on the following line:

_____

6. Click the **Properties** button in the Ethernet0 Status dialog box, and in the Ethernet0 Properties dialog box, click the **Configure** button under the Connect using text box.

7. Click the **Advanced** tab. In the Property list box, click **Speed & Duplex** (or a similar name). Figure 3-16 shows the connection options. Not all NICs have the same options, so you might see different options.

Figure 3-16   Settings for the Speed & Duplex property

8. The default setting is usually Auto Negotiation. Click **10 Mpbs Half Duplex** if this option is available, and then click **OK**. If you were able to set this option, what speed and variety of Ethernet is your computer running now?

   • Connection speed: _____

   • Ethernet variety: _____

9. After you and your partner have changed the connection speed to a lower value, repeat the ping command you used in Step 5. Write down the reply times on the following lines, and state whether they were different:

   _____

   _____

10. Figure 3-17 shows two sets of ping results. The first result was from two computers connected at 1 Gbps (1000 Mbps) in full-duplex mode. The average reply took 5 ms. The second result was with the same computers connected at 10 Mbps half-duplex, and the average reply took 103 ms. Change your connection speed and duplex mode back to Auto Negotiation, and then close all open windows. Leave your computer running for the next project.

```
Administrator: Command Prompt

C:\Users\gtomsho>ping -l 60000 172.31.210.2

Pinging 172.31.210.2 with 60000 bytes of data:
Reply from 172.31.210.2: bytes=60000 time=5ms TTL=128
Reply from 172.31.210.2: bytes=60000 time=5ms TTL=128
Reply from 172.31.210.2: bytes=60000 time=5ms TTL=128
Reply from 172.31.210.2: bytes=60000 time=5ms TTL=128

Ping statistics for 172.31.210.2:
    Packets: Sent = 4, Received = 4, Lost = 0 (0% loss),
Approximate round trip times in milli-seconds:
    Minimum = 5ms, Maximum = 5ms, Average = 5ms

C:\Users\gtomsho>ping -l 60000 172.31.210.2

Pinging 172.31.210.2 with 60000 bytes of data:
Reply from 172.31.210.2: bytes=60000 time=103ms TTL=128
Reply from 172.31.210.2: bytes=60000 time=103ms TTL=128
Reply from 172.31.210.2: bytes=60000 time=104ms TTL=128
Reply from 172.31.210.2: bytes=60000 time=103ms TTL=128

Ping statistics for 172.31.210.2:
    Packets: Sent = 4, Received = 4, Lost = 0 (0% loss),
Approximate round trip times in milli-seconds:
    Minimum = 103ms, Maximum = 104ms, Average = 103ms

C:\Users\gtomsho>
```

Figure 3-17   Ping results at different connection speeds

HANDS-ON PROJECTS

Hands-On Project 3-3: Viewing an Ethernet Frame

Time Required: 20 minutes

Objective: Capture packets and examine details of an Ethernet frame.

Required Tools and Equipment: Two lab computers, a switch, and two patch cables

Description: In this project, you capture some packets and then examine the frame and protocol headers.

1. If necessary, log on to your computer as **NetAdmin**.

2. Start Wireshark and click **Capture Options**. In the Capture Filter text box, type **icmp**, and then click **Start**.

3. Open a command prompt window, and then type `ping IPaddress` and press **Enter** (replacing *IPaddress* with the IP address of your partner's computer from Hands-On Project 3-2).

4. In Wireshark, click the **Stop the running live capture** toolbar icon to stop the capture.

5. Click a packet summary in the top pane with ICMP listed in the protocol field. In the middle pane, click to expand the **Ethernet II** row (see Figure 3-18).

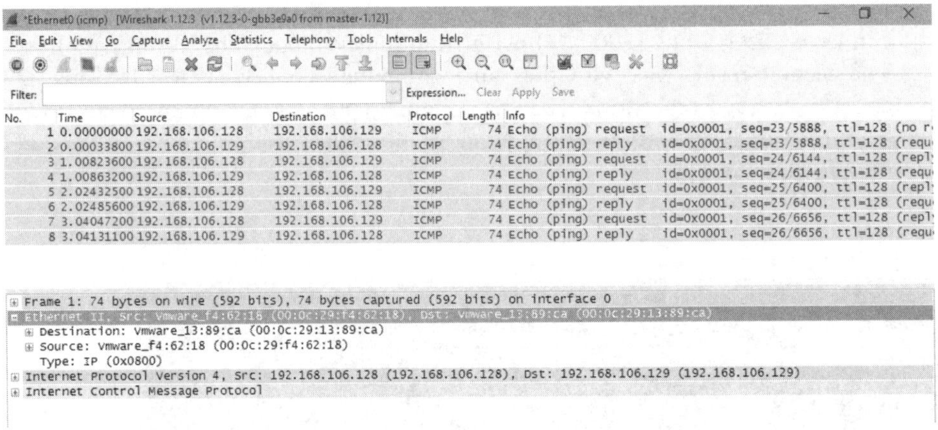

Figure 3-18   An Ethernet II frame in Wireshark

Source: Wireshark Foundation, *www.wireshark.org*

6. Notice the three fields in the Ethernet II frame: Destination, Source, and Type. The Destination and Source fields are the destination and source MAC addresses in the frame. In Figure 3-18, you see "Vmware" before the source and destination addresses because Wireshark attempts to resolve the NIC manufacturer coded in the MAC address's first six digits. The full MAC address (without manufacturer name) is shown in parentheses. The Type field has the value 0x800, which indicates that the protocol in the frame is IP. Click to expand the **Internet Protocol Version 4** row.

7. Under Internet Protocol Version 4, you see details of the IP header, including the destination and source IP addresses. Click to expand the **Internet Control Message Protocol** row to view details of the ICMP protocol header. (You learn more about IP-related protocols in Chapter 5.)

8. Click to expand the **Data** portion of the frame, and then click the **Data** field to see the ICMP message data in hexadecimal in the bottom pane (see Figure 3-19). The right side of this pane shows the translation from hexadecimal to ASCII (human-readable characters); as you can see, it's just portions of the alphabet repeated. Some `ping` programs include more clever data, such as "Hello, are you there?" The actual data in a ping message doesn't matter; what matters is that the reply contains the same data as the ping request.

*Ethernet0 (icmp) [Wireshark 1.12.3 (v1.12.3-0-gbb3e9a0 from master-1.12)]   — ☐ ✕

File Edit View Go Capture Analyze Statistics Telephony Tools Internals Help

Filter: ∨ Expression... Clear Apply Save

No.	Time	Source	Destination	Protocol	Length	Info
1	0.00000000	192.168.106.128	192.168.106.129	ICMP	74	Echo (ping) request id=0x0001, seq=23/5888, ttl=128 (no r
2	0.00033800	192.168.106.129	192.168.106.128	ICMP	74	Echo (ping) reply id=0x0001, seq=23/5888, ttl=128 (requ
3	1.00823600	192.168.106.128	192.168.106.129	ICMP	74	Echo (ping) request id=0x0001, seq=24/6144, ttl=128 (repl
4	1.00863200	192.168.106.129	192.168.106.128	ICMP	74	Echo (ping) reply id=0x0001, seq=24/6144, ttl=128 (requ
5	2.02432500	192.168.106.128	192.168.106.129	ICMP	74	Echo (ping) request id=0x0001, seq=25/6400, ttl=128 (repl
6	2.02485600	192.168.106.129	192.168.106.128	ICMP	74	Echo (ping) reply id=0x0001, seq=25/6400, ttl=128 (requ
7	3.04047200	192.168.106.128	192.168.106.129	ICMP	74	Echo (ping) request id=0x0001, seq=26/6656, ttl=128 (repl
8	3.04131100	192.168.106.129	192.168.106.128	ICMP	74	Echo (ping) reply id=0x0001, seq=26/6656, ttl=128 (requ

```
    Fragment offset: 0
    Time to live: 128
    Protocol: ICMP (1)
  ⊞ Header checksum: 0x0000 [validation disabled]
    Source: 192.168.106.128 (192.168.106.128)
    Destination: 192.168.106.129 (192.168.106.129)
    [Source GeoIP: Unknown]
    [Destination GeoIP: Unknown]
⊟ Internet Control Message Protocol
    Type: 8 (Echo (ping) request)
    Code: 0
    Checksum: 0x4d44 [correct]
    Identifier (BE): 1 (0x0001)
    Identifier (LE): 256 (0x0100)
    Sequence number (BE): 23 (0x0017)
    Sequence number (LE): 5888 (0x1700)
  ⊞ [No response seen]
  ⊟ Data (32 bytes)
      Data: 6162636465666768696a6b6c6d6e6f7071727374757677761...
      [Length: 32]
```

```
0000  00 0c 29 13 89 ca 00 0c  29 f4 62 18 08 00 45 00   ..)..... ).b...E.
0010  00 3c 14 d6 00 00 80 01  00 00 c0 a8 6a 80 c0 a8   .<...... ....j...
0020  6a 81 08 00 4d 44 00 01  00 17 61 62 63 64 65 66   j...MD.. ..abcdef
0030  67 68 69 6a 6b 6c 6d 6e  6f 70 71 72 73 74 75 76   ghijklmn opqrstuv
0040  77 61 62 63 64 65 66 67  68 69                     wabcdefg hi
```

○ 📄 | Data (data), 32 bytes | Packets: 8 · Displayed: 8 (100.0%) · Dropped: 0 (0.0%) | Profile: Default

Figure 3-19 The data portion of an ICMP message

Source: Wireshark Foundation, *www.wireshark.org*

9. Exit Wireshark and click **Quit without Saving** when prompted. Close the command prompt window. Stay logged on if you're going on to the next project; otherwise, shut down your computer.

802.11 Wi-Fi

The 1997 802.11 wireless networking standard, also referred to as **Wireless Fidelity (Wi-Fi)**, has continued to undergo development. With it, manufacturers of wireless networking devices have brought inexpensive, reliable wireless LANs (WLANs) to homes and businesses. In fact, Wi-Fi has become so affordable that some businesses give it away free. In most towns, you can usually find a public Wi-Fi network, called a **hotspot**, at a local library or McDonald's where you can connect with your tablet or smartphone.

Wi-Fi networks are also known as "wireless LANs (WLANs)," and the terms can be used interchangeably.

Essentially, 802.11 wireless is an extension to Ethernet, using airwaves instead of cabling as the medium, although most 802.11 networks incorporate some wired Ethernet segments. The 802.11 networks can extend from several feet to several thousand feet, depending on equipment (such as antennas) and environmental factors, such as obstructions and radio frequency interference. The following sections discuss these aspects of 802.11 Wi-Fi:

- Modes of operation
- Channels and frequencies
- Antennas
- Access methods and operation
- Signal characteristics
- Standards

Wi-Fi Modes of Operation

Wi-Fi networks can operate in one of two modes: infrastructure and ad hoc. Most Wi-Fi networks operate in **infrastructure mode**, meaning wireless stations connect through a wireless AP before they can begin communicating with other devices. Infrastructure mode uses a logical bus topology because all nodes hear all communications (in most cases). The physical topology is more difficult to describe because there are no physical wires; however, with a central device that all nodes communicate with, it most resembles a star topology. **Ad hoc mode**, sometimes called "peer-to-peer mode," is a wireless mode of operation typically used only in small or temporary installations. There's no central device, and data travels from one device to another in a line (more or less). If you want to describe ad hoc mode in terms of a physical and logical topology, it most resembles a physical and logical bus. Most of this chapter's discussion of Wi-Fi focuses on infrastructure mode.

NOTE Ad hoc mode shouldn't be used in public environments because it's less secure than infrastructure mode. Microsoft removed the capability to create an ad hoc wireless network in the Network and Sharing Center starting with Windows 8; however, you can still create one in Windows 8 and later by using the `netsh wlan hostednetwork` command at a command prompt.

Wi-Fi Channels and Frequencies

Wi-Fi networks operate at one of two radio frequencies: 2.4 GHz and 5.0 GHz. However, this frequency is not fixed. The 2.4 GHz Wi-Fi variety operates from 2.412 GHz through 2.484 GHz, divided into 14 channels spaced 5 MHz apart, with each channel being 22 MHz wide. Because of radio frequency use restrictions, only the first 11 channels are used in North America. Other regions have channel use restrictions, too, but Japan allows using all 14 channels. The 5.0 GHz Wi-Fi variety divides frequencies between 4.915 GHZ and 5.825 GHz into 42 channels of 10, 20, 40, 80, or 160 MHz each, depending on the Wi-Fi standard in use. The remainder of the discussion on Wi-Fi channels pertains to 2.4 GHz Wi-Fi because it's the most popular, but most points also apply to the 5.0 GHz varieties.

A wireless channel works somewhat like a TV channel, in which each channel works at a different frequency and can, therefore, carry different streams of data. When you configure a wireless AP, you can choose the channel in which it operates (see Figure 3-20). By choosing a channel that's not in heavy use, you can improve reception and throughput rate. However, 2.4 GHz channels are spaced 5 MHz apart, but each channel is actually 22 MHz wide,

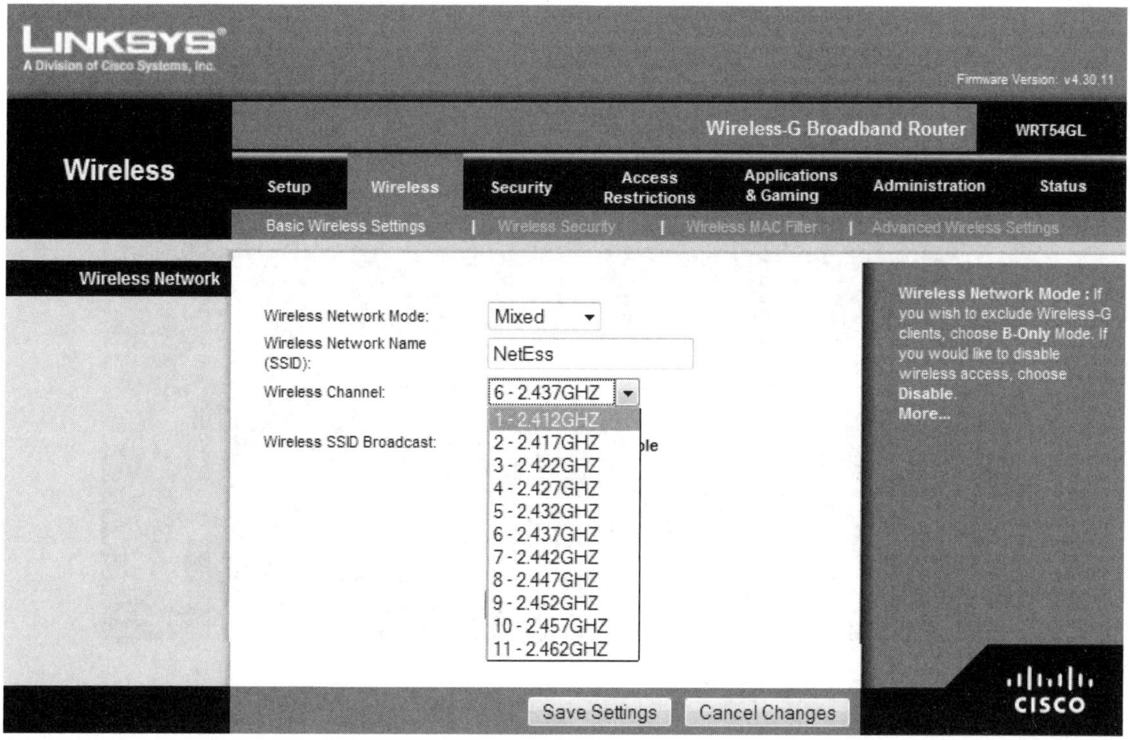

Figure 3-20 Selecting a Wi-Fi channel on an access point

Source: Cisco Systems, Inc.

resulting in channel overlap. So if you're configuring several Wi-Fi networks, you should choose channels that are five apart; for example, if you configure three Wi-Fi networks in close proximity, choose channels 1, 6, and 11 because those channels don't overlap one another.

Wi-Fi networks using the 5.0 GHz frequency have up to 24 nonoverlapping channels because the channels are spaced 20 MHz apart, and each channel has the option to use 20 MHz bandwidth. Access points operating in this frequency can be configured to use channels wider than 20 MHz, however, which then causes adjacent channels to overlap, a fact you should be aware of when configuring 5.0 GHz Wi-Fi networks. The newer Wi-Fi standards, such as 802.11ac, configure the channel and channel bandwidth automatically, so in most cases, configuring a channel manually isn't necessary.

Several tools are available that scan channels to see how much activity is on each channel. You can then configure the AP to operate on a less frequently used channel. Figure 3-21 is an example of the output of the inSSIDer program and shows that several Wi-Fi networks were detected. Each is labeled with its SSID and the channel it's set to.

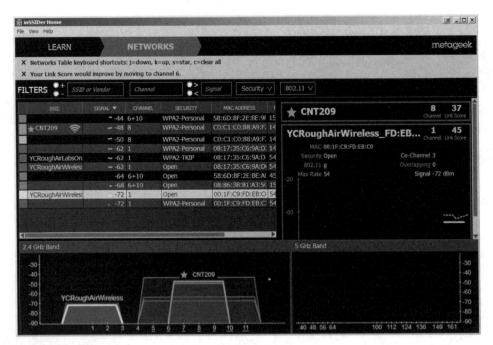

Figure 3-21 Wi-Fi network activity

Source: MetaGeek, LLC

Wi-Fi runs in the vast range of frequencies encompassed by microwave radio. For this reason, a microwave oven can cause interference in a Wi-Fi network. The result of this interference can vary from a slight loss in signal strength to disconnection from the network while the oven is running. A change in Wi-Fi channels can sometimes lessen the effects of microwave oven interference. In addition, some cordless phones use the same frequencies as Wi-Fi networks. If a cordless phone is causing interference, try changing the channel of the AP, the cordless phone (if possible), or both.

Wi-Fi Antennas

The antenna on a Wi-Fi device is both the transmitter and receiver. Its characteristics and placement determine how well a device transmits or receives Wi-Fi signals in an environment. Antennas are usually categorized by their radiation pattern, which describes how signals radiate out from the antenna:

- *Omnidirectional antenna*—In an **omnidirectional antenna**, the signals radiate out from the antenna with equal strength in all directions. If you had a perfect antenna, the radiation pattern would look like a sphere with the antenna in the center of the sphere. However, in the real world, the pattern looks more like a doughnut with the antenna situated in the center of the doughnut hole. This means signal strength is higher in spaces horizontal to the antenna's axis (see Figure 3-22) and weaker in spaces above and below the antenna. Omnidirectional antennas are used most often in WLANs because they cover a broad area. They should be placed in a central location where mobile devices are evenly situated in all directions horizontally around the antenna, such as on a single floor of a building. Omnidirectional antennas usually look like a pole and can often be articulated up or down to change the coverage area.

Figure 3-22 The radiation pattern of an omnidirectional antenna

- *Unidirectional antenna*—With a **unidirectional antenna**, signals are focused in a single direction, which makes them ideal for placement at one end of long, narrow spaces or to cover distances between buildings. Common unidirectional antennas include the Yagi, which looks like a cylinder and produces an egg-shaped radiation pattern extending in the direction the antenna is pointed. Another common example is a dish antenna, much like those used in satellite TV installations. With this type, the dish's parabolic shape focuses received signals toward the antenna, which sticks out from the center of the dish. Transmitted signals radiate out from the dish in a column focused in the direction the antenna is pointed.

Wi-Fi Access Methods and Operation

You have learned about CSMA/CD as the access method in wired forms of Ethernet, but wireless networks have a special problem with this access method. CSMA/CD requires that all stations be able to hear each other so that each station knows when another station is sending data. This requirement is reasonable, but if two stations try to send at the same time, a collision can occur. Fortunately, in a wired network, sending stations hear the collision and attempt to resend the data. If you've ever used a push-to-talk handheld radio, you know that when you're talking, you can't hear anybody else talking, and vice versa. 802.11 networks work the same way. If a station transmits data, it can't hear whether any other station is transmitting, so if a collision does occur, the sending station doesn't detect it. For this reason, 802.11 specifies the **Carrier Sense Multiple Access with Collision Avoidance (CSMA/CA)** access method, in which an acknowledgement is required for every packet sent, as explained in Chapter 2. With this requirement, if a collision occurs, the sending station knows the packet didn't arrive safely because there's no acknowledgement. Simulation 8 shows basic WLAN operation.

Simulation 8: Basic WLAN operation

Another problem exists in wireless networks that doesn't happen in wired networks. It's quite possible that in a three-station wireless network, all workstations can communicate with the AP: For example, workstation A can hear workstation B and workstation B can hear workstation C, but workstation A can't hear workstation C, perhaps because the two are out of range. This situation is called the "hidden node problem." CSMA/CA doesn't work because workstation A never knows whether workstation C is sending, and vice versa. To counteract this problem, the 802.11 standards specify another feature that uses handshaking before transmission. If this feature is enabled, a station must send the AP a request-to-send (RTS) packet requesting transmission. If it's okay to transmit, the AP sends a clear-to-send (CTS) message, and the workstation starts its communication. All other devices communicating with the AP hear the exchange of RTS and CTS messages, informing them that another device has control of the medium.

The 802.11b standard specifies a transmission rate of 11 Mbps, but this value isn't absolute. Environmental conditions can prevent transmission at this speed. Therefore, transmission speeds might be dropped incrementally from 11 Mbps to 5.5 Mbps to 2 Mbps and, finally, to 1 Mbps to make a reliable connection. In addition, there's no fixed segment length for wireless networks because reliable communication relies heavily on the environment—for example, the number of walls between stations and the AP. The other 802.11 standards behave similarly.

In general, an 802.11 network operating at 2.4 GHz has a maximum distance of 300 feet at full speed with no obstructions. However, this distance can be longer with 802.11n and large, high-quality antennas. Keep in mind that the data rate might suffer as the distance and number of obstructions increase.

For an excellent tutorial on wireless networking, visit *http://computer. howstuffworks.com/wireless-network3.htm.*

Wi-Fi Signal Characteristics

In a perfect world, Wi-Fi signals would be transmitted from a device and received directly by the destination device. However, in the real world, radio signals meet with all types of obstructions, from water droplets in the air to solid walls, that affect signal quality and can severely affect a WLAN's performance and reliability. The following list explains some common types of signal interference caused by physical objects lying in the path between the transmitter and receiver:

- *Absorption*—Wi-Fi signals can pass through solid objects, such as walls and trees, but they don't get through unscathed. Solid objects absorb radio signals, causing them to **attenuate** (weaken). The denser and thicker the material, the more signals attenuate, so a thick cinderblock wall, for example, absorbs more of the signal than a thin plywood wall. Other materials that cause absorption include water, so Wi-Fi installations outside can be affected by rain or even high humidity. The Wi-Fi signal's frequency also plays a part; the higher 5.0 GHz frequency is affected by solid objects more adversely than the 2.4 GHz frequency.

- *Refraction*—Refraction is the bending of a radio signal as it passes from a medium of one density through a medium of a different density, altering the angle of the signal's trajectory. It's similar to how light waves bend when they hit water, causing an underwater object to look like it's in a slightly different location than it actually is when viewed from outside the water. Refraction is most likely to have adverse effects with unidirectional antennas because the signals might not end up where you think they should, depending on where the antenna is pointed.

- *Diffraction*—Look at a Wi-Fi radio signal as a wave. When the wave runs into an object, it tries to bend around the object and come together on the other side.

However, the wave is slightly altered, or distorted, on the far side of the object. Think of a wave of water in the ocean as it hits a small boat. The boat doesn't cause the part of the wave that hits it to disappear, but it's not quite the same as it continues past the boat. This is diffraction. If the object is very large so that the signal can't travel around it on all sides, part of the signal is absorbed; what's not absorbed might change direction, resulting in signal loss. This type of diffraction is a problem especially with unidirectional signals because the change in direction could cause the signal to miss the targeted receiver.

- *Reflection*—Reflection occurs when a signal hits a dense, reflective material, such as a mirror or sheet of metal. Many metal objects, such as steel doors and furniture, can cause signal reflection, as can water or reflective glass. Reflection creates a copy of the original signal, like an echo. You don't notice an echo if the original sound and the copy arrive at your ear at the same time, but if they arrive at different times, the sound can be distorted. Signals arriving at different times (referred to as "out of phase") are called **multipath**. Multipath signals can cause distortion and errors in transmission that require the sender to retransmit.

- *Scattering*—Scattering is caused by small, irregular objects, such as leaves, chain-link fences, dust, water droplets, and so forth. The signal changes direction in unpredictable ways, causing a loss in signal strength.

Besides interference from physical obstacles, Wi-Fi signals can be degraded by other radio waves, also known as "noise." Wi-Fi signals are most susceptible to other signals in the same frequency range. Noise can come from equipment (such as microwave ovens), other wireless devices (such as cordless phones), and, of course, other wireless networks. Electrical equipment can also produce electromagnetic waves that interfere with a Wi-Fi signal. So although there's no escaping noise on a Wi-Fi network, what's important is the amount of noise compared with the signal strength, which is called the **signal-to-noise ratio**. Imagine you're having a conversation with someone in a small quiet room. You can both use normal speaking voices, but as more people enter the room and begin having conversations, you need to speak louder and louder so that you can be heard. In other words, you need to increase your signal (volume) to be heard over the noise of other conversations—increase your signal-to-noise ratio. If you don't, your conversation can no longer continue. Many wireless devices can increase the transmitter's power level (volume) to overcome noise and other types of interference.

All the preceding types of interference can cause signal degradation and errors that reduce the overall speed of data transfers over a wireless network. The actual amount of data transferred, not counting errors and acknowledgements, is called **throughput**. So even though a Wi-Fi standard has a bandwidth rating of 54 Mbps, for example, the actual amount of data sent and received over the network is considerably less, usually about half the rated speed.

The actual application-to-application data transfer speed is the **goodput**, which is essentially the throughput minus the protocol headers that don't contain application data. For example, if a file containing 5 MB of data is transferred across the network in 5 seconds, the goodput is calculated at 1 MB per second, even though 10 or more MB of information might have had to be transferred in that same 5 seconds. The extra 5 MB comes in the form of packet and frame headers, acknowledgements, and retransmissions, collectively known as **overhead**. The following example uses the maximum data transfer speed, throughput, and goodput values, with megabits instead of megabytes for easier computation:

File to be transferred: 45 megabits

Amount of nonfile data in packet and frame headers: 9 megabits

Total amount of data to be transferred: 54 megabits

Maximum data transfer speed: 54 Mbps

Amount lost to errors and acknowledgements: 27 Mbps

Throughput: 54 Mbps - 27 Mbps = 27 Mbps

Time it takes to transfer the entire file: 54 megabits/27 Mbps = 2 seconds

Goodput (size of the original file/time): 45 megabits/2 seconds = 22.5 Mbps

Wi-Fi Standards

Current Wi-Fi standards include 802.11a, 802.11b, 802.11g, 802.11n, and 802.11ac, with speeds starting at 11 Mbps for 802.11b up to more than 5 Gbps for some versions of 802.11ac. Besides the operating speeds, the properties that distinguish these standards include the frequency they operate at, the channel bandwidth, and support for multiple transmissions and receptions to occur simultaneously (data streams). Standards using the same frequency are generally backward-compatible with older and slower standards, so for example, an 802.11b device can still be used in an 802.11n network because both standards can operate at 2.4 GHz. Table 3-4 summarizes Wi-Fi standards and their properties.

Table 3-4   802.11 Wi-Fi standards

Wi-Fi standard	Operating frequency	Maximum data transfer speed	Indoor range[3]	Backward-compatibility	Channels, nonoverlapping	Data streams
802.11a	5.0 GHz	54 Mbps	75 ft	N/A	24 (8), 24[2]	N/A
802.11b	2.4 GHz	11 Mbps	150 ft	N/A	14 (11), 3[1]	N/A
802.11g	2.4 GHz	54 Mbps	150 ft	802.11b	14 (11), 3[1]	N/A
802.11n	5.0 and 2.4 GHz	600 Mbps	200 ft	802.11a, 802.11b, 802.11g	3 (2.4 GHz), 12 (5.0 GHz)	4
802.11ac	5.0 GHz	6 Gbps+	200 ft	802.11a, 802.11n	2, 2	Up to 8

[1]802.11b and 802.11g offer 14 channels, but only 11 can be used in North America.
[2]802.11a offers up to 24 channels with only 8 typically used in North America.
[3]Range is difficult to measure because it can be affected by obstacles and interference sources. This table represents only approximate average values. Also, keep in mind that transfer speed decreases as devices are farther apart.

Take a look at the advantages and disadvantages of each standard:

- *802.11a*—This 5.0 GHz standard came out in 1999; although it was released about the same time as 802.11b, it didn't see as much commercial success. The higher frequency requires more power and has a shorter indoor range because the signals are more easily absorbed by obstructions. This standard transfers data at 54 Mbps, and because it operates at 5.0 GHz, there aren't as many sources of interference as with 2.4 GHz networks.

- *802.11b*—Operating at 2.4 GHz, 802.11b was perhaps the most widely accepted Wi-Fi standard because of its low cost and comparatively good indoor range. However, because it operates at only 11 Mbps, the newer 802.11g and 802.11n standards running at much faster speeds have rapidly replaced it. The 2.4 GHz frequency range is crowded, however, with cordless phones, Bluetooth devices, and microwave ovens posing interference problems for these networks.

- *802.11g*—This 2.4 GHz standard is backward-compatible with 802.11b, so people looking to upgrade to 54 Mbps can do so easily without having to replace all their devices at the same time. However, it suffers from the same interference problems as 802.11b networks. Nonetheless, both standards fueled the Wi-Fi revolution and until recently were the most common devices used in Wi-Fi networks.

- *802.11n*—The 802.11n standard takes much of what works in the earlier standards and improves on it by adding **multiple-input/multiple-output** (**MIMO**) antennas. MIMO takes advantage of multipath signals by using a separate antenna to process signals as they arrive slightly out of phase. Each separately processed signal is called a "data stream." 802.11n can use up to four antennas and achieve data rates up to 600 Mbps. It can work in the 2.4 GHz or 5.0 GHz frequency range, but the 2.4 GHz range is used more often. In an 802.11n network, you might see a Wi-Fi client connect to an AP indicating a connection type of 802.11a-ht or 802.11g-ht. The "ht" stands for high throughput; some manufacturers use this term to indicate that the client is connected to the AP in 802.11n mode, using 5.0 GHz (802.11a-ht) or 2.4 GHz (802.11g-ht).

- *802.11ac*—The 802.11ac standard was ratified at the end of 2013, although products based on the standard were available a few years earlier. It operates in the 5.0 GHz range only and continues to undergo development. Current implementations have data transfer speeds of about 1 Gbps, but future implementations will have speeds up to 6.93 Gbps. 802.11ac hardware will be developed in "waves," with each wave having additional data streams and faster speeds. 802.11ac improves on the MIMO technology in 802.11n by providing up to eight data streams and introducing **multiuser MIMO** (**MU-MIMO**), which allows 802.11ac APs to send data to multiple client stations simultaneously. MU-MIMO works by using a process called "beamforming," in which the AP sends the signal in the direction of the receiving device instead of uniformly in all directions. Beamforming allows the AP to send data to multiple devices simultaneously if they aren't too close together. 802.11ac devices are still expensive compared with 802.11n devices and probably will be for several years, but with much faster speeds and multiuser support, 802.11ac is the standard for the future.

Wi-Fi Security

Because the network signals and, therefore, network data, of a Wi-Fi network aren't constrained by physical media, access to a Wi-Fi network *must* be secure. The signals from a Wi-Fi network can travel several hundred feet, which means Wi-Fi devices outside your home or business can detect them. A person with a Wi-Fi–enabled device sitting outside your home or business can connect to an unsecured network and use your Internet access to capture packets with a program such as Wireshark—or worse, access files on your computers.

At the least, a Wi-Fi network should be protected by an encryption protocol that makes the data unauthorized users capture extremely difficult to interpret. Wi-Fi devices typically support one of these encryption protocols, listed in order of effectiveness: Wired Equivalent Privacy (WEP), Wi-Fi Protected Access (WPA), and Wi-Fi Protected Access 2 (WPA2). Not all devices support all three protocols; in particular, older devices might support only WEP and/ or WPA. Wi-Fi encryption is configured on the AP, so to connect to the network, Wi-Fi devices connecting to the AP must be configured for the specific encryption protocol. Wi-Fi security is discussed in more depth in Chapters 8 and 11.

 WEP should be used only when it's the only option available because its encryption protocols can be broken easily.

Token Ring Networks

Developed by IBM in the mid-1980s, the **token ring** network technology provides reliable (albeit slow by current standards) transport of data. Based on the IEEE 802.5 standard, token ring networks are cabled in a physical star topology but function as a logical ring, as shown earlier in Figure 3-9. Token ring originally operated at 4 Mbps, but this speed increased to 16 Mbps and later to 100 Mbps. A 1000 Mbps standard was approved in 2001, but by that time, the token ring technology had clearly lost out to 100 Mbps Ethernet, and no 1000 Mbps products were ever manufactured in quantity. Most token ring networks used Category 4 or higher UTP.

Token Ring Media Access   Token ring uses the token-passing media access method, which is where the technology gets its name. Using this method, a special frame called the "token" passes from one computer to the next. Only the computer holding the token can send data, and a computer can keep the token for only a specific amount of time. If the computer with the token has no data to send, it passes the token to the next computer.

Because only the computer with the token can transmit data, this method prevents collisions. Computers no longer spend time waiting for collisions to be resolved, as they do in a CSMA/CD network. All computers have equal access to the medium, which makes token-passing networks best suited for time-sensitive environments, such as banking transactions and databases requiring precise timestamps. Also, because traffic moves in a specific "direction" around a ring topology, faster access methods (such as 100 Mbps token ring) can circulate two tokens at the same time without fear of collision. (By keeping the two sets of messages from overlapping, both tokens can circulate in order.)

However, token passing has two disadvantages. First, even if only one computer on the network has data to send, it must wait to receive the token. If its data is large enough to warrant two or more "turns" at the token, the computer must wait until the token makes a complete circuit before starting its second transmission. Second, the complicated process of creating and passing tokens requires more expensive equipment than what's used on CSMA/CD networks. This additional expense and complication is in part what led to token ring quickly becoming second best in LAN technologies, compared with 100 Mbps and switched Ethernet. Because token ring is no longer a widely used LAN technology, additional operating details are no longer covered.

Fiber Distributed Data Interface Technology

Fiber Distributed Data Interface (FDDI) uses the token-passing media access method and dual rings for redundancy. The rings in an FDDI network are usually a physical ring of fiber-optic cable. FDDI transmits at 100 Mbps and can include up to 500 nodes over a distance of 100 kilometers (60 miles). FDDI full-duplex technology, an extension to standard FDDI, can support up to 200 Mbps. Like token ring, FDDI uses token passing; however, FDDI's token-passing scheme is based on IEEE 802.4 rather than IEEE 802.5. An FDDI network has no hubs; devices generally connect directly to each other. However, devices called "concentrators" can serve as central connection points for buildings or sites in a campus setting.

Much like token ring, FDDI technology lost out to faster versions of Ethernet and is now obsolete for new network designs. It had its heyday in the early to mid-1990s when Ethernet was operating at only 10 Mbps and switched Ethernet was just being developed.

Chapter Summary

- Networks can be described by a physical and logical topology. The physical topology describes the arrangement of cabling that connects one device to another. The logical topology describes the path data travels between devices. The logical and physical topologies can be, and often are, different.

- The main physical topologies are the bus, star, ring, and point-to-point. A physical bus topology is simple but is no longer in common use because of a number of weaknesses. A star topology, along with the extended star, is the most common for implementing LANs. A physical ring topology isn't in widespread use now but was used mainly in network backbones. Point-to-point topologies are used primarily in WANs and with wireless bridges. Several point-to-point connections can create a mesh topology for the purpose of redundancy.

- The main logical topologies are bus, ring, and switched. A logical bus can be implemented as a physical star or a physical bus and is used with hub-based Ethernet and Wi-Fi networks. A logical ring can be implemented as a physical ring or a physical star and is most commonly seen in token ring and FDDI networks. The switched topology uses a physical star and is used with Ethernet networks using a switch in the center of a star physical topology.

- A network technology defines the structure of frames and how a network interface accesses the medium to send frames. It often defines the media types that must be used to operate correctly.

- The most common network technology for LANs is Ethernet. It's described in IEEE 802.3 and has many subcategories, including 10BaseT, 100BaseT, and 1000BaseT, that use twisted-pair copper cabling. Ethernet uses the CSMA/CD access method, which is turned off when a full-duplex connection is established. Other Ethernet standards include fiber-optic implementations, such as 100BaseFX and 1000BaseLX, among others.

- Wi-Fi is a wireless technology based on Ethernet, but it uses the CSMA/CA media access method. The most common Wi-Fi standards are 802.11b, 802.11g, 802.11a, 802.11n, and 802.11ac with speeds from 11 Mbps up to several Gbps.

- The antenna on a Wi-Fi device is both the transmitter and receiver. Its characteristics and placement determine how well a device transmits or receives Wi-Fi signals in an environment. Antennas are usually categorized by their radiation pattern: omnidirectional or unidirectional.

- Wi-Fi signal interference can severely affect a WLAN's performance and reliability. Common types of interference include absorption, refraction, diffraction, reflection, and scattering. Noise from equipment and other wireless devices and networks can also interfere with a Wi-Fi signal. This interference can cause signal degradation and errors that reduce the overall speed of data transfers over a wireless network.

■   Token ring and FDDI are obsolete technologies that used a token-passing access method. Token ring operated at speeds of 4 Mbps and 16 Mbps and ran over twisted-pair cabling, whereas FDDI ran over fiber-optic cabling at 100 Mbps.

Key Terms

1000BaseT Ethernet   A technology defined by the IEEE 802.3ab standard; supports 1000 Mbps Ethernet (usually called "Gigabit Ethernet") over Category 5 or higher UTP cable, using baseband signaling.

100BaseFX   100 Mbps Ethernet using baseband signaling over two strands of fiber-optic cabling.

100BaseTX   A technology defined by IEEE 802.3u, it's the most commonly used Ethernet variety today. It runs over Category 5 or higher UTP cable and uses two of the four wire pairs: one to transmit data and the other to receive data. It runs at 100 Mbps, using baseband signaling.

10BaseT   A technology defined by IEEE 802.3i, it's Ethernet running at 10 Mbps, using baseband signaling over Category 3 or higher twisted-pair cabling. Although still seen in older networks, newer networks use 100BaseT or faster technology.

10GBaseT   A technology defined by IEEE 802.3an, it's 10 Gigabit Ethernet running over four pairs of Category 6A UTP cabling, using baseband signaling. Unlike the other BaseT Ethernet standards, 10GBaseT operates only in full-duplex mode.

ad hoc mode   Sometimes called "peer-to-peer mode," it's a wireless mode of operation typically used only in small or temporary installations. There's no central device, and data travels from one device to another to reach the destination device.

attenuate   The weakening of a signal as it travels across network media.

baseband   A type of signaling used in networks, in which each bit of data is represented by a pulse of electricity (on copper media) or light (on fiber-optic media). These signals are sent at a single fixed frequency, using the medium's entire bandwidth. LAN technologies use baseband signaling.

broadband   A type of signaling that uses analog techniques to encode binary 1s and 0s across a continuous range of values. Broadband signals move across the medium in the form of continuous electromagnetic or optical waves rather than discrete pulses. Signals flow at a particular frequency, and each frequency represents a channel of data, allowing multiple streams of data on a single wire. TV and cable Internet use broadband signaling.

Carrier Sense Multiple Access with Collision Avoidance (CSMA/CA)   An access control method used by Wi-Fi networks, in which an acknowledgement is required for every packet sent, thereby avoiding most possibilities of a collision (collision avoidance).

Carrier Sense Multiple Access with Collision Detection (CSMA/CD)   A media access method in which a device must first listen (carrier sense) to the medium to be sure no other device is transmitting. If two devices transmit at the same time (multiple access), a collision occurs and is detected (collision detection). In this case, all devices involved in the collision wait for a random period of time before transmitting again.

collision   The result of two or more devices on the same medium transmitting simultaneously when CSMA/CD is the media access method in use. *See also* Carrier Sense Multiple Access with Collision Detection (CSMA/CD).

collision domain   The extent to which signals in an Ethernet bus topology network are propagated. All devices connected to a logical bus topology network are in the same collision domain. Switch and router ports delimit collision domains.

Cyclic Redundancy Check (CRC)   The error-checking code in an Ethernet frame's trailer; it's the result of a mathematical algorithm computed on the frame data. When the destination device receives the frame, the calculation is repeated. If the results of this calculation don't match the CRC in the frame, it indicates the data was altered in some way.

extended star topology   An extension of the physical star topology, in which a central switch or hub is the central connecting point for other switches or hubs that have computers and other network devices attached, forming a star of stars. *See also* physical star topology.

Fiber Distributed Data Interface (FDDI)   A technology that uses the token-passing media access method and dual rings for redundancy. The rings in an FDDI network are usually a physical ring of fiber-optic cable. FDDI transmits at 100 Mbps and can include up to 500 nodes over a distance of 100 kilometers.

goodput   The actual application-to-application data transfer speed.

hotspot   A public Wi-Fi network that can usually be accessed without an encryption or authentication code.

infrastructure mode   An operational mode for Wi-Fi networks, in which wireless stations connect through a wireless access point before they can begin communicating with other devices.

logical topology   The path data travels between computers on a network. The most common logical topologies are switched, bus, and ring.

media access method   A set of rules governing how and when the network medium can be accessed for transmission. The rules ensure that data is transmitted and received in an orderly fashion, and all stations have an opportunity to communicate. Also called "media access control."

mesh topology   A topology in which each device in the network is connected to every other device, providing multiple pathways in the event of a device or cable failure.

multipath   Signals that are copied because of reflection and scattering and arrive at the receiver at different times.

multiple-input/multiple-output (MIMO)   An antenna technology that uses multiple antennas to process more than one stream of data.

multiuser MIMO (MU-MIMO)   Uses a process called "beamforming" to send data to multiple clients simultaneously.

network backbone   The cabling used to communicate between LANs or between hubs or switches. The backbone cabling often runs at a faster speed than the cabling used to connect computers because the backbone must carry data from many computers to other parts of the network.

omnidirectional antenna   An antenna technology in which signals radiate out from the antenna with equal strength in all directions.

overhead   The amount of information in a network transmission (headers, acknowledgements, retransmissions) that isn't part of the application data.

physical bus topology   A network topology in which a continuous length of cable connects one computer to another in daisy-chain fashion. There's no central interconnecting device.

physical ring topology   A cabling arrangement in which each device is connected to another device in daisy-chain fashion, and the last device connects back to the first device forming a ring. Used by token ring and FDDI, the physical ring is rarely used now.

physical star topology   A network topology that uses a central device, such as a hub or switch, to interconnect computers in a LAN. Each computer has a single length of cable going from its NIC to the central device. It's the most common physical topology in LANs.

physical topology   The arrangement of cabling and how cables connect one device to another in a network. The most common physical topology is a star, but bus, ring, point-to-point, and mesh topologies are also used.

point-to-multipoint (PMP) topology   A topology in which a central device communicates with two or more other devices, and all communication goes through the central device. It's often used in WANs where a main office has connections to several branch offices via a router. *See also* point-to-point topology.

point-to-point topology   A topology in which cabling creates a direct link between two devices; used most often in WANs or in wireless networks to create a wireless bridge.

signal bounce   The result of electricity bouncing off the end of a cable and back in the other direction. It causes corruption of data as the bouncing signal collides with signals behind it. A terminator at each cable end is needed to prevent signal bounce. Also called "reflection."

signal propagation   Signals traveling across a medium and through any connectors and connecting devices until the signal weakens enough to be undetectable or is absorbed by a termination device.

signal-to-noise ratio   A ratio that measures the amount of valid signal compared with the amount of noise in a network transmission.

terminator   An electrical component called a "resistor," placed at the ends of a physical bus network to absorb the signal instead of allowing it to bounce back up the wire.

throughput   The actual amount of data transferred, not counting errors and acknowledgements.

token ring   A technology based on the IEEE 802.5 standard; its cabling is in a physical star topology, but it functions as a logical ring. It uses the token-passing media access method, and only the computer holding the token can send data.

unidirectional antenna   An antenna technology in which signals are focused in a single direction.

wireless bridge   An operational mode of wireless networking usually used to connect two wired LANs that are separated from each other in such a way that using physical media is impractical. Can also be used to extend the reach of a wireless network.

Wireless Fidelity (Wi-Fi)   The name given to the 802.11 series of IEEE standards that define five common varieties of wireless LANs: 802.11a, 802.11b, 802.11g, 802.11n, and 802.11ac.

Review Questions

1. Which of the following describes the arrangement of network cabling between devices?

   a. Logical topology

   b. Networking technology

   c. Physical topology

   d. Media access method

2. Which of the following is an advantage of a star topology? (Choose all that apply.)

   a. Allows faster technologies than a bus does

   b. Requires less cabling than a bus

   c. Centralized monitoring of network traffic

   d. No single point of failure

3. Which topology is likely to be deployed in a WAN where there's a central office and three branch offices, and you want all traffic from the branch offices to go through the central office network?

   a. Ring

   b. PMP

   c. Mesh

   d. Point-to-point

4. Which technology is likely to be implemented as a point-to-point physical topology?

   a. Wi-Fi infrastructure mode

   b. FDDI

   c. Ethernet

   d. Wireless bridge

5. Which of the following describes a hub-based Ethernet network?

   a. Physical bus

   b. Logical bus

   c. Physical switching

   d. Logical star

6. You're configuring a WLAN in a long narrow ballroom. The only place you can put the AP is at the far end of the room. Which type of antenna should you use?

   a. Unidirectional

   b. Bidirectional

   c. Omnidirectional

   d. Semidirectional

7. Which best describes a typical wireless LAN?

    a. Logical ring topology

    b. Logical switching topology

    c. Logical bus topology

    d. Logical star topology

8. Which of the following is a characteristic of a switched logical topology? (Choose all that apply.)

    a. Uses a physical bus topology

    b. Creates dynamic connections

    c. Sometimes called a shared-media topology

    d. Uses a physical star topology

9. Which of the following is a characteristic of unshielded twisted-pair cabling? (Choose all that apply.)

    a. Consists of four wires

    b. Commonly used in physical bus topologies

    c. Has a distance limitation of 100 meters

    d. Susceptible to electrical interference

10. Which of the following is a characteristic of fiber-optic cabling? (Choose all that apply.)

    a. Can be used in electrically noisy environments

    b. Requires only a single strand of fiber for network connections

    c. Carries data over longer distances than UTP does

    d. Lower bandwidth capability

11. Which topology most likely uses coaxial cabling?

    a. Physical star

    b. Logical ring

    c. Physical bus

    d. Logical switching

12. Which of the following is true of a MAC address?

    a. All binary 1s in the source address indicates a broadcast frame.

    b. It's sometimes called a logical address.

    c. A destination address of 12 hexadecimal Fs is a broadcast.

    d. It's composed of 12 bits.

13. Which type of Wi-Fi signal interference is most likely to be caused by leaves on trees?

    a. Diffraction

    b. Reflection

    c. Refraction

    d. Scattering

14. Which of the following is a field of the most common Ethernet frame type? (Choose all that apply.)

    a. ARP trailer

    b. FCS

    c. Destination MAC Address

    d. Data

    e. MAC type

15. Which access method uses a "listen before sending" strategy?

    a. Token passing

    b. CSMA/CD

    c. Token bus

    d. Polling

16. Which of the following is true about full-duplex Ethernet? (Choose all that apply.)

    a. Stations can transmit and receive but not at the same time.

    b. Collision detection is turned off.

    c. It's possible only with switches.

    d. It allows a physical bus to operate much faster.

17. Which of the following is defined by the extent to which signals in an Ethernet bus topology network are propagated?

    a. Physical domain

    b. Collision domain

    c. Broadcast domain

    d. Logical domain

18. Which of the following is considered a property of Ethernet? (Choose all that apply.)

    a. Scalable

    b. Best-effort delivery system

    c. Guaranteed delivery system

    d. Obsolete technology

19. Which of the following is true of IEEE 802.3an?

    a. Requires two pairs of wires

    b. Uses Category 5 or higher cabling

    c. Currently best for desktop computers

    d. Operates only in full-duplex mode

20. Which of the following is a feature of 100BaseFX? (Choose all that apply.)

    a. Often used as backbone cabling

    b. Best when only short cable runs are needed

    c. The fastest of the Ethernet standards

    d. Uses two strands of fiber

21. Which Wi-Fi standard can provide the highest bandwidth?

    a. 802.11ac

    b. 802.11b

    c. 802.11n

    d. 802.11g

22. Which of the following is true about infrastructure mode in wireless networks? (Choose all that apply.)

    a. Best used for temporary networks

    b. Uses a central device

    c. Resembles a physical bus and logical ring

    d. Most like a logical bus and physical star

23. How many channels can be used on an 802.11b network in North America?

    a. 7

    b. 9

    c. 11

    d. 13

24. Which media access method does Wi-Fi use?

    a. CSMA/CD

    b. Token bus

    c. Demand priority

    d. CSMA/CA

25. Which Wi-Fi standard uses beamforming to allow an AP to send data to multiple devices simultaneously?

    a. 802.11ac

    b. 802.11n

    c. 802.11a

    d. 802.11g

Critical Thinking

The following activities give you critical thinking challenges. Challenge labs give you an opportunity to use the skills you have learned to perform a task without step-by-step instructions. Case projects offer a practical networking setup for which you supply a written solution.

CHALLENGE LAB

Challenge Lab 3-1: Building an Extended Star Topology Network

Time Required: 30 minutes

Objective: Use hubs and switches to build an extended star topology network.

Required Tools and Equipment: Determine which type of devices and how many you need to build the network.

Description: In this lab, you build an extended star network, in which the computers are connected in a physical star and a logical bus topology, and the computers form the outer arms of the extended star. The center of the extended star should be a device that creates one collision domain per port. Build the network with as much equipment as you have available, distributing computers evenly around the outer edges of the extended star. Draw the final topology and label the devices. If you lack equipment, you can simply draw the topology without building the physical network. Then answer the following questions:

- What type of device are the computers attached to?

  _____

- What type of device is at the center of the extended star?

  _____

- How many collision domains are in this network?

  _____

CHALLENGE LAB

Challenge Lab 3-2: Add Wireless Access to the Extended Star Network

Time Required: 30 minutes

Objective: Add wireless networking to the extended star network you built in Challenge Lab 3-1.

Required Tools and Equipment: An access point or wireless router and some wireless NICs

Description: Add wireless networking to the extended star network you built in Challenge Lab 3-1. Expand the drawing you created to include the AP or wireless router. If you don't have the necessary equipment, just expand the drawing. Answer the following questions:

- Which device in your extended star did you connect the AP to and why?

  _____

- Which wireless mode are you using: ad hoc or infrastructure?

  _____

- What logical and physical topology does adding wireless bring to this network?

  _____

Challenge Lab 3-3: Download and Install inSSIDer

Time Required: 20 minutes

Objective: Install a wireless scanning tool and scan your network.

Required Tools and Equipment: A computer with a wireless NIC and access to the Internet or an already downloaded copy of inSSIDer

Description: In this lab, you download inSSIDer from *http://metageek.net* and install it on a computer with a wireless NIC. Your instructor might need to install it for you if you don't have the necessary permissions. After it's installed, start a scan of your network to look for access points. Answer the following questions:

- Approximately how many wireless networks did inSSIDer find?

  _____

- Which wireless channels are the most heavily used?

  _____

- If you were to set up a new wireless LAN based on what inSSIDer found, what channel would you use for the network?

  _____

Case Project 3-1

Old-Tech Corporation has 10 computers in its main office area, which is networked in a star topology using 10 Mbps Ethernet hubs, and wants to add five computers in the manufacturing area. One problem with the existing network is data throughput. Large files are transferred across the network regularly, and the transfers take quite a while. In addition, when two or more computers are transferring large files, the network becomes unbearably slow for users. Adding the manufacturing computers will only make this problem worse and result in another problem. Because the ceiling is more than 30 feet high, there's no easy way to run cables to computers, and providing a secure pathway for cables is next to impossible. Devise a solution to this company's networking problems. As part of your solution, answer the following questions:

- What changes in equipment are required to bring this company's network up to date to solve the shared-bandwidth problem?

_____

_____

- What topology and which type of device can be used in the manufacturing area to solve the cabling difficulties?

_____

_____

CASE PROJECTS

Case Project 3-2

EBiz.com has 250 networked computers and five servers and uses a star topology wired network to reach employees' offices, with a bus interconnecting three floors in its office building. Because of a staggering influx of Internet business, the network administrator's task is to boost network performance and availability as much as possible. The company also wants a network design that's easy to reconfigure and change because workgroups form and disband frequently, and their membership changes regularly. All computers must share sensitive data and control access to customer files and databases. Aside from the customer information and billing databases, which run on all servers, employees' desktop computers must run standard word-processing and spreadsheet programs.

Use the following write-on lines to evaluate the requirements for this network. After you finish, determine the best network topology or topology combination for the company. On a blank piece of paper, sketch the network design you think best suits EBiz.com's needs. Remember: High performance and easy reconfiguration are your primary design goals!

- What type of topology should be used in this network?

_____

_____

- Will the network be peer to peer or server based?

_____

_____

- How many computers will be attached to the network?

_____

_____

- What kind of networking device is easiest to reconfigure? What kind offers the best access to the network medium's bandwidth between pairs of devices?

_____

_____

Case Project 3-3

ENorm, Inc. has two sites in Pittsburgh that are four miles apart. Each site consists of a large factory with office space for 25 users at the front of the factory and up to 20 workstations in two work cells on each factory floor. All office users need access to an inventory database that runs on a server at the Allegheny Street location; they also need access to a billing application with data residing on a server at the Monongahela site. All factory floor users also need access to the inventory database at the Allegheny Street location.

Office space is permanently configured, but the manufacturing space must be reconfigured before each new manufacturing run begins. Wiring closets are available in the office space. Nothing but a concrete floor and overhead girders stay the same in the work cell areas. The computers must share sensitive data and control access to files. Aside from the two databases, which run on the two servers, office computers must run standard word-processing and spreadsheet programs. Work cell machines are used strictly for updating inventory and quality control information for the Allegheny Street inventory database. Workstations in the manufacturing cells are switched on only when they're in use, which might occur during different phases of a manufacturing run. Seldom is a machine in use constantly on the factory floor.

Use the following write-on lines to evaluate the requirements for this network. After you finish, determine the best network topology or topology combination for the company. On a blank piece of paper, sketch the network design you think best suits ENorm, Inc.'s needs.

- Will the network be peer to peer or server based?

  _____

  _____

- How many computers will be attached to the network?

  _____

  _____

  What topology works best for the offices, given the availability of wiring closets? What topology works best for the factory floor, given its need for constant reconfiguration?

  _____

  _____

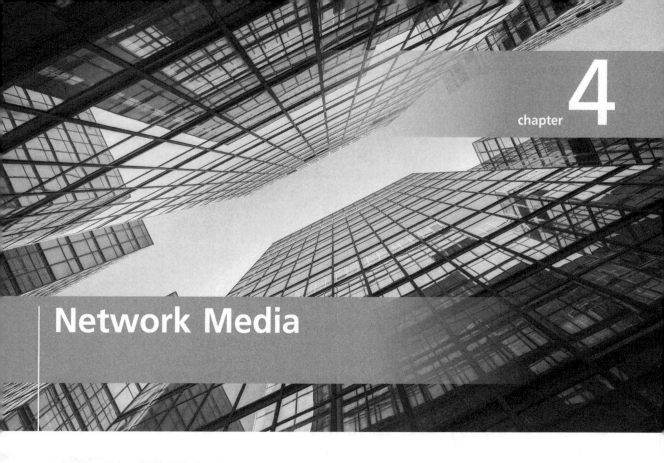

chapter 4

Network Media

After reading this chapter and completing the exercises, you will be able to:

- Define the primary cables used in wired networking
- Describe the characteristics of the major types of fiber-optic media
- Explain the technologies used for wireless networking

Network media are the materials through which network signals travel between devices. They can be a physical material, such as copper wire or glass fiber, or simply the air. When a physical material is used as the medium, it's usually referred to as "wired networking," and when signals are transmitted through the air, the medium is aptly called "wireless networking."

In this chapter, you learn about common options for wired and wireless networking and where these options make sense. You learn about the characteristics of wired media and how to choose a media type to suit a situation and environment. You also learn how to install and terminate the most common types of LAN media. In addition, you learn about transmission technologies for making wireless network links for both short-range Wi-Fi networks and long-range wireless networks.

Wired Networking

Table 4-1 summarizes what you need for the hands-on projects in this chapter.

Table 4-1   Hands-on project requirements

Hands-on project	Requirements	Time required	Notes
Hands-On Project 4-1: Making a Patch Cable	Wire cutter and cable stripper, RJ-45 crimping tool, 2 to 4 feet of Cat 5e or Cat 6 cable, two RJ-45 plugs, cable tester (optional)	20 minutes	
Hands-On Project 4-2: Terminating UTP Cable	Wire cutter and cable stripper, 2 to 4 feet of Cat 5e or Cat 6 cable, 110 punchdown tool, Cat 5e or Cat 6 patch panel, RJ-45 jack, cable tester (optional)	20 minutes	
Hands-On Project 4-3: Conducting End-to-End Testing	The patch cable you made, an additional patch cable, the patch panel and RJ-45 jack to which you terminated the cable, a lab computer , and a switch	10 minutes	

Wired networking uses tangible physical media called "cables." Cables used in networking come in two broad categories: copper wire and fiber optic. Regardless of the material used, all networking cables must support the basic tasks of sending and receiving bit signals. The composition of these signals (electricity or light), the speed at which these signals can be sent (bandwidth), and the distance they can effectively travel make up the main differences between cabling types. The following sections discuss cable characteristics, the criteria for choosing a particular type of cabling, and a variety of cable types, both copper and fiber optic.

Criteria for Choosing Network Media

All cables share certain fundamental characteristics you should know to understand their function and correct use. Even though copper cables differ radically from fiber-optic cables in composition and types of signals they carry, the characteristics described in the following sections apply equally to both types of cabling.

Bandwidth Rating Bandwidth, the number of bits per second that can be transmitted across a medium, is as much a function of the technology used to transmit bit signals as it is of the medium. For example, Category 5e UTP cabling was originally intended to support only up to 100 Mbps but was later upgraded to support up to 1000 Mbps when the 1000BaseT standard was developed.

What really determines the bandwidth of a cabling type is how fast a transmitting device, such as a NIC, can generate bit signals on the medium and whether these signals can be received accurately at the other end of the cable. Bit signals lose strength as they travel along the medium, so when judging whether a cabling type is suitable for a particular transmission speed, the maximum cable length must also be considered.

Another factor determining bandwidth is how bit signals are represented on the medium, a process called **encoding**. Different networking standards use different patterns of electrical or light pulses to represent a series of bits on the medium.

Although different media types and cable grades can support higher bandwidths than others, what's most important is choosing the media type and cable grade specified by the networking standard you want to run. Keep in mind that today's 1000BaseT network might be tomorrow's 10GBaseT network. So when possible, choose a cabling category that's compatible with the standard you want to implement now but will support the next level of speed your network is likely to need in the future.

Maximum Segment Length A **cable segment** is a length of cable between two network devices, such as a NIC and a switch. Any intermediate passive (unpowered) devices, such as wall jacks, are considered part of the total segment length.

Each cable type can transport data at a particular speed only so far before its signals begin to weaken past the point that a receiving station can read them accurately; this phenomenon is attenuation, as you learned in Chapter 3. In addition, electrical signals are affected by electromagnetic interference, or "noise." The longer a signal travels down a cable segment, the more likely it is that electrical noise impairs the signal to the point that data can be misinterpreted. (For example, a 0 bit is read as a 1 bit.) An internetwork can be constructed of several cable segments, as long as the hardware connecting them (such as switches and routers) can capture and regenerate the incoming signal at full strength.

Interference and Eavesdropping Susceptibility How well a media type resists signal interference from outside sources depends on the medium's construction and the type of signals it's designed to carry. Interference to electrical signals on copper media comes in the form of **electromagnetic interference (EMI)** and **radio frequency interference (RFI)**. Motors, transformers, fluorescent lights, and other sources of intense electrical activity can emit both EMI and RFI, but RFI problems are also associated with the proximity of strong broadcast sources in an environment (such as a nearby radio or TV station). RFI can also affect wireless networks if the frequencies are in the same range the wireless network is operating in.

Another type of interference in copper wires is a form of EMI called **crosstalk**, which is interference one wire generates on another wire when both wires are in a bundle (as all cabling in LANs is). When electrical signals travel across the medium, they create their own electromagnetic field. Although this field is weak, it can leak onto other wires, especially when their insulation is in contact with the other wire. Although it's not as common now, you might have experienced crosstalk while talking on a landline phone and hearing another conversation faintly. With phone wires, crosstalk is merely an annoyance because people can filter out this noise easily, but in networking, excessive crosstalk can render the network connection unusable.

Because electrical signals traveling down a copper wire create an electromagnetic field that can be detected outside the wires, copper wire is susceptible to electronic eavesdropping. It might sound like the stuff of spy movies, but with the right type of equipment, an eavesdropper simply needs to get close to a copper cable to extract data from it. In the absence of sensitive electronic equipment, if eavesdroppers have physical access to the connecting equipment and the copper wire is slightly exposed, they would have no problem installing a listening device directly on these wires.

Fiber-optic media carries light signals and is impervious to interference. In addition, because no magnetic field is present, eavesdropping is a difficult proposition with fiber-optic cable. To eavesdrop, someone needs access to the glass strands carrying the optical signals to install a device that captures data and prevents the connection from being broken. Not impossible, but extremely difficult.

When choosing a cable type, the environment the medium operates in is one of the most crucial factors in the decision. The choice is usually between copper cabling and fiber-optic cabling for high-performance applications and between copper cabling and wireless for less bandwidth-heavy applications.

Cable Grade Building and fire codes include specific cabling requirements, usually aimed at the combustibility and toxicity of the jacket and insulation covering most cables. Polyvinyl chloride (PVC) covers the cheapest and most common cables (for example, the 120-volt cord in lamps and other household appliances). Unfortunately, when this material burns, it gives off toxic fumes, which makes it unsuitable for cables strung in ceilings or inside walls.

The space between a false ceiling and the true ceiling in most office buildings, called the "plenum," is commonly used to aid air circulation for heating and cooling. Any cables in this space must be plenum-rated, which typically means they're coated with Teflon because of its low combustibility and the nontoxic fumes it produces when burned. These cables can be used in the plenum or inside walls without being enclosed in conduit. Although plenum-rated cable is nearly twice as expensive as non-plenum-rated cable, eliminating the need for conduit makes installing plenum-rated network cabling much cheaper. UTP cabling is usually marked as communications riser (CMR) or communications plenum (CMP). CMR is suitable only for building risers, such as elevator shafts or in cable trays, and can't be used in spaces that carry environmental air. CMP is suitable for use in plenum spaces. Before installing any type of cable, check all local fire and building codes because requirements vary widely.

Connection Hardware Every type of cable has connectors that influence the kinds of hardware the cable can connect to and affect the costs of the resulting network. Some connectors are fairly easy to attach, requiring only inexpensive tools, but others need specialized and often expensive equipment to make the correct termination and should be left to professionals. In this chapter, you learn how to install the connectors used in UTP cabling, which are the least expensive and most often used connectors. Fiber-optic connectors tend to be expensive, as are the tools used to attach them.

Other Media Considerations Additional media considerations include ease of installation, testability, and of course cost:

- *Ease of installation*—The difficulty of installing a cable plant has a bearing on your choice of media. **Cable plant** is the term for all the cables and connectors tying a network together. Sometimes you have to make a tradeoff between the highest quality available and the cost and time factors involved in installing the medium correctly. Some factors to consider are a medium's minimum bend radius, which limits the angle at which a cable can be bent to run around corners; the cost and time to terminate the medium, which involves installing connectors and attaching media to patch panels and jacks; and the physical environment. (Cinderblock or plaster walls, concrete floors, and high ceilings can make installing a cable plant cost prohibitive, for example.) You might decide to make parts of your network wireless because of some of these factors.

- *Testability*—How difficult and expensive is it to test the medium after it's installed? Declaring a cable installation successful just because computers can communicate doesn't really constitute a test. A network that "works" might be crippled by excessive transmission errors caused by poor cable termination. A true test of cabling, whether it's copper or fiber optic, is to install it, add the connectors and other termination points, and then test it with a device that can certify whether the cable meets the requirements for its category. Simple testers that check for basic electrical or optical connectivity are inexpensive (a few hundred dollars or less) but don't give you a true picture of your cable plant. Copper cable certifiers that do a full battery of Category 5e and above tests start at about $1000, and those capable of fiber-optic testing range up to more than $10,000.

- *Total cost*—When figuring the total cost for media, you must include the cabling, connectors, termination panels, wall jacks, termination tools, testing equipment, and, of course, time. The complexity of a large media installation (for a new building, for example) can be daunting, which is why there are companies specializing in media installation. In almost all cases, fiber-optic cabling costs considerably more than copper cabling for all components. When you need fiber-optic cabling, however, there's really no substitute. Some people opt for a wireless network because of the cost of wired components, but wireless networks are often not the solution when there are many users requiring high bandwidth. As a network administrator, you need to factor in all costs as well as users' needs before deciding which media types to use and in which situations. A combination of types tends to be the norm in today's networks.

Now that you know the general characteristics of cabling as well as which characteristics influence selecting cable types, you can understand the importance of the strengths and weaknesses of cabling types discussed in the following sections.

Coaxial Cable

For many years, coaxial cable—often called "coax" for short—was the predominant form of network cabling. Inexpensive and easy to install, coaxial cable was the networker's choice for many years, until the early 1990s. Now the main use for coaxial cable in networking is in connecting a cable modem to the wall outlet a cable TV/Internet provider installs. For this reason, details on coax cable used in LANs are no longer covered.

Twisted-Pair Cable

Twisted-pair (TP) cable comes in two types: unshielded and shielded. It consists of one or more pairs of insulated strands of copper wire twisted around one another and housed in an outer jacket or sheath (shown in Figure 4-1). These twists are important because they cause the electromagnetic fields that form around a wire carrying bit signals to wrap around one another and improve resistance to crosstalk and EMI from outside sources. In general, the more twists per unit length, the better the resistance to EMI and crosstalk. More expensive TP cable is usually more twisted than less expensive kinds and, therefore, provides a better pathway for higher bandwidth networks.

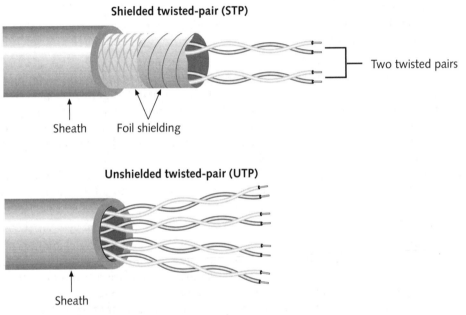

Figure 4-1 Twisted-pair cable

Unshielded Twisted-Pair Cable Most networks use UTP cabling, with STP used only where electrical noise is a major problem. The UTP cable used in LANs consists of four pairs of insulated wires; other UTP types contain fewer pairs. UTP is also used as phone wire, but because voice applications are much less demanding than networking in bandwidth and signal quality, the type of cable used for phone connections is usually unsuitable as network cabling.

UTP cabling is rated according to categories devised by the Telecommunications Industry Association (TIA) and the Electronic Industries Alliance (EIA); the American National Standards Institute (ANSI) has also endorsed these standards. The ANSI/TIA/EIA 568 Commercial Building Wiring Standard defines standards for the kinds of wiring used in commercial environments and helps ensure consistent performance from wiring products. Currently, the ANSI/TIA/EIA 568 standard includes eight categories for UTP wiring; these categories also govern the number of twists per foot or meter:

- *Category 1*—Applies to traditional UTP phone cabling, which is designed to carry voice but not data. This cabling is, therefore, labeled as **voicegrade**. Most UTP installed before 1982 falls into this category. This standard is no longer recognized by TIA/EIA.

- *Category 2*—Certifies UTP cabling for bandwidth up to 4 Mbps and consists of four pairs of wire. Because 4 Mbps is slower than most current networking technologies (except for older token ring installations), Category 2 is unlikely to be seen in networking environments and is no longer recognized by TIA/EIA.

- *Category 3*—Certifies UTP cabling for bandwidth up to 10 Mbps with signaling rates up to 16 MHz. This category supports 10BaseT Ethernet and 4 Mbps token ring networks with maximum segment lengths of 100 meters. Cat 3 consists of four pairs, with each pair having a minimum of three twists per foot (10 twists per meter). It remains in use in some older networks but should be replaced when networks are upgraded. Most networks have already migrated to 100 Mbps and 1000 Mbps speeds, and Cat 3 isn't suitable for these speeds.

- *Category 4*—Certifies UTP cabling for bandwidth up to 16 Mbps with signaling rates up to 20 MHz. This category supports mainly 10BaseT Ethernet and 16 Mbps token ring and is the first ANSI/TIA/EIA designation that labels cables as **datagrade** (capable of carrying data) rather than voicegrade. Cat 4 consists of four twisted pairs.

- *Category 5*—Certifies UTP cabling for bandwidth up to 100 Mbps with signaling rates up to 100 MHz. This category supports 100BaseTX, Asynchronous Transfer Mode (ATM) technologies at 25 and 155 Mbps, and Copper Distributed Data Interface (CDDI) at 100 Mbps. Category 5 also consists of four twisted pairs with an average of three to four twists per inch. This cabling has been superseded by Category 5e. It can be used in Gigabit Ethernet (1000BaseT), but Cat 5e is the minimum recommendation because of the additional tests required for it. Cat 5 cable is no longer widely available.

- *Category 5e*—The "e" means enhanced, so this category is an enhancement to Category 5 UTP. It differs mainly in the tests it must undergo and was designed to correct some shortcomings in Cat 5 cabling, particularly in Gigabit Ethernet and full-duplex operation. Cat 5e is an acceptable cable type for 1000BaseT Ethernet, but Category 6 should be considered for new installations. Cat 5e consists of four pairs and is rated for 100 MHz signaling rates; it comes in both shielded and unshielded versions.

- *Category 6*—This standard, published in June 2002 by the TIA/EIA, is the recommended UTP cabling standard for Ethernet applications over copper media at speeds up to 1 Gbps. Category 6 cabling uses the same type of modular jack as lower categories and is backward-compatible with Category 5 and Category 5e cable plants. It's specified to operate at signaling rates of 250 MHz. Some Cat 6 cabling includes a spline, or separator, in the jacket for additional separation between pairs of wires. However, this separator isn't a requirement. Cat 6 is the preferred cabling for 1000BaseT (Gigabit Ethernet) networks, but it can also support 10GBaseT for distances under 55 meters. It's a four-pair cable and comes in both shielded and unshielded versions

- *Category 6a*—Published in February 2008, Category 6a (Category 6 augmented) is suitable for signaling rates up to 500 MHz and is the category specified for 10GBaseT networks with segments up to 100 meters. It comes in both shielded and unshielded versions.

Two additional categories aren't yet TIA/EIA standards and might never be in the United States. However, Europe has accepted the Category 7 and Category 7a standards, which specify a fully shielded twisted-pair cable (each wire pair is shielded, as is the outer sheath) with performance characteristics well above earlier cabling standards. Signaling rates are specified at up to 600 MHz for Cat 7 and 1000 MHz for Cat 7a. Because of a different connecting hardware design, these cables and connectors aren't likely to be backward-compatible. Cat 7 and 7a are ISO/IEC 11801 standards, and their use in the upcoming 40 and 100 Gigabit Ethernet standards is uncertain. These two categories of cable might have a short life if they aren't specified in a widely adopted networking standard.

 A Category 8 standard is in draft form. It's reported to support operating frequencies up to 2000 MHz and speeds up to 40 Gbps over shielded twisted-pair wiring.

Categories 5, 5e, and 6 are by far the most popular types of UTP cabling. Their huge installed base guarantees that developers of new high-speed networking technologies will strive to make their technologies compatible with these categories. For example, Category 5 cable, originally designed for 10 Mbps Ethernet, is capable (although not recommended) of running at speeds up to 1 Gbps. Table 4-2 summarizes the characteristics of the two most common UTP cabling types.

Table 4-2   **Category 5e and 6 UTP cabling characteristics**

Characteristic	Value
Maximum cable length	100 m (328 ft.)
Bandwidth	Up to 1000 Mbps
Bend radius	Minimum four times the cable diameter or 1 inch
Installation and maintenance	Easy to install, no need to reroute; the most flexible
Cost	Least expensive of all cabling options
Connector type	RJ-45 plug, RJ-45 jack, and patch panels
Security	Moderately susceptible to eavesdropping
Signaling rates	100 MHz for Cat 5e; 250 MHz for Cat 6
Interference rating	Susceptible to EMI and crosstalk

Shielded Twisted-Pair Cable As its name indicates, STP includes shielding to reduce crosstalk and limit the effects of external interference. For most STP cables, this means the wiring includes a wire braid inside the cladding or sheath material as well as a foil wrap around each wire pair. This shielding improves the cable's transmission speed and resistance to interference, which allows using STP in electrically noisy environments or very high-bandwidth applications. Unfortunately, no standards for STP correspond to the ANSI/TIA/EIA 568 Standard for UTP, but you can readily find STP versions of Cat 5e (shown in Figure 4-2), Cat 6, and Cat 6a. These STP versions are sometimes referred to as "foiled twisted pair (FTP)," and the shielding surrounds all four wire pairs rather than each wire pair.

Figure 4-2 Cat 5e shielded twisted pair

Twisted-Pair Cable Plant Components
A twisted-pair cable plant requires more than just the cabling, which is usually sold in spools of 1000 feet. In addition, you find most of the following components:

- *RJ-45 connectors*—Whether STP or UTP, most twisted-pair cabling uses registered jack 45 (RJ-45) connectors to plug into network interfaces or other networked devices. This connector looks much like the RJ-11 connector on modular phone jacks, but it's larger and contains eight wire traces rather than the four or six in an RJ-11. An RJ-45 connector (see Figure 4-3), often called an **RJ-45 plug**, is most commonly used in patch cables, which are used to connect computers to hubs and switches and computers to RJ-45 wall jacks.

Figure 4-3 An RJ-45 plug

Source: Courtesy of Hyperline Systems

- *Patch cable*—A **patch cable** (see Figure 4-4) is a short cable for connecting a computer to an RJ-45 jack or connecting a patch-panel port to a switch or hub. Patch cables can be made with inexpensive tools, two RJ-45 plugs, and a length of TP cable, which you do later in Hands-On Project 4-1. Although making a patch cable is easy, most network administrators prefer buying ready-made cables to save time.

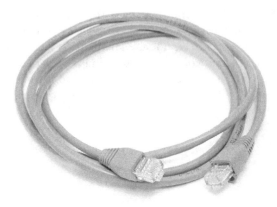

Figure 4-4   A patch cable

Source: © spillman/Shutterstock.com

- *RJ-45 jacks*—An **RJ-45 jack** (shown in Figure 4-5) is what you plug an RJ-45 connector into when the computer is in a work area away from hubs and switches. It has a receptacle for an RJ-45 plug on one side and a place to terminate, or "punch down," the TP cabling on the other side. RJ-45 jacks are usually placed behind wall plates when cables are run inside walls but can also be recessed into the floor or placed in surface-mounted boxes if the cabling runs on the outside of walls.

Figure 4-5   An RJ-45 jack

Source: Curtesy of Hyperline Systems

- *Patch panels*—Patch panels are used to terminate long runs of cable from the work area (where computers are) to the wiring closet (where switches are). Patch panels are like RJ-45 jacks, in that they have a receptacle on one end and punchdown terminals on the other, but a patch panel can usually accommodate 12, 24, or 48 cables. Figure 4-6 shows the front side of a patch panel, where a patch cable plugs in, and the back side, where long runs of cable are terminated.

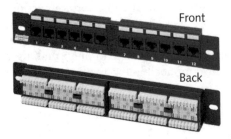
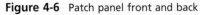

Figure 4-6   Patch panel front and back

Source: Courtesy of Hyperline Systems

- *Distribution racks*—Distribution racks (also called 19-inch racks because the upright rails are 19 inches apart) hold network equipment, such as routers and switches, plus patch panels and rack-mounted servers. They're usually found in wiring closets and equipment rooms. Figure 4-7 shows a typical distribution rack.

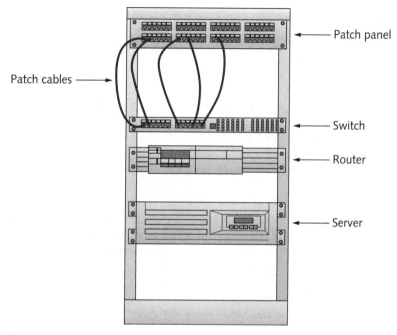

Patch panel

Patch cables

Switch

Router

Server

Figure 4-7   A distribution rack

The following sections explain how to use these components to construct a cable plant.

Structured Cabling: Managing and Installing a UTP Cable Plant

Entire books are written on cable installation and management, and the details are beyond the scope of this book. However, understanding some basic methods and terminology of cable installation and management gives you a good foundation. As mentioned, the TIA/EIA developed the document "568 Commercial Building Wiring Standard," which specifies how network media should be installed to maximize performance and efficiency. This standard defines what's often referred to as "structured cabling."

The 568 Commercial Building Wiring Standard covers all media types, but the discussion in this section focuses on UTP cabling, the most common media for LANs and internetworks.

Structured cabling specifies how cabling should be organized, regardless of the media type or network architecture. Although a variety of logical topologies can be used, structured cabling relies on an extended star physical topology. TIA/EIA 568 can be applied to any size network and divides the details of a cable plant into six components. A small LAN in a 10-computer business might need only two or three of these components, but large networks typically use most or all of these components:

- Work area
- Horizontal wiring
- Telecommunications closets
- Equipment rooms
- Backbone or vertical wiring
- Entrance facilities

Network cabling standards are designed to ensure that standards for equipment rooms and wiring closets, including limitations on media, are adhered to, which helps limit the possible reasons for network failure or poor performance. If the network cable plant is in good working order and meets standards, a network administrator's job is easier. Structured cabling facilitates troubleshooting as well as network upgrades and expansion.

Work Area   The **work area**, as the name suggests, is where workstations and other user devices are located—in short, the place where people work. Faceplates and wall jacks are installed in the work area, and patch cables connect computers and printers to wall jacks, which are connected to a nearby telecommunications closet. Patch cables in the work area should be limited to less than 6 meters long (about 20 feet). The TIA/EIA 568 standard calls for at least one voice and one data outlet on each faceplate in each work area. The connection between wall jack and telecommunications closet is made with horizontal wiring. Figure 4-8 shows the components of the work area.

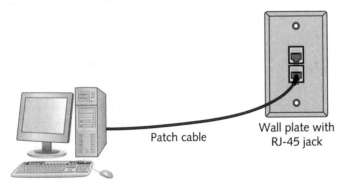

Patch cable   Wall plate with RJ-45 jack

Figure 4-8   Work area components

Horizontal Wiring   **Horizontal wiring** runs from the work area's wall jack to the telecommunications closet and is usually terminated at a patch panel. Acceptable horizontal wiring types include four-pair Cat 5e or Cat 6 or two fiber-optic cables. The total maximum distance for horizontal wiring is up to 100 meters, which includes the cable running from the wall jack to the patch panel plus all patch cables. However, horizontal wiring from the wall jack to the patch panel should be no longer than 90 meters to allow up to 10 meters for patch cables.

Telecommunications Closet The **telecommunications closet** (TC) provides connectivity to computer equipment in the nearby work area. In small installations, it can also serve as the entrance facility (explained later in "Entrance Facilities"). Typical equipment includes patch panels to terminate horizontal wiring runs, switches to provide network connectivity, and patch cables to connect patch panels to switches. In smaller installations, network servers can be housed in the TC. Larger installations usually have connections from the TC to an equipment room (discussed next). A telecommunications closet that houses the cabling and devices for work area computers is referred to as an **intermediate distribution frame (IDF)**. Figure 4-9 shows the relationship and connections between the work area, horizontal wiring, and IDF.

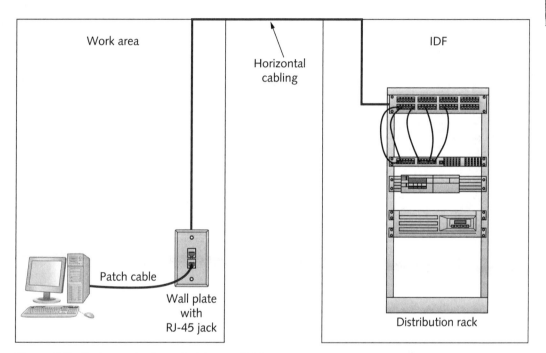

Figure 4-9 Work area, horizontal wiring, and IDF

Equipment Rooms The **equipment room** houses servers, routers, switches, and other major network equipment and serves as a connection point for backbone cabling running between IDFs. An equipment room that's the connection point between IDFs is called a **main distribution frame (MDF)** or "main cross-connect." An MDF can be the main cross-connect of backbone cabling for the entire network, or it might serve as the connecting point for backbone cabling between buildings. In multi-building installations, each building often has its own MDF.

Backbone Cabling Backbone cabling (or vertical cabling) interconnects IDFs and MDFs. This cabling runs between floors or wings of a building and between buildings to carry network traffic destined for devices outside the work area. It's often fiber-optic cable but can also be UTP if the distance between rooms is less than 90 meters. When it connects buildings, backbone cabling is almost always fiber optic because of UTP's distance limitations and because fiber doesn't propagate lightning strikes or electrical imbalances between buildings. Multimode fiber-optic cable can extend up to 2000 meters, whereas single-mode fiber can reach distances up to 3000 meters when used as backbone cabling between the MDF and IDFs. Figure 4-10 shows how backbone cabling can connect IDFs to an MDF.

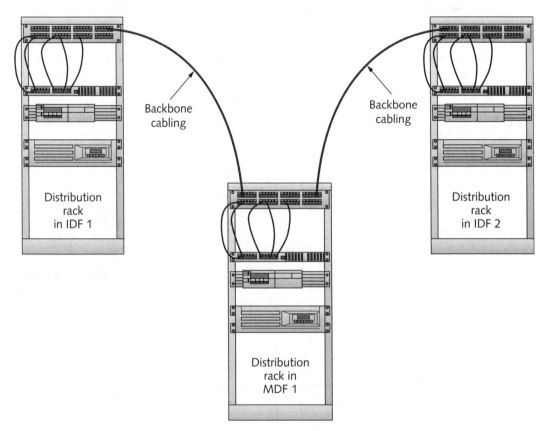

Figure 4-10   Backbone cabling connects IDFs and MDFs

Entrance Facilities   An **entrance facility** is the location of the cabling and equipment that connects an organization's network to a third-party telecommunications provider. It can also serve as an equipment room and the MDF for all backbone cabling. This location is also where a connection to a WAN is made and where an organization's LAN equipment ends and a third-party provider's equipment and cabling begins—also known as the **demarcation point.**

Installing UTP Cabling   One skill required of a network technician is terminating UTP cables. Cable **termination** means putting RJ-45 plugs on a cable to make a patch cable or punching down cable wires into terminal blocks on a jack or patch panel. To create a patch panel, a technician needs the following tools:

- Bulk UTP cabling
- Wire cutters or electrician's scissors
- Cable stripper
- Crimping tool
- Cable tester
- RJ-45 plugs

To terminate cable at an RJ-45 jack or a patch panel, you need the following tools:

- Bulk UTP cabling
- Wire cutters or electrician's scissors
- Cable stripper
- Type 110 punchdown tool
- Cable tester
- RJ-45 jack and patch panel

Some tools you need to perform these tasks are shown in Figure 4-11.

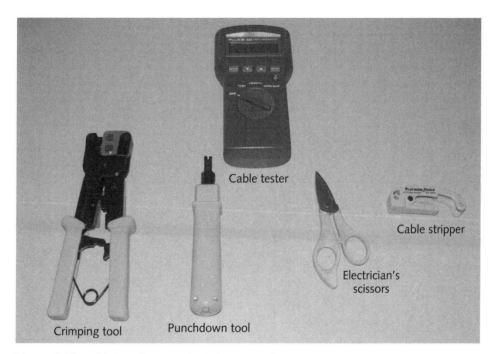

Figure 4-11 Cable installation and termination tools

The quality of the tools needed for cable installation varies considerably, usually according to cost. If you expect to be doing a lot of cable termination, it pays to invest in high-quality tools, particularly a cable tester. If you're installing only a few dozen to a few hundred cables, you might get away with less expensive tools and a basic cable tester. However, if you have a cable-installation business, you need high-quality tools, including a cable tester that certifies the cable plant for the category of cable installed.

Hands-On Project 4-1 walks you through making a patch cable. One of the most important aspects of making a cable or terminating a cable at a jack or patch panel is to get the colored wires arranged in the correct order. There are two competing standards for the arrangement of wires: TIA/EIA 568A and TIA/EIA 568B. Either standard is okay to follow, as long as you stick to one throughout your network. Figures 4-12 and 4-13 show the arrangement of wires for both standards.

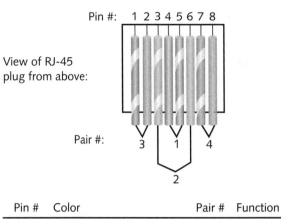

Pin #	Color	Pair #	Function
1	White with green stripe	3	Transmit +
2	Green	3	Transmit -
3	White with orange stripe	2	Receive +
4	Blue	1	Unused
5	White with blue stripe	1	Unused
6	Orange	2	Receive -
7	White with brown stripe	4	Unused
8	Brown	4	Unused

Figure 4-12 TIA/EIA 568A cable pinouts

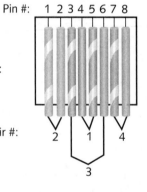

Pin #	Color	Pair #	Function
1	White with orange stripe	2	Transmit +
2	Orange	2	Transmit -
3	White with green stripe	3	Receive +
4	Blue	1	Unused
5	White with blue stripe	1	Unused
6	Green	3	Receive -
7	White with brown stripe	4	Unused
8	Brown	4	Unused

Figure 4-13 TIA/EIA 568B cable pinouts

The unused pins in the cable pinouts shown in Figures 4-12 and 4-13 are unused only on Ethernet networks up to 100BaseT. 1000BaseT Ethernet uses all eight wires for transmitting and receiving.

Straight-Through Versus Crossover Cable When you make a standard patch cable, you use the same wiring standards on both ends of the cable so that each wire is in the same corresponding location on both ends of the cable (pin 1 goes to pin 1, pin 2 to pin 2, and so forth). This type of cable is also called a **straight-through cable**. Another type of cable, called a **crossover cable**, uses the 586B standard on one end and the 586A standard on the other end. This arrangement crosses the transmit and receive wires so that transmit on one end connects to receive on the other end. This type of cable is often needed when you connect two devices of the same type to one another—for example, connecting a hub to a hub, a switch to a switch, a hub to a switch, or a PC to a PC. However, for a 1000BaseT crossover cable, you have to cross the blue and brown pins because they're used in 1000BaseT. Table 4-3 shows the pinout for a 1000BaseT crossover cable. This configuration also works for a 10BaseT or 100BaseT crossover cable, even though the brown and blue pins aren't used.

Table 4-3 Pinout for a 1000BaseT crossover cable

Pin	Connector 1	Connector 2
1	White with orange stripe	White with green stripe
2	Orange	Green
3	White with green stripe	White with orange stripe
4	Blue	White with brown stripe
5	White with blue stripe	Brown
6	Green	Orange
7	White with brown stripe	Blue
8	Brown	White with blue stripe

Medium Dependent Interface Network devices connecting with RJ-45 plugs over twisted-pair cabling are classified as **medium dependent interface (MDI) devices** or **MDI crossed (MDI-X) devices**. You might even see these abbreviations on some switches. For communication to take place between two devices, the wires one device transmits on must be connected to the wires the other device receives on, and vice versa. For example, the 568 standards have pins 1 and 2 labeled as transmit and pins 3 and 6 labeled as receive. Clearly, not all devices can transmit on pins 1 and 2 and receive on pins 3 and 6; otherwise a standard patch cable wouldn't work between these devices because one device's transmit signals would be going to the transmitter of the other device—like having a phone's earpiece at your mouth and the mouthpiece at your ear.

MDI devices transmit on pins 1 and 2 and receive on pins 3 and 6. Examples include PC NICs and routers. MDI-X devices, usually hubs and switches, receive on pins 1 and 2 and transmit on pins 3 and 6. Therefore, a straight-through patch cable works for the most common connection of a PC NIC to a switch. When a switch needs to be connected to a switch (or a PC to a PC), you use a crossover cable so that the transmit and receive wires get crossed, and you end up with transmit going to receive and vice versa. Thankfully, developers of NICs, switches, and routers have started doing this job for you by making ports on some devices auto-sensing. "Auto-sensing" means they can detect whether you're trying to connect transmit wires to transmit wires, and the port reconfigures its transmit and receive wires, thus making a crossover cable unnecessary. Not all devices support auto-sensing, so it's best to have crossover cables handy in case you need them.

Another type of cable you might run across is called a "rollover cable," which is designed to connect a PC's serial communication port and a Cisco device's console port for configuring the Cisco device. You use terminal emulation software, such as PuTTY, to get a command-line interface prompt from the Cisco device so that you can enter commands to view and change its configuration. A rollover cable reverses all eight wires where the wires on one end are connected to pins 1 through 8, and on the other end, they're connected to pins 8 through 1. So pin 1 goes to pin 8, pin 2 to pin 7, pin 3 to pin 6, and so forth.

Hands-On Project 4-1: Making a Patch Cable

Time Required: 20 minutes

Objective: Create a 568B straight-through patch cable.

Required Tools and Equipment: Wire cutter and cable stripper, RJ-45 crimping tool, 2 to 4 feet of Cat 5e or Cat 6 cable, two RJ-45 plugs, cable tester (optional)

Description: In this project, you make a patch cable according to the instructions. The instructor will inspect the cable for the correct wire order and strain relief. If possible, use a cable tester to test for conductivity and wiremap, at a minimum.

1. Strip approximately 2 inches of the outer jacket off one end of the cable with the cable stripper. Be careful not to nick the inner wires' insulation. Most UTP cable strippers are calibrated to score the cable's outer jacket so that you can simply break it off. Cable strippers differ in the techniques you use with them, so refer to the instructions that came with yours or ask your instructor.

2. Untwist the four pairs of wires.

3. Here comes the tricky part: Arrange the wires from left to right (as you're looking down on them) so that they're in the following order: white with orange stripe, orange, white with green stripe, blue, white with blue stripe, green, white with brown stripe, and brown. This order adheres to the 568B wiring standard (see Figure 4-14).

Figure 4-14 The correct arrangement of wires

4. Clip the eight wires so that a little more than a half-inch of wire extends beyond the outer jacket.

5. While holding the RJ-45 plug in one hand with the clip facing away from you, insert the eight wires into the connector, making sure the tops of wires extend to the front of the connector and the cable jacket goes far enough into the connector so that the jacket will be caught by the crimp bar (see Figure 4-15).

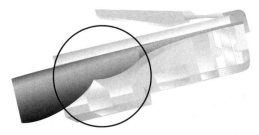

Figure 4-15 Correct RJ-45 plug installation

6. Now insert the RJ-45 connector into the crimping tool, and make sure the wires don't slip. Squeeze the handle on the crimping tool firmly. It might take a little hand strength

or using two hands, depending on the crimping tool's quality. This tool does two things. First, it forces the eight small contacts at the top of the plug down onto the wires; the contacts are pushed just far enough in that they slice through the insulation on each wire, thereby making an electrical contact with the wire. Second, the strain-relief bar is pushed in to grab the cable's outer jacket, making it more difficult to pull the wires out of the plug.

7. Repeat the process for the other end of the cable, and test with a cable tester, if available. Congratulations! You have made a patch cable. Where do you find patch cables in structure cabling installations? Describe the connections they make.

_____

_____

8. Keep your tools handy for the next project.

Hands-On Project 4-2: Terminating UTP Cable

Time Required: 20 minutes

Objective: Terminate UTP cable at a patch panel and an RJ-45 jack.

Required Tools and Equipment: Wire cutter and cable stripper, 2 to 4 feet of Cat 5e or Cat 6 cable, 110 punchdown tool, Cat 5e or Cat 6 patch panel (a 568A or 568B patch panel can be used; 568B panels are more common), RJ-45 jack, cable tester (optional).

Description: In this project, you punch down one end of a cable to the back of a patch panel.

1. Strip approximately 2 inches of the outer jacket off one end of the cable with the cable stripper. Be careful not to nick the inner wires.

2. Leave the wire pairs twisted. Arrange the wires according to the color coding on your patch panel. The color-coding will vary, depending on whether it's a 568A or 568B patch panel, and the wires might be arranged in a straight line or split between the two rows of terminals.

3. Center the cable so that each wire is equally distant from the terminal in which it will be placed. On each wire pair, separate the wires about one-half inch or less from the end of the jacket so that the two wires form an oval, and slip the pair over the middle terminal for that wire pair (see Figure 4-16). Pull each wire pair down firmly so that the wires stay in place.

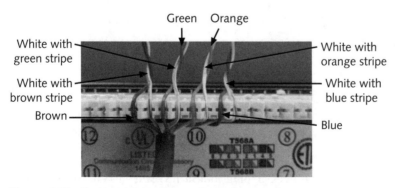

Figure 4-16 Placing wires on the patch panel terminals

4. Next, use the 110 punchdown tool. For each wire, place the tool over the wire so that the slot in the tool lines up with the wire. The tool's blade should be facing the end of the wires, not the cable jacket (see Figure 4-17).

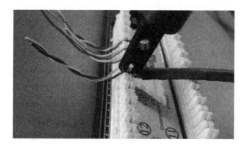

Figure 4-17 Positioning the punchdown tool

5. Push the punchdown tool down firmly until you hear it snap. Don't be afraid to give it a good hard push. The blade should cut the wire or at least score it so that you can gently twist the end off. Do this for all eight wires.

6. That's it! A correct termination should have no more than one-half inch of untwisted wire outside the jacket. Repeat this process for the other end of the cable, but this time, terminate the cable onto an RJ-45 jack. In structured cabling, what's the run of cable called that goes from a wall jack to a patch panel?

_____

7. Keep your cables and tools ready for the next project.

Hands-On Project 4-3: Conducting End-to-End Testing

Time Required: 10 minutes

HANDS-ON PROJECTS

Objective: Test your terminations and patch cable with a live connection.

Required Tools and Equipment: The patch cable you made, an additional patch cable, the patch panel and RJ-45 jack to which you terminated the cable, a lab computer, and a switch

Description: Working in groups of at least two, connect a lab computer, using the patch cable you made, to the RJ-45 jack you punched down. Using an additional patch cable, connect the patch panel to a switch. Then you use the `ping` command to verify connectivity between computers.

1. Using the patch cable you made in Hands-On Project 4-1, connect your lab computer's NIC to the RJ-45 jack you punched down in Hands-On Project 4-2.

2. Using the additional patch cable, connect the port on the patch panel you punched down to a switch.

3. Turn on the PC and the switch, if necessary.

4. Verify that you have a link light at the switch and at your lab computer's NIC. Log on to your computer, and give your computer's IP address to another student who's connected to the switch.

5. Ping another student's computer after getting his or her IP address. If the ping is successful, your cable termination was a success.

6. If you're sharing computers, allow the next group of students to test their cabling.

7. Shut down your computer if no one else is using it for testing.

Why Two Transmit and Two Receive Wires? As you can see from the cable pinout diagrams shown previously in Figures 4-12 and 4-13, one wire pair is used for transmit (labeled transmit+/transmit-) and one wire pair is used for receive (labeled receive+/receive-). The plus and minus symbols indicate that the wires carry a positive or negative signal. This **differential signal** mitigates the effects of crosstalk and noise on the cable. It does so because when a bit signal is transmitted, it's transmitted as a positive voltage and a negative voltage (v). For example, if a 1 bit is defined as +2v, the bit is transmitted as +2v on one wire and -2v on the other wire. The receiver reads the difference between the two values, which is 4v. EMI and crosstalk manifest as positive voltages, so what happens if the signal is hit by a burst of EMI that adds 1v to the signal? You have the following:

Original signal with no EMI:

Transmit+	Transmit+	Differential result
+2v	-2v	+4v

Signal with EMI adding 1v to both transmit+ and transmit- wires:

Transmit+	Transmit+	Differential result
+2v + 1v = 3v	-2v + 1v = -1v	+4v

As you can see, the result stays at +4v in both cases because the differential signal effectively cancels out the EMI. However, this canceling effect works only if the same amount of EMI is imposed on both wires. The closer the wires are, the more likely that EMI will affect both wires equally. This phenomenon is one reason for using twisted wires: The wires are so tightly coupled that both external EMI and crosstalk are likely to affect both wires equally and be canceled out.

Although UTP is the most common media type for LANs, it has its limitations in bandwidth, noise susceptibility, and length. In addition, UTP wiring shouldn't be used outside to connect between buildings. Copper wire is susceptible to the elements, and its electrical conducting properties change slightly depending on the temperature. A more important reason to not use any type of copper wire between buildings is that it can carry a harmful electrical charge based on the ground potential between buildings, if the buildings are fed from different transformers. When any of these limitations eliminate UTP as an option, fiber-optic cable, discussed in the next section, is the likely solution.

Fiber-Optic Cable

Fiber-optic cable trades electrical pulses for pulses of light to represent bits. Because no electrical signals ever pass through the cable, fiber-optic media is as immune to electrical interference as any medium can get. Therefore, light pulses are unaffected by EMI and RFI. This characteristic also makes fiber-optic cables highly secure. They emit no external signals that might be detected, unlike electrical or broadcast media, thereby eliminating the possibility of electronic eavesdropping. In particular, fiber-optic cable is a good medium for high-bandwidth, high-speed, long-distance data transmission because of its lower attenuation characteristics and vastly higher bandwidth potential. Commercial implementations at 10, 40, and 100 Gbps are currently in use.

Figure 4-18 shows a typical fiber-optic cable. A slender cylinder of glass fiber called the "core" is surrounded by a concentric layer of glass, the cladding. The fiber is then jacketed in a thin transparent plastic material called the "buffer." These three components make up what's labeled as the optical fiber in this figure. The fiber is optionally surrounded by an inner sheath made of colored plastic. A strengthening material, usually Kevlar, comes next, followed by an outer sheath. Sometimes the core consists of plastic rather than glass fibers; plastic is more flexible and less sensitive to damage than glass, but attenuation is more of a problem than with glass.

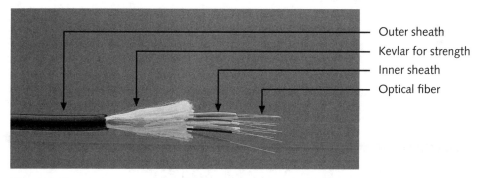

Figure 4-18   Fiber-optic cable

Each fiber-optic strand carries data in only one direction, meaning fiber-optic network connections consist of two or more strands, each in a separate inner sheath. However, these cables can be enclosed in a single sheath or can be two separate cables, each with its own sheath. Just as you have UTP patch cables, you also find fiber-optic patch cables, usually to connect from a fiber-optic patch panel to a switch or router. Fiber-optic cable used as backbone cabling often comes in bundles of 12 or more fiber strands. Even if you're using only two strands at first, it's a good idea to run cable containing more fiber than you need, in case a strand breaks during installation or you need additional strands for future growth.

Some testing has shown that glass fibers can carry several terabits (1000 gigabits) per second (Tbps). There's really no end in sight for the bandwidth capacity of optical fiber. As network bandwidth needs increase and the limits of copper wire are reached, fiber-optic cable might eventually replace copper for all types of network connections. Table 4-4 summarizes fiber-optic cable characteristics.

Table 4-4 Fiber-optic cable characteristics

Characteristic	Value
Maximum cable length	2 km (6562 ft.) to 100 km (62.14 miles)
Bandwidth	10, 40, and 100 Gbps and higher
Bend radius	30 degrees per foot
Installation and maintenance	Difficult to install and reroute; sensitive to strain and bending
Cost	Most expensive of all cabling options
Connector type	Several types (see bulleted list in the next section)
Security	Not susceptible to eavesdropping
Interference rating	None; least susceptible of all cable types

Fiber-Optic Connectors

A wide variety of connectors can be used with fiber-optic media, depending on the light-emitting sources used to generate light pulses and the corresponding light-detecting sensors used to detect them. Figure 4-19 shows some connectors described in the following list:

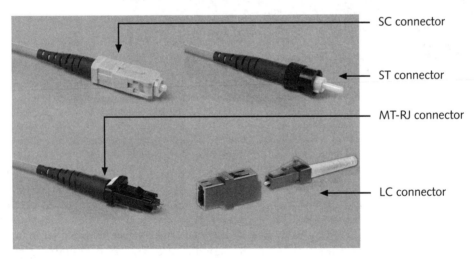

Figure 4-19 Fiber-optic connectors

- *Straight tip*—Straight tip (ST) connectors join fibers at cross-connects or to optical devices. They're used most often in Ethernet networks with fiber-optic cable as backbone cabling. An ST connector locks onto the jack when twisted.

- *Straight connection*—Straight connection (SC) connectors push on, which makes them easy to install and requires less space for an attachment. They make a strong connection and can be used when splicing fiber-optic cables. An SC connector is a one-piece component, with two receptacles for sending and receiving fibers. A notch in its jacket ensures the correct orientation when inserted.

- *Locking connection*—Locking connection (LC) connectors push on and pull off with an RJ-45-style latching mechanism. They're about half the size of SC connectors, which makes them good for high-density applications, in which many fibers are concentrated in one location.

- *Mechanical transfer registered jack*—A mechanical transfer registered jack (MT-RJ) connector looks a little like an RJ-45 connector. It provides a high-density fiber-optic connection by using two fiber-optic cables. Compared with other connector types, MT-RJ connectors take only half the space for the same number of cable terminations. They're also easy to install and require only one connector for a two-fiber termination.

- *Fiber channel*—A fiber channel or ferrule connector (FC) is used in some measurement equipment applications and with single-mode lasers. This type of connector is less common than most of the others in this list for LAN and WAN applications.

- *Medium interface connector*—A medium interface connector (MIC) is used for Fiber Distributed Data Interface (FDDI). Like SC connectors, MIC connectors are one-piece constructions.

- *Subminiature type A*—The company Amphenol originally designed subminiature type A (SMA) connectors for microwave use and later modified them for fiber-optic use. Two SMA versions are widely available: The 905 uses a straight ferrule, which is a metal sleeve for strengthening the connector, and the 906 uses a stepped ferrule with a plastic sleeve to ensure precise alignment of fibers. Like ST connectors, SMAs use two connectors for each fiber strand.

Fiber-Optic Installation

Installing fiber-optic networks is somewhat more difficult and time consuming than copper media installation. However, advances in connector technology have made field termination of fiber-optic cables almost as fast and easy as copper terminations. The connectors and test equipment for termination are still considerably more expensive than their copper counterparts, but the trend toward easier, more affordable fiber-optic networks continues. Fiber-optic cable to the desktop, although not common, is becoming a feasible option for more companies.

There are several methods for terminating fiber-optic cables because of the many connectors and cable types available, so installation details are beyond the scope of this book. Before embarking on a fiber-optic termination task, you need to purchase a fiber-optic termination kit, which can range from several hundred to several thousand dollars. Some tools in a typical fiber-optic termination kit include the following:

- *Buffer tube stripper*—A tightly calibrated tool designed for stripping buffer tubes off the glass fiber strand without breaking the fiber

- *Cable stripper*—Used to remove the fiber cable's outer sheath; much like the cable stripper used with UTP

- *Crimper*—Used with connectors that use crimping as the method to fix the connector to the cable, such as MT-RJ connectors

- *Diamond cleaver*—Used to cut glass fiber cleanly without shattering the end

- *Inspection scope*—Used for examining the end of a fiber strand to make sure it's clean and polished

- *Polishing tool*—Used to polish the end of a cleaved (cut) strand of fiber

Fiber-Optic Cable Types

Fiber-optic cables come in two main types: single-mode fiber (SMF) cables, which include a single extremely small-diameter fiber (typically 8 microns) at the core, and multimode fiber (MMF) cables, which use a considerably larger diameter fiber (50 and 62.5 microns are standard sizes) at the core. SMF cable costs more and generally works with laser-based emitters but spans the longest distances and is used in higher-bandwidth applications. MMF cables cost less and work with lower-power light emitting diodes (LEDs), which span shorter distances.

In the past, fiber-optic cable's high cost and difficult installation meant it was used only when a network required extremely high bandwidth or needed to span long distances between wired network segments. However, because of the falling costs of fiber and its advantages in immunity to interference, high-bandwidth capability, and increased security, it's now used almost exclusively for all network backbone connections. It's also the medium of choice for long-haul telecommunications, in which large amounts of voice and data traffic are aggregated, such as between telecommunication providers and ISPs.

Cable-Testing Equipment

Network cable installers should have a variety of testing and troubleshooting gadgets in their toolkits. Cable-testing tools are used to detect incorrect terminations, breaks, shorts, excessive noise or crosstalk, and cable length, among other problems and characteristics. The following list describes some common tools for testing and troubleshooting wired networks:

- *Cable certifier*—As mentioned, cable certifiers do a full battery of tests to certify that a cable installation meets a particular wiring standard, such as Cat 5e, Cat 6, Cat 6a, and so forth. These tools check for total segment length, crosstalk, noise, wiremap, resistance, impedance, and the capability to transfer data at the maximum frequency rated for the cable. They do the most complete testing of the tools discussed in this list and, therefore, cost the most.

- *Basic cable tester*—This device varies by capability and cost. Most cable testers check for wiremap, shorts, and opens, and some also check for length and crosstalk. They're mostly intended to let installers know that wires have been terminated correctly, but they don't certify a cable for a particular category. Basic cable testers sometimes come with several ID plugs that help you identify the cable end you're testing. You insert several ID plugs into patch panel ports, and the ID number (for example, 1, 2, 3) shows on the display of the cable tester at the other end of the cable, allowing you to quickly identify which cable goes to which patch panel port.

- *Tone generator*—This tool is used to locate both ends of the same wire. It issues a signal on one end of a wire, and a probe is used on the other end of the wire to verify continuity. The probe delivers an audible tone when it's touched to the same wire as the tone generator. In some installations, dozens or hundreds of cables are installed in the work area with the other end of the cables in an IDF. To match up the two ends of the cable, a technician places the tone generator on a wire in the work area, and the technician in the IDF touches each wire until the tone is heard. There are other methods to locate cables. For example, cable certifiers and some basic cable testers include remote ID plugs that are plugged into a patch panel's ports, and the end of the cable in the work area is plugged into the cable tester. The cable tester runs through its tests and displays the ID number of the remote ID plug to let the installer know to which patch panel port the cable is terminated.

- *Time domain reflectometer*—A TDR measures cable length by transmitting a signal on one end and measuring the time it takes for the reflection (signal bounce) to reach the end of the cable. TDRs are useful for finding a cable's total segment length and finding breaks. For example, if a cable is believed to be about 80 meters, but you don't have end-to-end continuity because of a break in the cable, a TDR can tell you approximately how far down the cable the break is located. A similar tool for fiber-optic cables, called an "optical time domain reflectometer (OTDR)," can also measure the location of breaks, bad connectors, and signal attenuation.

- *Multimeter*—This device can measure properties of electrical signals, such as voltage, resistance, impedance, and current. It's not often used to test communications cables but is handy for measuring DC and AC voltage and resistance levels on electrical circuits and power supplies. It can be used with some coaxial cable installations to measure impedance and test for shorts and opens.

- *Optical power meter*—An OPM measures the amount of light transmitted by a device on a fiber-optic cable and whether the amount of light on the cable's receiver meets the requirements for the device you're connecting. OPMs and OTDRs can be stand-alone devices but are also built into fiber-optic cable certifiers.

Wireless Networking

Wireless technologies are playing a bigger role in all kinds of networks. Since 1990, wireless options have increased, and the cost of these technologies continues to decrease. As wireless networking has become more affordable, demand has increased, and as demand increases, so does production of wireless equipment, which brings prices down even more. For this reason, wireless networks can now be found in most towns and cities in the form of hotspots, and many home users have turned to wireless networks so that their computers are no longer tethered to a network cable.

The adjective "wireless" might lead you to believe that wireless networks have no cabling of any kind. However, wireless networks are often used with wired networks to interconnect geographically dispersed LANs or groups of mobile users with wired servers and resources on a wired LAN. Networks including both wired and wireless components are called "hybrid networks." Indeed, even in home or small business networks with workstations connecting to a wireless AP or router, the AP or router usually connects to the Internet via a wired connection to a cable modem or similar device. Probably the only truly wireless networks are ad hoc networks or small infrastructure networks put together for the purpose of sharing files among a small group of people.

Wireless Benefits

Wireless networking has a lot of appeal in many circumstances and can offer the following capabilities:

- Create temporary connections to existing wired networks.
- Establish backup or contingency connectivity for existing wired networks.
- Extend a network's span beyond the reach of wire-based or fiber-optic cabling, especially in older buildings where rewiring might be too expensive.

- Allow businesses to provide customers with wireless networking easily, thereby offering a service that gets customers in and keeps them there.

- Enable users to roam around an organization or college campus with their devices.

Each capability supports uses that extend the benefits of networking beyond conventional limits. Common applications for wireless networking technologies include the following:

- Ready access to data for mobile workers, such as doctors and nurses in hospitals or delivery personnel. For instance, United Parcel Service (UPS) drivers maintain connections to a server at the home office; their handheld computers send and receive delivery updates and status information to a network server over a wireless phone connection. Doctors can carry lightweight mobile devices so that they have wireless access to patient information at all times.

- Delivering network access to isolated facilities or disaster-stricken areas. For example, the Federal Emergency Management Agency (FEMA) uses battery-powered wireless technologies to install field networks in areas where power and connections might be unavailable.

- Access in environments where layout and settings change constantly. For instance, film studios often include wireless network components on the set so that information is always available, no matter how the stage configuration changes.

- Improved customer services in busy areas, such as check-in or reception centers. For example, Hertz employees use handheld units to check in returned rental vehicles right in the parking lot.

- Network connectivity in structures, such as historical buildings, where in-wall wiring is impossible to install or prohibitively expensive.

- Home networks where running cables is inconvenient. More people who own multiple computers install inexpensive wireless networks so that family members can share Internet connections and files. Figure 4-20 shows an example of a home wireless network.

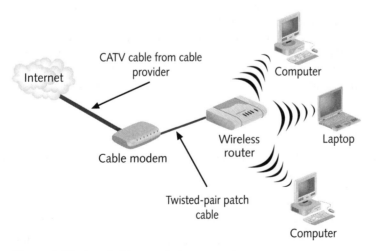

Figure 4-20 A typical home wireless network

Types of Wireless Networks

Depending on the role wireless components play in a network, wireless networks can be subdivided into the following categories:

- *Local area networks (LANs)*—In LANs, wireless components act as part of an ordinary LAN, usually to provide connectivity for mobile users or in changing environments or perhaps across areas that couldn't otherwise be networked. Examples include older buildings where installing wiring is impractical or areas encompassing public or common property where cabling might not be permitted.

- *Extended LANs*—In **extended LANs**, an organization might use wireless components to increase a LAN's span beyond normal distance limitations for wire-based or fiber-optic cables, using a point-to-point arrangement (described in Chapter 3).

- *Internet service*—A company that wants to be a high-speed ISP but doesn't have a media infrastructure available, as cable and phone companies do, can use wireless technologies to bring Internet access to homes and businesses.

- *Mobile computing*—With mobile computing, users communicate by using a wireless networking medium, such as a radio or cell phone frequency, that enables them to move around while remaining connected to a network.

Wireless LAN Components

The wireless components of most LANs behave like their wired counterparts, except for the media and related hardware. The operational principles are much the same: Attaching a network interface of some kind to a computer is still necessary, but the interface attaches to an antenna and an emitter rather than to a cable. Users can still access the network as though a cable connects them to it.

Another component is required to link wireless users with wired users or resources. At some point on a cabled network, a transmitter/receiver device, called a **transceiver** or an access point (AP), must be installed to translate between wired and wireless networks. This device broadcasts messages in wireless format that must be directed to wireless users and relays messages sent by wireless users to resources or users on the wired side of its connection. An AP includes an antenna and a transmitter to send and receive wireless traffic but also connects to the wired side of the network. This connection enables the device to shuttle traffic back and forth between a network's wired and wireless sides.

Wireless LAN Transmission

All wireless communication depends on sending and receiving signals broadcast through the air to carry information between network devices. These signals take the form of waves in the electromagnetic (EM) spectrum. The frequency of the wave forms used for communication is measured in cycles per second, usually expressed as **hertz (Hz)**. The entire EM spectrum starts with low-frequency waves, such as those used for electrical power (60 Hz in the United States) and telephone (0 to 3 kilohertz [KHz] for traditional voice systems), and goes all the way through the visible light frequencies to the highest frequencies in existence, at which gamma rays and other high-energy particles operate.

In wireless communication, frequency affects the amount and speed of data transmission. The transmission's strength or power determines the distance that broadcast data can travel and still remain intelligible. In general, however, the principles governing wireless transmissions dictate that lower-frequency transmissions can carry less data more slowly over longer distances, and higher-frequency transmissions can carry more data faster over shorter distances.

The middle part of the EM spectrum is commonly divided into several named frequency ranges (bands). The following are the most common frequencies for wireless data communication:

- *Radio*—10 KHz to 300 MHz
- *Microwave*—300 MHz to 300 GHz
- *Infrared*—300 GHz to 400 THz (terahertz)

 Wi-Fi networks operate in the microwave category of frequencies.

The important principles to remember about a broadcast medium are the inverse relationship between frequency and distance and the direct relationship between frequency and data transfer rate and bandwidth. It's also important to understand that higher-frequency technologies often use tight-beam broadcasts and require a clear line of sight between sender and receiver to ensure correct delivery.

Wireless LANs make use of four main technologies for transmitting and receiving data, discussed in the following sections:

- Infrared
- Laser
- Narrowband (single-frequency) radio
- Spread-spectrum radio

Infrared LAN Technologies Infrared (IR) wireless networks use infrared light beams to send signals between pairs of devices. These devices typically generate signals strong enough to prevent interference from light sources in most office environments. Infrared works well for LAN applications because of its high bandwidth, which makes 10 to 100 Mbps transmission rates easy to deliver. The four main kinds of infrared LANs include the following:

- Line-of-sight networks require an unobstructed view, or a clear line of sight, between the transmitter and receiver.
- Reflective wireless networks broadcast signals from optical transceivers near devices to a central hub, which then forwards signals to their intended recipients.
- Scatter infrared networks bounce transmissions off walls and ceilings to deliver signals from sender to receiver. TV remotes work in this fashion. This approach limits

maximum reception distances to approximately 30 meters (100 feet). Because bounce technologies introduce signal delays, scatter infrared results in lower bandwidth than line of sight.

- Broadband optical telepoint networks provide broadband services. This technology offers high speed and wide bandwidth, can handle high-end multimedia traffic, and matches the capabilities of most wired networks.

IR transmissions are sometimes used for virtual docking connections that enable portable computing devices to communicate with wired computers or peripheral devices, such as printers. Even though infrared offers reasonable networking speeds and convenience, infrared LANs are hampered by the typical 100-foot distance limitation. Because infrared light is close in frequency to visible light (and most visible light sources emit strongly in infrared frequencies), infrared is prone to interference problems from fluorescent and other light sources in most work environments. These devices are often called **IrDA devices,** named after the Infrared Device Association, a trade association for designers and manufacturers of infrared equipment.

Laser-Based LAN Technologies
Laser-based transmissions also require a clear line of sight between sender and receiver. Any solid object or person blocking a beam interrupts data transmissions. To protect people from injury and excess radiation, laser-based LAN devices are subject to many of the same limitations as infrared but aren't as susceptible to interference from visible light sources.

Narrowband Radio LAN Technologies
Narrowband radio (also called "single-frequency radio") LANs use low-powered, two-way radio communication, much like what's used in taxis, police radios, and other private radio systems. Receiver and transmitter must be tuned to the same frequency to handle incoming and outgoing data. Unlike light-based communications, such as infrared or laser, narrowband radio requires no line of sight between sender and receiver, as long as both parties stay within the broadcast range of these devices—typically, a maximum range of approximately 70 meters (230 feet).

In the United States, government agencies, such as the Federal Communications Commission (FCC), regulate nearly all radio frequencies. Organizations that want frequencies for their exclusive use in specific locales must complete a time-consuming, expensive application process before being granted the right to use them. Because of the difficulty in securing exclusive use, the FCC sets aside certain frequencies for unregulated use, such as the ones at which cell phones and remote-control toys operate. As wireless networking and other forms of wireless communication become more popular, crowding of these frequencies could become a problem.

Depending on the frequency, walls or other solid barriers can block signals and prevent transmission and reception. Interference from other radio sources is also possible, particularly if the devices broadcast in the unregulated frequency ranges, as most wireless LAN technologies do. As with any broadcast technology, anyone within range of the network devices could eavesdrop on communications. For narrowband radio technologies, this range is quite short. Table 4-5 summarizes the characteristics of narrowband wireless LAN technologies.

Table 4-5 Narrowband wireless LAN characteristics

Characteristic	Value
Frequency ranges	Unregulated: 902–928 MHz, 2.4 GHz, 5.72–5.85 GHz
Maximum distance	50–70 m (164–230 ft.)
Bandwidth	1–10 Mbps
Installation and maintenance	Easy to install and maintain
Interference	Highly susceptible
Cost	Moderate
Security	Highly susceptible to eavesdropping within range

Other single-frequency LAN technologies operate at higher power ratings. Networks of this type can usually transmit as far as the horizon and even farther by using repeater towers or signal-bouncing techniques. This kind of technology is well suited for communicating with mobile users but much more expensive than lower-powered alternatives. In addition, transmission equipment is more expensive and usually requires FCC licensing. Most users of this technology, even in the largest organizations, purchase this service from a communications carrier instead of operating their own facilities.

Lack of security can be a serious concern with this kind of networking technology. Anyone with the correct receiver can eavesdrop on communications, which explains why encryption of traffic is common for networks operating at these frequencies. Table 4-6 summarizes the characteristics of high-powered single-frequency radio networks.

Table 4-6 High-powered single-frequency LAN characteristics

Characteristic	Value
Frequency ranges	Unregulated: 902–928 MHz, 2.4 GHz, 5.72–5.85 GHz
Maximum distance	Line of sight, unless extension technologies are used
Bandwidth	1–10 Mbps
Installation and maintenance	Difficult, highly technical, requires licensing
Interference	Highly susceptible
Cost	Expensive to very expensive
Security	Highly susceptible to eavesdropping

Spread-Spectrum LAN Technologies Spread-spectrum radio addresses several weaknesses of single-frequency communications, whether high or low power. Instead of using a single frequency, spread-spectrum uses multiple frequencies simultaneously, thereby improving reliability and reducing susceptibility to interference. Also, using multiple frequencies makes eavesdropping more difficult.

The two main kinds of spread-spectrum communications are frequency hopping and direct-sequence modulation. Frequency hopping switches data between multiple frequencies at regular intervals. The transmitter and receiver must be tightly synchronized to maintain communication. The hardware handles the timing of hops and chooses the next frequency without sending any information about this activity, so eavesdropping is nearly impossible. Because frequency-hopping technologies use only one frequency at a time, however, their effective bandwidth is usually 1 Mbps or lower and seldom exceeds 2 Mbps.

Direct-sequence modulation breaks data into fixed-size segments called "chips" and transmits the data on several different frequencies at the same time. The receiving equipment knows what frequencies to monitor and how to reassemble the arriving chips into the correct sequences of data. It's even possible to transmit dummy data on one or more channels, along with real data on other channels, to make it more difficult for eavesdroppers to re-create the original data. Typically, these networks operate in unregulated frequencies and provide bandwidths from 2 to 6 Mbps, depending on the number of dummy channels used. The original 802.11 and 802.11b specifications use direct sequence spread spectrum (DSSS). Table 4-7 summarizes the characteristics of spread-spectrum LAN technologies.

Table 4-7 **Spread-spectrum LAN characteristics**

Characteristic	Value
Frequency ranges	Unregulated: 902–928 MHz or 2.4 GHz, 5 GHz
Maximum distance	Limited to cell boundaries but often extends over several miles
Bandwidth	1–2 Mbps for frequency hopping, 2–6 Mbps for direct-sequence modulation
Installation and maintenance	Depends on equipment; ranges from easy to difficult
Interference	Moderately resistant
Cost	Inexpensive to moderate
Security	Not very susceptible to eavesdropping

Orthogonal frequency divisional multiplexing (OFDM) is a spread-spectrum technology used by 802.11g and 802.11n running at 2.4 GHz and the 802.11a 5 GHz and 802.16 WiMAX standards.

The term "cell boundary," as used in Table 4-7, refers to the service area or the radius of a viable signal produced by a wireless transmitter.

LAN Media Selection Criteria

In LANs and internetworks, there are three main media choices: UTP, fiber optic, and wireless. For UTP, the choices are usually Cat 5e, Cat 6, or Cat 6a for most applications, although you might opt for a shielded version. Fiber-optic cabling is often the top choice for connecting wiring closets and buildings and possibly in electrically noisy environments and for ultra-high speed connections to servers. Wireless networks typically supplement a wired network to accommodate mobile users or are used for SOHO networks that don't need the higher bandwidth wired networks can provide. Following is a summary of criteria to explore when you're having difficulty choosing between media types:

- *Bandwidth*—How fast must the network be? Higher bandwidth means more expensive cable and higher installation costs, usually fiber-optic cable. However, if you need a 40 or 100 Gigabit Ethernet network, fiber optic is really your only choice.

- *Budget*—How much money can you spend on cabling? Sometimes budget alone dictates a choice. A typical UTP cable installation costs $100 to $200 per cable run, whereas fiber optic might cost twice as much. Wireless media have no physical installation costs, but you need to install access points and verify connectivity from all locations.

- *Environmental considerations*—How electrically noisy is the deployment environment? How important is data security? Sometimes high-EMI environments or security requirements can dictate cable choices, regardless of other factors. The more weight either factor has, the more likely a choice fiber-optic cable is (or in lower-bandwidth applications, a secure wireless network).

- *Span*—What kind of distance must the network span? Longer spans might require fiber-optic cabling or wireless technologies used between buildings. Strategic placement of small switches for use with UTP wiring gives UTP surprising reach in many office environments where workers tend to cluster in groups, even if these groups are widely scattered.

- *Existing cable plant*—For a new installation, only the previously listed criteria need to be considered, but for an upgrade, the existing cable plant must be considered. For example, if some existing cable is to remain, is it compatible with the speeds and new equipment that are planned?

Networks combining fiber-optic, UTP, and wireless media have almost become the norm, with fiber-optic cables providing a backbone that ties together clusters of devices networked with UTP cable through switches and wiring centers. With wireless networks, users can stay connected with their Wi-Fi–enabled phones, laptops, and tablets. Table 4-8 condenses the most important information for the cable types covered in this chapter.

Table 4-8 Comparison of LAN media characteristics

Type	Maximum cable length	Bandwidth	Installation	Interference	Cost
UTP	100 m	10–10000 Mbps	Easy	High	Cheapest
STP	100 m	16–10000 Mbps	Moderate	Moderate	Moderate
Fiber optic	2–100 km	100 Mbps–10 Gbps	Moderate	None	Most expensive
Wireless	100-300 feet	11 to 300 Mbps	Easy	Moderate	None for physical media

Chapter Summary

- Wired networking media come in two main categories: copper and fiber optic. Cable characteristics include bandwidth rating, maximum segment length, susceptibility to interference and eavesdropping, and cable grade.

- Twisted-pair cabling comes in shielded or unshielded varieties. Most networks use UTP, but STP can be used in electrically noisy environments. Cat 5e and Cat 6 are the most common cable types in networks today.

- Twisted-pair cabling components consist of connectors, patch cable, jacks, patch panels, and distribution racks. A structured cabling plant consists of work areas, horizontal wiring, telecommunications closets (IDFs), equipment rooms (MDFs), backbone cabling, and entrance facilities.

- Fiber-optic cable uses pulses of light to represent bits and is immune to EMI, RFI, and electronic eavesdropping. Commercial implementations of up to 100 Gbps are in use. Each network connection requires two strands of fiber-optic cable: one for transmitting and one for receiving. Fiber-optic cable comes in single-mode or multimode; single-mode uses lasers and can carry data longer distances, and multimode uses LEDs.

- Wireless networks can be subdivided into LANs, extended LANs, and mobile computing. The components of a wireless LAN are a NIC, an antenna, and a transceiver or an access point. Wireless networks send signals in the form of electromagnetic waves. Different network types use different frequencies for signal transmission.

- Different technologies are used to transmit and receive data, including infrared, laser, narrowband radio, and spread-spectrum radio. Infrared can deliver speeds up to 100 Mbps and is used in some LAN applications. Laser-based technologies require line of sight between sender and receiver, as does infrared, but laser isn't as susceptible to interference from other light sources. Narrowband radio uses low-power two-way radio communication and is highly susceptible to interference. Spread-spectrum LANs are the most common and are used for 802.11 b/g/n Wi-Fi networks.

- Criteria for choosing LAN media include needed bandwidth, budget, environmental factors, the distance the network must span, and the existing cable plant, if any. Networks combining fiber-optic cable, UTP, and wireless have become the norm.

Key Terms

backbone cabling   Network cabling that interconnects telecommunications closets (IDFs) and equipment rooms (MDFs). This cabling (also called "vertical cabling") runs between floors or wings of a building and between buildings to carry network traffic destined for devices outside the work area. It's often fiber-optic cable but can also be UTP.

cable plant   The collection of all cables and connectors tying a network together.

cable segment   A length of cable between two network devices, such as a NIC and a switch. Any intermediate passive (unpowered) devices, such as wall jacks, are considered part of the total segment length.

crossover cable A type of patch cable that uses the 586B standard on one end and the 586A standard on the other end. This arrangement crosses the transmit and receive wires so that transmit on one end connects to receive on the other end. Often used to connect two devices of the same type to one another—for example, connecting a switch to a switch.

crosstalk Interference one wire generates on another wire when both wires are in a bundle.

datagrade A grade of cable suitable for data networking.

demarcation point The location in the cable plant where a connection to a WAN is made and where an organization's LAN equipment ends and a third-party provider's equipment and cabling begins.

differential signal A method for transmitting data in which two wires of opposite polarity are used. One wire transmits using positive voltage and the other uses negative voltage. Differential signals enhance signal reliability by providing a canceling affect on EMI and crosstalk.

electromagnetic interference (EMI) A disturbance to the operation of an electronic circuit or its data, caused by devices that emit an electromagnetic field.

encoding The method used to represent bits on a medium.

entrance facility The location of cabling and equipment that connects an organization's network to a third-party telecommunications provider. It can also serve as an equipment room and the main cross-connect for all backbone cabling.

equipment room A room that houses servers, routers, switches, and other major network equipment and serves as a connection point for backbone cabling running between telecommunications closets (IDFs). When it's used to connect backbone cabling between buildings and IDFs, it's called a "main distribution frame." *See also* intermediate distribution frame (IDF) *and* main distribution frame (MDF).

extended LANs A LAN that's expanded beyond its normal distance limitations with wireless communication.

fiber-optic cable A cable type that carries data over thin strands of glass by using optical (light) pulses to represent bits.

hertz (Hz) A unit expressing how many times per second a signal or electromagnetic wave occurs.

horizontal wiring The network cabling running from the work area's wall jack to the telecommunications closet (IDF), usually terminated at a patch panel. The total maximum distance for horizontal wiring is 100 meters.

infrared (IR) A very long wavelength light source in the invisible spectrum that can be used to transmit data wirelessly.

intermediate distribution frame (IDF) A telecommunications closet that houses the cabling and devices for work area computers. *See also* telecommunications closet *and* work area.

IrDA devices Devices that use infrared signals to communicate. IrDA stands for Infrared Device Association.

main distribution frame (MDF) An equipment and cabling room that serves as the connecting point for backbone cabling between buildings and between IDFs; also called the "main cross-connect." *See also* equipment room.

MDI crossed (MDI-X) devices   Network devices that connect by using RJ-45 plugs over twisted-pair cabling; they transmit over pins 3 and 6 and receive over pins 1 and 2 of an RJ-45 connector.

medium dependent interface (MDI) devices   Network devices that connect by using RJ-45 plugs over twisted-pair cabling; they transmit on pins 1 and 2 and receive on pins 3 and 6 of an RJ-45 connector.

narrowband radio   Low-powered, two-way radio communication systems, such as those used in taxis, police radios, and other private radio systems; also called "single-frequency radio."

patch cable   A short cable for connecting a computer to an RJ-45 jack or connecting a patch-panel port to a switch. *See also* straight-through cable.

radio frequency interference (RFI)   Similar to EMI, but RFI is usually interference caused by strong broadcast sources. *See also* electromagnetic interference (EMI).

RJ-45 jack   A device used in the work area in wall plates and surface-mounted boxes to plug a patch cable that connects a computer to the horizontal wiring.

RJ-45 plug   A connector used to terminate twisted-pair cable for making patch cables. It has eight wire traces to accommodate a standard twisted-pair cable with four wire pairs.

spread-spectrum radio   A radio communication system that uses multiple frequencies simultaneously, thereby improving reliability and reducing susceptibility to interference over narrowband radio.

straight-through cable   A standard patch cable that uses the same wiring standards on both ends so that each wire is in the same location on both ends of the cable (pin 1 goes to pin 1, pin 2 to pin 2, and so forth). *See also* patch cable.

structured cabling   A specification for organizing cabling in data and voice networks, regardless of the media type or network architecture.

telecommunications closet (TC)   Usually an enclosed space or room that provides connectivity to computer equipment in the nearby work area; can also serve as the entrance facility in small installations. Typical equipment includes patch panels to terminate horizontal wiring runs and switches. When it houses the cabling and devices for work area computers, it's called an "intermediate distribution frame." *See also* intermediate distribution frame (IDF).

termination   The attachment of RJ-45 plugs on a cable to make a patch cable or punching down the cable wires into terminal blocks on a jack or patch panel.

transceiver   A device that transmits and receives. In wireless networking, an access point is a transceiver.

twisted-pair (TP) cable   A cable containing one or more pairs of insulated strands of copper wire twisted around one another and housed in an outer sheath.

voicegrade   A grade of cable that's not suitable for data networking but is suitable for voice communication.

work area   The location of workstations and other user devices—in short, the place where people work with computers and other network devices.

Review Questions

1. Which of the following is a common characteristic of a networking medium? (Choose all that apply.)

    a.   Bandwidth rating

    b.   Interference susceptibility

    c.   Broadband rating

    d.   Maximum segment length

2. Which of the following types of fiber-optic connectors provides high density and requires only one connector for two cables?

    a.   SC

    b.   ST

    c.   MT-RJ

    d.   RJ-45

3. Which of the following conditions requires cables not to exceed a recommended maximum length?

    a.   Diminution

    b.   Capacitance

    c.   Bandwidth

    d.   Attenuation

4. Which of the following is the process for representing bit signals on the medium?

    a.   Encryption

    b.   Encoding

    c.   Decryption

    d.   Decoding

5. What happens to signals as they travel the length of the medium?

    a.   They decode.

    b.   They amplify.

    c.   They attenuate.

    d.   They implode.

6. Which of the following is UTP susceptible to? (Choose all that apply.)

    a.   EMI

    b.   Crosstalk

    c.   Signal enhancement

    d.   LEDs

7. The space between a false ceiling and the true ceiling where heating and cooling air circulates is called the _____.
   a. duct-equivalent airspace
   b. conduit
   c. return air
   d. plenum

8. What type of connector is used most commonly with TP network wiring?
   a. RJ-11
   b. RJ-45
   c. BNC
   d. MT-RJ

9. You have been hired to install a network at a large government agency that wants to reduce the likelihood of electronic eavesdropping on its network. What type of cable is most resistant to eavesdropping?
   a. UTP
   b. STP
   c. Coaxial
   d. Fiber optic

10. Which of the following is a characteristic of unshielded twisted-pair cable? (Choose all that apply.)
   a. Consists of four wires
   b. Commonly used in physical bus topologies
   c. Has a distance limitation of 100 meters
   d. Is susceptible to electrical interference

11. Which of the following is a characteristic of fiber-optic cabling? (Choose all that apply.)
   a. Can be used in electrically noisy environments
   b. Requires only a single strand of fiber for network connections
   c. Carries data over longer distances than UTP does
   d. Has low bandwidth

12. You're preparing to install a conventional Ethernet network in your new office building, but your boss tells you to be ready to handle a switchover to 1 Gbps Ethernet next year. What types of cable could you install? (Choose all that apply.)
   a. Cat 5
   b. Fiber optic
   c. Cat 4
   d. Cat 6
   e. Coax

13. When two cables run side by side, signals traveling down one wire might interfere with signals traveling on the other wire. What is this phenomenon called?

    a. RFI

    b. Attenuation

    c. Impedance

    d. Crosstalk

14. What characteristic of twisted-pair cabling helps mitigate the effects of crosstalk?

    a. Differential signals

    b. Copper conductors

    c. Four pairs of wires

    d. 100-ohm impedance

15. Which of the following is a wiring standard for twisted-pair cable connections? (Choose all that apply.)

    a. IEEE 802.3a

    b. TIA/EIA 568A

    c. IEEE 802.3b

    d. TIA/EIA 568B

16. Which of the following is a component of a structured cabling system? (Choose all that apply.)

    a. Patch cables

    b. RJ-11 plugs

    c. Coax cable

    d. Horizontal wiring

17. Where are you most likely to find backbone cabling? (Choose all that apply.)

    a. MDF

    b. In the work area

    c. Between IDFs

    d. Connecting a work area to an IDF

18. Which of the following is a tool needed to make a patch cable? (Choose all that apply.)

    a. 110 punchdown tool

    b. Cable stripper

    c. Crimping tool

    d. RJ-45 jack

19. Which type of connection is most likely to require a crossover cable?

    a. PC to hub

    b. Hub to router

    c. Router to switch

    d. PC to router

20. Which UTP limitations can be solved by fiber-optic cable? (Choose all that apply.)

    a. Bandwidth

    b. EMI susceptibility

    c. Installation cost

    d. Segment length

21. How many strands of fiber-optic cable are needed for a network connection?

    a. 1

    b. 2

    c. 4

    d. 8

22. Which statement is true about fiber-optic cables?

    a. MMF uses lasers and has a thicker core.

    b. SMF uses lasers and has a thinner core.

    c. MMF uses LEDs and has a thinner core.

    d. SMF uses LEDs and has a thicker core.

23. When might you want to use a rollover cable?

    a. To connect a PC to another PC

    b. To connect a router to a switch

    c. To add a switch to a LAN

    d. To configure a Cisco device

24. Which of the following wireless technologies does a 802.11 wireless network using the 2.4 GHz frequency range use?

    a. Infrared

    b. Narrowband radio

    c. Frequency hopping

    d. Direct-sequence spread spectrum

Critical Thinking

The following activities give you critical thinking challenges. Challenge labs give you an opportunity to use the skills you have learned to perform a task without step-by-step instructions. Case projects offer a practical networking setup for which you supply a written solution.

Challenge Lab 4-1: Creating a 1000BaseT Crossover Cable

Time Required: 20 minutes

Objective: Create a 1000BaseT crossover cable.

Required Tools and Equipment: Wire cutter and cable stripper, RJ-45 crimping tool, 2 to 4 feet of Cat 5e or Cat 6 cable, two RJ-45 plugs, and two devices that support 1000BaseT (which can be two PCs with 1000BaseT NICs or two 1000BaseT switches)

Description: In this challenge lab, you create a crossover cable that supports 1000BaseT Ethernet and test it between two devices. Then you verify that the devices connect at 1000BaseT speed.

- How is a 1000BaseT crossover cable different from a 100BaseT crossover cable?

- How did you verify that the devices connected at 1000BaseT?

Challenge Lab 4-2: Creating a Rollover Cable

Time Required: 20 minutes

Objective: Create a rollover cable.

Required Tools and Equipment: Wire cutter and cable stripper, RJ-45 crimping tool, 2 to 4 feet of Cat 5e or Cat 6 cable, two RJ-45 plugs, a Cisco-managed device (such as a switch or a router with a console port), a PC with terminal emulation software installed (such as PuTTY), and a DB-9-to-RJ-45 adapter

Description: In this challenge lab, you create a rollover cable, using the DB-9-to-RJ-45 adapter to connect the PC's DB-9 serial port to one end of the rollover cable and the other end to the device's console port. If the PC doesn't have a DB-9 serial port, USB-to-RJ-45 serial port adapters are available. Run PuTTY to connect to the managed switch or router's console. You might need to research the PuTTY settings required to make the connection.

- Why might you need a rollover cable?

- What's the pinout for a rollover cable?

CASE PROJECTS

Case Project 4-1

During the design of most real-world networks, you'll discover that using more than one type of networking medium is common. The usual reasons for needing more than one type of medium include the following:

- Two or more areas must be interconnected, and the distance separating them is greater than the maximum segment length for the type of medium used in (or best suited for) each area.

- A connection must pass through a high-interference environment (across some large transformers, near heavy-duty electrical motors, and so on). Failure to use a different type of medium increases the risk of impeding data flow. This reason is especially common for choosing fiber-optic cable or wireless in many networks, particularly when connecting floors in an office building and the only available pathway is the elevator shaft.

- Certain parts of an internetwork might have to carry more traffic than other parts. Typically, the segment where traffic aggregates is the backbone, a common cable segment that interconnects subsidiary networks. (Think of a tree trunk as the backbone and its major branches as cable segments.) Often, a higher-capacity cable is used for a backbone (for example, fiber-optic cable or Cat 6 cable rated for Gigabit Ethernet), along with a higher-speed networking technology for attachments to the backbone. This arrangement means outlying segments might use conventional 10 or 100 Mbps Ethernet, and the backbone uses 1 Gbps or 10 Gbps Ethernet.

Using this information, suggest solutions that involve at least two types, if possible, of networking media to address the following problems:

- A—XYZ Corp. is planning a new network. Engineers in the design shop must have connections to accountants and salespeople in the front office, but all routes between the two areas must traverse the shop floor, where arc welders and metal-stamping equipment create potent amounts of EMI and RFI. Given that both the design shop and front office use 10BaseT (twisted-pair Ethernet), how might you interconnect these two areas? What medium guarantees immunity from interference?

- B—After the front-office network at XYZ Corp. is set up, an accountant realizes that if the loading dock connected to the network, dock workers could log incoming and outgoing shipments and keep the inventory more current. Even though the loading dock is nowhere near the shop floor, the dock is 1100 feet from the front office. What kinds of cable will work to make this connection? What kind would you choose and why?

- C—ABC Company occupies three floors in a 10-story building, where the elevator shaft provides the only path to all these floors. In addition, users on the 9th and 10th floors must access a collection of servers on the 8th floor.

Explain what kind of connections would work in the elevator shaft. If more than one choice is possible, pick the best option and explain the reasons for your choice. Assuming that interfloor connections might someday need to run at much higher speeds, reevaluate your choice. What's the best type of medium for open-ended bandwidth needs? Explain your answer.

Case Project 4-2

XYZ Corp.'s facilities in Nashua, New Hampshire, are two office buildings 400 feet apart, each with its own LAN. To connect the two networks, you plan to dig a trench and lay cable in conduit between the two buildings. You want to use fiber-optic cable, but your budget-conscious facilities manager wants to use 100 Mbps Ethernet over twisted-pair cable. Which of the following reasons can you use to justify fiber-optic cable in this case, and why?

- a: Twisted pair won't span a 400-foot distance.
- b: Fiber-optic cable is cheaper and easier to work with than twisted pair.
- c: Twisted pair is a conductive cable and can, therefore, carry current based on the difference in ground potential between the two buildings.
- d: Fiber-optic cable leaves more room for growth and future needs for increased bandwidth than twisted pair does.

Case Project 4-3

TVBCA has just occupied a historic building in downtown Pittsburgh where 15 employees will work. Because of codes for historic buildings, TVBCA isn't permitted to run cables inside walls or ceilings.

Required result: Employees must be able to share files and printers, as in a typical LAN environment, without using cables.

Optional desired results: Employees must be able to use their laptops or tablets and move freely throughout the office while maintaining a network connection. Because of the size of some computer-aided design (CAD) files employees use often, data transfer speeds should be at least 100 Mbps and the connection should be secure.

Proposed solution: Install an 802.11ac wireless access point and configure each mobile device to connect to the AP with WPA2 encryption. Which of the following results does the proposed solution deliver? Explain your answer.

- a: The proposed solution delivers the required result and both optional desired results.
- b: The proposed solution delivers the required result and only one of the two optional desired results.
- c: The proposed solution delivers the required result but neither optional desired result.
- d: The proposed solution does not deliver the required result.

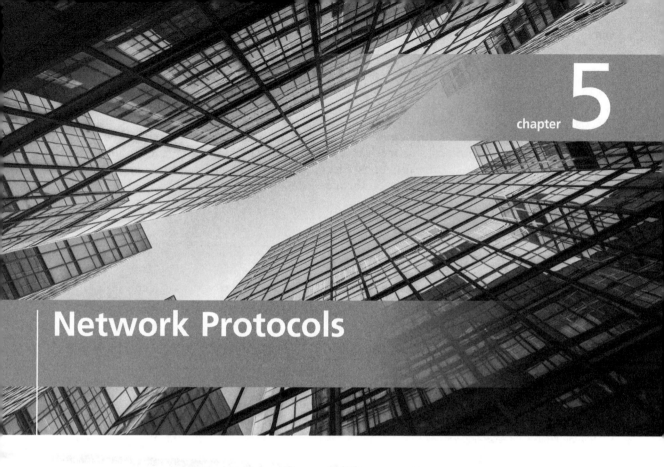

chapter 5

Network Protocols

After reading this chapter and completing the exercises, you will be able to:

- Describe the purpose of a network protocol and the layers in the TCP/IP architecture
- Describe TCP/IP Application-layer protocols
- Describe TCP/IP Transport-layer protocols
- Describe TCP/IP Internetwork-layer protocols
- Describe TCP/IP Network access–layer protocols

For effective communication across a network, computers must be capable of transmitting data reliably and efficiently. Network protocols are designed to accomplish this goal, with some protocols emphasizing reliability and others efficiency. Network protocols often work together at different layers of the network communication process to provide both reliability and efficiency. Network administrators must understand the role and function of protocols, as much of their time is spent configuring and troubleshooting the protocols used by the network's clients and servers. This chapter discusses network protocols in general but focuses on the most common suite of protocols used in networks: TCP/IP.

TCP/IP's Layered Architecture

Table 5-1 summarizes what you need for the hands-on projects in this chapter.

Table 5-1 Hands-on project requirements

Hands-on project	Requirements	Time required	Notes
Hands-On Project 5-1: Viewing TCP/IP Layers in Windows and Configuring Your IP Address	Net-*XX*	10 minutes	
Hands-On Project 5-2: Identifying the TCP/IP Layers in a Frame	Net-*XX*, Wireshark installed	10 minutes	
Hands-On Project 5-3: Working with DNS Tools	Net-*XX*	10 minutes	
Hands-On Project 5-4: Working with the DHCP Client	Net-*XX*	10 minutes	A configured DHCP server must be available.
Hands-On Project 5-5: Examining the Internetwork Layer	Net-*XX*, Wireshark installed	10 minutes	
Hands-On Project 5-6: Capturing ARP and ICMP Packets	Net-*XX*, Wireshark installed	10 minutes	
Hands-On Project 5-7: Using the `arp` Command	Net-*XX*	10 minutes	
Hands-On Project 5-8: Using the `netstat` Program	Net-*XX*	10 minutes	
Hands-On Project 5-9: Examining NIC Properties	Net-*XX*	10 minutes	

The term "protocol" isn't specific to the field of networking. In general, a **protocol** consists of rules and procedures for communication and behavior or etiquette. Just as two people must share a common set of rules for verbal communication—a language—computers must also "speak" the same language and agree on the rules of communication. You use protocols in other ways. Texting, e-mail, and Facebook communication, for example, have their own rules of etiquette and, especially for texting, their own language.

Until fairly recently, you had a choice of network protocols you could install on your computer, depending on the computing environment. A small network in the 1990s running Windows 3.1 or Windows 95 probably ran the Windows-specific NetBEUI protocol. A network with Novell NetWare 4.x servers typically ran IPX/SPX. Both these protocols are obsolete now and are found only in networks that haven't been upgraded in more than a decade. Today, you can focus on the TCP/IP protocol suite, the protocol of the Internet and the protocol all contemporary OSs run.

When a set of protocols works cooperatively, it's called a **protocol suite** (or "protocol stack"). The most common one is **Transmission Control Protocol/Internet Protocol (TCP/IP)**, the Internet protocol suite. Although you can see by its name that TCP/IP consists of at least two protocols—TCP and IP—this protocol suite is actually composed of more than a dozen protocols operating at different layers of the communication process.

Recall the communication process explained in Chapter 1 and animated in Simulation 1. This discussion was an introduction to the idea of communication taking place in layers. The protocols in TCP/IP can also be divided into four layers, with similar names and functions. Figure 5-1 shows the layers of the TCP/IP protocol suite and which protocols operate at each layer. This layered architecture is usually referred to as the "TCP/IP model."

Layer name	TCP/IP protocols			
Application	HTTP	FTP	DHCP	TFTP
	SMTP	POP3	DNS	SNMP
Transport	TCP		UDP	
Internetwork	ICMP	ARP		IPsec
	IPv4 and IPv6			
Network access	Ethernet, token ring, FDDI, WAN technologies			

Figure 5-1 The TCP/IP layered architecture

Many books and Web sites about TCP/IP call the Internetwork layer the "Internet layer," but the term "internetwork" describes the layer's function more accurately, especially because many people use the term "Internet" interchangeably with the term "World Wide Web." Also, the Network access layer is often referred to as the "Network interface layer." Although both terms describe this layer's function, "Network access" has been used in this book.

The TCP/IP protocol suite includes more protocols than the ones shown in this figure, but they're some of the most common protocols used in networks. Before you examine each layer and protocol more closely, take a look at an example of how the layers work together.

Suppose you start your Web browser and have configured your home page as *http://www.cengage.com*. The Web browser formats a request for a page on the *www.cengage.com* Web server by using the Application-layer protocol HTTP. The request looks something like Figure 5-2.

get the cengage.com home page

Figure 5-2 The Application layer creates data

You've learned about packets and frames, but the unit of information the Application layer works with is simply called "data." The Application-layer protocol HTTP passes the request down to the Transport-layer protocol: in this case, TCP. Notice that the four Application-layer protocols in the left column of Figure 5-1 use TCP as the Transport-layer protocol, and the Application-layer protocols in the right column use UDP. (The difference between TCP and UDP is explained later in "Role of the Transport Layer.") TCP has its own job to do, so it adds a header to the request that looks like Figure 5-3.

TCP header	get the cengage.com home page

Figure 5-3   The Transport layer adds its header to make a segment

The unit of information the Transport layer works with is called a **segment** (when using TCP) or a **datagram** (when using UDP). The Transport layer passes the segment or datagram to the Internetwork layer. The Internetwork layer has a number of subprotocols, but most operate by following the basic rules and format of IP. IP then places its header on the segment, making it a packet (see Figure 5-4).

IP header	TCP header	get the cengage.com home page

Figure 5-4   The Internetwork layer creates a packet

The packet is almost ready for delivery to the network medium, with one more stop at the Network access layer, where the NIC operates. As you know, NICs work with frames, so a frame header and trailer are added (see Figure 5-5).

Frame header	IP header	TCP header	get the cengage.com home page	Frame trailer

Figure 5-5   The frame is created and ready for delivery on the medium

The frame is then delivered to the network medium as bits on its way to the *www.cengage.com* server, where the Web server software processes it and returns a Web page to the computer that originated the request. Now that you have an idea of how all these protocols work together, examine the roles of these four layers more closely, starting from the top: the Application layer.

This chapter discusses the four layers of the TCP/IP model and the protocols operating at each one. Chapter 7 covers a more detailed, seven-layer model called the "OSI model." It isn't an actual protocol suite; it's a model that describes how network protocols should operate in a layered design. By seeing an actual protocol suite use the layered approach, you can better understand the concepts described in the seven-layer OSI model.

Hands-On Project 5-1: Viewing TCP/IP Layers in Windows and Configuring Your IP Address

Time Required: 10 minutes

Objective: View the properties of your computer's network connection, identify the TCP/IP layers, and configure your IP address.

Required Tools and Equipment: Net-*XX*

Description: In this project, you view the properties of your computer's local area connection and identify the TCP/IP layers. This project is similar to Hands-On Project 1-3, but you're viewing the TCP/IP protocol suite layers instead of the more general layers of the networking process. Next, you configure your IPv4 address.

1. Start your computer and log on as **NetAdmin**.

2. Right-click **Start** and click **Network Connections**. Right-click **Ethernet0** and click **Properties** to open the Ethernet0 Properties dialog box.

3. The "Connect using" text box displays the network interface card. In the list box under it, you see several items. Client for Microsoft Networks, File and Printer Sharing for Microsoft Networks, Internet Protocol Version 4, and Internet Protocol Version 6 are the items you're interested in right now, as they're the most necessary software components for making network communication work. For each component, write which TCP/IP layer or layers you think it operates in:

   - NIC displayed in the "Connect using" text box: _____
   - Client for Microsoft Networks: _____
   - File and Printer Sharing for Microsoft Networks: _____
   - Internet Protocol Version 4: _____
   - Internet Protocol Version 6: _____

4. Next, you configure your IP address settings. Click **Internet Protocol Version 4 (TCP/IPv4)** and click **Properties**.

5. f your IP settings have the "Obtain an IP address automatically" option enabled, click **Use the following IP address**. You use this option to set a static IP address. If your address is already static, make a note of it, and skip entering the information in Step 7. Click **OK**.

6. For the following IP address settings, enter the information shown unless your instructor tells you to use different values, and then click **OK** when you're finished:

   - IP address: **192.168.100.XX** (replacing *XX* with your student number)
   - Subnet mask: **255.255.255.0**
   - Default gateway: provided by your instructor
   - Preferred DNS server: provided by your instructor

7. Click **OK**. If you're prompted to set a network location, click **Work network**, and then click **Close**.

8. To test your configuration, open a command prompt window and try to ping the default gateway address and the preferred DNS server address. If either ping is unsuccessful, inform your instructor and troubleshoot your settings.

9. Close all open windows, but leave your computer running for the next project.

The following list recaps your IP address configuration and explains each item's purpose:

- The IP address provides your computer with a unique internetwork identity on a logical IP network.

- The subnet mask defines which part of the IP address is the network ID and which is the host ID.

- The default gateway is a router in your network that your computer sends packets to when the destination is a remote network.

- The preferred DNS server is the address of a DNS server that resolves computer names to IP addresses.

These items are explained in more detail in this chapter and throughout this book.

Hands-On Project 5-2: Identifying the TCP/IP Layers in a Frame

Time Required: 10 minutes

Objective: Capture packets and view the TCP/IP layers in the frame.

Required Tools and Equipment: Net-*XX* with Wireshark installed

Description: In this project, you capture some frames generated by your Web browser and examine the captured frames to identify the TCP/IP layers.

1. If necessary, log on to your computer as **NetAdmin**.

2. Start Wireshark and click **Capture Options**. In the Capture Filter text box, type **tcp port http**, and then click **Start**.

3. Start a Web browser, and after the home page loads, exit the browser.

4. In Wireshark, click the **Stop the running live capture** toolbar icon to stop the capture. Scroll up to the first packet summary line, if necessary.

5. Click a packet summary in the top pane with HTTP in the protocol field and an Info line beginning with GET. In the middle pane are summaries of each protocol header (see Figure 5-6). You can ignore the first line starting with Frame *X* (with *X* representing the frame number), as it gives information about the frame, such as the time it arrived, its length, protocols in the frame, and so forth.

```
Frame 4 (629 bytes on wire, 629 bytes captured)
Ethernet II, Src: Supermic_67:7e:6c (00:30:48:67:7e:6c), Dst: Cisco_42:22:c0 (00:0c:85:42:22:c0)
Internet Protocol, Src: 172.31.210.1 (172.31.210.1), Dst: 174.129.210.177 (174.129.210.177)
Transmission Control Protocol, Src Port: 52091 (52091), Dst Port: http (80), Seq: 1, Ack: 1, Len: 575
Hypertext Transfer Protocol
```

Figure 5-6 Summary of protocol headers in Wireshark

Source: Wireshark Foundation

6. Click to expand the line beginning with **Ethernet II**. Examine the information in this header (discussed in more detail in the following sections). Write which layer of the TCP/IP model the Ethernet II header represents, and then click again to collapse this header:

_____

7. Click to expand the line beginning with **Internet Protocol**. Examine the information in this header (discussed in more detail in the following sections). Write which layer of the TCP/IP model the Internet Protocol header represents, and then click again to collapse this header:

_____

8. Click to expand the line beginning with **Transmission Control Protocol**. Examine the information in this header (discussed in more detail in the following sections). Write which layer of the TCP/IP model the Transmission Control Protocol header represents, and then click again to collapse this header:

_____

9. Click to expand the line beginning with **Hypertext Transfer Protocol**, and examine the information. This data portion of the frame is what a Web server actually sees and responds to. In this case, the HTTP command is GET, which means HTTP is requesting a page (or part of a page) from the Web server. Write which layer of the TCP/IP model the HTTP protocol represents, and then click again to collapse this header:

_____

10. Exit Wireshark and click **Quit without Saving** when prompted.

11. Close all open windows, but leave your computer running for the next project.

Application-Layer Protocols

The Application layer provides network services to user applications that access network resources. For example, when you run Microsoft Word and need to open a file on a network server, Word contacts Client for Microsoft Networks, an Application-layer service, which provides the details of accessing files on the server. Client for Microsoft Networks implements an Application-layer protocol called Server Message Block (SMB), which is also known as Common Internet File System (CIFS). Linux uses NFS and Samba file-sharing Application-layer protocols.

In some cases, the Application-layer protocol or service is built into the user application, as with a Web browser or e-mail client. For example, a Web browser contains the software that implements Hypertext Transfer Protocol (HTTP). Whether the Application-layer protocol is implemented by the user application or by a network service, the process is the same: When data is ready to be sent, it's transferred from the Application-layer protocol to the Transport layer and down the protocol stack until a frame is transmitted as bits to the network medium.

Application-layer protocols also provide authentication and data-formatting services as needed. For example, if a client attempts to access a server that's password protected, the Application layer is responsible for handling the exchange of packets that allow user logon. If data needs to be formatted or translated in some way for the user application, as with some types of data encryption, the Application layer provides that service for user applications. For example, when you connect to a secure Web site with HTTPS, the authentication and encryption that occur with HTTPS are Application-layer functions.

Some functions of the TCP/IP model's Application layer are separated into additional layers in the OSI model discussed in Chapter 7. For example, the Session layer of the OSI model handles network logon, and the Presentation layer handles data encryption and decryption.

With most Application-layer protocols, both a client and a server version exist. For HTTP, the client is a Web browser and the server is a Web server, such as Microsoft Internet Information Services (IIS) or the popular Apache Web Server that's often used on Linux servers. For file sharing, Client for Microsoft Networks has File and Printer Sharing for Microsoft Networks as its server counterpart.

Most Application-layer protocols facilitate a client's access to data, such as an e-mail message or a document. However, the Application layer contains some specialized protocols for making a network easier to use and configure. Examples include protocols for name resolution and dynamic IP address assignment. Several Application-layer protocols are discussed in more detail in the next sections, but to sum up, the Application layer handles these functions:

- Access by applications to network services
- Client/server data access
- Name resolution
- Dynamic address assignment
- Authentication/user logon
- Data formatting and translation

HTTP: Protocol of the World Wide Web

HTTP is the protocol Web browsers use to access data on the World Wide Web. Originally, its main purpose was simply to transfer static Web pages written in HTML. Now HTTP is also used for general file transfer, downloading and displaying multimedia files, and delivering scripts for animated and interactive Web pages. Because it's often used to transfer large amounts of data over the Internet, it uses TCP as its Transport-layer protocol, and the default TCP port number is 80. Figure 5-7 shows a typical HTTP message as it might look at the Application layer before being sent to the Transport layer.

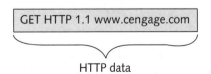

Figure 5-7   An HTTP message

E-mail Protocols: POP3, IMAP, and SMTP

E-mail clients use the **Post Office Protocol version 3 (POP3)** protocol to download incoming messages from an e-mail server to their local desktops. POP3 clients download e-mail from the mail server running at the user's ISP, and these message are then deleted from the server. POP3 uses TCP port 110.

Internet Message Access Protocol version 4 (IMAP4) has advanced message controls, including the capability to manage messages locally yet store them on a server, plus numerous fault-tolerance features. IMAP4 downloads only e-mail headers initially, and then downloads the message body and attachments when the message is selected. IMAP4 uses TCP port 143.

Simple Mail Transfer Protocol (SMTP) is the standard protocol for sending e-mail over the Internet. POP3 is used to retrieve e-mail, and SMTP is used to send it. SMTP uses TCP port 25. All three e-mail protocols use the TCP Transport-layer protocol to ensure reliable delivery of large messages.

FTP and TFTP

File Transfer Protocol (FTP), as the name suggests, is a client/server protocol used to transfer and manage files across a network. FTP uses TCP ports 20 and 21. Port 20 is for users sending control commands, and port 21 is for transferring file data. FTP is used to transfer files both within a private network and across the Internet. It's not a secure protocol, however, so using it to transfer files across the Internet is risky. Neither the data nor the username and password are encrypted, which means anyone who captures packets containing your logon information can see your username and password. Trivial File Transfer Protocol (TFTP) is a simple protocol for transferring files, but it has little file management capability. It uses UDP port 69, so it's not reliable for long file transfers across the Internet. It's used primarily in a LAN to transfer configuration and firmware files to network devices, such as managed routers and switches. TFTP is also used by some devices that boot an OS from a network server rather than local storage. Like FTP, TFTP isn't a secure protocol, but because it's rarely used across the Internet and doesn't require credentials, security isn't as much of a concern.

Server Message Block

Server Message Block (SMB) is the protocol Windows file and printer services use to share resources between Windows computers. For example, the Client for Microsoft Networks and File and Printer Sharing for Microsoft Networks listed in a network connection's properties in Windows use the SMB protocol to share files across a network. SMB is used almost exclusively in a private network instead of across the Internet. Linux and Mac OS X also support SMB with their own variations. SMB uses TCP port 445.

Remote Desktop Protocol

Remote Desktop Protocol (RDP) is used to access a Windows computer remotely by using the Windows graphical user interface (GUI). With RDP, you can access the desktop of another Windows computer across the network, allowing you to use the remote computer as though you were sitting at its monitor and using its keyboard and mouse. RDP is used to run Windows applications remotely, and network administrators use it to manage Windows workstations and servers remotely.

Telnet and SSH

Telnet and **Secure Shell (SSH)** are used to connect to a device across a network via a command-line interface. Network administrators might use Telnet or SSH to connect to a managed switch or router to view status information or perform configuration tasks by using the device's command-line interface. Telnet uses TCP port 23 and, like FTP, isn't a secure protocol, so it should be used with caution. SSH uses TCP port 22 and provides an encrypted channel between the client and server, so it's preferred over Telnet when both devices support it.

Simple Networking Management Protocol

Simple Network Management Protocol (SNMP) is used to monitor and manage network devices and gather statistics about network traffic. It's a client/server protocol in which software agents are installed on devices you want to monitor and manage. The SNMP agents collect data and transfer it to a network management station for storage and analysis. SNMP operates on UDP ports 161 and 162. More details are covered in Chapter 12.

Dynamic Host Configuration Protocol

Some drawbacks of using TCP/IP in a large network include detailed configuration of devices and keeping track of assigned addresses and to which machine they're assigned. To make these tasks easier, **Dynamic Host Configuration Protocol (DHCP)** was developed. To use DHCP, a server must be configured with a block of available IP addresses and other IP address configuration information. To receive its IP address from the server, each computer must be configured to request its address configuration. A computer requests IP address information from the DHCP server in the form of a broadcast message. Each time a computer requests an address, the server assigns one until it has no more addresses to assign. The following sections explain the operation of DHCP.

DHCP Server A DHCP server is composed of the following elements:

- *IP address scope*—An **IP address scope** is a range of IP addresses the server leases to clients that request an IP address. In Windows, a scope is specified with starting and ending IP addresses, a subnet mask, and the address lease time, which can range from one minute to unlimited (meaning the address lease never expires). After the scope is created, an administrator can further configure it by using the following:

  - *Scope options*—IP settings such as the router (the DHCP client's default gateway address), DNS servers, a domain name, and other address options are included in scope options. When a client requests an IP address, the client receives an address and a subnet mask from the scope and any options defined for the scope.

   DHCP servers can maintain multiple scopes if they service more than one subnet.

  - *Reservations*—A **reservation** is an IP address tied to a particular MAC address. When a client requests an IP address from the DHCP server, if the client's MAC address matches an address specified by a reservation, the reserved IP address is leased to the client instead of getting it from the scope. In addition, reservations can have their own options that differ from regular scope options.

- *Exclusions*—An **exclusion** is one or more IP addresses excluded from the IP address scope; for example, if the scope ranges from 192.168.1.1 to 192.168.1.100, you can exclude addresses 192.168.1.1 through 192.168.1.10 if these addresses have been assigned statically.

- *DHCP Server service*—This service runs in the background and listens on UDP port 69, the port reserved for client-to-server DHCP communication. It responds to DHCP client requests for new IP addresses and IP address release and renewal requests.

A computer leases the address the server assigns to it. After an address is leased, a record of the lease is stored in a database containing the IP address, the name and MAC address of the computer leasing the address, and the lease expiration time. Administrators can view the database's contents to determine which computers are leasing which addresses. Figure 5-8 shows the DHCP management console.

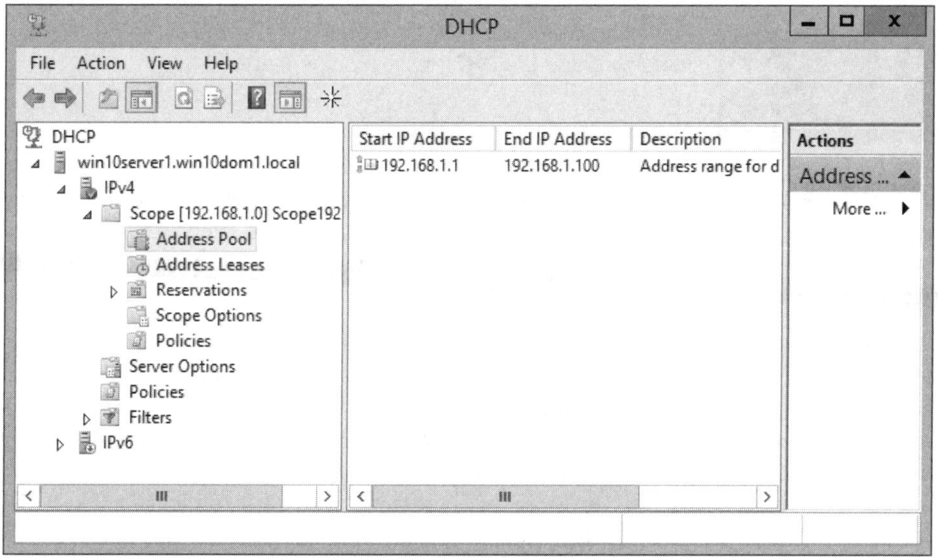

Figure 5-8 The DHCP management console in Windows Server 2016

The network administrator defines the lease time when the DHCP server is configured. It can be as little as a few minutes to an infinite period, in which case the lease never expires. A typical lease time is one day or a few days. When 50% of the lease time has elapsed, the computer attempts to renew the lease from the same DHCP server that responded to the original DHCP request. If there's no response, the computer waits until 87.5% of the lease time has elapsed and then sends a broadcast DHCP renewal request. If no response has been received when the lease expires, the computer broadcasts a DHCP request for a new IP address. If no DHCP server responds, one of two things happens: TCP/IP stops functioning, or the computer assigns itself an address from a special range of addresses beginning with 169.254.

These special addresses are reserved for **Automatic Private IP Addressing (APIPA)**. An address in the APIPA range is assigned automatically to an APIPA-enabled computer when an IP address is requested via DHCP, but no DHCP server responds to the request. Using APIPA rather than a DHCP server to assign addresses is recommended only for small networks that aren't attached to the Internet because APIPA addresses can't be routed.

A major benefit of using DHCP is how easily computers can be moved. When a computer is moved to a new network segment and turned on, it requests its configuration from a DHCP server on that segment. This type of address assignment shouldn't be used for systems requiring a static address, such as Web servers, DNS servers, and DHCP servers, because computers with these network services are usually expected to maintain the same IP address.

DHCP uses the UDP Transport-layer protocol because DHCP servers are usually located on the same network as the DHCP client, and DHCP messages are short. As you learn later in "Role of the Transport Layer," UDP is a connectionless protocol and provides few reliability features, so it works best when the amount of data in each transaction is small.

 All major OSs include a DHCP client service, and most server OSs and routers include the DHCP server component.

DHCP Client When an OS is first installed, IP address assignment is done through DHCP by default, so if a DHCP server is running on the network, the client OS gets an address and can then start running. If no DHCP server is operating, the client assigns itself an IP address with APIPA.

However, computers need more than just an IP address and subnet mask to operate in most networks. They need a default gateway if they access computers on other networks, including the Internet, and the address of a DNS server that can be queried to resolve computer and domain names to IP addresses. DHCP servers are configured to supply these additional addresses when a client requests an IP address. When a computer requests its IP address configuration, the process involves the following broadcast packets if the computer has no address assigned or its address lease has expired:

- *DHCPDiscover*—The client announces to the network that it's looking for a DHCP server from which to lease IP address settings.
- *DHCPOffer*—The server replies and offers the client an IP address for lease.
- *DHCPRequest*—The client wants the offered IP address.
- *DHCPAck*—The server acknowledges the transaction, and the client can now use the IP address.

After a client has the IP address configuration, it can begin using TCP/IP. The IP address is just a lease that must be renewed periodically. When half the lease is over, the client sends a unicast DHCPRequest packet to the server that leased it the address. The server sends a unicast DHCPAck packet to indicate that the address has been renewed.

When IP addresses are assigned with DHCP, a station's address can change periodically, especially if it's turned off when the lease time expires. You might want to manage IP address configurations with DHCP but still assign certain devices, such as network printers and some workstations, addresses that don't change. To do this, you configure a reservation address on the DHCP server.

The DHCP client software runs as a service that starts when the computer starts. In Windows, you can stop, start, restart, and view the status of the DHCP Client service (shown in Figure 5-9) by double-clicking DHCP Client in the Services control panel. This service runs even if your IP address is assigned statically. To prevent it from running, you can disable it in the DHCP Client Properties dialog box or from the command line with the net command.

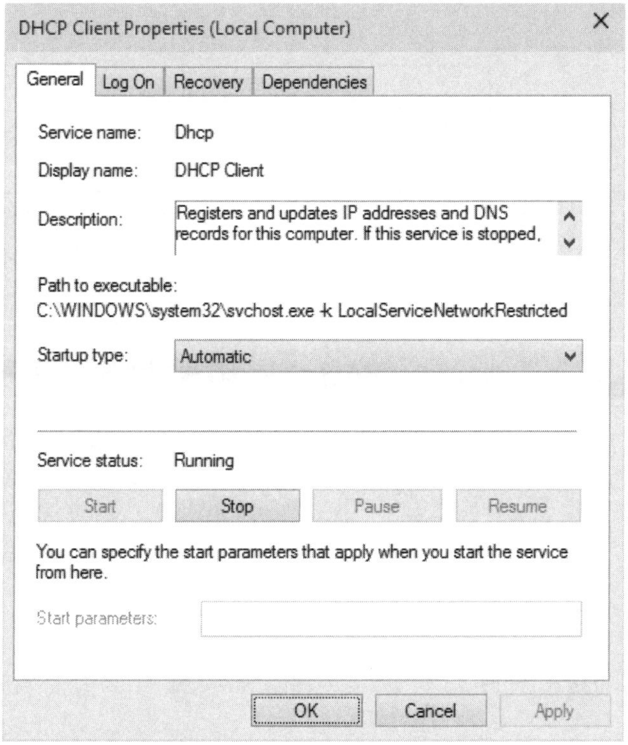

Figure 5-9 Configuring the DHCP Client service

Domain Name System

Domain Name System (DNS) is a name-to-address resolution protocol that keeps a list of computer names and their IP addresses. Through a correctly configured workstation, a user can use a computer's name—for instance, Server1 or www.cengage.com—rather than a numerical address, such as 203.0.113.189, to communicate with the computer. For example, when you enter "www.cengage.com" in your Web browser's address box, the Web browser contacts the DNS Client service on your computer. The DNS client contacts the DNS server specified in your OS's IP configuration and requests that the name "www.cengage.com" be resolved to an IP address. The DNS server responds with the IP address assigned to the computer named www at the cengage.com domain. Using this IP address, your Web browser application can contact the Web server to request a Web page.

DNS uses the UDP Transport-layer protocol because DNS messages usually consist of a single packet of data, so there's no need for the reliability measures TCP offers. The DNS system used throughout the Internet is organized as a treelike hierarchy (see Figure 5-10). The tree consists of these domain levels: root, top, second, subdomain, and host. All levels below the root level have branches, each of which has a name. When you put all the names of a branch together, separated by periods, you have the **fully qualified domain name (FQDN)** of the network resource, such as *www.cengage.com*.

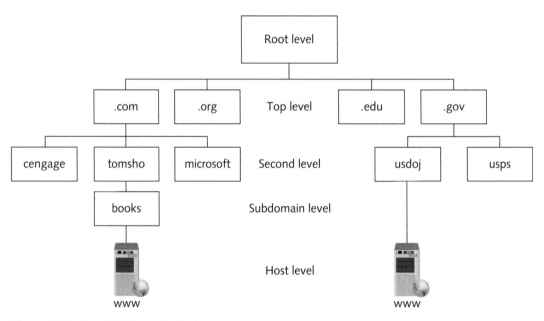

Figure 5-10 The DNS hierarchical tree structure

The top-level domains are organized into categories—such as commercial (.com), nonprofit organizations (.org), government (.gov), and education (.edu)—or country of origin, indicated by a two-letter country code. The second-level domains are usually the names of companies or institutions. The subdomain level is optional and can consist of several names separated by a period. An example is a department or branch of an organization. Finally, the host level represents individual computers hosting network services. For example, in *www.books.tomsho.com*, com is the top-level domain name, tomsho is the second-level domain, books is the subdomain, and www is the hostname.

Because of the hierarchical nature of DNS, not every DNS server needs to maintain a database of all domain names, computer names, and IP addresses for the entire Internet. Most DNS servers maintain addresses for the domain in which they're installed. The domain might be a single secondary-level domain, such as xyzcorp.com, or if you own a business hosting Web sites for other companies, you might maintain hundreds or thousands of domains, but this number is small compared with the entire Internet.

When a DNS server is installed, the administrator creates one or more domain names or zones. A zone is named by using the second-level and top-level domain names and the subdomain, if necessary. Most of the information a DNS zone contains consists of hostname–IP address pairs (for example, host records, mail server records, and name server records) and other data that allows people to find a domain's network resources. An administrator can create records manually, and they can be created dynamically with Dynamic DNS, which enables a computer to create its own DNS record.

In addition to host records, a DNS server database is loaded with a list of IP addresses that point to root servers around the world. These servers supply the addresses of top-level domain servers, which are used to provide addresses of second-level domain servers. This hierarchical organization allows any DNS client anywhere in the world to access the DNS servers for any domain.

You can view a map of the root servers around the world at
http://public-root.com/root-server-locations.htm.

To speed up communication, DNS clients in most OSs maintain a DNS cache, called a **resolver cache**, that stores name and IP address pairs along with other pertinent DNS data for names that have been resolved recently. This cache prevents the DNS client from having to request that a DNS server do a name lookup for a name that was resolved recently. Additionally, the cache contains a text file called `Hosts`, which stores name and IP address pairs. This file usually contains only the name "localhost" mapped to 127.0.0.1, but you can add entries manually by editing the file. If there are computers you access frequently by name and you don't expect their addresses to change, you can add an entry for them in the `Hosts` file, thereby preventing a network DNS lookup from occurring when you access them. You examine the `Hosts` file in Hands-On Project 5-3.

DNS Client Like the DHCP client, the DNS client runs as a service that can be configured in the Services control panel in Windows. It's responsible for communicating with a DNS server to resolve computer and domain names to IP addresses, so it's referred to as a "resolver." As discussed, DNS resolvers maintain a local cache of the results of recent DNS lookups. The resolver cache speeds communication because it eliminates the need to communicate with a DNS server for records looked up recently.

An OS must be configured to use DNS. At the very least, a client computer needs one address of a DNS server it can query. In Windows, the first DNS server configured is the preferred DNS server, and the second one is the alternate DNS server (see Figure 5-11).

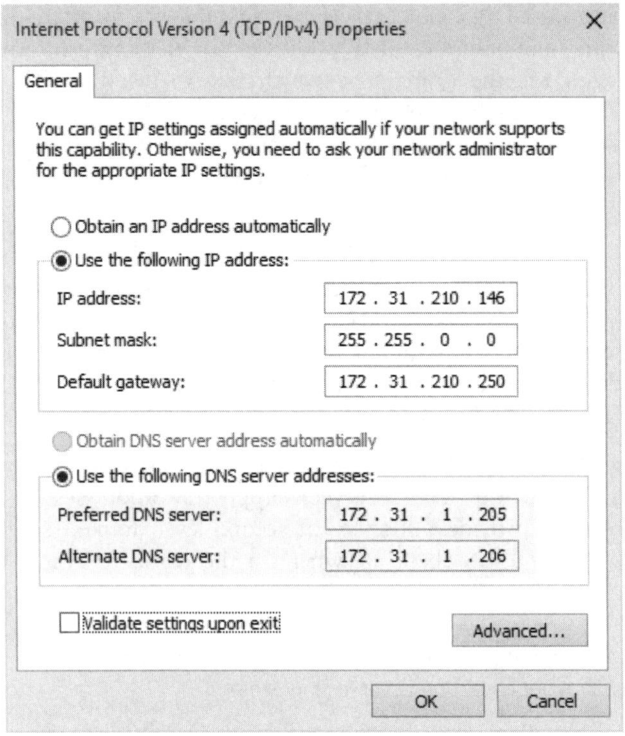

Figure 5-11   Preferred and alternate DNS servers in Windows

When a client computer tries to resolve a computer name to an address, the DNS resolver attempts to append a domain name to the computer name because DNS servers require a domain name in addition to a computer name. In Windows, the default domain appended to DNS lookups is called the "primary DNS suffix." This value is set when a computer is added as a member of a Windows domain, or it can be set manually. To view it, go to the Computer Name tab in the System Properties dialog box, click Change, and then click More to open the dialog box shown in Figure 5-12. For example, in this figure, if a user attempts to contact server1, the DNS resolver sends the query to the DNS server as server1.netess.local.

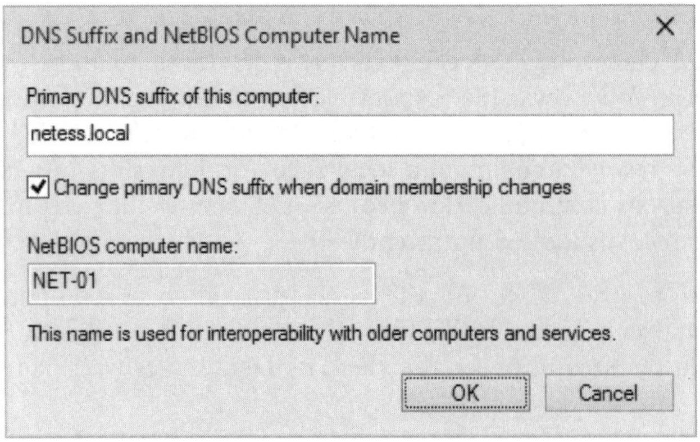

Figure 5-12   Viewing the primary DNS suffix

Some environments are more complicated, with multiple domains that are accessed frequently. If users should be able to access computers in different domains with only their usernames, the DNS resolver can append a list of domains, or DNS suffixes, to computer names automatically. If the first query isn't successful, the next suffix is tried, and so forth. You can create the list of DNS suffixes the DNS resolver uses in the DNS tab of the Advanced TCP/IP Settings dialog box (see Figure 5-13).

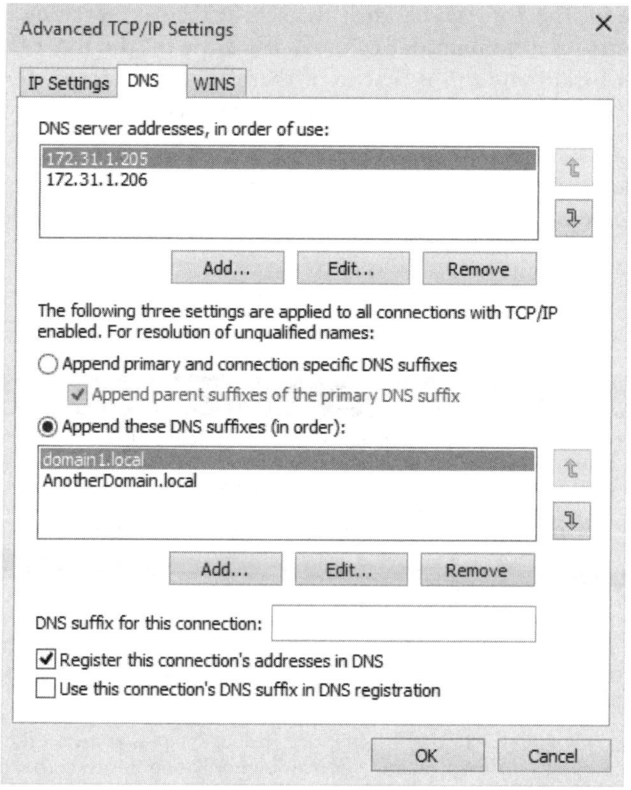

Figure 5-13   DNS suffixes used to resolve names to addresses

In this figure, notice the "Register this connection's addresses in DNS" check box. Windows supports **Dynamic DNS (DDNS)**, which allows computers and other devices to contact their primary DNS server whenever their name or address changes. If the contacted DNS server allows DDNS, the server creates or updates the DNS host record in its database automatically.

DNS Server   DNS is a central component of every network for both Internet name resolution and local resource name resolution. The Linux environment has long used DNS for name resolution; on Windows networks, DNS became the standard name resolution protocol starting with Windows 2000 Server. Before that time, Windows networks used Windows Internet Naming Server (WINS), a Windows-specific protocol for resolving Windows computer names. WINS is still supported in Windows Server 2016 but only as a legacy service for backward-compatibility with Windows 9x and older applications requiring WINS.

DNS servers are composed of the following elements:

- *DNS zones*—A **DNS zone** is a database of primarily hostname and IP address pairs that are related by membership in an Internet or a Windows domain. Each zone carries the name of the domain whose records it stores. Zone records are created manually by an administrator or dynamically by the host device. When a DNS client contacts a DNS server to resolve a name to an IP address, the domain name specified in the request is matched to the zones the DNS server manages. If a zone name matches the request, the zone is searched for a host record matching the hostname in the request. If the domain doesn't match a zone on the local DNS server, the server looks for a match in its cache. If there's still no match, the DNS server contacts other DNS servers by using its root hints (explained later in this list).

- *Resource records*—**Resource records** are the data contained in a zone, such as host records, but other resource record types can be found in a DNS zone, described in Table 5-2.

Table 5-2 DNS resource record types

Record type (code)	Description
Start of Authority (SOA)	Less a resource than an informational record, the SOA identifies the name server that's authoritative for the domain and includes a variety of timers, dynamic update configuration, and zone transfer information.
Host (A)	The most common resource record; consists of a computer name and an IPv4 address.
IPv6 Host (AAAA)	Like an A record but uses an IPv6 address.
Name Server (NS)	The FQDN of a name server that has authority over the domain. NS records are used by DNS servers to refer queries to another server that's authoritative for the requested domain.
Canonical Name (CNAME)	A record containing an alias for another record that enables you to refer to the same resource with different names yet maintain only one host record. For example, you could create an A record for a computer named "web" and a CNAME record that points to the A record but allows users to access the host with the name "www."
Mail Exchanger (MX)	Contains the address of an e-mail server for the domain. Because e-mail addresses are typically specified as user@domain.com, the mail server's name is not part of the e-mail address. To deliver a message to the mail server, an MX record query supplies the address of a mail server in the specified domain.
Pointer (PTR)	Used for reverse DNS lookups. Although DNS is used mainly to resolve a name to an address, it can also resolve an address to a name by using a reverse lookup. PTR records can be created automatically on Windows DNS servers.
Service Records (SRV)	Allows DNS clients to request the address of a server that provides a specific service instead of querying the server by name. This type of record is useful when an application doesn't know the name of the server it needs but does know what service is required. For example, in Windows domains, DNS servers contain SRV records with the addresses of domain controllers so that clients can request the logon service to authenticate to the domain.

- *Cache*—When the local DNS server contacts another DNS server to satisfy a client's DNS query, the results are saved or cached so that if the same query occurs again, the local DNS server can respond without having to contact another server. Cached records expire after a specified time to prevent stale records.

- *Root hints*—When a DNS query can't be resolved from local zone records or cached records, a DNS server consults the root hints file, which contains a list of IP addresses of Internet root servers. Root servers maintain records for the Internet top-level domain (TLD) servers. TLD servers maintain records for DNS servers that manage second-level domains. These servers maintain different levels of domain information that form the basis of the hierarchical nature of the DNS system. Figure 5-14 shows a DNS query involving root servers.

- *DNS Server service*—This service runs in the background and listens for DNS queries on UDP port 53.

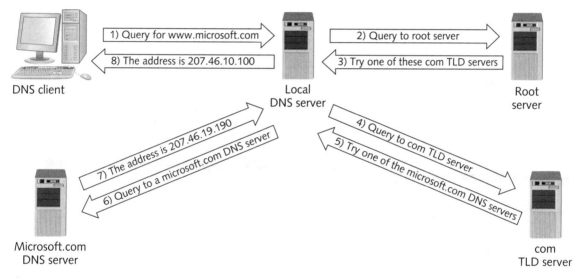

Figure 5-14 A DNS query making its way through the DNS hierarchy

DNS servers can also be configured with no zones at all—a configuration called a "caching-only server." A home or small business network that doesn't maintain its own domain can still install and use a DNS server. After DNS is installed on the server, clients can be configured to use the server for DNS queries. Initially, the server has to query root servers for most requests, but because the results are cached, it can resolve queries for frequently visited Web sites by using its stored results. A caching-only DNS server has the advantage of reducing traffic to the ISP's DNS servers, and your local DNS server can often respond to queries faster, especially if your ISP's DNS servers are busy or down. Figure 5-15 shows the DNS Manager console.

Many Linux systems use a DNS system called Berkeley Internet Name Daemon (BIND), which has been around since the 1980s and is the original widely used DNS system.

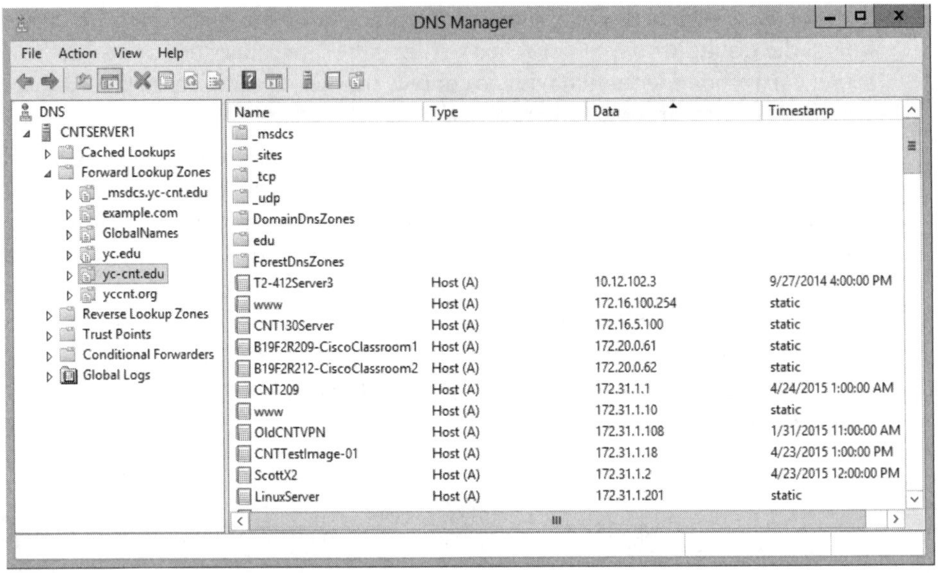

Figure 5-15 The DNS Manager console

Many other Application-layer protocols work with the TCP/IP protocol suite, but the protocols discussed in this chapter cover the ones used in most networks.

Hands-On Project 5-3: Working with DNS Tools

Time Required: 10 minutes

Objective: Use `ipconfig` and `nslookup` to work with DNS.

Required Tools and Equipment: Net-*XX*

Description: In this project, you use `ipconfig` to display and delete your DNS cache, and then view your `Hosts` file. You also use `nslookup` to query your DNS server.

1. If necessary, log on to your computer as **NetAdmin** and open a command prompt window. Start a Web browser and navigate to a Web site, such as **www.cengage.com**. Exit your browser.

2. To see the DNS resolver cache, type **ipconfig /displaydns** and press **Enter**. To delete the entries, type **ipconfig /flushdns** and press **Enter**. Display the DNS resolver cache again. Unless there are entries in your `Hosts` file, you should get the message "Could not display the DNS Resolver Cache."

At the command prompt, you can press the up and down arrow keys to access recent commands you have entered.

3. To perform a DNS lookup, type **ping www.cengage.com** and press **Enter**. Display the DNS cache again. You should see a DNS record for *www.cengage.com* that includes the IP address and other information. Another field in the DNS cache is a TTL value, which is different from the TTL in an IP packet. This DNS TTL value is sent by the DNS server maintaining the *www.cengage.com* record. It's measured in seconds and tells your DNS client how long to cache the DNS record as a safeguard against clients holding on to DNS records whose IP addresses might have changed.

4. To open your computer's hosts file, right-click **Start**, click **Run**, type **Notepad**, and press **Enter**. Click **File, Open** from the Notepad menu. In the Open dialog box, navigate to **C:\Windows\System32\Drivers\Etc**. In the File type drop-down list, click **All Files**. Double-click the **hosts** file to open it.

5. After the last line in the file, type **67.210.126.125 books**. Save the file by clicking **File, Save**, and in the File name text box, type **"hosts"**. (You must include the quotation marks so that Notepad doesn't save the file with the .txt extension.) Click **Desktop** in the Save As dialog box; you can't replace this file with Notepad because of Windows file protection. Click **Save**, and exit Notepad.

6. Open File Explorer, navigate to the desktop, and copy the hosts file you just saved. Then navigate to **C:\Windows\System32\Drivers\Etc** and paste the file there. When prompted to confirm, click **Replace the file in the destination**. When prompted, click **Continue**. Close File Explorer.

7. At the command prompt, type **ipconfig /displaydns** and press **Enter** to see that the entry is in your DNS cache. Type **ping books** and press **Enter**. Delete the DNS resolver cache (see Step 2), and then display it again. Notice that the books entry remains in the cache because the hosts file data always stays in the cache.

8. Type **nslookup www.cengage.com** and press **Enter**. Your DNS server's name and IP address are displayed along with the name and IP address of *www.cengage.com*. You use nslookup to look up a host's IP address without actually communicating with it.

9. Type **nslookup** and press **Enter**. You enter interactive mode. Type **www.yahoo.com** and press **Enter**. You might see more than one address along with one or more aliases (other names that *www.yahoo.com* goes by). Type **www.yahoo.com** again (or press the up arrow to repeat the last line you typed) and press **Enter**. You should see the IP addresses returned in a different order. (If you don't, keep trying, and the order will change.) The *www.yahoo.com* page can be reached by a number of different IP addresses, and the addresses are returned in a different order so that a different server is used each time, which is called "round-robin load balancing."

10. Type **198.60.123.100** and press **Enter**. Nslookup is also used to do reverse lookups, in which the IP address is given and the hostname is returned.

11. To set the DNS server that nslookup uses to a public DNS server run by Google, type **server 8.8.8.8** and press **Enter**. Type **www.microsoft.com** and press **Enter**. If you're ever concerned that your DNS server isn't working correctly, you can test it with nslookup and compare the results of your DNS server with the results from another server, such as Google's.

12. Type **exit** and press **Enter** to return to the command prompt. Leave the command prompt window open for the next project.

Hands-On Project 5-4: Working with the DHCP Client

Time Required: 10 minutes

Objective: Use `ipconfig` to work with your DHCP client.

Required Tools and Equipment: Net-*XX*, a configured DHCP server on the network

Description: In this project, you change your IP settings to use DHCP and then see how to work with DHCP by using `ipconfig`.

1. If necessary, log on to your computer as **NetAdmin**.

2. Right-click **Start** and click **Network Connections**. Right-click **Ethernet0** and click **Properties** to open the Ethernet0 Properties dialog box.

3. Click **Internet Protocol Version 4 (TCP/IPv4)** and click **Properties**. If your IP address settings were set manually in Hands-On Project 5-1, write these settings on the following lines. At the end of this project, you set your IP address again by using these settings.

   _____

   _____

4. Click **Obtain an IP address automatically**. Click **OK** and then **Close**.

5. Open a command prompt window, if necessary. Type **ipconfig /all** and press **Enter** to view detailed IP configuration information. Under Ethernet adapter Ethernet0, you see information about DHCP, including its status (enabled or not), the DHCP server's IP address, and lease information.

6. Occasionally, you might need to force your computer to renew its lease (for example, if changes are made on the DHCP server and you need to get the newest IP configuration). To renew a DHCP lease, type **ipconfig /renew** and press **Enter**. Display your detailed IP configuration again to see that the lease information has changed.

7. To release your IP address configuration, type **ipconfig /release** and press **Enter**. This command's output shows that your IP configuration has been deleted. To request a new IP address configuration, type **ipconfig /renew** and press **Enter**. (Note that you might not get the same IP address you had before.) Using these commands can help you troubleshoot DHCP-related problems.

8. Close the command prompt window, and set your IP configuration to the values you wrote down in Step 3.

Transport-Layer Protocols

Transport-layer protocols are used with most Application-layer protocols because they supply a header field to identify the Application layer and provide reliability and flow control for applications that typically transfer a large amount of data. The following sections explain the role of the Transport layer in TCP/IP along with the two protocols that work at this layer: TCP and UDP.

Role of the Transport Layer

Without the Transport layer in the TCP/IP protocol suite, large internetworks would be in big trouble. So many things can go wrong with complex, constantly changing networks that without some reliability measures, successful transfers of large amounts of data would be the exception rather than the norm. In environments such as the Internet, using only connectionless protocols (protocols that don't verify data was received) simply wouldn't work. The more robust protocols in the Transport layer provide the reliability needed to handle the unpredictable nature of the Internet (or any large internetwork, for that matter).

The Transport layer has two protocols. **Transmission Control Protocol (TCP)** is connection oriented and designed for reliable transfer of information in complex internetworks. **User Datagram Protocol (UDP)** is connectionless and designed for efficient communication of generally small amounts of data. Both protocols perform the following tasks:

- Work with segments (TCP) or datagrams (UDP).
- Provide a means to identify the source and destination applications involved in a communication.
- Protect data with a checksum.

Working with Segments and Datagrams

As discussed, TCP works with units of data called "segments," and UDP works with units of data called "datagrams." For outgoing data, in which the Application-layer protocol requires the services of a Transport-layer protocol, the Application layer passes data to TCP or UDP, depending on which protocol it was designed to use. Both TCP and UDP add a header to the data. The Transport-layer protocol then passes the segment or datagram to the Internetwork-layer protocol, usually IP.

With incoming data, the Internetwork-layer protocol deencapsulates the packet and forwards the resulting segment or datagram to the Transport-layer protocol. The Transport-layer protocol processes it, deencapsulates it, and sends the resulting data up to the Application layer.

Identifying Source and Destination Applications

Have you ever wondered how your computer keeps track of the myriad network applications you run? At any time, you might be running a Web browser, an e-mail application, and a chat program and have a file open on a file server. When one of these applications receives data from the network, a frame is received by the NIC, which sends a packet up to the IP protocol, which then sends a segment or datagram to TCP or UDP. Now what? Eventually, data that's received must go to an application or a network service.

The Transport-layer header provides the information needed to determine the application the received data is sent to. TCP and UDP use a **port number** to specify the source and destination Application-layer protocols. Using an envelope analogy, if the IP address is the zip code and the street number is the MAC address, the port number specifies the person in the house who should read the letter. In other words, the MAC address and IP address get the packet to the computer, and the port number gets the data to the application or service.

The IANA assigns a dedicated port number to every well-known network service. For example, Web servers are assigned port 80, so when your computer formats a message to a Web server, the destination port number in the TCP header is 80. Likewise, when your e-mail application requests messages from your mail server, it sends the request to port 110, the Post Office Protocol (POP3) port number. Most client applications are assigned a random port number when they make a request to a server. So when you start a Web browser, for example, the Web browser window is assigned a port number. When the request for a Web page goes out, the source port number in the TCP header contains the number assigned to that Web browser window so that the Web server knows which port the reply should be sent to. If you open another Web browser window or tab, another port number is assigned, and so forth. The port number is a 16-bit value, so you can open as many as 65,000 windows! Table 5-3 lists well-known port numbers along with the Transport-layer protocol that uses them most often.

Some Application-layer protocols can use TCP or UDP, but the following table shows the Transport-layer protocol most commonly used by the Application-layer protocol.

Table 5-3 Well-known port numbers

Application-layer protocol	Port number	Transport layer
FTP	20, 21	TCP
SSH	22	TCP
Telnet	23	TCP
SMTP	25	TCP
DNS	53	UDP
DHCP	67, 68	UDP
TFTP	69	UDP
HTTP	80	TCP
POP3	110	TCP
IMAP	143	TCP
SNMP	161	UDP
HTTPS	443	TCP
SMB	445	TCP
RDP	3389	TCP

You can see the complete list of well-known port numbers at *www.iana.org/assignments/port-numbers*.

An IP application that doesn't use a Transport-layer protocol, such as the `ping` program and routing protocols, can rely on the Internetwork layer to provide application information. As you see later in "Internetwork-Layer Protocols," the IP packet header includes the Protocol field for just this purpose.

Protecting Data with a Checksum To protect data integrity, TCP and UDP provide a **checksum** similar to the Cyclic Redundancy Check (CRC, the error-checking code explained in Chapter 3) in the Network access layer. However, the CRC isn't always a perfect mechanism for ensuring that data wasn't corrupted on the way to its destination. Routers and switches have been known to corrupt data, recalculate the CRC code, and send the corrupted data on its way. In this situation, the receiver has no way of knowing the data was corrupted because the CRC was calculated after the corruption. Intermediate devices don't recalculate the checksum in the Transport layer, so if data corruption occurs along the way, the final receiving station detects the checksum error and discards the data. To ensure reliability, calculating a checksum is as far as UDP goes. All other reliability features at the Transport layer are the domain of TCP.

TCP: The Reliable Transport Layer

If an application requires reliable data transfer, it uses TCP as the Transport-layer protocol. TCP provides reliability with the following features that aren't available in UDP:

- Establishing a connection
- Segmenting large chunks of data
- Ensuring flow control with acknowledgements

Each feature relies on TCP being a connection-oriented protocol. TCP establishes a connection with the destination, data is transferred, and the connection is broken.

Establishing a Connection: The TCP Handshake Establishing a connection with TCP is similar to making a phone call. You dial the number and wait for your party to answer, usually with a greeting. The caller then states his or her name and says who he or she wants to talk to. If everything is agreeable, a conversation begins.

A TCP session begins when a client sends a TCP synchronization (SYN) segment to the destination device, usually a server. A destination port number (typically a well-known port, such as 80) is specified, and a source port number is assigned dynamically. When the server receives the SYN segment, it usually responds by sending one of two segments: an acknowledgement-synchronization (ACK-SYN) segment or a reset connection (RST) segment. If an RST segment is returned, the server refused the request to open a session, possibly because the destination port is unknown. If an ACK-SYN segment is returned, the client completes the **three-way handshake** by sending an ACK segment back to the server. The client is then ready to begin sending or requesting data. You capture and examine a three-way handshake in Challenge Lab 5-1.

Segmenting Data One safeguard TCP provides is segmenting data before sending it to the Internetwork layer and reassembling data at the destination before sending it up to the Application layer. When TCP receives data from the Application layer, the size of the data might be too large to send to the Internetwork layer in one piece. Ethernet can send only frames that are a maximum of 1518 bytes. It's TCP's job to break the data into smaller segments before handing each segment to the Internetwork layer. Each segment is labeled with a sequence number so that if segments arrive at the destination out of order, they can be reassembled in the correct order by using the sequence number. Programs that work with large amounts of data, such as Web browsers and file transfer programs, use Application-layer protocols that work with TCP for this reason. Applications that work with small amounts of data can use UDP, which doesn't disassemble or reassemble data.

Ensuring Flow Control with Acknowledgements Another role of TCP is to provide **flow control**, which prevents a destination from becoming overwhelmed by data, resulting in dropped packets. TCP does this by establishing a maximum number of bytes, called the "window size," that can be sent before the destination must acknowledge receipt of the data. If a sending machine hasn't received an acknowledgement before sending the number of bytes established by the window size, it stops sending data. If no acknowledgement is received in a specified timeout period, the sender retransmits the data from the point at which an acknowledgement was last received.

After the Transport layer is finished with its job, a header is added to the data created by the Application layer, as shown in Figure 5-16, to create a segment (because TCP is used). This figure shows a destination port of 80 (the default for HTTP) and a source port of 4921, which is selected randomly for the Web browser window.

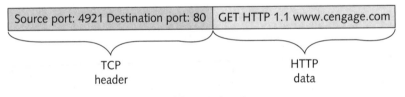

Figure 5-16   An HTTP message with a TCP header

Internetwork-Layer Protocols

The Internetwork layer is where administrators usually do the most network configuration. It's where the IP protocol operates, and it can be looked at as the heart of the TCP/IP protocol suite. IP addresses, of course, are defined here, and routing takes place in this layer, too. Without routing, the Internet and World Wide Web wouldn't exist. With all the complexity of configuring routing and managing IP addresses, this layer is also where most errors in network configuration occur. In a large internetwork, a lot of time is typically spent unraveling the intricacies of the Internetwork layer.

The Internetwork layer is responsible for four main tasks, discussed in the following sections:

- Defines and verifies IP addresses
- Routes packets through an internetwork
- Resolves MAC addresses from IP addresses
- Delivers packets efficiently

Defines and Verifies IP Addresses

An IP address is assigned to every computer and network device using TCP/IP for communication. IP addresses are used for two main purposes: to identify a network device at the Internetwork layer and to identify the network on which a device resides. When an IP address is assigned to a computer or network device (referred to as an "IP host" or just "host"), the host's Internetwork-layer identity is defined. When a host receives an IP packet, it compares the packet's destination IP address with its own address to verify that the packet was delivered correctly. If the destination address matches or is a broadcast or recognized multicast address, the packet is processed; otherwise, it's discarded. When a host sends a packet, the IP protocol places its own IP address in the packet header's source field before sending the packet to the network interface.

The IP address is also used to identify the network on which a host resides. Every IP address contains two parts: a network ID and a host ID. This format is similar to a 10-digit phone number, with a three-digit area code identifying the region of the country where the number was assigned and a seven-digit number identifying the particular phone. IP addresses aren't as straightforward in their format, as you discover in Chapter 6, but there's always a portion of an IP address that identifies the network the host resides on.

Routes Packets Through an Internetwork

The next task of the Internetwork layer is determining the best way to get a packet from network to network until it reaches its destination. If there were only one way for a packet to get from here to there, this aspect of the Internetwork layer's job would be pretty ho-hum. However, much like the nation's road system, most large networks, such as the Internet, have multiple paths for getting from location A to location B. Which path to take isn't always a clear-cut decision. Some paths are heavily traveled, and some are lightly traveled; some paths have construction or accidents, and others are clear sailing.

As mentioned, routers work at the Internetwork layer, and their job is to select the best path to the destination. If a path becomes unavailable or congested, they select an alternative, if available. Routers use the network ID portion of IP addresses along with their routing tables to determine on which network a destination device can be found and the best way to get packets to their destination. Chapter 8 discusses routers in more detail.

Resolves MAC Addresses from IP Addresses

As you've learned, every frame sent to the network medium contains both physical (MAC) and logical (IP) source and destination addresses. When a packet is ready to be sent to the Network access layer, the destination device's MAC address must be retrieved before the frame header can be constructed. TCP/IP uses Address Resolution Protocol (ARP) for this task. ARP is discussed in more detail later in "Address Resolution Protocol," but in a nutshell, it returns a computer's MAC address by querying the network to determine which computer is assigned a particular IP address.

Delivers Packets Efficiently

Internetwork-layer protocols focus mainly on efficient delivery of packets. The secret to achieving this efficiency is low processing overhead. Internetwork-layer protocols don't include features such as flow control, delivery confirmation, or message reassembly; these features require considerable overhead to ensure reliable delivery, at the cost of efficiency.

Internetwork protocols rely on protocols in the Transport and Application layers to provide advanced reliability features. Protocols at this layer are concerned with one packet at a time, with no concern for packets that came before or after it and with no confirmation that delivery was successful. This communication strategy is called "connectionless communication," and protocols using it are called "connectionless protocols."

When using a **connectionless protocol,** no lasting connection is made from source to destination. A connectionless protocol relies on an upper-layer protocol to ensure the packet's safe journey. This process is much like delivering a first-class letter via the U.S. mail. You drop the letter in a mailbox and hope it makes it to its destination. Usually it does, but when you want to be certain it was received (or notified if it wasn't), you must add a layer of complexity by sending the letter certified mail, which requires an acknowledgement that the letter was received. As you've learned, TCP provides this acknowledgement, so it's a connection-oriented protocol.

Protocols at the Internetwork Layer

IP is the underlying basis for most Internetwork-layer protocols, which means they just send specialized versions of IP packets. The protocols operating at this layer are too numerous to describe in this book, so the following sections focus on the most commonly used:

- IPv4
- IPv6
- ICMP
- ARP
- IPsec

Internet Protocol Version 4 Internet Protocol version 4 (IPv4), or just IP, is an Internetwork-layer protocol that provides source and destination addressing and routing for the TCP/IP protocol suite. IP is a connectionless protocol, so it's efficient but unreliable. Note that "unreliable" doesn't mean it fails often. In this context, it simply means IP has no method for ensuring that data is delivered to the destination. IP assumes the Transport or Application layer provides reliable data delivery in applications that require it.

IPv4 is the most common IP version in networks and the first version that was in widespread use. Earlier versions never really made it out of the lab. One of IP's most important functions is the definition of a logical address, called an **IP address.** IPv4 defines a 32-bit dotted decimal address: 172.31.149.10, for example. Each grouping of numbers separated by a dot (period) is an 8-bit value that can range from 0 to 255. Because an IP address has 32 bits, a total of 2^{32} addresses are possible, which is approximately 4 billion. That might seem like a lot of addresses, but as you learn in Chapter 6, many are wasted, and available addresses to assign to devices on the Internet are running out.

As mentioned, part of an IP address specifies the network where the computer assigned the address is located, and the rest of the address specifies a unique host ID in the network. For example, in the address 172.31.149.10, 172.31 is the network ID, and 149.10 is the host ID. This topic can be complex and is covered in more detail in Chapter 6.

IP works with packets, and when it receives a message from the layers above, it adds an IP header. So far in this chapter, only the destination (the intended recipient) and source (the sending machine) addresses of the IP header have been discussed. There's quite a bit more to an IP header, and the following list describes the more important fields in the order they appear in a packet:

- *Version*—This field simply indicates which version of IP is in use. Today, the possibilities are 4 and 6. Because computers can run both versions at the same time, the Version field tells the computer whether the packet should be processed by IPv4 or IPv6.

- *Time to live*—The TTL field is a safeguard that prevents a packet from wandering aimlessly through an internetwork, which can be caused by a network misconfiguration. Before a packet is sent to the network, the TTL field is given a value, usually 64, 128, or 255. As the packet travels through the internetwork, the TTL value is decremented at each router. If the TTL value reaches 0, the packet is deemed to have expired, and the router that decremented the packet to 0 discards it. Most routers also send a message back to the source address as notification that the packet expired.

The TTL can also be decremented by routers if a packet remains in the router's buffers. The router can decrement the TTL by one for each second the packet waits in the router's buffers. This can happen if a very large packet is fragmented into smaller packets and the packet fragment is buffered by the router waiting for the remaining fragments to arrive. It prevents packets that can't be delivered from remaining in the router's buffers forever.

- *Protocol*—This field is a numeric code specifying the type of IP packet or the next layer protocol contained in the packet. For example, the Protocol value in an ICMP packet (used by the `ping` program) is 1. If the packet contains a Transport-layer protocol, such as TCP, the value is 6. There are more than 140 different types of IP packets.

- *Checksum*—This field is a value produced by a mathematical calculation on data in the header that protects the IP header's contents. When a network device receives a packet, this value is recalculated and compared with the value in the Checksum field. If they match, the header hasn't been altered.

- *Source address*—This field is self-explanatory.

- *Destination address*—This field is self-explanatory, too, but it can be one of three types, as in a MAC address: unicast (intended for a single computer), broadcast (sent to all computers in the network), or multicast (sent to a group of computers).

After the Internetwork-layer protocol (in this case, IPv4) has done its job, a header is added to the segment TCP creates, and it becomes a packet (see Figure 5-17).

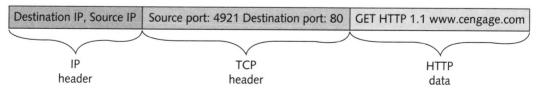

Figure 5-17 An HTTP message that's now a packet

Internet Protocol Version 6 IPv4 has been the driving force on the Internet for decades and continues to be the dominant protocol in use. However, it's showing its age as IPv4 address space becomes used up, and workarounds for security and quality of service must be put in place. IPv4 was developed more than 40 years ago, so it seems natural that as all other aspects of technology slowly get replaced, so will IPv4. This section discusses that replacement: **Internet Protocol version 6 (IPv6)**. IPv6 addresses look very different from IPv4 addresses, and unlike IPv4, IPv6 addresses have a built-in hierarchy and fields with a distinct purpose. Configuring an IPv6 address is clearly different from configuring an IPv4 address. The transition from IPv4 to IPv6 isn't going to happen overnight, so methods have been developed to allow IPv4 and IPv6 networks to coexist and communicate with one another.

This section doesn't attempt to give you a full explanation of IPv6 and its many complexities; there are entire books on this topic. However, it addresses the key aspects of the IPv6 protocol and what you need to know to configure and support a computer using IPv6. The Internet Engineering Task Force (IETF) started development on IPng (IP next generation) in 1994, and it was later named IPv6. IPv6 was developed to address IPv4's shortcomings. Some improvements and changes in IPv6 include the following:

- *Larger address space*—IPv4 addresses are 32 bits, which provide a theoretical four billion addresses. IPv6 addresses are 128 bits, so the number of possible addresses can be expressed as 34 followed by 37 0s, or 340 trillion trillion trillion. It's probably safe to say that running out of IPv6 addresses is unlikely.

- *Hierarchical address space*—Unlike IPv4, in which numbers in the address have little meaning other than the address class, network ID, and host ID, IPv6 addresses have a more defined structure. For example, the first part of an address can indicate a particular organization or site.

- *Autoconfiguration*—IPv6 can be self-configuring or autoconfigured from a router or server running IPv6 or through DHCPv6.

- *Built-in Quality of Service (QoS) support*—IPv6 includes built-in fields in packet headers to support QoS strategies (used to prioritize data packets based on the type or urgency of information they contain) without having to install additional protocol components, as IPv4 does.

- *Built-in support for security*—From the ground-up, IPv6 is built to support secure protocols, such as Internet Protocol Security (IPsec), whereas IPv4's support for IPsec is an add-on feature.

- *Support for mobility*—With built-in support for mobility, routing IPv6 packets generated by mobile devices over the Internet is more efficient than with IPv4.

- *Extensibility*—IPv6 uses extension headers instead of IPv4's fixed-size 40-byte header. Extension headers allow adding features to IPv6 simply by adding a new header.

The advantage of a layered approach to networking is that IPv6 can run on computers alongside IPv4 without needing to change the Transport layer or Network access layer. Most Application-layer protocols require no changes either, except those dealing directly with IP addresses, such as DHCP and DNS. Most of the intricacies of IPv6 lie in addressing, covered in Chapter 6.

Address Resolution Protocol Address Resolution Protocol (ARP) is used to resolve a logical (IP) address to a physical (MAC) address. When a system begins a conversation with a host and doesn't have its MAC address to create the frame header, it sends an ARP broadcast frame requesting the MAC address corresponding to the host's IP address. A network device configured with the specified IP address responds with an ARP reply message containing its MAC address. Then the packet is sent to the Network access layer, and the frame can be constructed.

This process requires more explanation, as you might be wondering what happens when the two computers are on separate networks of an internetwork or even miles apart on the Internet. As explained in Chapter 2, routers are responsible for getting packets from one network to another, and they don't forward broadcast packets, which makes them the delimiting device for broadcast domains. If routers did forward broadcasts, when any computer on the Internet sent a broadcast, the message would be forwarded to every LAN on the Internet, and the Internet would be overrun with broadcasts.

When a computer using TCP/IP wants to communicate with another computer, it must know the destination computer's IP address. Usually, the application sending the message knows the address, or it's resolved by using a name lookup. If the destination's IP address is on the same network as the source, the source computer sends an ARP request message in the form of a broadcast. All computers in the broadcast domain process the ARP request, and the computer with this IP address sends back an ARP reply containing its MAC address. After the MAC address is received, the frame header can be constructed, and the frame is delivered to the destination.

If a computer has to send an ARP broadcast every time it wants to send an IP packet to a particular destination, the network would have one broadcast ARP frame for every frame carrying actual data, which is a big waste of bandwidth. To avoid sending an ARP request every time an IP packet is sent, PCs and other devices store learned IP address–MAC address pairs in an **ARP cache**, a temporary location in RAM. (You viewed the ARP cache in Hands-On Project 1-4 with the `arp -a` command.) So a computer or router has to send an ARP broadcast only once for each destination host it communicates with on its network.

ARP cache entries aren't kept indefinitely. Most computers keep each entry for only a few minutes after it's last used to avoid storing inaccurate information, which could result from a changed NIC or IP address.

If the destination computer is on another network, the computer uses ARP to retrieve the MAC address of the router configured as its default gateway. The packet is delivered to the router, and the router determines where the packet should go next to get to its destination. When the packet gets to the destination network, the router on the destination network uses ARP to get the destination computer's MAC address. Figure 5-18 illustrates this process, and it's animated in Simulation 9. Notice that the destination MAC address in the original message is the MAC address of router R1, but the destination IP address remains the same throughout the journey. Only when the message gets to the destination network does the MAC address become Computer2's address. Notice also that the source MAC address in the frame going from router R3 to Computer2 has changed, showing that the frame is coming from router R3.

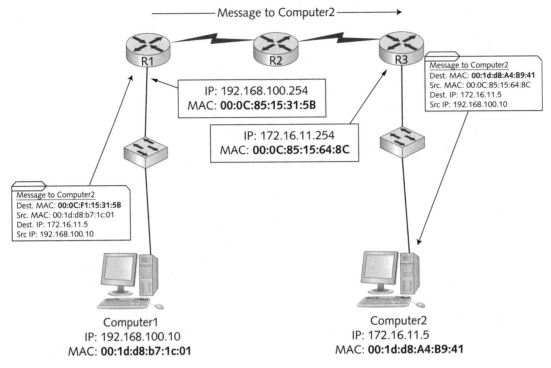

Figure 5-18 How MAC addresses are used in an internetwork

Simulation 9: The changing frame header

Internet Control Message Protocol Internet Control Message Protocol (ICMP) is used to send error, status, and control messages between systems or devices. It's an encapsulated IP protocol, meaning it's wrapped in an IP header. In essence, ICMP is just a specialized IP packet with its own header.

ICMP has many message types, but the two most people know are ICMP Echo (sent by the ping program) and ICMP Echo Reply (sent by the target of the ping). Ping uses ICMP Echo packets to request a response from another computer to verify whether it's available for communication. The response, if received, is an ICMP Echo Reply packet indicating not only that the remote host is reachable, but also how long the message's round trip from sender to receiver took.

The tracert program uses ICMP Echo packets to determine the route a packet takes through an internetwork. It sends an ICMP Echo packet with the TTL value in the IP header set to 1. When the packet reaches the first router on its way to the destination, the router decrements the TTL value to 0, discards the packet, and sends a TTL-Expired ICMP packet to the sending machine to notify it that the packet expired. Tracert receives the TTL-Expired message containing the router's IP address and then has the address of the first router in the path to the destination. Next, `tracert` sends an ICMP Echo packet with a TTL of 2. When the packet gets to the second router, it again expires, and the second router sends a TTL-Expired message. In this way, `tracert` discovers the IP address of every router between the source and destination computers.

These uses of ICMP are the most common, but ICMP has more than 20 message types, many of which are now obsolete. To learn more about ICMP message types, see *www.iana.org/assignments/icmp-parameters*. The Internet Assigned Numbers Authority (IANA) is in charge of everything related to numbers used in Internet protocols.

Internet Protocol Security Internet Protocol Security (IPsec) works with IPv4 to ensure secure delivery of packets. Most OSs now support IPsec as a feature that can be enabled for certain types of communication between specific computers. In other words, it can be used to secure sensitive network transmissions between computers needing the extra security.

This protocol provides security by using authentication and encryption. It authenticates the identity of computers transmitting data with a password or some other form of credentials, and it encrypts data so that if packets are captured, the data will be unintelligible. IPsec requires additional network and computer resources, so it should be enabled only for highly sensitive communication and in environments where security risks are high.

Hands-On Project 5-5: Examining the Internetwork Layer

Time Required: 10 minutes

Objective: Capture packets and view the Internetwork layer.

Required Tools and Equipment: Net-*XX* with Wireshark installed

Description: In this project, you capture some ICMP packets and examine the IP header information.

1. If necessary, log on to your computer as **NetAdmin**.
2. Start Wireshark and click **Capture Options**. In the Capture Filter text box, type **icmp**, and then click **Start**.
3. Ping your default gateway or DNS server. If you don't remember these IP addresses, use the `ipconfig` command to display them.
4. In Wireshark, click the **Stop the running live capture** toolbar icon to stop the capture. Scroll up to the first packet summary line, if necessary.
5. Click a packet summary in the top pane with ICMP in the Protocol field and "Echo (ping) request" in the Info field.
6. Click to expand the line beginning with **Internet Protocol**. In the header, find the fields discussed previously in "Internet Protocol Version 4." Write the values in the Version, Time to live, Protocol, and Checksum fields:

_____

_____

7. Click to expand the line beginning with **Internet Control Message Protocol**, and examine the information in the ICMP header. The Type field specifies the type of ICMP message. The data portion of the ICMP field is simply a string of letters. It doesn't matter what's in the data part of the Echo (ping) request message, as long as the reply contains the same data.

8. Exit Wireshark and click **Quit without Saving** when prompted.

9. Close all open windows, but leave your computer running for the next project.

Hands-On Project 5-6: Capturing ARP and ICMP Packets

Time Required: 10 minutes

Objective: Use Wireshark to capture packets created by the `tracert` program.

Required Tools and Equipment: Net-*XX* with Wireshark installed

Description: In this project, you use Wireshark to capture ARP and ICMP packets generated by the `tracert` program.

1. If necessary, log on to your computer as **NetAdmin**. Right-click **Start** and click **Command Prompt (Admin)**. In the UAC message box, click **Yes**.

2. Type **arp -d** and press **Enter** to clear your ARP cache.

3. Start Wireshark and click **Capture Options**. In the Capture Filter text box, type **arp or icmp**, and then click **Start**.

4. At the command prompt, type **tracert books.tomsho.com** and press **Enter**. When `tracert` is finished, click the **Stop the running live capture** toolbar icon in Wireshark to stop the capture. Scroll to the first packet summary line, if necessary.

5. Find the ARP packets your computer has generated by looking in the Info column for "Who has *A.B.C.D*, Tell 192.168.100.*XX*" (replacing *A.B.C.D* with the address of your default gateway and *XX* with your student number). Click this packet summary line.

6. Notice that the Dst (for destination) address is ff:ff:ff:ff:ff:ff, indicating a broadcast. In the middle pane, click to expand the **Ethernet II** line. Notice that the Type field is ARP (0x806), which tells the Network access layer which Internetwork-layer protocol should receive the packet. Click again to collapse this line.

7. Click to expand the **Address Resolution Protocol (request)** line. Examine the information in the ARP header. The ARP message has fields to indicate what technology is used in the Network access layer (Ethernet) and the protocol type that needs the MAC address (IP, in this case). Click again to collapse this line.

8. Next, in the top pane, click the ARP reply message immediately following the ARP request. The Info column should be similar to "*A.B.C.D* is at 0A:1B:2C:3D:4E:5F." The MAC address in the ARP reply is the MAC address of your default gateway. Explore the Network access and Internetwork headers for this frame. (*Note*: You might

also find an ARP request and ARP reply for your DNS server if it's in the same network as your computer.)

9. In the top pane, click the first **ICMP Echo (ping) request** message from your computer to the destination computer at *books.tomsho.com*. The IP address should be 67.210.126.125, but IP addresses can change, so it might be different.

10. In the middle pane, click to expand the **Internet Protocol** line. Notice that the value in the "Time to live" line is 1.

11. In the top pane, click the **ICMP Time-to-live exceeded** message that follows the ping request. This message was generated by the first router en route to *books.tomsho.com*. Notice that the source address is the address of your default gateway.

12. Find the next ICMP Echo (ping) request message and view the TTL value. Tracert sends three Echo (ping) request messages for each TTL value, so the first three messages have a TTL value of 1. Find the fourth ICMP Echo (ping) request message and view the TTL value, which should be 2. The "Time-to-live exceeded" message following it is from the next router down the line. Tracert follows this pattern until reaching the destination device (*books.tomsho.com*).

13. Exit Wireshark, but leave the command prompt window open if you're continuing to the next project.

Hands-On Project 5-7: Using the `arp` Command

Time Required: 10 minutes

Objective: Use the `arp` command to view and change the ARP cache.

Required Tools and Equipment: Net-*XX*

Description: In this project, you use the `arp` command to view and then delete the ARP cache, and you use the `ping` command to generate ARP cache entries.

1. If necessary, log on to your computer as **NetAdmin**.

2. Some tasks require opening the command prompt window as an administrator. To do this, right-click **Start** and click **Command Prompt (Admin)**. In the User Account Control (UAC) message box, click **Yes**.

3. To display the current ARP cache, type **arp -a** and press **Enter**. A list of IP address–MAC address pairs is displayed. The Type field (third column) indicates whether the entry is static or dynamic. Windows 10 generates static entries automatically, but dynamic entries are generated by network communication. If you don't have any entries, the message "No ARP Entries Found" is displayed.

4. To delete the ARP cache, type **arp -d** and press **Enter**. To verify that the entries have been deleted, type **arp -a** and press **Enter** again. (Some entries marked as "static" remain.)

5. Type **ping 192.168.100.XX** (replacing *XX* with the IP address of another computer in your network) and press **Enter**. Display your ARP cache again. You should see the IP address you pinged along with its MAC address.

6. Clear the ARP cache again. Type **ping www.cengage.com** and press **Enter**. Display the ARP cache again. You'll probably see two new entries in your ARP cache. On the following lines, list these two new entries and state why they were generated. Compare the entries in the ARP cache with the IP address of *www.cengage.com*. Do you see this IP address in the ARP cache? Write your answer along with an explanation.

_____

_____

_____

7. Leave the command prompt window open for the next project.

Hands-On Project 5-8: Using the `netstat` Program

Time Required: 10 minutes

Objective: Use the `netstat` program to view network interface and IP protocol status and statistics.

Required Tools and Equipment: Net-*XX*

Description: In this project, you use `netstat` to view statistics about your network interface and the IP protocol. Then you generate traffic with `ping` and `tracert` to see the statistics of different packet types change.

1. If necessary, log on to your computer as **NetAdmin**, and open a command prompt window.

2. To display statistics about your Ethernet interface, type **netstat -e** and press **Enter**. These statistics include the number of bytes and packets received and sent through the Ethernet interface. If any errors are indicated in the display, you might have problems with your network connection that are slowing the network down. If the error packets approach 1% of the total number of packets, something is probably wrong with your NIC or physical interface.

3. To see statistics for all protocols, type **netstat -s** and press **Enter**. To limit the display to just IP statistics, type **netstat -ps IP** and press **Enter**.

4. To see your network statistics updated every 5 seconds, type **netstat -ps IP 5** and press **Enter**. Press **Ctrl+C** to stop the program.

5. To display ICMP information, type **netstat -ps ICMP** and press **Enter**. A variety of ICMP message types are displayed along with how many of each type of message were received and sent. Most, if not all, will be Echo and Echo Reply messages.

6. Type **ping 5.5.5.5** and press **Enter**. This command should generate ICMP Destination Unreachable messages. To see whether the number of these messages has increased, type **netstat -ps ICMP** and press **Enter**.

7. The ICMP TTL-Expired messages used in `tracert` are called Time Exceeded messages in `netstat`. Type **tracert books.tomsho.com** and press **Enter**. To see whether the number of these messages has increased, type **netstat -ps ICMP** and press **Enter**.

8. To display your computer's routing table, type **netstat -r** and press **Enter**. Every computer has a routing table it uses to decide which interface to send packets to. The first entry lists the network destination as 0.0.0.0, which is the entry for your default gateway.

9. Close all windows, but stay logged on if you're continuing to the next project.

Network Access–Layer Protocols

Strictly speaking, the Network access layer isn't composed of TCP/IP protocols. As you saw in Figure 5-1, network technologies, such as Ethernet, operate at this layer. So this layer is part of the TCP/IP architecture only to the extent that the layer above—the Internetwork layer—has the capability to communicate with any network technologies following the rules of the Network access layer. Some tasks the Network access layer performs have already been discussed but are worth repeating here:

- Provides a physical (MAC) address for the network interface
- Verifies that incoming frames have the correct destination MAC address
- Defines and follows media access rules
- Receives packets from the Internetwork layer and encapsulates them to create frames
- Deencapsulates received frames and sends the resulting packets to the Internetwork layer
- Often provides frame error detection in the form of a CRC code
- Transmits and receives bit signals
- Defines the signaling needed to transmit bits, whether electrical, light pulses, or radio waves
- Defines the media and connectors needed to make a physical network connection

As you learn in Chapter 7, the last three items in this list are tasks the Physical layer performs in the more detailed OSI model, which splits the Network access layer into two separate layers.

Getting back to the HTTP message, after the Network access layer is finished with it, another header is added that includes the source and destination MAC addresses. Remember that the destination MAC address is the address of the next device to receive the packet, which might be the final destination or an intermediate device, such as a router. The packet is now a frame and ready for delivery onto the medium as bits (see Figure 5-19).

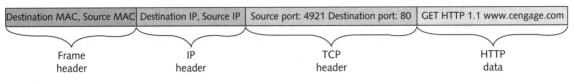

Destination MAC, Source MAC	Destination IP, Source IP	Source port: 4921 Destination port: 80	GET HTTP 1.1 www.cengage.com
Frame header	IP header	TCP header	HTTP data

Figure 5-19 An HTTP message that's now a frame and ready for delivery

Hands-On Project 5-9: Examining NIC Properties

Time Required: 15 minutes

Objective: View the properties of your NIC in Windows and look up its vendor by using the MAC address.

Required Tools and Equipment: Net-*XX*

Description: When describing a NIC as a component of networking, it means both the hardware NIC and its driver. NIC drivers are configured in the OS in which they're installed and control certain operational aspects of the network interface as a whole. In this project, you examine the properties of your installed NIC. You also use the NIC's MAC address to look up the vendor. Not all NICs or NIC drivers are equivalent in features, so your NIC might have more or fewer features than are described here.

1. Log on as **NetAdmin,** if necessary.

2. Right-click **Start** and click **Network Connections**. Right-click **Ethernet0** and click **Status**. The Ethernet0 Status window shows a summary of information about your network connection. To see more information, click **Details** to open the Network Connection Details window.

The `ipconfig /all` command shows much of the same information as what's in the Network Connection Details window.

3. The Network Connection Details window shows information about your connection, including the NIC model, the physical (MAC) address, and your IP address configuration. Write down your MAC address, which you use later to look up the NIC vendor. Review the remaining information, and then click **Close**.

   • MAC address: _____

4. In the Ethernet0 Status window, click **Properties**. In the Ethernet0 Properties dialog box, click the **Configure** button under the "Connect using" text box. In the Network Connection Properties dialog box, click the **Advanced** tab (see Figure 5-20). Your NIC might have fewer, more, or different options.

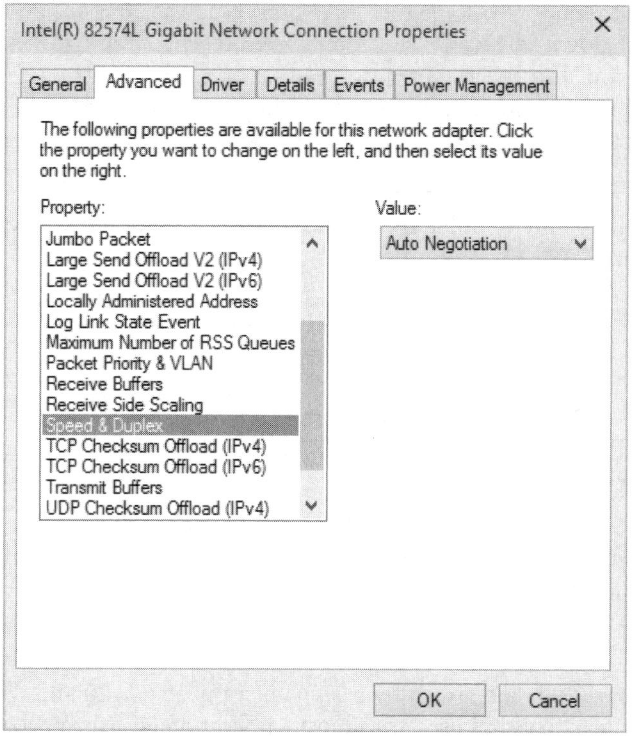

Figure 5-20 Viewing advanced settings in the Network Connection Properties dialog box

5. Review the available properties for your NIC. When you select a property, you can see its possible values in the Value drop-down list.

6. Click **Speed & Duplex** (or **Link Speed and Duplex**), and then click the **Value** list arrow to see the possible values. On most NICs, the default value is Auto Negotiation, which means the NIC and switch exchange signals to determine the optimum operational mode. Other modes usually include combinations of 10, 100, and 1000 Mbps and full-duplex and half-duplex. Normally, you don't need to change these values unless auto negotiation fails to work. If this happens, you'll probably see the link status light change from on to off repeatedly or never turn on at all.

7. Click the **Locally Administered Address** property. (It might also be listed as Network Address, Physical Address, or MAC Address.) In most cases, this property's value is set to Not Present. You can use this property to override the NIC's burned-in MAC address by entering a new address in the Value text box. Normally, however, you shouldn't override the burned-in MAC address because if you duplicate an existing address accidentally, it can cause a loss of communication. Click **Cancel** to close the Network Connection Properties dialog box.

8. Close the Ethernet0 Status window and the Network Connections window.

9. Start a Web browser, and go to **www.coffer.com/mac_find**.

10. In the "MAC Address or Vendor to look for" text box, type the first six digits of the MAC address you wrote down in Step 3. You don't need to enter the hyphen between each pair of digits, but you do need to enter the leading zeros. Click **string** to find the vendor of the MAC address. Knowing the vendor can help you track down devices that might be causing problems on your network. Write down the name of the vendor:

    • Vendor: _____

11. Close all open windows. If you aren't doing the Challenge Labs, shut down your computer; otherwise, stay logged on.

Chapter Summary

- TCP/IP is the main protocol suite used in networks. Like most facets of networking, TCP/IP takes a layered approach and is organized in these four layers: Application, Transport, Internetwork, and Network access.

- The Application layer consists of protocols such as HTTP and DNS and provides an interface for applications to access network services. Other Application-layer protocols include POP3, IMAP, and SMTP for e-mail; FTP, TFTP, and SMB for file transfer and sharing; Telnet and SSH for command-line remote access; and SNMP for device management.

- The Transport layer provides reliability and works with segments (TCP) and datagrams (UDP). Transport-layer protocols are used with most Application layer protocols because they supply a header field to identify the Application layer and provide reliability and flow control for applications that typically transfer a large amount of data.

- The Internetwork layer is where most network configuration occurs and is composed of IP, ICMP, and ARP. This layer is responsible for four main tasks: defining and verifying IP addresses, routing packets through an internetwork, resolving MAC addresses from IP addresses, and delivering packets efficiently.

- The Network access layer is composed of network technologies, such as Ethernet and WAN technologies. Some tasks it performs include providing a physical (MAC) address for the network interface, verifying that incoming frames have the correct destination MAC address, receiving packets from the Internetwork layer and encapsulating them to create frames, and transmitting and receiving bit signals.

Key Terms

Address Resolution Protocol (ARP)   An Internetwork-layer protocol used to resolve a host's IP address to its MAC address. ARP uses a broadcast frame containing the target host's IP address, and the host that's assigned the address responds with its MAC address.

ARP cache   A temporary storage location in an IP host's RAM that keeps recently learned IP address/MAC address pairs so that the ARP protocol isn't necessary for each packet sent to a host.

Automatic Private IP Addressing (APIPA)   A private range of IP addresses assigned to an APIPA-enabled computer automatically when an IP address is requested via DHCP but no DHCP server responds to the request. *See also* Dynamic Host Configuration Protocol (DHCP).

checksum   A field in the Transport-layer and Internetwork-layer headers that protects data integrity by providing a means for a receiving device to ensure that data hasn't been altered.

connectionless protocol   A type of network communication in which data is transferred without making a connection between communicating devices first, and the receiving station gives no acknowledgement that the data was received.

datagram   The unit of information used by UDP in the Transport layer. A datagram is passed up to the Application layer as data and passed down to the Internetwork layer, where it becomes a packet.

DNS zone   A database of primarily hostname and IP address pairs that are related by membership in an Internet or a Windows domain.

Domain Name System (DNS)   An Application-layer protocol that resolves computer and domain names to their IP addresses; uses UDP port 53.

Dynamic DNS (DDNS)   A DNS client and server option that allows a DNS client computer to register its hostname and IP address with a DNS server automatically. *See also* Domain Name System (DNS).

Dynamic Host Configuration Protocol (DHCP)   An Application-layer protocol used to configure a host's IP address settings dynamically; it uses UDP ports 67 and 68.

exclusion   A configuration option that excludes specified IP addresses from the DHCP IP address scope. *See also* IP address scope.

File Transfer Protocol (FTP)   An Application-layer protocol used to transfer and manage files across a network; uses TCP ports 20 and 21.

flow control   A mechanism network protocols use to prevent a destination device from becoming overwhelmed by data from a transmitting computer, resulting in dropped packets.

fully qualified domain name (FQDN)   A name that includes the hostname, subdomain names (if applicable), second-level domain name, and top-level domain name, separated by periods.

Internet Control Message Protocol (ICMP)   An Internetwork-layer protocol used to send error, status, and control messages between systems or devices. It's an encapsulated IP protocol, meaning it's wrapped in an IP header.

Internet Message Access Protocol version 4 (IMAP4)   An Application-layer protocol used by an e-mail client to download messages from an e-mail server; operates on TCP port 143. IMAP4 also provides fault-tolerance features. It downloads only message headers from the server initially, and then downloads the message body and attachments after the message is selected.

Internet Protocol Security (IPsec)   An extension to IP working at the Internetwork layer that provides security by using authentication and encryption. It authenticates the identity of computers transmitting data with a password or some other form of credentials, and it encrypts data so that if packets are captured, the data will be unintelligible.

Internet Protocol version 4 (IPv4)   A connectionless Internetwork-layer protocol that provides source and destination addressing and routing for the TCP/IP protocol suite; uses 32-bit dotted decimal addresses.

Internet Protocol version 6 (IPv6)   A connectionless Internetwork-layer protocol that provides source and destination addressing and routing for the TCP/IP protocol suite. Uses 128-bit hexadecimal addresses and has built-in security and QoS features.

IP address   A 32-bit dotted-decimal address used by IP to determine the network a host resides on and to identify hosts on the network at the Internetwork layer.

IP address scope   A component of a DHCP server, it's a range of IP addresses the server leases to clients requesting an IP address.

port number   A field in the Transport-layer protocol header that specifies the source and destination Application-layer protocols that are used to request data (the source) and are the target of the request (the destination).

Post Office Protocol version 3 (POP3)   An Application-layer protocol used by a client e-mail application to download messages from an e-mail server; uses TCP port 110.

protocol   Rules and procedures for communication and behavior. Computers must use a common protocol and agree on the rules of communication.

protocol suite   A set of protocols working cooperatively to provide network communication. Protocols are "stacked" in layers, and each layer performs a unique function required for successful communication. Also called a "protocol stack."

Remote Desktop Protocol (RDP)   An Application-layer protocol used to access a Windows computer remotely with the Windows GUI; uses TCP port 3389.

reservation   A configuration option for an IP address scope that ties an IP address to a MAC address. When a client requests an IP address from the DHCP server, if the client's MAC address matches an address specified by a reservation, the reserved IP address is leased to the client instead of getting it from the scope. *See also* IP address scope.

resolver cache   Storage for recently resolved DNS data on a DNS client; used so that clients don't have to perform DNS lookups if host were resolved recently.

resource records   The data contained in a DNS zone, such as host records, MX records, and NS records.

Secure Shell (SSH)   A secure Application-layer protocol used to connect to a device across a network via a command-line interface; uses TCP port 22.

segment   The unit of information used by TCP in the Transport layer. A segment is passed up to the Application layer as data and passed down to the Internetwork layer, where it becomes a packet.

Server Message Block (SMB)   An Application-layer protocol that Windows file and printer services use to share resources between Windows computers; uses TCP port 445.

Simple Mail Transfer Protocol (SMTP)   An Application-layer protocol used to send e-mail over the Internet; uses TCP port 25.

Simple Network Management Protocol (SNMP)   An Application-layer protocol used to monitor and manage network devices and gather statistics about network traffic. It operates on UDP ports 161 and 162.

Telnet   An unsecure Application-layer protocol used to connect to a device across a network via a command-line interface; uses TCP port 23.

three-way handshake   A series of three packets used between a client and server to create a TCP connection. After the three-way handshake has been completed successfully, a connection is established between client and server applications, and data can be transferred.

Transmission Control Protocol (TCP)   A connection-oriented Transport-layer protocol designed for reliable transfer of information in complex internetworks.

Transmission Control Protocol/Internet Protocol (TCP/IP)   The most common protocol suite, TCP/IP is the default protocol in contemporary OSs and the protocol of the Internet.

User Datagram Protocol (UDP)   A connectionless Transport-layer protocol designed for efficient communication of generally small amounts of data.

Review Questions

1. An IPv6 address is made up of how many bits?

   a. 32

   b. 48

   c. 64

   d. 128

   e. 256

2. Which Application-layer protocol provides remote access to a Windows computer via a GUI?

   a. Telnet

   b. RDP

   c. SSH

   d. FTP

3. If a protocol is routable, which TCP/IP layer does it operate at?

   a. Network access

   b. Internetwork

   c. Transport

   d. Application

4. Which Application-layer protocol is used to monitor and manage network devices, and what Transport-layer protocol does it use?

   a. SMTP, UDP

   b. SNMP, TCP

   c. SMTP, TCP

   d. SNMP, UDP

5. Which TCP/IP model layer takes a large chunk of data from the Application layer and breaks it into smaller segments?

    a.   Network access

    b.   Internetwork

    c.   Transport

    d.   Application

6. Which of the following protocols resolves logical addresses to physical addresses?

    a.   DHCP

    b.   TCP

    c.   IP

    d.   DNS

    e.   ARP

7. Which of the following protocols provides connectionless service? (Choose all that apply.)

    a.   IP

    b.   UDP

    c.   TCP

    d.   HTTP

8. If you want to design an Application-layer protocol that provides fast, efficient communication and doesn't work with large amounts of data, what Transport-layer protocol would you design it to use?

9. Which of the following is the term for identifying packets used by TCP to establish a connection?

    a.   Port number indicators

    b.   Multiwindow agreement

    c.   Three-way handshake

    d.   Sequencing establishment

10. What element of a DHCP server uses the client MAC address to ensure that the client is leased the same address each time it requests an IP address?

    a.   IP address scope

    b.   Address exclusion

    c.   Reservation

    d.   ARP mapping

11. Which of the following is the first packet sent when a computer wants to lease an IP address?

    a. DHCPAck

    b. DHCPDiscover

    c. DHCPRequest

    d. DHCPOffer

12. Which of the following IPv6 features is an enhancement to IPv4? (Choose all that apply.)

    a. Larger address space

    b. Works at the Internetwork and Transport layers

    c. Built-in security

    d. Connectionless communication

13. Which protocol can configure a computer's IP address and subnet mask automatically?

    a. TCP

    b. IP

    c. ARP

    d. DNS

    e. DHCP

14. What type of packets are transmitted between DHCP client and server when a client is initially leasing an IP address?

    a. Broadcast

    b. Multicast

    c. Unicast

    d. Anycast

15. Which of the following accurately describes the .edu in the FQDN www.yc.edu?

    a. Fully qualified domain name

    b. Top-level domain

    c. Root domain

    d. Second-level domain

16. What's another name for a DNS client?

    a. Alias

    b. Reservation

    c. DDNS

    d. Resolver

17. What type of resource record is an alias for another record?

    a. MX

    b. AAAA

    c. CNAME

    d. PTR

18. When a Windows computer is configured to use DHCP but no DHCP server is available, what type of address is configured automatically for it?

    a. PAT

    b. APIPA

    c. NAT

    d. Static

19. Where does a DNS server look when it can't resolve a query from its zone records or cache?

    a. Root hints

    b. Alternate server

    c. Top-level domain

    d. BIND

20. What does the Transport layer use to identify source and destination Application-layer protocols?

    a. Checksum

    b. TCP address

    c. Port number

    d. Root hints

21. Which of the following Application-layer protocols typically uses the UDP Transport-layer protocol? (Choose all that apply.)

    a. HTTP

    b. DNS

    c. DHCP

    d. FTP

22. Which is the correct order of headers, from left to right, in a completed frame?

    a. Frame, TCP, IP

    b. UDP, frame, IP

    c. TCP, IP, frame

    d. Frame, IP, UDP

23. Which of the following is a task performed by the Network access layer? (Choose all that apply.)

   a. Verifies that incoming frames have the correct destination MAC address

   b. Defines and verifies IP addresses

   c. Transmits and receives bit signals

   d. Resolves MAC addresses by using IP addresses

   e. Delivers packets efficiently

24. What field of the IP header does the `tracert` program use to get the IP address of routers in the path?

   a. Version

   b. TTL

   c. Checksum

   d. Protocol

25. Which of the following is *not* found in a connectionless Transport-layer protocol? (Choose all that apply.)

   a. Three-way handshake

   b. Port numbers

   c. Checksum

   d. Acknowledgements

Critical Thinking

The following activities give you critical thinking challenges. Challenge labs give you an opportunity to use the skills you have learned to perform a task without step-by-step instructions. Case projects offer a practical networking setup for which you supply a written solution.

CHALLENGE LAB

Challenge Lab 5-1: Capturing and Identifying the Three-way Handshake

Time Required: 30 minutes

Objective: Determine which packets create the three-way handshake used in establishing a communication session.

Required Tools and Equipment: Net-*XX* with Wireshark installed

Description: Using Wireshark and a suitable capture filter, capture the packets involved in an HTTP session that you start by opening a Web page. Find the three packets that constitute the three-way handshake. Perform the following tasks:

• What capture filter did you use to limit Wireshark to capturing only packets related to HTTP?

- Find the three-way handshake that immediately precedes the first HTTP packet. Which Transport-layer protocol was used to create the connection?

  _____

- Find the following fields in the Transport-layer header of the first packet in the three-way handshake and write down their value:
  - Source port: _____
  - Destination port: _____
  - Sequence number: _____
  - Flags: Syn: _____
  - Window size: _____
  - Maximum segment size: _____

- Find the following fields in the Transport-layer header of the third packet in the three-way handshake. Research their meanings, and then write down their values along with brief descriptions of them:
  - Window size: _____
  - Maximum segment size:

  _____

- How are the sequence number and acknowledgement used to make this protocol reliable?

  _____

CHALLENGE LAB

Challenge Lab 5-2: Capturing and Identifying DHCP Packets

Time Required: 30 minutes

Objective: Capture the packets used to lease a DHCP address to a client.

Required Tools and Equipment: Net-*XX* with Wireshark installed, a configured DHCP server

Description: Using Wireshark and a suitable capture filter, capture the packets involved in a DHCP IP address lease. Make sure your computer is configured to get an address via DHCP, and set your computer's IP address back to its original settings when you're finished. Answer the following questions:

- What commands did you use to cause your computer to request a new address lease?

  _____

- What capture filter did you use to limit Wireshark to capturing only packets related to DHCP?

  _____

- Find the four packets involved in the DHCP lease. In the Info column of Wireshark, what's the name shown for each of the four packets?

  _____

  _____

  _____

- Find the following fields in the Transport-layer header of the first packet in the DHCP lease, and write down their values:

  ○ Source port: _____

  ○ Destination port: _____

- What's the Internetwork-layer source address and destination address in the two packets sent by the client computer? Explain.

  _____

Case Project 5-1

You work at a help desk and have just received a call from an employee who says she can't access network resources. You want the employee to view her IP address configuration. Write an e-mail to the employee, explaining what command-line program to use and how she can use it to find the information you need. After following your instructions, the employee tells you that her IP address is 169.254.14.11 with the subnet mask 255.255.0.0. What conclusion can you make from this information?

Case Project 5-2

You have configured a LAN with 25 workstations, three network printers, and two servers. The workstations and printers will have dynamically assigned IP addresses, and the printers always need to have the same IP address assigned. The servers will have static IP addresses. What should you install on one of the servers, and what are some of the configuration options?

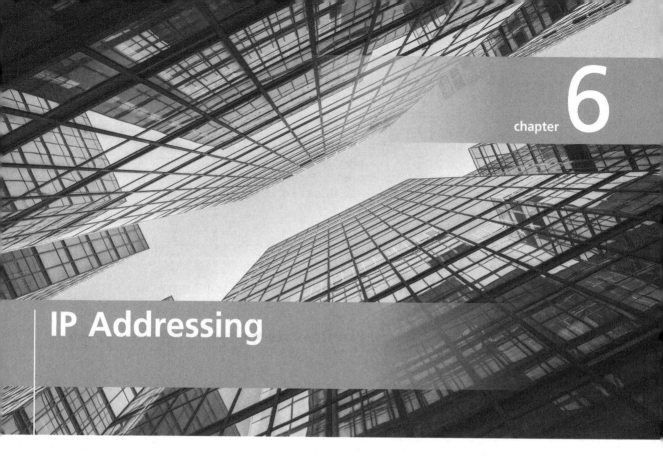

chapter **6**

IP Addressing

After reading this chapter and completing the exercises, you will be able to:

- Explain IPv4 addressing
- Use Classless Interdomain Routing Notation
- Perform subnetting calculations
- Configure IPv4 addresses
- Describe Network Address Translation
- Describe IPv6
- Recognize IPv6 address types
- Explain IPv6 autoconfiguration
- Describe IPv4 to IPv6 transitioning methods

A major task that network administrators must perform is setting up a Layer 3 addressing scheme. All devices must have a Layer 3 address to communicate in a TCP/IP network, and no two addresses can be the same throughout the internetwork. In a TCP/IP network, an administrator must be concerned with both IPv4 and IPv6 addresses, and a suitable design and method for address delivery must be developed for both. In this chapter, you learn about IPv4 addresses and how to design and use a suitable subnetting scheme in an internetwork. You also learn about IPv6, the different methods for autoconfiguring IPv6 addresses, and the IPv6 address structure, which differs substantially from IPv4's structure.

IPv4 Addressing

Table 6-1 summarizes what you need for the hands-on projects in this chapter.

Table 6-1 Hands-on project requirements

Hands-on project	Requirements	Time required	Notes
Hands-On Project 6-1: Converting Decimal Numbers to Binary	Paper and pencil	15 minutes	
Hands-On Project 6-2: Converting Binary Numbers to Decimal	Paper and pencil	15 minutes	
Hands-On Project 6-3: Working with CIDR Notation	Paper and pencil	20 minutes	
Hands-On Project 6-4: Determining the Correct Prefix	Paper and pencil	20 minutes	
Hands-On Project 6-5: Using the netsh Command	Net-XX	10 minutes	
Hands-On Project 6-6: Trying to Set an Invalid IP Address	Net-XX	10 minutes	
Hands-On Project 6-7: Setting IPv6 Static Addresses	Net-XX	10 minutes	
Hands-On Project 6-8: Working with IPv6	Net-XX	15 minutes	Need the address of one other computer with an IPv6 address

An **IPv4 address** is a 32-bit number divided into four 8-bit values called "octets." Each **octet** can have a value from 0 to 255. IPv4 addresses are written in **dotted decimal notation**. This format consists of four decimal numbers, each in the range 0 to 255, separated by a period. For example, in the IPv4 address 10.255.0.100, 10 is the first octet and 100 is the fourth octet.

Every IP address contains a network ID, which specifies the network on which the computer is found, and a host ID, which uniquely identifies the computer on that network. Determining which part of the IP address is the network ID and which part is the host ID depends on the **subnet mask**, another 32-bit dotted decimal number consisting of a contiguous series of binary 1 digits followed by a contiguous series of binary 0 digits. A contiguous series of eight binary 1s equals the decimal value 255. For example, a typical subnet mask is 255.0.0.0 or 255.255.0.0. In these two examples, for each 255 in the subnet mask, the corresponding octet of the IP address is part of the network ID.

Take a look at an example. In binary, the subnet mask 255.255.0.0 looks like 11111111.11111111.00000000.00000000. (Binary math is discussed in the next section.) Say you configured a Windows computer with the following IP address and subnet mask:

```
IP address: 10.1.221.101
Subnet mask: 255.0.0.0
```

Because the first octet of the subnet mask is 255 (a series of eight binary 1s), the first octet of the IP address is the network ID, which is 10. The network ID is written as 10.0.0.0, and the host ID is 1.221.101. Understand, however, that the network ID and host ID are used together when configuring a computer's IP address and when communicating with another computer. So the source address in a network packet being sent by the computer in this example is 10.1.221.101.

Now take this example:

```
IP address: 172.31.100.6
Subnet mask: 255.255.0.0
```

The first two octets of the subnet mask are 255 (a total of 16 contiguous binary 1s), so the network ID is 172.31, which is written as 172.31.0.0. The host ID is 100.6. When referring to the network ID, you always fill in the host part of the address with 0s.

Continuing with this pattern, say you have the following IP address and subnet mask:

```
IP address: 192.168.14.250
Subnet mask: 255.255.255.0
```

They give you the network ID 192.168.14.0 and the host ID 250. You can't have the subnet mask 255.0.255.0 because the network ID must be contiguous. However, you can have an IP address and a subnet mask such as 172.16.67.5 and 255.255.192.0. What's going on in the third octet of this subnet mask? Even though this subnet mask doesn't look like the other examples, with only the values 255 and 0, it's still a contiguous series of 1s followed by a contiguous series of 0s. In binary, this subnet mask looks like this:

```
11111111.11111111.11000000.00000000
```

The decimal equivalent of this binary number is 255.255.192.0, making the network ID of the 172.16.67.5 address equal to 172.16.64.0 and the host ID equal to 3.5. How is this information determined? Before you go any further, it helps to understand a little about binary math and how to convert between binary and decimal.

Binary Math

An important part of IP addressing is how the subnet mask is used to determine the network ID. As you've seen, it's not as simple as stating that "Anywhere there's a 255 in the subnet mask, the corresponding octet in the IP address is part of the network ID." In addition, computers don't reason that way; they perform calculations, specifically in binary math. To determine the network ID of an IP address, computers use a **logical AND operation**, which is an operation between two binary values that you can think of as binary multiplication. Because there are only two unique digits in binary numbers, the multiplication is easy. There are only four possible results when you combine two binary numbers with AND, and three of these results are 0:

```
0 AND 0 = 0
1 AND 0 = 0
0 AND 1 = 0
1 AND 1 = 1
```

To determine the network ID based on the IP address and subnet mask, a computer simply performs a logical AND between the binary digits in the IP address and the binary digits in the subnet mask, which looks something like this:

```
10101100.00011111.01100100.00000110 (binary for 172.31.100.6)
                 AND
11111111.11111111.00000000.00000000 (binary for 255.255.0.0)
_____
10101100.00011111.00000000.00000000 (binary for 172.31.0.0)
```

You simply take the binary digit from the IP address (top number) and perform a logical AND with the corresponding digit in the subnet mask (bottom number). The result is the network ID 172.31.0.0. Take a look at the last example in the previous section:

```
10101100.00010000.01000011.00000101 (binary for 172.16.67.5)
                 AND
11111111.11111111.11000000.00000000 (binary for 255.255.192.0)
_____
10101100.00010000.01000000.00000000 (binary for 172.16.64.0)
```

After you do the AND operation, you can see the network ID 172.16.64.0 (that is, if you know how to convert binary to decimal, discussed next). The remaining bits in the IP address that aren't part of the network ID are the host ID. In this case, it's 00000011.00000101, which is equal to decimal 3.5. Essentially, anywhere there's a 1 bit in the subnet mask, the corresponding bits in the IP address are part of the network ID, and anywhere there are 0 bits in the subnet mask, the corresponding bits are part of the host ID. This sure would be easier if you knew how to convert from decimal to binary and back, wouldn't it?

Converting Binary to Decimal Before you start converting from binary to decimal and back, you need to review how the decimal number system works. It's based on powers of 10 (which is where the word "decimal" comes from, with "dec" meaning "ten"). Ten different symbols, 0 through 9, are used to represent any possible number. Each place in a decimal number can have one of 10 possible values—again, 0 through 9. Furthermore, each place in a decimal number can be expressed as a power of 10. The ones place can be expressed as a number, 0 through 9, multiplied by 10 raised to the 0 power, or 10^0. (Any number raised to the 0 power equals 1.) The tens place can be expressed as a number multiplied by 10 to the 1 power, or 10^1. The hundreds place can be expressed as a number multiplied by 10^2, and so on. For example, the decimal number 249 can be expressed as either of the following:

$2 * 10^2 + 4 * 10^1 + 9 * 10^0 = 249$
$2 * 100 + 4 * 10 + 9 * 1 = 249$

When you see the number 249, you don't think of it in these terms because you grew up using the decimal number system, and recognizing the hundreds place, tens place, and ones place happens without conscious effort, as does the multiplication and addition that occurs. However, take a look at this number:

379420841249

A little more thought has to go into recognizing that the 3 represents 300 billion, the 7 represents 70 billion, and so forth. The binary number system works the same way, except everything is governed by twos. Two digits, 0 and 1, represent every possible number, and each place in a binary number is 0 or 1 multiplied by a power of 2. So instead of having the ones place, the tens place, the hundreds place, and so on, you have the ones place, the twos place, the fours place, and so on, based on 2^0, 2^1, 2^2, and so forth. For example, using the same method as for the decimal example, you can express the binary number 101 as either of the following. The numbers in bold are the binary digits.

1 $* 2^2 +$ **0** $* 2^1 +$ **1** $* 2^0 = 5$
1 $* 4 +$ **0** $* 2 +$ **1** $* 1 = 5$

Converting Decimal to Binary One way to convert from decimal to binary is shown in Table 6-2. The first two rows are the binary and exponent values of each bit position of an 8-bit number. You use 8 bits because in subnetting, most work can be done 8 bits at a time. The third row is what you fill in to determine the decimal number's binary representation.

Table 6-2 Decimal-to-binary conversion table

128	64	32	16	8	4	2	1
2^7	2^6	2^5	2^4	2^3	2^2	2^1	2^0
0	1	1	1	1	1	0	1

To use this method, start with the number you're trying to convert to binary, which is referred to as the "test number." In this example, you use 125. You compare the test number with the leftmost number in the preceding table (128). If it's equal to or greater than this number, you place a 1 in the column and subtract this column's number from your test number; otherwise, place a 0 in the column. Remember: Eight binary places or 8 bits can represent only a value up to 255. If you're converting a number greater than 255, simply extend the table to the left (256, 512, and so on). Here's the sequence of steps:

1. 125 is less than 128, so you place a **0** in the column under the 128. The test number remains 125.

2. 125 is greater than 64, so you place a **1** in the column under the 64 and subtract 64 from 125, leaving the new test number as 61.

3. 61 is greater than 32, so you place a **1** in the column under the 32 and subtract 32 from 61, leaving the new test number as 29.

4. 29 is greater than 16, so you place a **1** in the column under the 16 and subtract 16 from 29, leaving the new test number as 13.

5. 13 is greater than 8, so you place a **1** in the column under the 8 and subtract 8 from 13, leaving the new test number as 5.

6. 5 is greater than 4, so you place a **1** in the column under the 4 and subtract 4 from 5, leaving the new test number as 1.

7. 1 is less than 2, so you place a **0** in the column under the 2.

8. 1 is equal to 1, so you place a **1** in the column under the 1 and subtract 1 from 1, leaving the new test number as 0. When the test number is 0, you're done.

Now try this with 199, 221, and 24. You should get the following results:

```
199 = 11000111
221 = 11011101
24 = 00011000
```

Converting Binary to Decimal The easiest way to convert an 8-digit binary number (octet) is to use Table 6-3, as you did for the decimal-to-binary conversion. Of course, if your binary number is more than 8 bits, you can simply extend the table to the left as many places as necessary. Here's how to do it: Write your binary number in the third row of the table, as shown in this table. For every column with a 1 bit, write down the corresponding decimal number from the first row. For columns with a 0 bit, you can simply skip them or write down a 0. Using the binary number 11010011, you get the following:

$$128 + 64 + 0 + 16 + 0 + 0 + 2 + 1 = 211$$

Table 6-3 Converting 11010011 to 211

128	64	32	16	8	4	2	1
2^7	2^6	2^5	2^4	2^3	2^2	2^1	2^0
1	1	0	1	0	0	1	1

Plug in the binary values for 199, 221, and 24 to make sure you get the correct results.

Hands-On Project 6-1: Converting Decimal Numbers to Binary

Time Required: 15 minutes

Objective: Convert decimal numbers to binary.

Required Tools and Equipment: Paper and pencil

Description: Convert the following decimal numbers to binary without using a calculator. You can use Table 6-3 to help with the conversions or create your own table.

Decimal number	Binary number
167	
149	
252	
128	
64	
240	

Decimal number	Binary number
255	
14	
15	
63	
188	
224	

Hands-On Project 6-2: Converting Binary Numbers to Decimal

Time Required: 15 minutes

Objective: Convert binary numbers to decimal.

Required Tools and Equipment: Paper and pencil

Description: Convert the following binary numbers to decimal without using a calculator. You can use Table 6-3 to help with the conversions or create your own table.

Binary number	Decimal number
00110101	
11111000	
00011111	
10101010	
01010101	
11111110	
11111100	
00111011	
11001100	
00110011	
00000111	
00111100	

IP Address Classes

When you enter an IP address in the Internet Protocol Version 4 (TCP/IPv4) Properties dialog box shown in Figure 6-1, Windows fills in a subnet mask automatically, which you can change if needed. Windows bases the suggested subnet mask on the class of the IP address you enter.

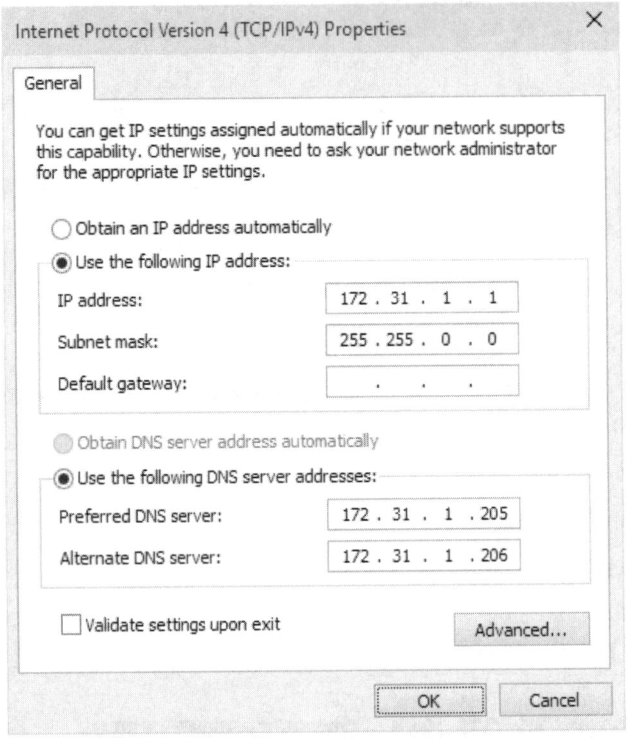

Figure 6-1 A subnet mask based on the address class

IP addresses are categorized in ranges referred to as Classes A, B, C, D, or E. Only IP addresses in the A, B, and C classes can be assigned to a network device (host). Although the IP address class system has been superseded by a more flexible way to manage IP addresses, called Classless Interdomain Routing (CIDR, discussed later in this chapter), the class system is a basis for determining which part of an IP address is the network ID and which part is the host ID. The first octet of an address denotes its class. Review the following facts about IP address classes:

- The value of the first octet for Class A addresses is between 1 and 127. Class A addresses were intended for use by large corporations and governments. An IP address registry assigns the first octet, leaving the last three octets for network administrators to assign to hosts. This allows 24 bits of address space or 16,777,214 hosts per network address. In a Class A IP address such as 10.159.44.201, for example, the network address is 10.0.0.0. So the first address in the 10.0.0.0 network is 10.0.0.1, and the last address is 10.255.255.254.

- Class B addresses begin with network IDs between 128 and 191 and were intended for use in medium to large networks. An IP address registry assigns the first two octets, leaving the third and fourth octets available for administrators to assign as host addresses. In the Class B address 172.17.11.4, for example, the network address is 172.17.0.0. Having two octets in the host ID allows 65,534 hosts per network address.

- Class C addresses were intended for small networks. An IP address registry assigns the first three octets, ranging from 192 to 223. In the Class C address 203.0.113.254, for example, the network address is 203.0.113.0. These networks are limited to 254 hosts per network.

- Class D addresses are reserved for **multicasting**, in which a packet is addressed so that more than one destination can receive it. Applications using this feature include videoconferencing and streaming media. In a Class D address, the first octet is in the range 224 to 239. Class D addresses can't be used to assign IP addresses to host computers.

- Class E addresses have a value from 240 to 255 in the first octet. This range of addresses is reserved for experimental use and can't be used for address assignment.

A couple of notes about this list: First, if you do the math, you would see that a Class C address provides 28 bits of **address space**, which yields 256 addresses, not 254. An address space is the total number of addresses in an IP network number that can be assigned to hosts. The number of addresses specified for Classes A and B are also two fewer than the address space suggests. This discrepancy happens because each network has two reserved addresses: the address in which all host ID bits are binary 0s and the address in which all host ID bits are binary 1s. For example, all the host bits in address 203.0.113.0 are binary 0s, and this address represents the network number and can't be assigned to a computer. The host bits in address 203.0.113.255 are binary 1s; this address is the broadcast address for the 203.0.113.0 network and can't be assigned to a computer.

The other note concerns the 127.0.0.0 network. Although technically a Class A address, it's reserved for the **loopback address**, which always refers to the local computer and is used to test the functioning of TCP/IP. A packet with a destination address starting with 127 is sent to the local device without reaching the network medium. Likewise, the reserved name **localhost** always corresponds to the IP address 127.0.0.1 so that a local machine can always be referenced by this name.

Even though localhost and the loopback address are usually associated with the address 127.0.0.1, any address in the 127.0.0.0 network (except 127.0.0.0 and 127.255.255.255) references the local machine in most OSs.

Table 6-4 summarizes address Classes A, B, and C and the default subnet masks.

Table 6-4 IPv4 address class summary

Class	A	B	C
Value of first octet	0–127	128–191	192–223
Default subnet mask	255.0.0.0	255.255.0.0	255.255.255.0
Number of network ID bits	8	16	24
Maximum number of hosts/network	16,777,214	65,534	254
Number of host bits	24	16	8

Private IP Addresses

Each device that accesses the Internet must do so by using a public IP address. Because of the popularity of TCP/IP and the Internet, unique IP addresses to assign to Internet-accessible devices are almost exhausted. To help alleviate this problem, TCP/IP's technical governing body reserved a series of addresses for private networks—that is, networks whose hosts can't be accessed directly through the Internet. The reserved addresses are as follows:

- Class A addresses beginning with 10 (one Class A network address)
- Class B addresses from 172.16 to 172.31 (16 Class B network addresses)
- Class C addresses from 192.168.0 to 192.168.255 (256 Class C network addresses)

The addresses in these ranges can't be routed across the Internet, which is why any organization can use them to assign IP addresses to their internal hosts. If access to the Internet is necessary, a process called Network Address Translation (NAT) is used, explained later in "Network Address Translation."

Another type of private IP address is a **link-local address**. It's not assigned manually or through DHCP; it's assigned automatically when a computer is configured to receive an IP address through DHCP but no DHCP service is available. Another term for this type of addressing is **Automatic Private IP Addressing (APIPA)**. APIPA addresses are assigned in the range 169.254.1.0 through 169.254.254.255 with the subnet mask 255.255.0.0. Computers that are assigned a link-local address can communicate only on the local LAN, as packets containing these addresses shouldn't be forwarded by routers.

Link-local IPv4 addresses don't use the first 256 or the last 256 addresses in the 169.254.0.0/16 range because these addresses are reserved for future use, according to RFC 3927.

Classless Interdomain Routing

If IP addresses have a default subnet mask assigned based on the value of the IP address's first octet, why do you even need to specify the subnet mask? The reason is the default subnet mask doesn't always suit your network's needs. Address classes and default subnet masks were designed when TCP/IP was in its infancy, and computer networks and the Internet were almost unheard of. They met the needs of the few government agencies and universities using TCP/IP in the late 1970s and 1980s. The use of IP addresses with their default subnet masks is referred to as **classful addressing**.

After computer networks were being installed in every business, and users wanted access to the new information source called the Internet, classful addressing clearly needed some flexibility—hence, subnet masks that could be configured regardless of the address class. This type of IP address configuration became what's known as **Classless Interdomain Routing (CIDR)**. For example, assigning the IP address 172.31.210.10 with a subnet mask of 255.255.255.0 (instead of the default of 255.255.0.0) is perfectly acceptable. In this case, the network ID is 172.31.210, and the host ID is 10. Why would you want to assign a subnet mask different from the default? Aren't the default subnet masks good enough? In some cases, they are, but not in others.

Take, for instance, the address 172.31.0.0 with the default subnet mask 255.255.0.0. As Table 6-4 showed, this subnet mask allows a 16-bit host ID, making it possible to assign more than 65,000 host addresses, starting with 172.31.0.1 and ending with 172.31.255.254. (Remember that you can't assign an address with all 0 bits or all 1 bits in the host ID, so you have to exclude 172.31.0.0 and 172.31.255.255 from the possible IP addresses you can assign to a host.) The exact calculation for the number of hosts is 2^n - 2; n is the number of bits in the host ID. Being able to assign this many addresses might seem like an advantage if you have a large network. However, having such a large address space assigned to a single network has two distinct disadvantages: If you're actually using the number of computers the address space affords (in this case, more than 65,000 computers), communication efficiency suffers, and if you aren't using the addresses, precious address space is wasted. The following sections explain these concepts in more detail.

CIDR Notation

Writing IP addresses with their subnet masks can be tedious and takes up a lot of space. What's important is how many bits of the IP address constitute the network ID. To that end, you can specify an IP address and its subnet mask with CIDR notation. **CIDR notation** uses the format A.B.C.D/n; n is the number of 1 bits in the subnet mask, or expressed another way, the number of bits in the network ID. It's referred to as the **IP prefix** (or just "prefix"). For example, 172.31.210.10 with a 255.255.255.0 subnet mask is expressed as 172.31.210.10/24 in CIDR notation. The network ID is 24 bits, leaving 8 bits for the host ID. As another example, 10.25.106.12 with the subnet mask 255.255.240.0 is expressed as 10.25.106.12/20. In this case, the network ID is 20 bits, leaving 12 bits for the host ID.

Broadcast Domains

All computers and devices with the same network ID in their IP address are said to be in the same broadcast domain. As you learned in Chapter 2, a **broadcast domain** defines which devices must receive a packet that's broadcast by any other device, and each port on a router constitutes a broadcast domain because routers don't forward broadcast packets. TCP/IP communication relies heavily on broadcast packets to perform a variety of functions. For example, DHCP and ARP use broadcasts to perform their tasks. Every time a computer receives a broadcast packet, the NIC generates an interrupt, causing the CPU to stop what it's doing to read the packet. If the broadcast isn't relevant to the computer, the packet is usually discarded.

Now imagine 65,000 computers on the same broadcast domain; at any moment, probably several thousand are sending broadcast packets. The amount of traffic generated and the additional CPU utilization would likely bring the network to a screeching halt. Preventing this problem is one of the reasons you might want to subnet.

Subnetting

If you do have 65,000 computers in your organization, instead of creating one large network with the network address 172.31.0.0/16, you can divide this very large network into many smaller **subnets**. For example, you can use 172.31.0.0/24, 172.31.1.0/24, and so forth up to

172.31.255.0/24. This addressing strategy, called **subnetting**, makes 256 smaller subnets with a maximum of 2^8 - 2, or 254, devices per subnet. If a computer on one subnet needs to communicate with a computer on another subnet, the packets are sent to a router that locates the subnet and forwards the data. Now the maximum size of your broadcast domain is only 254 computers, which is more manageable.

 When a classful network has been divided or subnetted into multiple smaller networks, the resulting networks are called "subnets." Functionally, however, there's no difference between a classful network and a subnet.

Another reason to subnet is to conserve IP addresses. Companies that maintain Internet-connected devices need public Internet addresses, which must be unique in the world—meaning a public address can be assigned to only one device on the Internet. In the past, if a company had four Web servers and two routers that needed public addresses, the only recourse an ISP had was to assign a class C network address consisting of 254 possible host addresses, thereby wasting 248 addresses. By subnetting a network, the ISP can assign an address such as 198.60.123.0/29 that uses only addresses 198.60.123.0 through 198.60.123.7, which satisfies the company's needs and still makes addresses 198.60.123.8 through 198.60.123.254 available for other customers.

A third reason to subnet is to divide a network into logical groups. When one large network is divided into two or more smaller subnets, a router is needed to allow hosts on one subnet to communicate with hosts on another subnet. A router serves as a natural security barrier between the two subnets because access control lists can be configured on it to restrict the type of network traffic traveling from one subnet to another. Being able to restrict access enables network administrators to, for example, place the Payroll Department computers and servers on their own subnet and disallow computers from other subnets to access any resources in the Payroll Department.

Calculating a Subnet Mask

There are usually two approaches to subnetting, and they depend on the answer to these questions: Am I subnetting to provide a network with a certain number of host addresses? Or am I subnetting to provide a network with a certain number of subnets? If you're working for an ISP, the answer is usually yes to the first question, and if you're a network administrator for an organization, the answer is more apt to be yes to the second question. Sometimes the answer is a combination of both.

Say you have a large internetwork and need to break an IP address space into several subnets. Follow this process:

1. First, decide how many subnets you need. You can figure out the number of subnets needed by seeing how many network cable segments are or will be connected to router interfaces. Each router interface connection indicates a required subnet.

2. Next, decide how many bits you need to meet or exceed the number of required subnets. To calculate this value, use the formula 2^n, with n representing the number of bits you must reallocate from the host ID to the network ID. For example, if your starting network number is the Class B address 172.20.0.0, its default subnet mask is

255.255.0.0, which is your starting point. The number of subnets you create is always a power of 2, so if you need 20 subnets, you must reallocate 5 bits ($2^5 = 32$) because reallocating 4 bits gives you only 2^4, or 16, subnets.

3. Reallocate bits from the host ID, starting from the most significant host bit (that is, from the left side of the host ID).

4. You must also make sure you have enough host bits available to assign to computers on each subnet. To determine the number of host addresses available, use the formula discussed previously: $2^n - 2$, with n representing the number of host (0) bits in the subnet mask.

Here's an example to help you put this formula to work: CSM Tech Publishing wants 60 subnets for its Class B address: 172.20.0.0/16. The nearest power of 2 to 60 is 64, which equals 2^6. This means you must reallocate 6 bits from the host portion of the original subnet mask (255.255.0.0) and make them subnet bits.

Reallocating 6 bits, starting from the leftmost bit of the third octet, creates a subnet mask with the bit pattern 11111100. The decimal value for this number is 252. This reallocating of bits changes the subnet mask from 255.255.0.0 to 255.255.**252**.0. Expressing it in CIDR notation gives you 172.20.0.0/22.

To calculate the number of host addresses for each subnet, just subtract the number of network ID bits from the total number of bits in an IP address: 32 - 22. The result is the number of bits left for the host ID. In this case, the number is 10. Again, the formula for determining the number of host addresses is $2^n - 2$, so you have $2^{10} - 2 = 1022$ addresses per subnet, which should be more than enough for most networks.

Now that you have a correct subnet mask, you need to determine what network numbers can be derived from using it. To do this, take the reallocated 6 bits, place them in the network number, and cycle the 6 bits through the possible combinations of values they represent. Table 6-5 shows the first 16 subnetwork numbers resulting from the preceding steps, with the third octet written in binary on the left and the resulting subnetwork address written in decimal on the right. The bits shown in bold are the 6 bits used to create the subnets. If you convert the third octet on the left side from binary to decimal, you'll see that it equals the third octet on the right.

Table 6-5   Subnetwork numbers and addresses

Subnetwork number in binary	Subnetwork address
172.20.**000000**00.0	172.20.0.0
172.20.**000001**00.0	172.20.4.0
172.20.**000010**00.0	172.20.8.0
172.20.**000011**00.0	172.20.12.0
172.20.**000100**00.0	172.20.16.0
172.20.**000101**00.0	172.20.20.0
172.20.**000110**00.0	172.20.24.0
172.20.**000111**00.0	172.20.28.0
172.20.**001000**00.0	172.20.32.0

(Continues)

Table 6-5   Subnetwork numbers and addresses (continued)

Subnetwork number in binary	Subnetwork address
172.20.**00100100**.0	172.20.36.0
172.20.**00101000**.0	172.20.40.0
172.20.**00101100**.0	172.20.44.0
172.20.**00110000**.0	172.20.48.0
172.20.**00110100**.0	172.20.52.0
172.20.**00111000**.0	172.20.56.0
172.20.**00111100**.0	172.20.60.0
...	...
172.20.**11111100**.0	172.20.252.0

A Pattern Emerges   Table 6-5 shows the first 16 of the possible 64 subnets and the last subnet created for network 172.20.0.0. As you can see, there's a pattern to the subnetwork numbers—they go in increments of 4. You can derive this pattern without having to list the subnets, however. Look at the octet where the subnet bits are reallocated, and then look at the rightmost reallocated bit. The subnet increment is determined by the binary place value of this bit: in this case, the 4s place.

You know when to stop counting subnets when all the subnet bits are binary 1s, as in the last entry in the table. You also know to stop counting when the subnet number equals the value of the changed octet in the subnet mask. In this case, the subnet mask 255.255.0.0 was changed to 255.255.252.0 after the bit reallocation. The 252 in the third octet of the subnet mask is the same value as the last subnet number.

Determining Host Addresses   Similarly, the host addresses in each subnet can be determined by cycling through the host bits. Therefore, the subnetwork 172.20.32.0 would have host addresses from 172.20.32.0 through 172.20.35.255. However, you can't use the IP address in which all host bits are 0s or 1s, so the actual range is 172.20.32.1 through 172.20.35.254, giving you 1022 host addresses. Table 6-6 shows this for the first five subnets and the last subnet.

Table 6-6   Host addresses per subnet

Subnetwork number	Beginning and ending host addresses in binary	Beginning and ending host addresses in decimal
172.20.0.0	172.20.**00000000**.00000001–172.20.**00000011**.11111110	172.20.0.1–172.20.3.254
172.20.4.0	172.20.**00000100**.00000001–172.20.**00000111**.11111110	172.20.4.1–172.20.7.254
172.20.8.0	172.20.**00001000**.00000001–172.20.**00001011**.11111110	172.20.8.1–172.20.11.254
172.20.12.0	172.20.**00001100**.00000001–172.20.**00001111**.11111110	172.20.12.1–172.20.15.254
172.20.16.0	172.20.**00010000**.00000001–172.20.**00010011**.11111110	172.20.16.1–172.20.19.254
...		...
172.20.252.0	172.20.**11111100**.00000001–172.20.**11111111**.11111110	172.20.252.1–172.20.255.254

Another Subnet Mask Example In Figure 6-2, the network number is 192.168.100.0, which is a Class C network address with the default subnet mask 255.255.255.0.

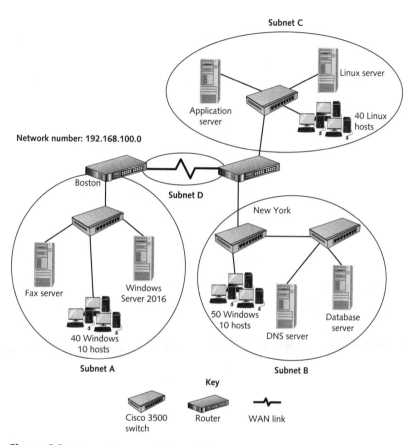

Figure 6-2 A sample network for calculating subnet mask requirements

The following steps show how to calculate a new subnet mask:

1. In this example, you can see that four cable segments are connected to router inter-faces. The WAN cable segment between the two routers counts as a single cable segment and, therefore, a single subnet. You have to account for the WAN subnet even if the network has no hosts because the router interfaces require an IP address. As you can see, there are four subnets. Subnet A requires 43 IP addresses (40 for the Windows 10 hosts, 2 for the servers, and 1 for the router interface). Subnet B requires 53 IP addresses, subnet C requires 43 IP addresses, and subnet D requires only 2 IP addresses.

2. To accommodate the required number of subnets (4), you need a power of 2 that's equal to or greater than 4. Because $2^2 = 4$, you need to reallocate 2 bits from the host ID to the network ID.

3. Reallocating 2 bits from the leftmost part of the host portion of the original subnet mask (255.255.255.0) gives the last octet of your new subnet mask the bit pattern 11000000. Converting to decimal and putting the entire subnet mask together yields 255.255.255.192.

4. To be sure you have enough host bits per subnet, use the formula $2^n - 2$, with n representing the number of 0 bits in the new subnet mask. The result is $2^6 - 2 = 62$. This number of host addresses satisfies your requirement of a maximum of 53 hosts per subnet.

Calculating a Subnet Mask Based on Needed Host Addresses Sometimes you need to know what prefix to assign an IP network based on the number of host addresses required for the network. This process is fairly straightforward. Suppose you're told that you need to determine the subnet mask to use with network ID 172.16.16.0, and the network will support 60 hosts. In this problem, simply determine how many host bits are needed to support the number of hosts specified, and subtract this number from 32, giving you the number of bits in the network ID. For this example of 60 hosts, you need 6 bits for the host ID because $2^6 = 64$, which is the closest power of 2 to 60. Therefore, the prefix is $32 - 6 = 26$, so in CIDR notation, the network ID is 172.16.16.0/26. Examine the examples in Table 6-7 to become more comfortable with this process.

Table 6-7 Examples for determining the correct CIDR notation

Network ID	Required hosts	Host bits required	Network ID bits	CIDR notation
10.19.32.0	900	10 ($2^{10} = 1024$)	22	10.19.32.0/22
172.25.110.0	505	9 ($2^9 = 512$)	23	172.25.110.0/23
192.168.100.32	28	5 ($2^5 = 32$)	27	192.168.100.32/27

To learn more about this topic and get plenty of subnetting practice problems, go to *www.subnetting.net*.

Hands-On Project 6-3: Working with CIDR Notation

Time Required: 20 minutes

Objective: Determine the subnet mask, number of host bits, and number of hosts for network numbers in CIDR notation.

Required Tools and Equipment: Paper and pencil

Description: Examine the IP addresses/prefixes specified in CIDR notation, and fill in the resulting subnet mask, number of host bits, and number of hosts possible in the network. The first row is completed for you, and the next two are partially completed.

Network/prefix	Subnet mask	Host bits	Number of hosts
172.16.1.0/24	255.255.255.0	8	254
10.1.100.128/26	255.255.255.192	6	
10.1.96.0/19	255.255.224.0		8190
192.168.1.0/24			
172.31.0.0/16			
10.255.255.252/30			
172.28.240.0/20			
10.44.108.0/22			
192.168.100.24/21			
172.23.64.0/18			
192.168.5.128/25			

Hands-On Project 6-4: Determining the Correct Prefix

Time Required: 20 minutes

Objective: Determine the correct prefix, given the required number of hosts per network.

Required Tools and Equipment: Paper and pencil

Description: Given the IP address and number of hosts in the first two columns, determine the number of host bits required and write the network number with the correct prefix. The first one is completed for you, and the next two are partially completed.

Network ID	Required hosts	Host bits needed	Network ID/prefix
172.16.1.0	254	8	172.16.1.0/24
10.1.100.128	62	6	
10.1.96.0	8190		10.1.96.0/19
192.168.1.0	200		
172.31.0.0	65,000		
10.255.255.252	2		
172.28.240.0	4000		
10.44.108.0	900		
192.168.240.0	2200		
172.23.64.0	16,000		
192.168.5.128	110		

Supernetting

Although not practiced as commonly as subnetting, **supernetting** is sometimes necessary to solve certain network configuration problems and to make routing tables more streamlined. When talking about routing tables, supernetting is usually referred to as "route aggregation" or "route summarization." Supernetting reallocates bits from the network portion of an IP address to the host portion, effectively making two or more smaller subnets a larger supernet. Supernets allow combining two or more consecutive IP network addresses and make them function as a single logical network. Here's how it works:

1. Suppose you have four Class C network addresses—192.168.0.0, 192.168.1.0, 192.168.2.0, and 192.168.3.0—available for your network design. You have a total of 900 hosts on your proposed network. You don't have four router interfaces that can use the four different network numbers, however. You can combine the four networks into one by reallocating 2 bits ($2^2 = 4$) from the network portion of the address and adding them to the host portion. You then have a network address of 192.168.0.0 with the subnet mask 255.255.252.0. The 252 in the third octet is derived from setting the last 2 bits of the original Class C subnet mask (255.255.255.0) to 0, thereby making them part of the host portion.

2. Instead of supporting only 8 bits for the host address portion, the supernet now supports 10 bits (8 + 2) for host addresses. This number of bits provides $2^{10} - 2$ host addresses on this supernet, or 1022, which satisfies your requirement for 900 hosts and allows you to assign all host addresses in a single network.

As mentioned, combining two or more small networks into one larger network is only one reason to supernet. Routers on the Internet can have enormous routing tables. The larger the routing table, the more work the router must do to determine where to send a packet. Route aggregation or summarization can combine multiple routing table entries into a single entry, which can drastically decrease the table's size on Internet routers. This reduction in routing table size increases routers' speed and efficiency. The procedure is similar to supernetting, except you configure routers.

Routing tables grow partly because routers communicate with one another by sending information about their routing tables to one another. If several networks can be represented by a single routing table entry, the routing tables are more efficient. Taking the previous example, suppose RouterA in a company network has the network addresses 192.168.0.0, 192.168.1.0, 192.168.2.0, and 192.168.3.0 in its routing table, and it communicates with RouterB (see Figure 6-3). Without supernetting/route summarization, RouterA sends all four network addresses to RouterB, each with its 255.255.255.0 subnet mask. Consequently, RouterB's routing table expands with these four additional routes. However, because all four routes lead to the same place (RouterA), these routes can be represented by a single entry. RouterA can summarize these routes by simply sending RouterB the address 192.168.0.0 with subnet mask 255.255.252.0, which tells RouterB that all networks from 192.168.0.0 through 192.168.3.0 can be reached through RouterA.

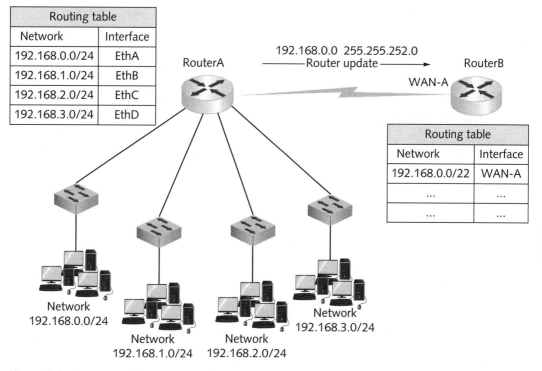

Figure 6-3 RouterA sends a summary of its routing table to RouterB

Configuring IPv4 Addresses

When you assign a computer an IP address, there are some rules to remember:

- A host can be assigned an IP address only in the range of Class A, Class B, or Class C addresses.
- Every IP address configuration must have a subnet mask.
- All hosts on the same network must have the same network ID in their IP addresses. The term "network" in this case means a group of computers connected to one or more switches (or access points), not separated by a router. Put another way, all computers are in the same broadcast domain.
- All host IDs on the same network must be unique.
- You can't assign an IP address in which all the host ID bits are binary 0. This type of IP address is reserved as the network ID. For example, IP address 10.1.0.0 with subnet mask 255.255.0.0 is reserved to identify network 10.1.
- You can't assign an IP address in which all the host ID bits are binary 1. This type of IP address is reserved as the network broadcast address. For example, IP address 10.1.255.255 with subnet mask 255.255.0.0 has all host ID bits set to binary 1 and is reserved as the broadcast address for the 10.1.0.0 network.

- Computers assigned different network IDs can communicate only by sending packets to a router, which forwards the packets to the destination network.

- The default gateway address assigned to a computer must have the same network ID as that computer. For example, if a computer's IP address is 10.1.0.100 with subnet mask 255.255.0.0, the default gateway address must be in the 10.1.0.0 network.

Configuring Multiple IP Addresses

Windows OSs allow assigning multiple IP addresses to a single network connection in the Advanced TCP/IP Settings dialog box shown in Figure 6-4. As long as the address isn't assigned via DHCP, you can click the Add button and enter a new IP address and subnet mask. Multiple IP addresses can be useful in these situations:

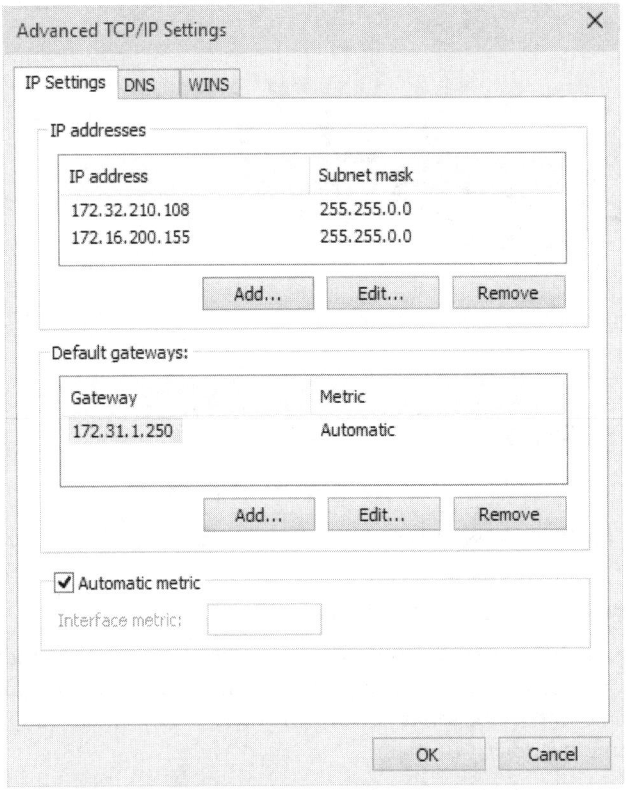

Figure 6-4   The Advanced TCP/IP Settings dialog box

- The computer is hosting a service that must be accessed by using different addresses. For example, a Web server can host multiple Web sites, each assigned a different IP address and domain name.

- The computer is connected to a physical network that hosts multiple IP networks. This situation can occur if your network addressing scheme is transitioning from one network ID to another, and you need a server to be available to both the old and the new IP networks until the transition is completed. It can also occur when you have multiple groups of computers (or hosts and virtual machines) connected to the same physical network but with different network addresses. If all the computers need access to server resources, the servers can be configured with IP addresses to serve all the IP networks.

 When multiple IP addresses are assigned to a Windows computer that uses a Windows DNS server supporting Dynamic DNS (the default DNS server configuration), the DNS server has a host entry for each IP address assigned to the computer.

You also have to configure more than one IP address on servers with multiple NICs, which are called "multihomed servers" (discussed later in "Using Multihomed Servers").

Configuring the Default Gateway

Almost all IP address configurations require a default gateway address. The default gateway, which is usually a router or a computer configured to act as a router, tells the computer where packets destined for another network should be sent. By definition, the default gateway's address must have the same network ID as the host's network ID.

Using the Subnet Mask to Know When to Send Packets to the Default Gateway So how does a computer know from the address whether the destination computer is on a different network? Is the address 172.19.44.211 on a different network from 172.19.46.188? The only way to know is by consulting the subnet mask. Using these two addresses, take a look at the sample network shown in Figure 6-5.

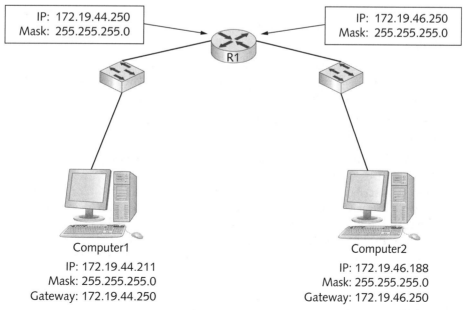

Figure 6-5 Determining the destination computer's network address with the subnet mask

Here's what happens when Computer1 has a packet to send to Computer2:

1. Computer1 must first know its network address. It determines this by doing a logical AND operation between its IP address and subnet mask, which results in the network address 172.19.44.0.

2. The next step is to determine whether Computer2's address is on the same network or a different network. The same AND calculation is done between Computer2's IP address and Computer1's subnet mask. (Computer1 has no way of knowing Computer2's subnet mask.) The resulting network address is 172.19.46.0.

3. Because Computer2 is on a different network, Computer1 knows that the packet must be sent to the router, which forwards it to Computer2's network.

Using Multiple Default Gateways You can configure multiple default gateways in the Advanced TCP/IP Settings dialog box, and then Windows attempts to select the gateway with the best metric automatically. A **metric** is a value assigned to the gateway based on the speed of the interface used to access the gateway. Multiple gateways provide fault tolerance to a computer, so if the primary default gateway is no longer responding, Windows switches to another gateway. By using a feature called "fail-back," Windows attempts periodically to communicate with the original default gateway. If the original gateway comes back online, Windows switches back to it.

Using Multihomed Servers A **multihomed server** has two or more NICs, each attached to a different IP network. Each NIC is assigned a network connection and requires its own IP address for the network it's connected to. This configuration can be used in the following situations:

- A server is accessed by internal clients (clients on the network) and external clients (clients on the Internet or an extranet). For example, you have a server for services such as file and printer sharing, DHCP, and DNS that also acts as a public Web server.

- A server provides resources for computers on multiple subnets of the network. Interfaces can be configured for each subnet, which provides more throughput than is possible with a single NIC.

- A server is configured as a router or virtual private network (VPN) server. Both functions often use multiple NICs.

For network connections to a LAN, Windows uses names such as Ethernet0, Ethernet1, and so forth, which aren't very descriptive. If a computer has two NICs, renaming each network connection to describe the network it connects to is recommended. For example, if a server is connected to internal and external networks, you might name one connection LAN-Internal and the other LAN-External. If the server is connected to two internal networks, you could use the network address in the names, such as LAN-172.31 and LAN-172.16. To rename a connection, right-click it in the Network Connections window and click Rename.

When a server is multihomed, it's usually connected to two physical as well as logical networks. Typically, each physical network has a router. Simply configuring a default gateway for each interface might be tempting. However, Windows always chooses only one default gateway for sending packets to remote networks. For example, a server could receive a packet through an interface connected to the internal network and send the reply to the default gateway on the external network. You probably don't want this to happen. To solve this problem, you can use the `route` command, explained in the next section.

Using the `route` Command   Windows computers maintain a routing table that dictates where a packet should be sent, based on the packet's destination address. The `route.exe` command-line program enables you to display and alter the routing table's contents. Figure 6-6 shows partial results of the `route print` command, which displays the contents of the routing table.

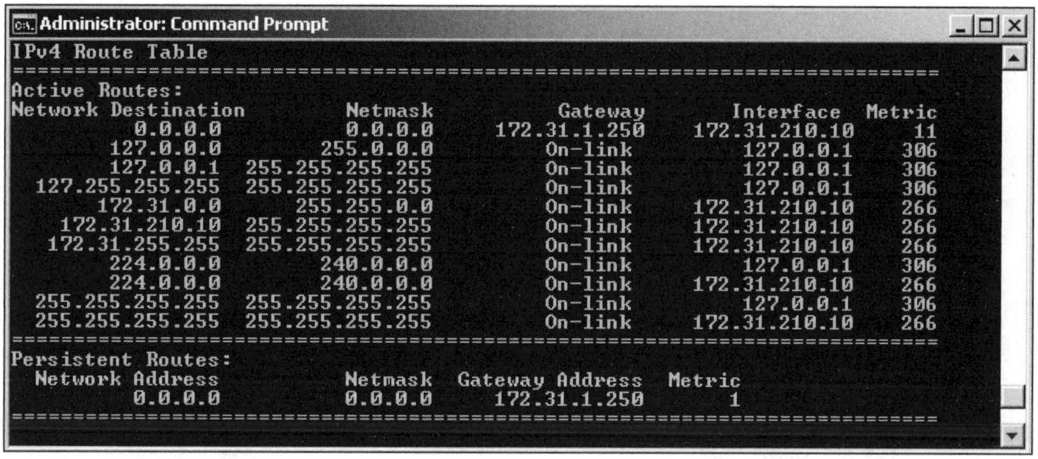

```
Administrator: Command Prompt                                          _ □ ×
IPv4 Route Table
===========================================================================
Active Routes:
Network Destination        Netmask          Gateway       Interface  Metric
          0.0.0.0          0.0.0.0     172.31.1.250    172.31.210.10      11
        127.0.0.0        255.0.0.0         On-link        127.0.0.1     306
        127.0.0.1  255.255.255.255         On-link        127.0.0.1     306
  127.255.255.255  255.255.255.255         On-link        127.0.0.1     306
       172.31.0.0      255.255.0.0         On-link    172.31.210.10     266
    172.31.210.10  255.255.255.255         On-link    172.31.210.10     266
   172.31.255.255  255.255.255.255         On-link    172.31.210.10     266
        224.0.0.0        240.0.0.0         On-link        127.0.0.1     306
        224.0.0.0        240.0.0.0         On-link    172.31.210.10     266
  255.255.255.255  255.255.255.255         On-link        127.0.0.1     306
  255.255.255.255  255.255.255.255         On-link    172.31.210.10     266
===========================================================================
Persistent Routes:
  Network Address          Netmask  Gateway Address  Metric
          0.0.0.0          0.0.0.0     172.31.1.250       1
===========================================================================
```

Figure 6-6   Results of the `route print` command

These results are displayed in five columns. The first column, Network Destination, is a network number compared against an IP packet's destination address. The Netmask column displays the subnet mask associated with the network destination. The Gateway column is the address of the router where packets with a destination address matching the network destination should be forwarded. The Interface column is the address of the NIC the packet should be sent through to reach the gateway. The Metric column is the value assigned to the route. If the routing table contains two or more entries that can reach the same destination, the one with the lowest metric is chosen.

In this figure, the entry with the network destination 0.0.0.0 and the netmask 0.0.0.0 indicates the default route or default gateway. A packet with a destination address that doesn't match any entries in the routing table is forwarded to the gateway address in the default route entry—in this case, 172.31.1.250. A gateway specified as "on-link" simply means the network destination is a network connected directly to one of the computer's interfaces. All Network Destination entries beginning with 127 indicate the computer's loopback address, which means "this computer." The Network Destination entries starting with 224 are multicast addresses, and entries starting with 255 are broadcast addresses. All packets with a multicast or broadcast destination address are sent to the local network, not to a router.

The route command can also be used to change the routing table. For instance, a multi-homed computer might have two or more possibilities for a default gateway. Best practices dictate configuring only one interface with a default gateway. However, suppose you have a server connected to two networks: 192.168.1.0/24 and 172.16.208.0/24, as shown in Figure 6-7. The 192.168.1.0 network connects to the Internet, and the 172.16.208.0 network is part of the internal network and is also connected to networks 172.16.200.0/24 through 172.16.207.0/24. In addition, the 192.168.1.0 network has no possible way to get to the 172.16 networks.

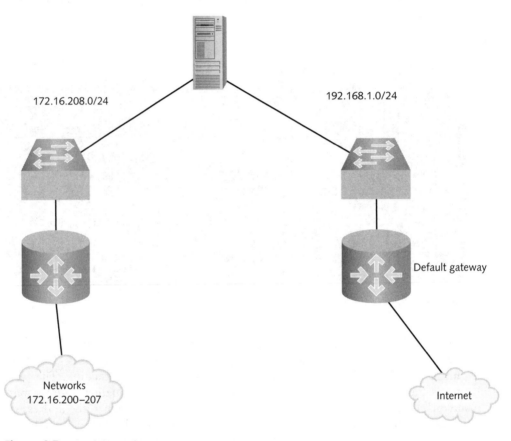

172.16.208.0/24

192.168.1.0/24

Default gateway

Networks
172.16.200–207

Internet

Figure 6-7 A multihomed server

If your default gateway is configured on the 192.168.1.0 network (as it should, because it's connected to the Internet), when your server replies to a packet from the 172.16.200.0 to 172.16.207.0 networks, it sends the reply out the 192.168.1.0 interface because that's where the default gateway is. Remember that by default, the routing table contains entries only for networks the computer is directly connected to plus the default route. So the server doesn't have an entry for the 172.16 networks, except 172.16.208.0. Any packets sent to these networks go to the default gateway, which can't deliver them to the destination network. To solve this problem, you can add routes to the routing table by using the following command:

```
route add 172.16.200.0 mask 255.255.255.0 172.16.208.250
```

This command creates a routing table entry for the 172.16.200.0 network with the subnet mask 255.255.255.0 and the gateway 172.16.208.250, which is the router on your server's network. You could make eight entries, one for each remote network, or a single entry, as shown:

```
route add 172.16.200.0 mask 255.255.248.0 172.16.208.250
```

This entry consolidates networks 172.16.200.0 through 172.16.207.0 into a single entry by using a modified subnet mask (the supernetting technique discussed previously). You use the `route` command in Chapter 8.

IP Configuration Command-Line Tools

Several command-line tools are available to help you troubleshoot, display, and configure IP addresses and related TCP/IP settings on a Windows computer. This section examines the following tools:

- `netsh`
- `ipconfig`
- `ping`
- `arp`
- `tracert`
- `nslookup`

Other network configuration and troubleshooting tools are available, but they're typically used to verify correct IP configuration settings and connectivity.

Using `netsh` You can use the `netsh` command for a wide variety of network configuration tasks, such as firewall configuration and IP address configuration. To see a list of `netsh` commands, type `netsh /?` at the command prompt. To configure the IP address of an interface named Ethernet0 to 10.1.1.1/16, use this command:

```
netsh interface ipv4 set address "Ethernet0"
   static 10.1.1.1 255.255.0.0
```

You can include the default gateway by adding the address to the end of the command:

```
netsh interface ipv4 set address "Ethernet0"
   static 10.1.1.1 255.255.0.0 10.1.1.250
```

To set the primary DNS server for the computer to 10.1.1.100, use the following command:

```
netsh interface ipv4 set dns "Ethernet0" static 10.1.1.100 primary
```

The `netsh` command has many options that are useful for network configuration tasks. You should spend some time with this command to discover what you can do with it.

Using `ipconfig` As you've learned, `ipconfig` is usually used to display a computer's IP address settings but can perform other tasks, depending on the options included:

- *No options*—Displays the basic IP configuration, including the IP address, subnet mask, and default gateway.

- `/all`—Displays extended IP configuration information, such as the computer name, domain name, network adapter description, physical (MAC) address, use of DHCP, and DNS address.

- `/release`—Releases the IP address back to the DHCP server if DHCP is used. If the address is released, the computer is assigned the invalid address of 0.0.0.0.

- `/renew`—Renews the IP address configuration lease.

- `/displaydns`—Windows caches the most recent DNS lookup request results, and this option displays the contents of the local DNS cache. If a computer recently did a DNS lookup for *www.cengage.com*, for example, it keeps that information in local memory so that the next time the address is needed, a DNS query is unnecessary.

- `/flushdns`—Deletes cached DNS information from memory. This option can be useful if a computer's IP address or hostname was changed recently, and the cache contains obsolete information.

- `/registerdns`—Requests new DHCP leases and registers these names again with a DNS server.

Using `ping` You have used `ping` to test connectivity between two computers. It sends an ICMP Echo Request packet to the destination IP address specified in the command. If the destination computer receives the ICMP Echo Request, it replies with an ICMP Echo Reply packet. When the computer receives the reply packet, the `ping` command displays a message similar to this one:

`reply from 192.168.100.201: bytes=32 time=<1ms TTL=128`

In this output, the IP address is the address of the computer that sent the reply. The `bytes=32` parameter specifies how many data bytes are in the ICMP message. You can change the number of data bytes with options in the `ping` command. The `time=<1ms` parameter indicates that the reply took less than a millisecond from the time the ICMP Echo Request was sent. The `TTL=128` indicates the message's time to live, which specifies how many routers a packet can go through before the packet should be expired and discarded. At each router, the TTL is decremented. If the TTL reaches 0, the router sends the source computer a message indicating that the TTL expired before reaching its destination.

To see the options available with this command, type `ping /?` at a command prompt. Some of the options are as follows:

- `-t`—Sends ICMP Echo Request packets until you press Ctrl+C to stop. By default, `ping` sends four packets.

- `-a`—Tries to resolve the IP address to a hostname. If the name can be resolved, it's printed in the first line of the ping output.

- `-n count`—The *count* parameter is the number of Echo Request packets to send.

- `-l size`—The *size* parameter is the number of data bytes to send in each Echo Request packet. The default is 32 bytes.

- `-i TTL`—Time to live is the number of routers the packet can go through on the way to the destination before the packet should be expired.

Using arp The arp command displays or makes changes to the Address Resolution Protocol (ARP) cache, which contains IP address–MAC address pairs. As discussed, when an IP packet is sent to a destination on the local network, the sending device must have the destination's MAC address. The source computer retrieves the MAC address by sending a broadcast ARP request packet to the local network. The ARP request packet essentially asks "Who has IP address A.B.C.D?" The computer on the local network that's assigned the IP address sends an ARP reply message containing its MAC address. When a computer learns another computer's MAC address, it keeps the address in its ARP cache temporarily so that it doesn't have to send another ARP request packet to communicate with that computer again. Entries in the ARP cache are kept for only a few minutes to prevent them from becoming obsolete. Some options for the arp command are as follows:

- -a *or* -g—Displays the contents of the ARP cache. These options perform the same function.

- -d—Deletes the entire contents of the ARP cache or a single entry specified by IP address. This option can be useful if a computer's NIC has changed recently, and the cache contains obsolete information.

- -s—Adds a permanent entry to the ARP cache by specifying a host's IP address and MAC address. This option should be used only if the address of a frequently accessed computer is unlikely to change. Remember that if the NIC is changed on a computer, its MAC address changes, too.

Using tracert The tracert command is usually called "trace route" because it displays the route packets take between two computers. It displays the address or DNS name of each router a packet travels through to reach the specified destination. It then sends a series of three ICMP Echo Request packets with a TTL value starting at 1 and increases the value until the destination is reached. Each router a packet encounters along the way to the destination decrements the TTL value by 1. If the TTL value reaches 0, the router sends a TTL-expired message back to the sending computer and drops the packet. When tracert receives the TTL-expired message, it records the sending router's IP address and the time to receive a reply and displays this information. Next, a new series of three ICMP Echo Request packets is sent with an incremented TTL value. This procedure continues until all routers between the source and destination have been recorded.

Tracert is useful for troubleshooting the routing topology of a complex network and finding the bottleneck between a computer and a destination network. Because it displays the time it took to receive a reply from each router, a router (or the link to this router) showing an inordinately long delay might be where the bottleneck lies.

Using nslookup The nslookup command is used to test and troubleshoot DNS operation and can be used in command mode or interactive mode. In command mode, you type nslookup *host*; *host* is the name of a computer in the local domain or a fully qualified domain name. Nslookup replies with the specified host's IP address. By default, it uses the DNS server address configured in the IP address settings. Following are some examples of using it in command mode:

```
nslookup server99
nslookup www.yahoo.com
nslookup www.google.com 172.31.1.200
```

The first two commands query the default DNS server. The last command queries a DNS server at address 172.31.1.200. Because you can specify a different DNS server, you can compare the results of different DNS servers to verify correct DNS operation.

To use interactive mode, type `nslookup` at the command prompt, and the output shows which server it's using to perform lookups. You can type a question mark at the interactive mode prompt to get a list of available options and commands.

Hands-On Project 6-5: Using the `netsh` Command

Time Required: 10 minutes

Objective: Use the `netsh` command to change IP address settings.

Required Tools and Equipment: Net-*XX*

Description: In this project, you use `netsh` to view and change your IP address settings.

1. Start Net-*XX* and log on as **NetAdmin**. Open an elevated command prompt window by right-clicking **Start** and clicking **Command Prompt (Admin)**. In the UAC message box, click **Yes**.

2. Type **netsh /?** and press **Enter** to see the available options for the `netsh` command. Type **netsh interface ipv4 show addresses** and press **Enter**. You see IPv4 configuration information for your interfaces. Notice that the loopback interface is included with the address 127.0.0.1.

3. Type **netsh interface ipv6 show addresses** and press **Enter**. You see information about IPv6 configuration. Make a note of your IP address and default gateway:

_____

4. To change your IP address to use DHCP, type **netsh interface ipv4 set address "Ethernet0" dhcp** and press **Enter**.

5. Type **netsh interface ipv4 show addresses** and press **Enter**. You see that the address has changed. If you don't have a DHCP server on the network, your computer assigns itself an APIPA address.

6. To change back to the original settings, type **netsh interface ipv4 set address "Ethernet0" static 192.168.100.XX 255.255.255.0 192.168.100.250** (replacing *XX* with your student number) and press **Enter**. (If these settings aren't correct for your network, ask your instructor what settings to use.)

7. Stay logged on to your computer if you're continuing to the next project.

Hands-On Project 6-6: Trying to Set an Invalid IP Address

Time Required: 10 minutes

Objective: Try to set an invalid IP address in Windows.

Required Tools and Equipment: Net-*XX*

Description: In this project, you use the Network Connection Properties dialog box to try to set an invalid IP address–subnet mask combination.

1. Log on Net-*XX* as **NetAdmin**, if necessary. Right-click **Start** and click **Network Connections**.

2. Right-click **Ethernet0** and click **Properties**. Double-click **Internet Protocol Version 4 (TCP/IPv4)**.

3. Make a note of your current IP address settings. In the IP address text box, type **192.168.100.0**, and in the Subnet mask text box, type **255.255.255.0**. Click **OK**. You see a message stating that the IP address and subnet mask combination is invalid because all the host bits are set to 0. Click **OK**.

4. In the IP address text box, type **192.168.100.16**, and in the Subnet mask text box, type **255.255.255.240**. Click **OK**. Again, you see a message stating that the IP address and subnet mask combination is invalid because all the host bits are set to 0. The *255.255.255.240* subnet mask specifies that there are 28 bits in the network ID and only 4 host bits. If you do a binary conversion on the last octet (16), you see that the last 4 bits are 0. Click **OK**.

5. In the IP address text box, type **192.168.100.255**, and in the Subnet mask text box, type **255.255.255.0**. Click **OK**. Now you see a message stating that the IP address and subnet mask combination is invalid because all the host bits are set to 1. Click **OK**.

6. In the IP address text box, type **192.168.100.63**, and in the Subnet mask text box, type **255.255.255.224**. Click **OK**. Again, you see a message stating that the IP address and subnet mask combination is invalid because all the host bits are set to 1. If you convert 63 to binary, you find that it's 00111111. Because the network ID is 27 bits, all 5 bits of the host ID are set to binary 1. Click **OK**.

7. Change the IP address back to the original settings, and click **OK** twice. Close all open windows. Stay logged on to your computer if you're continuing to the next project.

The `netsh` command allows you to enter invalid IP address–subnet mask combinations. If you do so, however, your computer can't communicate by using TCP/IP.

Network Address Translation

Although subnetting can alleviate the IP address shortage problem, it simply makes more efficient use of existing addresses. **Network Address Translation (NAT)** helps more by allowing an organization to use private IP addresses while connected to the Internet. As you've learned, the three ranges of private IP addresses (one range for each class) can't be used as source or destination addresses in packets on the Internet.

Anyone can use private IP addresses for address assignment to internal computers and devices, and because the addresses aren't sent to the Internet, there's no address conflict. What if you want your computers to have access to the Internet, however? That's where NAT comes in. For example, an organization with 1000 workstations can assign all its workstations' addresses in the 10.x.x.x private network. Although these addresses can't be used on the Internet, the NAT process translates a workstation address (as a packet leaves the organization's network) into a valid public Internet address. When data returns to the workstation, the address is translated back to the original 10.x.x.x address. NAT is usually handled by a network device that connects the organization to the Internet, such as a router. As shown in Figure 6-8, when station 10.0.0.1 sends a packet to the Internet, the NAT router intercepts the packet and replaces its source address with 198.60.123.101 (a public Internet address). When a reply comes back addressed to 198.60.123.101, the NAT router replaces the destination address with 10.0.0.1.

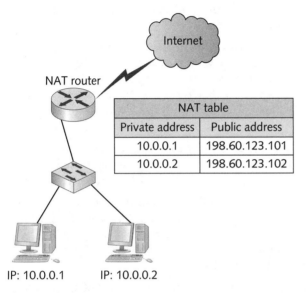

Figure 6-8   Private addresses translated to public addresses with NAT

This process allows any company to use private IP addresses in its own network and requires a public IP address only when a workstation attempts to access the Internet. NAT reduces the number of public IP addresses needed because a public address is required only if a computer accesses the Internet. NAT does have a drawback, in that one public address is required for every private address. However, it's usually used only for Web servers and other devices that must be accessed through the Internet.

An extension of NAT, called **Port Address Translation** (**PAT**), allows several hundred workstations to access the Internet with a single public Internet address. This process relies on each packet containing not only source and destination IP addresses, but also source and destination TCP or UDP port numbers. With PAT, the address is translated into a single public IP address for all workstations, but a different source port number (which can be any value from 1024 to 65,535) is used for each communication session, allowing a NAT device to differentiate between workstations. The typical router used in home and small business networks is already configured to use PAT.

Figure 6-9 shows an example of how PAT is used. Notice that the public address is the same for both entries; only the port number differs. When an Internet server responds to 198.60.123.100 on port 3105, however, the router knows to translate the destination address in the packet to 10.0.0.2 port 12441. Notice also that the public address in the NAT/PAT table is the same as the router's Internet-connected interface. Although this configuration isn't necessary, it's common in home and small office routers. Simulation 10 is an animation of how NAT and PAT work.

NAT/PAT table	
Private address: Port	Public address: Port
10.0.0.1:2562	198.60.123.100:5311
10.0.0.2:12441	198.60.123.100:3105

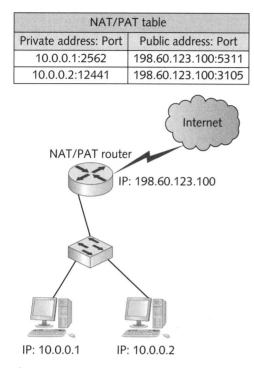

NAT/PAT router

IP: 198.60.123.100

IP: 10.0.0.1   IP: 10.0.0.2

Figure 6-9 PAT uses the port number to allow using a single public IP address

Simulation 10: Demonstrating NAT/PAT

For an excellent tutorial on NAT, see *www.howstuffworks. com/nat.htm.*

Internet Protocol Version 6

IPv4 has been the driving force on the Internet for decades and continues to be the dominant protocol. However, it's starting to show its age as its address space becomes used up, and work-arounds for security and quality of service must be put in place. IPv4 was developed more than 40 years ago, so it seems natural that as all other aspects of technology slowly get replaced, so will IPv4. This section discusses that replacement: IPv6. IPv6 addresses look different from IPv4 addresses, and unlike IPv4, they have a built-in hierarchy and fields with a distinct purpose. Configuring an IPv6 address is distinctly different from doing so for an IPv4 address. The transition from IPv4 to IPv6 is not going to happen overnight, so methods have been developed to allow IPv4 and IPv6 networks to coexist and communicate with one another.

This section doesn't attempt to give you a full explanation of IPv6 and its many complexities; there are entire books on this topic. However, it covers the key aspects of the IPv6 protocol and what you need to know to configure and support a computer using IPv6.

IPv6 Overview

The Internet Engineering Task Force (IETF) started development on IPng (IP next generation) in 1994, and it was later named IPv6. IPv6 was developed to address IPv4's shortcomings. Some improvements and changes in IPv6 include the following:

- *Larger address space*—IPv4 addresses are 32 bits, which provide a theoretical four billion addresses. IPv6 addresses are 128 bits, so the number of possible addresses can be expressed as 34 followed by 37 0s, or 340 trillion trillion trillion. It's probably safe to say that running out of IPv6 addresses is unlikely.

- *Hierarchical address space*—Unlike IPv4, in which numbers in the address have little meaning other than the address class, and the network ID and host ID, IPv6 addresses have a more defined structure. For example, the first part of an address can indicate a particular organization or site.

- *Autoconfiguration*—IPv6 can be self-configuring or autoconfigured from a router or server running IPv6 or through DHCPv6.

- *Built-in quality of service (QoS) support*—IPv6 includes built-in fields in packet headers to support QoS strategies (used to prioritize data packets based on the type or urgency of information they contain) without having to install additional protocol components, as IPv4 does.

- *Built-in support for security*—From the ground up, IPv6 is built to support secure protocols, such as Internet Protocol Security (IPsec), whereas IPv4's support for IPsec is an add-on feature.

- *Support for mobility*—With built-in support for mobility, routing IPv6 packets generated by mobile devices over the Internet is more efficient than with IPv4.

- *Extensibility*—IPv6 uses extension headers instead of IPv4's fixed-size 40-byte header. Extension headers allow adding features to IPv6 simply by adding a new header.

IPv6 Address Structure

The good news with IPv6 is that subnetting as it's done in IPv4 will be a thing of the past. The bad news is that you still need to work with binary numbers, and with 128 bits in the address, there are quite a few new things to learn. IPv6 addresses are written as eight 16-bit hexadecimal numbers separated by colons. There's no official name for each part of the address, so each 16-bit value is simply called a "field." A valid IPv6 address looks like this:

```
fe80:0:0:0:18ff:0024:8e5a:60
```

There are a few things to note in this address:

- IPv6 addresses often have several 0 values. One or more consecutive 0 values can be written as a double colon (::), so the preceding address can be written as `fe80::18ff:0024:8e5a:60`. However, you can have only one double colon in an IPv6 address.

- Leading 0s are optional. The value `0024` in the previous example could just as easily have been written as `24`, and the value `60` could have been written as `0060`.

- The hexadecimal numbering system was chosen to represent IPv6 addresses mostly because it's much easier to convert to binary than decimal is. Each hexadecimal digit represents 4 bits, so to convert an IPv6 address to binary, simply convert each hexadecimal digit (accounting for leading 0s) to its binary equivalent. For example, the first field in the preceding address (`fe80`) can be written as follows:

```
1111 1110 1000 0000
  f    e    8    0
```

In Windows, when you view an IPv6 address in the network connection's Status dialog box or after using `ipconfig`, you see a percent sign (`%`) followed by a number at the end of the address. The number following the percent sign is the interface index, used to identify the interface in some `netsh` and PowerShell commands. You don't see a subnet mask or even the prefix length, as you do with an IPv4 address. IPv6 addresses have a prefix length, however; it's just that it's always 64 for host addresses because in IPv6, all network IDs are 64 bits. So a typical IPv6 address can be written as follows:

```
fe80:0:0:0:18ff:0024:8e5a:60/64
```

However, because the prefix is always 64 for an IPv6 host address, the prefix is often omitted.

The IPv6 Interface ID Because the prefix length (network ID) of an IPv6 address is 64 bits, the interface ID (the host ID in IPv4) is 64 bits, too. So you can easily identify the network ID of an IPv6 address by looking at the first 64 bits (16 hex digits or four fields) and the interface ID by looking at the last 64 bits. For example, in the following address, the network ID is `fe80:0:0:0`, and the interface ID is `18ff:0024:8e5a:60`:

```
fe80:0:0:0:18ff:0024:8e5a:60
```

Because the prefix isn't a variable length, working with IPv6 addresses is somewhat easier because you don't have to do a binary calculation with a subnet mask to determine the network and interface IDs.

An IPv6 interface ID can be assigned to a host in these ways:

- *Using the 48-bit MAC address*—Because a MAC address is only 48 bits, the other 16 bits come from the value `fffe` inserted after the first 24 bits of the MAC address. In addition, the first two 0s that compose most MAC addresses are replaced with `02`. For example, given the MAC address 00-0C-29-7C-F9-C4, the host ID of an IPv6 address is `020c:29ff:fe7c:f9c4`. This autoconfigured 64-bit host ID is called an **Extended Unique Identifier (EUI)-64 interface ID**. This method is defined in RFC 4291.

- *A randomly generated permanent interface identifier*—The interface ID is generated randomly but is a permanent assignment maintained through system restarts. Windows Vista and later use this method by default for permanent interfaces, such as Ethernet ports. However, you can have Windows use EUI-64 addresses with this `netsh` command:

```
netsh interface ipv6 set global randomizeidentifiers=disabled
```

- *A temporary interface identifier*—Some connections, such as dial-up Point-to-Point Protocol (PPP) connections, might use this method for interface IPv6 address assignment, defined in RFC 4941, whereby the interface ID is assigned randomly and changes each time IPv6 is initialized to maintain anonymity.

- *Via DHCPv6*—Addresses are assigned via a DHCPv6 server to IPv6 interfaces when they're initialized.

- *Manually*—Similar to IPv4 configuration, the IPv6 address is entered manually in the interface's Properties dialog box.

In contrast to Windows, Linux does use EUI-64 IPv6 host addressing.

IPv6 Address Types

IPv4 defines unicast, multicast, and broadcast addresses, and IPv6 defines unicast, multicast, and anycast addresses. Unicast and multicast addresses in IPv6 perform much like their IPv4 counterparts, with a few exceptions. Anycast addresses are an altogether different animal.

IPv6 Unicast Addresses

A **unicast address** specifies a single interface on a device. To participate in an IPv6 network, every device must have at least one network interface that has been assigned a unicast IPv6 address. In most cases, each interface on a device is assigned a separate unicast address, but for load-balancing purposes, multiple interfaces on a device can share the same IPv6 unicast address. In the realm of IPv6 unicast addresses, there are three main types: link-local, unique local, and global. In addition, there are addresses reserved for special purposes and transition addresses, which were developed to help with the transition from IPv4 to IPv6.

Link-Local Addresses Addresses starting with `fe80` are called **link-local IPv6 addresses** and are self-configuring. Link-local addresses can't be routed and are somewhat equivalent to Automatic Private IP Addressing (APIPA) in IPv4. These addresses can be used for computer-to-computer communication in small networks where no routers are needed. In fact, a router doesn't forward packets with a link-local address destination or source address. Most often, however, the use of link-local addresses is simply one step in the process toward autoconfiguration of a different type of address by a router or DHCPv6 server.

Link-local addresses are defined by RFC 4291, which you can read about at *http://tools.ietf.org/html/rfc4291*.

Unique Local Addresses Unique local IPv6 addresses are analogous to the familiar private IPv4 addresses (discussed previously in "Private IP Addresses") that most companies use behind the network's firewall and are preconfigured on routers for use in small and medium networks. Unique local addresses, like private IPv4 addresses, can't be routed on the Internet (but can be routed inside the private network).

RFC 4193 at *http://tools.ietf.org/html/rfc4193* defines unique local addresses.

A unique local address begins with `fc` or `fd` and is usually expressed as `fc00::/7`. Its format is as follows:

`fdgg:gggg:gggg:ssss:iiii:iiii:iiii:iiii`

In this example, the string of `g` characters after the `fd` represents a 40-bit global ID, which identifies a specific site in an organization. The string of four `s` characters represents the subnet ID field, giving each site 16 bits for subnetting its unique local address. The string of `i` characters represents the 64-bit interface ID. This address format allows a whopping 65,536 subnets, each with a 64-bit interface ID field. With more than 65,000 subnets per site and more than 18 quintillion hosts per subnet, you can see that IPv6 solves the address space problem with IPv4.

This global ID is supposed to be set to a pseudo-random 40-bit value. RFC 4193 provides an algorithm for generating the pseudo-random global ID. It's set to a random number to ensure that organizations whose networks are connected still have unique IPv6 address prefixes. In practice, you can assign the 40-bit global ID manually if you aren't concerned about a future conflict with another network.

As mentioned, unique local addresses can begin with `fc` or `fd`. The global IDs of unique local addresses beginning with `fd` are called "locally assigned" and are the only type RFC 4193 defines. Those starting with `fc` aren't defined as of this writing but might be used later, with an address registrar assigning the 40-bit global ID. For now, you should use `fd` when assigning unique local IPv6 addresses.

Unique local addresses effectively replace an older addressing format called "site-local addresses," which have the format `fec0::/10`. Site-local addresses were defined by RFC 3879 but have been deprecated, and the IETF considers them reserved addresses.

Global Addresses Global unicast IPv6 addresses, defined by RFC 4291, are analogous to public IPv4 addresses. They are accessible on the public Internet and can be routed. Essentially, an IPv6 address is global if it doesn't fall into one of the other categories of address (special use, link-local, unique local, loopback, transition, and so forth).

IPv6 addresses have one sizable advantage over IPv4 addresses, aside from the much larger address space; a structure, or a hierarchy, can be built into them that allows more efficient routing on the Internet. Global addresses have the following formats:

`2ggg:gggg:gggg:ssss:iiii:iiii:iiii:iiii`
             or
`3ggg:gggg:gggg:ssss:iiii:iiii:iiii:iiii`

In early specifications of the IPv6 standard, a defined hierarchy was built into the global ID of IPv6 addresses. A top-level aggregator (TLA) was a 13-bit field that the IANA allocated to Internet registries, and a next-level aggregator was a 24-bit field that ISPs could use to allocate addresses to its customers. These identifiers have been deprecated as specified by RFC 4147 and are no longer used. It's expected, however, that large ISPs and Internet registries will use the 45 bits of the available global ID to form an address hierarchy for efficient routing.

As in the previous example, the g characters are the global ID or global routing prefix, the s characters are the subnet ID, and the i characters are the interface ID. As of this writing, only IPv6 addresses beginning with the binary bit pattern 0010 (decimal 2) or 0011 (decimal 3) are allocated for Internet use, which represent only one-eighth the total available address space. The rest of the address space is reserved. So the global unicast address space is often specified as 2000::/3, which means only the first three bits are a fixed value; the remaining part of the address is variable. Even with this constraint on the IPv6 address space, the 45 variable bits in the global ID allow more than 35 trillion different address prefixes, each with more than 65,000 subnets.

The global ID is typically 48 bits, and the subnet ID is 16 bits; however, this allocation isn't fixed. A larger global ID with a smaller subnet ID (or vice versa) is possible but not likely to be common. The interface ID is fixed at 64 bits.

RFC 4147 lists IPv6 prefixes and their use and includes a table showing that most of the address space is reserved by the IETF. The IPv6 address space has a tremendous amount of room to grow.

IPv6 Special-Purpose Addresses A few IPv6 addresses and prefixes have a special purpose:

- *Loopback address*—The loopback address in IPv6 is equivalent to the 127.0.0.1 used in IPv4 and is written as ::1. Like its IPv4 counterpart, the IPv6 loopback is used only for testing local IPv6 protocol operation; no packets actually leave the local computer.

- *Zero address*—The zero (or unspecified) address, which can be written simply as ::, is used as a placeholder in the source address field of an outgoing IPv6 packet when the sending computer doesn't yet have an IPv6 address assigned.

- *Documentation*—The global unicast address 2001:db8::/32 has been reserved for use in books and other documentation discussing IPv6. This address prefix can also be used for test labs, but it shouldn't be routed on a company network or the Internet.

- *IPv4-to-IPv6 transition*—A number of address prefixes are used for transitioning from IPv4 to IPv6 and to support both IPv4 and IPv6 on the same network. These addresses are discussed later in "Transitioning from IPv4 to IPv6."

Subnetting with IPv6 Although subnetting as done in IPv4 will be a thing of the past, it doesn't mean subnetting won't be used at all in IPv6 networks. Typically, ISPs allocated IPv4 addresses to businesses in groups specified by a network address and IP prefix. ISPs try to give a business only the number of addresses it requires. However, with IPv6 having such a large address space, most address allocations will have a /48 prefix, even for small home networks. This means the network ID is 48 bits, and the network administrator has 80 bits for assigning subnets and host IDs. Because the host ID is 64 bits, 16 bits are left for creating subnets. This number of bits allows for 65,536 subnets, more than enough for all but the largest organizations. Large conglomerates can get multiple /48 or /47 prefix addresses, which provide more than 130,000 subnets. A typical IPv6 address assigned by an ISP looks like Figure 6-10.

Global routing prefix (48 bits)	Subnet ID (16 bits)	Interface ID (64 bits)

Figure 6-10 Structure of a typical IPv6 address

With 16 bits available to subnet, there are many strategies you can use. A small network that doesn't have multiple subnets can simply leave the subnet ID as all 0s, for example, and an address in this situation might look like this:

```
2001:DB8:A00:0000:020C:29FF:FE7C:F9C4/64
```

The first two fields (2001:DB8) use the reserved documentation prefix mentioned previously. The A00 in the address is the last 16 bits of the network prefix and was chosen randomly for this example. The 0s following the A00 are the subnet ID, and the last 64 bits are the computer's interface ID. The /64 just indicates that the network portion of the address is the first 64 bits (network prefix plus subnet ID), although the prefix for an interface ID is unnecessary.

A network that does need to subnet could just take the 16 bits for the subnet ID and start counting. For example, a company could make the first three subnets as follows; the bold part of the address is the subnet ID, and the 64-bit interface ID has been omitted.

```
2001:DB8:A00:0000
2001:DB8:A00:0001
2001:DB8:A00:0002
```

Large organizations with multiple locations could take a more structured approach and assign each location a bank of subnets as in the following:

- 2001:DB8:A00:0000—Assigned to New York location
- 2001:DB8:A00:4000—Assigned to London location
- 2001:DB8:A00:8000—Assigned to Shanghai location

With this strategy, each location has 4000 hexadecimal subnet IDs to work with. For example, New York can make subnets 2001:DB8:A00:0000, 2001:DB8:A00:0001, 2001:DB8:A00:0002, and so forth, up to 2001:DB8:A00:3FFF. Put another way, each location can configure up to 16,384 subnets. As you can see, subnetting does still exist in IPv6, but it's a more straightforward process than in IPv4.

Multicast Addresses

A **multicast address** in IPv6 performs the same function as its IPv4 counterpart. A multicast address isn't assigned to an interface, but a node can listen for packets with multicast addresses to participate in a multicast application. Multicast addresses can be identified easily because they begin with `ff` (first 8 bits of the address set to 1). Beyond that, multicast addresses have the following structure:

`ffxy:zzzz:zzzz:zzzz:zzzz:zzzz:zzzz:zzzz`

- *Flags*—The 4-bit flags field, indicated by the x, uses the three low-order bits. The high-order bit is reserved and must be 0. The next high-order bit is the R (rendezvous point) flag; when set, it indicates that the address contains a rendezvous point. The next high-order bit is the P (prefix) flag; when set, it indicates that the multicast address is based on the network prefix. The last bit, called the T (transient) bit, indicates a permanently assigned or well-known address assigned by IANA when it's 0. If the T bit is 1, the multicast address isn't permanently assigned—in other words, "transient." If the R flag is set to 1, the P and T flags must also be set to 1. If the P flag is set to 1, the T bit must also be set. Common values for this field, therefore, are 0, 1, 3, and 7.

- *Scope*—The scope field, indicated by the y, specifies whether and where the multicast packet can be routed. Common values and scopes for this field are as follows:

    o   1: Interface-local scope, which is essentially a multicast loopback address because the packet can't be sent across the network; it must stay with the current node.

    o   2: Link-local scope, which means the packet must stay on the current network and can't be routed.

    o   5: Site-local scope, meaning this scope can be targeted at specific devices on the network, such as routers and DHCP servers.

    o   8: Organization-local, which means the packet can't be routed beyond the organization's network.

    o   E: Global scope, meaning these multicast packets can be routed on the public Internet.

- *Group ID*—This field, represented by the z characters, identifies a multicast group, which is the group of computers listening to the stream of multicast packets. In essence, this 112-bit field identifies the unique multicast application that's transmitting the multicast packets. RFC 2375 lists the well-known multicast address assignments.

Anycast Addresses

Anycast addresses are unique to IPv6, so they don't have an IPv4 counterpart. Anycast addressing is a cross between unicast and multicast. Multiple nodes are assigned the same address, and packets sent to that address are delivered to the "closest" node. So although packets sent with a multicast address are delivered to multiple destinations, the anycast address is sent to only one of a group of nodes sharing the same anycast address. This addressing is often defined as a one-to-one-of-many association because there are potentially many destinations, but the packet is delivered to only one.

Anycast addressing is used when there are multiple nodes providing the same service and the client computer doesn't care which device actually provides the service. Examples include routers and DNS servers. Anycast addresses don't have a special format because they're just unicast addresses used in a special way.

IPv6 Autoconfiguration

As mentioned, IPv6 can configure its address settings automatically. IPv6 autoconfiguration occurs by these two methods:

- *Stateless autoconfiguration*—The node listens for router advertisement messages from a local router. If the Autonomous flag in the router advertisement message is set, the node uses the prefix information contained in the message. In this case, the node uses the advertised prefix and its 64-bit interface ID to generate the IPv6 address. If the Autonomous flag isn't set, the prefix information is ignored, and the node can attempt to use DHCPv6 for address configuration or an automatically generated link-local address.

- *Stateful autoconfiguration*—The node uses an autoconfiguration protocol, such as DHCPv6, to get its IPv6 address and other configuration information. A node attempts to use DHCPv6 to get IPv6 address configuration information if there are no routers on the network providing router advertisements or if the Autonomous flag in router advertisements isn't set.

Autoconfiguration on Windows Hosts

The Windows autoconfiguration process involves the following steps in Windows 8 and later:

1. At initialization, a link-local address is determined.
2. The link-local address is verified as unique by using duplicate address detection.
3. If the address is verified as unique, the address is assigned to the interface; otherwise, a new address is generated and Step 2 is repeated.
4. The host transmits a router solicitation message. This message is addressed to the all-routers multicast address.
5. If no router advertisement messages are received in response to the solicitation message, the host attempts to use DHCPv6 to get an address.
6. If a router advertisement message is received and has an Autonomous flag set, the prefix in the router advertisement is used along with the interface ID to configure the IPv6 address on the interface. The host can also use a DHCPv6 server to acquire other IPv6 configuration parameters if specified in the router advertisement. If the Autonomous flag isn't set, the host uses DHCPv6 to acquire the address.

Transitioning from IPv4 to IPv6

The move from IPv4 to IPv6 isn't happening on a particular date worldwide; rather, the transition is under way and will continue over several years. However, whether it's a small business with just a few Internet-connected computers or a 100,000-computer global enterprise, the switch to IPv6 is inevitable. Thankfully, both protocols can coexist easily on the same computer and the same network, allowing network administrators to ease into the transition instead of having to change from IPv4 to IPv6 instantly.

Transitioning an entire network from IPv4 to IPv6 successfully while maintaining compatibility with IPv4 requires a variety of transition technologies. These technologies and special address types, discussed in the following sections, help ease the transition to IPv6 while maintaining compatibility with IPv4:

- Dual IP layer architecture
- IPv6-over-IPv4 tunneling
- Intra-Site Automatic Tunnel Addressing Protocol (ISATAP)
- 6to4
- Teredo

Dual IP Layer Architecture

A **dual IP layer architecture** (or dual-stack architecture) means that both IPv4 and IPv6 are running, and the computer can communicate directly with both IPv4 and IPv6 devices by using the native packet types. In addition, computers running both IPv4 and IPv6 can encapsulate IPv6 packets in an IPv4 header, a process called "tunneling."

IPv6-over-IPv4 Tunneling

Tunneling is a network protocol technique that allows transmitting a packet in a format that's otherwise incompatible with the network architecture by encapsulating the packet in a compatible header format. In other words, it's needed when packets must traverse a network in which their protocol isn't used. For example, VPNs use tunneling to send encrypted data across the Internet by encapsulating an encrypted packet in a standard unencrypted IP header (see Figure 6-11).

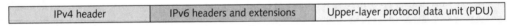

| IPv4 header | IPv6 headers and extensions | Upper-layer protocol data unit (PDU) |

Figure 6-11 IPv6 packet encapsulated in an IPv4 header

IPv6-over-IPv4 tunneling allows a host to send an IPv6 packet over an IPv4 network to an IPv6 device. How is this feature useful? Suppose your network runs a dual IP layer architecture, and you need to access a server across the Internet that's running an IPv6-only application. Unfortunately, your ISP is still using IPv4-only routers. The only way to get IPv6 packets to the IPv6 application is to encapsulate them in IPv4 headers, allowing them to traverse the Internet as IPv4 packets. At the destination network, the packets are deencapsulated and delivered to the server as IPv6 packets. Figure 6-12 illustrates this process. Some details are left out because a variety of methods are used to create tunnels.

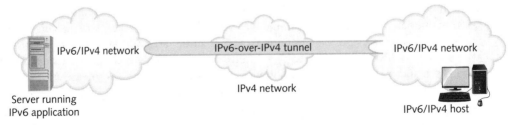

Figure 6-12 IPv6-over-IPv4 tunneling

One common method is creating the tunnel from router to router so that the IPv6 packet is encapsulated when it gets to a router in the source network and deencapsulated at the router connected to the destination network (see Figure 6-13). Tunnels can also be created between two hosts and between a host and a router.

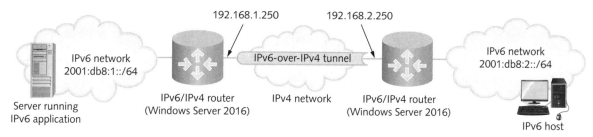

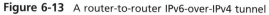

Figure 6-13 A router-to-router IPv6-over-IPv4 tunnel

Intra-Site Automatic Tunnel Addressing Protocol

Intra-Site Automatic Tunnel Addressing Protocol (ISATAP) is used to transmit IPv6 packets between dual IP layer hosts across an IPv4 network. This automatic tunneling protocol doesn't require manual configuration, as IPv6-over-IPv4 tunneling does. ISATAP is enabled by default on Windows computers starting with Vista SP1.

In Windows, ISATAP interfaces are created for each LAN interface. ISATAP addresses have the following format:

```
fe80::5efe:n:n:n:n
```

The first 64 bits of an ISATAP address are the link-local IPv6 address `fe80` followed by 48 0 bits. The next 16 bits are typically 0 unless the globally unique flag is set, in which case the next 16 bits in hexadecimal are `0200`. The next 16 bits are `5efe`. ISATAP embeds the IPv4 address in the last 32 bits of the IPv6 address. For example, if a LAN interface has the IPv4 address 172.31.210.200, the ISATAP address is as follows:

```
fe80::5efe:172.31.210.200
```

6to4 Tunneling

6to4 provides automatic tunneling of IPv6 traffic over an IPv4 network. It can provide host-to-router or router-to-host tunneling but is most often used to create a router-to-router tunnel. The key to 6to4 tunneling is the `2002::/16` prefix. Routers configured to perform 6to4 tunneling recognize the `2002` prefix as a 6to4 address, just as `fe80::5efe` is recognized as an ISATAP address. When an IPv6 packet with addresses using the `2002` prefix arrives at a 6to4-configured router, the router knows to encapsulate the packet in an IPv4 header. A 6to4 address has the following format:

```
2002:xxxx:xxxx::/48
```

The first 16 bits are always `2002`, and the next 32 bits, represented by the x characters, are the hexadecimal representation of the 32-bit IPv4 address. The remaining bits are the subnet ID and 64-bit interface ID. The IPv4 address embedded in the 6to4 address must be a public address, which limits the use of this tunneling technology because it can't traverse a router interface that uses NAT.

Teredo Tunneling

Teredo is an automatic IPv6-over-IPv4 tunneling protocol that solves the problem of 6to4's requirement of a public IPv4 address and the inability to traverse NAT routers. Teredo allows the tunnel endpoints to exist behind a NAT firewall by tunneling IPv6 packets between hosts instead of requiring a router as an endpoint.

Teredo achieves NAT traversal by encapsulating IPv6 packets in IPv4 UDP messages, which can traverse most NAT routers. It has the added benefit of allowing IPv4 applications to communicate through a NAT router that otherwise might not be able to. A Teredo address can be identified by the Teredo prefix `2001::/32` and has the following format:

`2001:tttt:tttt:gggg:pppp:xxxx:xxxx`

The first 16 bits are always the Teredo prefix `2001`. The next 32 bits, represented by t characters, are the Teredo server's IPv4 public address. The next 16 bits, shown as g characters, are Teredo flags that specify processing options. The p characters represent an obscured UDP port the client uses for Teredo traffic. The port is obscured to prevent certain types of NATs from attempting to translate the port. The last 32 bits are the obscured IPv4 address the client uses for Teredo traffic.

For more information on IPv6 transition technologies, see
http://technet.microsoft.com/en-us/library/dd379548(v=ws.10).aspx.

Hands-On Project 6-7: Setting IPv6 Static Addresses

Time Required: 10 minutes

Objective: Set IPv6 static addresses.

Required Tools and Equipment: Net-*XX*

Description: Before you begin using common tools with IPv6, such as `ipconfig` and `ping`, you configure static IPv6 addresses to work with.

1. Log on Net-*XX* as **NetAdmin,** if necessary. Right-click **Start** and click **Network Connections.**
2. Right-click **Ethernet0** and click **Status,** and then click the **Details** button. Look for the row "Link-local IPv6 Address." You'll see an address beginning with `fe80`, which is always the first 16 bits of a link-local IPv6 address. Click **Close.**
3. Click **Properties,** and double-click **Internet Protocol Version 6 (TCP/IPv6).** By default, your IPv6 address is set to get an IP address automatically.
4. Click **Use the following IPv6 address.** In the IPv6 address text box, type **2001:db8::XX** (replacing *XX* with your student number). In the Subnet prefix length text box, type **64.** Click **OK** twice, and then click **Close.**
5. Open a command prompt window. Type **netsh interface ipv6 show addresses** and press **Enter.** This command shows address information for all IPv6 interfaces, including the transitioning interfaces ISATAP and Teredo.
6. Stay logged on if you're continuing to the next project.

Hands-On Project 6-8: Working with IPv6

Time Required: 15 minutes

Objective: Use `ipconfig` and `ping` with IPv6 and change an IPv6 interface address.

Required Tools and Equipment: Net-*XX*, the address of another computer with an IPv6 address

Description: Your company has plans to move to IPv6. Because you haven't used IPv6, you want to become comfortable with using common tools, such as `ipconfig` and `ping`.

1. Log on to Net-*XX* as **NetAdmin,** and open an elevated (admin) command prompt window, if necessary.

2. Type **ipconfig** and press **Enter**. Find the output line starting with "Link-local IPv6 Address." Notice that the assigned address starts with `fe80::`. The `fe80` indicates a link-local IPv6 address, and the `::` indicates a string of 0 values—in this case, three consecutive 0 values. The rest of the address (64 bits) has been assigned randomly by Windows.

3. Type **ping ::1** and press **Enter**. Windows replies because you just pinged your own computer. Type **ping -a ::1** and press **Enter**. The `-a` option tells Windows to display the hostname for the `::1` address, which is the name of your computer.

4. Type **ping 2001:db8::*XX*** (replacing *XX* with the address of another computer on the network) and press **Enter**. You should get a reply from the other computer. Type **ping -6 Net-*XX*** (replacing *XX* with the name of another computer on the network) and press **Enter**. The `-6` option tells `ping` to use IPv6 addresses. You should get a reply from the other computer, but it will probably come from the other computer's link-local (`fe80`) address.

5. Type **getmac** and press **Enter** to display your computer's MAC address. Make a note of this address:

   _____

6. Type **netsh interface ipv6 set global randomizeidentifiers=disabled** and press **Enter**. The interface is now using the EUI-64 format to assign the link-local IPv6 address.

7. Type **ipconfig** and press **Enter**. Notice that the last 64 bits of the IPv6 address now look like your MAC address, with the addition of `fffe` after the first 24 bits and `02` instead of the first `00` of your MAC address.

8. Close the command prompt window, and log off.

Chapter Summary

- An IPv4 address is a 32-bit dotted decimal number separated into four octets. Every IP address must have a subnet mask to indicate which part of the IP address is the network ID and which part is the host ID.

- There are three main address classes: A, B, and C. Address classes determine the default network ID and host ID portions of an IP address. Each class has a range of private IP addresses that can't be used on the Internet; they're used to address private networks.

- CIDR largely replaces the IP address class system; it uses a prefix number or subnet mask to determine the network and host IDs of an IP address.

- Subnetting enables an administrator to divide a large network into smaller networks that require a router for communication. It also allows an ISP to allocate only the number of public IP addresses a company requires instead of assigning an entire address class, thereby conserving public IP addresses. Subnetting also allows dividing networks into logical groups for security and efficiency.

- There are several rules for IP address assignment. Only Class A, B, and C addresses can be assigned to a host; every IP address must have a subnet mask; all host IDs on the same network must be unique; you can't assign the network number or broadcast address to a host; computers with different network IDs can only communicate through a router; and the default gateway must have the same network ID as the host.

- Commands for working with IP address configurations include `netsh`, `ipconfig`, `ping`, `arp`, `route`, `tracert`, and `nslookup`.

- Network Address Translation (NAT) enables an organization to use private IP addresses while connected to the Internet. Port Address Translation (PAT) allows several hundred workstations to access the Internet with a single public Internet address.

- IPv6 will eventually replace IPv4 because of advantages such as a larger address space, a hierarchical address space, autoconfiguration, built-in QoS, and built-in security. IPv6 addresses are expressed as eight four-digit hexadecimal values.

- IPv6 defines unicast, multicast, and anycast addresses. Unicast address types include link-local addresses, unique local addresses, and global addresses.

- IPv6 can configure address settings automatically. IPv6 autoconfiguration occurs by using stateful or stateless autoconfiguration. With stateless autoconfiguration, the node listens for router advertisement messages from a local router. With stateful autoconfiguration, the node uses an autoconfiguration protocol, such as DHCPv6.

- Transitioning an entire network from IPv4 to IPv6 successfully while maintaining compatibility with IPv4 requires a variety of transition technologies, including dual IP layer architecture, IPv6-over-IPv4 tunneling, ISATAP, 6to4, and Teredo.

Key Terms

6to4   An IPv4-to-IPv6 transition protocol that provides automatic tunneling of IPv6 traffic over an IPv4 network. It can handle host-to-router or router-to-host tunneling but is most often used to create a router-to-router tunnel.

address space   The number of addresses available in an IP network number that can be assigned to hosts.

anycast addresses   An address type used in IPv6 to allow a one-to-many relationship between source and destination; the packet is delivered to only one of the possible destination computers.

Automatic Private IP Addressing (APIPA)   A private range of IP addresses assigned to an APIPA-enabled computer automatically when an IP address is requested via DHCP but no DHCP server responds to the request.

broadcast domain   The bounds of a network that defines which devices must receive a packet that's broadcast by any other device; usually an IP subnet.

CIDR notation   A method of expressing an IP address in the format A.B.C.D/*n*; *n* is the number of 1 bits in the subnet mask or the number of bits in the network ID. *See also* Classless Interdomain Routing (CIDR).

classful addressing   The use of IP addresses with their default subnet masks according to their address class: A, B, or C.

Classless Interdomain Routing (CIDR)   A method of IP addressing in which the network and host IDs are determined by a prefix number that specifies how many bits of the IP address are network bits; the remaining bits are host bits.

dotted decimal notation   The format for expressing an IPv4 address; it's four decimal numbers separated by periods.

dual IP layer architecture   The current architecture of the IPv6 protocol in Windows, in which both IPv4 and IPv6 share the other components of the stack.

Extended Unique Identifier (EUI)-64 interface ID   An autoconfigured IPv6 host address that uses the MAC address of the host plus an additional 16 bits.

Intra-Site Automatic Tunnel Addressing Protocol (ISATAP)   An automatic tunneling protocol used to transmit IPv6 packets between dual IP layer hosts across an IPv4 network. *See also* dual IP layer architecture.

IP prefix   A value used to express how many bits of an IP address are network ID bits. Usually expressed preceded by a / symbol, as in 192.168.1.24/27; in this example, 27 is the IP prefix.

IPv4 address   A 32-bit dotted-decimal address containing a network ID, which specifies the network the computer is on, and a host ID, which uniquely identifies the computer on that network.

link-local address   An IP address that can be used to communicate only on the local subnet. It can't be routed to other networks.

link-local IPv6 address   Similar in function to the IPv4 APIPA addresses, link-local IPv6 addresses begin with `fe80`, are self-configuring, and can't be routed. *See also* Automatic Private IP Addressing (APIPA).

localhost   A reserved name that corresponds to the loopback address in an IP network. *See also* loopback address.

logical AND operation   A binary operation in which there are two operands; the result is 0 if either operand is 0 and 1 if both operands are 1.

loopback address   An address that always refers to the local computer; in IPv4, it's 127.0.0.1, and in IPv6 it's `::1`. This address is used to test TCP/IP functionality on the local computer.

metric   A value assigned to the gateway based on the speed of the interface used to access the gateway.

multicast address   An address that identifies a group of computers running a multicast application.

multicasting   A network communication in which a packet is addressed so that more than one destination can receive it.

multihomed server   A server with two or more NICs, each attached to a different IP network. Each NIC is assigned a network connection and requires its own IP address.

Network Address Translation (NAT)   A service that translates a private IP address to a public IP address in packets destined for the Internet, and then translates the public IP address in the reply to the private address. Often used to allow using private IP addresses while connected to the Internet.

octet   An 8-bit value; a number from 0 to 255 that's one of the four numbers in a dotted decimal IP address.

Port Address Translation (PAT)   An extension of NAT, a service that allows several hundred workstations to access the Internet with a single public Internet address by using Transport-layer port numbers to differentiate each host conversation. *See also* Network Address Translation (NAT).

subnet mask   A 32-bit dotted decimal number, consisting of a contiguous series of binary 1 digits followed by a contiguous series of binary 0 digits, that determines which part of an IP address is the network ID and which part is the host ID.

subnets   Subdivisions of an IP network address space.

subnetting   A process that reallocates bits from an IP address's host portion to the network portion, creating multiple smaller address spaces. *See also* subnets.

supernetting   A process that reallocates bits from an IP address's network portion to the host portion, effectively combining smaller subnets into a larger supernet.

Teredo   An automatic IPv6-over-IPv4 tunneling protocol that solves the problem of 6to4's requirement of a public IPv4 address and the inability to traverse NAT routers. *See also* 6to4.

tunneling   A common network protocol technique that allows transmitting a packet in a format that would otherwise be incompatible for the network architecture by encapsulating the packet in a compatible header format.

unicast address   An address in a unit of network data intended for a single destination device.

unique local IPv6 address   An address for devices on a private network that can't be routed on the Internet.

Review Questions

1. An IPv6 address is made up of how many bits?

   a.   32

   b.   48

   c.   64

   d.   128

   e.   256

2. The subnet mask of an IP address does which of the following?.

 a. Provides encryption in a TCP/IP network

 b. Defines network and host portions of an IP address

 c. Allows automated IP address configuration

 d. Allows users to use a computer's name rather than its address

3. Which of the following is needed if a computer with the IP address 172.31.210.10/24 wants to communicate with a computer with the IP address 172.31.209.122/24?

 a. Hub

 b. Router

 c. Switch

 d. Server

4. Which of the following is a private IP address and can't be routed across the Internet?

 a. 192.156.90.100

 b. 172.19.243.254

 c. 11.200.99.180

 d. 221.24.250.207

 e. 12.12.12.12

5. Which command should you use with a dual-homed server to make sure the server sends packets out the correct interface?

 a. `ipconfig`

 b. `ping`

 c. `tracert`

 d. `route`

6. Which command should you use to configure the primary DNS server on your computer?

 a. `ipconfig`

 b. `netsh`

 c. `nslookup`

 d. `arp`

7. Which IP address expressed in CIDR notation has the subnet mask 255.255.255.0?

 a. 10.100.44.123/24

 b. 172.16.88.222/16

 c. 192.168.100.1/26

 d. 172.29.111.201/18

8. Which IP network address expressed in CIDR notation can support a maximum of 1022 hosts?

    a.   10.100.44.0/24

    b.   172.16.4.0/22

    c.   192.168.100.64/26

    d.   172.29.128.0/18

9. The IP address 10.240.0.0/8 can't be assigned to a host. True or False?

10. What's the term for each grouping of 8 bits in an IP address?

    a.   Quartet

    b.   Quintet

    c.   Hexadecimal

    d.   Octet

11. When using TCP/IP, which of the following must computers on the same logical network have in common? (Choose all that apply.)

    a.   Network ID

    b.   Host ID

    c.   Subnet mask

    d.   Computer name

12. Which of the following IPv6 features is an enhancement to IPv4? (Choose all that apply.)

    a.   Larger address space

    b.   Works at the Internetwork and Transport layers

    c.   Built-in security

    d.   Connectionless communication

13. Which protocol can configure a computer's IP address and subnet mask automatically?

    a.   TCP

    b.   IP

    c.   ARP

    d.   DNS

    e.   DHCP

14. How many bits must be reallocated from host ID to network ID to create 16 subnets?

    a.   6

    b.   4

    c.   16

    d.   28

15. For the Class C network address 192.168.10.0, which of the following subnet masks provides 32 subnets?

    a. 255.255.255.252

    b. 255.255.255.248

    c. 255.255.255.240

    d. 255.255.255.224

16. How many host bits are necessary to assign addresses to 62 hosts?

    a. 6

    b. 5

    c. 4

    d. 3

17. Which IP addressing process enables workstations to use private IP addresses to access the Internet?

    a. Supernetting

    b. NAT

    c. DHCP

    d. Subnetting

18. When a Windows computer is configured to use DHCP but no DHCP server is available, what type of address is configured automatically for it?

    a. PAT

    b. APIPA

    c. NAT

    d. Static

19. Which of the following represents a valid IPv6 address?

    a. `2001:345:abcd:0:230:44`

    b. `2001:345:abcd::BEEF:44`

    c. `2001:345::abcd:0:79f::230:44`

    d. `2001:345:abcd:0:FEED:230:44`

20. Which of the following is a reason to subnet? (Choose all that apply.)

    a. Networks can be divided into logical groups.

    b. Subnetting eliminates the need for routers.

    c. Subnetting can decrease the size of broadcast domains.

    d. There's no need to assign static IP addresses to each computer.

21. Which of the following IP addresses has 12 bits in the host ID?

    a. 172.31.21.12/16

    b. 172.31.89.100/12

    c. 12.49.127.88/8

    d. 12.156.109.252/20

22. You have a server with two NICs, each attached to a different IP network. You're having problems communicating with devices on remote networks that send packets to one of the interfaces. The server receives the packets fine, but the server's replies never reach the intended destination network. Replies to packets that come in through the other interface seem to reach their destination without any problems. What can you do that will most likely solve the problem?

    a. Configure a second default gateway on the interface exhibiting problems.

    b. Change the default gateway to use the router that's on the network of the interface exhibiting problems.

    c. Use the route command to add routes to the networks that aren't receiving replies.

    d. Replace the NIC that's having problems replying to packets.

23. You have just changed the IP address on a computer named computer5 in your domain from 172.31.1.10/24 to 172.31.1.110/24. You were communicating with this computer from your workstation fine right before you changed the address. Now when you try the command ping computer5 from your workstation, you don't get a successful reply. Other computers on the network aren't having a problem communicating with the computer. Which command might help solve the problem?

    a. arp -d

    b. ipconfig /flushdns

    c. tracert computer5

    d. ping -6 172.31.1.110

24. Which address can't be assigned to a host computer?

    a. 10.100.44.16/24

    b. 172.16.7.255/22

    c. 192.168.100.66/26

    d. 172.29.132.0/18

25. Which IPv6 transition technology can be used with NAT routers and has the address prefix 2001::/32?

    a. Teredo

    b. ISATAP

    c. 6to4

    d. IPv6-over-IPv4

26. How many bits are in the interface ID of an IPv6 address?

   a. 32

   b. 64

   c. 16

   d. 48

27. What address should you ping if you want to test local IPv6 operation but don't want to actually send any packets on the network?

   a. `1::f`

   b. `2001::db8`

   c. `fe80::ffff`

   d. `::1`

Critical Thinking

The following activities give you critical thinking challenges. Challenge labs give you an opportunity to use the skills you have learned to perform a task without step-by-step instructions. Case projects offer a practical networking setup for which you supply a written solution.

Challenge Lab 6-1 Creating a Subnet Mask

Time Required: 30 minutes

Objective: Create a suitable subnet mask and list the resulting networks and host address ranges.

Required Tools and Equipment: Pen and paper or a word-processing document

Description: Review the network diagram in Figure 6-14. Given this information, devise a subnet mask that works for this network if the original network address is 192.168.10.0/24. Write the subnet mask and number of subnets, and fill in the chart with the network numbers in CIDR and the host address ranges you need. (*Hint*: The chart has more rows than you need.)

- Number of subnets needed: _____

- Subnet mask: _____

- Number of subnets created: _____

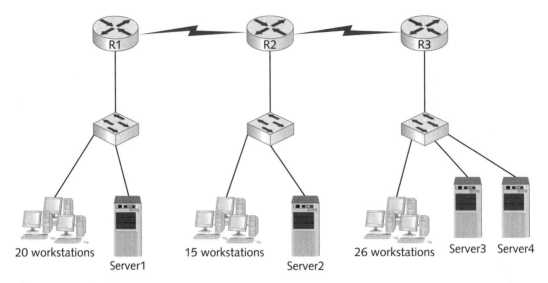

Figure 6-14 Network diagram for Challenge Lab 6-1

Network number in CIDR	Host address range

Case Project 6-1

As the network administrator for a growing ISP, you want to make efficient use of your network addresses. One of the network addresses IANA assigned to you is a Class C network of 197.14.88.0. You have decided to use the addresses in this Class C network to satisfy the IP address requirements of 16 corporate customers who need between 10 and 14 addresses each. Calculate a subnet mask that meets their needs. List the subnet mask and the first four subnet addresses the mask will create.

Case Project 6-2

You're the head network administrator for a large manufacturing enterprise that's completing its support for IPv6. The company has six major locations with network administrators and several thousand users in each location. You're using a base IPv6 address of 2001:DB8:FAB/48 and want network administrators to be able to subnet their networks however they see fit. You also want to maintain a reserve of address spaces for a possible 6 to 10 additional locations in the future. Each network administrator should be able to construct at least 200 subnets from the addresses you supply, and each location should have the same amount of available address space. What IPv6 addresses should you assign to each location? When constructing your answer, list each location as Location 1, Location 2, and so forth.

Case Project 6-3

You must install 125 computers for a new business that wants to run TCP/IP and have access to the Internet. The ISP in town will assign you only four public IP addresses, so you decide to assign the computers addresses in the range 172.16.1.1/16 through 172.16.1.125/16. What else must you do to allow these computers to access the Internet?

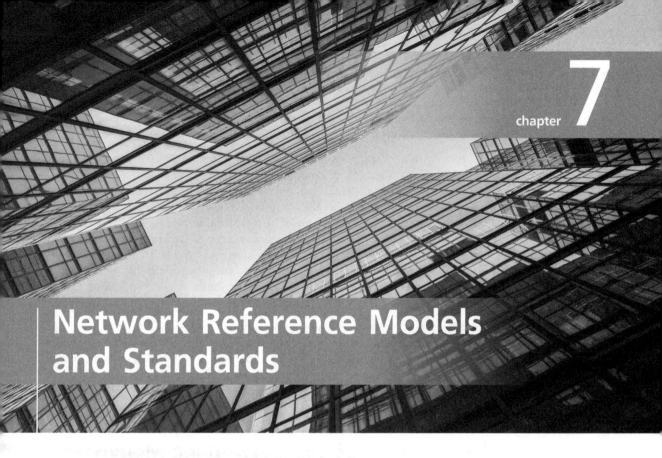

chapter 7

Network Reference Models and Standards

After reading this chapter and completing the exercises, you will be able to:

- Describe the OSI and IEEE 802 networking models
- Summarize the IEEE 802 networking standards

The Open Systems Interconnection (OSI) reference model for networking explains how networks behave within an orderly, seven-layered model for networked communication. The OSI model isn't specific to a protocol suite and can be applied to most networking protocols past and present. Many of the networking hardware and software components discussed in this book can be identified as working in one or more of the OSI model layers.

Although the OSI model isn't specific to one protocol suite, it's the standard model for discussing, teaching, and learning the field of computer networking. It's unlikely you'll have a course in networking that doesn't at least mention the OSI model, and some courses you take might cover it in more detail than in this chapter. Because you have already learned about the layered architecture of the TCP/IP model, some of the information in this chapter has already been introduced. However, the concept of a layered architecture in network communication is so vital to understanding how to configure and troubleshoot networks, the repetition should be worthwhile. In addition, descriptions of network devices refer to the layers of the OSI model rather than the TCP/IP model; for example, a switch might be called a "Layer 2 switch."

The OSI model is a general framework for how networking systems should operate, and the IEEE 802 networking standards are formal specifications for how to implement particular networking technologies. The IEEE standards are most important if you're designing network hardware or writing network drivers or protocols, as these standards define how vendors of networking products should implement certain technologies.

Introducing the OSI and IEEE 802 Networking Models

Table 7-1 summarizes what you need for the hands-on projects in this chapter.

Table 7-1 Hands-on project requirements

Hands-on project	Requirements	Time required	Notes
Hands-On Project 7-1: Viewing Your MAC Address	Net-XX	10 minutes	
Hands-On Project 7-2: Dragging and Dropping the OSI Model Layers	A computer with a Web browser	10 minutes	Follow instructions in this book's Introduction to access the simulations.
Hands-On Project 7-3: Matching OSI Model Descriptions to Layer Numbers	A computer with a Web browser	10 minutes	Follow instructions in this book's Introduction to access the simulations.
Hands-On Project 7-4: Creating a Frame	A computer with a Web browser	10 minutes	Follow instructions in this book's Introduction to access the simulations.

Several networking models have sought to create an intellectual framework for clarifying network concepts and activities, but none has been as successful as the **Open Systems Interconnection (OSI) reference model** proposed by the **International Organization for Standardization (ISO)**. This model is sometimes called the "ISO/OSI reference model."

ISO isn't an acronym; it comes from the Greek prefix iso, which means "equal" or "the same." The ISO, based in Geneva, Switzerland, is a network of national standards institutes from 140 countries. The expanded name differs from language to language. For example, in France the organization is the Organisation Internationale de Normalisation. The term "ISO" gives the network of institutes a common name.

The OSI reference model has become a key part of networking, in large part because it's a common framework for developers and students of networking to work with and learn from. The attempt to develop a working set of protocols and technologies based on the OSI model and put these efforts into common use never materialized, partly because existing protocols, such as TCP/IP, were already entrenched in the marketplace. However, the OSI reference model has a prominent place in networking as a model and teaching tool. This chapter covers the model's seven-layer organization, the function of each layer, and the networking devices and components operating at each layer.

The set of protocols developed to conform to the OSI model is called "ISO." You can view the fruits of these labors at *www.protocols. com/pbook/iso.htm*.

This IEEE 802 networking model provides detailed implementation specifications for a number of networking technologies. As you learned in Chapter 3, the IEEE standards define Ethernet standards from 10 Mbps up to 100 Gbps. In fact, the 802 specification encompasses most types of networking and allows adding new types of networks (such as the 40 Gigabit and 100 Gigabit standards) as needed. This chapter briefly discusses how the IEEE 802 standards relate to the OSI model.

Role of a Reference Model

You might wonder why a reference model for networking is needed and why the layer concept in particular is so valuable. To see the value of a layered model outside the field of networking, take a look at the process of a letter being created, sent, and delivered via the U.S. Postal Service:

1. Tom, who lives in New York, writes a letter to Cindy, who lives in San Francisco. When the letter is finished, it's ready for Cindy to read, but Tom needs to get the letter to Cindy, so he decides to use the U.S. mail.

2. Tom folds the letter and places it in an envelope, which is the container required by the U.S. mail letter-sending protocols. Tom can't send the letter yet, however; first he must address the envelope.

3. Tom addresses the envelope by putting Cindy's name and address in the middle of the front of the envelope, which is where the post office expects to find the destination address. Tom also puts his return address on the envelope's upper-left corner.

4. Before Tom can send the envelope, per post office protocol, he must place a stamp on the envelope's upper-right corner.

5. Tom then walks to the post office and drops the letter in the mailbox. At this point, Tom's job is done; it's up to the post office (the next layer) to take care of getting the letter to its destination.

6. The mail carrier picks up the mail in the mailbox at the prescribed time and brings it to the central office for sorting. The mail carrier's job is done, and now it's up to other post office workers (the next layer) to get the letter to its destination.

7. The mail is sorted according to zip code, which identifies the part of the country the mail is destined for. After sorting, the letter goes into the pile headed for the West Coast of the United States. The mail is put on a plane, and the job of the post office worker in New York is completed.

8. After the mail arrives in San Francisco, it's sorted by zip code to determine which area of San Francisco to deliver it to. After the letter has been sorted, a mail carrier takes it on his or her route.

9. The mail carrier uses the street address to determine which house to deliver the letter to, and he or she leaves the letter in Cindy's mailbox. At this point, the mail carrier's job is done.

10. Cindy receives the letter, opens the envelope, and now has exactly what Tom had in his hand before he placed the letter in the envelope. Mission accomplished.

As you can see, a number of tasks have to be completed to deliver this message. Each task is separate, but for one task to be completed, the previous task (or layer) must be completed correctly:

- The letter has to be written.
- The letter has to be placed in an envelope and addressed in the correct format.
- The local post office in New York has to sort the letter correctly and get it on the right plane to San Francisco.
- The post office in San Francisco has to sort the letter correctly for the right part of town.
- The local carrier has to deliver the letter to the correct house.
- The recipient has to receive the letter, open it, and read it.

A layered approach to what might otherwise be a daunting process for a single person reduces its complexity and turns it into a series of interconnected and well-defined tasks. Each task or activity can be handled separately and its issues solved independently, often without affecting the procedures of other tasks. This approach creates a method for solving big problems by reducing them to a series of smaller problems with separate solutions.

To further exemplify the value of layers in this analogy, consider the effect of having the mail carrier switch from walking the mail route to driving a delivery truck. In fact, the only step that's affected is the mail carrier's job—his or her job gets done faster. Addressing the envelope is still done in the same way, and post office workers still follow the same procedure to sort the mail. In short, people involved in these steps don't even have to know that the mail carrier is using a truck to get from house to house. As you can see, with a layered approach, one part of the process can change, sometimes drastically, but the rest of the process remains unchanged. Now think about what's necessary to upgrade from 100 Mbps Ethernet to 1000 Mbps Ethernet: Change the NICs and/or the switch, and you're done. There's no need to change the protocols or applications. By the same token, IPv6 can replace IPv4 without having to change the Transport layer or Network access layer in the TCP/IP model.

Structure of the OSI Model

The OSI model divides network communication into the seven layers shown in Figure 7-1.

TIP Here are two mnemonics to remember the seven layers of the OSI reference model. From the bottom up, starting with the Physical layer, the mnemonic is "People Do Not Throw Sausage Pizza Away." From the top down, starting with the Application layer, try "All People Studying This Need Drastic Psychotherapy" or "All People Seem To Need Data Processing."

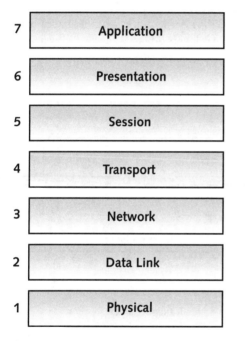

7	Application
6	Presentation
5	Session
4	Transport
3	Network
2	Data Link
1	Physical

Figure 7-1 The seven layers of the OSI reference model

At the top, the Application layer provides interfaces that enable user applications—such as File Explorer or Microsoft Word—to access network services. These user applications aren't part of the OSI model but communicate with its top layer. On the other hand, some user applications, such as Web browsers and e-mail programs, are integrated with functions of the Application layer (as well as the Presentation and Session layers).

At the bottom of the OSI model, the Physical layer is where the network medium and the signals traversing it reside. All the activities needed to handle network communication occur between the top and bottom layers. To comprehend how a network works as a whole, you simply need to understand how each layer functions, what networking components and devices operate at each layer, and how the layers interact with one another.

Each layer in the OSI model has its own well-defined functions, and the functions of each layer communicate and interact with the layers immediately above and below it. For example, the Transport layer works with the Network layer below it and the Session layer above it. The Physical layer doesn't have a layer below it, and the Application layer, although not having a layer above it, interacts with user applications and network services.

Because you're already familiar with the TCP/IP model, now is a good time to compare the two models. Your understanding of how the TCP/IP layers work gives you a context for the OSI model's more detailed layers. Figure 7-2 shows this relationship. Notice that both models contain an Application layer, but the TCP/IP model combines the functions of the OSI model's Application, Presentation, and Session layers. It's not that TCP/IP doesn't perform the function of these layers; it's just that a single TCP/IP Application-layer protocol performs all three functions. The Transport layer in both models is equivalent in name and function; however, the TCP/IP suite contains the connectionless Transport-layer protocol UDP, which doesn't perform many of the functions defined at the OSI model's Transport layer. The OSI model's Network layer is equivalent to the TCP/IP Internetwork layer. The OSI model divides the function of the Network access layer into two layers—Data Link and Physical—that have distinct jobs.

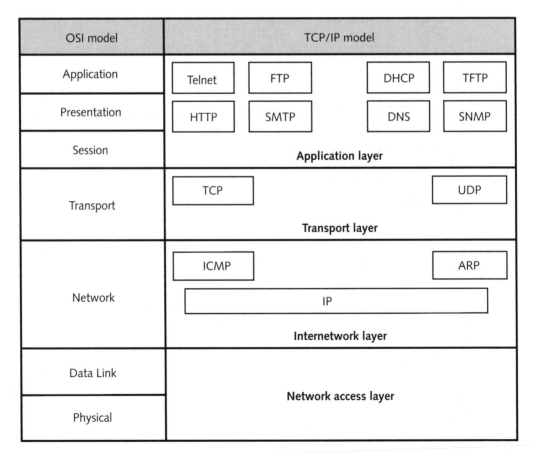

Figure 7-2 Comparing the OSI model and the TCP/IP model

The familiar network connection properties in a Windows OS are used again to show the layers in an OS context (see Figure 7-3). The Ethernet adapter shown in the "Connect using" text box represents the model's two bottom layers: Physical and Data Link. Internet Protocol (TCP/IP) represents the next two layers: Network and Transport. Client for Microsoft Networks and File and Printer Sharing for Microsoft Networks represent the top three layers: Session, Presentation, and Application. All these components (layers) are required for Windows network communication to work, but any component can be replaced with a suitable substitute (for example, replacing the NIC and its driver with a different NIC and driver) without affecting the other components.

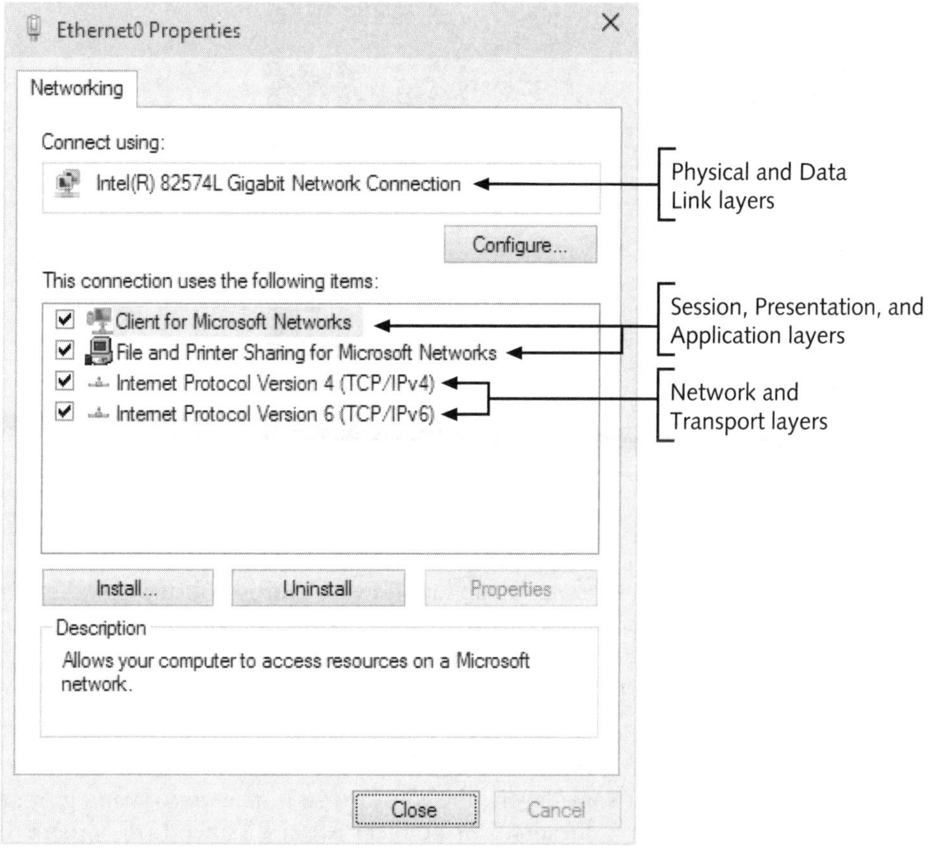

Figure 7-3 Layers of the OSI model in the Ethernet0 Properties dialog box

Each layer in the model provides services to the next higher layer until you get to the Application layer, which has the job of providing network services to user applications. In the layered approach, each layer on one computer behaves as though it were communicating with its counterpart on the other computer. This means each layer on the receiving computer sees network data in the same format its counterpart on the sending computer did. This behavior is called **peer communication** between layers, as shown in Figure 7-4. Returning to the U.S. mail analogy, the receiver of the letter, Cindy, sees the letter in the same format Tom saw it before he placed it in an envelope. Likewise, the mail carrier in San Francisco saw the envelope (with the letter in it) in the same format the letter carrier in New York did.

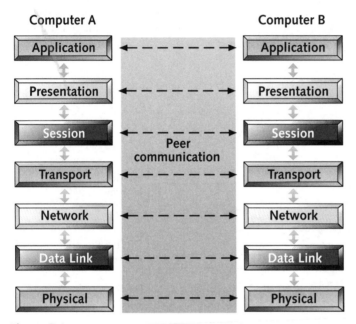

Figure 7-4 Peer communication between OSI layers

In network communication, data passes up and down the protocol stacks on both machines. Operations occurring on the way down the stack on the transmitting machine are largely reversed on the way up the stack on the receiving machine, so data on one layer of the sender is nearly identical to data arriving on that layer for the receiver.

On data's way down the stack, it's divided into data units suitable for each layer. Each unit, called a **protocol data unit** (**PDU**), is passed from one layer to another on its way up or down the protocol stack. At some layers, the software adds its own formatting or addressing to the PDU, which is called a "header." As you learned in Chapter 1, the process of adding this header is called "encapsulation." In the mail delivery analogy, the sender must put the letter (data) into an envelope (encapsulation) and address the envelope.

When data arrives at the receiving end, the packet travels up the stack from the Physical layer through the Application layer. At each layer, the software reads its PDU data and performs any additional processing that's required. It then strips its header information from the PDU (a process called **deencapsulation**) and passes the PDU to the next higher layer. When the packet leaves the Application layer, data is in a form that the receiving application can read and has been stripped of all the network addressing and packaging instructions needed to move the data from sender to receiver. Again, using the mail delivery analogy, the deencapsulation process is analogous to the letter recipient reading the envelope and verifying the address before opening and discarding the envelope to finally read the letter.

Simulation 11 shows how data generated from an application travels down through the OSI model layers, with encapsulations added where necessary, and how the process is reversed on the receiving computer.

Simulation 11: Peer communication with the OSI model

The following sections describe the layers of the OSI model and the services each one provides. After reading this material, you should have a good idea of each layer's functions, how each layer interacts with adjacent layers, and some problems that can occur at each layer. Protocols and software components are listed for each layer. When applicable, devices that operate at a layer are listed. When a device is said to operate at a layer, it means the highest layer in which the device operates. For example, a PC operates at Layer 7, so it's considered a Layer 7 device, but clearly, a PC also operates at Layers 6 through 1.

Both the name and number of the layer are listed. When discussing devices or protocols in relation to the OSI model, the OSI layer number rather than its name is often used. For example, you hear terms such as "Layer 3 switch" or "Layer 7 gateway."

Application Layer

The **Application layer** (Layer 7) provides interfaces for applications to access network services, such as file sharing, message handling, and database access. It also handles error recovery for applications, as needed. The PDU at this layer (and the Presentation and Session layers) is referred to simply as "data."

Generally, components at the Application layer have both a client component and a server component. An example of this client/server pairing is a Web browser (client component) that accesses a Web server (server component), and both provide access to the Application-layer protocol HTTP. Other examples are Client for Microsoft Networks, used to access Windows network services (such as File and Printer Sharing), and the UNIX/Linux Network File System (NFS) client, which provides access to shared file resources. Common protocols at the Application layer include HTTP, FTP, SMB/CIFS, TFTP, and SMTP. Computers with network OSs and some security devices operate at Layer 7 because they work with these Application-layer protocols.

Possible problems at this layer include missing or misconfigured client or server software and incompatible or obsolete commands used to communicate between a client and server. In addition, Application-layer protocols that use a connectionless Transport-layer protocol are more susceptible to network disruptions and must provide their own error recovery or rely on error recovery from the user application.

Presentation Layer

The **Presentation layer** (Layer 6) handles data formatting and translation. For outgoing messages, it converts data into a format specified by the Application layer, if necessary; for incoming messages, it reverses the conversion if required by the receiving application. In short, Layer 6 "presents" data in a suitable format to the Application layer. The Presentation layer handles protocol conversion, data encryption and decryption, data compression and decompression, data representation incompatibilities between OSs, and graphics commands.

An example of functionality at this level is a Web browser displaying graphics files embedded in a Web page. In this situation, the Presentation-layer component informs the Application layer what type of data or graphics format to display. Yet another example involves character conversion. For example, PCs represent the carriage return/line feed combination in text files differently than Linux and UNIX systems do. If no conversion takes place, a text file created on a Linux system looks like one long string of sentences when read by Notepad on a PC. However, if the file is transferred from Linux to a PC with a file transfer program that can convert the codes, the Presentation-layer component of the file transfer program handles the conversion. As another example, a Web browser that connects to a secure Web server with encryption protocols must encrypt data before it's transferred to the server and decrypt data arriving from the Web server, which is a Presentation-layer function.

A software component known as a "redirector" operates at this layer. It intercepts requests for service from the computer; requests that can't be handled locally are redirected across the network to a network resource that can handle the request. Software components operating at this layer are usually built into the Application-layer component. These components include FTP clients and servers, HTTP clients and servers, and OS-specific clients and servers, such as Client for Microsoft Networks and File and Printer Sharing for Microsoft Networks.

Possible problems occurring at this layer include incompatible or missing translation software, in which the Presentation layer on one system doesn't have the necessary decryption, decompression, graphics-processing, or data-translation software to interpret received data correctly.

Session Layer

Layer 5, the **Session layer**, permits two computers to hold ongoing communications—called a "session"—across a network, so applications on either end of the session can exchange data for as long as the session lasts. The Session layer handles communication setup ahead of data transfers when necessary and session teardown when the session ends. Some common network functions this layer handles include name lookup and user logon and logoff. Therefore, DNS and other name resolution protocols work in part at this layer, as do the logon/logoff function and some authentication protocols built into most client software, such as FTP, Client for Microsoft Networks, and NFS.

The Session layer also manages the mechanics of ongoing conversations, such as identifying which side can transmit data when, and for how long. In addition, a process called "checkpointing" is performed at this layer. Checkpointing is a synchronization process between two related streams of data, such as an audio and a video stream in a Web-conferencing application. The Session layer keeps the audio in sync with the video.

Transport Layer

The **Transport layer** (Layer 4) manages data transfer from one application to another across a network. It breaks long data streams into smaller chunks called "segments." Segmenting the data is important because every network technology has a maximum frame size called the **maximum transmission unit (MTU)**. For Ethernet, the MTU is 1518 bytes, which means segments must be small enough to allow for the Network-layer and Data Link–layer headers and still be no larger than 1518 bytes. If segmenting doesn't occur, as with UDP, the Network layer must fragment the packets it creates, leading to inefficient and possibly unreliable communication. Figure 7-5 shows a simplified example of what the original data might look like and what each segment might look like after data is broken up into smaller pieces and the header is added.

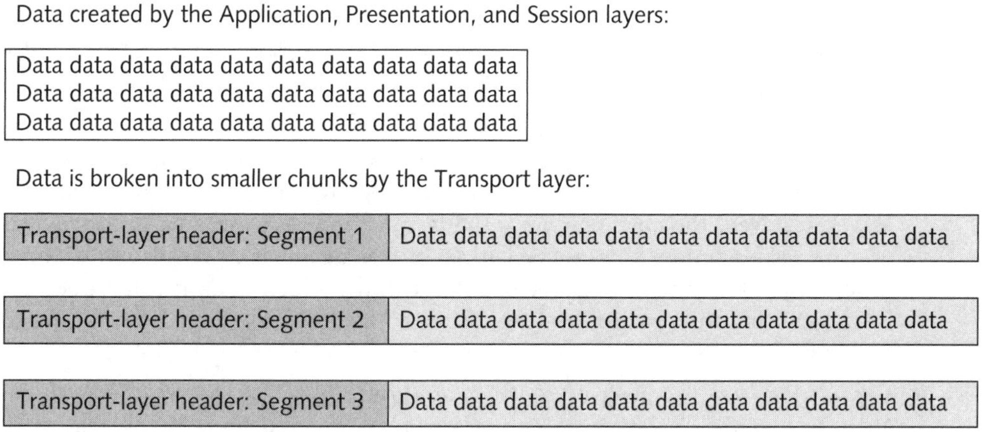

Data created by the Application, Presentation, and Session layers:

Data data data data data data data data data data
Data data data data data data data data data data
Data data data data data data data data data data

Data is broken into smaller chunks by the Transport layer:

Transport-layer header: Segment 1	Data data data data data data data data data data data

Transport-layer header: Segment 2	Data data data data data data data data data data data

Transport-layer header: Segment 3	Data data data data data data data data data data data

Figure 7-5 The Transport layer breaks data into segments

To ensure reliable delivery, the Transport layer includes flow control and acknowledgements and handles resequencing segments into the original data on receipt. Flow control ensures that the recipient isn't overwhelmed with more data than it can handle, which could result in dropped packets.

The PDU at this layer is a segment (see Figure 7-6). The components working at this layer include TCP and UDP from the TCP/IP protocol suite. As you learned in Chapter 5, however, UDP doesn't perform all the functions expected of an OSI model's Transport-layer protocol. Therefore, it's sometimes called a "pseudo-Transport-layer protocol" and UDP's PDU is often called a "datagram" rather than a segment.

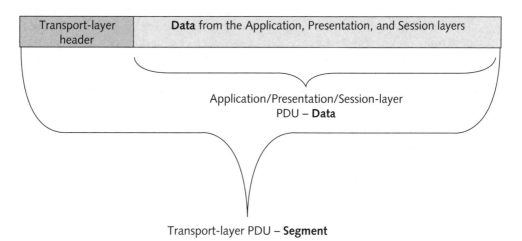

Figure 7-6 The Transport-layer PDU: a segment

Some key fields in the Transport-layer header include the following:

- *Source and destination port numbers*—As discussed in Chapter 5, port numbers identify the application or service the segment should be delivered to. Each application or service is assigned a unique port number so that when data arrives, the Transport-layer protocol (TCP or UDP) knows which application it should be transferred to.

- *Sequence and acknowledgement numbers*—These fields, found in TCP headers but not UDP headers, are used to ensure that all data sent was received; if segments arrive out of order, the sequence number is used to reorder them.

- *Window size*—This field specifies the maximum amount of data in bytes that can be transferred before the sender requires an acknowledgement. If an acknowledgement isn't received, the data sent since the last acknowledgement was received is sent again. The window size, along with acknowledgements, provides flow control because if a computer is overwhelmed with too much data, it can reduce the window size, causing the sending computer to send fewer segments before waiting for an acknowledgement.

Problems that can occur at this layer include segments that are too large for the medium between source and destination networks. This situation forces the Network layer to fragment the segments, which causes performance degradation. In addition, hackers can exploit TCP's handshaking feature with a half-open SYN attack, discussed in Chapter 9.

Network Layer

Layer 3, the **Network layer**, handles logical addressing, translates logical network addresses (IP addresses) into physical addresses (MAC addresses), and performs best path selection and routing in an internetwork. A router performs best path selection when multiple pathways, or routes, are available to reach a destination network; the router attempts to choose the best, or fastest, path.

As you can see, this layer performs the same tasks as TCP/IP's Internetwork layer. It's also the traffic cop for network activity because it provides access control. **Access control** is handled at the Network layer during the routing process; the router consults a list of rules before forwarding an incoming packet to determine whether a packet meeting certain criteria (such as source and destination address) should be permitted to reach the intended destination. This feature of routers is one reason to divide large networks into smaller subnets. By creating several logical groups of computers, you can control which users have access to which resources, using routers as gatekeeper.

The PDU at the Network layer is a packet, as shown in Figure 7-7. The software components working at this layer include IP, ARP, ICMP, and several routing protocols from the TCP/IP suite. Routers, of course, work at this layer, as do firewalls and certain remote access devices, such as virtual private network (VPN) servers. A switch with routing capabilities, called a "Layer 3 switch," also works at the Network layer. Essentially, any device that works mainly with packets and their source and destination IP addresses is said to be a Network-layer device or Layer 3 device.

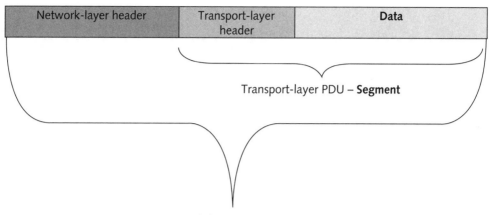

Network-layer header	Transport-layer header	Data

Transport-layer PDU – **Segment**

Network-layer PDU – **Packet**

Figure 7-7 The Network-layer PDU: a packet

A mostly obsolete protocol called Reverse Address Resolution Protocol (RARP) also works at the Network layer. It resolves a known MAC address to an IP address.

Many problems can occur at the Network layer and often include incorrect IP addresses or subnet masks, incorrect router configuration, and router operation errors.

Data Link Layer

Layer 2, the **Data Link layer,** works with frames and is the intermediary between the Network layer and Physical layer. It defines how computers access the network medium—also called "media access control," which is why the MAC address is defined at this layer. As you've learned, media access control methods include CSMA/CD and token passing, among others.

As shown in Figure 7-8, a frame consists of both a header and a trailer component. The trailer component labeled "FCS" (frame check sequence) contains the CRC error-checking code discussed in Chapter 3. The CRC value is recalculated on the receiving end, and if the sent and recalculated values agree, the assumption is that data wasn't altered during transmission. If they differ, the frame is discarded in most networking technologies. Note that the CRC is recalculated at every intermediary device (usually a router) between the source and destination computer. For example, if the frame is delivered to a router, the router recalculates the CRC and compares it with the original to make sure the frame wasn't damaged in transport. Next, the router changes the source MAC address to its own MAC address and the destination MAC address to the next device (which might be another router or the final destination device). Therefore, the router must recalculate the CRC and place it in the frame trailer because the frame's contents were changed. Simulation 9, which you saw in Chapter 5, shows how a frame header changes during its journey through an internetwork.

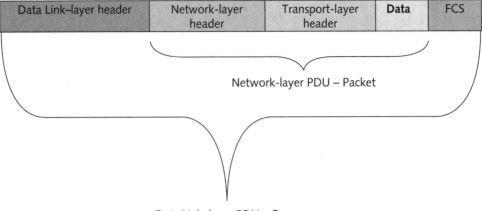

Figure 7-8 The Data Link–layer PDU: a frame

Simulation 9: The changing frame header

The Data Link header contains fields for source and destination addresses. The destination address is the hardware (MAC) address of the computer the frame should be delivered to or an intermediate device, such as a router. The source address is the MAC address of the sending computer or intermediary device and tells the recipient where to send a reply.

After receiving a frame from the Physical layer and verifying the destination MAC address and the CRC, the Data Link layer strips its header and trailer information from the frame and sends the resulting packet up to the Network layer for further processing. In most networking technologies, the Data Link layer discards frames containing CRC and other frame errors. However, it's the responsibility of the upper layers (usually the Transport layer) to retransmit data that has been discarded because of errors. TCP, for example, detects missing segments caused by discarded frames because of the sequence numbers it uses to keep track of all segments.

The software component operating at this layer is the NIC driver, and the hardware components include NICs and switches. A NIC operates at this layer because it contains the MAC address and is responsible for media access control. Switches operate at this layer because they do their job by examining MAC addresses in the frame header and using this information to switch packets from incoming ports to outgoing ports. Because media access control is defined in this layer, networking technologies such as Ethernet and token ring operate at this layer. Problems occurring in the Data Link layer include collisions and invalid frames, which can be caused by collisions, poor network design, line noise, or NIC driver problems. Another problem at this layer results from trying to use incompatible network technologies, such as token ring and Ethernet, on the same LAN.

Physical Layer

Last but not least, the job of the **Physical layer** (Layer 1) is to convert bits into signals for outgoing messages and signals into bits for incoming messages. The type of signals generated depend on the medium; for example, wire media, such as twisted-pair cable, use electrical pulses, fiber-optic media use pulses of light, and wireless media use radio waves. At this layer, details for creating a physical network connection are specified, such as the type of connectors used to attach the medium to the NIC.

The Physical layer also specifies how to encode 1s and 0s. **Encoding** is representing 0s and 1s by a physical signal, such as electrical voltage or a light pulse. For example, a 1 bit might be represented on a copper wire by the transition from a 0-volt to 5-volt signal, whereas a 0 bit might be represented by the transition from a 5-volt signal to a 0-volt signal.

The network components working at the Physical layer include all the cables and connectors used on the medium plus repeaters and hubs. Problems occurring here are often related to incorrect media termination, EMI or noise that scrambles the signals, and NICs and hubs that are misconfigured or don't work correctly.

Summary of the OSI Model

The OSI model is a helpful way to categorize and compartmentalize networking activities, and most discussions of protocol suites and networking software use its terminology. Table 7-2 summarizes the actions occurring at each layer. Even though most protocol suites don't adhere strictly to this model (perhaps because so many of them were already implemented in some form before the model's development), they still incorporate its outlook on networking.

 ARP is said to reside between Layers 2 and 3, as it provides Layer 3 services to Layer 2 protocols.

 Although not all networking protocols adhere to the OSI model, a network administrator's clear understanding of the functions at each layer is essential in troubleshooting networks and network equipment and in understanding how network devices operate.

Table 7-2 OSI model summary

Layer	PDU	Protocols/software	Devices	Function
7. Application	Data	HTTP, FTP, SMTP, DHCP	Computers	Provides programs with access to network services
6. Presentation	Data	Redirectors	N/A	Handles data representation to application and data conversions, ensures that data can be read by the receiving system, and handles encryption and decryption
5. Session	Data	DNS, authentication protocols	N/A	Establishes, maintains, and coordinates communication between applications

(Continues)

Table 7-2 OSI model summary (continued)

Layer	PDU	Protocols/ software	Devices	Function
4. Transport	Segment	TCP, UDP	N/A	Ensures reliable delivery of data, breaks data into segments, handles sequencing and acknowledgements, and provides flow control
3. Network	Packet	IP, ICMP, ARP	Routers, firewalls, Layer 3 switches	Handles packet routing, logical addressing, and access control through packet inspection
2. Data Link	Frame	Ethernet, token ring, FDDI, NIC drivers	Switches, NICs	Provides physical device addressing, device-to-device delivery of frames, media access control, and MAC addresses
1. Physical	Bits	N/A	Network media, hubs/repeaters, connectors	Manages hardware connections, handles sending and receiving binary signals, and handles encoding of bits

The OSI model helps explain how data is formatted and moves up and down the proto-col stack and from computer to computer. Although TCP/IP was developed long before the OSI model, you can see how the TCP/IP model adheres to the OSI concept of a lay-ered architecture. Understanding both models and their relationship to each other is important, but when discussing devices and software that work at particular layers, the OSI model's layer names and numbers are the most pertinent.

IEEE 802 Networking Standards

The Institute of Electrical and Electronics Engineers (IEEE) defined LAN standards to ensure that network interfaces and cabling from multiple manufacturers would be compatible as long as they adhered to the same IEEE specification. This effort was called Project 802 to indicate the year (1980) and month (February) of its inception. Since then, the IEEE 802 specifications have taken firm root in the networking world. Because the OSI model wasn't standardized until 1983 to 1984, the IEEE 802 standards predate the model, as did TCP/IP. Nevertheless, the two were developed in collaboration and are compatible with one another. (The IEEE is one of the U.S. participants in the ISO.)

For more information on the IEEE and its standards, visit
www.ieee.org.

Project 802 concentrates its efforts on standards that describe a network's physical elements (the topics of Chapters 3 and 4), including NICs, cables, connectors, signaling technologies, media access control, and the like. Most of these elements reside in the lower two layers of the OSI model: Data Link and Physical. In particular, the 802 specification describes how NICs can access and transfer data across a variety of network media and what's involved in attaching, managing, and detaching these devices in a network environment.

IEEE 802 Specifications

The IEEE numbers the collection of 802 documents starting with 802.1, 802.2, and so forth. Each number after the dot represents a different technology or subset of a technology. When a technology is enhanced, such as Ethernet going from 10 Mbps to 100 Mbps, each enhancement is usually specified by letters after the number. For example, 802.3 is the original Ethernet standard, and 802.3u specifies 100BaseT Ethernet.

Table 7-3 lists the major 802 categories. For the purposes of this book, standards 802.3 and 802.11 are of the most interest because they define the most widely used technologies of Ethernet and Wi-Fi, although 802.15 and 802.16 warrant some attention, too. The 802 standards aren't a static set of documents. New technologies and enhancements are added often, as with the newest 802.11ac Wi-Fi standard.

You can access IEEE 802 standards at *www.ieee.org/publications_standards/index.html#IEEE_Standards*. Most require a fee or subscription membership.

Table 7-3 IEEE 802 standards

Standard	Name	Explanation
802.1	Internetworking	Covers routing, bridging, and internetwork communication
802.2	Logical Link Control	Covers error control and flow control over data frames (inactive)
802.3	Ethernet LAN	Covers all forms of Ethernet media and interfaces, from 10 Mbps to 10 Gbps (10 Gigabit Ethernet)
802.4	Token Bus LAN	Covers all forms of token bus media and interfaces (disbanded)
802.5	Token Ring LAN	Covers all forms of token ring media and interfaces
802.6	Metropolitan Area Network	Covers MAN technologies, addressing, and services (disbanded)
802.7	Broadband Technical Advisory Group	Covers broadband networking media, interfaces, and other equipment (disbanded)
802.8	Fiber-Optic Technical Advisory Group	Covers use of fiber-optic media and technologies for various networking types (disbanded)
802.9	Integrated Voice/Data Networks	Covers integration of voice and data traffic over a single network medium (disbanded)
802.10	Network Security	Covers network access controls, encryption, certification, and other security topics (disbanded)
802.11	Wireless Networks	Sets standards for wireless networking for many different broadcast frequencies and techniques
802.12	High-Speed Networking	Covers a variety of 100 Mbps-plus technologies, including 100VG-AnyLAN (disbanded)
802.13	Unused	
802.14	Cable modems	Specifies data transport over cable TV (disbanded)
802.15	Wireless PAN	Covers standards for wireless personal area networks

(Continues)

Table 7-3 IEEE 802 standards (continued)

Standard	Name	Explanation
802.16	Wireless MAN (WiMAX)	Covers wireless metropolitan area networks
802.17	Resilient Packet Ring	Covers emerging standards for very high-speed, ring-based LANs and MANs
802.18	Wireless Advisory Group	A technical advisory group that monitors radio-based wireless standards
802.19	Coexistence Advisory Group	A group that addresses issues of coexistence with current and developing standards
802.20	Mobile Broadband Wireless	A group working to enable always-on multivendor mobile broadband wireless access
802.21	Media Independent Handoff	A group working to enable handoff between wireless networks of the same or different types
802.22	Wireless Regional Area Network	Working to bring broadband access to hard-to-reach low-population areas
802.23	Emergency Services Working Group	A new group (March 2010) working to facilitate civil authority communication systems

IEEE 802 Extensions to the OSI Reference Model

The two lowest layers of the OSI model—the Physical and Data Link layers—define how computers attach to specific network media and specify how more than one computer can access the network without causing interference with other computers on the network. Project 802 took this work further to create the specifications (mainly 802.1 through 802.5) that define the most successful LAN technologies, including Ethernet and token ring, which together dominated the LAN world. Token ring, however, is now an obsolete LAN technology.

The IEEE 802 specification expanded the OSI model at the Physical and Data Link layers. Figure 7-9 shows how the 802 standards provide more detail by separating the Data Link layer into these sublayers:

- Logical Link Control (LLC) for error recovery and flow control
- Media Access Control (MAC) for controlling access to network media

The **Logical Link Control (LLC) sublayer** (defined by 802.2) controls data-link communication and defines the use of logical interface points, called "service access points (SAPs)," that other computers can use to transfer information from this sublayer to the upper OSI layers. It's also responsible for error recovery in some situations and is the sublayer that communicates with the Network layer. There are several modes of LLC operation; some modes require the LLC to detect and recover from errors in transmission and provide flow control. This function is largely carried out in hardware on the NIC.

The **Media Access Control (MAC) sublayer** manages access to the physical medium and, therefore, communicates with the Physical layer. It communicates directly with a computer's NIC and is responsible for physical addressing. The physical address burned into every NIC is called a "MAC address" because it operates at this sublayer of the 802.2 specification. The MAC sublayer of the Data Link layer is where networking technologies such as Ethernet, token ring, FDDI, and so forth do their work.

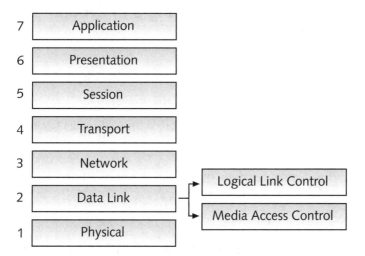

Figure 7-9 The IEEE 802 standard divides the OSI Data Link layer into two sublayers

Hands-On Project 7-1: Viewing Your MAC Address

Time Required: 10 minutes

Objective: Use different methods to view your MAC address.

Required Tools and Equipment: Net-*XX*

Description: In this project, you use the Ethernet0 Status dialog box and the `ipconfig` and `getmac` commands to view your MAC address.

1. Start your computer, and log on as **NetAdmin**, if necessary.

2. Right-click **Start** and click **Network Connections**. Right-click **Ethernet0** and click **Status** to open the Ethernet0 Status dialog box.

3. Click **Details**. In the Network Connection Details list box, the physical address of your NIC (its MAC address) is the third item from the top. Write down the MAC address, and then click **Close** twice.

4. Open a command prompt window. Type **`ipconfig /all`** and press **Enter**. Your MAC address is listed under Ethernet0 as "Physical Address." If you have more than one interface, each interface is listed along with the physical address.

5. Type **`getmac`** and press **Enter**. Your MAC address is listed along with the Windows internal name for the interface. The `getmac` command displays the MAC address for all interfaces. Verify that the address it displays is the same as in Step 3.

6. Close all open windows, but leave your computer running for the next project.

Hands-On Project 7-2: Dragging and Dropping the OSI Model Layers

Time Required: 10 minutes

Objective: Put the OSI model layers in the correct order by using Simulation 12.

Required Tools and Equipment: A computer with a Web browser

Description: In this project, you run Simulation 12 to place the OSI model layers in order.

1. Start your computer, and log on, if necessary.
2. Access Simulation 12 by following the instructions in this book's introduction.
3. Drag and drop the OSI model layers in their correct order.
4. Click **Menu** to go back to the simulation menu, and leave it open for the next project.

Hands-On Project 7-3: Matching OSI Model Descriptions to Layer Numbers

Time Required: 10 minutes

Objective: Match the OSI model layer descriptions to the correct layer numbers by using Simulation 13.

Required Tools and Equipment: A computer with a Web browser

Description: In this project, you run Simulation 13 to place the OSI model layer description in the correct layer number.

1. Start your computer, and log on if necessary.
2. Access Simulation 13 by following the instructions in this book's introduction.
3. Drag the OSI model layer description into their correct order by layer number.
4. Click **Menu** to go back to the simulation menu, and leave it open for the next project.

Hands-On Project 7-4: Creating a Frame

Time Required: 10 minutes

Objective: Create a frame by dragging and dropping frame headers in Simulation 14.

Required Tools and Equipment: A computer with a Web browser

Description: In this project, you run Simulation 14 to create a frame based on the information displayed.

1. Start your computer, and log on if necessary.
2. Access Simulation 14 by following the instructions in this book's introduction.
3. Given the information in the simulation, drag frame headers to the correct places in the target frame placeholder.
4. Close all open windows.

Chapter Summary

- The OSI reference model and IEEE Project 802 define a frame of reference for networking and specify the operation of most networking technologies in current use. Together, these models describe the complex processes and operations involved in sending and receiving information across a network.

- The OSI reference model separates networking into seven layers, each with its own purposes and activities. From the top down, the layers are Application, Presentation, Session, Transport, Network, Data Link, and Physical. Most network products and technologies are also specified in terms of the layers at which they operate. The layers help describe the features and functions the products and technologies deliver.

- Following is a summary of the functions of each OSI model layer:

  - *Application*—Provides access to network resources
  - *Presentation*—Handles data formatting and translation
  - *Session*—Manages ongoing conversations between two computers
  - *Transport*—Breaks long data streams into smaller chunks (segments)
  - *Network*—Provides best path selection and IP addressing
  - *Data Link*—Defines how computers access the media
  - *Physical*—Converts bits into signals and defines media and connectors

- The IEEE 802 project defines networking standards in more than 20 categories to ensure that network interfaces and cabling from different manufacturers are compatible. The IEEE 802.2 standard specifies the functions of a network's Physical and Data Link layers by dividing the Data Link layer into two sublayers: Logical Link Control (LLC) and Media Access Control (MAC). Together, these sublayers handle media access, addressing, and access control and provide reliable, error-free delivery of frames from one computer to another.

Key Terms

access control   In the context of the Network layer and routing, the process by which a router consults a list of rules before forwarding an incoming packet. The rules determine whether a packet meeting certain criteria (such as source and destination address) should be permitted to reach the intended destination.

Application layer   Layer 7 in the OSI model provides interfaces that enable applications to request and receive network services. *See also* Open Systems Interconnection (OSI) reference model.

Data Link layer   Layer 2 in the OSI model is responsible for managing access to the network medium and delivery of data frames from sender to receiver or from sender to an intermediate device, such as a router. *See also* Open Systems Interconnection (OSI) reference model.

deencapsulation   The process of stripping the header from a PDU as it makes its way up the communication layers before being passed to the next higher layer. *See also* protocol data unit (PDU).

encoding   Representing 0s and 1s as a physical signal, such as electrical voltage or a light pulse.

International Organization for Standardization (ISO)   The international standards-setting body based in Geneva, Switzerland, that sets worldwide technology standards.

Logical Link Control (LLC) sublayer   The upper sublayer of the IEEE Project 802 model for the OSI model's Data Link layer. It handles error-free delivery and controls the flow of frames between sender and receiver across a network.

maximum transmission unit (MTU)   The maximum frame size allowed to be transmitted across a network medium.

Media Access Control (MAC) sublayer   The lower sublayer of the IEEE Project 802 model for the OSI model's Data Link layer. It handles accessing network media and mapping between logical and physical network addresses for NICs.

Network layer   Layer 3 of the OSI model handles logical addressing and routing of PDUs across internetworks. *See also* Open Systems Interconnection (OSI) reference model *and* protocol data unit (PDU).

Open Systems Interconnection (OSI) reference model   ISO Standard 7498 defines a frame of reference for understanding networks by dividing the process of network communication into seven layers. Each layer is defined in terms of the services and data it handles on behalf of the layer above it and the services and data it needs from the layer below it.

peer communication   In the layered approach, each layer on one computer behaves as though it were communicating with its counterpart on the other computer. This means each layer on the receiving computer sees network data in the same format its counterpart on the sending computer did.

Physical layer   Layer 1, the bottom layer of the OSI model, transmits and receives signals and specifies the physical details of cables, NICs, connectors, and hardware behavior. *See also* Open Systems Interconnection (OSI) reference model.

Presentation layer   At Layer 6 of the OSI model, data can be encrypted and/or compressed to facilitate delivery. Platform-specific application formats are translated into generic data formats for transmission or from generic data formats into platform-specific application formats for delivery to the Application layer. *See also* Open Systems Interconnection (OSI) reference model.

protocol data unit (PDU)   A unit of information passed as a self-contained data structure from one layer to another on its way up or down the network protocol stack.

Session layer   Layer 5 of the OSI model is responsible for setting up, maintaining, and ending communication sequences (called sessions) across a network. *See also* Open Systems Interconnection (OSI) reference model.

Transport layer   Layer 4 of the OSI model is responsible for reliable delivery of data streams across a network. Layer 4 protocols break large streams of data into smaller chunks and use sequence numbers and acknowledgements to provide communication and flow control. *See also* Open Systems Interconnection (OSI) reference model *and* protocol data unit (PDU).

Review Questions

1. The original commercial version of Ethernet supported 10 Mbps bandwidth; the version introduced in the early 1990s supports 100 Mbps; and in 1998, Gigabit Ethernet was introduced. All versions use the same data frame formats, with the same maximum PDU sizes, so they can interoperate freely. Given this information and what you know of layered technologies, which of the following statements is true? (Choose all that apply.)

   a. Ethernet works at the Data Link and Physical layers of the OSI model, and upgrades to newer, faster versions of Ethernet can be made by changing only the components that work at these layers.

   b. Ethernet spans several layers and requires a new protocol stack to upgrade to new versions.

   c. Changes in technology at one layer of the OSI model don't usually affect the operation of other layers.

   d. Ethernet isn't considered a scalable technology.

2. The addition of information to a PDU as it's passed from one layer to the next is called which of the following?

   a. PDI transforming

   b. Encapsulation

   c. Deencapsulation

   d. Converting

3. Layers acting as though they communicate directly with each other across the network are called which of the following?

   a. Partners

   b. Synchronous

   c. Interchangeable

   d. Peers

4. Place the following letters in the correct order to represent the OSI model from Layer 7 to Layer 1:

   a. Presentation

   b. Data Link

   c. Session

   d. Physical

   e. Application

   f. Transport

   g. Network

5. Which OSI layer creates and processes frames?

6. Which OSI layer handles flow control, data segmentation, and reliability?

    a. Application

    b. Physical

    c. Transport

    d. Data Link

7. Which OSI layer governs how a NIC is attached to the network medium?

8. Which OSI layer determines the route a packet takes from sender to receiver?

    a. 7

    b. 1

    c. 3

    d. 4

9. Which OSI layer is responsible for setting up, maintaining, and ending ongoing information exchanges across a network?

    a. 6

    b. 3

    c. 2

    d. 5

10. Which of the following elements might the Data Link layer add to its PDU? (Choose all that apply.)

    a. Physical addresses

    b. Logical addresses

    c. Data

    d. CRC

11. When and how many times is a CRC calculated?

    a. Once, before transmission

    b. Once, after receipt

    c. Twice, once before transmission and again on receipt

    d. At the source and destination and at each intermediary device

12. Which layer of the OSI model does Project 802 divide into two sublayers?

    a. Physical

    b. Data Link

    c. Network

    d. Session

13. What are the names of the sublayers specified as part of Project 802? (Choose all that apply.)

    a. Data Link Control (DLC)

    b. Logical Link Control (LLC)

    c. Carrier Sense Multiple Access/Collision Detection (CSMA/CD)

    d. Media Access Control (MAC)

14. Which term refers to stripping header information as a PDU is passed from one layer to a higher layer?

    a. Deencapsulation

    b. Encapsulation

    c. PDU stripping

    d. Packetization

15. Which IEEE 802 standard applies to Ethernet?

    a. 802.2

    b. 802.3

    c. 802.4

    d. 802.5

    e. 802.11

16. Which IEEE 802 standard applies to wireless LANs?

    a. 802.2

    b. 802.3

    c. 802.4

    d. 802.5

    e. 802.11

17. What's the name of the PDU at the Transport layer?

    a. Bit

    b. Packet

    c. Segment

    d. Data

18. At which OSI layer does the PDU contain sequence and acknowledgement numbers?

    a. Application

    b. 4

    c. Data Link

    d. 6

19. Which of the following is an example of software found at the Application layer? (Choose all that apply.)

    a. FTP

    b. TCP

    c. HTTP

    d. ICMP

20. At which Data Link sublayer does the physical address reside?

    a. Media Access Control (MAC)

    b. Logical Link Control (LLC)

    c. Data Access Control (DAC)

    d. Network Access Control (NAC)

21. Which of the following problems can occur at the Physical layer?

    a. NIC driver problems

    b. Incorrect IP addresses

    c. Signal errors caused by noise

    d. Incorrect segment size

Critical Thinking

The following activities give you critical thinking challenges. Challenge labs give you an opportunity to use the skills you have learned to perform a task without step-by-step instructions. Case projects offer a practical networking setup for which you supply a written solution.

CHALLENGE LAB

Challenge Lab 7-1: Identifying OSI Model Layers from Captured Packets

Time Required: 15 minutes

Objective: Use Wireshark to capture the packets generated from an HTTP communication session. Identify the OSI model layers represented by the headers in the captured files.

Required Tools and Equipment: Net-XX with Wireshark installed and Internet access

Description: Using Wireshark and an appropriate capture filter, capture the packets involved in an HTTP session that you start by opening a Web page. Select an HTTP packet, and using the headers in the middle pane, perform the following tasks:

• Map the header names in the captured packet to the layers of the OSI model.

• For each header, find two fields you can identify as pertaining to that OSI layer's function, and be prepared to explain why.

- Write the information you derived from the previous items and be prepared to turn it in to your instructor or discuss it in class.

Challenge Lab 7-2: Listing MAC Addresses in Your Network

Time Required: 15 minutes

Objective: Find MAC addresses for the computers, printers, routers, and other devices on your network.

Required Tools and Equipment: Net-*XX*

Description: Your boss has asked you to get a list of MAC addresses in your network. He has told you that the addresses of all devices are in the range 192.168.100.1 through 192.168.100.20. (If these addresses aren't the ones you're using, substitute the actual addresses.) Because people are working at their computers, he expects you to accomplish this task without leaving your computer. List the steps you took to get all the MAC addresses.

Case Project 7-1

The OSI model is a useful tool in troubleshooting a network because it enables you to isolate a problem to a particular software module or piece of hardware. In this project, after reading the description of a problem, identify the OSI model layer or layers that are most likely involved.

- A computer won't connect to the network. After some investigation, you find that the patch cable isn't terminated correctly.

_____

- A computer can access resources on the local LAN but not on a different subnet. You find that the computer's default gateway isn't configured correctly.

_____

- You can ping a computer you're trying to transfer files to via FTP, but you can't communicate by using FTP.

_____

- All computers connected to a particular hub have lost network connectivity. You determine that the hub is the problem.

_____

- You receive an encrypted text file, but when you open it, the text is unreadable. You determine that decryption didn't take place as it should have.

_____

- You check some statistics generated by a network-monitoring program and discover that an abnormally high number of CRC errors were detected.

   _____

- One of your servers has been exhibiting sluggish network performance. You use a network-monitoring program to try to evaluate the problem. You find considerable TCP retries occurring because the server is being overwhelmed by data, and packets are being discarded.

   _____

- A user is trying to connect to another computer, but the logon attempt is continually rejected.

   _____

- You try to access a Linux server to share files by using NFS. You can communicate with the server, but the shared files don't appear to be available.

   _____

- You inspect a computer that isn't able to communicate with other computers. You find that IPv6 instead of IPv4 is installed on that computer.

   _____

Case Project 7-2

Your instructor might want you to organize in groups for this project. This chapter included a few real-world examples that use a layered approach to describing a process. See whether you can come up with another process that can be described in layers. You should give a presentation to the class with a detailed description of the layered process you decide on.

Case Project 7-3

You want to transfer a document from one computer to another, and *you want the document to be encrypted*. The destination computer is on another network, so you know *data has to travel through one or more routers*. The network technology on *your network is Ethernet*, but the technology on *the destination network is Wi-Fi*. From what you have learned about networking, should this document transfer work? Why or why not? Which layers of the OSI model are involved in the italicized parts of this description?

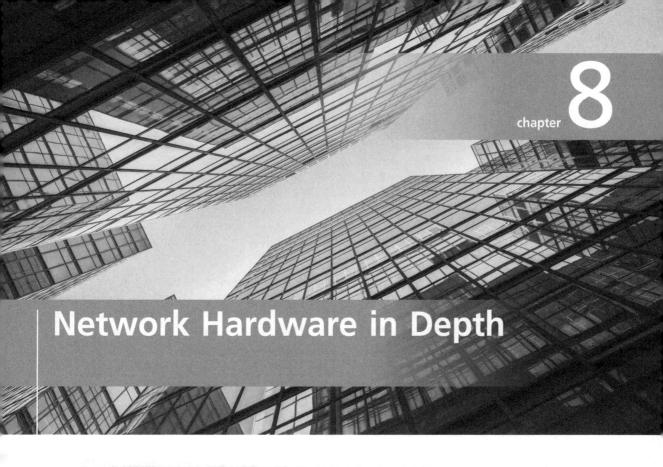

chapter 8

Network Hardware in Depth

After reading this chapter and completing the exercises, you will be able to:

- Describe the advanced features and operation of network switches
- Describe routing table properties and discuss routing protocols
- Explain basic and advanced wireless access point features
- Select the most suitable NIC bus and features for a computer

Network packets travel through a variety of network devices on their journey between sender and receiver. These devices vary from the simplest of hubs requiring no configuration to complex routers and switches that have a multitude of configuration settings and fine-tuning options.

This chapter begins with switches because although some high-end hubs can be configured for the purposes of network management, hubs are declining in use to the point of near obsolescence. Routers and routing protocols are discussed next, and you learn more about a routing table and the protocols used to build it. In the section on wireless access points, you learn about some configuration and security options available for wireless networks. Finally, the discussion of NICs focuses on some high-performance and enterprise features you might see on server NICs and workstation NICs in a large internetwork.

Although there are many other types of network devices, the devices discussed in this chapter form the core of most networks. Network security devices, such as firewalls and intrusion detection systems, are discussed in Chapter 9, and network performance-enhancing devices, such as load balancers and packet shapers, are discussed in Chapter 12.

Network Switches in Depth

Table 8-1 summarizes what you need for the hands-on projects in this chapter.

Table 8-1   Hands-on project requirements

Hands-on project	Requirements	Time required	Notes
Hands-On Project 8-1: Observing a Switching Loop	Two lab computers, two switches, two patch cables, two crossover cables	20 minutes	
Hands-On Project 8-2: Viewing and Changing Your Computer's Routing Table	Net-XX	5 minutes	

Network switches at their simplest are plug-and-play devices. Apply power to a switch, and it's ready to move frames from one device to another. However, advanced features on some switches enable administrators to fine-tune their networks for optimal operation. Before getting into these features, reviewing some properties common to all switches is helpful:

- Switches work at the Data Link layer (Layer 2) of the OSI model. At this layer, physical addresses are defined, and the PDU at this layer is the frame. Switches receive frames on one port and forward the frames out the port where the destination device can be found.

- Switches **flood** broadcast frames out all ports. When a switch receives a broadcast frame (defined as a destination address of all binary 1s, or FF:FF:FF:FF:FF:FF), it forwards the incoming frame out all connected ports except the port where the frame was received. When a switch forwards a frame out all ports, it's referred to as "flooding the frame."

- Each switch port is considered a collision domain (see the circled areas in Figure 8-1). If a collision occurs between the switch port and the devices connected to a switch port, the switch doesn't forward collision information to any of its other ports. This behavior limits a collision's effects to only the devices connected to the port, so each port is called a collision domain.

- Switch ports can operate in full-duplex mode, allowing connected devices that also support full-duplex to transmit and receive simultaneously, thereby eliminating the possibility of a collision. However, even though a collision can't occur on a port in full-duplex mode, each port is still referred to as a collision domain.

NOTE With switches, collisions can occur only if a switch port is connected to a computer running in half-duplex mode or if the switch port is connected to a hub.

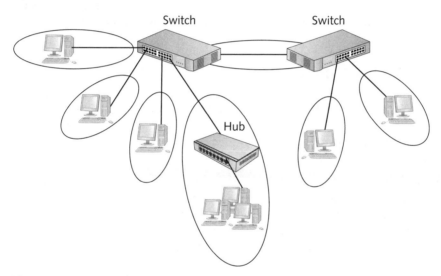

Figure 8-1 Each switch connection is a collision domain

Now that you have the basics of switch operation, the following sections cover a few properties of switches in more detail.

Switch Port Modes of Operation

Most switches have the capability to work in multiple modes. Ports on a switch, for instance, can usually operate at multiple speeds and multiple duplex modes. For example, ports on a typical 10/100 megabits per second (Mbps) switch can usually operate in these modes:

- 10 Mbps half-duplex
- 100 Mbps half-duplex
- 10 Mbps full-duplex
- 100 Mbps full-duplex

Most inexpensive switches run in **auto-negotiate mode**, which means the switch exchanges information with a device connected to a port and attempts to set the port's operating mode to the highest performance setting the device supports. If the device is set to operate at a particular speed and duplex mode (a setting configured in a NIC's properties, for example), the switch sets the port to match the connected device's settings. Occasionally, auto-negotiate fails and a link is never achieved. In this case, one or both devices should be set to a particular mode instead of relying on auto-negotiate. Mid-range and high-end switches allow configuring each port to the mode that works best for the connected device.

Another option you sometimes find is **auto-MDIX** (media-dependent interface crossed), in which the switch port detects the type of device and cable it's connected to. If necessary, the port swaps its transmit and receive pins, which enables you to use a straight-through or crossover cable regardless of the type of device you're connecting to the port. If each port on the switch can be configured separately, the auto-MDIX feature can usually be enabled or disabled.

If port configuration on switches is important in your environment, you need to invest more money than if you simply want to rely on switches' capability to configure their ports automatically.

Creating the Switching Table

Chapter 2 discussed the basics of a switching table. This section explains more details of creating and maintaining the table. A switching table is composed primarily of MAC address/port pairs that tell the switch where to forward a frame, based on the frame's destination MAC address. When a switch is first powered on, however, the switching table is empty because the switch hasn't yet learned which devices are connected to which ports.

As network devices begin to send frames throughout the network, the switch reads each frame's source address and adds it to the switching table along with the port it was received from. Each frame's destination address is searched for in the switching table and, if found, is forwarded out the corresponding port. However, what if the frame's destination address isn't found in the switching table? The switch does the reasonable thing and floods the frame.

The switching table isn't limited to a single MAC address per port. The technical specifications for most switches usually include the number of MAC addresses the switch supports. This number is usually in the thousands and is often expressed with K, as in "8K MAC addresses supported." For example, if your network looks something like Figure 8-2, Switch1's switching table would be similar to the table in this figure. In the figure, the two switches are connected, so Switch1 must forward frames destined for any computers connected to Switch2 out the port where Switch1 is connected to Switch2 (in this case, port 1).

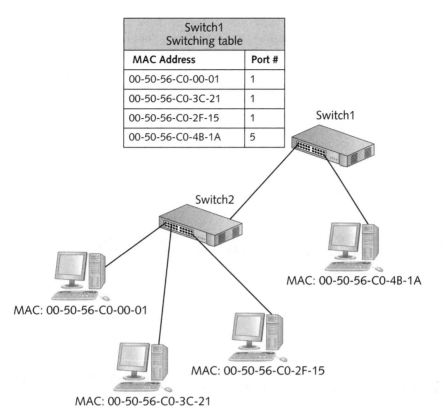

Switch1 Switching table	
MAC Address	**Port #**
00-50-56-C0-00-01	1
00-50-56-C0-3C-21	1
00-50-56-C0-2F-15	1
00-50-56-C0-4B-1A	5

Figure 8-2 Switching tables can contain multiple MAC addresses per port

As you learned in Chapter 2, a switching table prevents stale entries by including a time-stamp when a switching table entry is created. When a switch receives a frame, the entry for the frame's source address is updated with a new timestamp. Periodically, the switch inspects its switching table for expired entries. Switches typically maintain a MAC address for a period called the **aging time**, which is usually several minutes. If an entry's timestamp isn't updated within the aging time, it expires and is removed from the table.

Frame Forwarding Methods

Switches receive a frame on one port and forward it out another port with a variety of methods. The simplest and fastest is **cut-through switching**, in which the switch reads only enough of the incoming frame (in Ethernet, 12 bytes) to determine the frame's source and destination addresses. After the forwarding location is determined, the frame is switched internally from the incoming port to the outgoing port, and the switch is free to handle additional frames. The benefit of cut-through switching is speed. A typical Ethernet frame can be up to 1518 bytes. With cut-through switching, the switch reads only a small portion of the frame's contents before sending the frame on its way. The disadvantage of this switching method is that the switch indiscriminately forwards frames containing errors, so it ties up bandwidth needlessly with frames that will be discarded.

On the other hand, **store-and-forward switching** requires that the switch read the entire frame into its buffers before forwarding it. The switch first examines the frame's frame check sequence

(FCS) field to make sure it contains no errors before it's forwarded. If an error is found, the switch discards the frame. This method has the advantage of conserving bandwidth when many frames contain errors. The disadvantage is that the entire frame must be read, stored in memory, and examined before it can be forwarded. This process takes time and slows the network slightly.

A third popular switching method is **fragment-free switching**, in which the switch reads enough of the frame to guarantee that it's at least the minimum size for the network type. For Ethernet, it's 64 bytes. One type of frame error that can occur in a network is a **frame fragment**, meaning the frame is damaged because of a collision or a malfunctioning device, such as a NIC or hub. When this type of damage occurs, the frame might be truncated to less than the minimum allowable size. A switch operating in fragment-free mode detects this problem and discards the frame without forwarding it. Table 8-2 summarizes these switching methods.

Table 8-2 Switching method summary

Switching method	Switching performance	Errors forwarded
Cut-through	Fastest	All errors forwarded
Fragment-free	Medium	All errors except frame fragments forwarded
Store-and-forward	Slowest	No error frames forwarded

High-end switches can combine the best features of these switching methods. For example, they can initially operate in cut-through mode for the best performance. However, if they detect frequent errors, they can change to store-and-forward mode, thereby decreasing the number of propagated errors. If the error rate decreases enough, the switch can be put in cut-through mode again.

Advanced Switch Features

All switches have a main objective: to receive frames on one port and forward them out another port to arrive at the destination device eventually. As you have learned, there are different methods for performing this task and different speeds at which it's accomplished. However, high-end switches, often referred to as "smart switches" and "managed switches," can offer more features to help you design an efficient, reliable network. **Managed switches** have too many advanced options to cover all of them in this book, but this section gives you an overview of their most common features:

- Multicast processing
- Spanning Tree Protocol
- Virtual local area networks
- Port security

Multicast Processing You know how a switch handles unicast and broadcast frames, but how does it handle a multicast frame? A multicast frame contains as its destination a special address that signifies one or more computers or devices. The application waiting for the frame determines this address. For example, some disk-imaging programs can use multicast frames. When a computer classroom or lab is configured, one computer can be configured with all the applications the classroom needs. Then an exact copy of the disk is made and stored on a server. Next, the image is transferred by using multicast frames to only the computers that require it and are running the application that's "listening" for a particular multicast address. The image is sent only once, and only the computers running the disk-imaging program receive the frames.

Now that you have an idea how multicast frames can be used, there are two ways switches can process them:

- By treating them as broadcasts and flooding them to all ports
- By forwarding the frames only to ports that have registered the multicast address

The first method is used by low-end switches that don't have multicast support and by switches that support multicast but haven't been configured for it. The second method is used by switches that support Internet Group Management Protocol (IGMP), specifically IGMP "snooping." Multicast MAC addresses always begin with 01:00:5E, leaving the rest of the MAC address to identify a particular multicast application. When a switch sees MAC addresses containing 01:00:5e as the first 24 bits arriving on a port, it registers that port as belonging to the multicast group (specified by the remaining 24 bits of the multicast MAC address). When the switch sees a multicast frame, it forwards it out only registered ports. The details of IGMP are beyond the scope of this book, but you should know that the protocol also allows a computer to "unregister" the multicast application so that the switch can remove it from the switching table.

Spanning Tree Protocol Some switches, unlike hubs, are designed to accommodate redundancy, or multiple paths, in the network. However, using redundant switches can also cause a network administrator's worse nightmare: a **switching loop** (also called a "bridging loop"). A switching loop occurs when switches are connected in such a way that it's possible for frames to be forwarded endlessly from switch to switch in an infinite loop. Figure 8-3 shows a network configuration in which this problem could happen.

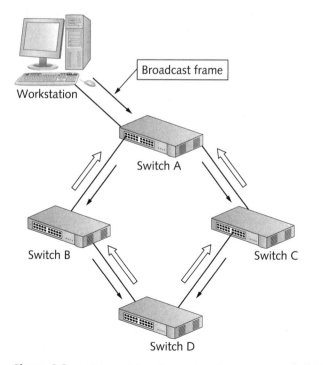

Figure 8-3 Switches with redundant paths can create a switching loop

Because a switch forwards broadcast frames out every port except the port the frame was received on, a broadcast frame originating from a computer attached to Switch A is forwarded to Switches B and C. Switches B and C forward the frame to Switch D. Switch D forwards the frame received from Switch B to Switch C and the frame received from Switch C to Switch B. Switches B and C then forward the frame to Switch A, which starts the process again. It continues until the switches are just forwarding the same broadcast frame repeatedly while causing every computer in the network to process the frame. If this type of loop occurs with a broadcast frame, it's referred to as a **broadcast storm**.

Luckily, this problem doesn't usually happen. IEEE 802.1D specifies the Spanning Tree Algorithm to prevent this behavior. It requires that switches communicate with one another. The protocol used to communicate between switches is **Spanning Tree Protocol (STP)**, which enables switches to detect when there's a potential for a loop. When this happens, one of the switch ports goes into **blocking mode**, preventing it from forwarding frames that would create a loop. If the loop configuration is broken, perhaps because of a switch failing or the connection between two switches failing, the switch that was in blocking mode resumes forwarding frames. In this way, redundancy is achieved, allowing frames to reach their destination in the event of a switch or media failure but preventing the disastrous effect of switching loops. Simulation 15 shows how a switch uses STP to prevent a switching loop.

Simulation 15: STP prevents switching loops

STP is an integral part of most mid-range to high-end switches. Beware of SOHO (small office/home office) products, as most of these lower-end switches don't support STP. Before using a switch in a configuration that could form a loop, be certain that all involved switches support the 802.1D standard for STP.

One side effect of STP is that devices take a bit longer to create a link with a switch that runs the protocol. The reason is that after the switch detects that a new device is plugged into a port, STP begins transferring packets to determine whether the new device is another switch that could cause a loop. When the switch determines that the new device won't cause a switching loop, the link can be established. This process usually takes several seconds. With many mid-range to high-end switches supporting STP, administrators can disable the protocol on specific ports, so if you know that certain ports will never be used to connect another switch, it's safe to turn STP off on these ports.

Rapid Spanning Tree Protocol (RSTP), an enhancement to STP that's defined in 802.1w, provides faster convergence when the topology changes. STP can take more than 30 seconds to respond to changes in the switch topology (a switch link coming up or going down), but RSTP can respond in fewer than 10 seconds. RSTP is preferred if all the switches connected together support it.

Virtual Local Area Networks Switches that support **virtual local area networks (VLANs)** enable you to configure one or more switch ports into separate broadcast domains. A switch with two or more VLANs configured is effectively divided into logically disconnected networks. In other words, it's like separating the switch into two or more switches that aren't connected to one another. So how do you communicate between these virtual networks or broadcast domains? A router is needed to communicate between VLANs.

A switch that enables you to create multiple broadcast domains can offer many benefits for your network. A switch with VLAN capability can optimize your network configuration by creating broadcast domains without having to add switches. This capability can be an advantage for your network, as it improves management and security of the network and gives you more control of broadcast frames.

Because a VLAN divides the network into more broadcast domains, devices on switch ports belonging to different VLANs must have logical addresses (IP addresses, for example) on different networks. Furthermore, if devices on one VLAN are to communicate with devices on another VLAN, a Layer 3 device (typically a router) is required to route packets between VLANs. Because routers are slower devices than switches or hubs, you should plan your network so that most resource accesses occur within a VLAN. Figure 8-4 shows a network divided into two VLANs, with a router communicating between them. Notice that there's a server on each VLAN so that workstation traffic doesn't need to cross the router for access to a server. You must consider the ramifications of moving a workstation from one switch port to another. When adding a workstation to your network, you need to know which VLAN the workstation should belong in before choosing a switch port to connect the station and a logical address to assign to the workstation.

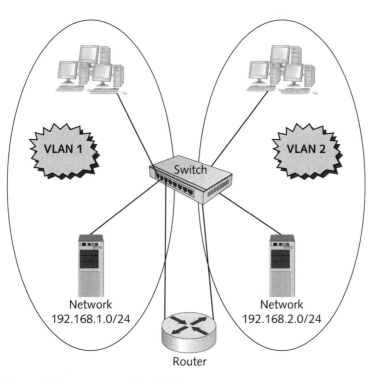

Figure 8-4 A network using VLANs

In addition to dividing a network into multiple broadcast domains, VLANs make it possible for network administrators to group users and resources logically instead of by physical location. With conventional networks, a user or resource's location dictates which network it's assigned to. This limitation sometimes makes resource sharing inefficient because ideally, users are assigned to the same network as the resources they access most often.

A switch supporting VLANs allows assigning any switch port or group of ports to a VLAN. Suppose you have a group of employees from different departments working on a long-term project. A new server has been allocated for this project, but the employees working on the project are scattered in different buildings. To solve this problem, you can assign switch ports in each building to the same VLAN in which the server is configured. In this way, these employees and the resources they share, although physically separated, are logically grouped by using VLANs. Figure 8-5 shows how users and resources from different physical locations can be assigned to the same VLAN.

Although the details of implementing VLANs are beyond the scope of this book, you can read a good overview on the subject at *http://computer.howstuffworks.com/lan-switch16.htm*.

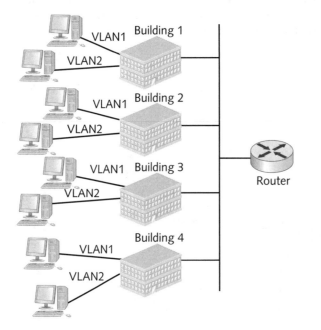

Figure 8-5 VLANs logically group users and resources from different physical locations

VLAN Trunks If you study Figure 8-5, you realize there must be a way to communicate between devices in the same VLAN. There are two possible configurations for doing so. One method is connecting a cable from a port in each VLAN on one switch to a port in each VLAN on another switch. This method is impractical because of the amount of cabling and the number of ports needed to make the VLAN connections. VLAN trunk ports take care of this problem. A **trunk port** is a switch port configured to carry traffic from all VLANs to another switch or router. The switch or router port must also be configured as a trunk port. IEEE 802.1Q defines how to configure a trunk port, which involves the switch adding a tag to each frame that must traverse the trunk port. The VLAN tag identifies which VLAN the traffic originated from, so the traffic stays in that VLAN unless it's being routed. After the switch or router connected to the other side of the trunk cable receives the frame, the tag is removed from the frame before it's forwarded. Simulation 16 demonstrates how trunk ports work to allow VLAN traffic to travel from switch to switch.

Simulation 16: How switches use trunk ports with VLANs

Factors to Consider Before Using VLANs You might be tempted to use VLANs because the prospect of optimizing your network is enticing. However, the overuse of VLANs can end up costing you more than it benefits you. In addition, because more VLANs mean more logical networks, your network will be more complex. Furthermore, they can actually slow down your network when your intention is to increase performance.

Because VLANs need a router for communication, every VLAN you create requires a corresponding router interface, which usually increases costs. More router interfaces mean additional IP networks, which is likely to require subnetting your existing network, and this task can become quite complex. If you need to change your existing network addressing scheme, you'll probably have to reconfigure many devices to reflect the new addressing scheme, which can take a lot of time. Finally, having more smaller VLANs can slow your network unless workstations and the network resources they access most of the time are in the same VLAN. So although VLANs can help optimize and organize your network, make sure you have a carefully planned network design before using them.

Remember that for a workstation to communicate outside its VLAN, it must go through a router, and communication through a router is always slower than through a switch.

Switch Port Security In some public buildings, such as libraries and schools, controlling network access is difficult sometimes. In particular, network jacks with connections to switches are often available to public users who can plug in a laptop that could contain viruses, hacker tools, and other malware. A switch with port security features can help prevent this type of connection.

Port security on most switches enables an administrator to limit how many and which MAC addresses can connect to a port. If an unauthorized computer with an unauthorized MAC address attempts to connect to the switch port, the port can be disabled and a message can be generated to indicate the violation. Alternatively, administrators can disable switch ports entirely until they're needed, giving them complete control over when a port can be used and by whom.

Hands-On Project 8-1: Observing a Switching Loop

Time Required: 20 minutes

Objective: Observe what happens in a network where two switches are connected in a way that creates a switching loop.

Required Tools and Equipment: Two lab computers (one with Wireshark installed), two switches that don't have STP enabled, two patch cables, and two crossover cables (or four patch cables if your switches support auto-MDIX)

Description: In this project, you connect two computers to two separate switches. First, you connect the two switches with a single cable and verify that you can ping from one computer to the other. Next, you connect the switches with a second cable, which creates the switching loop. Then you clear the ARP cache so that an ARP broadcast is created and ping from one computer to another while capturing ARP packets. This project can be done as a demonstration by the instructor or in groups.

1. Configure the network as shown in Figure 8-6. Use a crossover cable between switches unless the switches support auto-MDIX, in which case a regular patch cable works. Designate one computer as Computer1 and the other as Computer2. Start both computers and log on with an administrator account.

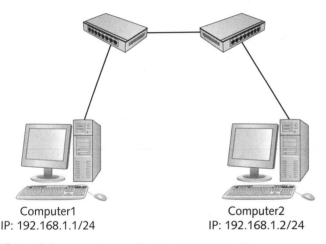

Computer1
IP: 192.168.1.1/24

Computer2
IP: 192.168.1.2/24

Figure 8-6 Network setup for Hands-On Project 8-1

2. Configure Computer1 with the IP address 192.168.1.1/24 and Computer2 with the IP address 192.168.1.2/24. No default gateway or DNS server address is required.

3. On both computers, turn off the firewall to prevent ping messages from being blocked. To do so, right-click **Start** and click **Control Panel**. Click **System and Security**, and then click **Windows Firewall**. In the left pane, click **Turn Windows Firewall on or off**, and then click **Turn off Windows Firewall (not recommended)** under both "Private network settings" and "Public network settings." Click **OK**, and then close all windows.

4. On Computer1, open a command prompt window as administrator. To do so, right-click **Start** and click **Command Prompt (Admin)**, and click **Yes** in the UAC message box.

5. Ping Computer2 (192.168.1.2) to verify that your network is working correctly. If the ping isn't successful, check all connections and settings and verify that the firewall is turned off on both computers. After you have pinged Computer2 successfully, continue to Step 6.

6. On Computer1, type **arp -d** at the command prompt and press **Enter** to delete the current ARP cache.

7. Using the second crossover cable (or patch cable), connect the two switches a second time to create a switching loop on switches that don't support (or haven't enabled) STP.

8. On Computer1, ping Computer2. You should see Wireshark begin to capture packets—many of the same packets over and over. Your computer might even freeze. What you're seeing is a broadcast storm caused by a switching loop. Depending on your switches, you might see the number of ARP packets captured slow or stop, but you'll likely see hundreds or thousands of ARP packets caused by the loop. The ping probably won't be successful.

9. Accidental switching loops can be created by cabling errors, and if they do occur, you can see how this condition can bring a network down or slow it dramatically. If you need redundant switch paths, using switches that support STP is critical, but even if you don't need redundant paths, switches equipped with STP can prevent an accidental loop. Disassemble the network and turn off the computers.

Multilayer Switches

When people are discussing a switch, a Layer 2 device is usually what's meant. However, some advanced devices have all the functions of a managed switch but add Layer 3 capabilities. So you might hear of a Layer 3 switch or a multilayer switch with most of the same capabilities as a traditional router. Multilayer switches are typically used in the interior of networks to route between VLANs instead of being placed on the network perimeter to route packets between WANs and external networks. They can offer a substantial performance advantage over traditional routers because packet routing between VLANs is done within the switch instead of having to exit the switch to a router. Figure 8-7 is

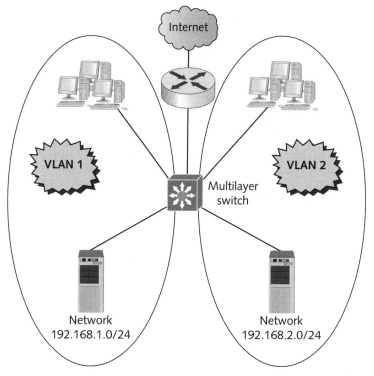

Figure 8-7 Multilayer switches route between VLANs

similar to Figure 8-4, except that all the devices in VLAN 1 and VLAN 2 are connected to a multilayer switch and the routing between VLANs occurs within the switch. The connection to the Internet still goes through a traditional router.

Routers in Depth

As you know, routers operate at the Network layer (Layer 3) and work with packets as the PDU. These advanced devices connect separate logical networks to form an internetwork. A router can be used to facilitate exchanging data between networks, but broadcast frames are kept in their respective networks. The Internet uses routers to interconnect thousands of networks around the world. If it interconnected networks with bridges or switches, which forward broadcast frames, any broadcast frame generated by any computer connected to the Internet would be forwarded to and processed by every other computer on the Internet. If this happened, the only traffic flowing on the Internet would be broadcasts!

In addition to dividing large networks into smaller broadcast domains, routers are used to create complex internetworks so that LANs in a large international corporation, for example, can communicate efficiently. As shown in Figure 8-8, you can use routers to create complex internetworks with multiple paths between networks; these multiple paths are used for fault tolerance and load sharing. If a network link goes down, an alternate path can be chosen to get a packet to its destination. Furthermore, if a path becomes congested, additional paths can be used to ease congestion.

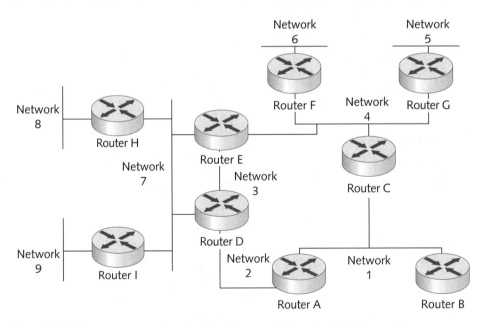

Figure 8-8 Routers can connect networks with many different paths between them

Routers are also used to control network access by inspecting source and destination address information of packets they handle. Based on rules an administrator defines, a router can forward a packet or discard it. The processing done by routers depends on the following features found on most routers:

- Router interfaces
- Routing tables
- Routing protocols
- Access control lists

The following sections describe these features and how routers use them to create effective internetworks.

Router Interfaces

Routers must have two or more interfaces, or ports, to be able to take packets coming from one network and forward them to another network. Each interface on a router has full Layer 3 functionality, including both an IP address and a MAC address. In fact, you can look at a router interface as just a NIC with the IP protocol bound to it.

When a router interface receives a frame, it performs the Data Link layer function of comparing the destination MAC address with the interface's MAC address. If they match, the router reads the frame and strips the frame header and trailer; if they don't match, the router discards the frame. Next, the router checks the resulting packet's destination IP address. If this address matches the IP address of the interface on which the packet was received, the packet was intended for the router, which simply processes the packet. If the destination IP address's network ID doesn't match the interface address's network ID, the router knows the packet should be routed to another network.

It then consults its routing table to determine how to get the packet to its destination and moves the packet from the incoming interface to the interface that will get the packet to its destination—the outgoing interface. The process of moving a packet from the incoming interface to the outgoing interface is called **packet forwarding**, or just "forwarding." Before the packet can be sent out the outgoing interface, however, it must be encapsulated in a new frame header and trailer. The new frame header contains the outgoing interface's MAC address as the source and the MAC address of the destination computer or the next router in the path as the destination. In addition, a new CRC is calculated and placed in the FCS field of the frame trailer. This process is shown in Figure 8-9 and demonstrated in Simulation 9, which you first saw in Chapter 5.

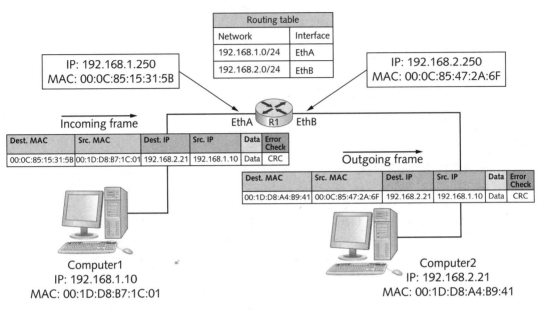

Figure 8-9 Packets are forwarded from one network to another

Simulation: 9 The changing frame header

The following steps summarize how a router uses its interface to forward packets from one network to another:

1. A router receives a frame on an interface.
2. The router checks the frame's destination MAC address.
3. If the destination MAC address matches the interface's address, the router reads the frame; otherwise, the frame is discarded.
4. The frame header and trailer are stripped to create a packet.
5. The destination IP address is checked.
6. If the IP address's network ID is different from the interface's network ID, the packet should be routed.
7. The router consults the routing table to determine to which of its interfaces the packet should be forwarded.
8. The packet is encapsulated in a new frame header and trailer.
9. The packet is forwarded to the destination computer or the next router in the path.

A configuration called "a router on a stick" is sometimes used when a router is routing between VLANs on a switch. In this configuration, a single router interface is used to connect to a switch trunk port that carries traffic going from one VLAN to another. The router interface is configured with multiple IP addresses, each in a different network. In this setup, the router has multiple logical interfaces, but the incoming and outgoing interfaces are physically the same.

Routing Tables

As discussed in Chapter 2, routing tables are composed mainly of network address and interface pairs that tell the router which interface a packet should be forwarded to so that it gets to its destination network. Of course, there's more to the story than the overview in Chapter 2. The routing table in most routers contains the following information for each table entry:

- *Destination network*—The network address of a network to which the router can forward packets is called the **destination network**. It's usually expressed in CIDR notation, such as 172.16.0.0/16. When a router receives a packet on one of its interfaces, it compares the packet's destination address with the list of destination networks in its routing table. If it finds a match, the packet is forwarded as specified by the information in the next hop field.

- *Next hop*—The **next hop** (or gateway, as specified in Windows routing tables) indicates an interface name or the address of the next router in the path to the destination. If an interface name is specified, such as Ethernet 0 or Fast Ethernet 1, the destination network is usually connected directly to the router. In this case, the router gets the destination device's MAC address from its ARP cache or an ARP request broadcast. After the destination MAC address is retrieved, the frame is delivered. If an address is specified, indicating that the packet must be forwarded to the next router in the path, the router retrieves the MAC address of the next router and forwards the frame on its way. When a packet must be sent to a router to get to its destination, it's called a **hop**. The total number of routers a packet must travel through is called the **hop count**.

- *Metric*—The **metric** is a numeric value that tells the router how "far away" the destination network is. Other terms for metric are cost and distance. The metric doesn't have anything to do with actual distance measured in feet or miles. It can be composed of a number of values, including the bandwidth of links between the source and destination, the hop count, the link's reliability, and so forth. If the destination network is connected directly, the metric is usually 0. The values used to determine the metric depend on how routes get into the table, discussed next.

- *How the route is derived*—This field tells you how the route gets into the routing table. A route is added to the routing table in three main ways: The destination network is connected directly; an administrator enters the route information manually (called a **static route**); or the route information is entered dynamically, via a routing protocol. The first two are somewhat self-explanatory, and the third is discussed later in "Routing Protocols."

- *Timestamp*—Just as switching table entries need timestamps, so do routing table entries, but only those that are created dynamically. A timestamp tells the router how long it has been since the routing protocol updated the dynamic route. Not all routing protocols require a timestamp.

Figure 8-10 shows a network of several Cisco routers running a routing protocol. The table shown is the actual routing table of RouterB. The top part of the table lists codes that indicate how a route is derived. Take a look at the first row of the routing table, starting from the leftmost column:

- R—The route was derived from the RIP routing protocol.
- 192.168.8.0/24—The destination network.
- [120/2]—The 120 indicates a reliability value for the RIP routing protocol called the **administrative distance**. This value is assigned to a routing protocol to indicate its reliability compared with other routing protocols that might be in use on the same router. If a route is derived by using two different routing protocols, the one with the least administrative distance is used. The 2 indicates a metric of 2, meaning the route can be reached by traversing two routers (in this case, RouterC and RouterD).

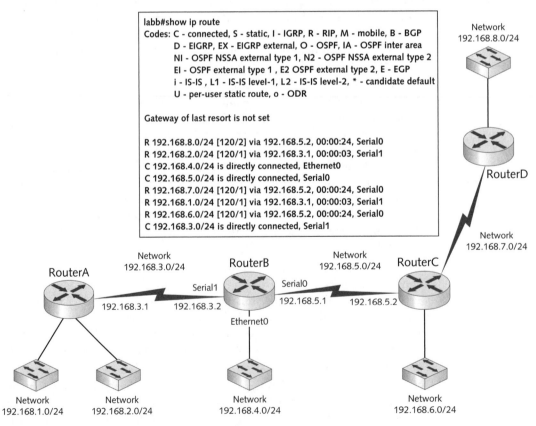

Figure 8-10 An internetwork and a router's routing table

- via 192.168.5.2—The next hop address; the address of the next router (RouterC) in the path.

- 00:00:24—The age of the route; because RIP updates every 30 seconds, this value is usually less than that unless there's a problem.

- Serial0—The interface the packet should be sent out to reach the next hop.

In the network configuration shown in Figure 8-10, there's only one path from any network to any other network. To provide fault tolerance and load balancing, network administrators often design networks with multiple paths to critical networks. If the network is designed purely for fault tolerance, a router keeps only the shortest path to a destination network in its routing table. However, if the shortest path route goes down, the router can use the next shortest path as a backup. In other cases, a router can use two or more paths to a network to spread the traffic load over multiple network links. Simulation 17 shows what happens when a link goes down in an internetwork and the router automatically chooses an alternate path to get to the destination network.

Simulation 17: Routers use multiple paths in an internetwork

Routing Protocols

As mentioned, routing tables can be populated in three ways: directly connected networks, manually added static routes, and dynamically added routes via routing protocols. A **routing protocol** is a set of rules that routers use to exchange information so that all routers have accurate information about an internetwork to populate their routing tables. When an internetwork changes because of new networks coming online and going offline and network addresses changing, routers affected by these changes pass the information on to other routers so that all routers have an up-to-date picture of the entire internetwork. By having accurate status information on the internetwork, routers can choose the best path for routing packets they receive.

There are two main types of routing protocols; the type of protocol, in part, determines the algorithm a router uses to choose the best path to a destination when more than one exists:

- **Distance-vector protocols** share information about an internetwork's status by copying a router's routing table to other routers with which they share a network. Routers sharing a network are called **neighbors**. In a large internetwork, changes to the network are passed from one router to another until all routers have received them. Distance-vector protocols use metrics based on factors such as hop count, bandwidth of the links between networks, network congestion, and delays. The best path is determined by identifying the route with the lowest metric. **Routing Information Protocol (RIP)** and **Routing Information Protocol version 2 (RIPv2)** are the most well-known distance-vector routing protocols. RIP and RIPv2 consider only hop count in path selection, which works fine if the speeds of all internetwork links are equivalent. However, if multiple paths exist, a path that uses slower links but has a lower hop count is selected over a path with faster links but a higher hop count. Figure 8-11 shows this setup. Two paths from RouterB to network

192.168.9.0 are available. One path goes directly to RouterD through network 192.168.7.0, and the other goes through RouterC via networks 192.168.5.0 and 192.168.8.0. However, each link between RouterB and RouterC and RouterC and RouterD is 45 Mbps, whereas the link between RouterB and RouterD is only 1.5 Mbps. Clearly, the path with the faster links is the better choice, but RIP and RIPv2 nonetheless choose the path from RouterB to RouterD based on a hop count of 1 versus 2.

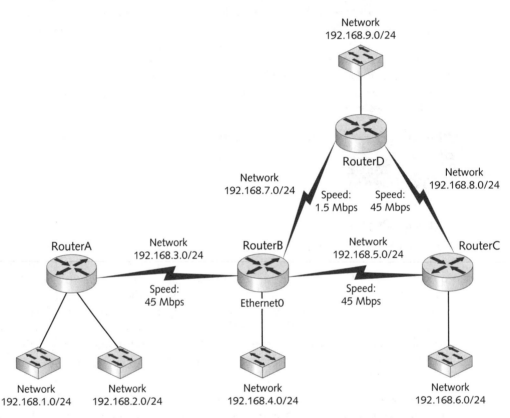

Figure 8-11 When using RIP, a router always chooses the path with the lower hop count

- **Link-state protocols** share information with other routers by sending the status of all their interface links to other routers in the internetwork. The status includes link speed, whether the link is up or down, and the link's network number. This exchange of information takes place only when a change occurs in the network. When a router receives information from other routers, an algorithm is run on the information gathered to determine the best path to all networks in the internetwork. This algorithm requires more processing power than a distance-vector protocol does, but because the metric is based mainly on link speed, better choices are made in a complex internetwork. Open Shortest Path First (OSPF) is one of the most common link-state routing protocols. Referring again to Figure 8-11, if OSPF were the routing protocol, RouterB would choose the route through RouterC to get to network 192.168.9.0.

Another link-state protocol that has been gaining popularity because of its ability to scale to support very large internetworks is Intermediate System to Intermediate System (IS-IS). OSPF is tied to IPv4, but IS-IS is a separate Layer 3 protocol that can be adapted easily to IPv4 or IPv6 networks.

A version of OSPF named OSPFv3 was developed to support both IPv4 and IPv6.

Table 8-3 summarizes the differences between distance-vector and link-state routing protocols.

Table 8-3 Distance-vector versus link-state routing protocols

Protocol type	CPU use	Network use	Memory use	Speed of convergence	Size of network	When is routing data transferred?
Distance-vector	Lower	Higher	Lower	Slower	Small	Periodically
Link-state	Higher	Lower	Higher	Faster	Large	Only when a change occurs

A note of explanation for one column in Table 8-3: The speed of **convergence** refers to how fast the routing tables of all routers in an internetwork are updated with accurate information when a change in the network occurs. Because distance-vector protocols pass routing tables from one router to the next, based on a periodic timer, convergence can take quite a bit of time. However, when a router is running a link-state protocol and a network change occurs, information about the change is sent immediately to all routers in the internetwork.

A third type of routing protocol called a "hybrid protocol" combines some features of distance-vector and link-state protocols. The most common example of a hybrid protocol is Cisco's proprietary Enhanced Interior Gateway Routing Protocol (EIGRP).

Interior Gateway Versus Exterior Gateway Routing protocols come in two categories: **interior gateway protocol (IGP)** and **exterior gateway protocol (EGP)**. IGPs are used in an **autonomous system,** which is an internetwork managed by a single organization. EGPs are used between autonomous systems, such as between an organization's network and an ISP or between two ISPs. The routing protocols discussed so far are IGPs. The only widely used EGP is **Border Gateway Protocol (BGP)**. It's used to route between autonomous systems and includes an autonomous system (AS) number in its configuration parameters. BGP is the routing protocol used by ISPs, and it's what makes the Internet work.

BGP is classified as a **path-vector routing protocol,** which analyzes the characteristics of all autonomous systems lying in the path between the router and each destination network so that it can form a nonlooping routing topology. BGP is used between ISPs, but it can also be used on border routers of large organizations' networks. A **border router** connects one autonomous system to another—for example, from an organization's network to an ISP. An organization network that maintains multiple data centers for high availability might use BGP in each data center to ensure that if one becomes unavailable, BGP routes requests to another data center.

Routing Protocol or Static Routes? You might wonder whether your network should run a routing protocol at all. Routing protocols aren't a necessity in all situations, as static routes can be entered in a routing table manually. Some factors to consider when deciding whether to use a routing protocol or static routes include the following:

- Does the network change often, with new networks being added or networks going offline frequently? If so, a routing protocol is probably a good choice. If not, static routes should suffice.

- Are there several alternate paths to many of the networks in the internetwork? If so, a routing protocol can reroute around down links or congested routes automatically, but with static routes, an administrator must change the routing table manually after the problem is discovered.

- Is the internetwork large, with many networks and remote sites? If so, keeping up with the status of all networks might prove to be more work than you bargained for if you're using static routes. A routing protocol builds and maintains routing tables automatically, freeing you to do more important tasks.

Keep in mind that there's no reason you can't combine static routing with routing protocols in your internetwork. Some areas of the internetwork might be simple and straightforward and, therefore, be suitable for static routes, and the more complex areas might benefit from using routing protocols.

Access Control Lists

One advantage of using routers in an internetwork is that you can group users who need access to common resources into subnets. A router facilitates users in one subnet being able to access resources on another subnet, but it can also be used to block access. Routers use access control lists to determine which network traffic passes through and which traffic doesn't. An **access control list (ACL)** is a set of rules configured on a router's interface for specifying which addresses and which protocols can pass through the interface and to which destinations. When an access control list blocks a packet, it's called **packet filtering**. ACLs are usually configured to filter traffic based on the following:

- Inbound or outbound traffic
- Source address
- Destination address
- Protocol

When an administrator applies an ACL to a router interface, it specifies the direction of the traffic, inbound or outbound. The router inspects and filters only traffic traveling in the specified direction. The source and destination addresses can be specific IP addresses or network numbers. Filtering can be done on just the source address, just the destination address, or both. The ACL can specify anything from the entire IP protocol suite to a particular Transport-layer protocol to a specific TCP or UDP port.

ACLs as defined here can usually be configured only on mid-range to high-end routers. These routers are shipped without any configuration, and an administrator must configure all aspects of the router, including its interfaces, routing protocols, and ACLs, before the router is operational.

SOHO routers, used mainly to give a small group of computers Internet access, are usually configured already. The default access control configuration on these routers typically allows all network traffic from the private network to pass to the Internet and allows only network traffic from the Internet that was initiated from the private network to pass to the private network. An example of traffic allowed from the Internet is a Web server's response to a Web browser's request for a page. An example of traffic that's blocked is any packet coming from the Internet to the private network that the private network didn't request.

Hands-On Project 8-2: Viewing and Changing Your Computer's Routing Table

Time Required: 5 minutes

Objective: View your computer's routing table with the `route` command.

Required Tools and Equipment: Net-*XX*

Description: In this project, you use the `route` command to view and change your computer's internal routing table. Even though your computer isn't a router, it maintains an internal routing table with entries for the network interface network, the loopback network, and a variety of other internal networks.

1. Start your computer and log on as **NetAdmin**, if necessary.

2. Open a command prompt window as an administrator. (See Step 4 of Hands-On Project 8-1, if you don't remember how.)

3. To view your routing table, type **route print | more** and press **Enter**. The | more after the `route print` command causes output to be displayed one screen at a time. Your output should look similar to Figure 8-12.

```
===========================================================================
Interface List
 11...00 0c 29 f5 3e 97 ......Intel(R) PRO/1000 MT Network Connection
  1...........................Software Loopback Interface 1
 13...00 00 00 00 00 00 00 e0 Microsoft ISATAP Adapter
 12...00 00 00 00 00 00 00 e0 Teredo Tunneling Pseudo-Interface
===========================================================================

IPv4 Route Table
===========================================================================
Active Routes:
Network Destination        Netmask          Gateway       Interface  Metric
          0.0.0.0          0.0.0.0      192.168.100.1  192.168.100.100    266
        127.0.0.0        255.0.0.0         On-link         127.0.0.1    306
        127.0.0.1  255.255.255.255         On-link         127.0.0.1    306
  127.255.255.255  255.255.255.255         On-link         127.0.0.1    306
    192.168.100.0    255.255.255.0         On-link   192.168.100.100    266
  192.168.100.100  255.255.255.255         On-link   192.168.100.100    266
  192.168.100.255  255.255.255.255         On-link   192.168.100.100    266
        224.0.0.0        240.0.0.0         On-link         127.0.0.1    306
        224.0.0.0        240.0.0.0         On-link   192.168.100.100    266
  255.255.255.255  255.255.255.255         On-link         127.0.0.1    306
  255.255.255.255  255.255.255.255         On-link   192.168.100.100    266
===========================================================================
-- More --
```

Figure 8-12 Output of the `route print` command

4. Next, examine the output of the `route print` command. Your computer's network interfaces are listed at the top, and the IPv4 Route Table lists entries in the routing table, which has five columns:

   - *Network Destination*—The network destination your computer compares with the destination IP address of outgoing packets to determine where to send them.

   - *Netmask*—The subnet mask of the network destination. A value of 255.255.255.255 indicates that the address in the Network Destination column is a specific IP address rather than a network address; it's referred to as a "host route." A value of 0.0.0.0 is used when the network destination is 0.0.0.0, indicating the default route or gateway.

   - *Gateway*—The next hop address or on-link, which means the network destination is connected directly to an interface. Make a note of the value in this column for the 0.0.0.0 network destination because you need it later:

   - *Interface*—The address of the interface Windows uses to send the packet to the network destination.

   - *Metric*—The metric assigned to the route. If there are two entries for the same network destination, the lower metric is the route chosen.

     Press the **spacebar** one or more times to display the rest of the output. You'll see a row of output labeled "Persistent Routes." If you create a route manually and want it to stay in the table between reboots, it's listed here.

5. To verify that you can communicate with the Internet, type **ping www.cengage.com** and press **Enter**. If the ping is successful, your default network is working correctly.

6. Type **route delete 0.0.0.0** and press **Enter** to delete your default route. Type **ping www.cengage.com** and press **Enter** again. The ping will fail. Type **route print | more** and press **Enter** to verify that the 0.0.0.0 network destination is no longer in the table. Press the **spacebar** as needed to display the rest of the output.

7. To create the default route entry, type **route add -p 0.0.0.0 mask 0.0.0.0** *default-gateway* and press **Enter** (replacing *default-gateway* with the address you noted in Step 4).

8. Display the routing table again to verify that your default route is in the table. Ping **www.cengage.com** to verify that you can do so again.

9. Close all open windows, and stay logged on if you're going on to the next project.

Wireless Access Points in Depth

You learned about the basic operation of wireless access points (APs) in Chapter 2 and Wi-Fi technology in Chapter 3. This section discusses some configuration options available on most wireless APs and wireless routers, regardless of the 802.11 networking standard in use. First you look at wireless network configuration options, and in the next section, you explore options available on wireless routers. Remember that a wireless router, as it's usually marketed, is actually three devices in one: a wireless AP, a router, and a switch. So when you examine the features of an AP, the discussion also applies to the AP built into a wireless router. The following sections explain these AP options and settings: basic wireless settings, wireless security options, and advanced wireless settings.

Basic Wireless Settings

Basic wireless settings on most APs define the settings a client wireless device needs to connect to an AP:

- Wireless network mode
- Wireless network name (SSID)
- Wireless channel
- SSID broadcast status

Figure 8-13 is an example of where these settings can be configured.

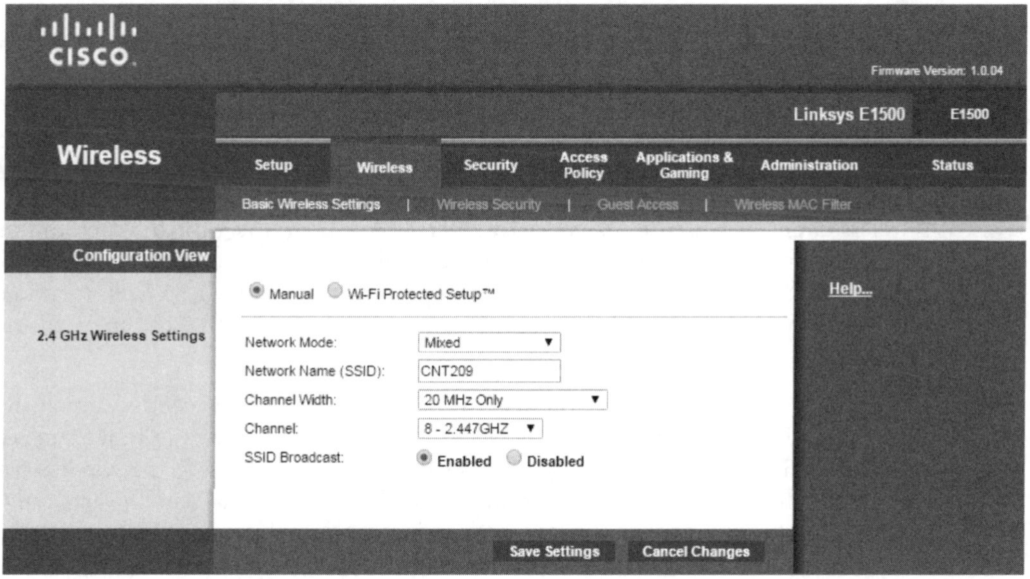

Figure 8-13 Basic wireless settings

Source: Cisco Systems, Inc.

The wireless network mode allows you to choose which 8021.11 standard the AP should operate under. If an AP supports multiple modes, it can generally operate in all or some combination of the supported modes. For example, if the AP supports 802.11n, 802.11g, and 802.11b, the options are as follows:

- *Mixed*—In mixed mode, the AP supports client connections by using any of the three standards.
- *Wireless-B/G only*—Both 802.11b and 802.11g client connections are supported.
- *Wireless-N only*—Only 802.11n client connections are possible.

- *Wireless-G only*—Only 802.11g client connections are possible.

- *Wireless-B only*—Only 802.11b client connections are possible.

- *Disabled*—On wireless routers, you can disable the AP portion if you have only wired devices. If you don't have wireless devices, you should use this setting.

APs generally work best when only one standard is enabled. So if your wireless network has only clients with 802.11n NICs, choose N only mode. Mixed mode is useful when you're transitioning clients from an older standard, such as 802.11b, to a newer and faster standard, such as 802.11n.

The wireless network name refers to the service set identifier (SSID) discussed in Chapter 2. When an AP is shipped, the SSID is set to a default value, such as "default" or "linksys" for a Linksys AP. You can leave the name as is, but doing so is a sure giveaway to wardrivers that your network is probably not secure. An SSID can be up to 32 characters. If you're running a wireless network in your home in an area with other wireless networks operating, it's best not to set the SSID to a name that obviously identifies you. The more hackers know about a network and its users, the more easily they can infiltrate it.

A wardriver is someone who drives around neighborhoods with a wireless scanning device looking for unsecured wireless networks. After finding one, a wardriver might simply use the network for free Internet access—or worse, break into the computers connected to the network.

Wireless channels were discussed in Chapter 3. An AP in the United States can usually be set to operate in channels 1 through 11. Recall that the channels overlap, so if you set your AP to channel 3, data is being transferred over channels 1 to 5. For optimal operation when multiple APs are in use, choose channels that are five channels apart, such as 1, 6, and 11.

The option to enable or disable the SSID broadcast is a low-end security option. By default, APs are configured to transmit the SSID so that any wireless device in range can see the network. If the SSID isn't broadcast, wireless devices can still connect to the wireless network by entering the SSID manually, if it's known. Disabling SSID broadcasts thwarts only the least sophisticated wardrivers because wireless packet-capturing programs can still intercept and view SSIDs transmitted between clients and the AP.

Wireless Security Options

Enabling wireless security options on your AP is a critical step of setting up a wireless LAN. Most APs offer the following security options:

- Encryption

- Authentication

- MAC filtering

- AP isolation

All private wireless networks should use encryption at a minimum to secure communication. With encryption enabled, even if a hacker captures transmitted data, it's unintelligible.

Encryption protocols vary in strengths, and the most common protocols are listed from weaker to stronger:

- Wired Equivalent Privacy (WEP)
- Wi-Fi Protected Access (WPA)
- Wi-Fi Protected Access 2 (WPA2)

These protocols are described in more detail in Chapter 9. What you need to know in practice is that you should use the highest level of security your systems support. Be aware that older APs and wireless NICs might not support the stronger WPA and WPA2 protocols. Because all devices must use the same protocol, you have to set your wireless security to a protocol supported by all your wireless devices.

If authentication is used on an AP, users must enter a username and password to access the wireless network. Authentication is most likely to be used on wireless networks that allow limited public access, such as at colleges, libraries, and other organizations that allow wireless access by members who can be identified with a username or some other credential. APs that support authentication usually support the Remote Authentication Dial-In User Service (RADIUS) protocol, in which the AP contacts your network servers that store user account information to provide authentication. Often, if a wireless network is protected by authentication, it's also protected by encryption.

MAC filtering, a feature available on most APs, enables you to restrict which devices can connect to your AP. To use MAC filtering, you add the MAC addresses of the wireless devices allowed to access your network to a list on the AP. After this configuration, only computers with wireless NICs that have a MAC address in the list can connect to the wireless network. MAC filtering should be used *only* in combination with encryption because a sophisticated user could capture packets that include the MAC addresses of authorized devices. These captured MAC addresses can then be used to impersonate authorized computers, a technique called "spoofing," discussed more in Chapter 9.

AP isolation mode creates a separate virtual network for each client connection. If this mode is enabled, clients connecting to the AP can access the Internet but can't communicate with each other. This mode is a good option for Internet cafés and other establishments that offer wireless Internet access.

Advanced Wireless Settings

Many advanced settings are available on high-end APs to help you manage a wireless network. The following are some common settings:

- *Adjustable transmit power*—This setting lets you control the power and, therefore, the range of the wireless network signal. For example, if you place your AP near the center of your building, you can adjust the power so that clients inside the building can connect, but clients outside the building can't.
- *Multiple SSIDs*—Two or more wireless networks can be created with different security settings, such as when you want to create a private network and a guest network.
- *VLAN support*—Enable VLAN support to assign wireless networks to wired VLANs.
- *Traffic priority*—If your AP is configured for multiple SSIDs and, therefore, multiple wireless networks, you can assign a priority to packets coming from each network.

- *Wi-Fi Multimedia*—Defined by 802.11e, this standard provides quality of service (QoS) settings for multimedia traffic, giving priority to streaming audio or video, for example.

- *AP modes*—An AP can be set to operate as a traditional access point, a repeater, or a wireless bridge. In repeater mode, the AP is used to extend the range of an existing AP, making two or more APs essentially act as a single AP. A repeater configuration also enables users to roam the wireless network. When a client passes out of one AP's range, it connects to another AP automatically. Bridge mode is used to connect physically separate wired networks by using two or more APs. For example, wired networks in separate buildings can be connected by using APs in bridge mode so that wired clients in each building can communicate with one another.

Network Interface Cards in Depth

A NIC makes the connection between a computer and the network medium, so the performance and reliability of a computer's NIC are crucial to the computer's network performance. Chapter 2 introduced a NIC's operation and basic factors for choosing a NIC. This section covers the PC bus options and advanced features to look for in a NIC when purchasing one for a workstation or server.

PC Bus Options

A bus makes the connections between a computer's vital components, such as the CPU, RAM, and I/O devices. The faster the bus, the faster data can be transferred between these components, which makes for a faster overall system. NICs are considered I/O devices, and whether they're built into the motherboard or added as an expansion card, they still communicate with the rest of the components via the bus. PC bus options have changed over the years with older, and usually slower, technologies fading into obsolescence and being replaced by newer, faster technologies. The following list describes the most common PC bus architectures in current use:

- *Peripheral Component Interconnect Express*—**PCI Express** (PCIe) uses a high-speed serial communication protocol of one or more lines or lanes. Each lane of PCIe 1.0 can operate at 250 megabytes per second (MBps) in each direction. PCIe 2.0 provides data rates of 500 MBps, and the current PCIe 3.0 provides speeds up to 984 MBps on each lane. PCIe 4.0, due in 2016, will provide up to 1969 MBps on each lane. Because PCIe can be set up in lanes, several lanes can be combined, resulting in tremendous transfer speeds, up to almost 32 GBps. PCIe boards are specified with notations such as x1, x4, x8, x16, and x32. The number following the "x" is the number of lanes. The more lanes, the higher the bandwidth. For example, a PCIe 1.0 x1 board supports data transfer rates up to 250 MBps, and a PCIe 2.0 x32 board supports transfer rates up to 16 GBps. PCIe is now the dominant bus technology, particularly for high-bandwidth devices such as NICs, disk controllers, and video cards. Figure 8-14 shows a PCIe x1 NIC.

- *PCI*—Several local bus standards appeared in the early 1990s as computers became faster, but by 1995, Intel's **Peripheral Component Interconnect** (PCI) bus became the default bus standard. You can still buy PCs and motherboards that have a PCI slot or two, but this bus, at more than 20 years old, is coming to the end of its lifetime.

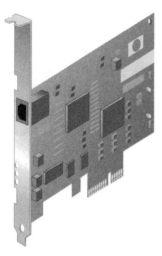

Figure 8-14 A PCIe x1 NIC

- *PCI-X*—**Peripheral Component Interconnect-Extended (PCI-X)** is backward-compatible with PCI but supports 32-bit or 64-bit bus widths, providing superior performance over PCI. However, most computer manufacturers have moved to PCIe for higher performance cards, and PCI-X is rarely found in systems today.

- *PCMCIA*—**PCMCIA cards** are credit card–sized expansion cards used mainly to add functionality to laptop computers. Two main standards are in common use: Cardbus and ExpressCard. Cardbus is the more mature standard, having been around since the mid-1990s. It operates at 33 MHz and supports a 32-bit bus, providing up to 132 MBps data transfer rates. ExpressCard was developed as computer users' thirst for faster data transfer speeds continued to grow. It uses PCIe technology to provide data transfer rates up to 500 MBps, with future versions expected to reach 4 GBps. A variety of NICs are available in these formats, including wireless NICs. Figure 8-15 shows a Cardbus NIC with an RJ-45 connector. Because laptops are typically equipped with both wired and wireless network connections, PCMCIA cards are usually necessary only if you want to upgrade a laptop's network connection or replace a faulty interface.

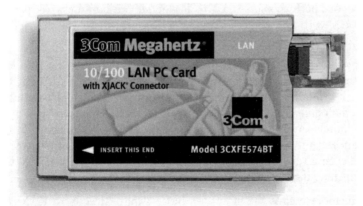

Figure 8-15 A Cardbus NIC

- *USB*—**Universal Serial Bus (USB)** comes in three versions: USB 1.0, USB 2.0, and USB 3.0. USB 1.0 is a low-speed serial interface operating at a maximum bandwidth of 12 Mbps. It's used mostly for low-speed peripheral devices, such as mice, keyboards, and joysticks, but can also be used to connect printers, scanners, phones, and some video devices to a computer. USB is now a standard interface on both PCs and Macintoshes for these uses. In networking, USB is usually used as an interface for wireless network adapters or as an attachment for cable or DSL modems. Because USB is an external interface on PCs, it offers the advantage of being able to add a NIC to a system without opening the computer case or even shutting down the computer. USB 2.0 can operate at up to 480 Mbps (60 MBps, 40 times faster than USB 1.0), and USB 3.0 (or SuperSpeed USB) provides speeds up to 5 Gbps or 625 MBps. This interface is used for external hard drives, CD/DVD burners, flash memory card readers, high-speed scanners, wired and wireless network adapters, and digital cameras.

Table 8-4 compares several bus types used for networking.

Table 8-4   Common bus types

Bus type	Maximum transfer rate	Bus size	Use
PCI	533 MBps	32 and 64 bits	Declining; absent on most servers
PCI-X	4 GBps	32 and 64 bits	Declining use on servers and high-end workstations
PCI Express (PCIe)	32 GBps	1 to 32 serial lanes	Standard on all types of computers
PCMCIA	500 MBps	1 serial lane	Laptops
USB 3.0	625 MBps	N/A	Laptops and easy addition of NICs to desktops

Advanced Features of NICs

Because NICs are the focus of network traffic on workstations and large volumes of traffic on network servers (even those with more than one network interface), they can have a major influence on network performance. If a NIC is slow, it can limit network performance. Particularly on networks with shared media, slow NICs anywhere on the network can decrease performance for all users.

When selecting a network adapter, first identify the physical characteristics the card must match. They include the type of bus the card will connect with (PCI or PCMCIA, for example), the type of network technology in use, and the kind of connector or physical attachment the adapter must accommodate. After you determine these basic characteristics, it's equally important to consider purchasing other options that can seriously affect a card's speed and data-handling capabilities. Some of these options suit servers better, and others work equally well for servers and clients; all help improve overall network performance. These hardware-enhancement options include the following:

- **Shared adapter memory** means the adapter's buffers map directly to RAM on the computer. A computer actually writes to buffers on the NIC instead of writing to its own memory. In this instance, the computer treats adapter RAM as its own RAM.

- **Shared system memory** means a NIC's onboard processor selects a region of RAM on the computer and writes to it as though it were buffer space on the adapter. In this instance, the adapter treats computer RAM as its own RAM.

- **Bus mastering** permits a network adapter to take control of the computer's bus to initiate and manage data transfers to and from the computer's memory, independent of the CPU. This feature lets the CPU concentrate on other tasks and can improve network performance.

- **RAM buffering** means a NIC includes additional memory to provide temporary storage for incoming and outgoing data that arrives at the NIC faster than it can be shipped out. This option speeds overall performance because it lets the NIC process data as quickly as it can, without having to pause occasionally to grab (or send) more data.

- **Onboard co-processors** included on most NICs enable the card to process incoming and outgoing network data without requiring service from the CPU.

- Security features available on some high-end NICs allow them to handle several protocol functions, including IP Security (IPsec) and other encryption services related to authentication and payload protection. IPsec is a secure transport mechanism that protects network traffic from unwanted snooping.

- Quality of service (QoS) allows prioritizing time-sensitive data, such as streaming video and voice.

- **Automatic link aggregation** enables you to install multiple NICs in one computer and aggregate the bandwidth so that, for example, you can install two 1 Gbps NICs and have a total bandwidth of 2 Gbps to and from that computer. This feature is found most commonly on NICs designed for servers.

- Improved **fault tolerance**, in the form of redundant NICs with failover capabilities, is available on some high-end NICs. By installing a second NIC in a PC, failure of the primary NIC shifts network traffic to the second NIC instead of cutting off the PC from the network. Hot-pluggable NICs are also an option for fault tolerance because a NIC can be installed or removed without turning off the server. NICs with dual ports provide added bandwidth and fault tolerance. These NICs have two media connectors, both of which can be active, which doubles bandwidth and fault tolerance in case one media connection fails.

- Advanced Configuration Power Management Interface (ACPI)–compliant cards provide features such as **wake-on-LAN (WoL)**, which allows an administrator to power on a PC remotely by accessing the NIC through the network. In addition, Simple Network Management Protocol (SNMP) is built in on some NICs to allow remote configuration and management.

- **Preboot Execution Environment (PXE)**–compliant adapters allow a computer to download an OS instead of booting it from a local hard drive. This feature is used on diskless workstations ("thin clients") that don't store an OS locally. PXE-compliant adapters are also useful when network administrators use disk-imaging software to install the OS and applications on a number of computers on the network. A computer configured to boot from its PXE-enabled NIC announces to the network that it's trying to boot, and a server responds by sending a disk image to the PC. After the image is written to the hard drive, the PC boots from the local OS.

For a typical desktop computer, a standard PCIe NIC with basic features is usually adequate. Servers, however, warrant some of the high-end features discussed in the preceding list. Servers get network requests from multiple clients, so they benefit from having buffer space to hold incoming frames temporarily while other frames are processed. Virtualized environments benefit from NICs with multiple ports so that virtual machines don't have to share bandwidth with their host computer. You'll find when you investigate purchasing a NIC that prices can vary wildly from a few dollars to several hundred dollars. A $3.99 NIC on clearance might work fine in your desktop computer but definitely shouldn't be installed in mission-critical servers.

Chapter Summary

- Network switches use auto-negotiate mode to determine the link speed and duplex mode. Auto-MDIX allows a switch to swap transmit and receive pins negating the need for crossover cables.

- Switching tables can hold many more MAC addresses than ports. Several MAC addresses can be mapped to a single port. The aging time prevents stale switching table entries.

- Switches forward frames by using a variety of methods. In order of fastest to slowest and least reliable to most reliable, they're cut-through, fragment-free, and store-and-forward. Some switches can use a combination of these methods; fragment-free is used until a number of errors occur, and then store-and-forward is used until the errors decrease.

- Advanced features, such as VLANs, STP, multicast support, and port security, are found on smart or managed switches. VLANs create multiple broadcast domains but require a router to communicate between them. STP can prevent broadcast storms in a redundant configuration. Multicast support prevents the switch from simply flooding multicast frames. Port security prevents unauthorized MAC addresses from connecting to the switch.

- Multilayer switches can perform some of the same tasks as routers and offer a substantial performance advantage. Multilayer (or Layer 3) switches are usually used only in the interior of an internetwork; traditional routers are used on the perimeter.

- Routing tables contain destination networks, next hop addresses, metrics, methods used to derive routes, and timestamps. They can be populated statically or with a routing protocol.

- Routing protocols populate routing tables dynamically. The most common types of routing protocols are distance-vector and link-state. RIP, an example of a distance-vector protocol, is best used in smaller networks without redundant links. OSPF and IS-IS are examples of link-state protocols suitable for large complex networks.

- Routing protocols can be interior gateway protocols or exterior gateway protocols. RIP, OSPF, and IS-IS are IGPs, and Border Gateway Protocol (BGP) is an EGP.

- Access points have the following basic settings: wireless mode, SSID, and wireless channel. APs support security protocols that encrypt wireless data. From least secure to most secure, these protocols are WEP, WPA, and WPA2. Other security features include authentication, MAC filtering, and AP isolation.

- Higher-end APs can support advanced features, such as multiple SSIDs, adjustable transmit power, VLANs, QoS, and repeater and bridge modes.

- NIC selection includes the PC bus. PCI, PCI-X, and PCIe are the most common for internal NICs; USB can be used for external NICs. PCIe provides the fastest bus interface and is the standard PC bus.

- Some advanced NIC features to consider include RAM buffering, onboard co-processors, automatic link aggregation, multiple ports for fault tolerance, ACPI, and PXE.

Key Terms

access control list (ACL) A set of rules configured on a router's interface for specifying which addresses and protocols can pass through the interface and to which destinations.

administrative distance A value assigned to a routing protocol that indicates its reliability compared with other routing protocols that might be in use on the same router. If a route is derived by using two different routing protocols, the one with the least administrative distance is used.

aging time The amount of time a switch maintains a switching table entry that hasn't been updated.

auto-MDIX A switch port option used to detect the type of device and cable the switch port is connected to; if necessary, the port swaps its transmit and receive pins, which enables you to use a straight-through or crossover cable regardless of the type of device you're connecting to the port.

auto-negotiate mode Communication between a switch and a device connected to a switch port, in which the switch attempts to set the port's operating mode to the highest performance setting the device supports.

automatic link aggregation A feature that enables you to install multiple NICs in one computer and aggregate the bandwidth so that, for example, you can install two 1 Gbps NICs and have a total bandwidth of 2 Gbps to and from that computer.

autonomous system A network under the control of a single administrative entity, such as an organization's internetwork or an ISP's network.

blocking mode A mode on a switch port that prevents the switch from forwarding frames out the blocked port, thereby preventing a switching loop. *See also* switching loop.

Border Gateway Protocol (BGP) An exterior gateway routing protocol used to exchange routing information between two autonomous systems. *See also* autonomous system and exterior gateway protocol (EGP).

border router A router that connects one autonomous system to another—for example, an organization's network to an ISP. *See also* autonomous system.

broadcast storm A condition that occurs when a broadcast frame is forwarded endlessly in a switching loop. *See also* switching loop.

bus mastering A feature that allows a network adapter to take control of the computer's bus to initiate and manage data transfers to and from the computer's memory, independent of the CPU.

convergence Refers to how fast the routing tables of all routers in an internetwork are updated with accurate information when a change in the network occurs.

cut-through switching With this switching method, the switch reads only enough of the incoming frame to determine its source and destination addresses. After the forwarding location is determined, the frame is switched internally from the incoming port to the outgoing port, and the switch is free to handle additional frames.

destination network The network address of a network to which the router can forward packets.

distance-vector protocol A routing protocol that routers use to share information about an internetwork's status by copying their routing table to other routers with which they share a network.

exterior gateway protocol (EGP) A routing protocol category in which the routing protocol is used to exchange routing information between autonomous systems. *See also* autonomous system.

fault tolerance A feature available on some high-end NICs. By installing a second NIC in a PC, failure of the primary NIC shifts network traffic to the second NIC instead of cutting off the PC from the network.

flood The process whereby a switch forwards a frame out all connected ports.

fragment-free switching With this switching method, the switch reads enough of the frame to guarantee that it's at least the minimum size for the network type, reducing the possibility that the switch will forward a frame fragment.

frame fragment An invalid frame that's damaged because of a collision or a malfunctioning device.

hop Each router a packet must go through to get to the destination network.

hop count The total number of routers a packet must travel through to get to its destination network.

interior gateway protocol (IGP) A routing protocol category in which the routing protocol is used to exchange routing information within an autonomous system. *See also* autonomous system.

link-state protocol A routing protocol that a router uses to share information with other routers by sending the status of all its interface links to all other routers in the internetwork. The status includes link speed, whether the link is up or down, and the link's network number.

managed switch A high-end switch with many advanced features that can be configured.

metric A numeric value that tells the router how "far away" the destination network is. It can be composed of values such as the bandwidth of links between the source and destination, the hop count, and the link's reliability.

neighbor In an internetwork, routers sharing a common network.

next hop An interface name or the address of the next router in the path to the destination network.

onboard co-processors   A feature included on most NICs that enables the card to process incoming and outgoing network data without requiring service from the CPU.

packet filtering   A process whereby a router blocks a packet from being forwarded based on rules specified by an access control list. *See also* access control list (ACL).

packet forwarding   The process of a router receiving a packet on one port and forwarding it out another port based on the packet's destination network address and information in the routing table.

path-vector routing protocol   A routing protocol that analyzes the path to each destination network so that it can form a nonlooping routing topology.

PCI Express (PCIe)   A bus standard that uses a high-speed serial communication protocol of one or more lines or lanes. Each lane of PCIe 1.0 can operate at 250 MBps in each direction. *See also* Peripheral Component Interconnect (PCI).

PCMCIA cards   Credit card–sized expansion cards used mainly to add functionality to laptop computers. The main standards are Cardbus and ExpressCard. Cardbus operates at 33 MHz and supports a 32-bit bus; ExpressCard uses PCIe technology to provide data transfer speeds up to 500 MBps.

Peripheral Component Interconnect (PCI)   A bus standard used to connect I/O devices to the memory and CPU of a PC motherboard. PCI is implemented in both 32-bit and 64-bit versions at speeds of 33 and 66 MHz, respectively, and is rapidly becoming obsolete.

Peripheral Component Interconnect-Extended (PCI-X)   A bus standard that's backward-compatible with PCI and supports speeds of 66 to 533 MHz with 32-bit or 64-bit bus widths. *See also* Peripheral Component Interconnect (PCI).

Preboot Execution Environment (PXE)   A feature on some NICs that allows remotely booting an OS stored on a server through the PC's NIC instead of from local storage.

RAM buffering   A NIC feature for including additional memory to provide temporary storage for incoming and outgoing data.

Rapid Spanning Tree Protocol (RSTP)   Defined in 802.1w, this enhancement to the older, slower Spanning Tree Protocol (STP) provides much faster convergence when the switch topology changes. *See also* convergence *and* Spanning Tree Protocol (STP).

Routing Information Protocol (RIP)   A distance-vector protocol that uses hop count as the metric to determine the best path to a destination network.

Routing Information Protocol version 2 (RIPv2)   A newer version of RIP that supports a more complex IP addressing scheme and uses multicast packets rather than broadcasts to transmit routing table updates. *See also* Routing Information Protocol (RIP).

routing protocol   A set of rules routers use to exchange information so that all routers have accurate information about an internetwork to populate their routing tables.

shared adapter memory   A feature on some NICs in which the NIC's buffers map directly to RAM on the computer. A computer actually writes to buffers on the NIC instead of writing to its own memory.

shared system memory   A feature on some NICs in which a NIC's onboard processor selects a region of RAM on the computer and writes to it as though it were buffer space on the adapter.

Spanning Tree Protocol (STP)   A communication protocol switches use to ensure that they aren't connected in a way that creates a switching loop. *See also* switching loop.

static route   A routing table entry that's entered manually by an administrator.

store-and-forward switching   This switching method requires the switch to read the entire frame into its buffers before forwarding it. It examines the frame check sequence (FCS) field to be sure the frame contains no errors before it's forwarded.

switching loop   A condition that occurs when switches are connected in such a way that frames can be forwarded endlessly from switch to switch in an infinite loop.

trunk port   A switch port configured to carry traffic from all VLANs to another switch or router. *See also* virtual local area networks (VLANs).

Universal Serial Bus (USB)   An external PC bus interface for connecting I/O devices. Speeds range from 12 Mbps in USB 1.0 to 3.2 Gbps in USB 3.0.

virtual local area networks (VLANs)   A feature on some switches that allows configuring one or more switch ports into separate broadcast domains.

wake-on-LAN (WoL)   A feature on many NICs that allows an administrator to power on a computer remotely by sending a special packet, called a "magic packet," to the NIC's MAC address.

Review Questions

1. When a switch receives a frame on a port and floods the frame, what does it do with the frame?

   a.   Discards it

   b.   Changes the destination address to FF:FF:FF:FF:FF:FF

   c.   Forwards it out all other connected ports

   d.   Clears the switching table and adds the frame source address to the table

2. You have two eight-port switches. On each switch, seven stations are connected to ports, and the two switches are connected with the eighth port. How many collisions domains are there?

   a.   16

   b.   15

   c.   14

   d.   8

   e.   1

3. Which of the following is considered a Layer 2 device?

   a.   Computer

   b.   Switch

   c.   Router

   d.   Hub

4. You just purchased some new switches for your company's network. Your junior technicians are doing most of the work connecting switches to workstations and to each other, and you don't want to confuse them by requiring them to use both patch cables and crossover cables. How can you test the switches to determine whether you need both types of cable, and what's the feature for using only one type of cable for all connections?

   a. Connect the switch to a PC NIC and configure different speeds on the NIC by using the NIC driver. You're okay if the switch links at all speeds. It's called auto-MDIX.

   b. Connect two switches by using a crossover cable. If the connection works, the switch supports auto-negotiate.

   c. Connect the switch to a PC NIC and configure different speeds on the NIC by using the NIC driver. You're okay if the switch links at all speeds. It's called auto-negotiate.

   d. Connect two switches by using a patch cable. If the connection works, the switch supports auto-MDIX.

5. What feature of a switch keeps switching table entries from becoming stale?

6. Which is the fastest switching method?

   a. Store-and-forward

   b. Fragment-free

   c. Cut-through

   d. Forward-free

7. There can be only one MAC address per port in a switching table. True or False?

8. What does it mean if the first 24 bits of a MAC address are 01:00:5E?

   a. The NIC was manufactured by Intel.

   b. It's a multicast frame.

   c. It's an invalid CRC.

   d. The frame will be flooded.

9. What feature should you look for in switches if your network is cabled like the one in Figure 8-16?

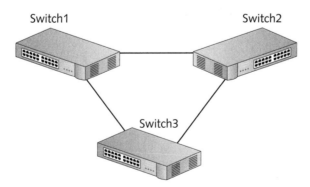

Figure 8-16 Network diagram for review question 9

    a. VLANs

    b. Auto-negotiate

    c. STP

    d. Auto-MDIX

10. What should you configure on a switch that's connected to three broadcast domains?

    a. IGMP

    b. VLANs

    c. Port security

    d. STP

11. Which of the following is a Layer 3 device? (Choose all that apply.)

    a. Router

    b. NIC

    c. Switch

    d. Multilayer switch

12. What does a router do after receiving a frame on one of its interfaces? (Choose all that apply.)

    a. Deencapsulates the frame to create a packet

    b. Deencapsulates the packet to create a segment

    c. Encapsulates the frame to create a new packet

    d. Encapsulates the packet to create a new frame

13. Which of the following is found in a routing table? (Choose all that apply.)

    a. Destination MAC address

    b. Port number

    c. Metric

    d. Next hop

    e. Domain name

14. Which of the following accurately describes a distance-vector routing protocol?

    a. OSPF is an example.

    b. It learns from its neighbors.

    c. It sends the status of its interface links to other routers.

    d. It converges the fastest.

15. Which of the following is a characteristic of routing protocols? (Choose all that apply.)

   a. They populate routing tables statically.

   b. Network changes are reflected in the routing table automatically.

   c. They're not a good solution with redundant routes.

   d. They add routing table entries dynamically.

16. Which of the following is the best routing solution for a network that includes redundant links?

   a. RIP

   b. STP

   c. OSPF

   d. Static

17. If you don't want wireless clients to view the name of your wireless network, what feature should you use?

   a. WEP

   b. Disabling SSID broadcasts

   c. MAC filtering

   d. AP isolation

18. To prevent a wardriver from being able to interpret captured wireless network data, you should enable which of the following?

   a. MAC filtering

   b. AP isolation

   c. WPA or WPA2

   d. Repeater mode

19. What feature can you use to wirelessly connect the wired networks in two buildings?

   a. Repeater mode

   b. AP isolation

   c. Bridge mode

   d. VLAN mode

20. Which AP feature is useful when you have many guests accessing your network and you don't want them to be able to access the computers of other guests?

   a. MAC filtering

   b. AP isolation

   c. Bridge mode

   d. VLAN mode

21. Which PC bus uses up to 32 lanes to achieve very high data transfer rates?

    a. PCI

    b. PCI-X

    c. USB

    d. PCIe

22. Which PC bus allows you to connect a NIC to your computer easily without powering off?

    a. PCI

    b. PCI-X

    c. USB

    d. PCIe

23. Which NIC feature do you need to configure on a thin client?

    a. QoS

    b. PXE

    c. IPsec

    d. ACPI

24. Which device is used to communicate between broadcast domains?

    a. Repeater

    b. Switch with VLANs

    c. Router

    d. Switch with STP

25. What feature should you configure to prevent users on one subnet from accessing the Web server on another subnet?

    a. MAC filtering

    b. Access control lists

    c. Dynamic routing

    d. Spanning Tree Protocol

Critical Thinking

The following activities give you critical thinking challenges. Challenge labs give you an opportunity to use the skills you have learned to perform a task without step-by-step instructions. Case projects offer a practical networking setup for which you supply a written solution.

Challenge Lab 8-1: Configuring a Wireless Network for Security

Time Required: 40 minutes

Objective: Install a wireless NIC (if necessary), connect to an access point, and configure security options.

Required Tools and Equipment: Two or more computers with 802.11 wireless NICs installed; USB wireless NICs work well because they don't require opening the computer case, and laptops with built-in wireless NICs will also do. One wireless AP or wireless router configured with the SSID NetEss. The 802.11 standard supported doesn't matter as long as the AP is compatible with the NICs. The computers shouldn't be connected to a hub or switch.

Description: In this challenge lab, you connect to a wireless access point and then configure security and other options. You can work in groups or have the instructor configure the AP and the students configure the NICs. If you work in groups, each group should choose a different SSID and channel. Perform the following tasks:

- Install the wireless NIC in each computer, if necessary.

- Configure the AP SSID as NetEss, if necessary.

- Connect to the AP from each computer.

- Configure the AP for the following security protocols, if available: WEP, WPA, and WPA2. After you configure the AP for a security protocol, change the wireless NIC configuration to use the same security protocol. Use as many of these protocols as your hardware supports.

- Change the AP's configuration to not use a security protocol and verify that all computers can connect before continuing.

- Configure these options on the AP to see how they affect your client connections; reset each option after you have tested it before moving on to the next option:

  o Disable SSID broadcasts.

  o MAC filtering: Configure filtering to allow only one or two computers to connect, and verify that the others can't connect.

- Answer the following questions:

  o Which security protocol was the easiest to configure? Which protocol is the most secure?

  _____

  o How did disabling the SSID broadcast affect your ability to connect to the AP?

  _____

  o How did MAC filtering affect your ability to connect to the AP?

  _____

Challenge Lab 8-2: Filling in Routing Tables

Time Required: 45 minutes

Objective: Fill in routing tables.

Required Tools and Equipment: None

Description: In this lab, you fill out routing tables for the network shown in Figure 8-17, using the following charts. The network is running the RIP routing protocol. RouterA's table has been started for you. Assume all networks are Class C networks.

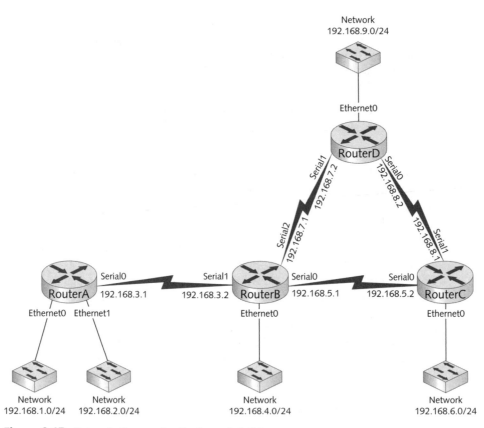

Figure 8-17 Network diagram for Challenge Lab 8-2

Key for the How column: C = directly connected network; R = RIP.

Router A

How	Network	Via/next hop	Metric	Interface
C	192.168.1.0/24	Connected	0	Ethernet0
	192.168.2.0/24			
	192.168.3.0/24			
	192.168.4.0/24			
	192.168.5.0/24			
R	192.168.6.0/24	192.168.3.2	2	Serial0
	192.168.7.0/24			
R	192.168.8.0/24	192.168.3.2		
	192.168.9.0/24			

Router B

How	Network	Via/next hop	Metric	Interface
	192.168.1.0/24			
	192.168.2.0/24			
	192.168.3.0/24			
	192.168.4.0/24			
	192.168.5.0/24			
	192.168.6.0/24			
	192.168.7.0/24			
	192.168.8.0/24			
	192.168.9.0/24			

Router C

How	Network	Via/next hop	Metric	Interface
	192.168.1.0/24			
	192.168.2.0/24			
	192.168.3.0/24			
	192.168.4.0/24			
	192.168.5.0/24			
	192.168.6.0/24			
	192.168.7.0/24			
	192.168.8.0/24			
	192.168.9.0/24			

Router D

How	Network	Via/next hop	Metric	Interface
	192.168.1.0/24			
	192.168.2.0/24			
	192.168.3.0/24			
	192.168.4.0/24			
	192.168.5.0/24			
	192.168.6.0/24			
	192.168.7.0/24			
	192.168.8.0/24			
	192.168.9.0/24			

CHALLENGE LAB

Challenge Lab 8-3: Configuring VLANs on a Cisco Switch

Time Required: 40 minutes

Objective: Configure VLANs on a Cisco switch.

Required Tools and Equipment: Four computers, one Cisco managed switch (Catalyst 2900 series work well, but other models that run Cisco IOS should work), a rollover cable

Description: In this challenge lab, you configure VLANs on a switch and demonstrate that the computers on each VLAN are on separate broadcast domains. Basic instructions for creating VLANs are given, but for detailed instructions on configuring Cisco VLANs, see *www. cisco.com/c/en/us/td/docs/switches/lan/catalyst2960/software/release/12-2_55_se/configuration/guide/scg_2960/swvlan.html#wp1274626*. The following instructions assume the switch isn't configured.

1. Connect a PC to the Cisco console port with the rollover cable. You need a COM (serial) port on your computer or a USB-to–serial port adapter.
2. Start a terminal emulation program, such as PuTTY, and open a terminal connection on the corresponding serial connection (usually COM1, COM2, or COM3). The speed should be set at 9600.
3. Next, you enter commands at the switch prompt. Log on to the switch and enter enable mode by typing **enable** at the switch prompt and pressing **Enter**.
4. Enter configuration mode by typing **config terminal** at the switch prompt and pressing **Enter**.
5. Type **vlan 10** and press **Enter** to create VLAN number 10. Type **vlan 20** and press **Enter** to create VLAN 20.

6. Now you verify that these VLANs are created. First, exit configuration mode by pressing **Ctrl+z**.

7. Type **show vlan brief** and press **Enter**. You see a list of VLANs, including several default VLANs, such as VLAN 1 and VLAN 1002. You also see the two VLANs you created (see Figure 8-18). You might need to press the spacebar one or more times to view all the output.

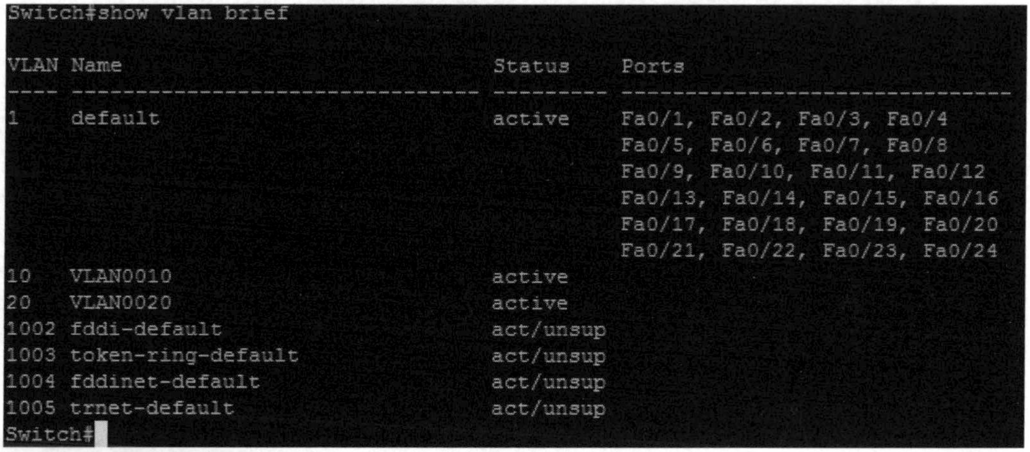

```
Switch#show vlan brief

VLAN Name                             Status    Ports
---- -------------------------------- --------- -------------------------------
1    default                          active    Fa0/1, Fa0/2, Fa0/3, Fa0/4
                                                 Fa0/5, Fa0/6, Fa0/7, Fa0/8
                                                 Fa0/9, Fa0/10, Fa0/11, Fa0/12
                                                 Fa0/13, Fa0/14, Fa0/15, Fa0/16
                                                 Fa0/17, Fa0/18, Fa0/19, Fa0/20
                                                 Fa0/21, Fa0/22, Fa0/23, Fa0/24
10   VLAN0010                         active
20   VLAN0020                         active
1002 fddi-default                     act/unsup
1003 token-ring-default               act/unsup
1004 fddinet-default                  act/unsup
1005 trnet-default                    act/unsup
Switch#
```

Figure 8-18 The output of the show vlan brief command

Source: Cisco Systems, Inc.

8. Enter configuration mode again by typing **config terminal** at the switch prompt and pressing **Enter**. Now you need to assign ports to the new VLANs you created. Figure 8-18 shows that all the switch ports are currently assigned to the default VLAN 1. You need to assign ports 2 through 4 to VLAN 10 and ports 10 through 12 to VLAN 20.

9. Type **interface fa0/2** and press **Enter** to enter configuration mode for port 2. Type **switchport mode access** and press **Enter**, and then type **switchport access vlan 10** and press **Enter**. Repeat these steps for Fa0/3 and Fa0/4 and again for Fa0/10, Fa0/11, and Fa0/12. Make sure you change the VLAN number to 20 for Fa0/10 through Fa0/12. When you're finished, press **Ctrl+z** to exit configuration mode.

10. Type **show vlan brief** and press **Enter** to see the new VLAN configuration, shown in Figure 8-19. Ports Fa0/2 through Fa0/4 are assigned to VLAN 10, and ports Fa0/10 through Fa0/12 are assigned to VLAN 20.

```
Switch#copy run start
Destination filename [startup-config]?
Building configuration...
[OK]
Switch#show vlan brief

VLAN Name                             Status     Ports
---- -------------------------------- ---------  -------------------------------
1    default                          active     Fa0/1, Fa0/5, Fa0/6, Fa0/7
                                                 Fa0/8, Fa0/9, Fa0/13, Fa0/14
                                                 Fa0/15, Fa0/16, Fa0/17, Fa0/18
                                                 Fa0/19, Fa0/20, Fa0/21, Fa0/22
                                                 Fa0/23, Fa0/24
10   VLAN0010                         active     Fa0/2, Fa0/3, Fa0/4
20   VLAN0020                         active     Fa0/10, Fa0/11, Fa0/12
1002 fddi-default                     act/unsup
1003 token-ring-default               act/unsup
1004 fddinet-default                  act/unsup
1005 trnet-default                    act/unsup
Switch#copy run start
Destination filename [startup-config]?
Building configuration...
[OK]
Switch#
```

Figure 8-19 Viewing the new VLAN configuration

Source: Cisco Systems, Inc.

11. To ensure that your configuration is saved for the next time the switch boots, type
copy run start at the switch prompt and press **Enter** to confirm. In the next
challenge lab, you connect computers to the VLAN 10 and VLAN 20 ports and
then configure a router to route between the VLANs.

CHALLENGE LAB

Challenge Lab 8-4: Configuring a Router to Communicate Between VLANs

Time Required: 40 minutes

Objective: Configure a router to communicate between VLANs.

Required Tools and Equipment: Four computers, the switch used in Challenge Lab 8-3, a
Cisco router with two Ethernet interfaces, a rollover cable, six patch cables

Description: In this challenge lab, you configure a router to route between VLANs. This lab
uses a Cisco 2600 series router with two Ethernet interfaces, but other router models will
work as long as they have two Ethernet interfaces. The following instructions assume the
router isn't configured. The four computers should be named Computer1, Computer2, Computer3, and Computer4.

1. Connect Computer1 and Computer2 to switch ports 3 and 4 and Computer3 and Computer4 to switch ports 11 and 12 with the patch cables.
2. Configure Computer1 and Computer2 with IP addresses 192.168.10.1/24 and
192.168.10.2/24.

3. Configure Computer3 and Computer4 with IP addresses 192.168.20.1/24 and 192.168.20.2/24.

4. From Computer1, verify that you can ping Computer2. From Computer3, verify that you can ping Computer4. Next, from Computer1, try to ping Computer3 or Computer4. The ping isn't successful. Why not?

_____

_____

5. Connect the Fa0/1 interface on the router to switch port 2 with one of the patch cables. Connect the Fa0/2 interface on the router to switch port 10. Connect a PC to the Cisco console port on the router with the rollover cable.

6. Start a terminal emulation program, such as PuTTY, and open a terminal connection on the corresponding serial connection (usually COM1, COM2, or COM3). The speed should be set at 9600.

7. Log on to the router and enter enable mode by typing **enable** at the router prompt and pressing **Enter**.

8. Enter configuration mode by typing **config terminal** at the router prompt and pressing **Enter**.

9. Type **interface fa0/1** and press **Enter** to enter interface configuration mode for the first Ethernet port. Type **no shutdown** and press **Enter** to enable the interface. Type **ip address 192.168.10.250 255.255.255.0** and press **Enter** to set the interface address. Repeat this command for fa0/2, using **192.168.20.250** for the IP address.

10. Now you verify that the interfaces are configured. First, exit configuration mode by pressing **Ctrl+z**. Type **show ip interface brief** and press **Enter**. You see a list of interfaces and their configured IP addresses.

11. Type **show ip route** and press **Enter**. You see the routing table that includes the two configured interfaces.

12. Now that you have a router to communicate between VLANs, from Computer1, try to ping Computer3. The ping is still not successful. Why not?

_____

13. Configure the default gateway address on all four computers. What's the correct default gateway address for each computer?

_____

14. Everything should be configured correctly now. From Computer1, try to ping Computer3. The ping should be successful. Try to ping to all computers from any computer. (_Note_: If the pings still aren't successful, verify that the firewall on the computers isn't blocking the ping messages and all the IP address settings are correct.)

Case Project 8-1

You have been called in to consult on a new network design for CNT Books. The requirements of this design are summarized as follows:

- The building has three floors.
- There are 300 user workstations and 10 servers.
- Users must be grouped according to the projects they're working on, but the users for each project are located on all three floors.
- There must be fault tolerance for communicating between the floors.

What features would you look for on the switches you purchase for this design? Explain why you would want each feature. Do you need to include any other devices in this design? Write a memo to your instructor with the answers to these questions or be prepared to discuss your answers.

Case Project 8-2

The CNT Books network described in Case Project 8-1 is expanding. There are 200 more user stations in the building, and a total of five floors are in use by the network. You have kept up with the design so far with a network of five subnets, each with its own router. The company leased a building across the street. You expect at least four subnets to be added to the design. The owner is concerned about how to connect to the building across the street, as he thinks the cost of contracting with a communications provider is too expensive for such a short distance. What solution can you suggest for connecting the building across the street with the existing building?

Case Project 8-3

Three years later, you're still consulting for CNT Books. The network has more than 15 subnets and 10 routers in several buildings and locations. You have been keeping up with the network by configuring the routers statically. However, users have had problems with downtime in the past year because of network links going offline, as there's only one route to reach every subnet. The owner wants fault tolerance built into the network to include backup links in case a primary link goes offline. You're concerned that the current router configuration method will still cause some downtime, even if the backup links operate correctly. Why might there be downtime if a primary link goes offline but the backup link is okay? What can you do to reduce the possibility of downtime?

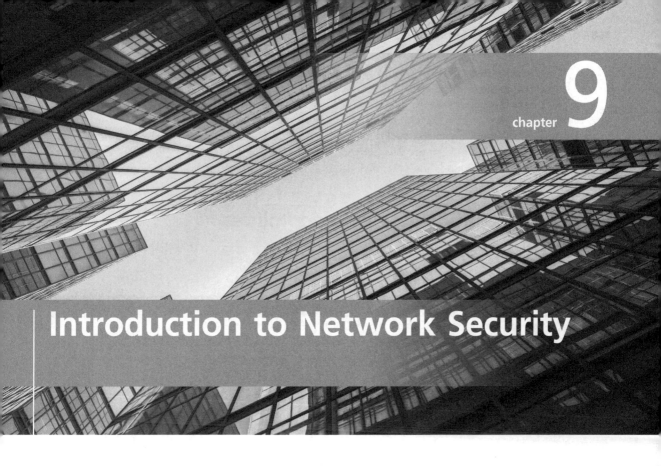

chapter 9

Introduction to Network Security

After reading this chapter and completing the exercises, you will be able to:

- Develop a network security policy
- Secure physical access to network equipment
- Secure access to network data
- Describe network security devices
- Protect a network from malware
- Use attackers' tools to find network security weaknesses

You have learned how to make wise choices about which network technologies to use and how to configure networking protocols for your network. Although you're off to a good start, you have plenty to do before you can bring a network online because of all the security risks that can make networks fail: Trojan horses, worms, spammers, denial-of-service attacks, spyware, network attackers, backdoors, and on and on. Understanding and preventing attacks that can infiltrate or disrupt your network are what network security is all about. This chapter gives you a solid foundation of knowledge and tools for protecting your network and its users.

Network Security Overview and Policies

Table 9-1 summarizes what you need for the hands-on projects in this chapter.

Table 9-1   Hands-on project requirements

Hands-on project	Requirements	Time required	Notes
Hands-On Project 9-1: Setting Password and Lockout Policies in Windows	Net-*XX*	20 minutes	
Hands-On Project 9-2: Exploring Windows Firewall	Net-*XX*	15 minutes	
Hands-On Project 9-3: Testing Your Firewall with ShieldsUP!	Net-*XX*	15 minutes	Internet access required
Hands-On Project 9-4: Configuring Windows Defender	Net-*XX*	15 minutes	Internet access required
Hands-On Project 9-5: Using NetInfo to Collect Computer and Network Information	Net-*XX*	15 minutes	Internet access required

Network security can mean different things to different people. To network users, network security is sometimes considered a necessary evil that takes the form of hard-to-remember passwords that must be changed frequently and cryptic terms, such as "VPN" and "IPsec," to describe methods they use to access the network. To other users, network security means the comfort of knowing that if they erase their hard drives accidentally, the friendly network administrator will gladly restore their data from the most recent system backup.

Perceptions about network security also vary depending on the industry a person is in or the job a person does. A chemical engineer might perceive network security to mean that the compound he has just developed is safe from the competition's eyes. A lawyer might describe network security as a means of safeguarding against illegal activities, such as unlawful distribution of copyrighted materials. To a network engineer, network security might simply mean she can get a good night's sleep, secure in the knowledge that the network is safe from the latest threats—at least until tomorrow. To a chief security officer (CSO), however, network security means more than job-specific tasks. A CSO knows that the goal of network security is to protect the organization and its users, customers, and business partners from any threat to the integrity of information passing through or residing on the organization's network.

Ideally, network security should be as unobtrusive as possible, allowing network users to concentrate on the tasks they want to perform instead of how to get to the data they need for those tasks. Achieving this goal enables an organization to go about its business confidently and efficiently. In the current security-conscious world, a company that can demonstrate its information systems are secure is more likely to attract customers, partners, and investors. That's where a network security policy comes in.

Developing a Network Security Policy

The lofty goal of good, unobtrusive security encompasses many dimensions, so where do you start? With a security policy that reflects your organization's attitude toward securing network resources. A network **security policy** is a document that describes the rules governing access to an organization's information resources, enforcement of these rules, and steps taken if rules are breached. The document should describe not only who can have access to which resources, but also how these resources are allowed to be used after they're accessed. In addition, it should follow these basic guidelines:

- A security policy should be easy for ordinary users to understand and reasonably easy to comply with. If you make the policy too difficult to understand or follow, users resist adhering to it. A policy requiring users to change their passwords every week, for example, is too difficult to follow. Users who must change their passwords too frequently often select easy-to-remember passwords that are based on common words and, therefore, are easy to crack. In addition, users who must change their passwords often are more likely to write them down somewhere, which is a security risk.

- A security policy should be enforceable. A rule that can't be reasonably enforced will almost always be broken. For example, you shouldn't prohibit use of the Internet during certain hours of the day unless you have a method of monitoring or restricting this use.

- A security policy should clearly state the objective of each policy so that everyone understands its purpose. For example, a policy that states "Misuse of the network is forbidden" doesn't define misuse, making this policy useless because of its lack of specificity.

The preceding guidelines explain how a security policy should be written. Now you need to know what information should be included in a security policy.

Determining Elements of a Network Security Policy

Explaining all the elements of a security policy is beyond the scope of this book, but the following items give you a solid start:

- *Privacy policy*—Describes what staff, customers, and business partners can expect for monitoring and reporting network use.

- *Acceptable use policy*—Explains for what purposes network resources can be used.

- *Authentication policy*—Describes how users identify themselves to gain access to network resources. Logon names, password conventions, and authentication methods should be described.

- *Internet use policy*—Explains what constitutes proper or improper use of Internet resources.

- *Access policy*—Specifies how and when users are allowed to access network resources. Policies should exist for both onsite and remote access to the network.

- *Auditing policy*—Explains the manner in which security compliance or violations can be verified and the consequences for violations.

- *Data protection*—Outlines the policies for backup procedures, virus protection, and disaster recovery.

To learn more about security policies and see a list of templates for different types of policies, refer to the System Administration, Networking, and Security (SANS) institute at *www.sans.org/security-resources/policies/*.

Your security policy might have other elements, depending on the type of organization it's being created for and the level of security required, but the preceding list is usually the minimum for most networks. Keep in mind that a well-thought-out security policy also protects the organization legally. If no policy exists, disciplining or prosecuting people who misuse or intrude on the network is more difficult. Unfortunately, after you create a security policy, your work isn't done. A security policy should be a constant work in progress, with modifications made as needed to reflect changing technology and business practices.

Understanding Levels of Security

Before starting to design a network security policy, you need to be aware of the relationship between the level of security imposed on a network and the cost and difficulty of supporting the network. Security doesn't come without a cost. If you're the network administrator for the security department of government offices, for example, price is likely no object in determining the extent of security measures. However, if you're setting up a network for a small manufacturer of household items, you might need to scale back on security measures. Before determining the level of security your network needs, answer these questions:

- What must be protected? Is there information on the network that would compromise the viability of the company or its customers if it fell into the wrong hands?

- From whom should data be protected? Is the biggest threat from people inside or outside the company?

- What costs are associated with security being breached and data being lost or stolen?

- How likely is it that a threat will actually occur? Do you have a high-profile business, or do you have known competitors who are likely to want to sabotage your business or steal trade secrets?

- What's the likelihood of a natural disaster, and what would the losses to your business be if your information systems were down for a day, a week, or longer?

- Are the costs to implement security and train personnel to use a secure network outweighed by the need to create an efficient, user-friendly environment?

Depending on your answers, you'll likely decide to use one of these security levels or some combination of them: highly restrictive, moderately restrictive, and open.

Highly Restrictive Security Policies
Highly restrictive security policies usually include features such as data encryption, complex password requirements, detailed auditing and monitoring of computer and network access, intricate authentication methods, and strict policies governing use of the Internet and e-mail. Some features of this type of policy might require third-party hardware and software. The high expense of implementing these restrictive policies comes in the form of design and configuration costs for software and hardware,

staffing to support security policies, and lost productivity caused by a steep learning curve for users. However, if you need highly restrictive security, it's probably because the cost of a security breach would be more expensive than implementing the security policy.

Moderately Restrictive Security Policies Most organizations can probably opt for a moderately restrictive security policy. These policies require passwords for each user but not overly complex passwords. Auditing is geared toward detecting unauthorized logon attempts, misuse of network resources, and network attacker activity. Most network OSs contain satisfactory authentication, monitoring, and auditing features to carry out these policies. The network infrastructure can be secured with moderately priced off-the-shelf hardware and software, such as firewalls and access control lists. The costs of moderate security policies are mainly in initial configuration and support. This type of policy is used in a typical business setting, in which users have personal files that require moderate security and users in some departments are responsible for files that might need additional security measures, such as data encryption.

Open Security Policies A company that uses an open network security policy might have simple or no passwords, unrestricted access to resources, and probably no monitoring and auditing. This type of policy might make sense for a small company with the main goal of making access to network resources easy. The company might not want to spend additional funds for the employee training often required for more restrictive policies.

In an open security environment, Internet access probably shouldn't be possible via the company LAN because it invites too many possibilities for outside mischief or inside abuse. If companywide Internet access is available, a more restrictive policy is probably warranted. In an open security environment, sensitive data, if it exists, might be kept on workstations that are backed up regularly and physically inaccessible to other employees.

Common Elements of Security Policies No matter which type of security policy your company uses, some common elements should be present. Antivirus software and other malware protection for servers and desktop computers are musts for every computing environment, and there should be policies aimed at preventing malware from being downloaded or spread. Backup procedures for all data that can't be reproduced easily should be in place, and a disaster recovery procedure must be devised and carried out. Remember: Security is aimed not only at preventing improper use of or access to network resources, but also at safeguarding the company's information, which is often more valuable than its physical assets. Before you turn to methods and practices for securing data, however, one often neglected aspect of security must be discussed: physical security of servers and network devices.

Securing Physical Access to the Network

A common guideline in discussing network security is "If there's physical access to the equipment, there's no security." This guideline applies to servers, desktop computers, network devices (such as routers and switches), and even network media. No matter how strong your logon name and password schemes are, if a person has physical access to a device, access to data isn't far behind.

There are numerous ways to break into an unprotected computer or networking device. A computer left alone with a user logged on is particularly vulnerable. A person walking by could access all the files the logged-on user has access to. If the computer is a server and an administrator account is logged on, that person has full reign of the network and can even give his or her account administrator control. Even if no user is logged on, people could log on to the computer with their own accounts and access files they wouldn't normally have access to. Failing that, the computer could be restarted and booted from removable media, thereby bypassing the normal OS security. Last, if a person is desperate, the entire computer or its hard drives could be stolen and later cracked. The following sections describe best practices for preventing a physical assault on your network.

Physical Security Best Practices

The following list is an overview of best practices to secure your network from physical assault:

- When planning your network, make sure rooms are available to house servers and equipment. These rooms should have locks to prevent unauthorized access and be suitable for the equipment being housed, including having enough power receptacles, adequate cooling measures, and an environment clear of electromagnetic interference (EMI) sources. In addition, rooms should be inaccessible through false ceilings.

- If a suitable room isn't available, locking cabinets (freestanding or wall mounted) can be purchased to house servers and equipment in public areas. Wall-mounted cabinets are particularly useful for hubs, switches, and patch panels. You must be certain cabinets have suitable ventilation for the devices they're housing.

- Wiring from workstations to wiring cabinets should be inaccessible to eavesdropping equipment. Wiring that's not concealed in floors or ceilings should be concealed in raceways or other channeling devices to discourage access.

- Your physical security plan should include procedures for recovery from natural disasters, such as fires or floods.

Physical Security of Servers Securing servers from physical access should be a high priority in any security plan. This goal can be achieved in several ways, and sometimes a combination of methods works best, depending on your environment. Many servers are stashed away in a lockable wiring closet along with the switch the servers are connected to. This setup is fine as long as the environment is suitable for the server, and the same people who have authority to access wiring and switches also have authority to access the servers, although this isn't always the case.

Servers often require more tightly controlled environmental conditions than patch panels and switches do. They can generate a substantial amount of heat and, therefore, need adequate cooling. The lack of cooling can damage hard drives, cause CPUs to shut down or malfunction, and damage power supplies, among other consequences.

In addition to adequate cooling, server rooms should be equipped with power that's preferably on a circuit separate from other electrical devices. Enough power outlets should be installed to eliminate the need for extension cords. Because you'll be putting servers on uninterruptible power supplies (UPSs), you need to verify power requirements for UPSs. Some UPSs require special twist-lock outlet plugs rated for high currents. Nothing is more frustrating than getting a brand-new UPS and preparing to plug in your servers, only to find that the wall outlets are incompatible with the UPS requirements.

Sometimes putting your servers in a place that's accessible to people who should *not* have physical access to servers is unavoidable. For example, you might have different teams maintaining internetworking equipment and servers, and you don't want internetworking maintenance teams to have access to servers. If you don't have the facilities to separate the two types of equipment physically, however, you can still take some steps to provide a measure of physical security. Many servers come with locking cabinets to prevent access to the inside of the case. Some also have lockable covers that protect the drives and power buttons from unauthorized access. You can also place the keyboard, mouse, and monitor in an area separate from the actual server by using long-distance cable extenders or network-based keyboard, mouse, video (KVM) switches. Last, you can place the server in a freestanding locking cabinet.

If you're forced to place servers in a public access area, locking cabinets are a must. Even if no users have malicious intentions, someone is sure to kick the server, spill coffee on it, unplug it, or inflict some sort of accidental damage. You can purchase rack-mountable servers, which are designed to bolt to a standard 19-inch equipment rack. To conserve space, you can purchase a freestanding cabinet with a built-in 19-inch rack, allowing you to store several servers. Make sure the cabinet you purchase is well ventilated or allows adding fans for ventilation. These cabinets typically start at about $1000. Like everything else, security comes with a price.

Security of Internetworking Devices
Routers and switches contain critical configuration information and perform tasks essential to your network's operation. A user with physical access to these devices needs only a laptop or handheld device and a few easily discovered keystrokes to get into the router or switch, change passwords, and view or change the device's configuration. In addition, a person who has access to a switch port can attach a laptop with a protocol analyzer installed. From that point, it's simply a matter of waiting for the right data to be captured to gain access to critical or sensitive information.

Clearly, internetworking devices should be given as much attention to physical security as servers. These devices give potential network infiltrators access to the network and an opportunity to wreak havoc. Unauthorized configuration changes made to routers and switches can have disastrous consequences. In addition, access to routers can reveal network topology information you might not want everyone to know. The more troublemakers know about a network's configuration, the more tools they have to break into the network or cause problems on it.

A room with a lock is the best place for internetworking devices, but a wall-mounted enclosure with a lock is the next best thing. These cabinets are usually heavy-duty units with doors that swing out and built-in 19-inch racks. Wall-mounted cabinets are expensive, so budget between $300 and $1000 for them, depending on the features and size you need. Some cabinets have a built-in fan or a mounting hole for a fan. The racks also come with convenient channels to run wiring.

Securing Access to Network Data

Physically securing network assets is only one part of the security puzzle. Networks are designed to give users working from remote locations access to data, whether the remote location is the next room or the other side of the world. Securing data on a network has many facets:

- *Authentication and authorization*—Identifying who's permitted to access which network resources

- *Encryption*—Making data unusable to anyone except authorized users

- *Virtual private networks (VPNs)*—Allowing authorized remote access to a private network via the public Internet

- *Wireless security*—Implementing measures for protecting data and authorizing access to a wireless network

- *Network security devices*—A hardware device or software (including firewalls, intrusion detection and prevention systems, and content filters) that protects a computer or network from unauthorized access and attacks designed to cripple network or computer performance

- *Malware protection*—Securing data from software designed to destroy data or make computers and networks operate inefficiently

The following sections discuss some of these areas of security and explore features of network OSs that help secure a network. Later in this chapter, you learn about network security devices, such as firewalls and intrusion detection systems, and security threats, such as viruses and other malware.

Setting Up Authentication and Authorization

Authentication and authorization are security features that enable administrators to control who has access to the network (authentication) and what users can do after they're logged on to the network (authorization). Authentication protocols used by OSs and network devices offer varying levels of secure authentication, some of which are discussed in the following list:

- *Kerberos*—**Kerberos** is the authentication protocol used in a Windows domain environment to authenticate logons and grant accounts access to domain resources. An account can be a user or a computer because computers must also authenticate to the domain. Kerberos provides mutual authentication between a client and server or between two servers. **Mutual authentication** means the identity of both parties is verified. Kerberos is also the basis for authorization to network resources in a Windows domain. It uses shared secret key encryption to ensure privacy, and passwords are never sent across the network.

- *Remote Authentication Dial In User Service*—RADIUS is an industry-standard client/server protocol that centralizes authentication, authorization, and accounting (AAA) for a network. It's often used to authenticate remote access and wireless access to a network when there's a variety of clients using different entry points. RADIUS is also used to authenticate administrative access to network devices for configuration and monitoring purposes. For example, a RADIUS client can be configured on a Cisco router that allows network administrators to use their Windows domain credentials to log on to the router instead of requiring different credentials. Another AAA protocol, TACACS+, developed by Cisco, is similar to RADIUS but has features designed for network device authentication and is arguably more secure than RADIUS. For example, TACACS+ encrypts the entire packet exchanged between client and server, whereas RADIUS encrypts only the password, leaving the username and other AAA parameters unencrypted and vulnerable.

- *Extensible Authentication Protocol*—**Extensible Authentication Protocol (EAP)** is not a self-contained authentication protocol; rather, it's a framework for other protocols that provide encryption and authentication. For example, EAP-TLS uses the Transport Layer Security (TLS) authentication protocol, which uses certificates for authentication. EAP-Tunneled Transport Layer Security (TTLS) adds tunneling to EAP-TLS, and EAP over LAN (EAPoL) is the IEEE 802.lX standard often used for authentication with wireless networks. EAP is flexible and can work with smart cards and biometric authentication methods as well as traditional username and password methods.

- *Microsoft Challenge Handshake Authentication Protocol version 2*—MS-CHAP v2 is a mutual authentication protocol that encrypts both authentication information and data. A different encryption key is used each time a connection is made and on both ends of the connection. MS-CHAP v2 is compatible with most Windows clients, going back to Windows 98. It's sometimes used with remote access protocols but should be used only when a stronger protocol, such as EAP, isn't available.

- *Microsoft Challenge Handshake Authentication Protocol*—MS-CHAP is an earlier version of MS-CHAP v2 that's easier to crack and doesn't provide mutual authentication.

- *Password Authentication Protocol*—PAP is not a secure protocol because the username and password are transmitted in cleartext, making it easy for someone to capture packets and access a user's credentials.

Multifactor Authentication It's always a good idea to use a secure authentication protocol, such as Kerberos or some form of EAP, but sometimes usernames and passwords aren't enough to protect highly sensitive information. In these cases, many organizations use **multifactor authentication (MFA)**, which requires a user to supply two or more types of authentication drawn from these credential categories:

- *Knowledge*—What the user knows, such as a username and password

- *Possession*—What the user has, or possesses, such as a smart card or key

- *Inherence*—What the user is; a unique biometric identifying trait, such as a fingerprint, retina scan, or voice pattern

As biometric authentication becomes more reliable and less expensive, using MFA will be more common. Passwords are often considered a weak link in security systems because users can write them down or tell other people, so biometric methods combined with some type of smart card are likely to replace passwords in the future.

Configuring Password Requirements in a Windows Environment Network OSs include tools that enable administrators to specify options and restrictions on how and when users can log on to the network. There are options for password complexity requirements, logon hours, logon locations, and remote logons, among others. After a user is logged on, file system access controls and user permission settings determine what a user can access on a network and what actions a user can perform (such as installing software or shutting down a system) on the network.

Administrators can specify whether a password is required for all users, how many characters a password must be, and whether the password should meet certain complexity requirements. Windows OSs allow passwords up to 128 characters, but a minimum of five to eight characters is typical. A password minimum length of zero means blank passwords are allowed, a setting that might be adequate for networks with open security policies but should never be used for networks requiring more security. A password policy with complexity requirements means user passwords must have three of these four characteristics: lowercase letters, uppercase letters, numbers, and special (nonalphanumeric) characters.

Other password options include:

- *Maximum password age*—Specifies, in days, how often users must change their passwords
- *Minimum password age*—Specifies the minimum number of days that must pass before users can change their passwords
- *Enforce password history*—Determines how many different passwords must be used before a password can be used again

One word of caution on password settings: Don't make your password requirements so stringent that well-meaning users feel forced to write their passwords down so that they can remember them. Password policies should make it difficult for would-be attackers to gain access to the system but not so difficult that your users have trouble adhering to the policies.

When a user fails to enter a correct password, a policy can be set to lock the user account, preventing that account from logging on. This account lockout option, used to prevent intruders from guessing a password, can be enabled or disabled. If it's enabled, the administrator can specify how many times an incorrect password can be entered before the account is locked. After it's locked, the administrator can require manual unlocking or automatic unlocking of the account after a certain amount of time has expired.

Password policies for a single Windows computer can be set in the Local Security Policy console (via Administrative Tools in the Control Panel). Figure 9-1 shows the Local Security

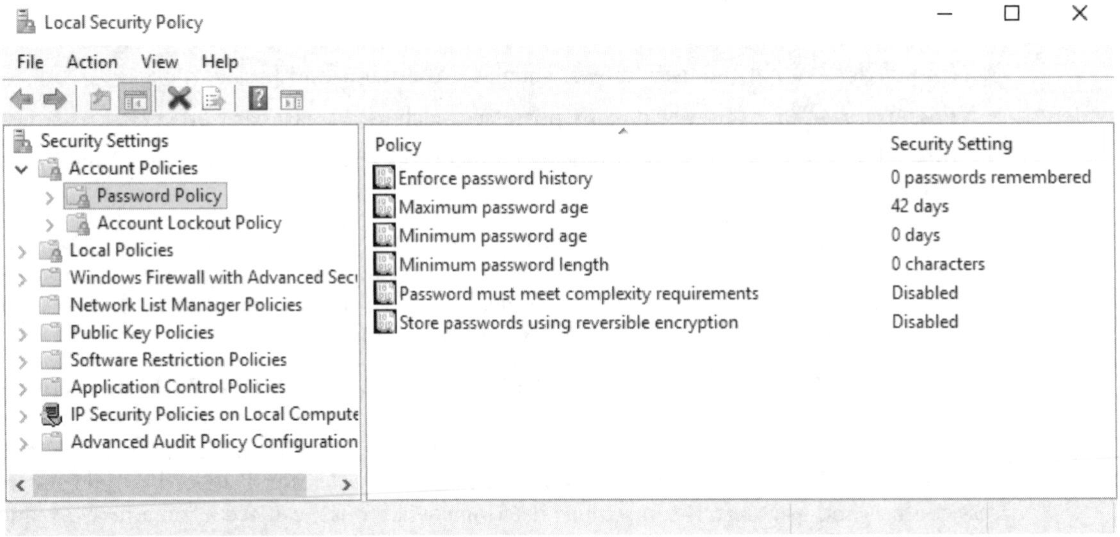

Figure 9-1 Password policy settings in Windows 10

Policy console with Password Policy selected. In a domain environment, password policies are set by using group policies on a domain controller.

Reviewing Password Dos and Don'ts Some general rules for creating passwords include the following:

- Do use a combination of uppercase letters, lowercase letters, numbers, and special characters, such as periods, dollar signs, exclamation points, and question marks.

- Do consider using a phrase, such as NetW@rk1ng !s C00l. Phrases are easy to remember but generally difficult to crack, especially if you mix in special characters and numbers.

- Don't use passwords based on your logon name, your family members' names, or even your pet's name. Users often use these types of passwords, but unfortunately, they're easy to guess after attackers discover personal information about users.

- Don't use common dictionary words unless they're part of a phrase, and substitute special characters and numbers for letters.

- Don't make your password so complex that you forget it or need to write it down somewhere.

Hands-On Project 9-1: Setting Password and Lockout Policies in Windows

Time Required: 15 minutes

Objective: Set password and lockout policies in the Windows Local Security Policy console.

Required Tools and Equipment: Net-*XX*

Description: This project shows you how to use the Local Security Policy console in Windows 10. You set a password policy that specifies the following:

- Users must use 10 different passwords before reusing a password.

- Users must change their password every 30 days.

- Users can't change their password more often than every seven days.

- The minimum password length is six characters.

- The password must contain three of these characteristics: uppercase letters, lowercase letters, numbers, or special characters.

You set the account lockout policy to enforce the following:

- User accounts are locked out after four invalid logon attempts.

- Locked accounts are unlocked automatically after 60 minutes.

- The counter is reset 15 minutes after each invalid logon attempt.

1. Log on to your computer as **NetAdmin**.

2. On the taskbar, click the **Search the web and Windows** text box, type **secpol.msc**, and press **Enter**.

3. Click to expand **Account Policies** and click **Password Policy**. In the right pane, double-click **Enforce password history**. Set the value to **10** passwords remembered, and then click **OK**.

4. Double-click **Maximum password age**, set the value to **30** days, and click **OK**.

5. Double-click **Minimum password age**, set the value to **7** days, and click **OK**.

6. Double-click **Minimum password length**. Notice that by default, the minimum password length is 0, which means blank passwords are allowed by default. Set the value to **0**, and click **OK**.

7. Double-click **Password must meet complexity requirements**, click the **Enabled** option button, and click **OK**. The settings should look similar to Figure 9-2 when you're finished.

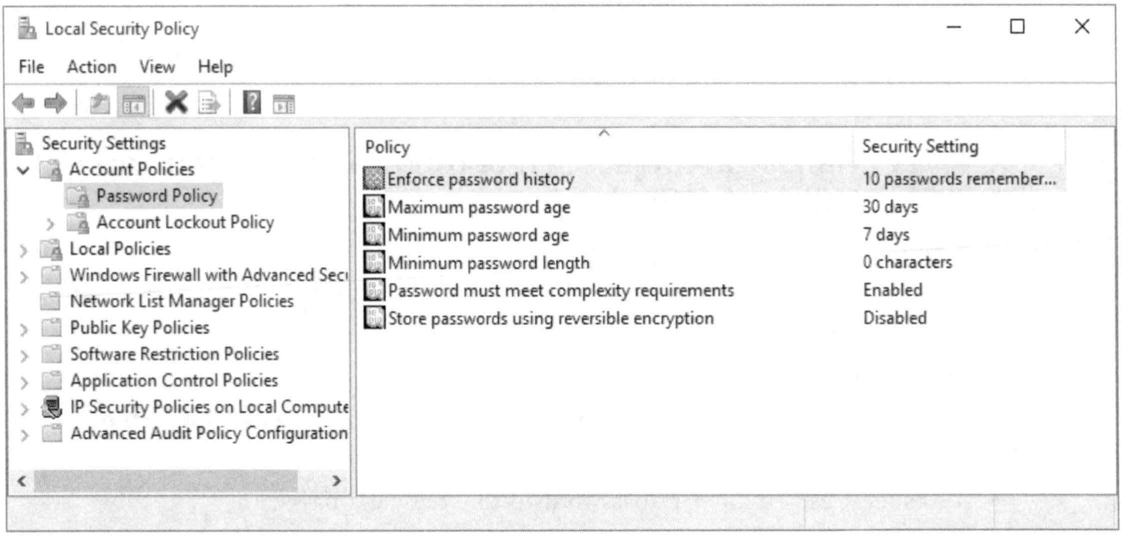

Figure 9-2   Viewing password policy settings

8. Next, you set the account lockout policy. Under Account Policies, click **Account Lockout Policy**. In the right pane, double-click **Account lockout threshold**. Notice that by default, it's set to 0, which means accounts are never locked out. Set the value to **4**, and then click **OK**. Windows fills in the other policies automatically with default values. Click **OK** again.

9. Double-click **Account lockout duration**, set the value to **60** minutes, and click **OK**.

10. Double-click **Reset account lockout counter after**, set the value to **15** minutes, and click **OK**. The Local Security Policy console should look similar to Figure 9-3 when you're finished.

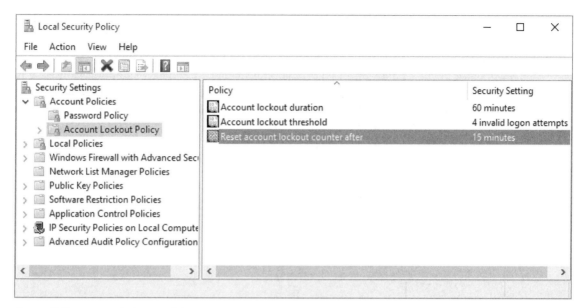

Figure 9-3 Account lockout policies

11. You test these settings later in Challenge Lab 9-1. Close the Local Security Policy console, and log off Windows for the next project.

Restricting Logon Hours and Logon Location Some network administrators allow users to log on any time of the day and any day of the week, but if your security policy states otherwise, most OSs have solutions to restrict logon by time of day, day of the week, and location.

In a Windows domain environment, allowed logon times can be set for each user account, as shown in Figure 9-4. The default settings allow logon 24 hours per day, seven days a week. A common use of restricting logon hours is to disallow logon during system backup, which usually takes place in the middle of the night. In this figure, the dark boxes indicate times that the user can log on, and the white boxes indicate hours the user can't log on. In this example,

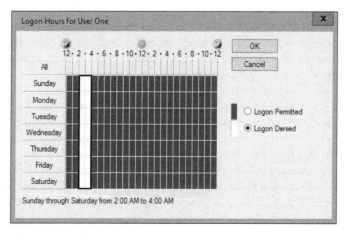

Figure 9-4 Setting logon hours for a user

logging on from 2 a.m. to 4 a.m. is not allowed. Note that the logon hours option is available only in a Windows domain environment, not for a stand-alone Windows computer.

Sometimes users log on to the network from computers that aren't their regular workstations. This practice might be allowed in your environment, but extending this option to users who have access to sensitive data can be dangerous. If a user logs on at a workstation in a coworker's office and then walks away from that machine, the coworker now has access to the sensitive data. To prevent this problem, users can be restricted to logging on only from particular workstations. Figure 9-5 shows the Windows user account settings for logon location; the user can log on only to the computers named jriley01 and engineering. As with logon hours, this option is available only in a Windows domain environment.

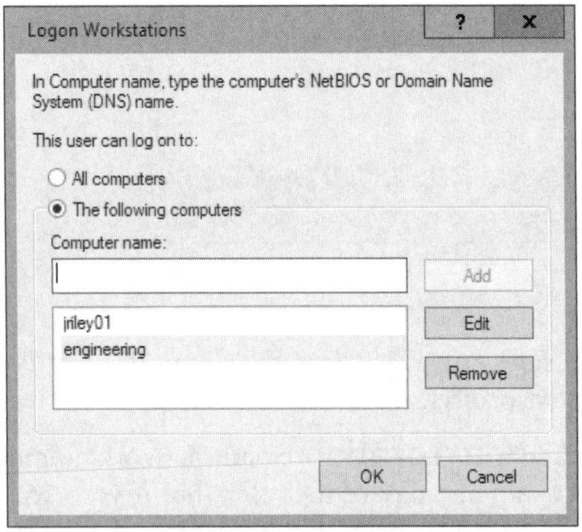

Figure 9-5 The Logon Workstations dialog box

Giving employees remote access to networks has become essential in many businesses, especially with secure, high-speed network connections. However, remote access isn't an all-or-nothing proposition because you can restrict remote access by user or by creating remote access policies that permit or deny user access based on criteria such as a user's group memberships and time of day.

Authorizing Access to Files and Folders After users have logged on to a network or computer, they must be authorized to access network resources. A common network resource is shared files, which are controlled by the OS file system security. File system security allows administrators to assign file and folder permissions to users or groups of users. Permissions define the level of access a user has to the file system, ranging from read access to full control, with permissions such as write and delete in between. Read access allows a user to open and view the contents of a file, and write access allows the user to change the file's contents. Some file systems have a separate delete permission. A user with full control access can read, write, delete, and change permissions. Different OSs and file systems might use different terms, but these permissions are typically available on most file systems. Another concept of file and folder permissions is ownership. Most file systems include a file property that specifies a user or group who owns the file; by default, it's usually the user who created the file. A file can also be owned by the system if the OS creates and maintains the file. File systems and file system permissions are discussed in more detail in Chapter 11.

File and folder permissions are a necessary tool administrators use to make network resources secure and still give users access to the resources they're permitted to use. However, permissions don't protect data traversing the network media, nor do they protect data in files if file system security has been compromised—which is where data encryption comes in.

Securing Data with Encryption

Many network administrators use **encryption** technologies to safeguard data as it travels across the Internet and even within the company network. This security measure prevents people from using eavesdropping technology, such as a protocol analyzer (or packet sniffer), to capture packets and use data in them for malicious purposes. Data stored on disks can also be secured with encryption to prevent someone who has gained physical access to the computer from being able to use the data.

Using IPsec to Secure Network Data
The most widely used method for encrypting data as it travels the internetwork is IP Security (IPsec), an extension to the IP protocol. It works by establishing an association between two communicating devices. An association is formed by two devices authenticating their identities via a preshared key, Kerberos authentication, or digital certificates.

A **preshared key** is a series of letters, numbers, and special characters, much like a password, that both communicating devices use to authenticate each other's identity. A network administrator must enter the same preshared key in the IPsec configuration settings on both devices. Kerberos is used in a Windows domain environment or on a Linux system to authenticate users and computers. It also uses keys, but the OS generates the keys, which makes this method more secure than having an administrator enter keys. **Digital certificates** involve a certification authority (CA). Someone wanting to send encrypted data must acquire a digital certificate from a CA, which is responsible for verifying the applicant's authenticity. When an IPsec communication session begins, the communicating parties exchange certificates, and each party sends the certificate to the CA electronically to verify its authenticity. Windows servers can be configured as CAs when certificates are used on computers in a private network. Public CAs, such as Symantec and Comodo, sell certificates to companies wanting to have secure communication sessions across public networks.

After the communicating parties are authenticated, encrypted communication can commence. Data sent across the network, even if it's captured by an eavesdropper, is unreadable to all but the intended recipient. Only the message recipient has the information needed to decrypt the message.

Although IPsec is an excellent way to secure data as it travels across a network, it doesn't secure data on disk drives if someone gains unauthorized access to the computer. Other security methods, discussed in the next section, are available for addressing this possibility.

Securing Data on Disk Drives
Sometimes file system permissions aren't enough to stop an attacker who's determined to gain access to data on your system. If someone can access the hard disk where sensitive data is stored or compromise system security, your data could be vulnerable. Data stored on a disk drive can be encrypted, however, so that only the person who created the encrypted file can read the data, even if the hard disk is read sector by sector, therefore bypassing file system security.

In Windows OSs, Encrypting File System (EFS) is a standard feature on NTFS-formatted disks. To encrypt a file or the files in a folder, you simply select the "Encrypt contents to secure data" option in the Advanced Attributes dialog box, which is opened via the file's Properties dialog box. Encrypted files provide an extra layer of security that file permissions alone can't provide. Someone with physical access to a computer can boot the system into an OS on a CD/DVD, effectively bypassing normal file access controls. By doing so, all files on the computer's hard drive are accessible regardless of the permissions. However, encrypted files are still inaccessible because an EFS certificate file matching the account of the user who encrypted the file must be available to the user trying to open the file. Even if someone is able to extract an encrypted file's contents, the data would be gibberish.

EFS encrypts only files or folders with the Encrypt attribute set, and it can't be used on Windows system files. Windows also offers BitLocker for full disk encryption. It can protect the entire system volume as well as other volumes and works in one of three modes:

- *Transparent mode*—Requires hardware with Trusted Platform Module (TPM) support. TPM hardware determines whether any changes have been made to the initial boot environment; if so, the user is prompted for a recovery key on a USB device or a recovery password. If no changes have been detected, the system boots normally. This method protects the system if someone tries to boot with a different OS.

- *USB key mode*—This mode is the most common method for booting a system configured with BitLocker that doesn't have TPM support. An encryption key is stored on a USB drive that the user inserts before starting the system.

- *User authentication mode*—The system requires a user password before it decrypts the OS files and boots. It's considered the fail-safe mode if TPM detects that the boot environment was compromised or if the USB key isn't detected.

BitLocker is a good security enhancement for servers that aren't physically secure and for mobile devices at risk of being lost or stolen. There are also third-party and open-source solutions for whole disk encryption for both Windows and Linux systems. One widely used open-source drive encryption solution called TrueCrypt ceased development in April 2015, so its continued use isn't recommended. Linux Unified Key Setup (LUKS) is a popular Linux alternative, and Mac OS X has a tool called FileVault.

The BitLocker To Go feature, which started in Windows 7, can protect the contents of removable storage, such as USB drives.

Securing Communication with Virtual Private Networks

A **virtual private network (VPN)** is a network connection that uses the Internet to give users or branch offices secure access to a company's network resources. VPNs use encryption technology to ensure that communication is private and secure, so while data travels through the public Internet, the connection remains private—hence the name "virtual private network." Privacy is achieved by creating a "tunnel" between the VPN client and VPN server. A tunnel is created by encapsulation, in which the inner packet containing the data is encrypted, and the outer headers contain the unencapsulated addresses that Internet devices need to route the packets correctly.

To use another mail delivery analogy, suppose you have an ultra-secure package to deliver, but you must use a courier. In a separate transaction, you deliver a key to the office manager at the package recipient's location. Next, you place the secret package containing the recipient's name in a lockbox. You put the lockbox inside an envelope and address the envelope to the office manager of the company where the recipient works. The courier can read the addressing on the envelope, but if the envelope is opened, the package contents are inaccessible without the key to the lockbox. The envelope is delivered, and the office manager removes the lockbox from the envelope and opens it with the key delivered earlier. The office manager can then deliver the package to the final recipient. In this analogy, the lockbox and outer envelope make up the VPN tunnel, and the office manager is the VPN server to which messages are delivered.

Figure 9-6 shows a VPN between a client computer and an organization's network. The tunnel connection is made between the client computer and the VPN server. After the VPN server opens the packet, the inner packet is decrypted (unlocked) and delivered to the resource the client requested.

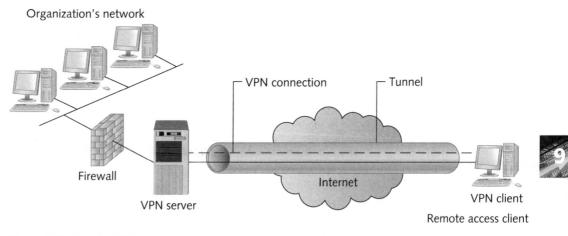

Figure 9-6 A typical VPN connection

VPN servers can be configured on server OSs, such as Windows Server 2016 and Linux. They can also be in the form of a dedicated device, such as a **VPN concentrator** or a VPN router. A VPN concentrator is a dedicated VPN device that can handle many VPN connections and tunnels. Whatever solution is used, the VPN server must have at least two network interfaces: one for the internal or company network and one that connects to the external or public network.

VPNs in a Windows Environment Windows server OSs include a VPN server solution with the Remote Access server role and support three implementations of VPNs:

- *Point-to-Point Tunneling Protocol (PPTP)*—A commonly used VPN protocol in Windows OSs with client support for Linux and Mac OS X, too. Most OSs that support VPN clients support PPTP.

- *Layer 2 Tunneling Protocol with IPsec (L2TP/IPsec)*—Developed in cooperation with Cisco Systems and Microsoft, L2TP/IPsec generally provides a higher level of security than PPTP. In addition to data security through encryption, it provides data integrity and identity verification.

- *Secure Socket Tunneling Protocol (SSTP)*—SSTP has the advantage of working behind most firewalls without firewall administrators needing to configure the firewall to allow VPN. It uses the standard port 443 used for SSL communication (HTTPS). SSTP is supported on Windows clients starting with Vista SP1 and as a VPN server starting with Windows Server 2008. It requires the VPN server to have a valid digital certificate issued by a CA for server identification.

All three implementations are enabled by default when you configure the Windows VPN server component, so any type of client that tries to connect will be successful.

VPN Remote Access Modes Two VPN modes are available with most VPN servers, including VPN concentrators and small office/home office (SOHO) VPN devices:

- *Site-to-site*—In the **site-to-site VPN mode** (also called "gateway-to-gateway"), a VPN connection is established between two VPN devices. No software needs to be installed on the computers using the VPN. This mode is used mostly between offices connected to the Internet through a VPN router. The VPN router can be a dedicated VPN device, a router with VPN software installed, or a server running, for example, Windows Server 2016 with the VPN service installed. In this setup, all communication between the two offices is private, even though data travels across the public Internet. This configuration is an affordable way for small businesses to create a secure WAN connection between a main office and a branch office.

- *Client-to-site*—The **client-to-site VPN mode** (also called "client-to-gateway") establishes a VPN connection between a single client computer and a VPN device. This mode requires configuring a VPN client on each computer participating in the VPN and a VPN server that clients connect to. This mode is best for providing private communication to a company network for employees working from home or employees who must connect to the network while traveling. In this setup, users connect to the Internet through their ISPs, and then run the VPN client software to create a private connection with their company network.

Many SOHO equipment manufacturers, such as Linksys, NetGear, and D-Link, have fairly inexpensive VPN routers that support either VPN mode. Prices for this equipment range from less than $100 for a VPN router that supports eight or fewer VPN connections to several hundred dollars for a VPN router that supports as many as 30 or 40 connections. Be aware of terminology when purchasing a router for VPN connections. Some routers claim to support VPN "pass-through," which enables a VPN client to connect to a remote VPN device but doesn't actually create a VPN connection. This type of router is best for users who have a small network at home and want to connect to the company network by using client-to-site VPN mode. The home router doesn't participate in the VPN connection; it simply allows the VPN connection to pass through it.

When outfitting your business with a router that supports VPN connections from remote clients, look for one that supports VPN tunnels. The number of tunnels or endpoints the VPN router supports tells you how many VPN connections can be established. In client-to-site VPN mode, one VPN tunnel per user connection is required. In site-to-site VPN mode, in which a connection is made from LAN to LAN, one tunnel per LAN connection is required.

VPN Benefits VPNs enable organizations to use the Internet as a private network to connect mobile users and telecommuters to their networks securely. Organizations can also use VPNs to connect headquarters to branch offices with permanent connections without the expense of leased lines and WAN links. To summarize, VPN benefits include the following:

- Enable mobile users to connect with organizations' networks securely wherever an Internet connection is available.

- Allow multiple sites to maintain permanent secure connections via the Internet instead of using expensive WAN links.

- Reduce costs by using the ISP's support services instead of paying for more expensive WAN support.

Securing Wireless Networks

The explosion of wireless networking devices creates a new problem for network administrators. Because wireless signals aren't bound by physical cables, an attacker doesn't need physical access to network cabling to compromise a network. Anyone with a wireless scanner and some software who gets within range of a wireless network's signals can intercept data or access wireless devices. What's worse is that because most wireless networks eventually tie into a wired network, an attacker could potentially access an entire network infrastructure while sitting in a car outside the organization's office. Attackers who drive around looking for wireless LANs (WLANs) to intercept are called **wardrivers**.

To foil would-be wireless attackers, wireless security must be enabled on all networking devices by using one or more of the following methods:

- *Wireless encryption*—Every wireless network should be protected by wireless encryption because it prevents unauthorized users from connecting and prevents someone who captures wireless network packets from being able to interpret the data they contain. The following list of wireless encryption protocols goes from strongest to weakest. You should always use the strongest encryption your devices support, and both the wireless access point and client device must support the same protocol.

    o *Wi-Fi Protected Access 2*—**Wi-Fi Protected Access 2 (WPA2)** is the strongest encryption standard as of this writing. It uses Advanced Encryption Standard (AES) algorithms, which have been determined strong enough to protect classified information up to the top-secret level, as defined by the U.S. government. WPA2 has two major variations. WPA2-Personal (also known as WPA2-PSK) is designed for SOHO networks and doesn't require an authentication server. WPA2-Enterprise (also known as WPA2-802.1X) is more suited for larger networks because it requires an authentication server, such as a RADIUS server. WPA2 is backward-compatible with WPA if you select the option to use TKIP encryption along with AES encryption. If you have only WPA2 devices, you should use AES encryption only. WPA2-Personal uses 256-bit keys derived from a user-created passphrase between 8 and 63 characters; in general, the longer the better, but one of 12 to 16 characters is thought to be ideal. A passphrase is essentially a password that may or may not contain spaces. The user must enter the passphrase on the access point when setting up the wireless network and then for each client device that connects to the network. Because the user must create and enter a passphrase, the wireless network is only as secure as the passphrase's strength, so when creating a passphrase, you should follow rules similar to password creation to prevent brute-force or guessing attacks.

○ *Wi-Fi Protected Access*—**Wi-Fi Protected Access (WPA)**, the predecessor to WPA2, uses Temporal Key Integrity Protocol (TKIP), which is a somewhat less effective encryption protocol than AES. WPA also has two modes: WPA-Personal (WPA-PSK) and WPA-Enterprise, which uses a RADIUS server for authentication. WPA is an upgrade compared with WEP, discussed next, but it still has some vulnerabilities that are carryovers from WEP. WPA-Personal also uses 256-bit keys generated from a passphrase.

○ *Wired Equivalent Privacy*—**Wired Equivalent Privacy (WEP)** provides data encryption so that a casual attacker who gains access to your wireless signals sees only encrypted data. However, WEP has its flaws, and a determined attacker can crack the encryption code fairly quickly. You shouldn't use WEP because it's not considered secure; however, old Wi-Fi devices might have WEP as the only option, and it's better than no encryption at all.

- *MAC address filtering*—If your wireless network is fairly small and only certain computers are to have access to it, you can use the **MAC address filtering** feature on APs to restrict network access to computers with specific MAC addresses. This security measure isn't viable in a large or nonstatic network where new laptops and PDAs access it frequently. In addition, it shouldn't be used without encryption because experienced wardrivers can thwart it fairly easily by capturing packets, noting the MAC address of allowed devices, and then spoofing the MAC address to gain entry. If the Wi-Fi network also has encryption enabled, the attacker would have to then crack the encryption.

- *Service set identifier (SSID)*—An SSID is an alphanumeric label configured on the AP that identifies one WLAN from another. Each client must configure its wireless NIC with the SSID to connect to the AP. A private WLAN should set the SSID to a value that's not too easy to guess, and the SSID shouldn't be set to broadcast. When an SSID is broadcast, wireless software can scan the network to look for available SSIDs, allowing an attacker to gain the first piece of information required to access your WLAN. Hiding the SSID doesn't stop a seasoned wardriver, but it can at least discourage neighbors from accidentally or purposely trying to connect to your network. For true Wi-Fi security, always use the strongest encryption protocol available and consider using MAC address filtering.

A final word about wireless networking security: Using a strong encryption protocol doesn't mean you're completely safe. Using social engineering and brute-force techniques, determined attackers might still be able to access your network. With that in mind, you should follow some policies for additional protection of your network:

- Do a site survey, and try to position APs so that only required areas are covered by the signal; limit signal access outside the building whenever possible.

- If you're using WEP, change the encryption key manually on a regular basis; better yet, upgrade your devices so that all support WPA2.

- When possible, use MAC address filtering, allowing only known addresses access to the network.

Remember that the benefit of a wireless network is having easy access to an organization's LAN or a home LAN without being tethered to a cable, but this access also applies to attackers wanting to harm your network.

Network Security Devices

Although a router can provide a layer of network security by using access control lists (ACLs), a router's main job is to route packets from one network to another and control access to resources in an internetwork. To protect against threats from external networks, you can use specialized devices on the network perimeter. The following sections discuss firewalls and intrusion detection and prevention systems.

Protecting Networks with Firewalls

A **firewall** is a hardware device or software program that inspects packets going into or out of a network or computer, and then discards or forwards these packets based on a set of rules. A hardware firewall is configured with two or more network interfaces, typically placed between a LAN and the WAN connection. The WAN link can connect to an ISP, another LAN in another city, or even the network of a partner organization. The type of firewall you use and how it's configured are determined by what's at the other end of the WAN link. For example, you might want to allow a remote sales office to access the company's database, but you should deny this access to Internet users and perhaps restrict it for users in a partner network.

A software firewall is installed in an OS and inspects all packets coming into or leaving the computer. Based on predefined rules, the packets are discarded or forwarded for further processing. Software firewalls are an integral part of Windows, Linux, and Mac OS X, but third-party solutions are also available that sometimes have more features or more user-friendly interfaces.

A network administrator is courting disaster if a firewall isn't installed between the network and the Internet. Firewalls protect against outside attempts to access unauthorized resources, and they protect against malicious packets intended to disable or cripple a network and its resources. A second use of firewalls placed between the Internet and the network is to restrict users' access to Internet resources. This type of restriction is usually intended to prevent users from accessing offensive Web sites or bandwidth-heavy content, such as streaming audio or video, which might not be the best use of an employee's time or the network's bandwidth.

Hardware firewalls installed on a network are usually dedicated devices with preinstalled software that must be configured by a knowledgeable administrator. This type of firewall, however, usually isn't suitable for home Internet users trying to protect their computers from would-be attackers. Because of the widespread availability of fast, always-on Internet connections for home users, personal (or host-based) firewalls were developed to guard a single workstation against Internet attacks. You install these personal firewalls to guard your computer from attempts to access your resources and services through the Internet. Personal firewalls are not just for the home, however. Because many attacks occur inside networks, these lightweight firewalls can also be used in the office to prevent other users from infiltrating workstations or prevent the spread of network-based malware, such as worms.

Firewall devices vary quite a bit in configuration details, but all are based on one premise: Rules are created to determine what type of traffic is allowed to enter and exit the network. A firewall, by default, is usually a closed device. After the firewall is installed and its interfaces are configured, it stops all incoming packets (and sometimes all outgoing packets, depending on the firewall). To configure a firewall, the network administrator must build rules that allow only certain packets to enter or exit the network. The rules are based on a variety of packet properties, including source and destination addresses; protocols such as IP, TCP, ICMP, and HTTP; and sometimes even a packet's context.

Source and destination addresses can be examined to determine whether the packet is coming from an approved network or device to an approved network or device. For example, a network might have a restricted segment where no external traffic is permitted. The firewall can examine all incoming packets and discard those with a destination address of the network's restricted segment. The protocol in the packet can also be examined to determine whether it's a type that should be permitted into the network. For example, you might want to deny certain ICMP packets from entering the network. ICMP packets are generated by the ping command, among others, and can be used to saturate a network's bandwidth or tie up a network server, thereby denying legitimate users access to the network. This is a denial-of-service attack (discussed later in "Disabling Network Resources"). Firewalls can also attempt to determine a packet's context; this process is called **stateful packet inspection (SPI)**. SPI helps ensure that a packet is denied if it's not part of an ongoing legitimate conversation. Attackers can insert rogue packets into a data stream in an attempt to hijack a legitimate connection or tie up network services. Examining a packet's context can reduce the success of these attacks.

Firewalls can go a step further and examine the actual data in a packet and filter packets containing malicious data or objectionable material. This type of firewall, called a **content filter**, looks for key words or phrases in the data portion of each packet to determine whether to allow it into the network. Content filters can also look for malware signatures to block certain types of malware as well as key words indicating that the content might be illegal or otherwise undesirable.

Firewalls perform other functions not covered here, but the functions discussed in this section are typically universal of all firewalls.

Using a Router as a Firewall Conceptually, a firewall is just a router with specialized software for creating rules to permit or deny packets. Many routers have capabilities similar to firewalls but with one key difference: Routers, by default, are open systems. After a router is first configured, all packets are permitted into and out of the network. Therefore, a network administrator must create rules called access control lists (ACLs) that deny certain types of packets. Typically, an administrator builds ACLs so that all packets are denied, and then creates rules that make exceptions. ACLs can examine many of the same packet properties that firewalls can.

Routers intended for SOHO use often combine a wireless AP, router, and switch into a single unit and have a preconfigured firewall. These routers are designed to connect a small LAN to the Internet and configured by default to allow all traffic to leave the network and deny traffic coming into the network that isn't part of a communication session initiated by a computer inside the LAN.

Using Network Address Translation to Improve Security Network Address Translation (NAT) was discussed in Chapter 6 in the context of alleviating the IP address shortage. An additional benefit of NAT is that an internal network resource's real address is hidden and inaccessible to the outside world. Because most networks use NAT with private IP addresses, devices configured with private addresses can't be accessed directly from outside the network. In fact, when NAT is used, the only way an Internet device can send a message to a device in the internal network is in response to a message from the internal device. That is, an Internet device can't initiate a network conversation with an internal device, thus limiting an attacker's options. NAT is usually an integral part of a network firewall positioned between the network and the Internet or another outside network.

Using Intrusion Detection and Prevention Systems

An **intrusion detection system (IDS)** monitors network traffic for malicious packets or traffic patterns and reports identified security breaches to a management station. A firewall is considered an active device because it inspects and filters packets entering and leaving the network, but an IDS is a passive device because its role is strictly monitoring packets. If suspicious activity is detected, an IDS can generate alerts so that an administrator can determine whether an attack is taking place. In addition, administrators can create reports to see whether any patterns are developing that indicate an attacker is probing the network for weaknesses.

An IDS can be network-based (NIDS) or host-based (HIDS). An NIDS protects an entire network and can be placed on the network perimeter, in the **demilitarized zone (DMZ)**, or both. The DMZ is part of a network that contains publicly accessible devices, such as Web servers and VPN servers, but is still protected by a firewall, as shown in Figure 9-7. An IDS is an invaluable tool that helps administrators know how often their network is under attack and devise security policies aimed at thwarting threats before they have a chance to succeed.

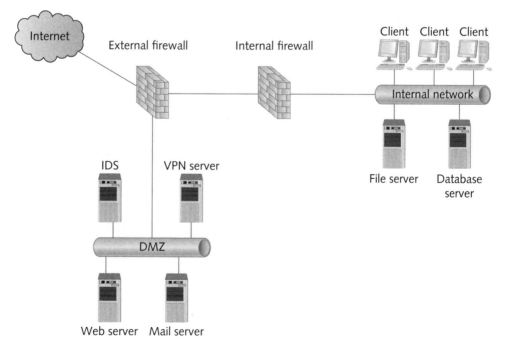

Figure 9-7 A DMZ with a network-based IDS

An HIDS is a software application used to protect a single computer, usually a critical server. An HIDS can also be installed on a **honeypot**, which is a network device, such as a server, installed as a decoy to lure potential attackers. It's configured to look like an enticing target to attackers, but because it has HIDS software installed, a network administrator can get information about the nature of the attacker and the attack techniques so that he or she can install countermeasures to protect legitimate network assets.

A variation on an IDS is an **intrusion prevention system (IPS)**, which can take countermeasures if an attack is in progress. These countermeasures include reconfiguring a firewall to prevent suspicious packets from entering the network, resetting the connection between source and destination devices, or even disabling the link between inside and outside networks.

Hands-On Project 9-2: Exploring Windows Firewall

Time Required: 15 minutes

Objective: Explore the Windows 10 firewall.

Required Tools and Equipment: Net-*XX*

Description: In this project, you learn how to configure the Windows 10 firewall.

1. Log on to your computer as **NetAdmin**.
2. In the search box on the taskbar, type **firewall**. Click **Windows Firewall** in the search results.
3. Figure 9-8 shows the Windows Firewall summary window, which displays the current state of the firewall for connected networks. Firewall rules are different for private networks (home or work networks) and public networks.

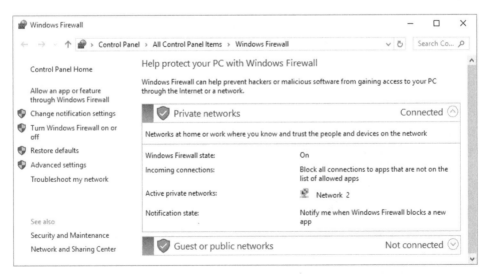

Figure 9-8 The Windows Firewall summary window

4. The "Change notification settings" and "Turn Windows Firewall on or off" links in the left pane bring you to the Customize Settings window. In the left pane, click **Turn Windows Firewall on or off**. In the "Customize settings for each type of network" window, you can turn the firewall on or off for the public and private network. If the firewall is on, you can block all incoming connections and select whether you should be notified when the firewall blocks a program. Click **Cancel**.

5. Click **Restore defaults** to return the firewall settings to their original status. Click **Restore defaults** again, and click **Yes** in the Restore Defaults Confirmation message box.

6. Click **Advanced settings** in the left pane to open the Windows Firewall with Advanced Security console (see Figure 9-9). You can also open this console from Administrative Tools. The middle pane shows an overview of your current settings.

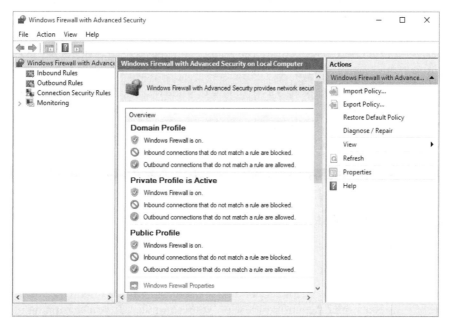

Figure 9-9   The Windows Firewall with Advanced Security console

7. In the Overview section, click the **Windows Firewall Properties** link. You see four tabs. The first three tabs are used to configure the Windows Firewall domain, private, and public profiles. The fourth tab has IPsec settings. Click each profile tab. Notice that inbound connections are set to Block and outbound connections are set to Allow. These settings allow any traffic out of your computer but deny unsolicited attempts from the outside to connect to your computer. Click **Cancel**.

8. In the Windows Firewall with Advanced Security console, click **Inbound Rules** in the left pane. A list of rules is displayed in the middle pane. Each rule has a name describing the type of network activity the rule pertains to, a group, a profile in which the rule is defined, a status (enabled or disabled), an action, and several other properties.

9. Scroll down the Inbound rules pane until you see File and Printer Sharing (Echo Request - ICMPv4-In). This rule controls whether another computer can ping your machine and is

disabled by default. You should see the same rule for both the Private and Domain profiles. Ask a partner to try to ping your computer. The attempt should be unsuccessful because the default inbound setting is to block inbound traffic, such as Echo Requests (the type of packet `ping` produces).

10. Double-click the **File and Printer Sharing (Echo Request - ICMPv4-In)** option with Private listed in the Profile column. Click **Enabled**, and then click **OK** to enable the rule and allow ICMP (`ping`) packets. Have a partner try to ping you again. This time it should be successful. (On a domain-based network, you would enable the rule for the Domain profile.)

11. Windows Firewall has dozens of predefined rules, and you can create your own rules. In the Actions pane, click **New Rule**.

12. In the Rule Type window, click **Port**, and then click **Next**. In the Protocol and Ports window, leave **TCP** selected. In the "Specific local ports" text box, type **80**, and then click **Next**. This setting allows other computers to connect to your computer via TCP port 80, which is the standard Web server port.

13. In the Action window, leave **Allow the connection** selected, and then click **Next**. In the Profile window, leave all three profiles selected, and then click **Next**.

14. In the Name window, type **Web Server In** in the Name text box, and then click **Finish**. Scroll to the top of the Inbound Rules section to see your new rule. If you installed a Web server now, such as Windows Internet Information Services, users would be able to connect to it.

15. Close all open windows, but leave your computer running for the next project.

Hands-On Project 9-3: Testing Your Firewall with ShieldsUP!

Time Required: 15 minutes

Objective: Connect to a Web site to run a free Internet vulnerability test.

Required Tools and Equipment: Net-*XX* with access to the Internet

Description: In this project, you connect to a Web site to run a free Internet vulnerability test. This Web site does a simple penetration test on your computer. If you're running it behind a NAT firewall that assigns a single public IP address to all outside connections, only one person at a time can run the ShieldsUP! test. The instructor might want to do this project as a demonstration and encourage students to run this test on their home computers.

1. Log on to your computer as **NetAdmin**, if necessary.

2. Start your Web browser, and go to **www.grc.com**. Click the **ShieldsUP!!** graphic. Scroll down and click the **ShieldsUP!** link.

3. Read the information that's displayed. ShieldsUP! attempts to resolve the name of the computer you're connecting from. You should see this name in the box labeled "The text below might uniquely identify you on the Internet." Click the **Proceed** button. (Click **Continue** if prompted.)

4. In the ShieldsUP!! Services section (see Figure 9-10), click **File Sharing**. ShieldsUP! displays your IP address or the translated IP address, and then attempts to connect to your computer. Port 139 should not be available; if it is, you have a serious security problem because this port is used to access files on your computer.

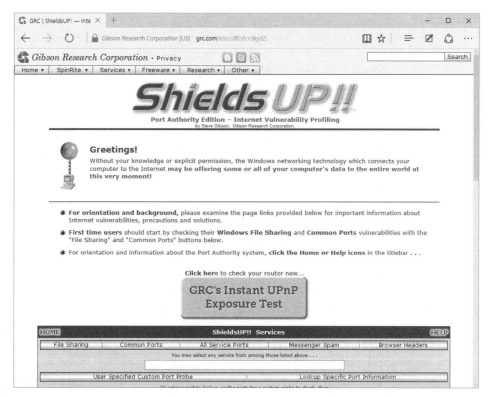

Figure 9-10 ShieldsUP! vulnerability testing

Source: © 2014 Gibson Research Corporation, *www.grc.com*

5. Next, scroll down and click **Common Ports,** and see whether any other ports are available through the Internet. You might see that the Ping Reply test failed because your computer replied to the ping requests. Remember that in Hands-On Project 9-2, you enabled incoming ping messages, so if your firewall allows these messages, ShieldsUP! gets a reply.

6. Continue clicking available ShieldsUP! options, and write a summary of your findings on the following lines. If ShieldsUP! finds any security vulnerabilities, it makes recommendations for securing your computer.

_____

_____

7. Exit your Web browser, and leave your computer running for the next project.

Protecting a Network from Malware

In Internet-connected networks, malware is an ever-present concern. **Malware** is any type of software that presents a nuisance to users or a threat to the integrity of a system or network. Users download programs, bring files from home, open e-mail attachments, and browse unsafe Web sites. Most of these actions are normal computing activities, but they can also bring viruses and other malware into the network.

Viruses

A **virus** is a program that spreads by replicating itself into other programs or documents. To spread, a virus requires a file to be opened, a program to be run, or the computer to be booted. Its sole purpose is to disrupt computer or network operation by deleting or corrupting files, formatting disks, or using large amounts of computer resources. There are many virus types, and some are more nefarious than others:

- *File infector virus*—This common virus attaches itself to an existing executable file, and when the OS loads that file, the virus is loaded with it. After it's loaded into memory, the virus can infect other files, alter data, delete files, and wreak other types of havoc. Virus scanners find this virus type by scanning executable files on a computer's disks looking for the **virus signature**, which is a pattern of computer code that's unique to a virus.

- *Boot sector virus*—This dangerous type of virus infects the code that's loaded when a system is powered on. The results can be an inability to boot the system and the destruction of system files. These viruses spread to every writeable disk that's accessed by the system. To clean a boot sector virus, you must boot the system from a read-only disk and then run antimalware software to remove the virus from all infected disks. Examples of boot sector viruses include Stoned, Brain, Michelangelo, and Parity Boot.

- *Polymorphic virus*—This type of virus is difficult to detect because it changes itself by using encryption techniques every time it infects a computer. Antivirus software detects most viruses by finding a telltale signature that identifies the virus, but a polymorphic virus changes its signature so that it can't be detected easily. An example of a polymorphic virus is Win32.Virut, which infects executable (.exe) files and can open a backdoor into a computer by connecting to an Internet Relay Chat (IRC) server.

- *Macro virus*—These viruses infect documents containing macros. A **macro** is a command or keystroke that executes a series of actions in a document. Many documents created with Microsoft Office applications can contain macros, and macro viruses are spread by simply opening a Word or an Excel file, for example. They're often spread as e-mail attachments, so do not open attachments unless you're certain of their source. You can protect yourself by disabling macros in office applications unless you know the document you're using uses them.

- *Overwrite virus*—This virus deletes data in the file it infects and replaces it with the virus code, making the original file useless. Deleting the file usually removes the virus, but the original file data is lost.

- *Browser hijacker virus*—This virus typically works by redirecting your Web browser to URLs you didn't intend to go to. It's often installed as a plug-in and is particularly frustrating. It often uses a technique called **ransomware** that redirects to a Web site warning that your system is infected, and you must install the vendor's software or call a phone number to clean it.

Worms

A **worm** is a type of malware that, unlike a virus, doesn't require another file to spread to other computers; it's a self-contained program that just needs the computer to be connected to a network. Worms are commonly spread by e-mail attachments, instant messaging, IRC channels, and network file sharing. The main difference between a worm and a virus is how it's spread, but both types of malware can perform the same types of destruction: altering data, deleting files, formatting disks, and using excessive resources. Worms can also create backdoors into computers. A **backdoor** is a program installed on a computer that permits access to the computer, bypassing the normal authentication process. A common use of backdoors is to allow spammers to send e-mail from computers on which they're installed, thereby hiding a spammer's true identity. Well-known worms include the ILOVEYOU or Love Bug worm, Code Red, Nimda, Melissa, Sobig, Stuxnet, and Flame. Some of these worms infected tens of millions of computers. Both Code Red and Melissa are estimated to have caused more than a billion dollars in damages.

Other Forms of Malware

Another type of malware that's not technically a virus because it's usually not self-replicating is a **Trojan horse**. It appears to be something useful, such as a free utility, but in reality contains some type of malware. What's unfortunate about a Trojan horse is that users willingly run the software and don't even know that it's the cause of problems on their systems. The most dangerous Trojan horses are also keyloggers that record every keystroke you enter, including usernames and passwords, and then use your e-mail program to send the contents of keystrokes to an attacker.

A **rootkit** is a form of malware that can monitor traffic to and from a computer, monitor keystrokes, and capture passwords. It's the ultimate backdoor into a system and is among the most insidious forms of malware because it can mask that a system has been compromised by altering system files and drivers required for normal computer operation. Rootkits aren't specific to an OS and can be found for Windows, Linux, and forms of UNIX. They're notoriously difficult to detect because they hide themselves so well and integrate into the OS they have infected. Typically, detection requires restarting the system and booting to another medium, such as a CD or flash drive, with tools that can scan for and detect a rootkit's presence. Removal is even more difficult because rootkits often alter system files and drivers the system depends on to run normally. Many experts agree that the time and effort required to remove a rootkit is better spent backing up critical data files, reformatting the disk, and reinstalling the OS.

A **hoax virus** is one of the worst kinds of viruses because it preys on people's good intentions. With a hoax virus, someone sends an e-mail proclaiming that Microsoft, the government, or another well-known entity has just discovered a new virus that reformats your hard drive or performs another nefarious deed. The hoax message goes on to say that you should forward this e-mail immediately to everyone you know to inform them of this terrible virus. The flood of e-mail from people actually falling for this hoax *is* the virus! It clogs e-mail servers, decreases productivity, and generally wastes time. Although a hoax virus doesn't actually destroy data, it uses a tactic called **social engineering**, in which attackers get users to do their bidding without being aware of the consequences. If you're concerned that the warning might be real, check the Web site of the organization the message references or the Web site of your antivirus software. If the supposed virus isn't mentioned at these sites, stop this type of virus in its tracks and delete the e-mail without forwarding it to innocent friends and acquaintances.

In the Computer section of the *www.snopes.com* Web site, you can find a list of real and hoax viruses.

A **logic bomb** is time-dependent malware that can come in different forms. Its main characteristic is that it's activated when a particular event occurs, such as a specific date and time, or when a particular file is accessed. Logic bombs aren't always destructive, however; sometimes the developers just want to send a message to show how clever they are.

Spyware and Spam

Spyware and spam aren't that similar in function, but both affect your privacy, and their main goal is to get you to buy something or get taken by a fraud. **Spyware** is a type of malware that monitors or controls part of your computer at the expense of your privacy and the gain of some third party. The result of spyware is usually a decrease in computer performance and an increase in pop-up Internet messages and spam. The goal is to monitor your Internet activity, such as which Web sites you visit and how often. The data the spyware gathers is then used by advertisers, spammers, and perhaps even more malicious third parties for the sole purpose of extracting money from your wallet.

Unlike a virus or worm, spyware isn't usually self-replicating. Typically, it's installed on a system when a user installs some legitimate software or is too quick to click OK when a message pops up on a Web site offering to install a program. Many free peer-to-peer file-sharing applications install spyware on your computer as a condition of being free. Nonetheless, millions of users install the software (*and* the spyware) because the prospect of being able to download free music and software is just too compelling.

Spam, like spyware, is more a nuisance than a threat to your computer. It's simply unsolicited e-mail. Although spam doesn't delete files or format disks, it's a thief of e-mail storage space, network bandwidth, and, most important, people's time. For those naive enough to click where spam leads, it can also be a thief of your hard-earned cash if you end up purchasing products or fall for frauds. Like spyware and virus protection, spam detection and prevention are uphill battles because for every rule or filter antispam software places on your e-mail account, spammers find a way to get around them.

Malware Protection

To help prevent the spread of viruses and worms, every desktop and server should have antimalware software running, which should include antivirus and antispyware. Most virus-protection software is also designed to detect and prevent worms. A virus scanner residing in memory should be used so that every program file or document that's accessed is scanned. Documents should be scanned if the document type might contain macros, and servers should run virus-protection software that scans every file read from or written to servers' drives. If a server file accessed by other users gets infected, the malware can spread through the network in a matter of seconds. Some firewalls or specialized content-filtering devices scan for malware at the network's perimeter, with the goal of preventing malware from entering the network. However, even if network-based malware is in place, servers and computers should be equipped with antimalware protection to catch malware brought into the network on removable storage.

Viruses and worms that spread through e-mail attachments have been common for years. They're simple to avoid; just don't open any e-mail attachments sent by someone you're not expecting a message from. Even if you know the sender, be cautious. Malware can use an e-mail program's address book to send messages, which might lure you into believing a message is safe. Most virus scanners actually detect a virus or worm contained in an e-mail message and often delete the attachment before it ever reaches your inbox, but if the virus is very new, it might not be detected. Some public e-mail servers, such as Gmail, contain anti-malware software that filters e-mail suspected of containing malware.

Malware protection can be expensive, although many quite capable freeware or shareware packages are available. Microsoft includes Windows Defender with Windows 8 and later; it contains both antivirus and antispyware protection. It's installed and enabled by default and updated automatically on a regular basis. However, malware developers are always looking for new and clever ways to wreak havoc on networks, so just because you have antimalware software installed doesn't mean your computer is safe.

Probably one of the best ways to avoid spam is to not give your e-mail address to anyone but trusted parties. If you must register on a Web site with an e-mail address, use one from a free e-mail service that you never use for personal mail. That way, you can simply log on to the free e-mail Web site periodically and delete all the messages. Unfortunately, this method still doesn't guarantee your protection from spam, as even legitimate organizations you communicate with regularly can sell their e-mail lists or have them stolen. In addition, worms and spyware can use the address books of people you know to get access to your e-mail address.

It should be clear by now that the Internet, with its wealth of information and its avenues of entertainment and business, is also a dangerous place. The best advice, in lieu of pulling the plug on your Internet connection, is to be dutiful in keeping anti-everything software up to date, and use common sense when opening e-mails or responding to Web-based solicitations. Network security is effective only when users understand the risks of installing and using certain types of software and have a solid understanding of the organization's security policies. A well-educated workforce is a safe workforce.

Before purchasing or downloading antimalware software, it's best to read reviews published by reputable print or Internet publishers. Some software billed as antimalware is actually malware that can disable your existing antimalware software and thwart your attempts to uninstall it or install legitimate antimalware software.

Hands-On Project 9-4: Configuring Windows Defender

Time Required: 15 to 25 minutes

Objective: Configure Windows Defender.

Required Tools and Equipment: Net-*XX* with access to the Internet

Description: Windows 10 comes with Windows Defender installed and enabled. In this project, you examine some options for configuring it.

1. Log on to your computer as **NetAdmin**.

2. In the search box on the taskbar, type **windows defender**. Click **Windows Defender** in the search results to open Windows Defender (see Figure 9-11).

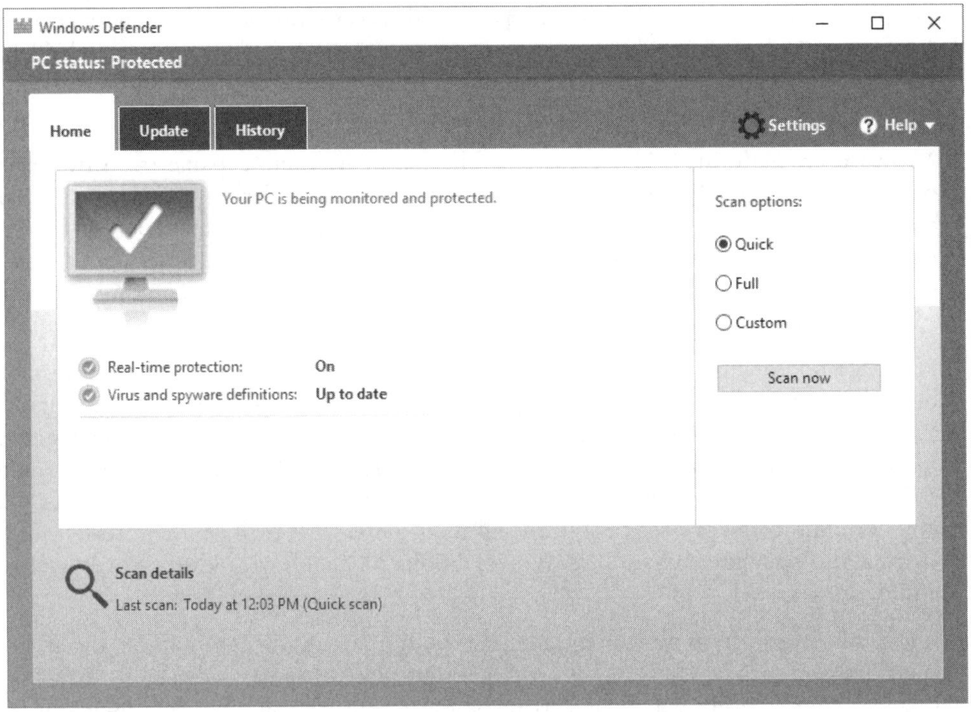

Figure 9-11 The Windows Defender main window

3. Review the options in the Home tab. Click the **Scan now** button to do a quick scan of your system. If any problems are found, Windows Defender lists them along with recommended actions.

4. Click the **Update** tab. Your virus and spyware definitions should be up to date. Click the **Update** button just to be sure. Windows Defender searches for new definition files.

5. Click the **History** tab. Click each option (**Quarantined, Allowed,** and **All detected**), and then click the **View details** button to see whether any of these items have been found.

6. Click the **Settings** icon. In this window, you can turn settings on and off and exclude files from the scanning process. Close the Settings window.

7. Close all open windows, and leave your computer running for the next project.

Using an Attacker's Tools to Stop Network Attacks

If you want to design a good, solid network infrastructure, hire a security consultant who knows the tools of the network attacker's trade. The terms "black hats" and "white hats" are sometimes used to describe people skilled in breaking into or disabling a network. A black hat is, as the analogy implies, the bad guy, and a white hat is the good guy. White hats often use the term **penetration tester** for their consulting services. In fact, a certification has been developed for white hats called Certified Ethical Hacker (CEH; *www.eccouncil.org*). This section approaches the subject of network security from the white hat's perspective. The goal is to see what type of holes exist in a network's security and close them.

NOTE The term "cracker" is sometimes used to describe a person who attempts to break in, disable, or otherwise attack a network. Sometimes confused with a hacker, a cracker attempts to compromise a network or computer for personal gain or to cause harm. Contrast this term with "hacker," which has had several meanings over the years. It's sometimes a derogatory term to describe an unskilled or undisciplined programmer. It can also mean someone who's highly skilled with computer systems and programs and can use some of the same tools crackers use to poke around networks or systems, but not for evil purposes. For simplicity's sake, the term "attacker" is used in this book to mean a person who tries to compromise a network for nefarious purposes.

Discovering Network Resources

Before attackers can gain access to or cause problems with your network, they must get information about the network configuration and available resources. Some tools they use are command-line utilities, such as `ping`, `tracert`, `finger`, and `nslookup`. These commands can help you determine which devices are available, identify name information for these devices, and possibly learn user information. The `ping` command, as you have learned, can be used to determine whether a computer is responding on the network. Because you can ping a computer by name and have its IP address returned, it can also be used to resolve a computer name to an IP address. The `tracert` command provides information about the route a packet takes from one computer to another, which can help determine an internetwork's structure. With `finger`, you can query a computer and determine who's logged on to it and its address. The `nslookup` command is used to query DNS servers. Depending on how well a DNS server is secured, you can use it to retrieve a list of all computer names and mail servers on a domain.

Other tools of the trade include ping scanners and port scanners. A **ping scanner** is an automated method for pinging a range of IP addresses. A **port scanner** determines which TCP and UDP ports are available on a computer or device. With a ping scanner, you can enter a network address, and the program queries all IP addresses in that network (or a range of IP addresses). Many ping scanners also look up the DNS name of any computer that responds. Attackers use this information to see what computers are available on a network, and the DNS name can provide useful information because most network administrators name devices to describe their purpose or location, such as naming a database server SQL-Server or a router Router-3rdFloor. Figure 9-12 shows the results of a ping scan.

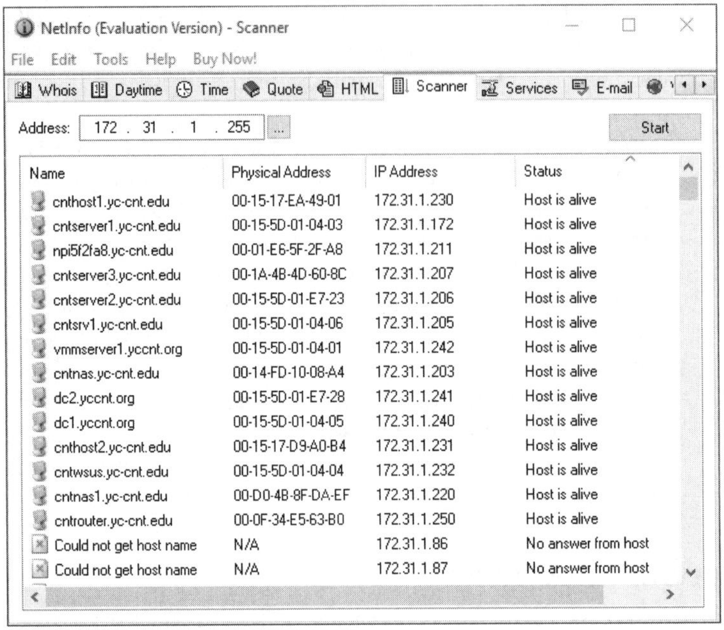

Figure 9-12   The results of a ping scan on a network

Source: © 2015 Tsarfin Computing Ltd.

A ping scan be done from the Windows command line by using the command FOR /L %I IN (1,1,254) DO PING -n 1 -w 100 192.168.1.%I > pingresults.txt. The results are sent to the pingresults.txt file.

A port scanner, by determining which ports are active, can tell you what services are enabled on a computer. Figure 9-13 shows running a port scan on a computer with the IP address 172.31.1.205. Most services are closed, but several are open. A network administrator should use this information to be sure ports listed as open are necessary for the computer's

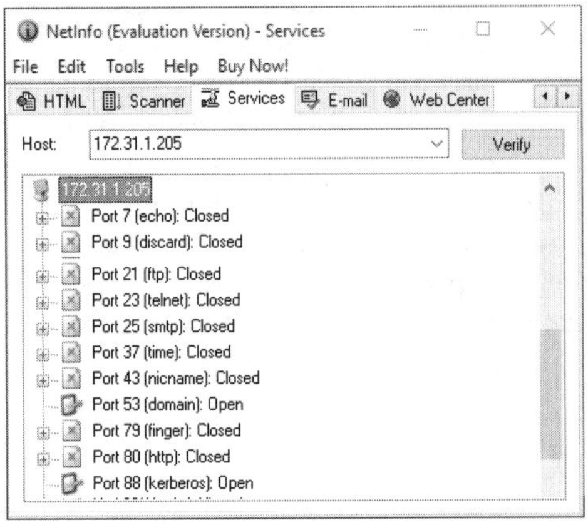

Figure 9-13   The results of a port scan on a computer

Source: © 2015 Tsarfin Computing Ltd.

operation. Any unnecessary ports should be closed, which usually involves stopping a service or an application from running or configuring Windows Firewall to deny access to the port.

Whois is a handy utility for discovering information about an Internet domain. You can find the name and address of the domain owner, contact information for the domain, and the DNS servers managing the domain (see Figure 9-14). The information that can be gathered from a Whois query includes IP address information and names and addresses of DNS servers used by that domain. DNS servers can also be queried to determine names and addresses of computers in that domain.

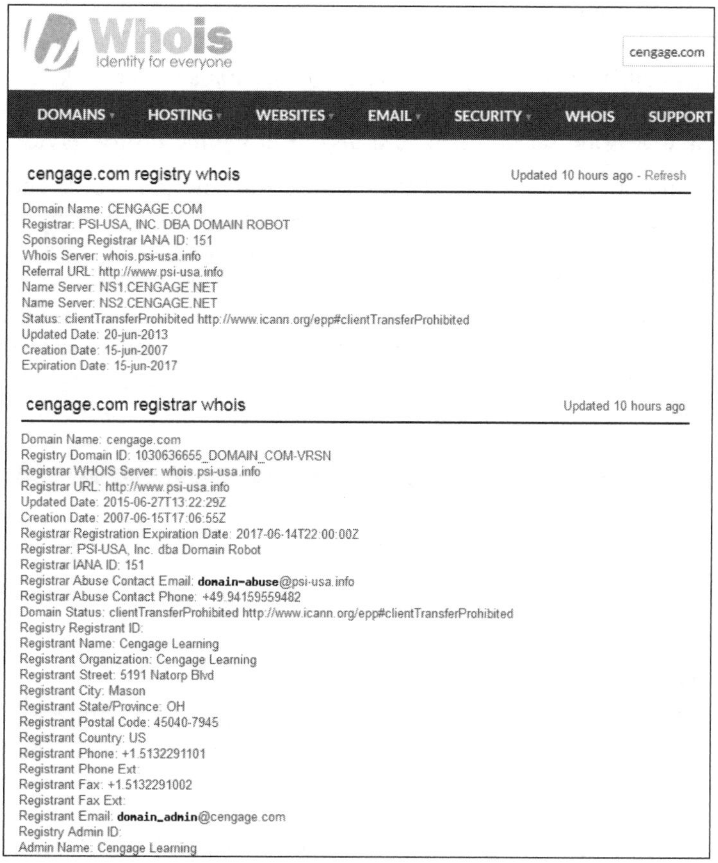

Figure 9-14 Results returned from a Whois query

Source: © Verio, Inc., *www.whois.net*

Protocol analyzers are also useful for resource discovery because they enable you to capture packets and determine which protocols services are running. They require access to the network medium and are, therefore, effective tools only if the attacker is an internal user or has gained access to the internal or wireless network.

To protect your network from some of these utilities, you can take a variety of actions. Some utilities, such as `finger`, can be rendered useless if they're turned off on all devices that support them. Some Linux and UNIX systems as well as some routers often leave the `finger` service on by default. A port scan should be run on all network devices to see which services are on, and then services that aren't needed should be turned off. This process is a white-hat use of a port scanner.

Access lists on routers and firewalls, including personal firewalls, can block pings to prevent the use of ping scanners. To protect the network from internal users of protocol analyzers, all hubs and switches should be secured to prevent an unauthorized user from hooking up a laptop or other device to the network.

Gaining Access to Network Resources

After an attacker has discovered the resources available on a network, the next step might be gaining access to these resources for the purposes of viewing, stealing, or destroying data. One of the easiest resources to access is one for which no password is set. Believe it or not, this situation happens more often than you think, and numerous routers and switches with no passwords set are available through the Internet or on a company network. The remedy to this problem is, of course, to check all devices supporting Telnet, FTP, e-mail, and Web services, verify that passwords are set on them, and disable any unnecessary services.

Often an attacker runs into a resource that requires a username and password. The finger command can be used in some cases to discover usernames, and Linux and Windows servers have default administrator names that are often left unchanged—a fact that an attacker with a password-cracking tool can exploit easily. Some password-cracking tools use a systematic method of guessing passwords from a dictionary of words or from an algorithm that uses all combinations of letters, numbers, and symbols. This type of tool can be extremely time and CPU intensive. If passwords are strong, these tools are often impractical because guessing complex passwords can take days. Using a password-cracking tool on your own system is recommended to see whether your passwords are complex enough.

For an extensive list of penetration-testing tools and more information about penetration testing, visit *www.softwaretestinghelp.com/ penetration-testing-tools/*.

Disabling Network Resources

A **denial-of-service (DoS) attack** is an attacker's attempt to tie up network bandwidth or network services so that it renders resources useless to legitimate users. Some attackers launch a DoS attack for fun; others do it to satisfy a grudge or even gain a leg up on the competition. Three common types of DoS attacks focus on tying up a server or network service: packet storms, half-open SYN attacks, and ping floods. Programs that can create these attacks are readily available for download.

Packet storms typically use the UDP protocol because it's not connection oriented. One packet storm program called Pepsi5 sends a stream of UDP packets that have spoofed host addresses, causing the host to be unavailable to respond to other packets. A **spoofed address** is a source address inserted into the packet that isn't the sender's actual address.

Half-open SYN attacks use the TCP three-way handshake to tie up a server with invalid TCP sessions, thereby preventing real sessions from being started. The attacker sends a series of packets with a valid port number and a request to start a conversation. These packets, called SYN packets, cause the server to respond with SYN-ACK packets. The original SYN packet contains a spoofed source address, resulting in the server waiting for the final packet in the three-way handshake until it times out. If enough SYN packets are sent, the server uses all available connections and, therefore, can't respond to legitimate attempts to a make a connection. Several programs that create this type of attack are available.

A ping flood is exactly what it sounds like. A program sends a large number of ping packets to a host. They cause the host to reply, which ties up CPU cycles and bandwidth. A variation is the smurf attack, in which pings are sent to a broadcast address. All the requests contain the spoofed source address of the host to be smurfed. When computers respond to the broadcast ping, they send their replies to the single host whose address is spoofed. The host is then flooded with ping responses, causing it to slow down or even freeze while it processes all the packets.

Distributed denial-of-service (DDoS) attacks use many systems to attack a single network or resource. Often the attacking systems are unaware they're involved because the attack software is installed as malware and set to activate on a certain date and time. MyDoom, the fastest-spreading worm ever at the time, is a well-known example of a DDoS attack; it targeted *www.sco.com*, among other sites.

There's no end to the methods for wreaking havoc on a network. Becoming familiar with the tools and methods that can be used against your network is essential so that you can prepare defenses against network attacks. You can also use these tools to test the integrity of your network security. Firewalls, access lists, virus scanners, and strong OS security are some ways to prevent these attacks or reduce their effects. In addition, using an IDS or IPS helps you analyze attempts to breach network security and track down and close potential holes in your security measures. Regardless of your tools, you should always start by devising a sound security policy that maps out your overall network security plan and contains provisions for auditing and revising the policy as your needs and technology change. Implementing your policies and using the tools available to protect your network keep your data safe and keep you sleeping well at night.

NOTE Network security is a complex topic. You're encouraged to take the knowledge you have learned in this book and study network security in more depth by reading books or taking a security class. Several network security certifications can be earned, such as the CompTIA Security+, Certified Ethical Hacker (CEH), Certified Information Systems Security Professional (CISSP), and many others.

HANDS-ON PROJECTS

Hands-On Project 9-5: Using NetInfo to Collect Computer and Network Information

Time Required: 15 minutes

Objective: Install the NetInfo program to collect information about a network.

Required Tools and Equipment: Net-XX with Internet access

Description: In this project, you download and install an evaluation version of NetInfo, used to scan computers for open ports and scan a network for IP addresses. The download is a zip file containing a Microsoft installer (.msi) file that must be extracted to run it. Alternatively, the instructor can download the file, extract the installer, and make it available to students on the local network. The software can also be preinstalled on students' computers, and students can begin this project at Step 3.

1. Log on to your computer as **NetAdmin**, if necessary.

2. Start your Web browser and go to **http://netinfo.tsarfin.com**. Click the **download** link, and then click **Download Now**. When you're directed to the Cnet download page, click **Download Now** again. Follow the instructions to download and install NetInfo.

3. To find out about other computers on your network, open a command prompt window, and then type **net view** and press **Enter**. Write down several of the computer names this command returns:

_____

_____

4. Choose a computer name from Step 3. Type **ping computername** (replacing *computername* with the name of the computer you chose) and press Enter. Write down the IP address of the computer returned by the ping command:

_____

5. To start NetInfo, double-click the **NetInfo** desktop shortcut. Click **No** in the message box stating you can try NetInfo for 14 days, and then click **I Agree**. If the Tip of the Day dialog box opens, click to clear the **Show tips at startup** check box, and then click **Close**. Maximize the NetInfo window on your desktop so that you can see all the tabs.

6. Click the **Services** tab. In the Host text box, type the IP address you wrote down in Step 4 and click **Verify**. (If you're doing this project yourself, you can type 127.0.0.1 in the Host text box to scan your own computer.)

7. Find ports that show a status of Open (see Figure 9-15). Open ports represent network services the computer offers but can also represent vulnerabilities that attackers can exploit. Write the name and number of these ports:

_____

_____

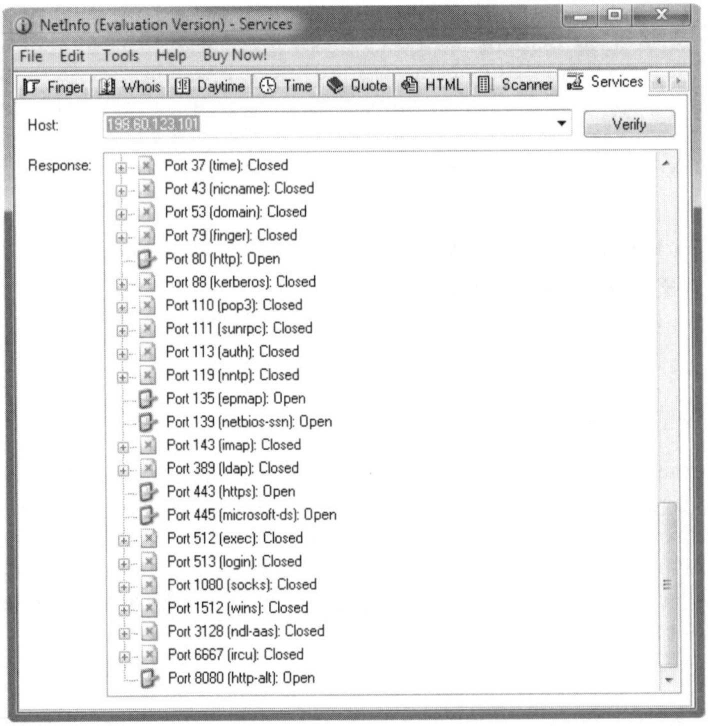

Figure 9-15 NetInfo scans for open ports or services

Source: © 2015 Tsarfin Computing Ltd.

8. You use the information from Step 7 in Case Project 9-2 at the end of this chapter. Clear the output from the last command by right-clicking in NetInfo, pointing to **Clear**, and clicking **All**. Next, you scan a range of IP addresses to see which computers are available on the network.

9. Click the **Scanner** tab. In the Address text box, type the first three octets of the IP address you used in Step 6, followed by a 0 for the last octet. For example, if the address you used was 192.168.1.55, type 192.168.1.0. This setting scans all addresses from 192.168.1.0 through 192.168.1.255.

10. Click **Start**. Write down the name and address of the first three computers for which NetInfo indicated the status "Host is alive." (You can sort the results by clicking the **Status** column.)

_____

_____

11. In the Name column, right-click one of the computers, point to **Send To**, and click **Services**. In the Services tab, click **Verify** to see a list of services this computer provides.

12. Write a short explanation of how NetInfo's Scanner and Services features could help an attacker:

_____

_____

_____

13. Close NetInfo and all other open windows. You can shut down the computer.

Chapter Summary

- A network security policy is a document that describes the rules governing access to a company's information resources. A security policy should be easy to understand and enforce and should state each policy objective clearly.

- A security policy should contain these types of policies: privacy policy, acceptable use policy, authentication policy, Internet use policy, auditing policy, and data protection policy.

- Securing physical access to network resources is paramount. Separate rooms or locking cabinets should be available to house network servers and equipment. Wiring should be inaccessible to eavesdroppers. Physical security includes procedures to recover from natural disasters.

- Securing access to data includes authentication and authorization, encryption, VPNs, wireless security, security devices (such as firewalls and IDSs), and malware protection.

- Authentication and authorization are security features that enable administrators to control who has access to the network (authentication) and what users can do after they're logged on to the network (authorization). A number of authentication protocols can be used, such as Kerberos, RADIUS, and EAP. Authorization includes restricting logon hours and locations and setting file access permissions.

- Many network administrators use encryption technologies to safeguard data as it travels across the Internet and even within a company network. This security measure prevents people from using eavesdropping technology, such as a protocol analyzer, to capture packets and use data in them for malicious purposes.

- VPNs are an important aspect of network security because they secure remote access to a private network via the Internet.

- Wireless security involves configuring a wireless network's SSID correctly, configuring and using wireless security protocols (such as WPA2 and WPA), and using MAC address filtering.

- To protect against threats from external networks, you can deploy specialized devices on the network perimeter: firewalls, IDSs, and IPSs. A firewall is a hardware device or software program that inspects packets going into or out of a network or computer, and then discards or forwards these packets based on a set of rules. An intrusion detection system monitors network traffic for malicious packets or traffic patterns and reports identified security breaches to a management station. An intrusion prevention system can take countermeasures if an attack is in progress.

- Malware encompasses viruses, worms, Trojan horses, rootkits, and spyware. Malware protection should be a required element on every computer and network.

- Tools that attackers use to compromise a network, such as ping scanners, port scanners, and protocol analyzers, can also be used to determine whether a network is secure.

- Denial of service is one method attackers use to disrupt network operation. Three types of DoS attacks include half-open SYN attacks, ping floods, and packet storms.

Key Terms

backdoor   A program installed on a computer that permits access to the computer, thus bypassing the normal authentication process.

client-to-site VPN mode   This VPN mode establishes a VPN connection between a single client computer and a VPN device.

content filter   A type of firewall or security device that looks for key words or phrases in the data portion of each packet to determine whether to allow it into the network.

demilitarized zone (DMZ)   The part of a network that contains publicly accessible devices, such as Web servers and VPN servers, but is still protected by a firewall.

denial-of-service (DoS) attack   An attempt to tie up network bandwidth or services so that network resources are rendered useless to legitimate users.

digital certificates   Digital documents used in encryption and authentication protocols that identify a person or computer and can be verified by a certification authority.

encryption   A technology used to make data unusable and unreadable to anyone except authorized users of the data.

Extensible Authentication Protocol (EAP)   A framework for other authentication protocols that provides encryption and authentication.

firewall   A hardware device or software program that inspects packets going into or out of a network or computer and then discards or forwards packets based on a set of rules.

hoax virus   A type of virus that's not really a virus but simply an e-mail announcement of a made-up virus. Its harm lies in people believing the announcement and forwarding the e-mail on to others.

honeypot   A network device, such as a server, that has been installed as a decoy to lure potential attackers.

intrusion detection system (IDS)   Usually a component of a firewall, a hardware device or software that detects an attempted security breach and notifies the network administrator. An IDS can also take countermeasures to stop an attack in progress.

intrusion prevention system   A variation of an IDS that can take countermeasures if an attack is in progress. *See also* intrusion detection system (IDS).

Kerberos   The authentication protocol used in a Windows domain environment to authenticate logons and grant accounts access to domain resources. It provides mutual authentication between a client and server or between two servers.

logic bomb   Time-dependent malware that can come in different forms. Its main characteristic is that it's activated when a particular event occurs, such as a specific date and time, or when a particular file is accessed.

MAC address filtering   A security method often used in wireless networks, in which only devices with MAC addresses specified by the administrator can gain access to the wireless network.

macro   A command or keystroke that executes a series of actions in a document.

malware   Any software designed to cause harm or disruption to a computer system or otherwise perform activities on a computer without the consent of the computer's owner.

multifactor authentication (MFA)   A type of authentication in which a user must supply two or more types of authentication, drawn from these credential categories: knowledge, possession, and inherence.

mutual authentication   A type of authentication in which the identity of both parties is verified.

penetration tester   A term used to describe a security consultant who detects holes in a system's security for the purpose of correcting these vulnerabilities.

ping scanner   An automated method for pinging a range of IP addresses.

port scanner   Software that determines which TCP and UDP ports are available on a computer or device.

preshared key   A series of letters, numbers, and special characters, much like a password, that both communicating devices use to authenticate each other's identity.

protocol analyzers   Programs or devices that can capture packets traversing a network and display packet contents in a form useful to the user.

ransomware   A type of malware that redirects you to a Web site warning that your system is infected and you must install the vendor's software or call a phone number to clean it.

rootkit   A form of malware that can monitor traffic to and from a computer, monitor keystrokes, and capture passwords. It's among the most insidious forms of malware because it can mask that a system has been compromised by altering system files and drivers required for normal computer operation.

security policy   A document that describes the rules governing access to an organization's information resources, enforcement of these rules, and steps taken if rules are breached.

site-to-site VPN mode   This VPN mode establishes a connection between two routers that support VPNs.

social engineering   A tactic attackers use to get users to perform an action, such as opening an infected e-mail attachment, sending a hoax virus, or providing a password, without being aware that they're aiding the attacker. *See also* hoax virus.

spam   Unsolicited e-mail. The harm in spam is the loss of productivity when people receive dozens or hundreds of spam messages daily and the use of resources to receive and store spam on e-mail servers.

spoofed address   A source address inserted into a packet that's not the sender's actual address.

spyware   A type of malware that monitors or controls part of your computer at the expense of your privacy and the gain of some third party. *See also* malware.

stateful packet inspection (SPI)   A filtering method used in a firewall, whereby packets aren't simply filtered based on packet properties but are checked for the context in which they're being transmitted. If a packet isn't part of a legitimate, ongoing data conversation, it's denied.

Trojan horse   A program that appears to be useful, such as a free utility, but in reality contains some type of malware. *See also* malware.

virtual private network (VPN)   A temporary or permanent connection across a public network that uses encryption technology to transmit and receive data. *See also* encryption.

virus   A malicious program that spreads by replicating itself into other programs or documents; usually aims to disrupt computer or network functions by deleting and corrupting files.

virus signature   A pattern of computer code that's unique to a virus and is used to identify it on an infected system.

VPN concentrator   A dedicated VPN device that can handle many VPN connections and tunnels.

wardrivers   Attackers who drive around with a laptop or PDA looking for wireless LANs to access.

Wi-Fi Protected Access (WPA)   A wireless security protocol that's the successor to Wired Equivalent Privacy and has enhancements that make cracking the encryption code more difficult. *See also* Wired Equivalent Privacy (WEP).

Wi-Fi Protected Access 2 (WPA2)   The successor to Wi-Fi Protected Access that uses Advanced Encryption Standard for the highest level of encryption; currently the strongest security protocol for wireless networks. *See also* Wi-Fi Protected Access (WPA).

Wired Equivalent Privacy (WEP)   A wireless security protocol that encrypts data so that unauthorized people receiving wireless network signals can't interpret the data easily.

worm   A self-replicating program, similar to a virus, that uses network services such as e-mail to spread to other systems. *See also* virus.

Review Questions

1. Which of the following passwords is best to use on a system containing highly sensitive information?
   a. BillySmith
   b. 0OxqH}ml2-wO
   c. H@ckAt!ack23
   d. MySecretPassword

2. Which of the following is a technique you can use to help secure a wireless network? (Choose all that apply.)
   a. IP subnetting
   b. MAC address filtering
   c. WPA2
   d. SSID broadcast

3. Which of these protocols is used for VPNs? (Choose all that apply.)
   a. PPTP
   b. WEP
   c. SSTP
   d. L2TP
   e. ICMP

4. How do VPNs accomplish the "private" part of a virtual private network?
   a. Tunneling
   b. Concentrating
   c. Encapsulating
   d. Authenticating

5. Which of the following terms refers to attacking a Web server by forcing it to respond to a flood of ping packets so that the server can't respond to normal traffic?
   a. DDR
   b. ICMP
   c. DoS
   d. Worm

6. Which of the following is a guideline for creating a security policy?
   a. A security policy should be cryptic so that attackers can't understand it.
   b. A security policy should be general enough so that rules can be added as needed.
   c. A security policy should be enforceable.
   d. A security policy should have different provisions depending on the user.

7. Which of the following is a component of a security policy? (Choose all that apply.)

   a. Authentication policy

   b. Privacy policy

   c. Network configuration policy

   d. Computer specification policy

8. Which of the following questions must be answered before determining what level of security a network requires? (Choose all that apply.)

   a. What tools are used to attack the network?

   b. What's being protected?

   c. From whom should data be protected?

   d. How much data is on the network?

9. Which of the following should be a common element in any level of security policy? (Choose all that apply.)

   a. Complex passwords

   b. Backup procedures

   c. Data encryption

   d. Virus protection

10. Which phrase from the following list best completes this sentence? If there's access to the equipment, there's no _____.

    a. physical security

    b. network monitoring

    c. data integrity

    d. security policy

11. Which of the following is a requirement for rooms housing network servers?

    a. Separate heating system

    b. Adequate cooling

    c. False ceilings

    d. Shared electrical circuit

12. Which procedure specifies what resources users can access and the tasks they can perform on a network?

    a. Authentication

    b. Auditing

    c. Authorization

    d. Logon

13. If you want to allow a blank password on a Windows computer, which of the following do you set the password minimum length to?

    a. Blank

    b. 0

    c. −1

    d. Nothing

14. If you want to prevent password guessing to foil intruders, you should enable which of the following?

    a. Account lockout

    b. Password expiration

    c. Password disabling

    d. Account policies

15. Which authentication protocol is used in a Windows domain environment?

    a. AES

    b. Kerberos

    c. EAP

    d. MS-CHAP v2

16. Which of the following is a credential category? (Choose all that apply.)

    a. Knowledge

    b. Inherence

    c. Encryption

    d. Possession

    e. Authentication

17. Which of the following is a method IPsec uses to authenticate the identity of communicating devices? (Choose all that apply.)

    a. Multishared key

    b. Kerberos

    c. PAM

    d. Digital certificates

18. To encrypt data stored on a hard drive on a Windows Server computer, you should use which of the following?

    a. EFS

    b. AES

    c. NTFS

    d. PAP

19. Firewalls can filter packets based on which of the following? (Choose all that apply.)

    a. Source address

    b. Protocol

    c. OS

    d. Context

20. If network administrators want to be informed when an attempt has been made to compromise the network, what should they use?

    a. VPN

    b. AES

    c. IDS

    d. EFS

21. Which VPN mode should you use if you want to establish a secure tunnel between a main office and a branch office?

    a. Client-to-gateway

    b. Site-to-site

    c. Site to gateway

    d. Host to site

22. Where's a common place to install an NIDS?

    a. In the DMZ

    b. On an isolated host

    c. On a honeypot

    d. In the ISP

23. What device should you consider installing if you want countermeasures to take place when an attack is detected?

    a. Content filter

    b. IPS

    c. Antivirus software

    d. HIDS

Critical Thinking

The following activities give you critical thinking challenges. Challenge labs give you an opportunity to use the skills you have learned to perform a task without step-by-step instructions. Case projects offer a practical networking setup for which you supply a written solution.

Challenge Lab 9-1: Testing Password and Account Lockout Settings

Time Required: 1 hour or longer, unless some times are modified to decrease the amount of waiting time

Objective: Test the password and account lockout policy settings you configured in Hands-On Project 9-1.

Required Tools and Equipment: Net-*XX*

Description: Whenever configuration changes are made that affect a system's security, they should be tested thoroughly. Review the password and account lockout policies you set in Hands-On Project 9-1, and devise a method to test these policies to be sure they have the effect you wanted. For each password policy and account lockout policy setting, write a short description of how you plan to test the setting, and then follow your testing instructions to verify that the instructions are correct and the settings are working as intended. You can use the following lines to write the testing instructions or create a document to give to your instructor.

Password policy settings:

- Users must use 10 different passwords before reusing a password.

  _____

- Users must change their passwords every 30 days.

  _____

- Users can't change their password more often than every 7 days.

  _____

- The minimum password length is six characters.

  _____

- The password must contain three of these characteristics: uppercase letters, lowercase letters, numbers, or special characters.

  _____

Account lockout policy settings:

- User accounts are locked out after four invalid logon attempts.

  _____

- Locked accounts are unlocked automatically after 60 minutes.

  _____

- The counter is reset 15 minutes after each invalid logon attempt.

  _____

Challenge Lab 9-2: Using Windows Firewall with Advanced Security to Limit Access to Your Computer

Time Required: 15 to 30 minutes

Objective: Limit access to your computer's Remote Desktop service to other computers in your network and allow computers outside your network to send ICMP Echo Request messages (`ping`).

Required Tools and Equipment: Net-*XX*

Description: This lab can be done in groups. You want to be able to allow Remote Desktop connections from users in your network, but you want your firewall to block attempts from outside your network. *Note*: If you want to test this setting, you need to enable Remote Desktop connections in the System control panel. You also want users in your network and outside your network to be able to ping your computer. You need to edit existing rules in the Windows Firewall with Advanced Security console. After you have edited the rules, answer the following questions:

- Which rule did you edit to allow Remote Desktop connections to your computer?

  _____

- What did you do to limit Remote Desktop access to your network only?

  _____

  _____

- Which rule did you edit to change the ICMP Echo Request settings?

  _____

- What did you do to allow pings from outside your network?

  _____

Challenge Lab 9-3: Creating a Network Diagram

Time Required: 30 minutes or longer

Objective: Create a network diagram that includes firewalls and other security devices.

Required Tools and Equipment: Net-*XX* with an Internet connection

Description: Create a network diagram by using an online diagramming tool called Gliffy. Go to *www.gliffy.com* and create a free account, which allows you to save five diagrams. Gliffy has templates for network diagrams, so you can choose from several icons representing network devices. You're creating a diagram for a network that has a main office and a branch office, both connected to the Internet. Only the main office requires a detailed diagram. Figure 9-16 shows a sample drawing with the Gliffy tool. Keep in mind that it's only an example; your drawing will be more detailed. It should meet the following requirements:

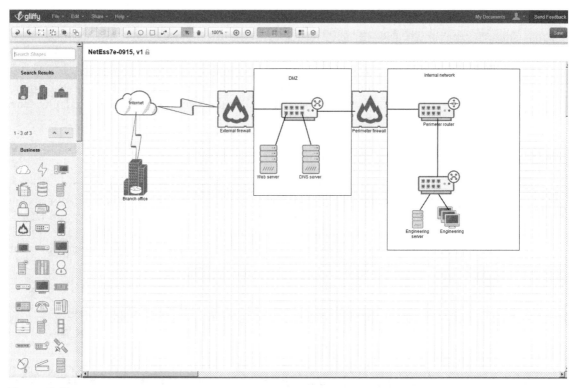

Figure 9-16   A sample drawing with the Gliffy tool

Source: © 2015 Gliffy, Inc., *www.gliffy.com*

You can use other drawing tools, such as Microsoft Visio, if you like.

- You don't want the expense of a dedicated WAN connection between offices, but you want the connection to be secure.

- The company is concerned about attacks from the Internet and wants to monitor incoming traffic. Alerts should be generated when suspicious traffic is detected.

- To determine the methods used to perpetrate attacks, you should include a device that's easily accessible to potential attackers and can be monitored.

- The company has a Web presence and runs a Windows Server 2016 domain. It has four departments: Management, Engineering, Accounting, and Operations. Each department has its own server, and it should be possible to limit access from one department to another.

- The internal network has four enterprise servers: database server, file server, mail server, and internal Web server. These servers should be placed so that access to them can be controlled.

As you create your drawing, add suitable labels, and include as much detail as possible. Think of other elements you should include that aren't specified in this project's requirements. Print or publish your drawing (with the Publish option in Gliffy) and give your instructor the printout or the URL to the published drawing.

Case Project 9-1

DoS attacks are one of the easier attacks to perpetrate on a network, so they're often used by people who have a grudge against a company or are out to commit acts of vandalism. To read about recent trends in DoS and DDoS attacks, do a Web search for "continued rise of ddos attacks" and read the paper by Symantec. Read the first eight pages, and write a summary of what you found, including answers to these questions:

- What's the largest attack volume (in Gbps) as of the paper's writing?
- What percentage of companies were hit by a DDoS attack in 2013?
- What's the trend for the current method attackers use to perpetrate DDoS attacks?
- Using the chart on page 7 of the report, what's the trend for the type of attacks being perpetrated?

Case Project 9-2

Using the information on open ports you found with NetInfo in Hands-On Project 9-5, research these ports to determine their function and whether leaving them open is safe. A Google search is a good place to begin your research. Write a summary of what you found and list which open ports pose a security risk.

Case Project 9-3

Search for security policy templates on the Internet. A good place to start is the SANS Institute (*www.sans.org*). Using one or more of the templates you find, develop a security policy for your school or a business, and present it to the class. This project can also be assigned to groups of students.

Case Project 9-4

A small research company in Pittsburgh is working to develop a new method of mass storage to replace current storage technology. Four engineers and an office manager work there. The engineers are highly skilled professionals, and the office manager is a capable computer user. The company has a high-bandwidth Internet connection because employees must conduct research frequently. The employees have hopes of making a breakthrough and bringing the company public within the next two years. You have been hired as a security consultant to assess the company's needs. Write a paper recommending what type of security policy should be used (open, moderately restrictive, or highly restrictive) and what security technologies should be used. On what areas should the security policy focus (physical security, data security, auditing, passwords, and so forth), and what technologies should be used to secure these areas?

Case Project 9-5

An architectural firm of eight employees, each with a networked desktop computer, wants you to develop a security policy for the company. Management has emphasized that ease of use is paramount, and little time is available for training. Working in small groups, each group should write a list of questions aimed at getting enough information for developing the policy. After determining the questions, each group should interview another group, with the other group posing as the architectural firm and answering the list of questions. What level of security should the policy reflect? Use one of the templates you found in Case Project 9-3 to develop a policy based on the answers the other group supplies.

chapter 10

Wide Area Networking and Cloud Computing

After reading this chapter and completing the exercises, you will be able to:

- Describe the fundamentals of WAN operation and devices
- Discuss the methods used to connect to WANs
- Configure and describe remote access protocols
- Describe the three major areas of cloud computing

Wide area networks connect LANs to LANs over a large geographic area. The Internet is the ultimate WAN, essentially connecting every LAN to every other LAN across the entire globe. Whether a company wants to connect its LAN to the Internet or to another private LAN across town or across the country, WAN technologies are used. This chapter discusses some devices used in WANs and the main methods of making a WAN connection. WAN technology has its own terms and acronyms, and this chapter explains some of the language used. Wide area networking is a vast topic because so many technologies can be used for WAN connections. This chapter gives you a brief introduction to some of these technologies to prepare you for further study of this complex topic.

Remote access is an extension of WAN communication, in which a network provides methods for remote users to connect to the LAN, and this chapter discusses the most common methods of remote access. Finally, this chapter gives you an overview of a growing trend in networking called cloud computing, which uses WANs to offer companies a range of services, including application services and infrastructure services.

Wide Area Network Fundamentals

Table 10-1 summarizes what you need for the hands-on projects in this chapter.

Table 10-1 Hands-on project requirements

Hands-on project	Requirements	Time required	Notes
Hands-On Project 10-1: Creating a Dial-up Connection	Net-*XX*	10 minutes	
Hands-On Project 10-2: Creating a VPN Connection	Net-*XX*	10 minutes	The instructor can configure a VPN server that enables students to test the connection.

Large, and sometimes even small, businesses often have multiple sites. For example, a company might have sales offices in New York and Los Angeles and a manufacturing plant in Chicago. Facilitating communication between geographically dispersed sites requires a WAN, which is simply an internetwork spanning a large geographical area.

From a user's perspective, WANs provide access to network resources the same way LANs do, albeit sometimes slower depending on the technology used. As you have learned, both internetworks and WANs can be described as two or more LANs connected. The most obvious difference between internetworks and WANs is the distance between the LANs being connected. However, aside from distance, WANs differ from internetworks in two other critical areas:

- WANs use the services of carriers or service providers, such as phone companies and ISPs, for network connections, whereas internetworks are confined to a building or campus where the internetwork's owner owns and operates all the technology.

- WANs use serial communication technologies that can span distances measured in miles compared with typical LAN technologies that span distances measured in hundreds of meters.

WAN technologies provide the same function in a network as LAN technologies, such as Ethernet. In the two layered architectures discussed in this book, WAN technologies operate at the Network access layer of the TCP/IP model and the Data Link and Physical layers of the OSI model (see Figure 10-1). The top layers are unchanged when WAN technologies are part of the network. Network protocols and applications are unaware whether data's traveling over a WAN connection across thousands of miles or over a 1 GB Ethernet connection across the room.

OSI model	TCP/IP model	
Application	Application	
Presentation		
Session		
Transport	Transport	
Network	Internetwork	
Data Link	Network access	WAN technologies
Physical		

Figure 10-1 WAN technologies operate at the lower layers

WAN Devices

Because WANs operate at the layers involving media access and WAN signals must traverse long distances, it follows that WANs use different methods for accessing network media and transmitting bit signals. Several types of devices are likely to be used in WANs for media access, signal transmission and reception, and connecting a WAN to a LAN:

- Modems
- Channel service units/data service units
- Routers

Modems A **modem** is a device that allows a computer, which works with digital information, to communicate over lines that use analog signals. For example, the telephone system and cable Internet networks use analog communication. A modem converts a digital signal from a computer into an analog signal to be transmitted over phone or cable lines. This conversion is called "modulation." A modem modulates the digital signal into an analog signal, and at the other end of the line, another modem demodulates the analog signal back to digital. The term "modem" is just a shortened form of "modulator/demodulator."

A **digital signal** is a series of binary 1s and 0s represented by some type of signal that has two possible states. For example, on copper media, two voltage levels, such as 5v and 0v, might be used, with 5v representing a 1 bit and 0v representing a 0 bit. On fiber-optic media, a 1 bit can be represented as a pulse of light and a 0 bit by the absence of light. Figure 10-2 shows a digital signal represented as a square wave.

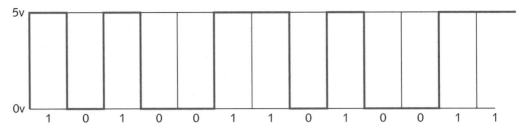

Figure 10-2   A digital signal represented as a square wave

An **analog signal** is a signal that varies over time continually and smoothly. Whereas a digital signal is 0v or 5v (with no value between these two used), an analog signal in the same voltage range transitions smoothly from 0v to 5v and every voltage value in between. You can look at a digital signal as a light bulb controlled by a typical light switch: It's either off, giving no light, or on at full brightness. An analog signal, on the other hand, is like a light bulb controlled by a dimmer switch that transitions from off to full brightness after passing through every other level of brightness. An analog signal is represented by a sine wave, as shown in Figure 10-3.

Figure 10-3   An analog signal varies continually

Modems used in WAN communications are most closely associated with dial-up communication over the public switched telephone network (PSTN). Dial-up networking over the PSTN was once the most common method of accessing the Internet and giving mobile users remote access to a private network. However, broadband networks have mostly supplanted dial-up Internet access, and remote access to private networks is usually handled through a VPN over a broadband Internet connection.

Even though cable Internet and DSL provide digital data, the digital signals are still transmitted by using analog carrier waves. So a cable modem still demodulates the analog signal to extract the encoded digital data for delivery to a computer or router and modulates the signal from the computer or router for delivery to the cable or DSL connection.

CSUs/DSUs   A channel service unit/data service unit (CSU/DSU) is a device (actually two devices that are usually combined) that creates a digital connection between a LAN device, such as a router, and the WAN link from the service provider. The WAN link is usually a T-carrier technology, such a T1 or T3 (discussed later in "Leased Lines"). A CSU/DSU performs a function similar to a modem's—converting WAN signals into a form a LAN can use and vice versa—but in this case, all the signals are digital, so a CSU/DSU converts one type of digital signal to another type of digital signal.

In a typical WAN connection, the incoming signal from a service provider (the T-carrier) is connected to the CSU, and the DSU converts the T-carrier frames into frames the router can understand. For outgoing signals, data from the router is converted into T-carrier frames for delivery back to the service provider. The DSU usually contains a multiplexer that separates a single signal stream into multiple signals that can have separate destinations. For example, a single T-1 connection might carry voice and data, and the multiplexer separates the signals for delivery to different devices.

Routers As you know, a router is responsible for getting packets from one network to another. In a WAN, it's usually the device connecting a LAN to the WAN service provider. In most cases, it connects to the modem or CSU/DSU, which then connects to the link from the WAN provider. Figure 10-4 shows a typical arrangement in which a LAN connects to the WAN through a router and a CSU/DSU or modem.

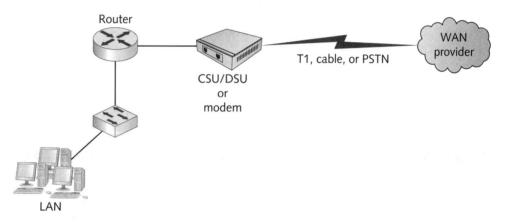

Figure 10-4 A typical LAN-to-WAN connection

The three types of devices discussed in this section are instrumental in making WAN connections of all types, and one or more of these devices is part of any type of WAN. In the following section, you take a look at the main methods of making a WAN connection.

WAN Connection Methods

Numerous WAN technologies are available that differ in speed, level of security and reliability, and cost. The methods of making a WAN connection often dictate the technologies that can be used and the connection's properties. The four most common connection methods are as follows:

- Circuit-switched
- Leased line
- Packet-switched
- VPN over the Internet

Each method has its strengths and weaknesses and works with different underlying WAN technologies. To make an informed decision, a network administrator must weigh each method's cost, speed, reliability, level of security, and available underlying technologies. The following sections explain these methods along with the technologies they work with.

Circuit-Switched WANs

A **circuit-switched WAN** creates a temporary dedicated connection between sender and receiver on demand. The main example is nothing fancier than a phone line connection from the PSTN, also known as plain old telephone service (POTS). When you pick up the phone, there's no connection until you dial the destination. If the destination is available, a circuit is created that's maintained until one party ends the communication session. A major drawback of using POTS for a network connection is that at least part of the connection is always analog, which limits the connection speed. Another circuit-switched technology that's all digital is Integrated Services Digital Network (ISDN).

Both POTS and ISDN have lost out to faster technologies for network access, but they're still in use in parts of the world where faster technologies are unavailable or too expensive. So both these circuit-switched technologies are covered in the following sections to give you some familiarity with how they work and what their limitations are.

Plain Old Telephone Service Circuit-switched connections over POTS are limited in bandwidth, partly because of the phone system's analog nature. Even when most of the connection is digital, a digital-to-analog conversion is still done by modems and usually the phone carrier's network. The conversion process degrades signal quality and limits data transfer speeds over POTS to about 56 Kbps. If both ends of the connection use a traditional modem, which requires another set of analog-to-digital conversions, the connection speed is limited to about 33 Kbps.

The most common modem standard for connecting to the Internet or a remote office is V.92, which allows connection speeds up to 56 Kbps by eliminating one of the modulation/demodulation steps in traditional modem communication. As shown in Figure 10-5, traditional modem communication converts a computer's digital data into analog data. The analog signal travels over phone lines until it reaches the telephone company ("telco"), where the signal is converted to digital. The telco must then convert the signal back to analog for the receiving modem at the ISP, which converts the signal to digital for the Internet. This two-way conversion limits transfer speeds to 33.6 Kbps because each conversion degrades signal quality.

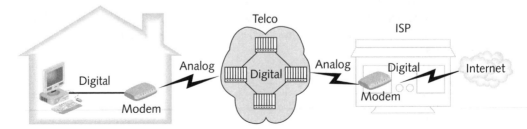

Figure 10-5   Modem communication with two analog-to-digital conversions

V.92 modems assume that the network from the telco to the ISP and then to the Internet is all digital. Therefore, instead of modulating analog data into digital data as it's received from the telco, a V.92 modem uses a technique called "pulse code modulation (PCM)" that digitizes analog signals. It introduces less noise into the signal than traditional modulation/demodulation techniques do, so it boosts the total number of bits per second at which data can be transferred. As shown in Figure 10-6, there's only one analog connection—from the home to the telco. From the telco to the ISP and then to the Internet, the signal is digital.

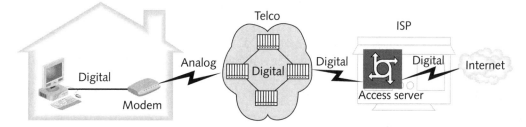

Figure 10-6 Modem communication with the V.92 standard

Two caveats with V.92 communication: There must be only one analog circuit between the modem and the Internet, and 56 Kbps communication works in only one direction—the download direction. This means data from the modem to the ISP travels at about 48 Kbps, but data from the ISP to the modem travels at the V.92 speed of 56 Kbps. Although V.92 technology is capable of data transfer speeds up to 56 Kbps, actual transfer rates depend on line conditions.

Integrated Services Digital Network Integrated Services Digital Network (ISDN) is a digital communication technology developed in 1984 to replace the analog phone system. Not as widely deployed as expected, it's rarely used in the United States now, and most European and Asian countries still using it have plans to retire it within a decade. The ISDN specification defines communication channels of 64 Kbps. When dial-up was the standard access method during the 1980s, ISDN seemed attractive, but with broadband access widely available at speeds up to 10 Mbps and faster, ISDN has no major benefits in most places. If not for private and SOHO use to establish Internet connections, ISDN might never have been deployed, although it was once used widely in corporate WANs as a backup line. Because ISDN charges are often based on connect time, a company can use ISDN in standby mode so that the WAN connection is established only if the primary connection fails.

ISDN offers speeds two to four times that of a standard POTS modem—not an overwhelming increase in speed but a vast improvement for SOHO users when faster technologies, such as DSL or cable modem, aren't available. ISDN is available in two formats or rates:

- *BRI*—The **Basic Rate Interface (BRI)** format consists of two B-channels (64 Kbps) and a D-channel (16 Kbps). Each B-channel can transmit and receive voice or data independently of the other or bonded together at a speed of 128 Kbps. This arrangement allows a user to talk on the phone with one B-channel and stay connected to the Internet with the second channel. The D-channel is used for call setup and control.

- *PRI*—The **Primary Rate Interface (PRI)** format consists of 23 B-channels and a D-channel. Each B-channel can be used independently or aggregated to provide up to 1.544 Mbps. As with BRI, the B-channels are 64 Kbps channels, but the D-channel is also 64 Kbps, compared with only 16 Kbps in a BRI.

ISDN connects to a network by using a device called a "terminal adapter," which performs similar functions as a CSU/DSU. It creates a circuit-switched network in a similar manner to POTS, but the call setup time is less than a second compared with several seconds for POTS. Sometimes you hear the term "ISDN modem," but because the signals are digital, no modulation/demodulation of analog signals takes place, so "modem" doesn't apply. ISDN is a nearly obsolete technology; DSL and broadband services have largely replaced it as an Internet access technology.

In general, circuit-switched networks for WAN access have been passed over by faster, more reliable technologies. Their biggest advantage is low cost, and as much as you trust your phone line, they're secure. However, bandwidth is low, and because they run over existing phone lines that may or may not be in good condition, their reliability is suspect.

Leased Lines

A leased line provides a dedicated point-to-point connection from the customer's LAN through the provider's network and to the destination network. It provides permanent, secure, and dedicated bandwidth limited only by the provider's technology and how much the customer is willing to spend. In essence, customers rent the network connection. A line is leased to the customer, who has the full benefits of a dedicated connection to the remote network until the customer (or provider) terminates the lease.

Leased lines are the most expensive way to get WAN connectivity because of the dedicated nature of the link. However, a leased line should be considered in these circumstances:

- When high-quality, 24/7 access is needed
- For mission-critical applications
- When fast upstream *and* downstream communication speeds are required

Leased lines are typically based on one of two types of digital technology: T-carriers and SONET, discussed in the following sections.

T-Carriers T-carriers originated when the dominant phone company at the time, AT&T, wanted to be able to carry multiple phone conversations over the same pair of wires and over longer distances. By digitizing voice data and organizing phone conversations into time slots on the media, AT&T could do just that, and the T-carrier technology was born.

Typical T-carrier lines are T1 and T3 that operate at 1.544 Mbps and 44 Mbps, respectively. **T-carrier lines** are derived from multiple 64 Kbps channels, making a T1 connection a grouping of 24 64-Kbps channels. A T3 line groups 672 64-Kbps channels. The channels aren't carried over separate wires, although this might be the best way to think of how they work. A T-carrier line uses a single pair of wires for transmitting data and another pair for receiving data. It uses the signaling method **time division multiplexing (TDM)**, which allocates a time slot for each channel, making it possible to extract any number of the channels for a particular purpose. If a portion of a T-carrier line is used for one purpose and a different portion for another purpose, the line has been **fractionalized**. So you hear the term "fractional T1" or "fractional T3" to mean some but not all of the line is being used for a specific purpose. For example, a T1 line can be fractionalized to use half the channels for a teleconferencing application and the other half for other network traffic traveling the WAN.

 Each 64 Kbps channel is called a "DS0," which means digital signal level 0. The next DS level is DS1, which is 24 64-Kbps channels, equivalent to a T1 carrier.

Multiplexing, or "muxing," enables several communication streams to travel simultaneously over the same cable segment. Through multiplexing, a T-carrier network supports simultaneous communication links over the same set of cables. T1 uses multiplexing to combine data transmissions from several sources and deliver them over a single cable. After a transmission is received, it's demultiplexed (demuxed) into its constituent channels, as shown in Figure 10-7, where three 64 Kbps channels are multiplexed into a single 192 Kbps channel and then demuxed into the original three channels.

Figure 10-7 Multiplexing/demultiplexing

The capability to mux/demux multiple channels makes T-carriers enormously flexible. Customers can pay for a fractional T1 or T3 link if their bandwidth needs are modest and later upgrade to additional channels if their needs increase.

T-carrier lines require a CSU/DSU at each end of the link to convert the signals used by the T-carrier line into signals used by the LAN and to mux/demux the DS0 signals as needed. As Figure 10-4 showed previously, a CSU/DSU usually connects to the customer's router on one side and the T-carrier line (WAN connection) on the other side. T-carriers can use shielded twisted-pair cabling for carrying up to T1 speeds. Multiple T1s or T3s require coaxial or fiber-optic cabling and can also be carried via microwave and satellite transmitters.

T1 lines are the most common WAN connection method in the United States. The equivalent of T-carrier lines in Europe are E-carrier lines with E1 (30 64-Kbps channels) and E3 (480 64-Kbps channels) lines. Japan uses J1 (24 64-Kbps channels) and J3 connections (480 64-Kbps channels). T1 connections over twisted pair are terminated with RJ-48 connectors, which look like RJ-45 connectors but use a different pinout. For a more advanced connection, T1 lines can be connected to a **smart jack,** which is a network interface device (NID) that serves as the termination point for a T1 connection and provides diagnostics, such as loopback testing, for troubleshooting the connection.

SONET Networks Synchronous Optical Network (SONET) is a flexible, highly fault-tolerant technology that can carry signals of different capacities over a fiber-optic network. It defines optical carrier (OC) levels from OC-1 to OC-3072, in which each OC level is a multiple of the base OC-1 rate of 51.84 Mbps. Typical SONET data rates are OC-3, OC-12, OC-48, OC-192, and OC-768. An OC-3 SONET connection (155 Mbps) is often used by Asynchronous Transfer Mode (ATM) networks, discussed next in "Packet-Switched WANs."

Because of the tremendous speeds SONET offers and its consequently high cost, it's rarely used above OC-3 levels by companies other than ISPs and telcos. For example, OC-12 (622 Mbps) is a common SONET speed used by regional or local ISPs and Web hosting providers for their Internet backbone connections. OC-48 (almost 2.5 Gbps) and higher speeds are typical of large regional ISPs, and large ISPs use OC-192 and even OC-768 SONET networks.

One of SONET's greatest benefits is its flexibility. SONET networks can carry traffic from a variety of other network types, such as T-carrier, ATM, and so forth, by using multiplexing techniques. SONET can also be arranged in a variety of physical topologies, including point-to-point, point-to-multipoint, star, and ring. The ring topology is the most popular because it provides fault tolerance. SONET uses a dual-ring topology, such as FDDI, that's self-healing if a portion of one ring fails.

 SONET is a North American term. In the rest of the world, the same technology is referred to as "Synchronous Digital Hierarchy (SDH)."

Although SONET can be used as a leased-line technology in which a customer has dedicated use of the bandwidth between sites or as an Internet connection, it's often used as the underlying technology of other connection types, such as packet-switched WANs.

Packet-Switched WANs

A **packet-switched WAN** doesn't create a dedicated connection between sender and receiver; instead, data is transmitted in frames or packets, and each packet is transmitted through the provider's network independently. This process works much like frame transmission in a LAN that uses switches to deliver each frame from its source to its destination. Changing network conditions could cause frames to be transmitted over different paths in a large network, and instead of having a dedicated circuit over which data travels, data shares bandwidth with a provider's other customers. At first glance, this sharing might not seem to be a good thing, but most network customers don't use all the bandwidth a dedicated circuit provides, which means they're paying for more bandwidth than they use.

Packet-switched networks should be nothing new to you because all LANs and internetworks use a similar procedure to get packets from a source computer to a destination computer. The biggest difference is the technologies that are used. Remember that WANs are defined at the Data Link and Physical layers of the OSI model, so these layers are where the differences lie. The most common packet-switched networks are X.25, frame relay, ATM, and MPLS, discussed in the following sections.

Virtual Circuits Before learning about the specific technologies, it's important to understand that packet-switched WANs use a virtual circuit to ensure that packets are delivered reliably and at the agreed-on bandwidth level. A **virtual circuit** is a logical connection created between two devices in a shared network. No single cable exists between the two endpoints; instead, a virtual circuit maps the path through the network of switches between the two devices and allocates the specified bandwidth throughout the circuit. This pathway between sender and receiver is created after devices at both ends of the connection agree on bandwidth requirements and request a pathway.

There are two types of virtual circuits: switched and permanent. **Switched virtual circuits (SVCs)** are established when needed and then terminated when the transmission is completed. The path between two communication points is maintained only as long as it's in active use. SVCs are best when communication between the two points is somewhat intermittent, allowing the circuit's bandwidth to be released for use by other SVCs. **Permanent virtual circuits (PVCs)** are similar to leased lines, in that the pathway between two communication points is established as a permanent logical connection; therefore, the pathway exists even when data isn't being transferred. PVCs are more expensive than SVCs because the circuit's bandwidth stays allocated even if data isn't being transferred, making PVCs a good choice only if communication between endpoints is fairly constant.

X.25 Networks

X.25 is a packet-switching technology developed in the mid-1970s that has the advantage of running effectively over older copper phone lines. The X.25 specification provides an interface between public packet-switching networks and their customers. X.25 networks offer both SVCs and PVCs, although not all X.25 providers offer PVCs.

Early X.25 networks used standard phone lines as communication links, which resulted in numerous errors and lost data. Adding error checking and retransmission schemes improved the success of X.25 transmissions but severely reduced speed. With its extensive level of error control, X.25 could deliver only 64 Kbps transmission rates. A 1992 specification revision improved the maximum throughput of X.25 to 2 Mbps per connection, but this new version wasn't widely deployed.

X.25 is usually associated with public data networks (PDNs) and was used to access these online services in the 1970s and 1980s. It remains popular in developing countries, where digital communication is less available and more expensive than in the North America and Europe. Using data terminal equipment (DTE) and data circuit-terminating equipment (DCE), explained later in "WAN Implementation Basics," connecting to an X.25 network can be done in one of three ways:

- An X.25 NIC in a computer
- A packet assembler/disassembler (PAD) that supports X.25 communication for low-speed, character-based terminals
- A LAN/WAN X.25 gateway

Even though X.25 networks offer reliable and error-free communication, this technology has mostly been replaced by other higher-speed technologies, such as frame relay and ATM.

Frame Relay Networks

Frame relay is a PVC packet-switching technology that offers WAN communication over a fast, reliable, digital link. It was developed from X.25 and ISDN technology. Error checking isn't required on the digital fiber-optic links most frame relay connections use, so overall throughput is improved. Instead, the devices on each end of the communication perform error checking.

Frame relay uses a PVC between communication points, so the same pathway carries all communications, which ensures correct delivery and higher bandwidth rates. A PVC is similar to a dedicated line, in that communication devices aren't concerned with route management and error checking. Instead, all the resources of devices are dedicated to moving data. This is why frame relay technology can maintain transmission rates from 64 Kbps to

44 Mbps (T3 speed). It fills the bandwidth gap between ISDN, which operates at a maximum of 128 Kbps, and ATM, which operates at 155 Mbps.

Frame relay services have grown in popularity. They're inexpensive (compared with leased lines) and allow customers to specify the bandwidth needed. Charges depend on the PVC's bandwidth allocation, also known as its **Committed Information Rate (CIR)**. CIR is the guaranteed minimum transmission rate the service provider offers. Customers can purchase frame relay services in CIR increments of 64 Kbps. Because customers can pay for a customized bandwidth solution, frame relay is sometimes preferred to T1 because it's generally less expensive.

A frame relay connection is established by using a pair of CSU/DSU devices—as with T1 lines—with a router or bridge at each end to direct traffic on and off the WAN link. An important difference between a frame relay connection and a T1 connection is that T1 is a point-to-point link, which means a T1 customer gets full-time bandwidth to the destination. However, frame relay connections are virtual circuits that go through a switch. This arrangement makes it possible to reach multiple destinations with a single connection. Therefore, a corporate customer can, for example, have a frame relay link to each of its branch offices as well as one to the Internet yet require only a single frame relay connection. Figure 10-8 shows a WAN using leased lines, and Figure 10-9 shows the same WAN using frame relay

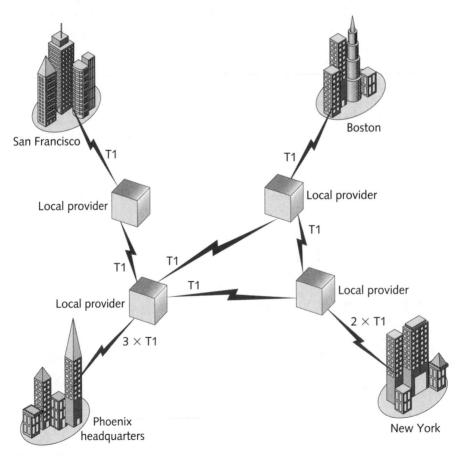

Figure 10-8 A leased-line network

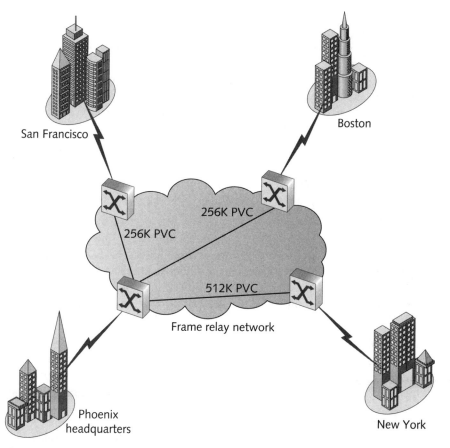

Figure 10-9 A frame relay network

connections. The leased-line network has dedicated bandwidth extending from the corporate site to the local provider to the other sites. An additional connection between New York and Boston provides redundancy. The frame relay network allows the company to pay for only the bandwidth it needs between sites and can be configured to create redundant PVCs if necessary, precluding the need for customers to pay for the additional connection.

ATM Networks Asynchronous Transfer Mode (ATM) is a high-speed network technology designed for both LAN and WAN use. ATM is a Data Link–layer technology, so it specifies the format of data frames and the media access method. ATM can run over fiber-optic SONET networks and T-carrier connections in WANs and Cat 5 or higher UTP and STP cable in LANs. Because it specifies only the Data Link layer, the Physical layer doesn't matter, as long as it supports the bandwidth the ATM application requires. Fiber-optic media is used most commonly in WAN applications. ATM bandwidth can be as low as a few Mbps up to 622 Mbps (OC-12), but the most common speed is 155 Mbps, an OC-3 SONET connection.

ATM is a cell-based packet-switching technology, in which the cells are a fixed length instead of the variable-length packets used in typical packet-based systems. In an ATM environment, data travels in short, 53-byte cells: 5 bytes of header information and 48 bytes of data. If a transmission (or the last cell in a transmission) is fewer than 53 bytes, the cell is padded to make up the difference. Fixed-length cells can be switched more efficiently than variable-length packets and are more predictable for time-sensitive data, such as voice and video. The predictable nature of fixed-length cells means a higher level of QoS for video and audio streaming and teleconferencing applications, among others.

Like frame relay, ATM uses virtual circuits created between the source and destination before cells are transferred, making ATM a connection-oriented technology that has the reliability of a circuit-switched technology and the flexibility and cost-effectiveness of a packet-switching technology. Conceptually, an ATM WAN looks much like the frame relay WAN shown previously in Figure 10-9.

ATM originated as a telephone company technology and is used quite heavily for the backbone and infrastructure in large communication companies. The wide availability and low cost of Gigabit and faster Ethernet speeds have diminished ATM's role as a LAN technology. When it's used in LANs, a service called "LAN Emulation (LANE)" must be used that encapsulates Ethernet frames into the correct cell format for transmission on an ATM network.

Because of Gigabit Ethernet's popularity, ATM is best suited for LAN applications in which voice, data, and time-sensitive information travel on the same media. ATM is also a solid choice, along with frame relay, for any type of high-bandwidth WAN application.

MPLS Networks Multiprotocol Label Switching (MPLS) has become a popular WAN technology because of its scalability and flexibility. It works with any Network-layer protocol and is independent of the Data Link–layer technology. Consequently, MPLS runs over ATM, frame relay, SONET, and even Ethernet, among other Layer 2 technologies. Because MPLS works as a sort of go-between for Layers 2 and 3, it's often referred to as a "Layer 2.5 technology."

MPLS creates a connection-oriented virtual circuit with labels assigned to each packet. These labels are used to make packet-forwarding decisions in the MPLS network, making it unnecessary to view packet contents. Other technologies, such as frame relay and ATM, have used similar techniques, but MPLS has the advantage of using the best of these technologies.

Although MPLS is capable of supporting different Layer 3 protocols, currently it's used exclusively in IP networks, supporting both IPv4 and IPv6. It was first envisioned as a technology targeted at improving routing speed because of the simpler function of routing based on labels rather than IP addresses. However, faster routing technologies have made this reason a moot point. Nonetheless, MPLS has evolved into a crucial technology for large-scale IP WANs. Some applications include network traffic engineering (because it enables network engineers to better control the path traffic takes through a network) and high-speed VPNs. Being able to finely control the path of traffic allows network engineers to implement quality of service (QoS) more easily. MPLS simplifies VPN deployment in large multisite VPN applications.

For an overview of MPLS, see *www.protocols.com/papers/mpls.htm*.

WANs over the Internet

Using VPN connections over inexpensive Internet connections is a popular WAN alternative to the methods already discussed. VPN connections can be used for secure communication from branch offices to the main office. In addition, VPNs aren't limited to broadband connections; a branch office that needs the dedicated bandwidth of a T1 or T3 connection can use a leased line as its gateway to the Internet and run a VPN over it to establish a secure connection with the main office. VPNs offer the following advantages over other WAN methods:

- *Inexpensive*—The cost of Internet access is much lower than leased lines or packet-switched WAN connections, particularly if broadband Internet is used.

- *Convenience*—A VPN can be configured as soon as Internet access is established, which can usually be done much faster than the sometimes complex installation and configuration of a traditional WAN connection.

- *Security*—Advanced authentication and encryption protocols protect the integrity and privacy of VPN traffic. Leased lines and packet-switched WANs, although usually considered secure, are still vulnerable to prying eyes while moving through the provider's network.

- *Flexibility*—After a VPN infrastructure is in place, it's available for WAN connections from branch offices as well as mobile users and telecommuters.

Although using a VPN for WAN connections has plenty of advantages, there are some drawbacks, most notably the unpredictable nature of the Internet. A VPN probably isn't a good solution for mission-critical applications because unlike a traditional WAN, you're paying only for the connection between your site and your ISP. After the data goes outside your ISP's network, the connection's speed and reliability are out of the ISP's hands and out of your control. With a traditional WAN, you're paying for an end-to-end connection, and your provider is responsible for your data throughout its entire journey.

VPNs are made secure through encryption and authentication protocols, but the data nonetheless travels through the public Internet. Given enough time and resources, almost any encryption protocol can be broken, and some companies dealing with highly sensitive data might prefer that their data travel on a private dedicated network.

Table 10-2 summarizes the WAN connection methods discussed in this section.

Table 10-2   WAN connection methods

WAN connection method	Description	Technologies	Advantages	Disadvantages
Circuit switched	Creates a temporary dedicated connection between sender and receiver	POTS, ISDN	Inexpensive, available everywhere, dedicated bandwidth	Low bandwidth; nonpermanent connect requires setup time; suspect reliability
Leased line	Provides a dedicated, permanent point-to-point link from end to end	T-carriers, SONET	Secure, reliable, dedicated bandwidth for mission-critical applications	Expensive
Packet switched	Packets travel through virtual circuits created in the provider's switches	X.25, frame relay, ATM	Pay only for bandwidth you need; less expensive than leased lines	Bandwidth shared with other customers; potential security concerns
VPN over Internet	Uses an Internet connection with authentication and encryption to provide a secure connection to the LAN	Broadband cable modem and DSL, dial-up Internet, FiOS, leased lines	Convenient and inexpensive; uses existing Internet connections; available anywhere an Internet connection is available	Unpredictable service level because of the nature of the Internet

As Internet access speeds become faster, with technologies such as Fiber Optic Service (FiOS) offered by Verizon bringing them up to 500 Mbps speeds, VPN over Internet becomes a more attractive WAN option than ever.

WAN Equipment

You have already learned some terms for the technologies that make WANs work, such as ISDN, ATM, and frame relay. The following sections explain how WANs are implemented.

Customer Equipment   When an organization must build a WAN to connect geographically dispersed resources, some equipment is the organization's responsibility, and some is the provider's responsibility. The organization requiring a WAN's services is always referred to as the "customer," and the equipment at the customer site that's usually the customer's responsibility is called the **customer premises equipment** (CPE). The customer might own or lease the equipment from the provider. CPE usually includes devices such as routers, modems, and CSUs/DSUs. Modems are needed when some type of analog connectivity is involved, and CSUs/DSUs are required for digital circuits.

Every WAN has a connection from the customer equipment (usually a cable from the CSU/DSU or modem) to a junction panel called the **demarcation point**: the point at which the CPE ends and the provider's responsibility begins. This junction is where the physical WAN connection is made from the customer to the telco or ISP (the provider).

Provider Equipment   The provider location nearest the customer site is usually referred to as the "central office (CO)," and the network medium runs from the customer site demarcation point to the CO of the WAN service provider. The medium is usually coaxial copper or fiber-optic cable and is the provider's responsibility. For a wireless connection to the provider, a wireless transmitter is usually mounted on the customer's building. The connection between the demarcation point and the CO is called the **local loop** (or "last mile"). The equipment specific to the WAN technology is usually placed at the CO. This equipment might be a frame relay switch, an ATM switch, a CSU/DSU, or another WAN device, depending on the type of WAN connection.

Going the Last Mile The CPE must be able to send data in the correct format to the connection that makes up the local loop and receive data coming from this connection. This requirement is where the CSU/DSU or modem comes in. The device that sends data to (and receives data from) the local loop is called **data circuit-terminating equipment (DCE)** or sometimes "data communication equipment," and the CSU/DSU or modem is called the "DCE device." The device that passes data from the customer's LAN to the DCE is called **data terminal equipment (DTE)**. A typical DTE is a router or bridge that has one connection to the customer's LAN and another connection to the DCE that makes the WAN connection. Figure 10-10 illustrates this arrangement.

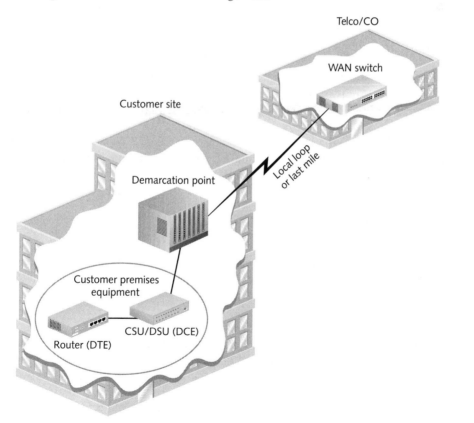

Figure 10-10 A WAN connection showing the CPE, demarcation point, and local loop

As you can see, getting all these definitions straight is half the struggle of understanding how to specify, design, and support these technologies.

Wireless WAN Technologies

Most WANs used to connect LANs have a wired technology, such as those discussed earlier in this chapter. Wireless WANs are used mostly for last-mile communication where wired WAN technologies aren't available or for mobile Internet connections, such as those used for Internet access on smartphones. Here are the three most common technologies for wireless WAN connections:

- *802.16 WiMAX*—IEEE 802.16 defines the Worldwide Interoperability for Microwave Access (WiMAX) standard, which was originally designed as a wireless MAN technology to bring Internet access to outlying areas. WiMAX is available as 802.16-2004 (fixed WiMAX, previously named 802.16d) or 802.16e (mobile WiMAX). These standards provide wireless broadband to outlying and rural areas, where last-mile wired connections are too expensive or impractical because of rough terrain, and to mobile users so that they can maintain a high-speed connection while on the road. Fixed WiMAX delivers up to 70 Mbps of bandwidth at distances up to 30 miles, and mobile WiMAX has a coverage area of 3 to 10 miles. Besides providing wireless network service to outlying areas, fixed WiMAX can be used to deliver wireless Internet access to entire metropolitan areas instead of the limited-area hotspots available with 802.11. It can blanket an area up to a mile in radius, compared with just a few hundred feet for 802.11. A newer standard, WiMAX 2 (802.16m, released in 2011), offers up to 100 Mbps speeds. Despite the promise of the WiMAX technology, it has largely lost out to newer 4G technologies—most notably LTE, discussed next.

- *LTE*—Long Term Evolution and its successor, LTE-Advanced, have largely cornered the mobile Internet access market. In the United States, all major cell phone carriers use LTE for smartphone data service, with download speeds reaching more than 30 Mbps and upload speeds more than 20 Mbps for some carriers. LTE-Advanced has theoretical speeds up to 3 Gbps for download and 1.5 Gbps for upload, although in practice, download speeds for fixed (non-mobile) devices is closer to about 1 Gbps and 100 Mbps for mobile devices. LTE is evolving quickly and is poised to be the wireless Internet standard for the foreseeable future.

 The term "4G," which simply means "fourth generation," is used to describe wireless standards, such as WiMAX and LTE. If your smartphone has an LTE connection, it probably indicates it with a 4G icon in the status bar. 3G technologies maxed out at 384 Kbps, 2G technologies delivered up to 240 Kbps, and 1G technology was voice only.

- *Satellite*—Satellite Internet access is offered by a few providers to customers who don't have access to wired or land-based wireless solutions. It requires a dish antenna mounted with a clear view of the southern sky (in North America). Satellite services are provided by geosynchronous satellites orbiting about 22,000 miles above the Earth. These satellites travel at the same rate as the earth rotates, so after an antenna is pointed in the right direction to make a connection, the connection is maintained. One problem with satellite communication is that it's affected by weather events, such as snow and rain. Satellite Internet providers can deliver up to 3 Mbps download and 1 Mbps upload. These rates are satisfactory compared with dial-up but fall short of most wired and other wireless options. In addition, for time-sensitive applications, such as voice, latency can be a problem caused by the distance the signal must travel.

Remote Access Networking

Large and small businesses alike are using fast, affordable remote access technologies that enable employees to access their office desktops and company resources from home and while on the road. VPNs are the favored method for remote access connections, but dial-up access is still widely supported by client and server OSs.

Windows Server includes the Routing and Remote Access feature, which supports both dial-up remote access and VPN remote access. Windows client OSs can create dial-up or VPN network connections to a remote access server. Figure 10-11 shows how a Windows remote access server might interact with a LAN to handle VPN and dial-up access for a private LAN. Windows offers local area routing services as well as the capability to route between one or more remote or local connections.

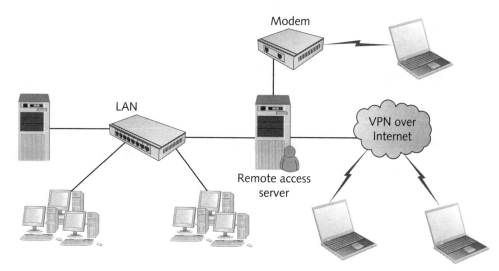

Figure 10-11   Windows Server provides remote connectivity to clients

With a remote access server configured on the LAN, users can dial in over POTS or use a VPN with any type of Internet connection. After the remote access connection is established, the remotely connected computer acts as though it were connected directly to the network, albeit more slowly.

The option for users to connect to a Windows remote access server is disabled by default for security reasons. This feature must be enabled in a user's account settings and/or set by configuring remote access policies on the Windows server.

Making a VPN Connection in Windows

Configuring a VPN connection in Windows is a straightforward process. In Windows, you create a new connection in the Network and Sharing Center by selecting "Set up a new connection or network," which starts the Set Up a Connection or Network Wizard (see Figure 10-12). To set up a VPN connection, click "Connect to a workplace."

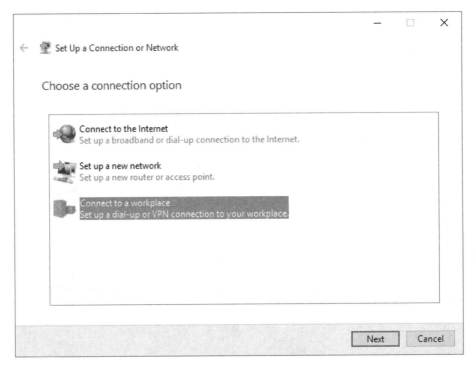

Figure 10-12   The Set Up a Connection or Network Wizard

In the next window, you specify using an Internet connection or dialing in directly. For a VPN, choose "Use my Internet connection (VPN)." From there, you simply enter the name or address of the VPN server along with your username and password. Windows attempts to make the connection by using the PPTP, L2TP, and SSTP protocols until a connection is made. Alternatively, you can select a specific VPN protocol in the VPN Connection Properties dialog box (see Figure 10-13).

As you can see, there are a number of options for authenticating to the VPN. The default settings usually work when connecting to a remote access server, but other authentication options might be necessary to connect to third-party VPN servers. After the VPN connection is made, the client connection is assigned an IP address on the network.

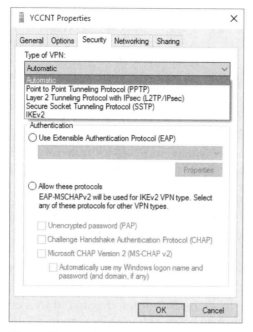

Figure 10-13 Selecting a VPN protocol

Making a Dial-Up Connection

All versions of Windows include **Dial-Up Networking** (DUN) software to make a remote connection. The DUN client also connects computers to ISPs for dial-up Internet access. The protocol that makes dial-up and most VPN connections possible is **Point-to-Point Protocol** (PPP). It operates at the Data Link and Network layers and is used to carry a variety of protocols over different types of network connections. Although PPP is best known for use in dial-up networks, it also provides advanced features (authentication and IP address assignment, for example) to other types of WAN connections, such as leased lines and ISDN.

PPP allows WAN connections to use a variety of network protocols, including TCP/IP and IPX/SPX, and includes advanced authentication services. Its flexibility comes from the two protocols that are integral to PPP:

- *Link Control Protocol (LCP)*—LCP sets up the PPP connection, defines communication parameters and authentication protocols, and terminates the link when a call or connection is ended. It works at the Data Link layer of the OSI model.

- *Network Control Protocol (NCP)*—NCP encapsulates higher-layer protocols, such as IP, and provides services such as dynamic IP addressing. It can carry multiple protocols because it contains a field to indicate which protocol is encapsulated in each packet. NCP works at both the Data Link and Network layers.

In Windows, dial-up connections are made much like VPN connections. The main difference is that you select "Dial directly" instead of "Use my Internet connection" and enter the phone number of the remote access server instead of its Internet address. Obviously, you must have a dial-up modem installed to make a dial-up connection.

 Serial Line Internet Protocol (SLIP) is an older protocol that PCs use to connect to the Internet via a modem. It provides connectivity across phone lines with no error correction and no secure authentication and doesn't support dynamic IP address assignment. SLIP is not a secure protocol and is no longer supported in Windows client OSs or remote access services.

Remote Access Networking via the Web

Dial-up networking and VPN connect your computer to a network, making it behave as though it were located on the LAN. Another remote access model in common use is remote control of your desktop via a Web browser. Several online services are available for connecting your Web browser to your desktop, including LogMeIn and GoToMyPC. Using these services, you install a client component on your computer and then log on to the online service, which connects your Web browser to your computer's desktop. These services use authentication and encryption to maintain a secure connection. No-frills versions of these services are available free, and you can purchase services offering advanced features, such as remote file transfer and desktop sharing with other users, for a monthly or annual fee.

Using a third-party remote desktop solution is convenient and frees IT staff from having to support dial-up or VPN servers. However, not all networks permit this type of remote access for security reasons. Microsoft has a solution called Remote Desktop Gateway that allows remote desktop connections via Secure Sockets Layer (SSL), the protocol that secures communication between Web browsers and Web servers. It doesn't use a Web browser to make the remote desktop connection. Instead, remote users use the standard Remote Desktop Protocol (RDP) client to access their desktops without having to establish a VPN or dial-up connection. After the gateway is set up, remote users just specify the Remote Desktop Gateway server settings in the RDP client (see Figure 10-14).

Figure 10-14 Remote Desktop Gateway server settings on the RDP client

Enter ↵

HANDS-ON PROJECTS

Hands-On Project 10-1: Creating a Dial-up Connection

Time Required: 10 minutes

Objective: Create a dial-up connection in Windows 10.

Required Tools and Equipment: Net-*XX*

Description: In this project, you configure a dial-up connection in Windows 10. You probably don't have a modem installed, so you simply go through the steps with an invalid phone number.

1. Log on to your computer as **NetAdmin**.

2. Open the Network and Sharing Center, and click **Set up a new connection or network**.

3. In the "Choose a connection option" window, click **Connect to a workplace**, and then click **Next**.

4. In the "How do you want to connect?" window (see Figure 10-15), click **Dial directly**. If your computer has no modem installed, you see the message "Windows could not detect a dial-up modem." Click **Set up a connection anyway**.

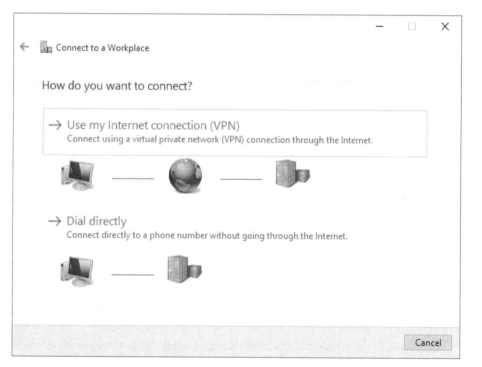

Figure 10-15 Selecting a connection type

5. In the "Type the telephone number to connect to" window, type **555-1234** in the Telephone number text box, and then click **Next**.

6. In the "Type your user name and password" window, type **RemoteUser** in the User name text box and **Password01** in the Password text box. If you're dialing into a

Windows domain network, you can also enter the domain where your user account resides. Click **Create**.

7. Click **Change adapter settings** in the Network and Sharing Center. Right-click **Dial-up Connection** and click **Properties**.

8. Click the **Options** tab, and review the settings you can configure. Click **PPP Settings**.

9. In the PPP Settings dialog box, review the options you can configure for PPP, and then click **Cancel**.

10. In the Dial-up Connection Properties dialog box, click the **Security** tab, and review the encryption and authentication options.

11. In the Dial-up Connection Properties dialog box, click the **Networking** tab. Notice that all protocols except File and Printer Sharing for Microsoft Networks are selected. This protocol is disabled for remote access connections to prevent remote users from accessing your shared files. Click **Cancel**, and stay logged on for the next project.

Hands-On Project 10-2: Creating a VPN Connection

Time Required: 10 minutes

Objective: Create a VPN connection in Windows 10.

Required Tools and Equipment: Net-XX and, if possible, a VPN server set up by the instructor

Description: In this project, you configure a VPN connection in Windows 10. If you have a VPN server to connect to, ask your instructor for the correct address, which you need in Step 5. You also need a username and password.

1. Log on to your computer as **NetAdmin**, if necessary.

2. Open the Network and Sharing Center, and click **Set up a new connection or network**.

3. In the "Choose a connection option" window, click **Connect to a workplace**, and then click **Next**. In the "Do you want to use a connection that you already have?" window, make sure **No, create a new connection** is selected, and then click **Next**.

4. In the "How do you want to connect?" window, click **Use my Internet connection (VPN)**.

5. In the "Type the Internet address to connect to" window, type **vpn.mydomain.com** in the Internet address text box if you don't have an actual VPN server to connect to. If your instructor gave you a VPN server's name or IP address, enter this information instead. Click **Create**.

6. Click **Change adapter settings**, and then double-click **VPN Connection**. In the Network & Internet control panel, click **VPN Connection** (shown in Figure 10-16), and then click **Connect**. In the Sign in dialog box, type **VPNUser** in the User name text box and **Password01** in the Password text box, unless your instructor gives you a different user-name and password. If you're connecting to a Windows domain network, you can also enter the domain where your user account resides.

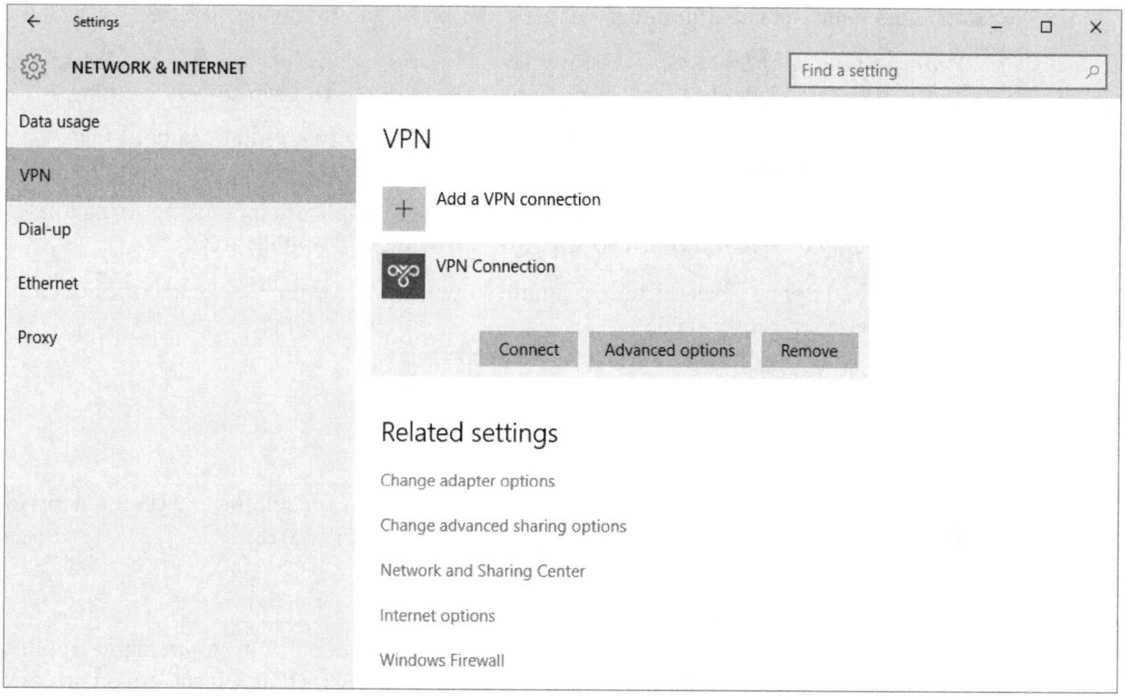

Figure 10-16 Making a VPN connection

7. If you're connecting to an actual VPN server, click **OK**; otherwise, click **Cancel**.

8. If you connected to an actual VPN server, open a command prompt window, and then type `ipconfig/all` and press **Enter** to view the address settings assigned to your VPN connection. The assigned IP address is an address on the VPN server's network. Close the command prompt window and all other open windows.

Cloud Computing

Many people rely on the Internet's services for communication, research, and entertainment. This trend has continued to the point that many functions once handled in a company's IT center are now handled by servers on the Internet—what's referred to as "cloud computing." **Cloud computing** is a networking model in which data, applications, and processing power are managed by servers on the Internet, and users of these resources pay for what they use rather than for the equipment and software needed to provide resources. It's like paying only for cell phone minutes you use instead of paying for the cell phone towers and switching equipment needed to make your phone work.

The word "cloud" is used to indicate obscuring the details of equipment and software that actually provide resources. For the most part, customers don't care whether equipment consists of Windows or Linux servers, large tower computers, or rack-mounted computers, just as you don't care how your cell phone makes a call, as long as it works.

For some companies, cloud computing's allure is based on the following benefits:

- *Reduced physical plant costs*—Having fewer servers means less space is needed to house them, and less electricity and cooling are required to keep servers running.

- *Reduced upfront costs*—Paying only for services and software that are used means a company can avoid the startup costs of purchasing hardware and software.

- *Reduced personnel costs*—Having fewer servers and applications to support means fewer IT employees are needed to support hardware and applications.

Although cloud computing has seemingly limitless applications, three main categories of cloud computing have taken center stage:

- Software as a service

- Platform as a service

- Infrastructure as a service

The phrase "as a service" simply means the resource resides on another server or network than the one using the resource, and customers use it as a paid service.

Software as a Service

Software as a service (SaaS) is also called "hosted applications" or "on-demand applications" because the customer doesn't actually buy any software that's installed on its own equipment. Instead, the customer pays for the use of applications that run on a service provider's network. The most well-known examples are Google Apps and Microsoft Office 365, which a business or a home user can use to run hosted applications, such as e-mail, calendar, word-processing, and spreadsheet programs. More complex applications involve large database systems, such as payroll services from ADP and customer relationship management software offered by companies such as Salesforce.com.

SaaS is usually offered as a subscription based on the number of users using the application. It takes the burden of installation and maintenance off the customer so that companies can focus on maintaining their LANs and Internet access instead of maintaining hundreds of copies of an installed application. In addition, customers can take advantage of new software editions much faster than the standard deployment times of traditional application upgrades. Some application upgrades require client computer or OS upgrades, but with SaaS, the vendor handles infrastructure upgrades when needed.

In addition, SaaS is available anywhere the customer has a connection to the Internet. Mobile users and telecommuters have access to the same applications they use in the office without having to install the software on their laptops or home computers. Some applications can't even be installed on home computers, but with SaaS, the software runs on remote servers, so local installations aren't necessary.

Platform as a Service

Platform as a service (PaaS)—also called "hosted platform"—is similar to SaaS, but the customer develops applications with the service provider's tools and infrastructure. After applications are developed, they can be delivered to the customer's users from the provider's servers. This setup differs from SaaS, in which the service provider owns the applications delivered to users; with PaaS, the customer develops and owns the application and then delivers it to a third party.

Developers who use PaaS can take advantage of many of the same benefits as users of SaaS. In addition, after an application is developed with PaaS, the developer can usually deploy the application immediately to customers who access it as a hosted application. The same operating environment used to develop the application is used to run it, which bypasses the sometimes complex and problem-prone process of migrating from a traditional development environment to a production environment.

The most common PaaS products are Salesforce.com's Apex, Azure for Windows, Google's AppEngine for Python and Java, WaveMaker for Ajax, and Engine Yard for Ruby on Rails. Others are available, but details on these development platforms are beyond the scope of this book. PaaS is still an evolving model for application development, and platforms will come and go as developers weed out what works and what doesn't. Developing in the cloud is likely here to stay because it offers benefits that aren't usually available in a locally managed environment. In addition, because small businesses and individual developers have access to expensive, full-featured development environments, entrepreneurs can be on an equal footing with the big boys, which increases competition and innovation—and that's always a good thing.

Infrastructure as a Service

Infrastructure as a service (IaaS), or "hosted infrastructure," allows companies to use a vendor's storage or even entire virtual servers as needed. Traditionally, if a company needs another 100 GB of storage to house a new database, it has to buy a new hard drive—assuming the server can accommodate a new hard drive. By using IaaS, the company simply pays for another 100 GB of space without worrying about how that space is actually provided. In addition, if a customer needs another server to handle its application workload, it simply pays for the amount of processing and storage the additional server actually requires instead of the physical device. In most cases, IaaS servers are virtualized (as discussed in Chapter 11), meaning they run as virtual machines on more powerful physical servers.

IaaS differs from other hosted services because customers mostly rent the resources they're using but are still responsible for application installation and upgrade. So although IT staff can be reduced because the IaaS vendor handles physical device upkeep, customers still need IT staff to configure and manage applications and server OSs.

IaaS isn't just for server infrastructure. Companies can "upgrade" to the latest OSs and desktop applications by using virtualized desktops through their IaaS providers. By accessing desktops remotely, IaaS customers can use thin clients (client computers with minimal hardware resources) or computers with older OSs to make use of the latest desktop OSs and applications. This IaaS feature—called "virtual desktop infrastructure (VDI)"—is becoming a popular way for companies to deliver desktop OSs and applications instead of using traditional methods of installing OSs and applications locally.

Cloud computing isn't for every company or situation, but it offers a flexible array of services that can complement an IT department's existing resources and sometimes replace them. The trend toward cloud computing is growing with no abatement in sight. Only time will tell whether it's a flash-in-the-pan model or one that will become an integral part of daily computing.

Private Cloud Versus Public Cloud

The cloud technologies covered in this section have been discussed in the context of a third party providing services to customers via the Internet. However, many companies deliver cloud services to their own employees through the use of virtualization technologies, such as VMware and Microsoft Hyper-V. VDI, cloud storage, and SaaS are commonly accessed as **private cloud** services, deployed from the company's own data center instead of using a third party—a **public cloud** service. This setup gives a company more control and more security yet still gives its employees many of the benefits of cloud computing.

Chapter Summary

- The most obvious difference between internetworks and WANs is the distance between the LANs being connected. WANs differ from internetworks in two other critical areas: the use of carriers or service providers and the use of serial communication technologies that can span long distances.

- Several types of devices are typically used in WANs for media access, signal transmission, and reception and to connect a WAN to a LAN: modems, channel service units/data service units, and routers.

- The methods of creating a WAN connection often dictate the technologies that can be used and the connection's properties. The most common connection methods are circuit-switched WANs, leased lines, packet-switched WANs, and VPN over the Internet.

- WAN equipment can be categorized as customer equipment, provider equipment, and the circuit that makes the connection between the demarcation point and the central office.

- Wireless WAN technologies include 802.16 WiMAX, LTE provided by cell phone carriers, and satellite. These technologies are used mainly for access to the Internet rather than LAN-to-LAN connections.

- Large and small businesses alike are using fast, affordable remote access technologies that enable employees to access their desktops and company resources from home and while on the road. VPNs are the favored method for remote access connections, but dial-up access is still supported by client and server OSs.

- Cloud computing is a networking model in which data, applications, and processing power are managed by servers on the Internet, and users of these resources pay for what they use instead of the equipment and software needed to provide resources.

- There are three main categories of cloud computing: SaaS (hosted applications), PaaS (hosted platforms), and IaaS (hosted infrastructure). Cloud computing can be further categorized as private cloud or public cloud. With a private cloud, a company delivers cloud services to its employees; public cloud services use a third-party provider.

Key Terms

analog signal   A signal, represented by a sine wave, that varies over time continually and smoothly.

Asynchronous Transfer Mode (ATM)   A high-speed, cell-based packet-switching technology designed for both LAN and WAN use; uses connection-oriented switches to allow senders and receivers to communicate over a network.

Basic Rate Interface (BRI)   An ISDN format that consists of two 64-Kbps B-channels and a 16-Kbps D channel; generally used for remote connections. *See also* Integrated Services Digital Network (ISDN).

channel service unit/data service unit (CSU/DSU)   A device that creates a digital connection between a LAN device, such as a router, and the WAN link from the service provider.

circuit-switched WAN   A type of WAN connection in which a temporary dedicated connection is established between sender and receiver on demand.

cloud computing   A networking model in which data, applications, and processing power are managed by servers on the Internet, and users of these resources pay for what they use rather than the equipment and software needed to provide resources.

Committed Information Rate (CIR)   A guaranteed minimum transmission rate offered by the service provider.

customer premises equipment (CPE)   The equipment at the customer site that's usually the responsibility of the customer.

data circuit-terminating equipment (DCE)   The device that sends data to (and receives data from) the last mile; usually a CSU/DSU or modem. *See also* channel service unit/data service unit (CSU/DSU) *and* local loop.

data terminal equipment (DTE)   The device that passes data from the customer LAN to the DCE; usually a router. *See also* data circuit-terminating equipment (DCE).

demarcation point   The point at which the CPE ends and the provider's responsibility begins. *See also* customer premises equipment (CPE).

Dial-Up Networking (DUN)   The Windows software component (beginning with Windows 95) for setting up a connection to an RRAS server or connecting computers to ISPs for dial-up Internet access.

digital signal   Represented as a square wave, a signal that uses binary 1s and 0s to represent two possible states.

fractionalized   The term used to describe a T-carrier line in which portions are dedicated for different purposes. *See also* T-carrier lines.

frame relay   A PVC packet-switching technology that offers WAN communication over a fast, reliable, digital link. Throughput is usually improved because error checking is done on endpoint devices instead of on the digital link. *See also* permanent virtual circuits (PVCs).

infrastructure as a service (IaaS)   A category of cloud computing in which a company can use a provider's storage or virtual servers as its needs demand; also called "hosted infrastructure."

Integrated Services Digital Network (ISDN) A digital WAN technology developed to replace the analog phone system. It defines communication channels of 64 Kbps and is most often used by SOHO users.

local loop The connection between a WAN's demarcation point and the central office (CO); also called the "last mile." *See also* demarcation point.

modem A device that converts a sending computer's digital signals to analog signals for transmission over phone lines and then converts analog signals to digital signals for the receiving computer.

multiplexing A technology that supports simultaneous communication links over the same set of cables, so data transmissions from several sources can be combined and delivered over a single cable.

Multiprotocol Label Switching (MPLS) A highly scalable, flexible WAN technology that works with any Network-layer protocol and is independent of the Data Link layer technology; used exclusively in IP networks. It creates a connection-oriented virtual circuit, using labels assigned to each packet that make it unnecessary to view packet contents.

packet-switched WAN A type of WAN network in which data is transmitted in frames or packets, and each packet is transmitted through the provider's network independently. Instead of having a dedicated circuit over which data travels, a provider's customers share the bandwidth.

permanent virtual circuits (PVCs) Pathways between two communication points that are established as permanent logical connections; therefore, the pathway exists even when it's not in use. *See also* virtual circuit.

platform as a service (PaaS) A category of cloud computing in which a customer develops applications with the service provider's development tools and infrastructure; also called "hosted platform." After applications are developed, they can be delivered to the customer's users from the provider's servers.

Point-to-Point Protocol (PPP) A remote access protocol that supports many protocols and is used to carry data over a variety of network connections.

Primary Rate Interface (PRI) An ISDN format that consists of 23 64-Kbps B-channels and one 64-Kbps D-channel. *See also* Integrated Services Digital Network (ISDN).

private cloud Cloud services that a company delivers to its own employees.

public cloud Cloud services delivered by a third-party provider.

smart jack A type of connector for terminating a T1 line that provides diagnostic testing for troubleshooting the connection.

software as a service (SaaS) A category of cloud computing in which a customer pays for the use of applications that run on a service provider's network; also called "hosted applications."

switched virtual circuits (SVCs) A communication circuit that's established when needed and then terminated when the transmission is completed. *See also* virtual circuit.

Synchronous Optical Network (SONET) A flexible, highly fault-tolerant technology that can carry signals of different capacities over a fiber-optic network at high speeds. It defines optical carrier (OC) levels for incrementally increasing data rates, and SONET networks can be arranged in a variety of physical topologies.

T-carrier lines Communication lines that use one pair of wires for transmitting data and another pair for receiving data. They use the TDM signaling method, making it possible to extract any number of channels for a particular purpose. *See also* time division multiplexing (TDM).

time division multiplexing (TDM) A signaling method that allocates a time slot for each channel, making it possible to transmit multiple streams, or channels, of data on a single physical medium.

virtual circuit A logical connection created between two devices in a shared network, with bandwidth allocated for a specific transmission pathway through the network.

X.25 A packet-switching technology that provides an interface between public packet-switching networks and their customers; it has the advantage of running effectively over older copper phone lines. X.25 networks are SVC networks, meaning they create the best available pathway at the time of transmission. *See also* switched virtual circuits (SVCs).

Review Questions

1. In which of the following areas does a WAN differ from an internetwork? (Choose all that apply.)
   a. WANs use service providers for the network connection.
   b. WANs can't transport Network-layer protocols.
   c. WANs use serial communication technologies that can span miles.
   d. WANs don't use routers.

2. Which of the following is a device used to make WAN connections? (Choose all that apply.)
   a. 10BaseT hub
   b. CSU/DSU
   c. Router
   d. Ethernet repeater

3. Which of the following best describes a digital signal?
   a. A signal that varies over time continually and smoothly
   b. A signal whose states vary much like a lamp controlled by a dimmer switch
   c. A channel service unit
   d. A series of binary values

4. For what purpose is a CSU/DSU used?
   a. Modulates a digital signal into an analog signal
   b. Creates a digital connection between a LAN device and the WAN link
   c. Routes packets from the LAN to the WAN
   d. Creates a WAN connection over the public switched telephone network

5. Which of the following is a common WAN connection method? (Choose all that apply.)

  a. Circuit switched

  b. Packet leased

  c. VPN over POTS

  d. Packet switched

6. Which of the following is true about ISDN?

  a. It uses a modem to modulate/demodulate the signal.

  b. Its BRI format consists of two B-channels and one D-channel.

  c. Its PRI format provides bandwidth up to 128 Kbps.

  d. It uses a terminal adapter to connect to the network.

7. Which of the following is a typical situation in which leased lines should be considered? (Choose all that apply.)

  a. Occasional use of the WAN link is needed.

  b. 24/7 access is required.

  c. Fast upstream and downstream communications are needed.

  d. You want to pay for only the bandwidth you use.

8. Which of the following combines several communication streams into a single faster communication stream?

  a. Multiplexing

  b. Demultiplexing

  c. CSU

  d. DSU

9. Which physical topology does SONET readily support? (Choose all that apply.)

  a. Point-to-point

  b. Star

  c. Ring

  d. Bus

10. Which of the following technologies uses packet-switching? (Choose all that apply.)

  a. ISDN

  b. Frame relay

  c. T1

  d. X.25

11. Which of the following technologies provides permanent virtual circuits? (Choose all that apply.)

    a. PSTN

    b. Frame relay

    c. X.25

    d. ISDN

12. Which technology uses 53-byte cells?

    a. POTS

    b. ATM

    c. Frame relay

    d. X.25

13. To maintain security, WAN connections over the Internet should use which of the following?

    a. BRI

    b. LANE

    c. OC-3

    d. VPN

14. What type of device is required to connect to a dedicated digital communication line?

    a. modem

    b. NIC

    c. CSU/DSU

    d. LANE

15. Which term best describes the place in a WAN connection where the customer's responsibility ends and the provider's responsibility begins?

    a. Data circuit-terminating equipment

    b. Demarcation point

    c. CPE

    d. Central office

16. Which of the following places data on the local loop?

    a. DCE

    b. DTE

    c. Router

    d. CPE

17. Which of the following is the equipment at the customer site that's the responsibility of the customer?

    a. DTE

    b. DCE

    c. Demarcation point

    d. CPE

18. Which of the following is a VPN protocol supported by Windows remote access? (Choose all that apply.)

    a. PPTP

    b. L2TP

    c. HTTP

    d. SSTP

19. Which of the following is a component of the PPP protocol? (Choose all that apply.)

    a. Link Control Protocol

    b. NCP

    c. VPN

    d. RDP

20. Which of the following can best be described as developing applications by using a service provider's development tools and infrastructure?

    a. Hosted applications

    b. Hosted networking

    c. Hosted platforms

    d. Hosted infrastructure

21. Which wireless WAN technology has a standard for fixed and mobile devices?

    a. WiMAX

    b. LTE

    c. Satellite

    d. LTE-Advanced

22. Which wireless WAN technology might not be suitable for voice applications because of latency?

    a. WiMAX

    b. LTE

    c. Satellite

    d. LTE-Advanced

Critical Thinking

The following activities give you critical thinking challenges. Challenge labs give you an opportunity to use the skills you have learned to perform a task without step-by-step instructions. Case projects offer a practical networking setup for which you supply a written solution.

Challenge Lab 10-1: Configuring a Windows Server to Accept VPN Connections

Time Required: 1 hour or more

Objective: Configure a Windows server to accept VPN connections.

Required Tools and Equipment: A Windows client computer, such as Windows 10, and a Windows Server 2016, 2012, or 2008 server. The server can be installed as a virtual machine in VMware Player or another virtualization program. You can download an evaluation version of Windows Server 2012 at *https://www.microsoft.com/en-us/evalcenter/evaluate-windows-server-2012*.

Description: In this lab, which can be done in groups, you configure a remote access server in Windows Server 2008 or later. To learn more about installing and configuring remote access in Windows Server, go to *https://technet.microsoft.com/en-us/network/dd420463*. Configure the server to assign IP addresses dynamically to VPN clients. For all other settings, use the Routing and Remote Access defaults. Then configure a Windows client to connect to the VPN server. Verify the connection by viewing connection details with the `ipconfig` command. When you have made a successful connection, answer the following questions:

- What tunneling protocol was used to make the VPN connection?

  _____

- What authentication protocol was used to authenticate the remote user?

  _____

- What property did you have to configure on the user account to allow the user to make the remote access connection?

  _____

Case Project 10-1

As the network administrator for a growing company, you're asked to solve a remote access dilemma. The 12 employees who work from home complain about not being connected to the network except by e-mail. The company also has several employees who travel and would benefit from remote access connections. The director of marketing is responsible for part of the cost and wants only the best solution. Currently, you run a Windows Server 2016 network, and users want access to all systems. Develop a plan to connect these remote users. Your solution can involve more than one remote access type.

Case Project 10-2

CNT-Books wants an affordable way to establish remote connections for its salespeople, who log on from customer sites all over the country, and its three branch offices. The company's main office is in Phoenix, Arizona, and its branch offices are in Los Angeles, California; Chicago, Illinois; and Orlando, Florida. Explain what kind of connections the salespeople and branch offices should use and what kinds of services should be installed on the main office's network to keep communication costs to a minimum.

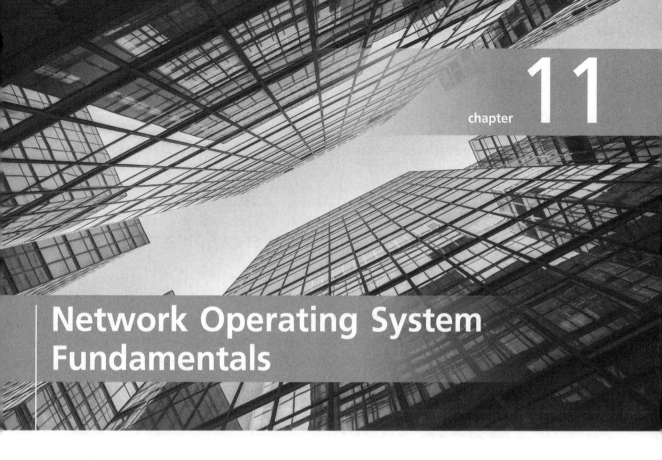

chapter 11

Network Operating System Fundamentals

After reading this chapter and completing the exercises, you will be able to:

- Explain the major components of an OS, including the file system, processes, and the kernel
- Describe client and server operating systems and compare client and server OSs
- Describe the components of virtualization and virtualization products
- Plan for an OS installation and perform postinstallation tasks

From a user's standpoint, the network operating system is the focal point of a network. A computer's OS is what users interact with when accessing a network's resources. Indeed, operating systems hide the details of network access so well that users often realize they're connected to a network only when access to network resources fails. As a network administrator, you know the network operating system (NOS) is only one piece of the network puzzle, but you're likely to spend quite a bit of time with this piece because of all the network-specific services you must install and configure.

This chapter discusses components common to almost every OS, networked or not, and then describes specific network services that network operating systems provide. In addition, virtualization, a technology that's integral to most medium and large networks and even many small networks, is introduced. Finally, the specifics of installing Windows Server 2016 and Linux are described.

Operating System Fundamentals

Table 11-1 summarizes what you need for the hands-on projects in this chapter.

Table 11-1 Hands-on project requirements

Hands-on project	Requirements	Time required	Notes
Hands-On Project 11-1: Navigating the Windows File System from the Command Prompt	Net-*XX*	20 minutes	
Hands-On Project 11-2: Navigating the Linux File System (Optional)	Net-*XX*	20 minutes	Need a Linux Live disk or a computer with Linux already installed
Hands-On Project 11-3: Using Windows Task Manager	Net-*XX*	10 minutes	
Hands-On Project 11-4: Displaying Linux Processes (Optional)	Net-*XX*	10 minutes	Need a Linux Live disk or a computer with Linux already installed
Hands-On Project 11-5: Mapping a Drive Letter	Net-*XX*	10 minutes	
Hands-On Project 11-6: Creating and Connecting to a Shared Printer	Net-*XX*	10 minutes	A computer with a shared printer that all student computers can connect to, or students can connect to each other's shared printers.
Hands-On Project 11-7: Downloading and Installing VMware Player	Net-*XX*	20 minutes	Internet access
Hands-On Project 11-8: Creating a Virtual Machine in VMware Player	Net-*XX*	15 minutes	
Hands-On Project 11-9: Installing Windows Server 2012 in a VM	Net-*XX*	30 minutes or longer	The Windows Server 2012 R2 ISO file (evaluation) downloaded from the Microsoft evaluation center

A computer's OS provides a convenient interface for users and applications to access computer hardware components. It controls access to memory, CPU, storage devices, and external input/output (I/O) devices (such as printers, webcams, scanners, and so forth). To understand the network services and tasks a contemporary NOS provides, you need a solid grasp of how an NOS manages its local resources. The following sections expand on these OS concepts introduced in Chapter 1:

- File systems
- Processes and services
- Kernel

The File System

A **file system** is the method by which an OS stores and organizes files and manages access to files on a storage device, such as a hard drive. File systems differ in how they allocate space for files, how files are located on a disk, what level of fault tolerance is built into the system, and how access to files is secured. Regardless of how these tasks are accomplished, contemporary file systems have the following objectives:

- Provide a convenient interface for users and applications to open and save files.
- Provide an efficient method to organize space on a drive.
- Provide a hierarchical filing method to store files.
- Provide an indexing system for fast retrieval of files.
- Provide secure access to files for authorized users.

User Interface When a user double-clicks a file to open it, the user interface calls the file system with a request to open the file. The file type determines exactly how the file is opened. If the file is an application, the application is loaded into memory and run by the CPU. If the file is a document, the application associated with the document type is loaded into memory and opens the file. For example, on Windows computers, if you double-click the Budget.xls file, the Excel application is loaded into memory and then opens this file. If a user creates a file or changes an existing file and wants to save it, the application calls the file system to store the new or changed file on the disk. Most users of an OS interact with the file system by using a file manager program, such as File Explorer in Windows. As a future computer or network professional, you need to have a deeper understanding of how a file system works so that you can make informed choices when you need to install a file system or troubleshoot file system–related problems.

Disk Drive Space Organization The storage space on a disk drive is divided into manageable chunks called "sectors." On most disk drives, each sector is 512 bytes. To make storage processing more efficient, sectors are grouped to make a disk cluster (also called a "block"). A **disk cluster** is the smallest amount of space that can be occupied by a file stored on the disk. For example, if you have a file system that groups four sectors to make a cluster, each cluster is 2048 (2K) bytes. So if you store a file that's 148 bytes, it occupies one cluster of 2048 bytes, which wastes 1900 bytes of storage. The waste occurs because no other file can occupy any part of a cluster already occupied by another file. If you store a file that's 10,000 bytes, it occupies five clusters, with about 240 bytes of unused, wasted space.

 Some file systems use optimization techniques to reduce wasted file space by allowing files to occupy unused sectors that are part of a cluster already in use.

You might think that having a smaller cluster size is the optimal way to organize your disk. This is true in some cases but only when mostly small files are stored on the disk because data is read from and written to the disk in cluster-sized chunks. So the smaller the clusters, the more read/write operations are required when using a file. Each read/write operation takes time, so the more operations required, the slower the system runs. If you store mostly large files on the disk, a larger cluster size usually results in better performance because fewer read/write operations need to be performed. In addition, smaller cluster sizes can lead to a fragmented disk, in which files are spread out all over the disk instead of being stored in consecutive locations. Fragmentation causes many more disk seek operations, which slows file access. Recall from Chapter 1 that the disk seek time is the amount of time required to move a drive's read/write heads to the correct position on disk platters to read or write clusters.

A disk's cluster size is selected when the disk is formatted. Most OSs set the cluster size to a medium value by default; for example, Windows sets the cluster size on NTFS-formatted disks to 4 KB. However, if you know you're going to be storing many files under 2 KB, choose a smaller cluster size when you format to reduce wasted space. If you know you're going to store mostly files larger than 16 KB, choose a larger cluster size.

The formatting process groups sectors into clusters and maps all disk clusters for fast access. In addition, clusters are marked as unused. When you format a disk containing files, the data is actually still there, but the file system can no longer access the data because it doesn't know how to find it. Third-party disk recovery programs can often recover data from a formatted disk by bypassing the file system and reading the data in each cluster.

Hierarchical Filing Method   Most file systems organize files in a hierarchy of folders or directories; the top of the hierarchy is called the "root" of the file system. ("Directory" is an older term for folder but is still used, particularly when discussing Linux file systems; however, the term "folder" is generally used in this book.) The root of the file system often represents a disk drive or other mass storage device, such as a flash drive. Off the root of the file system can be files and folders, with folders containing files and additional folders usually referred to as "subfolders." To navigate the file system and see its hierarchy with a GUI tool, such as File Explorer, users simply double-click folders and subfolders to open them and view their contents. Figure 11-1 shows a logical diagram of a typical Windows file system.

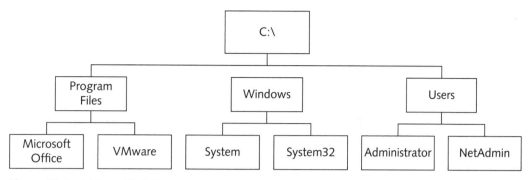

Figure 11-1 A hierarchical file system

Navigating the file system from a command prompt is a different proposition. Because users must enter the exact syntax with no typos, those who began using computers when a GUI was the standard user interface are often frustrated when trying to navigate the file system at the command prompt. However, mastering the command prompt (or shell prompt in Linux) is a valuable skill to have as a Windows administrator and essential for Linux administrators.

Commercial routers and switches are often configured with their own command-line user interfaces, so skill at the command line extends beyond working with desktop and server OSs.

File-Indexing System With today's large disk drives, more files can be stored on a hard drive, making it harder for users to find the files they need. To help solve this problem, most file systems include an indexing system that enables users to search for a file based on all or part of its filename or its contents. Users don't need to know where in the file system's hierarchy the file they need is stored; they just need to know some or all of the filename or some keywords in the file. The indexing system maintains a database that's updated as files are created, modified, and deleted. File-indexing systems can take considerable processing power, as they usually work in the background to monitor the file system and update the index as changes are made. However, they're usually configured to wait until the system is idle before performing operations. In Windows, you can configure aspects of the file system's index by clicking Indexing Options in Control Panel. Then you can select which types of files are indexed, which volumes and folders should be indexed, and whether file contents as well as file properties should be indexed. You can also change the default location of the index database, which is C:\ProgramData\Microsoft.

Secure Access to Files Computers are often shared at home or in the workplace. Each user might want to maintain a separate set of files and documents that other users can't access. In addition, files on a computer that's part of a network are potentially accessible to all users on the network. A file system's access controls, or permissions, can be used to allow only authorized users to access certain files or folders. In addition, access controls can be used to secure OS files from accidental corruption or deletion. Not all file systems have access controls, but the ones installed by default on current OSs do. Notably, the NTFS file system in Windows supports file and folder permissions, as do Linux file systems, such as Ext3. The older FAT16 and FAT32 file systems don't support file and folder permissions, so any user logged on to the system console has full access to all files stored on these file systems. The details of how these file systems work are beyond the scope of this book, but you learn more about using permissions in Windows and Linux in Chapter 12.

Hands-On Project 11-1: Navigating the Windows File System from the Command Prompt

Time Required: 20 minutes

Objective: Navigate the Windows file system from the command prompt.

Required Tools and Equipment: Net-XX

Description: In this project, you open a command prompt window and practice navigating the Windows file system from the command prompt.

1. Log on to your computer as **NetAdmin**.

2. Open a command prompt window. The prompt indicates your current file system context. Usually, when you open a command prompt window, you're placed in the file system context of your user profile. For example, if you log on as NetAdmin, the prompt is C:\Users\NetAdmin>. In this prompt, C: indicates the drive letter, and the path is \Users\NetAdmin. Type **dir** and press **Enter** to see the list of files in this folder (see Figure 11-2). The dir command displays the same information as having the NetAdmin folder open in File Explorer (see Figure 11-3).

```
Command Prompt                                    —   □   ×
C:\Users\NetAdmin>dir
 Volume in drive C has no label.
 Volume Serial Number is D0BA-D592

 Directory of C:\Users\NetAdmin

07/10/2015  02:43 PM    <DIR>          .
07/10/2015  02:43 PM    <DIR>          ..
05/23/2015  06:06 AM    <DIR>          3D Objects
05/22/2015  09:29 AM             7,752 certenroll.lo
g
07/02/2015  11:30 AM    <DIR>          Contacts
07/02/2015  11:30 AM    <DIR>          Desktop
07/07/2015  09:28 AM    <DIR>          Documents
07/02/2015  01:29 PM    <DIR>          Downloads
07/02/2015  11:30 AM    <DIR>          Favorites
07/02/2015  11:30 AM    <DIR>          Links
07/02/2015  11:30 AM    <DIR>          Music
07/02/2015  11:33 AM    <DIR>          OneDrive
07/02/2015  11:30 AM    <DIR>          Pictures
07/02/2015  11:30 AM    <DIR>          Saved Games
07/02/2015  11:30 AM    <DIR>          Searches
07/02/2015  11:30 AM    <DIR>          Videos
               1 File(s)          7,752 bytes
              15 Dir(s)  36,462,493,696 bytes free

C:\Users\NetAdmin>
```

Figure 11-2 Viewing the files in C:\Users\NetAdmin

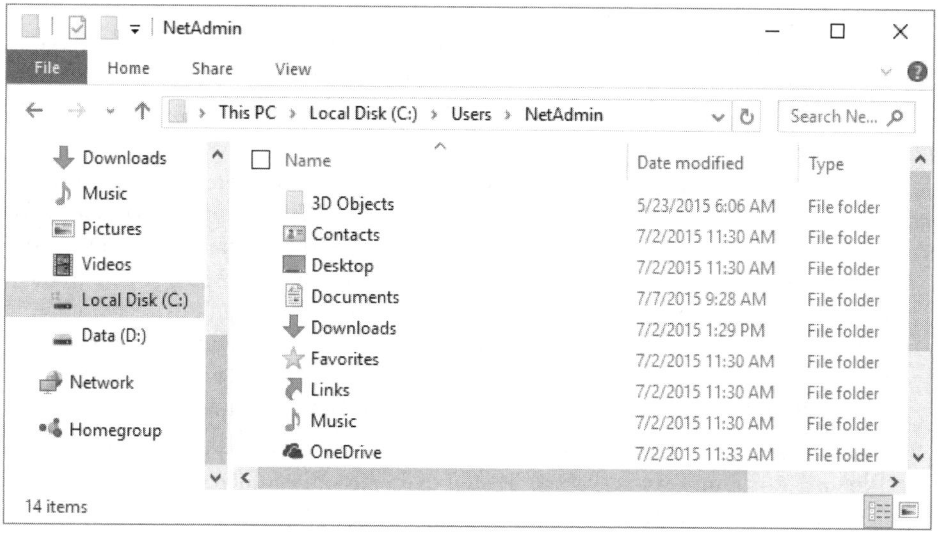

Figure 11-3   Viewing the contents of C:\Users\NetAdmin in File Explorer

3. In Windows file systems, the backslash (\) has two meanings. At the beginning of a path, it indicates the root or top of the file system. Anywhere else, it's used as a separator between folders, subfolders, and files. The forward slash (/) is used in many command-line programs to denote options for the command. The dir command means "directory," which is the term used before Windows started using the word "folder," and it lists the files and subfolders in the folder. As in File Explorer, the dir command doesn't display hidden files. To see hidden files, type **dir /ah** and press **Enter**. The /ah option tells dir to display files with the hidden attribute set. Type **dir /a** and press **Enter** to see all files. To see more options for the dir command, type **dir /?** and press **Enter**.

Remember to enter a space before any options you add to a command. Although not all commands require a space, many do, so it's best to get in the habit of entering one after the command.

4. To move to the root of the file system, type **cd ** and press **Enter**. The cd command means "change directory." Your prompt should now be C:\>. Type **dir** and press **Enter**. To go to C:\Windows\System32, type **cd \windows\system32** and press **Enter**. Notice that the prompt changes to C:\Windows\System32>. Type **dir** and press **Enter**. Several files scroll by quickly. To view them page by page, type **dir /p** and press **Enter**. (The /p option paginates the output.) Press any key to see the next page of files, or press **Ctrl+C** to terminate the output if you don't want to page through all the files.

5. Navigate back to the root of the file system. If you have more than one drive, you can switch drives by typing the drive letter and a colon and pressing Enter. For example, if you have a D drive, type **D:** and press **Enter**. The prompt changes to D:\>. If you don't have a D drive, you get an error stating that the drive can't be found. Type **c:** and press **Enter** to get back to the C drive, if necessary.

6. Next, create a folder by typing **mkdir TestDocs** and pressing **Enter**. The mkdir command means "make directory." To verify that the folder was created, type **dir** and press **Enter**, and then go to the new folder by typing **cd TestDocs** and pressing **Enter**. (*Note*: In Windows file systems, capitalization of filenames is ignored, so TestDocs is the same as testdocs; however, filenames are case sensitive in Linux.)

7. To create a subfolder, type **mkdir SubDocs1** and press **Enter**. Change to this subfolder by typing **cd SubDocs1** and pressing **Enter**. To go back to the TestDocs folder, type **cd \TestDocs** and press **Enter**. You must include the \ character because you're telling the file system that TestDocs is located directly under the root. To navigate to the SubDocs1 subfolder again, type **cd SubDocs1** and press **Enter**. You don't use the \ character in this command because SubDocs1 is located directly under your current location. To go up one level in the file hierarchy, use the .. notation: Type **cd ..** and press **Enter**, which takes you to the TestDocs folder. Type **cd ..** and press **Enter** again to get to the root.

8. Sometimes folder names are long and easy to mistype, so using a shortcut can be handy. Type **cd test** and press **Tab**. If TestDocs is the only folder name starting with "Test," the command prompt fills in the rest of the name for you. If more than one folder begins with "Test," the command prompt displays the first one in alphabetical order. Pressing Tab repeatedly cycles through all folders beginning with "Test." Press **Enter**.

9. The command prompt maintains a history of commands you've used since the window has been open. If you've been entering long commands that you need to repeat, you can scroll through the history by pressing the up arrow. Press the **up arrow** repeatedly to scroll through your recent commands. Press Esc when you're finished to cancel the command.

10. Type **mkdir ARealLongFolderName** and press **Enter**. Next, you make a mistake on purpose: misspelling the folder name. Type **cd ARealLongFoldName** (omitting the "er" in "Folder") and press **Enter**. You see the message "The system cannot find the path specified." To correct this error, press the **up arrow**. Press the **left arrow** until the cursor is under the "N" in Name. Type **er** and press **Enter**. Making a correction in this fashion is called "command-line editing."

11. To create a text file in your current folder, type **notepad myfile.txt** and press **Enter**. When prompted to create the file, click **Yes**. Type whatever you like in the file, and then click **File, Exit** from the menu. When prompted to save the file, click **Save**. Type **dir** and press **Enter** to verify that the file exists. To rename it, type **ren myfile.txt newfile.txt** and press **Enter**. To copy the file, type **copy newfile.txt newfile1.txt** and press **Enter**. Type **ren newfile.txt newfile.old** and press **Enter**. Press the **up arrow** until you see the dir command, and then press **Enter**.

12. To view only files with a .txt extension, type **dir *.txt** and press **Enter**. To see all files starting with "new," type **dir new*** and press **Enter**. To delete newfile.old, type **del newfile.old** and press **Enter**. To delete all files in the ARealLongFolderName folder, type **del *** and press **Enter**. Type **y** and press **Enter** when prompted. Press the **up arrow** until you see the dir command, and then press **Enter** to verify that all the files are deleted.

13. Write the commands to create a folder named **NewFolder**, move to this folder, and then list all files with the .doc extension:

_____

_____

_____

14. This project has shown you the basics of using the command line to navigate the file system in Windows. As a future network administrator, you'll find yourself using the command line often. Close the command prompt window and log off Windows for the next project.

Hands-On Project 11-2: Navigating the Linux File System (Optional)

Time Required: 20 minutes

Objective: Learn basic navigation of the Linux file system with the GUI and command line.

Required Tools and Equipment: A computer with Linux installed or Net-XX and a Linux Live disk (the Fedora Live Desktop DVD in this project, but others can be used)

Description: In this project, you use the Linux GUI and command line to navigate the file system. Linux distributions use different graphical desktop interfaces, and you might need to adjust the instructions in this project to accommodate the Linux distribution and version you're using.

1. Start Linux. If you're using the Fedora Live Desktop DVD, click **Try Fedora** in the Welcome to Fedora window. If necessary, click **Close**.

2. Click **Activities** at the top of the window. To begin navigating the file system, click the **file cabinet** icon to open a file browser window, which looks similar to File Explorer. Click **Computer** in the left pane (see Figure 11-4). You're now at the root of the file system.

Figure 11-4 The Fedora desktop with the file browser open

Remember that the file system in Linux doesn't use drive letters. All available drives are accessed as folders off the root of the file system, which in Linux is designated with a forward slash (/).

3. In the right pane, double-click the **home** folder. Home folders for all users on the system are in this folder. If you're using Fedora Live, you see a folder named liveuser, which is the user you're currently logged on as. Double-click **liveuser** (or the home folder for your installation and logon account). You see folders similar to the ones created for each user in Windows. Close the file browser window.

4. Open a command prompt window (called a "terminal window" or "shell prompt" in Linux) by clicking **Activities**, clicking the **Show Applications** icon, clicking **Utilities**, and then clicking **Terminal**. The prompt in a terminal window is different from the Windows command prompt. In Figure 11-5, the prompt is `[liveuser@localhost ~]$`. In the prompt, `liveuser` is the username, and `localhost` after the @ is the computer name, which is `localhost` by default. The tilde (~) following the computer name indicates the user's home folder, and $ is the end of the prompt. When you open a Linux terminal window, you're usually placed in your home folder.

```
liveuser@localhost:~                                    ✕

File  Edit  View  Search  Terminal  Help
[liveuser@localhost ~]$ █
```

Figure 11-5 A Linux terminal window

© 2015 Red Hat, Inc.

5. Besides the terminal prompt, there are other ways to see the logged-on user's name and the computer name. To see your username, type **whoami** and press **Enter**. To view the computer name, type **hostname** and press **Enter**.

6. To move to the root of the file system, type **cd /** and press **Enter**. Remember that Linux uses forward slashes, and Windows uses backslashes.

If you type a backslash accidentally, Linux thinks you're continuing the command on the next line and displays a > prompt. If this happens, press Enter to get back to the normal prompt, and then type the command again.

7. To view a list of files in the root, type **ls** (which means "list") and press **Enter**. You can get back to your home folder in three ways. Type **cd /home/liveuser** and press **Enter** (replacing liveuser with your logon name if you aren't using Fedora Live). A second way to get to the home folder is to type **cd** and press **Enter**, and a third way is to type **cd ~** and press **Enter**.

8. Create a folder in your home folder by typing **mkdir newfolder** and pressing **Enter**. Type **ls** and press **Enter** to verify that the new folder has been created.

9. You see other folders in your home folder, including one named Documents. Type **cd documents** and press **Enter**. Typing documents with a lowercase "d" causes an error because the Linux file system is case sensitive, so Documents is different from documents. Press the **up arrow** to repeat the command. Press the **left arrow** until the cursor is over the "o" in documents and press **Backspace**. Type **D** and press **Enter**.

10. To create an empty file, type **touch newfile** and press **Enter**. Verify that the file was created.

11. Type **gedit newfile** and press **Enter** to open newfile in gedit, a Notepad-like editor. Type whatever you like, click **Save**, and then close the gedit window.

12. To view newfile's contents from the command line, type **cat newfile** and press **Enter**. With a long file, you can use the more command to paginate the output. Type **more /etc/protocols** and press **Enter** to see a long file. Press the **spacebar** to page through the file, and type **q** to quit.

13. If you can't remember the complete name of a command, you can use the Tab key to perform command completion. If the command can be found by using the letters you typed, Linux completes the command. If there's more than one match, press Tab a second time to display all matches. Type **ge** and press **Tab** twice. A list of commands beginning with "ge" is displayed. Press **backspace** twice to delete ge, and then type **cd ..** and press **Enter** to move back one folder. Type **ls Doc** and press **Tab**. Linux completes the command. Press **Enter**. You see newfile and newfile~, which is a backup of newfile made automatically when you changed it with gedit.

14. Type **cd Doc** and press **Tab** and then **Enter**. The mv command is used to rename or move files. To rename the backup file that was created, type **mv newfile~ newfile.bak** and press **Enter**.

15. The rm command means "remove." To remove the file you just renamed, type **rm newfile.bak** and press **Enter**. Type **ls** and press **Enter** to see that only newfile remains in the folder.

16. Write two commands to get to the home directory in Linux:

_____

_____

17. To shut down Linux from the terminal, type **shutdown -h now** and press **Enter**. The -h option tells Linux to shut down and halt, and the now option means "do it now." (You use -r to restart the computer.) You can also specify a number of minutes to delay before the system shuts down by using +m instead of now, replacing m with the number of minutes to delay. If you get the message "Must be root," you have to be an administrator to shut down the computer. The root user is the default administrator account in Linux. If this happens, type **sudo shutdown -h now** and press **Enter**. The sudo command means "do this as superuser."

Processes and Services

A **process** is a program that's loaded into memory and run by the CPU. It can be an application a user interacts with, such as a word-processing program or a Web browser, or a program with no user interface that communicates with and provides services to other processes. This type of process is usually called a **service** in Windows and a "daemon" in Linux and is said to run in the background because there's no user interface. Examples of services include Client for Microsoft Networks and File and Printer Sharing for Microsoft Networks, which provide the client and server sides of Windows file sharing. Many TCP/IP Application-layer protocols, such as DNS and DHCP, also run as services.

Some OSs refer to processes as "tasks."

Network services are important because they allow your computer and applications to perform tasks they otherwise couldn't, or would need additional built-in functionality to handle. For example, a Web browser is designed to request Web pages from a Web server and display them. However, because most people use the Web server's name rather than its address, a name lookup is required before a Web browser can do its main job. If it weren't for the DNS client service running on the computer, the Web browser would have to know how to perform DNS functions. Instead, as you learned in Chapter 5, the Web browser simply sends the DNS service a request for a name lookup, and DNS returns the IP address to the Web browser. The same is true of almost every network application. Most network access is initiated by using the server name, and DNS is always running as a process to provide the name lookup service, so the application is free to do what it was designed to do. In Windows, you can use a handy tool called Task Manager to see processes and services running on your computer, check how much CPU time and memory each process is using, and stop a process from running, if necessary. In Linux, you use the System Monitor application for these tasks.

An OS can run 2, 10, 100, or more processes seemingly at once by using multitasking. **Multitasking** is an OS's capability to run more than one application or process at a time. It's what allows you to listen to a music file while browsing the Web, for example. Whether a computer has one or multiple CPUs, it multitasks by using a method called **time slicing**, which occurs when a CPU's computing cycles are divided between more than one process. Each process receives a limited number of processor cycles before the OS suspends it and activates the next process. The act of changing to another process is called **context switching**.

When a process has work to do, as when a user types at the keyboard or a Web browser submits a request for a Web page, the CPU is notified. If it already has other processes waiting, the new request is put into a queue. If this process has a higher priority than others in the queue, it jumps to the front of the line. Because a CPU can execute many billions of instructions per second, processes waiting in the queue are usually scheduled to run quickly. This activity is perceived as many applications operating simultaneously because each time slice is a very short period. People can't distinguish instances of such a brief time period, so it creates the illusion that the CPU and OS are performing several tasks at once. There are two types of multitasking:

- *Preemptive*—With **preemptive multitasking**, the OS controls which process gets access to the CPU and for how long; when the assigned time slice expires or a higher priority task has work to do, the current process is suspended, and the next process gets access to the CPU.

- *Cooperative*—With **cooperative multitasking,** the OS can't stop a process; when a process gets control of the CPU, it maintains control until it satisfies its computing needs. No other process can access the CPU until the current process releases it.

Cooperative multitasking was used in older OSs, such as Windows 3.1. An application that stopped working because of an infinite loop could bring the entire system to a screeching halt because it never gave up control of the CPU. Thankfully, all current OSs use preemptive multitasking, so the OS or the user can terminate misbehaving applications.

Many applications are now designed so that different parts can be scheduled to run separately, almost as though they were different processes. Each part that can be scheduled to run is called a **thread,** which is the smallest unit of software that can be scheduled. A **multithreaded application** has two or more threads that can be scheduled separately for execution by the CPU. For example, a multithreaded word-processing program might have one thread that waits for keyboard entry and then formats and displays the characters as they're typed and another thread that checks the spelling of each word as it's typed.

A multithreaded application benefits most when the OS and hardware support **multiprocessing,** which allows performing multiple tasks or threads simultaneously, each by a different CPU or CPU core. All current OSs support multiprocessing. Windows 10 supports up to two physical CPUs; a physical CPU is a chip installed in a socket on the motherboard. This means Windows 10 supports two CPUs, but each CPU can have one, two, four, or more cores. Windows Server OSs support up to 64 CPUs, depending on the edition. Most Linux OSs can support up to 32 or more CPUs.

The Kernel

If the CPU is the brain of a computer, the kernel is the office manager of the OS. Just as an office manager schedules everyone and everything and manages office resources, the kernel schedules processes to run, making sure high-priority processes are taken care of first; manages memory to ensure that two applications don't attempt to use the same memory space; and makes sure I/O devices are accessed by only one process at a time, in addition to other tasks. Because the kernel performs these important tasks, its efficiency and reliability are paramount to the OS's overall efficiency and reliability. Of course, the kernel is a process like any application, but it has the highest priority of any process, so when it needs to run, it takes precedence. You can't view it in Task Manager, and you certainly can't stop it, or the whole system would come crashing down.

Operating systems are designed in layers, as network protocols are, and the kernel is usually shown as the layer just above the hardware. This structure means nothing goes in or out without passing through the kernel—or at least without the kernel's approval. Figure 11-6 is a simplified illustration of the Windows OS structure, with the kernel near the bottom of the stack and above the hardware.

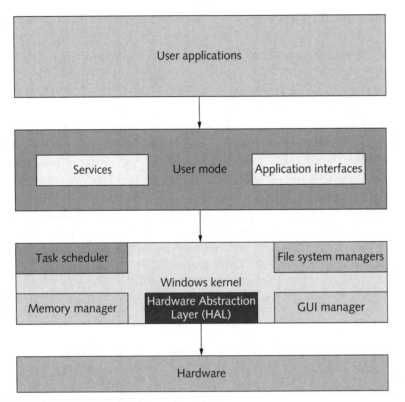

Figure 11-6   The Windows OS structure

Hands-On Project 11-3: Using Windows Task Manager

Time Required: 10 minutes

Objective: Use Windows Task Manager to view running processes, services, and real-time performance.

Required Tools and Equipment: Net-*XX*

Description: In this project, you use Task Manager to view processes and services.

1. Log on to your computer as **NetAdmin**.
2. Start Task Manager by right-clicking the **taskbar** and clicking **Task Manager**. You see a basic view of currently open windows. If you have no other windows open, you see the message "There are no running apps." Click the Search text box on the taskbar, type **notepad**, and press **Enter** to start Notepad. Switch to the Task Manager window to see Notepad in the list of running apps.
3. Click **More details** to see a more detailed view (see Figure 11-7). Right-click **Notepad** in Task Manager and click **Go to details**. The Details tab opens, and the notepad.exe process is selected.

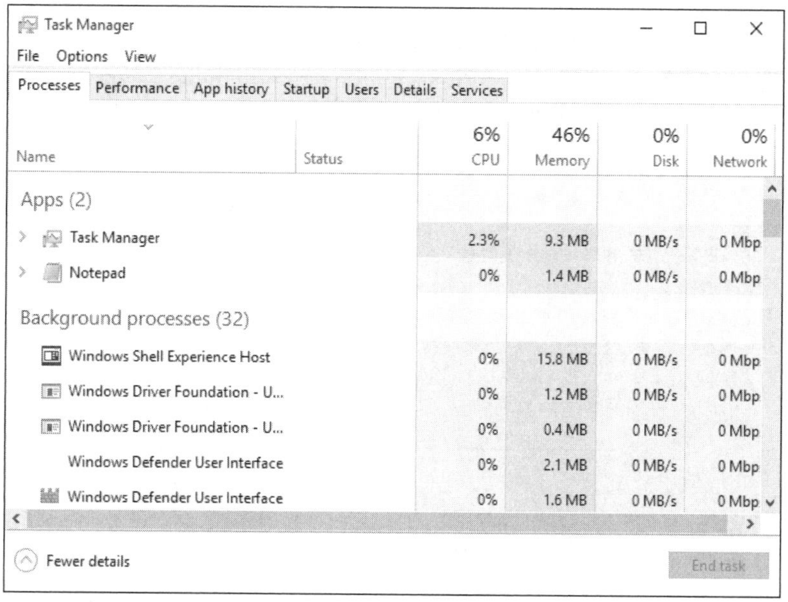

Figure 11-7 The Task Manager detailed view

4. To sort running processes by the percentage of CPU time they're using, click the **CPU** column. If necessary, scroll to the top of the window. You'll probably see System Idle Process at the top, and its CPU percentage will be in the high 90s. When a Windows OS has no real work to do, the kernel schedules the System Idle Process with CPU time. When the CPU percentage for System Idle Process is a high value, the computer isn't very busy; if it's a low value, other processes are using the CPU a lot.

5. Right-click the **CPU** column and click **Select columns,** and then click the **CPU time** check box. This column shows you the total CPU time a process has used since it was started. Next, scroll down and click **Command line.** This column shows you the name of the actual command that loaded the process. Click **OK.**

6. Click the **CPU time** column to sort entries by overall amount of CPU time in *hours:minutes:seconds* format. Notice that several processes are named svchost.exe, which is used to start many services in Windows. The Command line column gives you a better idea of which service each svchost.exe entry refers to and can also help you track down what application a process belongs to, based on the path to the application.

7. Find one of the svchost.exe entries ending with "LocalSystemNetworkRestricted" in the Command line column. Right-click the **svchost.exe** entry and click **Go to Service(s).** The Services tab opens, and the services started by that process are highlighted. Scroll through the Services tab to see all the highlighted services.

8. In the Services tab, click the **Status** column to sort services by status. Running services are listed first, and stopped services are listed next. Scroll through the services to see how many are running. Clearly, a lot is going on behind the scenes on your computer.

9. Click and then right-click the **Dhcp** service and click **Go to details.** The Details tab opens with the svchost.exe process that started the Dhcp service highlighted.

10. Click the **Performance** tab. The CPU box at the top left shows the total CPU % currently being used, and on the right is a line graph showing a one-minute history of CPU use. Figure 11-8 shows the Performance tab, which includes boxes for CPU utilization, memory use, disk utilization, and network utilization.

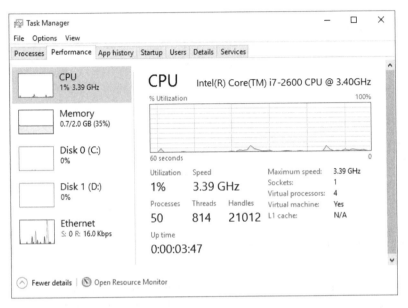

Figure 11-8   The Performance tab

11. Click the **Processes** tab. Right-click **notepad.exe** and click **End task** to close Notepad. You can use this feature to close an application that no longer responds to the mouse or keyboard.

12. In the Details tab of Task Manager, what's the difference between the CPU column and the CPU Time column?

_____

_____

13. Close Task Manager, and log off Windows for the next project.

Hands-On Project 11-4: Displaying Linux Processes (Optional)

Time Required: 10 minutes

Objective: View processes running in Linux.

Required Tools and Equipment: A computer with Linux installed or a Linux Live disk (Fedora Live Desktop in this project but others can be used)

Description: In this project, you use Linux System Monitor and the ps command to view processes and performance information.

1. Start Linux, and access the desktop. Click **Activities**, and then click the **Show Applications** icon.

2. Start System Monitor by clicking **Utilities** and then **System Monitor**. Click the **Processes** tab, if necessary, and then click the **% CPU** column to sort from highest to lowest CPU %. Linux doesn't show a system idle process. System Monitor itself is probably the biggest user of the CPU now.

3. Click the **Settings** icon, and then click **Active Processes** to see only currently active processes. System Monitor is probably the only process shown. Click the **Settings** icon, and then click **My Processes** to show all processes started by the currently logged-on user.

4. Click the **Resources** tab, which shows information similar to the Performance tab in Task Manager.

5. Start Firefox by clicking **Activities** and then the **Firefox** icon (orange and blue globe). You should see the CPU utilization and network utilization spike higher. Close Firefox and System Monitor.

6. Click **Activities, Show Applications, Utilities,** and **Terminal.** To see all currently running processes, type **ps -A** and press **Enter**. Type **ps -A | less** and press **Enter** to paginate the output. You can use the up and down arrows and Page Up and Page Down keys to scroll through the output. Type **q** to quit.

7. Type **top** and press **Enter** to see a real-time view of the top CPU users and other statistics. Type **q** to quit.

8. To shut down Linux, type **sudo shutdown -h now** and press **Enter**.

Client and Server Operating System Overview

Client OSs, such as Windows 10 and Mac OS X, now include many features once reserved for a server OS, such as file and printer sharing and file system security. Indeed, a client OS can perform as a basic server because it has these networking features built in, but an OS designed to be installed as a server still contains many additional networking and fault-tolerance features not found in client OSs. The determining factor of whether you need a server OS or a client OS is what role the computer will play in your network.

As you know, computers in a network usually play one of two roles: a client or a server. Although contemporary OSs allow servers to perform client tasks and clients to perform server tasks, most vendors have specific versions of their OSs to fulfill these roles. The client version generally comes configured with client software, such as Web browsers, DNS and DHCP clients, and file-sharing clients. Most server versions also include client software but have server components, such as Web servers, DNS and DHCP servers, and file-sharing servers. In addition, advanced server OSs usually include directory services, remote access services, fault-tolerance features, and virtualization.

The Role of a Client Operating System

The client OS is where network users spend all their time. Its purpose is to run applications, which often access network resources. Most desktop computers run a client OS equipped with the following network client software:

- DHCP client
- DNS client

- HTTP client (Web browser)
- File-sharing client
- E-mail client

Other client software can be installed on a client OS, such as the client side of a client/server database application, but these specialized applications are beyond the scope of this book. The preceding list of client software is installed on most OSs and used by most users. The DHCP, DNS, and HTTP clients were discussed in Chapter 5, so this chapter focuses on file-sharing and e-mail clients.

File-Sharing Client A file-sharing client allows the computer to access files and printers on the network. When a user or an application requests a resource—such as a printer or a data file—a **redirector** intercepts the request and then examines it to determine whether the resource is local (on the computer) or remote (on the network). If the resource is local, the redirector sends the request to the local software component for processing. If the resource is remote, the redirector sends the request over the network to the server hosting the resource.

With redirectors, network resources can be accessed as though they were local. For example, a user or user application doesn't distinguish between a printer connected to a local USB port and one connected to the network. In addition, with drive mapping, shared network folders are accessed just like a drive that's physically attached to the system—at least from the user's point of view. In Windows, the redirector component is part of Client for Microsoft Networks (listed in the network connection properties). This client software is designed to access shared folders and files on servers by using the Server Message Block (SMB) protocol. In Windows, the two most common ways to access a shared resource are using the UNC path or mapping a drive.

In Chapter 1, you used the UNC path to access a shared folder, which has the syntax *\\server-name\sharename*. The *server-name* is the name of the computer where the shared resource resides. You can also use the server's IP address in place of its name. The *share-name* is the name given to the folder or printer when it was shared. (Sharing folders and printers is discussed later in "The Role of a Server Operating System.") Typing a UNC path in the Search text box on the taskbar opens a File Explorer window showing the shared folder's contents. You can access a subfolder or file in the share directly by continuing the UNC path, as in *\\server-name\sharename\subfolder\file.extension*.

Linux systems also use the UNC path to access shared resources, but on Linux systems, forward slashes are used in place of backslashes.

TIP

You can use the UNC path to access shared folders and printers, but you must type the path every time you need it or create a shortcut with the UNC path as the target. One common method of making access to shared files easier (particularly those that are used often) is drive mapping, which associates a drive letter with the UNC path to a shared folder. Drives are usually mapped by using File Explorer or the net command. To use File Explorer, simply type the server portion of the UNC path in the Search text box on the taskbar to see a list of shared folders and printers the server is hosting. Right-click a shared folder and click Map network drive, as shown in Figure 11-9. You can then pick a drive letter (one that's not already in use) and choose to have Windows reconnect to the share with the same drive letter every time you log on.

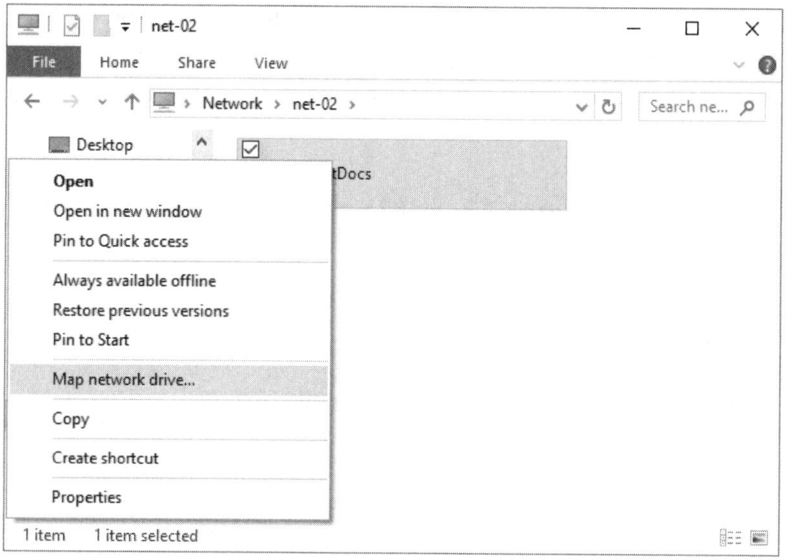

Figure 11-9   Mapping a drive in File Explorer

Another method of mapping a drive is using the `net` command. This method is often used by administrators in a **logon script**, which consists of commands that run when a user logs on to a Windows domain. To map a drive, for example, use the following command:
`net use` *`drive-letter`*`: \\`*`server-name`*`\`*`sharename`*

The *`drive-letter`* is an unused drive letter and must be followed by a colon (`:`). The command can be entered at the command prompt or placed in a batch file. A **batch file** is a text file containing a list of commands you ordinarily type at the command prompt. To run a batch file, enter its name at the command prompt or double-click the file in File Explorer. Batch files are useful for storing long complex commands that are used often or a series of commands that are always used together.

For the sake of comparison, Linux doesn't use drive letters at all. Instead, Linux file systems are based on the concept of a file system root designator, which is simply the / character. All local and network drives and folders are accessed from the root as folders (or directories, as most Linux users call them). A drive or network share is mounted into an empty directory so that it becomes part of the file system hierarchy. So to access a shared folder in Linux, you create a new directory at the root of the file system or in a subdirectory, and then mount the shared folder in the new directory.

The protocol used in Windows to share files and printers is SMB, also known as Common Internet File System (CIFS). Aside from file and printer sharing, SMB also provides a mechanism for interprocess communication between computers. Interprocess communication allows processes running on computers to communicate with one another for configuring and administering a computer over the network, for example.

Linux also supports SMB implemented as an installation option called Samba, but the native file-sharing protocol in the Linux environment is Network File System (NFS). NFS works much like SMB, in that NFS clients mount the shared folder into their local file system so that it appears as a local resource to both users and applications accessing it.

Using shared printers in Windows is even easier than mapping a drive. Simply right-click the shared printer in the File Explorer window and click Connect. A new printer is created in the Printers folder.

Hands-On Project 11-5: Mapping a Drive Letter

Time Required: 10 minutes

Objective: Map a drive letter by using different methods.

Required Tools and Equipment: Net-*XX*

Description: In this project, you create a shared folder, and then map a drive letter to it. You wouldn't normally map a drive letter to a share on your own computer, but this project shows you how to perform the process without using a second computer.

1. Log on to your computer as **NetAdmin.**

2. Click **Start, File Explorer.** Click **This PC** in the left pane, and then click **Local Disk (C:).**

3. Create a folder named **MyShare.** Right-click **MyShare,** point to **Share with,** and click **Specific people.** You see that NetAdmin is listed with the permission level Owner. You can add users who can access the share in this dialog box, but because only NetAdmin will access it, click **Share.** You're notified that the folder is shared, and you see the path listed as \\Net-*XX*\MyShare. Click **Done.**

4. Click in the Search text box on the taskbar, type **\\localhost,** and press **Enter.** The \\localhost refers to your own computer, so a window opens showing available shares, including MyShare. Normally, you wouldn't map a drive to a folder on your own computer, and you would replace "localhost" with the name of a server hosting the share. You're using localhost just for practice. Right-click **MyShare** and click **Map network drive.**

5. You can choose the drive letter to map to this share. Click the **Drive** list arrow and click **X:.** Click to clear the **Reconnect at sign-in** check box. If you leave this option selected, the drive is mapped to the share each time you log on. Notice that you can also choose to connect the share with different credentials (username and password). Click **Finish.**

6. A File Explorer window opens, showing the share's contents. Close all windows. Click **Start, File Explorer.** You see the drive letter and share name listed under This PC. Right-click **MyShare (\\localhost) (X:)** and click **Disconnect** to delete the drive mapping. (You might need to press F5 to refresh the File Explorer window to see that the drive mapping has been deleted.)

7. Open a command prompt window. To map a drive letter from the command line, type **net use x: \\localhost\MyShare** and press **Enter.** You should see the message

"The command completed successfully." To display current connections to shared resources, type **net use** and press **Enter**.

8. Click in the File Explorer window. The X drive letter is listed under This PC again.

9. At the command prompt, type **net use /?** and press **Enter** to see a list of options for the net use command. You can use the /persistent option to make a drive mapping reconnect each time you log on. You can also connect with a different set of credentials. Type **net use x: /delete** and press **Enter** to delete the drive mapping, and close the command prompt window.

10. To create a batch file for mapping a drive, open Notepad, and type the following two lines:

```
net use x: /delete
net use x: \\localhost\Myshare
```

11. The first command deletes any existing drive mappings for the X drive. Click **File, Save As** from the menu. In the left pane of the Save As dialog box, click **Desktop**. Click the **Save as type** list arrow, and click **All Files**. In the File name text box, type **mapX.bat** and click **Save**. Close Notepad.

12. On your desktop, double-click **mapX**. In File Explorer, verify that the X drive mapping has been created. Right-click **Myshare (\\localhost) (X:)** and click **Disconnect**.

13. Write the command to map drive letter G to a share named Accounting on a server named Finance:

_____

14. Batch files can come in handy if you need to connect to another computer periodically but don't want a permanent drive mapping. They're especially useful if you often need to enter a long command because they save you the time of having to remember and enter the command each time you need it. Close all open windows, and leave Windows running for the next project.

To learn more about creating and using batch files in Windows, read the TechNet article at *https://technet.microsoft.com/en-us/library/bb490869.aspx*.

Hands-On Project 11-6: Creating and Connecting to a Shared Printer

Time Required: 10 minutes

Objective: Create and connect to a shared printer.

Required Tools and Equipment: Net-*XX*, a computer with a shared printer that all student computers can connect to (or students can connect to each other's shared printers)

Description: In this project, you create a shared printer and then connect to it. You don't connect to an actual printer device, but this project walks you through the process of creating a printer, sharing it, and then connecting to a shared printer.

1. If necessary, log on to your computer as **NetAdmin**.

2. Click in the Search text box on the taskbar, type **Devices and Printers**, and press **Enter**. Click **Add a printer** in the Devices and Printers window. Windows searches for devices. Click **The printer that I want isn't listed**.

3. Click **Add a local printer or network printer with manual settings**, and then click **Next**. In the "Choose a printer port" window, leave the default option **Use an existing port** selected, and then click **Next**. In the "Install the printer driver" window, normally you select the printer's manufacturer and model, but because there's no physical printer, just accept the default selection, and then click **Next**.

4. In the "Type a printer name" window, click **Next**. In the Printer Sharing window, make sure **Share this printer so that others on your network can find and use it** is selected. For the share name, type **MyPrinter**, and then click **Next**. Click to clear the **Set as the default printer** check box. If you were actually installing a printer, you would click "Print a test page," but for this project, just click **Finish**.

5. To connect to a shared printer, ask your instructor whether a printer share is set up, or you can use another student's shared printer. In Windows, you can't connect to your own printer, as you did with the shared folder. Click in the Search text box on the taskbar, type *computer*, and press **Enter** (replacing *computer* with the name of the computer sharing the printer, such as net-01 or net-instr).

6. When the window opens, right-click the shared printer and click **Connect**. In the Devices and Printers window, verify that the printer was created. It's listed as "*Printer make and model* on computer."

7. Close all open windows.

E-mail Client E-mail is the lifeblood of communication for most businesses and the people who work in them. Its complexity and importance combine to make it one of an IT department's biggest headaches. Most users, however, simply see e-mail clients as one of several communication tools they use every day and don't think much about how it works.

There's more to e-mail than just typing a message, attaching a file, and sending it to a colleague. E-mail is based on its own set of protocols, just as Web browsing and file sharing are. The most common e-mail protocols are as follows:

- *Post Office Protocol version 3 (POP3)*—E-mail clients use this protocol to download incoming messages from an e-mail server to their local desktops. POP3 clients must manage messages locally (not on the server, as they can with IMAP).

- *Simple Mail Transport Protocol (SMTP)*—This protocol is the standard protocol for sending Internet and other TCP/IP-based e-mail. POP3 is used to retrieve e-mail, and SMTP is used to send e-mail.

- *Internet Message Access Protocol (IMAP)*—This standard has advanced message controls, including the capability to manage messages locally yet store them on a server and fault-tolerance features.

Sending an e-mail involves a series of steps. After a message has been written and the user clicks the Send button, the e-mail client software contacts an SMTP server. The SMTP server's address is part of the e-mail client's configuration. The SMTP server receives the message, looks up the domain of the destination address, and contacts an SMTP server at the destination domain. The destination SMTP server sends the message to the POP3 server containing the recipient's mailbox. The POP3 server deposits the message in the recipient's mailbox, where it sits until the mailbox owner instructs the e-mail client software to retrieve messages.

When you start your e-mail client or click the Get Mail (or equivalent) button in your client, the client uses POP3 to contact the POP3 server containing your mailbox. The POP3 server forwards waiting messages to the client software and usually deletes them from the server. If you're using IMAP instead of POP3, only the message headers are sent, which include sender information and the subject. Only when you click the message header is the body of the e-mail sent. Messages aren't deleted from the server until you delete them with the client software. With IMAP, you have the advantage of being able to open and read e-mail on one computer and download the same messages on another computer. Because IMAP doesn't delete messages on the server automatically, they can be downloaded and opened from multiple locations. In addition, users' mailboxes can be backed up on the server so that users don't have to back up e-mail on client computers. Simulation 18 shows how e-mail works with SMTP and POP3.

Simulation 18: How e-mail works

Some ISPs support IMAP and some don't because of the extra space undeleted messages use on their servers. Also, POP3 has an option to leave downloaded messages on the server until they're deleted from the client computer, but most ISPs don't support this feature.

Although the use of e-mail client and server software is still the norm in medium and large businesses, many small businesses and home users access their e-mail by using a Web browser interface from sites such as Gmail.com and Outlook.com. In this case, the same processes occur when transmitting and receiving e-mail, except the Web server you connect to for accessing your mail performs these tasks instead of a locally installed e-mail client.

The Role of a Server Operating System

In the past, server OSs installed on servers in PC networks were dedicated to providing network services to client computers and couldn't run user applications and client network software. The OS installed on a desktop computer is now largely the same as that installed on a server, however, with the differences being the number and type of network services available and how server resources are used. For example, Windows Server 2016 is configured with Client for Microsoft Networks and DHCP and DNS client services. However, you can install DHCP and DNS server components on Windows Server 2016 as well as the Active Directory directory service; these services are unavailable in Windows client OSs. In Linux distributions, some installation programs let you choose a desktop or server configuration, but some distributions, such as Red Hat Enterprise, are designed as server OSs.

Memory, CPU, and disk use in client OSs are optimized to run user applications and client network software. In server OSs, use of these resources is typically optimized to run network services in the background to speed up responses to client requests. In addition, server OSs have more security and fault-tolerance features. The following is a list (but by no means an exhaustive list) of the features and functions most server OSs provide in a typical network:

- Centralized user account and computer management
- Centralized storage
- Infrastructure services, such as name resolution and address assignment
- Server and network fault tolerance
- Additional server features

Name resolution (DNS) and address assignment (DHCP) have already been covered in Chapter 5. The other server OS features are discussed in the following sections.

Centralized User Account and Computer Management

Among the most compelling reasons to design a network, even a small one, as a server-based network is centralized management of network resources, which includes the following functions:

- User authentication and authorization
- Account management
- Security policy management

User Authentication and Authorization
Authentication is the process of identifying who has access to the network. The most common form of authentication is a logon with a username and password. Other forms include digital certificates, smart cards, and biometric scanners.

Authorization is the process of granting or denying an authenticated user's access to network resources. Both authentication and authorization require users (and sometimes devices) to have a user account that stores properties about the user, such as a logon name and password. A user account is also used to grant permissions for the user to access network resources.

Account Management
Most OSs, including those designed as client OSs, now incorporate account management for the purposes of authentication and authorization, but account management is centralized in the server OS. To better understand centralized account management and, therefore, centralized authentication and authorization, consider a network in which account management is decentralized, as in a Windows workgroup network. As discussed in Chapter 1, each computer in this type of network maintains its own list of user accounts and controls access to its own resources. In a network of 10 computers, if each computer shares resources that are accessed by users on other computers, each user account must be created 10 times, once on each computer. The password for each user must also be maintained on each computer. If a user's password is changed on one computer, he or she has to remember a different password to access that computer or have the password changed on all 10 computers. You can see how keeping up with this system could become tiresome quickly.

The server version of Windows OSs includes a centralized account management, authentication, and authorization system called Active Directory. Active Directory is a directory service that allows users to log on to the network once with their username and password and access resources they're authorized for regardless of which computer stores the resource. When Active Directory is installed on a server, the server becomes a domain controller, and users and computers with accounts in Active Directory are referred to as domain members. Figure 11-10 shows the Active Directory Users and Computers management console. In the left pane are folders used to organize accounts and resources for easier management. In the right pane are user and computer accounts, distinguished by different icons.

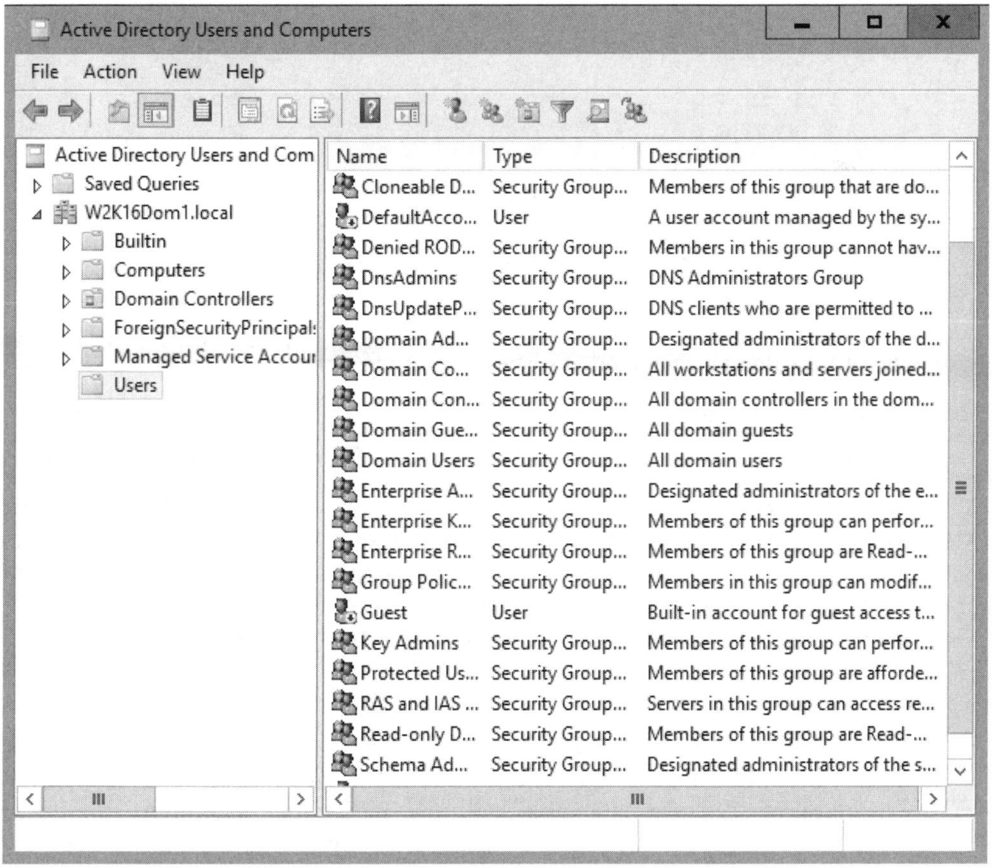

Figure 11-10   The Active Directory Users and Computers management console

When a computer running a desktop or server version of Windows becomes a domain member, an account is created for the computer in Active Directory. A computer becomes a domain member by changing its membership type from Workgroup to Domain in the Computer Name/Domain Changes dialog box accessed via the System Properties dialog box (see Figure 11-11). You work with accounts in Chapter 12.

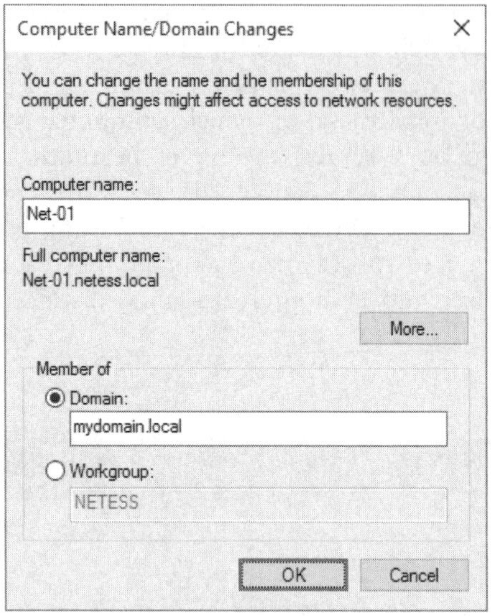

Figure 11-11 Making a computer a domain member

Security Policy Management Aside from authentication and authorization, accounts in Active Directory are used to distribute and enforce policies for network use and security. These policies, called "group policies" in a Windows domain environment, can be applied to all domain members. Policies can range from user interface policies controlling what icons appear on the desktop and Start menu to security policies controlling password restrictions and what applications a user can run on a computer. They're just a few examples of the power of group policies; hundreds of different policy settings are available.

Linux OSs have a basic directory service for centralized logon called Network Information Service (NIS), but Lightweight Directory Access Protocol (LDAP), which Active Directory is based on, is also commonly used in the Linux community. LDAP has the advantage of supporting both Windows and Linux user authentication and authorization. Chapter 9 covered some details of setting password and account lockout policies in Windows.

Centralized Storage

With huge multimedia files being such a large portion of the data stored and processed on networks, network administrators are in a constant quest to better manage and maintain storage resources. Network storage includes file sharing, in which users store documents on network servers that other users can access. It also includes storing e-mail, user files, application databases, and data backups, among many other resources.

Traditional servers use locally attached disk drives to store the installed OS and applications as well as user files. However, the amount of data stored in even small to medium networks is measured in dozens of terabytes, quite a burden for servers juggling numerous other network tasks. Although locally attached storage is still in common use, many network administrators are turning to specialized devices to help manage their storage requirements, including the following:

- Network-attached storage devices

- Storage area networks
- Cloud-based storage

Network-Attached Storage A **network-attached storage** (NAS) device is a dedicated server device designed solely for providing shared storage for network users. An NAS could be a regular server with NAS software installed or it could be a **network appliance,** a device equipped with specialized software that performs a limited task, such as file sharing. Network appliances are often packaged without video interfaces, so you don't configure them with an attached keyboard and monitor. They have a built-in Web server that you connect to with a Web browser to configure and manage the device. Many NASs integrate with Active Directory or an LDAP-based system for user authentication and authorization.

Storage Area Network A **storage area network** (SAN) is a high-speed, high-cost network storage solution that largely replaces locally attached drives on servers. SAN technology allows multiple servers to access an enormous amount of shared storage that appears as locally attached drives from the server and user's perspective. Servers can even boot their OSs from a SAN instead of booting from local disks. This level of centralized storage offers better reliability and fault tolerance than traditional storage methods. Additionally, because storage is shared among several servers, power requirements for maintaining these systems are lower than those needed to maintain several servers with their own locally attached storage. The most common network technologies in SANs are Fibre Channel and iSCSI. They're designed to connect large arrays of hard drive storage that can be accessed and shared by servers. Client computers access the shared data by contacting the servers via the usual method, and the servers retrieve the requested data from the SAN devices and pass it along to the client computer. Figure 11-12 shows a LAN with three servers connected to a SAN.

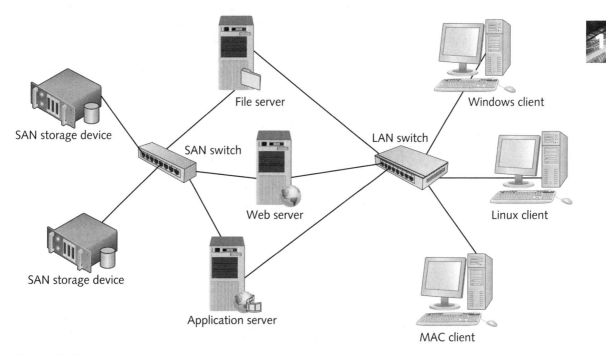

Figure 11-12 A storage area network

Cloud-Based Storage When a company's storage needs have outgrown its storage capabilities, whether because of physical capacity limits or the lack of personnel to maintain in-house storage, the company can turn to the cloud, as you learned in Chapter 10. In this case, the computing solution is network storage. With **cloud storage**, some or all of an organization's data is stored on servers located offsite and maintained by a storage hosting company. The customer can manage storage by assigning permissions for user access and allocating storage for network applications and so forth without having to physically maintain the servers. If more storage is needed, the customer simply pays the storage hosting company for the additional space. The advantage of this approach is that the details of managing and backing up storage on local servers are offloaded to a third party, which enables a company to focus its monetary and personnel resources on business rather than IT tasks. Cloud-based storage isn't for everyone. The data a company maintains might be too sensitive to trust to a third party, the data access speed might not be sufficient, or a host of other reasons. Cloud storage is a rather new model in network storage, but it's one that's here to stay.

Server and Network Fault Tolerance By now, you know that a server is defined by the type of software installed on it. For example, Windows Server 2016 and most Linux distributions can be installed on an inexpensive laptop just as easily as they can on a $20,000 server, but laptops are rarely adequate for an enterprise-level network. A network's servers can be critical to business operations, so keeping them running at peak performance is essential for user productivity and business transactions. For this reason, certain fault-tolerance features are built into server OSs, and only servers designed to use these features can access them. Some fault-tolerance features on a server OS that aren't usually available on client OSs include the following:

- *Support for hot-swappable devices*—A **hot-swappable device** can be removed, replaced, or added to a server while it's running. Many low-end servers support hot-swappable disk drives, but only high-end servers are likely to support hot-swappable memory and CPUs. Windows Server 2012 and later support hot-swappable disks, memory, and CPUs. Red Hat and other Linux distributions support hot-swappable devices (called "hotplug" in the Linux world), too.

- *Server clustering*—A **server cluster** is two or more servers configured to operate as a single unit. The most common types of server clusters are failover clusters and load-balancing clusters. A **failover cluster** is used to provide fault tolerance so that if one server fails, the other immediately takes over its functions with no or little downtime. A **load-balancing cluster** provides high-performance computing and data access by spreading the workload among multiple computers. Physically, there are multiple servers, but logically, they work as one unit. Load-balancing clusters have the added advantage that if one server fails, the others still operate, which ensures fault tolerance.

- *Redundant/high-end disk systems*—Hard drives are a critical component of a computer and one of the few moving parts in a computer, making them more susceptible to failure than other components. Most high-end servers support enterprise-class Serial Attached SCSI (SAS) disks designed for an around-the-clock duty cycle. Low-end servers and desktop computers support only Serial ATA (SATA) disks, which lack some of the performance properties of SAS. However, even high-end disk drives can fail, so most servers incorporate disk controllers capable of a disk arrangement known as **redundant array of independent disks (RAID)**. With RAID, you can configure disks in a fault-tolerant arrangement so that if one disk fails, the data is preserved and the server can continue to operate. Even some desktop computers support variations of RAID, but the variations with higher performance and fault tolerance are standard on servers. RAID is discussed more in Chapter 12.

Additional Server Features

As mentioned, OS vendors reserve many high-end applications and network services for the server version of the OS. Some applications and services usually found only on servers includes the following:

- *Remote access*—A mobile workforce needs convenient access to the company network from anywhere in the world. Most server OSs support virtual private networks (VPNs) and, if necessary, the older dial-up method of remote access.

- *Database server*—Many applications rely on a database to store and retrieve vast amounts of data. Server OSs support advanced database systems, such as MySQL, SQL Server, and Oracle.

- *Client/server applications*—Client/server applications, such as e-mail systems (Microsoft Exchange, for example), must run on a server OS. Web-based applications, too, need a server OS to handle the computing and network workload of these applications.

- *Virtualization*—Virtualization is an integral part of most IT data centers. Virtualization software runs on desktop systems, but for virtualizing production servers, you need a server-based product, such as Microsoft Hyper-V or VMware vSphere. For open-source fans, XenServer (*http://xenserver.org*) might be a good fit with your data center. Virtualization is such an important aspect of the computing environment that the next section focuses on this topic.

The list of applications and services usually reserved for servers and server OSs continues to grow as networks play an increasingly important role in personal and work activities. For now, turn your attention to OS virtualization, one of the hottest topics in computing.

Operating System Virtualization

OS virtualization has become a mainstream technology in both small and large networks. **Virtualization** is a process that creates a software environment to emulate a computer's hardware and BIOS, allowing multiple OSs to run on the same physical computer at the same time. This environment can be installed on most current OSs, from Windows to Linux to MAC OS. In this case, a picture is worth a thousand words, so examine Figure 11-13. It shows a Windows 10 client running a Windows Server 2016 (technical preview) virtual machine, using VMware Workstation virtualization software. Notice that there are two Start buttons: one on the host desktop and one on the VM.

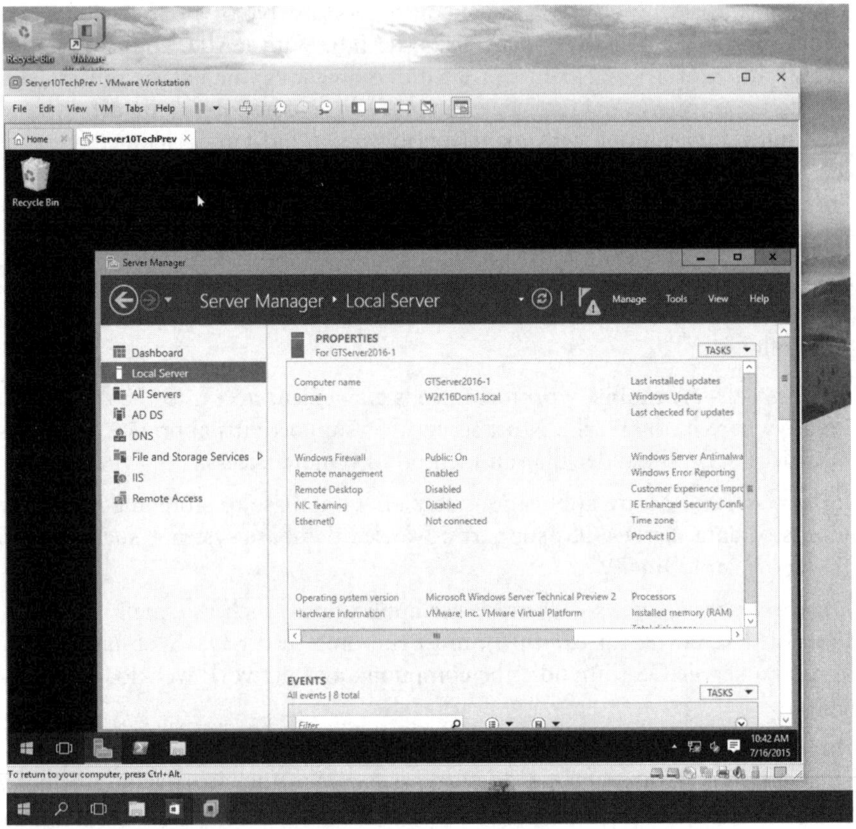

Figure 11-13 Windows Server 2016 running as a virtual machine in Windows 10

Source: VMware, Inc., *www.vmware.com*

Like all technologies, virtualization has a collection of terms that define its operation and components:

- A **virtual machine (VM)** is the virtual environment that emulates a physical computer's hardware and BIOS. A **guest OS** is the operating system installed on a VM.

- A **host computer** is the physical computer on which VM software is installed and VMs run.

- Virtualization software is the software for creating and managing VMs and creating the virtual environment in which a guest OS is installed. Examples are VMware Workstation, Oracle VirtualBox, and Microsoft Hyper-V.

- The **hypervisor** is the virtualization software component that creates and monitors the virtual hardware environment, which allows multiple VMs to share physical hardware resources. On a host computer, it acts somewhat like an OS kernel, but instead of scheduling processes for access to the CPU and other devices, it schedules VMs. It's sometimes called the "virtual machine monitor (VMM)." There are two types of hypervisors:

  - A type 1 hypervisor implements OS virtualization by running directly on the host computer's hardware and controls and monitors guest OSs. It also controls access to the host's hardware and provides device drivers for guest OSs. Also called **bare-metal virtualization**, it's used mainly for server virtualization in data centers. Examples include VMware ESX Server, Citrix XenServer, and Microsoft Hyper-V Server.

○ A type 2 hypervisor implements OS virtualization by being installed in a general-purpose host OS, such as Windows 10 or Linux, and the host OS accesses host hardware on behalf of the guest OS. Also called **hosted virtualization**, it's used mostly for desktop virtualization solutions. Examples include VMware Player and Workstation, Oracle VirtualBox, and OpenVZ for Linux.

• A **virtual disk** consists of files residing on the host computer that represent a virtual machine's hard drive.

• A **virtual network** is a network configuration created by virtualization software and used by virtual machines for network communication.

• A **snapshot** is a partial copy of a VM made at a particular moment; it contains changes made since the VM was created or since the last snapshot was made and is used to restore the VM to its state when the snapshot was taken.

Figure 11-14 illustrates the virtualization process, with a host computer connected to a physical network. The hypervisor on the host is running two VMs connected to a virtual network, which has a connection to the physical network so that the VMs can communicate on the physical network.

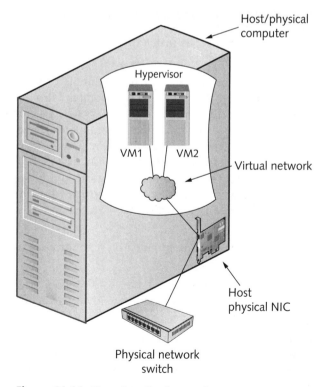

Figure 11-14 How virtualization works

One of the best ways to understand a technology is to understand the reasons it's used. The reasons to use virtualization are many and varied and are best discussed by splitting the topic into the two main types of virtualization: hosted and bare-metal.

Hosted Virtualization

As mentioned, hosted virtualization uses a type 2 hypervisor, which is installed in a standard desktop or server OS. It has the advantage of supporting a wider variety of guest OSs than bare-metal virtualization does, mostly because the guest OS uses the host OS to access host hardware, so there are few incompatibility problems between the guest OS and hardware. For example, you can run a distribution of Linux in a virtual machine on a host computer, even if you can't install Linux directly on the physical machine because of driver incompatibilities.

Another advantage of hosted virtualization is that it's easy and straightforward to use. With hosted virtualization, you install the virtualization software on your computer and begin creating virtual machines. There are few hardware requirements, and most products run on Windows versions starting with Windows XP as well as MAC OS X and most Linux distributions. All that's required are enough memory to support the host and guest OSs, adequate CPU power, and enough free disk space to store the virtual disk. A system running Windows 10 with 4 GB RAM, a 2.0 GHz CPU, and 40 GB free hard drive space can run Linux and Windows Server 2016 virtual machine at the same time. Performance might not be stellar, but the virtual machines should work well enough for experimenting or training (one of the main reasons for using hosted virtualization).

Hosted Virtualization Applications Hosted virtualization is so flexible and easy to use that its uses are varied and continuing to grow as people find different applications for it. Some common applications include the following:

- *OS training*—Whether in the classroom or at home, learning multiple OSs has often been a problem of not having enough computers or a lack of compatibility between the OS and available computers. With virtualization, a computer can have a host OS installed, such as Windows 10, and have virtual machines for numerous Linux distributions, Windows 7, Windows Server 2016, and even Novell NetWare. If you want to learn about the past, you can install Windows 3.11, DOS, or OS/2 (if you can find installation media for these very old OSs). In addition, you can run multiple VMs at the same time by using a virtual network, which enables you to work with both client and server OSs in situations that would normally take two or more physical computers.

- *Software training*—Students and employees can be trained on new software packages by giving them VMs with preinstalled software.

- *Application isolation*—Not all software plays well together, so if an application conflicts with other installed software, it can be installed in its own VM, effectively isolating it from the host machine's installed software.

- *Network isolation*—Installing some networking services, such as DHCP, can wreak havoc with an existing network. Virtual networks can be isolated from the rest of the network, however, so you can experiment with these services without causing the IT department to pay you a visit.

- *Software development*—Software developers often need to design software that works on multiple OSs and OS versions. Testing on VMs makes this process easier, compared with using a physical computer for each OS to be tested.

- *What-if scenarios*—If you want to try out a software package or see whether a configuration option you read about will actually improve performance on your computer, you might not want to risk destabilizing your physical computer. You can install software and make configuration changes safely on a VM before making the commitment on your host computer.

- *Use of legacy applications*—If you have a favorite application that won't run on a newer OS, you don't have to forgo the latest hardware technology because of one application. You can install the old OS in a VM and run your legacy application on it.

- *Physical-to-virtual conversion*—Your six-year-old machine is getting slow and unreliable, so you bought a new desktop computer. However, you have several applications on your old computer and no longer have the installation media. You can convert your old computer to a virtual machine, and then maintain all the software and run it on your new desktop computer as a VM. You'll probably even see a speed boost.

As you can see, virtualization can bring plenty of benefits to your computing experience. You have many choices of products in this category, and the good news is that most are free. The following section describes some products for hosted virtualization.

Hosted Virtualization Products Several hosted virtualization products are available. The following are the most well known:

- *VMware Workstation*—VMware, the virtualization pioneer in the PC world, released VMware Workstation in 1999. It's the only product in this list that isn't free, but it offers the most features, including multiple snapshots, nested virtualization (the capability to run a virtual machine inside another virtual machine), and extensive guest OS support.

- *VMware Player*—This free download from VMware has a streamlined user interface and fewer advanced features than Workstation, but maintains excellent guest OS support.

- *Microsoft Virtual PC*—This free download from Microsoft enables you to create and run virtual machines. XP mode is a new feature available only in Windows 7 Professional or Ultimate that integrates Windows XP virtual machine applications with the Windows 7 desktop. Virtual PC is no longer available in Windows 8 and later.

- *VirtualBox*—Originally developed by Innotek, it's now developed by Oracle Corporation. Two versions are available: a proprietary version that's free for home users and can be purchased for enterprise use and a free open-source version with a reduced feature set. VirtualBox runs on Linux, Mac OS X, or Windows hosts, and the proprietary version has features similar to VMware Workstation.

For more information on virtualization products, the platforms they run on, and supported guest OSs, review the article at *http://en. wikipedia.org/wiki/Comparison_of_platform_virtual_machines*.

These products have their strengths and weaknesses; the best approach is to work with different products to see which best serves your needs. The following sections discuss using these products.

Using VMware Workstation

VMware Workstation isn't free, but you can download a trial version at no cost and try it for 60 days. Not-for-profit educational institutions can join the VMware Academic program to give students and faculty free downloads of VMware Workstation and other VMware products.

After VMware Workstation is installed, a wizard takes you through the steps of creating a virtual machine. You can choose the size for the virtual disk and set other hardware options or just accept the defaults.

One convenience of installing a guest OS in a VM is being able to boot to the installation program with an ISO file rather than a DVD disk. This way, if you download the ISO file, burning a DVD to do the OS installation is unnecessary. In addition, the ISO file can be stored on a server and used by multiple users for VM installations.

An advanced feature of VMware Workstation is flexible networking options. You can configure the NIC on your VM to use one of the three virtual network options or you can create your own custom virtual network. VMware Workstation supports VMs with multiple NICs, and each NIC can be connected to a different virtual network. The three preconfigured options are as follows (see Figure 11-15):

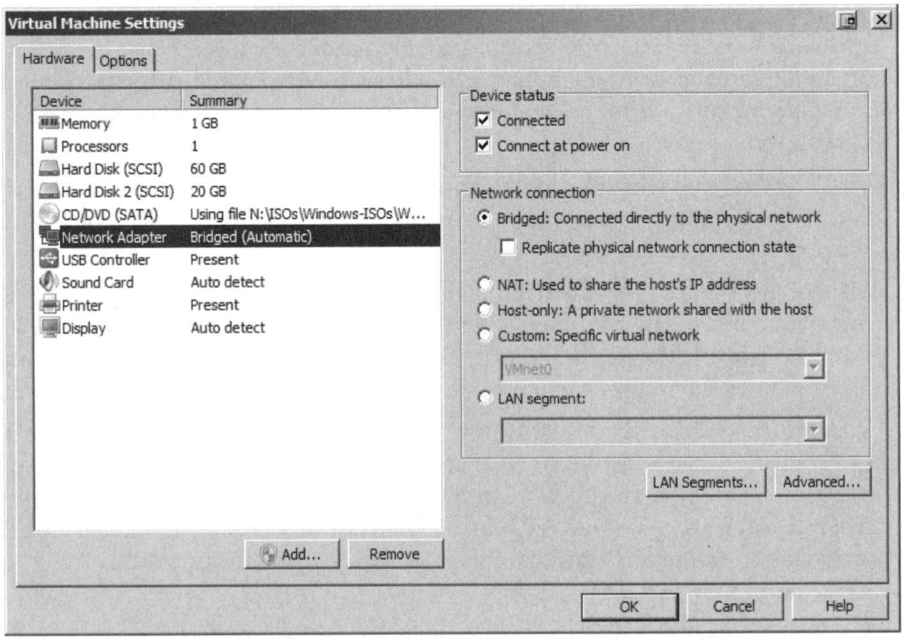

Figure 11-15   VMware virtual network options

- *Bridged*—This option connects the VM's virtual network to the physical network, and the VM acts like any other computer on the physical network, including having an IP address on the physical network. This option is illustrated in Figure 11-14, shown previously, in which the virtual network has a (virtual) connection to the host's physical NIC.

- *NAT*—With this default option, the host computer's IP address is shared with the VM by using Network Address Translation (NAT). The main difference between the NAT and Bridged options is that VMs are assigned an IP address from the host computer rather than the physical network, and the host translates the address for incoming and outgoing packets. This option is more secure than the Bridged option because the VM isn't directly accessible. However, it's not a viable option for a VM providing server functions to the host network.

- *Host-only*—This option isolates the VM from the host network and allows network communication only between VMs running on the host and the host computer. It's the most secure configuration and has the lowest risk of the VM causing problems with the host network. This configuration works well when you have multiple VMs that must communicate with one another but don't need to access computers or devices outside the host.

 Other virtualization software vendors use different terms to describe virtual networks, but the concepts are the same.

After the virtual machine is installed, you use it as you would any computer, except there are no physical on/off buttons.

VMware Tools, which is a collection of tools and drivers, should be installed in the guest OS for the best performance and ease of use. It adds optimized network, video, and disk drivers and guest-host integration tools that allow dragging and dropping files and cut and paste between the guest OS and host OS.

Other advanced features targeted to developers are available, which is why VMware Workstation is generally considered the flagship hosted virtualization product. However, if you don't need all the bells and whistles and simpler is better, try VMware Player.

Using VMware Player VMware Player is a stripped-down version of VMware Workstation but still offers the basics of desktop virtualization in a streamlined and easy-to-use interface. You can download it free from the VMware Web site, and it's also included with the VMware Workstation package. The opening window of VMware Player gives you an idea of its clean interface (see Figure 11-16).

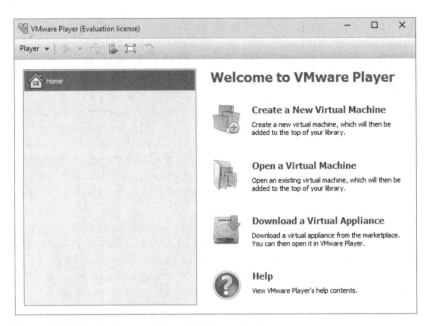

Figure 11-16 The VMware Player Welcome window

Source: VMware, Inc., *www.vmware.com*

Creating a VM in VMware Player is a wizard-based affair, nearly identical to the one in VMware Workstation. Notice in Figure 11-16 the option to download a virtual appliance. Virtual appliances are ready-to-use VMs from OS and software vendors that contain a guest OS with preconfigured applications or network services. In some cases, a virtual appliance is just a preinstalled guest OS. A virtual appliance is an easy way to use and evaluate a product or configuration without having to install it yourself. Virtual appliances can be run by VMware Player or Workstation and sometimes by VMware's bare-metal virtualization products.

VMware Player offers many of the same features as VMware Workstation, with the exception of snapshots, customized virtual networks (although the three preconfigured network options are available), and some advanced network and virtual hardware settings. It's a good choice for new virtualization users and for classroom and training centers where the interface's simplicity is an advantage.

Using Microsoft Virtual PC The VMware products just discussed can be installed on both Windows and Linux OSs (another desktop product called VMware Fusion runs in Mac OS), but Virtual PC is a Windows-only product and it runs only in Windows 7 Professional, Enterprise, or Ultimate. Because this product is no longer supported in Windows 8 and later, it's not discussed in detail. Instead, Microsoft has made its Hyper-V product a configurable option in Windows 8 and later. Hyper-V was introduced in Windows Server 2008 and originally supported only in Windows Server OSs. Hyper-V is discussed in more detail later in "Bare-Metal Virtualization."

Using VirtualBox VirtualBox can be installed on Windows, Mac OS X, Linux, and Solaris hosts and supports a wide range of Windows, Linux, and other guest OSs, making it the most versatile of the products discussed. Like the other products, virtual machines are created with a wizard that walks you through selecting the guest OS and the VM's hard disk and RAM configuration; however, you can change all these settings after the VM is created. The VirtualBox user interface consists of a console where you can create VMs and view the status of all VMs. VirtualBox supports unlimited snapshots, so you can save a VM's state as you work with it and restore its state from any of the snapshots you make. You can even jump forward and backward in snapshots, meaning that if you have three snapshots, you could revert to the first snapshot and later go back to the third snapshot.

Virtualization Software Summary All the virtualization products discussed so far provide a type 2 hypervisor (hosted virtualization). Table 11-2 summarizes some major features and differences in these products. Flash Movie 1: Using VMware Workstation shows creating a virtual machine in VMware Workstation and using this product's features.

Flash Movie 1: Using VMware Workstation

Table 11-2 Comparing features of hosted virtualization software

	VMware Workstation	**VMware Player**	**Microsoft Virtual PC**	**Oracle VirtualBox**
Price	$249 or free with Academic Program membership	Free	Free	Free
Host OS support	Windows, Linux, Mac OS X (with VMware Fusion)	Windows, Linux	Windows	Windows, Linux, Mac OS X, Solaris
Guest OS support	Windows, several Linux distributions, NetWare, Solaris, DOS	Same as Workstation	Windows XP and later	Windows, several Linux distributions, Solaris, Mac OS X Server, DOS, OS/2, others
Snapshots	Unlimited	None	One (with Disk Undo enabled)	Unlimited
Virtual network options	Bridged, NAT, host-only, custom	Bridged, NAT, host-only	Bridged, NAT, internal (guest-to-guest only)	Bridged, NAT, host-only, internal
Host integration tools	VMware Tools, Unity	VMware Tools, Unity	Integration Services, XP mode	Guest additions, seamless mode
Other features	Virtual teams, screen capture and screen movie capture, physical-to-VM conversion, developer tools			Command-line management interface, built-in remote desktop, developer programming interface, open-source edition

A benefit of these virtualization products is that you can install all of them and run them at the same time on a single host computer, so you can download and install each one and evaluate it for yourself.

Hands-On Project 11-7: Downloading and Installing VMware Player

Time Required: 20 minutes

Objective: Download and install VMware Player.

Required Tools and Equipment: Net-*XX*, access to the Internet

Description: In this project, you download and install VMware Player.

1. If necessary, log on to your computer as **NetAdmin**.

2. Start a Web browser, and go to **www.vmware.com**. Click **Downloads**, and under Free Product Downloads, click **Player**.

3. Click the **Download** button next to VMware Player for Windows 64-bit operating systems. After downloading the file, start the installation of VMware Player, and follow the prompts, using the default options.

4. When the installation is finished, double-click the **VMware Player** shortcut on your desktop to start VMware Player. In the Welcome to VMware Player window, type your e-mail address to use VMware Player for non-commercial use, click **Continue**, and then click **Finish**.

5. You're ready to create a virtual machine. Leave VMware Player running for the next project.

Hands-On Project 11-8: Creating a Virtual Machine in VMware Player

Time Required: 15 minutes

Objective: Create a virtual machine in VMware Player.

Required Tools and Equipment: Net-*XX*

Description: In this project, you create a virtual machine in VMware Player. In Hands-On Project 11-9, you install an evaluation copy of Windows Server 2012 in the virtual machine.

If you're running Net-*XX* as a virtual machine, you might not be able to run a virtual machine inside another virtual machine. If you're using VMware Workstation 10 and later, you can run a VM inside a VM (nested virtualization) by turning off the Net-*XX* VM, and then clicking VM, Settings from the VMware Workstation menu. Click Processors, and then click Virtualize Intel VT-x/EPT or AMD-V/RVI. Restart the Net-*XX* VM, and then run VMware Player.

1. If necessary, log on to your computer as **NetAdmin,** and start VMware Player.

2. In the VMware Player Welcome window, click **Create a New Virtual Machine** to start the New Virtual Machine Wizard.

3. In the Welcome window of the New Virtual Machine Wizard, click the **I will install the operating system later** option button (see Figure 11-17), and then click **Next**.

New Virtual Machine Wizard   ✕

Welcome to the New Virtual Machine Wizard
A virtual machine is like a physical computer; it needs an operating system. How will you install the guest operating system?

Install from:

○ Installer disc:

   📀 DVD Drive (D:) J_CCSA_X64FRE_EN-US_DV5   ∨

○ Installer disc image file (iso):

   [∨]   Browse...

● I will install the operating system later.
The virtual machine will be created with a blank hard disk.

   Help   < Back   Next >   Cancel

Figure 11-17 The New Virtual Machine Wizard

Source: VMware, Inc., *www.vmware.com*

4. In the Select a Guest Operating System window, make sure **Microsoft Windows** is selected, click the list arrow, and then click **Windows Server 2012**. Click **Next**.

5. In the Name the Virtual Machine window, accept the default name **Windows Server 2012** and the default path, and then click **Next**.

6. In the Specify Disk Capacity window, accept the default **60.0** GB, and then click **Next**.

7. In the Ready to Create Virtual Machine window, review the options. If you wanted to change hardware options, you could click Customize Hardware, but for now, click **Finish**.

8. Before you install an OS in the virtual machine, take a look at some of VMware Player's features and options. Click **Play virtual machine**. If you're running VMware Player in another VM, you see a message stating that performance will be degraded; click **OK**. If you see a message about removable devices, click **OK**. If you see a message about software updates, click **Remind me later**. Your VM attempts to boot. If you have an installation DVD in the host computer's DVD drive, the VM tries to boot to the DVD; otherwise, it tries to boot from the network. Finally, it displays a message stating that the OS can't be found.

 If you click in the VM window and your mouse pointer disappears, it has been captured by the VM. To release it, press Ctrl+Alt.

9. Click **Player** on the VMware Player menu, point to **Power**, and click **Shut Down Guest**, and then click **Yes** to exit VMware Player.

10. Start VMware Player again. The Windows Server 2012 VM is shown in the left pane of the Welcome window. Click to select **Windows Server 2012**, and in the right pane, click **Edit virtual machine settings** to open the Virtual Machine Settings dialog box (see Figure 11-18).

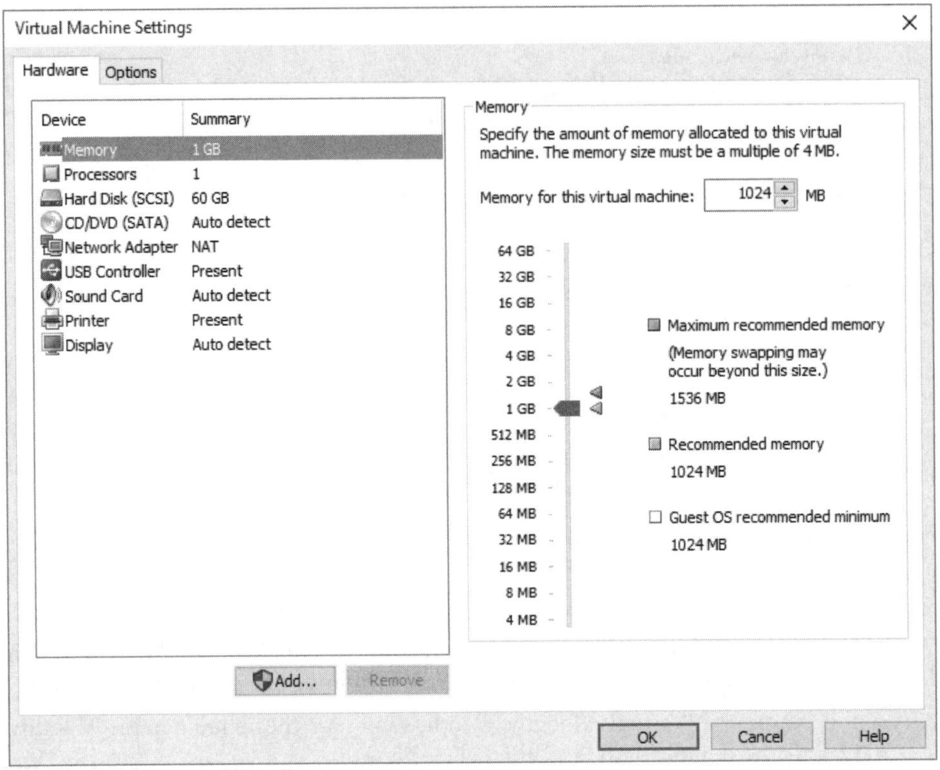

Figure 11-18 The Virtual Machine Settings dialog box

Source: VMware, Inc., *www.vmware.com*

11. In this dialog box, you can change the amount of memory allocated to the VM, change processor options, access disk utilities, change the virtual network settings, and configure many more settings. You can also add virtual hardware, such as hard disks, network adapters, and so forth. Click **Network Adapter** in the list on the left. The default option is NAT, which means the VM gets an IP address from the host computer, and VMware performs NAT so that the VM can access the physical network. Click **Advanced** to see advanced network settings (see Figure 11-19). Notice that the VM is assigned a MAC address, just like a computer with a physical NIC. Click **Cancel**.

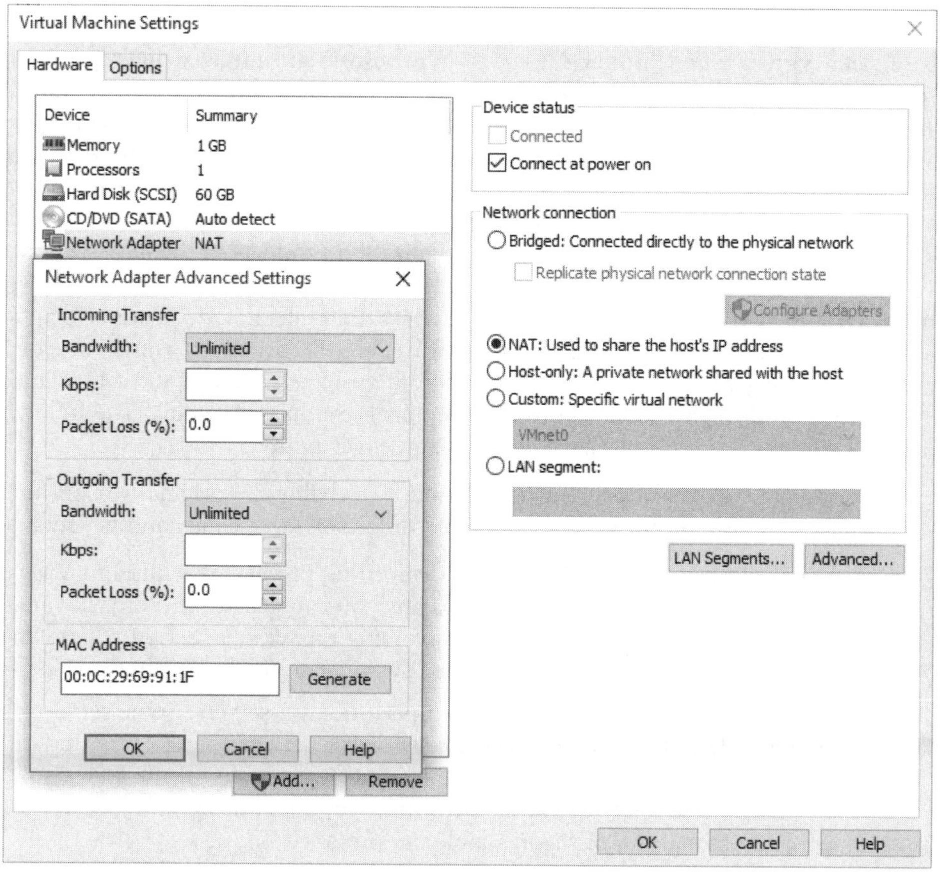

Figure 11-19 Advanced settings for network adapters

12. In the Virtual Machine Settings dialog box, click **Add**. Click **Yes** in the UAC message box, if necessary. The Add Hardware Wizard lists virtual hardware you can add to the VM. Click **Cancel**.

13. In the Virtual Machine Settings dialog box, click the **Options** tab, where you can change options such as the VM name, the guest OS to install, power options, and shared folders. Click **Shared Folders**. If you enable shared folders, you can copy files from the host computer to the VM without having to create a network share. Click **Cancel** to close the Virtual Machine Settings dialog box.

14. Which virtual network setting should you use in VMware Player if you want the VM to be able to get an IP address from a DHCP server on the physical network?

_____

15. If you're continuing to the next project, leave VMware Player open; otherwise, log off or shut down your computer.

Bare-Metal Virtualization

Bare-metal virtualization products (type 1 hypervisors) are targeted mainly for production virtualization in data centers. These products are installed directly on hardware and have more stringent host machine requirements than hosted products do. Because they're targeted for IT departments, they have more features for managing VMs and have a performance advantage over hosted virtualization products. Their installation and use tend to require more sophisticated, knowledgeable users, too. Before learning about specific products, take a look at some applications for bare-metal virtualization products in the next section.

Bare-Metal Virtualization Applications   Bare-metal virtualization products come with a price tag for the virtualization software, the hardware to run it on, or both. So when considering whether to use virtualization in an IT data center, most IT managers look for a return on their investment in real money or in productivity gains. The following applications show that bare-metal virtualization can deliver both:

- *Consolidate servers*—Server consolidation is probably the original reason for using bare-metal virtualization and is done for the following reasons and benefits:

  o Retire old or unreliable hardware: Converting physical machines to VMs and running them on the latest hardware means you can get rid of old hardware, thereby gaining a reliability advantage and avoiding the tedious task of reinstalling and reconfiguring a server OS on new hardware. You might also improve performance.

  o Make optimal use of multicore, high-performance servers: Some server roles, such as Active Directory, should be the only major network service running on a server. With multicore server CPUs, you're likely to waste a lot of the server's power if you install a single-role OS. Instead, run two, three, or more VMs on the server, making optimal use of the available performance.

  o Maintain application separation: Some applications and services run best when they're the only major application installed on an OS. You avoid OS resource conflicts and gain stability and reliability.

  o Reclaim rack or floor space: By consolidating a dozen physical servers into three or four host servers, you're no longer tripping over a plethora of towers or wondering whether your rack can handle one more server. You can even clear enough room for an easy chair and a reading lamp so that you can catch up on the latest technical journals in comfort!

  o Reduce cooling and power requirements: In most cases, by reducing the number of servers (even with higher performance machines), you save money on cooling and powering a data center, especially when you reduce hundreds of servers down to dozens of hosts.

- *Test installations and upgrades*—Before you install a major software package or upgrade on your server, create a copy of the VM (referred to as "cloning" in some products), and go through a test run to iron out any potential problems or conflicts. If something still goes wrong on the production VM, you can revert to a snapshot.

- *Test a preconfigured application*—Not sure whether the application the vendor is trying to sell you is right for your company? Some vendors offer virtual appliances you can use to evaluate the application without the trouble of installing it.

- *Test what-if scenarios*—You can create a virtual network and run clones of your production VMs to test ideas for improving your network's performance, functionality, and reliability. This type of testing on live production systems is never a good idea, but it's ideal on virtual machines.

- *Live migration*—Virtual machines can be migrated to new hardware while they're running for performance or reliability improvements with practically no downtime. Live migration features also ensure VM fault tolerance in clustered server environments.

- *Dynamic provisioning*—Advanced VM management systems can deploy VMs and storage dynamically to meet application requirements. This advanced feature has uses in clustered computing and cloud computing.

CAUTION

VMs that run distributed server applications, such as Active Directory, in which multiple servers synchronize a common database with one another, shouldn't be backed up or moved by copying the virtual hard disk, as it might result in database inconsistencies. Use only backup and migration tools approved for the virtualization software.

Bare-Metal Virtualization Products

VMware dominated the type 1 hypervisor category for years, but now you have a choice of products. The following are the most common bare-metal virtualization products:

- *Microsoft Hyper-V*—Hyper-V was introduced with Windows Server 2008 and can be installed as a server role, in which case the hypervisor is installed as a layer of software between Windows Server and the server hardware. Windows Server acts as a parent or management OS for VMs installed with Hyper-V. Hyper-V is included with Windows Server at no additional cost, or you can download the stand-alone Hyper-V Server free from the Microsoft Web site. (You can install Hyper-V Server directly on the server, with only a command-line interface available for rudimentary management tasks; it's managed remotely by another Windows Server computer.) Hyper-V supports advanced features, such as host server clustering and live migration, and requires a 64-bit CPU with virtualization extensions enabled on the host system. Virtualization extensions offload some virtualization work to the CPU and are available on most current CPUs.

  A big advantage of using Hyper-V is that Microsoft provides virtual instances of the OS with no additional licensing fees. For example, Windows Server 2012 Standard Edition allows you to run two virtual instances (or two VMs) of the OS at no additional cost. Datacenter Edition allows an unlimited number of virtual instances. Hyper-V has guest OS support for Windows Server OSs (Windows 2000 Server and later), SUSE and Red Hat Enterprise Linux distributions, Windows client OSs (Windows XP and later), and more.

  Microsoft has made Hyper-V available with Windows client OSs, too. You can enable Hyper-V in Windows 8 and later by going to Programs and Features in Control Panel, and clicking "Turn Windows features on or off." After Hyper-V is installed, you need to restart your computer and open Hyper-V Manager (see Figure 11-20) from Administrative Tools in Control Panel.

11

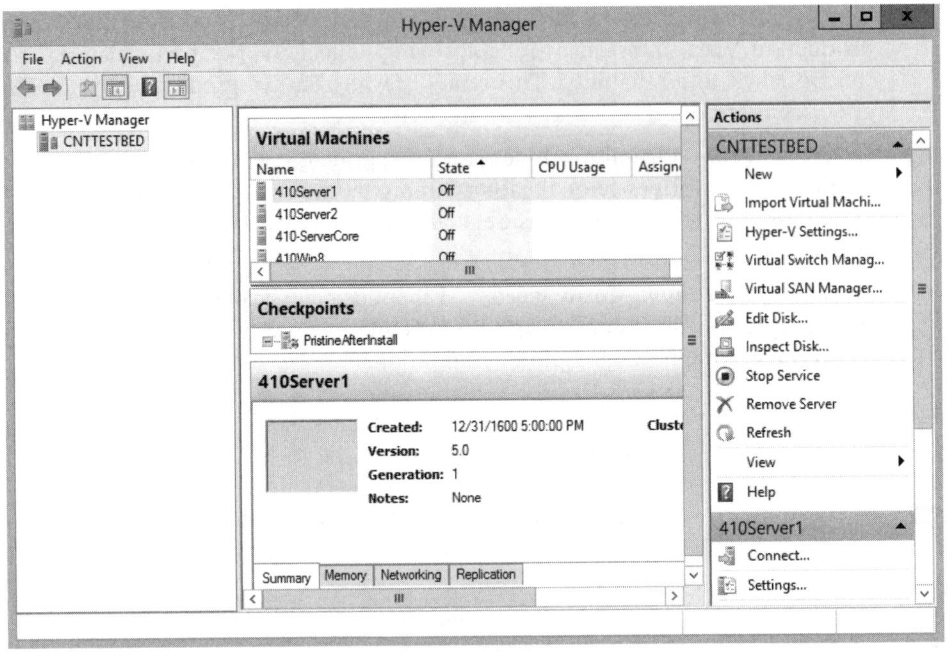

Figure 11-20   The Hyper-V Manager console

- *Citrix XenServer*—This open-source hypervisor uses Linux as a management OS on the host. It's available free or as a commercial edition that adds enterprise-level features, such as fault tolerance, performance management, and host power management. A number of modified Linux versions and Solaris can run as the management OS, and like Hyper-V, a XenServer host computer requires a 64-bit CPU with virtualization extensions to run Windows guest OSs. Guest OS support includes most Windows OSs starting with Windows XP and SUSE, Red Hat, and CentOS Linux distributions. To manage your host and VMs, you download and install XenCenter on a Windows computer.

- *VMware vSphere*—vSphere includes VMware ESX Server, which is installed directly on the physical server without a management OS. After ESX Server is installed, a basic command-line console based on Linux is available for simple configuration tasks, such as IP address configuration. Most configuration tasks are done from a remote client OS, using vSphere Client that's downloaded and installed on a Windows or Linux OS. You can also create, manage, and access VMs via a Web browser. ESX Server has the broadest guest OS support, including Windows versions back to Windows 3.1, more than a dozen Linux distributions, Novell NetWare, Solaris, and others.

All these products have extensive management tools for managing up to hundreds of hosts and a wide array of storage resources. These tools are available for a fee from virtualization software vendors. For example, Microsoft has System Center Virtual Machine Manager (SCVMM) for managing Hyper-V and ESX Server hosts. XenServer offers versions with different levels of management, depending on which product you purchase, and VMware sells vCloud Suite to manage an infrastructure as a service (IaaS) cloud computing environment.

All these products are designed to provide a secure, reliable, and highly available virtualization infrastructure.

The basic tasks of creating and accessing VMs on bare-metal virtualization software are similar to using desktop products: a wizard that walks you through the procedures. The real differences lie in host and resource management and the capability to give IT managers the tools needed to virtualize a data center, not just one or two servers. This section serves as an introduction to the available products so that you have a starting point for doing your own research in the expanding field of virtualization.

Installing an OS

Installing an OS, whether it's a desktop or server version, has become a no-brainer. Essentially, OSs install themselves, and all you have to do is click Next and OK a few times and perhaps enter a license key and accept the license agreement. Even most Linux distributions, which in the past could stymie novices with a frustrating array of choices and options, are mostly hands-off installations now.

The real work of installing an OS, particularly on a network server, involves preinstallation and postinstallation tasks. The prerequisites for installing any OS are a copy of the installation medium and a computer that meets the installation requirements, including enough free (preferably unallocated) disk space, a CPU that meets minimum performance requirements, and enough RAM. The following sections explain the preinstallation planning process, the installation, and common postinstallation tasks for Windows Server and a common distribution of Linux.

Planning for and Installing Windows Server

This section applies to most versions of Windows Server, starting with Windows Server 2008.

The role a server will play on the network is a key consideration in planning Windows Server installations. A server used only for file and printer sharing that supports a dozen users has different minimum hardware requirements than a server running Active Directory, a Web server, and a database and supporting a few hundred users. Windows Server is available in several editions with different costs and capabilities, so you need to determine which edition best fits your needs. After Windows is installed, you need to perform some postinstallation tasks immediately before installing additional features or applications.

Selecting Server Hardware for Windows Server
The minimum requirements for a server OS, although adequate for testing and training, are rarely satisfactory for a production server. So a major factor to consider for a server OS installation is the server's

hardware features. The following list describes a few features to consider before purchasing a server:

- *CPU architecture*—The minimum requirement is a 1.4 GHz CPU. CPUs are available in speeds well over 3 GHz, and major CPU manufacturers typically have a workstation line and a server line of processors. Depending on the expected server workload, you must also consider how many physical processors and how many cores each processor should have. Although Windows Server can run on just about any CPU meeting the minimum requirements, a CPU designed for servers (such as the Intel Xeon line of processors) usually has other server-specific components on the motherboard, such as high-end disk controllers and memory slots.

Windows Server 2008 R2 is the first Microsoft OS that no longer supports a 32-bit CPU; you must use a 64-bit system for Windows Server 2008 R2 and later.

- *Disk subsystem*—For entry-level or departmental servers, SATA is a good choice because it's inexpensive and offers excellent performance. For enterprise servers or servers accessed around the clock, SAS disks have better performance and reliability but are more expensive than SATA. SAS disks are generally designed for continuous use; SATA drives tend to be designed more for consumer use, although most manufacturers have an enterprise line of SATA hard drives designed for servers. Researching current technology and your network's needs before deciding is best. RAID configurations that provide fault tolerance are inexpensive and highly recommended, considering their usefulness in the event of a disk failure. Windows Server requires only about 60 GB of free disk space, but you need additional space for data you store on the server. The OS should be installed on one disk (or RAID set), and at least one other disk (or RAID set) should be used for data and application storage.

- *Memory*—The minimum requirement is 512 MB RAM. For testing or training purposes, Windows Server runs capably with this amount, at least until you have more than a couple of users accessing the server or want to install several server roles. Server motherboards are typically equipped with more RAM slots than desktop systems are—and for good reason. After you start running database-driven Web applications, maintaining a few thousand users in Active Directory, or using virtualization on your servers, often you need 32, 64, or 128 GB (or even more) RAM. Also, be aware that server memory usually costs more than desktop memory because it has features such as buffering and error correcting code (ECC) that make it more reliable.

This list covers just a few server hardware configurations you should consider before installing a server OS. The best advice is to forge a good relationship with a knowledgeable vendor you can consult when you need to make a purchase. This way, you can focus on managing your server, and your vendor can focus on keeping up with the latest hardware options.

To make sure hardware selections are compatible with Windows Server, check the Windows Server Catalog at *www.windowsservercatalog.com*.

Selecting the Right Windows Edition Windows Server 2012 comes in four main editions that target different types or sizes of customers. These editions can be summarized as follows:

- Both Datacenter and Standard editions are full-featured server OSs that support up to 4 TB of RAM, up to 64 physical processors, and server clusters with up to 64 nodes per cluster. Only the virtual use limits set them apart. For organizations using virtualization on a large scale, Datacenter Edition is clearly the best fit. A Datacenter Edition license allows you to install an unlimited number of virtual instances of the OS, meaning you can install Datacenter Edition with Hyper-V on a physical server and then install as many instances of Windows Server 2012 Datacenter Edition in virtual machines as you need. You must purchase one Datacenter Edition license for every two physical processors installed on a server. So if you have a physical server with one or two populated CPU sockets, you need one Datacenter Edition license. If your server has three or four populated CPU sockets, you need two Datacenter Edition licenses, and so forth. The number of CPU cores is irrelevant in the licensing; only physical CPU sockets are counted. So, for example, if your server has two eight-core processors installed, you still need just one Datacenter Edition license.

- Standard Edition has all the features of Datacenter Edition and the same processor licensing conditions. The only distinction (aside from price) is that a Standard Edition license permits only two virtual instances, so when you purchase Standard Edition, you can install it on a server with up to two populated CPU sockets, install the Hyper-V role, and then install Standard Edition on up to two virtual machines. If you want to install it on a server with more than two processors or on additional virtual machines, you must purchase additional licenses.

- Essentials Edition is aimed at small businesses with 25 or fewer users. It supports most of the roles and features in Standard and Datacenter editions, but some roles have restrictions or limited functions. In the original release of Windows Server 2012, the Hyper-V role couldn't be installed on Essentials Edition, but it's available in the R2 release. For the price of the license (typically around $500), you can install Essentials Edition one time on a physical server or a virtual machine, but not both. Essentials Edition is automatically configured as a domain controller. During installation, you're asked for the domain name, and Active Directory is installed automatically. Several other services are configured automatically in this edition: Active Directory Certificate Services, DNS, File Services, Web Server (IIS), Network Policy Server, and Remote Desktop Services. In addition, it comes with a front-end management interface called Dashboard that serves as a simplified server manager. Other features particular to this edition include client backups and Remote Web Access. This edition supports up to two physical processors and 64 GB RAM. In the R2 release of this edition, Office 365 integration and touch-enabled Remote Web Access have been added.

- Foundation Edition, the entry-level Windows Server 2012 edition, is suitable for small businesses that need to purchase a complete server solution for file and printer sharing, centralized control over user accounts and network resources, and common services used in most networks, such as Web services, DNS, and DHCP. Foundation Edition is available as an OEM version only, installed on a server by the manufacturer. The licensing is limited to 15 users. It supports a single physical processor; like the other editions, the number of CPU cores is irrelevant. It supports up to 32 GB RAM and can be configured as a stand-alone server or a domain controller. This edition can't be installed in a virtual machine and doesn't support Hyper-V.

Windows Server Preinstallation Decisions When installing a new server in a network, you must make some decisions shortly after finishing the installation. Many of these configuration decisions should be made before you actually begin the installation so that you can dive right into postinstallation tasks. Some are fairly straightforward, but others take some thought and consultation. Here's a list of some decisions you need to make:

- What should you name the server? This decision is more important than it sounds. Every computer needs a name so that it can be identified on the network. A server name must be unique on the network and should include some description, such as its location or primary function. Server names should also be simple and easy to remember because users often access servers by name.

- Which network protocols and addresses should you use? By default, Windows installs both TCP/IPv4 and TCP/IPv6. You can't uninstall them, but you can disable them in a network connection's Properties dialog box. Disabling TCP/IPv6 or TCP/IPv4 isn't recommended, however, as some network services depend on these protocols. Windows has no additional protocol or client options, so if you need something that isn't already installed, you must find a third-party solution.

- How should I assign an IP address to the server? By default, Windows Server is configured to use DHCP, but a server should have a static IP address. Some server roles, such as DHCP, actually require assigning a static address. If you haven't devised an addressing scheme, now is the time to do that. You might want to reserve a bank of addresses in the beginning or end of the address range for your servers, such as 192.168.1.1 to 192.168.1.20 or 192.168.1.230 to 192.168.1.250. Whatever you decide, be consistent so that when more servers are added, you can assign addresses easily.

- Setting the correct time zone isn't really a decision but a task you must complete because having the wrong time zone can cause all manner of problems, particularly in a domain environment. Certain functions in a domain network, such as user authentication, depend on client and server computers having their clocks synchronized within a few minutes of each other.

- Should I use the workgroup or domain model? The Windows domain model has a number of advantages in usability, manageability, and security. If you've invested in a Windows server OS, it makes sense to get the most out of it by using the domain model and installing Active Directory. With a small network of fewer than 10 users, however, the workgroup model is a viable option, particularly if the main administrator isn't familiar with Active Directory. With either model, you need a workgroup or domain name, unless you're using the workgroup model and keep the default name "Workgroup." If you're using the domain model, you need to decide whether the domain name will be registered on the Internet. If it isn't, many Active

Directory administrators use the top-level domain name "local," such as mycompany.local.

- What services should you install? This decision is one of the most important because it determines how the server will be used and what network services will be available to users. Windows Server refers to services such as Active Directory, DNS, and DHCP as "server roles." With the domain model, you must install Active Directory on at least one server. Active Directory requires DNS, so the DNS Server role is installed automatically. Other basic roles to consider on a first server include DHCP (for IP address configuration) and File and Storage Services, which include tools for sharing and managing file storage. Many other roles and features can be installed to meet your network and business needs.

After you have a plan, it's time to move on to the actual installation of Windows Server. Instead of reviewing installation steps here, you can run Flash Movie 2: Installing Windows Server 2012 to see these steps in action.

Flash Movie 2: Installing Windows Server 2012

Windows Server Postinstallation Tasks Now that Windows Server is installed, it's time to attend to some postinstallation tasks. Some were discussed earlier, such as naming the server and configuring protocols and addresses. Here's a summary of the tasks you should perform immediately after installation:

- Activate Windows Server.
- Set the correct date, time, and time zone.
- Assign a static IP address.
- Assign a computer name.
- Configure automatic updates.
- Download and install available updates.
- Add and configure roles and features.

Windows Server requires activation within 60 days after installation. After 60 days, you can't log on until you do so. Windows Server activates automatically after several days, or you can activate it manually by clicking "Activate Windows now" in the System Properties dialog box. As you can see, most of the work of installing Windows Server is in the planning and postinstallation tasks. The same is true of most Linux installations, covered next.

Planning for and Installing Linux

Planning for a Linux server installation isn't much different from a Windows Server installation. Minimum hardware requirements must be met, and more important, hardware requirements for the role the server will play in your network must be met. Linux has come a long way in hardware compatibility but still doesn't have the broad support for different hardware that Windows does.

To research hardware compatibility for Linux distributions, go to *www.linux-drivers.org*.

One of the biggest decisions to make before you install Linux is which distribution to use. There are so many distributions, each with its own target audience, that making a recommendation without knowing the intended environment is impossible. A Web site called DistroWatch.com lists dozens of distributions along with descriptions and links to get more information. Most Linux distributions are open source and governed by the GNU General Public License (GPL), which allows users to run the program for any purpose, make changes to the program, and redistribute the program to others under the same GPL license terms.

After deciding on a Linux distribution, the next step is downloading a disk image of the installation medium and burning it to a DVD. Many Linux distributions are offered as a Live install that you can use to boot your system (physical or virtual) from the DVD and run the OS without having to install it on a hard drive. Running a Live install isn't a replacement for installing the OS on a disk, but it's a good way to evaluate a distribution. In addition, many specialized Linux distributions are available as Live installs and contain disk and system repair utilities to help you fix a Linux or Windows installation.

You can find a list of Live Linux installs at *www.livecdlist.com.*

The preinstallation and postinstallation tasks for a Linux OS aren't very different from those for Windows Server, except there's no need to activate Linux and most tasks, such as IP address assignment and time zone selection, are done during the Linux installation. For demonstration purposes, the procedure for installing CentOS version 5.4, a popular Linux distribution used for server deployment, is shown in Flash Movie 3: Installing CentOS 5.4.

Flash Movie 3: Installing CentOS 5.4

Although installing Linux isn't difficult, it requires more input and decision-making during installation, whereas almost all configuration decisions in Windows are made after installation. Linux is a popular server OS, particularly for running Web applications and applications that use server-based databases. Compared with Windows, it offers all the basic infrastructure services, such as DHCP and DNS, but lacks a comprehensive directory service, such as Active Directory. Also, although more Linux services can be managed in a GUI, Linux still tends to make heavy use of the command line, which can be a drawback for administrators who are more at home with a GUI. Most large network environments use a combination of Windows and Linux servers, placing them in roles where they excel.

Hands-On Project 11-9: Installing Windows Server 2012 in a VM

Time Required: 30 minutes or longer

Objective: Install Windows Server 2012 in a VM.

Required Tools and Equipment: Net-*XX*, the Windows Server 2012 R2 ISO file

Description: In this project, you download and install the trial version of Windows Server 2012 R2 in the VM you created earlier. You need the Windows Server 2012 R2 ISO file (which contains an image of a DVD). Your instructor can make this file available to you, or you can download it at *https://www.microsoft.com/en-us/evalcenter/evaluate-windows-server-2012-r2*. You need to sign into the Microsoft Web site with a Microsoft account before you can download the file.

You can use Windows Server 2016, if it's available, for this project. Only the preview was available at the time of this writing, so Windows Server 2012 was used.

1. If necessary, log on to your computer as **NetAdmin**, and start VMware Player. In the left pane of the Welcome window, click **Windows Server 2012**, and then click **Edit virtual machine settings**. Click **CD/DVD**, and then click **Use ISO image file** (see Figure 11-21). Click the **Browse** button, navigate to where the ISO file is stored on your computer, click the ISO file, and then click **Open**.

Virtual Machine Settings	✕
Hardware Options	

Device	Summary
▥ Memory	1 GB
▢ Processors	1
▤ Hard Disk (SCSI)	60 GB
◉ CD/DVD (SATA)	Auto detect
▦ Network Adapter	NAT
▣ USB Controller	Present
◉ Sound Card	Auto detect
▥ Printer	Present
▥ Display	Auto detect

Device status
☐ Connected
☑ Connect at power on

Connection
○ Use physical drive:
　Auto detect
◉ Use ISO image file:
　C:\Users\NetAdmin\Desktop\W2K1 ⌄   [Browse...]

[Advanced...]

[Add...] [Remove]

[OK] [Cancel] [Help]

Figure 11-21 Using an ISO file to install Windows Server 2012 R2

Source: VMware, Inc., *www.vmware.com*

2. Click **OK** to close the Virtual Machine Settings window, and then click **Play virtual machine**. The VM boots to the Windows Server 2012 R2 installation ISO file, and you see the Windows Setup window (shown in Figure 11-22).

Figure 11-22   The Windows Setup window

Source: VMware, Inc., *www.vmware.com*

3. Accept the default options or change the language options, if necessary. Click **Next**, and then click **Install now**.

4. In the "Select the operating system you want to install" window, click **Windows Server 2012 R2 Standard Evaluation (Server with a GUI)**, which is the second installation option. Click **Next**.

5. In the "License terms" window, click **I accept the license terms**, and then click **Next**.

6. In the "Which type of installation do you want?" window, click **Custom: Install Windows only (advanced)**.

7. In the "Where do you want to install Windows?" window, accept the default option, and then click **Next**. Windows begins copying files. The installation might take 10 minutes or more.

8. After the installation is finished, the VM restarts, and the Settings dialog box opens. Set the Administrator password by typing **Password01** twice, and then clicking **Finish**. You see a message that Windows is finalizing your settings, and you're asked to log on.

9. When prompted to press Ctrl+Alt+Delete to sign in, instead press **Ctrl+Alt+Insert** or click the **Ctrl+Alt+Delete** icon on the VMware Player menu. Type **Password01** and press **Enter**. After a short time, you see the desktop, and Server Manager opens, and then you're ready to go. If you see a Network prompt, click **Yes**.

10. Now you're ready to perform postinstallation tasks, such as setting the computer name, IP address, time zone, and so forth. In Server Manager, click **Local Server** to see the default settings.

11. You can configure the server in Challenge Lab 11-1. For now, right-click **Start** on your virtual machine, point to **Shut down or sign out,** and click **Shut down**. Click **Continue,** and the VM shuts down and VMware Player closes. Log off or shut down your computer, unless you're going on to the challenge labs.

Chapter Summary

- A computer's OS provides services that enable users and devices to interact with the computer and manage the computer's resources. These services include a file system, process and service management, and the kernel.

- File systems provide a method for storing, organizing, and managing access to files on a storage device, such as a hard drive. In addition, they provide an indexing system for fast file retrieval and permissions for securing access to files.

- A process is a program that's loaded into memory and run by the CPU. It can be an application a user interacts with or a program with no user interface that communicates with and provides services to other processes. The latter type of process is called a service.

- The kernel schedules processes to run, making sure high-priority processes are taken care of first; manages memory to ensure that two applications don't attempt to use the same memory space; and makes sure I/O devices are accessed by only one process at a time, in addition to other tasks.

- Client OSs include many features once reserved for a server OS, such as file and printer sharing and file system security, but an OS designed to be installed as a server still contains many additional networking and fault-tolerance features not found in client OSs.

- Virtualization can be divided into two categories: hosted virtualization and bare-metal virtualization. Hosted virtualization products are installed on a desktop OS and include VMware Workstation, Virtual PC, and VirtualBox. Bare-metal virtualization software is used in data centers, is installed on servers, and includes products such as Microsoft Hyper-V, VMware vSphere, and Citrix XenServer.

- The real work of installing an OS consists of preinstallation and postinstallation tasks. The prerequisites for installing any OS are a copy of the installation medium and a computer that meets the hardware requirements, including enough free (preferably unallocated) disk space, a CPU meeting minimum performance requirements, and enough RAM.

- Some features to look for in a server system include CPU architecture, disk subsystem, and amount of memory. You must also be sure to select the correct edition of the OS you're going to install.

- Preinstallation decisions include the server name, the protocols to use, the networking model (domain or workgroup) you should use, and the services should be installed. Postinstallation tasks include activating the OS if necessary, setting the correct date and time, configuring IP settings, configuring the computer name, installing updates, and installing roles and features.

Key Terms

authentication   The process of identifying who has access to the network. The most common form of authentication is a logon with a username and password.

authorization   The process of granting or denying an authenticated user's access to network resources.

bare-metal virtualization   The hypervisor implements OS virtualization by running directly on the host computer's hardware and controls and monitors guest OSs. *See also* virtualization.

batch file   A text file containing a list of commands usually typed at a command prompt.

cloud storage   A data storage method in which some or all of an organization's data is stored on servers located offsite and maintained by a storage hosting company.

context switching   Occurs when the OS suspends one process and activates another process.

cooperative multitasking   In this form of multitasking, the OS can't stop a process; when a process gets control of the CPU, it maintains control until it satisfies its computing needs and informs the OS that another process can be activated.

disk cluster   A group of sectors; the smallest amount of space that can be occupied by a file stored on the disk.

failover cluster   A server cluster configuration used for fault tolerance so that if one server fails, the other takes over its functions immediately, with no or little downtime.

file system   The method by which an OS stores, organizes, and manages access to files on a storage device, such as a hard drive.

guest OS   The operating system installed on a virtual machine.

host computer   The physical computer on which virtual machine software is installed and virtual machines run.

hosted virtualization   The hypervisor implements OS virtualization by being installed in a general-purpose host OS, such as Windows 10 or Linux, and the host OS accesses host hardware on behalf of the guest OS. *See also* virtualization.

hot-swappable device   A computer device that can be removed, replaced, or added to a server while it's running.

hypervisor   The component of virtualization software that creates and monitors the virtual hardware environment, which allows multiple VMs to share physical hardware resources.

load-balancing cluster   A server cluster configuration that provides high-performance computing and data access by spreading the workload among multiple computers.

logon script   Commands typed into a file that run when a user logs on to a Windows domain.

multiprocessing   A feature of some OSs that allow two or more threads to be run concurrently by separate CPUs or CPU cores. *See also* thread.

multitasking   An operating system's capability to run more than one application or process at the same time.

multithreaded application   An application that has two or more threads that can be scheduled separately for execution by the CPU. *See also* thread.

network appliance   A device equipped with specialized software that performs a limited task, such as file sharing. Network appliances are often packaged without video interfaces, so you don't configure them with an attached keyboard and monitor.

network-attached storage (NAS)   A dedicated server device designed solely for providing shared storage for network users.

preemptive multitasking   A form of multitasking in which the OS controls which process gets access to the CPU and for how long.

process   A program that's loaded into memory and run by the CPU. It can be an application a user interacts with or a program with no user interface that communicates with and provides services to other processes.

redirector   An OS client component that intercepts resource requests and determines whether the resource is local or remote.

redundant array of independent disks (RAID)   A storage configuration of two or more disks, usually in a fault-tolerant arrangement so that if one disk fails, data is preserved and the server can continue to operate.

server cluster   Two or more servers configured to operate as a single unit. The most common types of server clusters are failover clusters and load-balancing clusters.

service   A process that runs in the background and provides services to other processes; for example, DNS client and server components are services.

snapshot   A partial copy of a virtual machine made at a particular moment, used to restore the virtual machine to its state when the snapshot was taken. *See also* virtual machine (VM).

storage area network (SAN)   A high-speed, high-cost network storage solution for replacing locally attached drives on servers.

thread   The smallest unit of software that can be scheduled to run.

time slicing   The process by which a CPU's computing cycles are divided between more than one process. *See also* multitasking.

virtual disk   Files stored on the host computer that represent a virtual machine's hard disk.

virtual machine (VM)   A software environment that emulates a physical computer's hardware and BIOS.

virtual network   A network configuration created by virtualization software and used by virtual machines for network communication.

virtualization   A process that creates a software environment to emulate a computer's hardware and BIOS, allowing multiple OSs to run on the same physical computer at the same time.

Review Questions

1. Which of the following is an objective of a file system? (Choose all that apply.)

    a. Organize space on a drive.

    b. Organize files hierarchically.

    c. Schedule access to applications.

    d. Secure access to files.

2. A cluster is composed of which of the following?

    a. One or more 512-bit blocks

    b. Two or more 2K-byte sectors

    c. One or more 512-byte sectors

    d. One or more 2K-byte blocks

3. Large cluster sizes can result in which of the following on a disk drive?

    a. Faster performance for large files, more wasted space for small files

    b. Faster performance for small files, less wasted space for small files

    c. More fragmentation, faster performance for large files

    d. Less fragmentation, more wasted space for large files

4. Which of these file systems includes file and folder permissions? (Choose all that apply.)

    a. FAT32

    b. FAT16

    c. NTFS

    d. Ext3

5. What feature of a file system makes it possible to find a file based on keywords in it?

6. Which of the following is best described as a program loaded into memory that has no user interface but communicates with other programs?

    a. Process

    b. Task

    c. Service

    d. Application

7. The DNS function is built into most applications. True or False?

8. Which best describes context switching?

    a. Dividing computing cycles equally among processes

    b. The OS suspending the running process and activating another process

    c. Cooperative multitasking

    d. Changing from one OS to another in a virtual environment

9. The most common form of multitasking in current OSs is cooperative multitasking. True or False?

10. Which OS component schedules processes to run?

    a. File system

    b. User interface

    c. Memory manager

    d. Kernel

11. Which best describes a thread?

    a. A process you can view in Task Manager

    b. The smallest schedulable unit of software

    c. A process in a preemptive multitasking OS

    d. A multiprocessing computer

12. Which of the following is true about the kernel?

    a. The kernel is positioned just above the hardware.

    b. The kernel provides the user interface.

    c. The kernel sets user permissions.

    d. The kernel is an optional part of the OS.

13. Which component of a file-sharing client intercepts requests to determine whether the requested resource is local or remote?

    a. Disk sector

    b. NTFS

    c. Redirector

    d. SMB

14. Which of the following is a high-speed network storage solution that can replace locally attached storage on a server?

    a. NAS

    b. SAN

    c. Cloud-based

    d. SMB

15. What should you use to provide fault tolerance so that if one server fails, the other immediately takes over its functions with no or little downtime?

    a. Failover cluster

    b. Storage area network

    c. Round-robin load balancing

    d. Load-balancing cluster

16. Which is the correct syntax for mapping drive letter W to a shared folder named Accounting on the Finance server?

    a.   `net use W: \\Finance\Accounting`

    b.   `net share W: \\Accounting\Finance`

    c.   `net use W: \\Accounting\Finance`

    d.   `net share W: \\Finance\Accounting`

17. A text file containing a list of commands is called which of the following?

    a.   Logon process file

    b.   Service file

    c.   Task file

    d.   Batch file

18. The default protocol Windows uses to share folders is which of the following?

    a.   NFS

    b.   SMB

    c.   WPA

    d.   FTP

19. Which of the following refers to a Windows server with Active Directory installed?

    a.   Member server

    b.   NIS server

    c.   Domain controller

    d.   LDAP controller

20. Which of the following best describes an NAS?

    a.   A dedicated device designed to provide shared storage for network users

    b.   A high-speed network storage solution that can replace locally attached drives on servers

    c.   A storage solution in which some or all data is stored on offsite servers

    d.   A SATA or SCSI drive connected to a server

21. Which of the following is a partial copy of a VM made at a particular moment that enables you to restore the VM's state?

    a.   Incremental backup

    b.   Virtual disk

    c.   Load balancing

    d.   Snapshot

22. If you want to configure disks on a server so that data is preserved if a disk fails, what should you use?

    a. RAID

    b. Failover cluster

    c. Redundant array of servers

    d. Load-balancing disk system

23. Software that creates and monitors the virtual hardware environment is called what?

    a. Host computer

    b. Hypervisor

    c. Snapshot

    d. Guest OS

24. Bare-metal virtualization is best for desktop virtualization. True or False?

25. If you want your virtual machine to have direct access to the physical network, which virtual network option should you configure?

    a. Bridged

    b. NAT

    c. Host-only

    d. Internal

Critical Thinking

The following activities give you critical thinking challenges. Challenge labs give you an opportunity to use the skills you have learned to perform a task without step-by-step instructions. Case projects offer a practical networking setup for which you supply a written solution.

CHALLENGE LAB

Challenge Lab 11-1: Configuring a Server

Time Required: 20 minutes

Objective: Configure the server installed in the VM in Hands-On Project 11-9.

Required Tools and Equipment: Net-XX with the server VM from Hands-On Project 11-9

Description: Your Windows Server 2012 server is installed and ready for postinstallation tasks. Based on the description in this chapter, configure your server. Because the server will be used for testing purposes and shouldn't have access to the physical network, configure the virtual network accordingly. Assume it's a test server for the IT Department, and give it a suitable name. Answer these questions:

• What virtual network setting did you use?

- List the configuration tasks you performed and state the values and settings you used:

_____

_____

_____

_____

Challenge Lab 11-2: Working with the Command Line

Time Required: 30 minutes

Objective: Navigate and use the Windows command line.

Required Tools and Equipment: Net-*XX* with the server VM installed in Hands-On Project 11-9 and configured in Challenge Lab 11-1. (*Note*: If you didn't install the server in Hands-On Project 11-9, you can use Net-*XX* for this challenge lab.)

Description: In this challenge lab, you create a folder hierarchy and work with the command line. Using the commands available at the command prompt, create a folder hierarchy on your Windows Server 2012 VM that could be used to store documents for the users in a company. This company has the following departments and subdepartments:

In this challenge lab, you create a file hierarchy; in a challenge lab in Chapter 12, you share folders, create users and groups, and assign permissions to the folders.

- Management
- Accounting
  - Billing
  - Accounts Payable
- Operations
  - Manufacturing
  - Design
- Customer Service
- Human Resources
- Information Technology
  - Network Engineering
  - Helpdesk

Each department and subdepartment should have its own folder to store files. In addition, create a folder containing company documents, such as policies and procedures, that all employees can access.

In each folder, create a file named ReadMe `DeptName`.txt (with `DeptName` indicating the name of the department). The file should explain the folder's purpose and contents. Rather than create the file again for each department, create it once, add the text, and copy and rename it for the other folders. When you're done, take a screenshot of the file hierarchy in File Explorer and hand it in to your instructor. In addition, answer the following questions:

- List the commands you used to navigate the file system and create the folder hierarchy. What's the function of each command?

_____

_____

- List the commands you used to create the master ReadMe file and the commands you used to copy the file to each department folder with the correct name.

_____

_____

_____

CHALLENGE LAB

Challenge Lab 11-3: Installing Linux in a Virtual Machine

Time Required: 1 hour or longer, depending on download and installation time

Objective: Download the latest Ubuntu Linux distribution and install it as a VM in VMware Player.

Required Tools/Equipment: Net-*XX* with VMware Player installed and Internet access to download the Linux distribution (or access to it on the local network)

Description: In this lab, you create a virtual machine for Ubuntu Linux, and then download the latest Ubuntu Linux distribution (at *www.ubuntu.com/download*) and install it in the VM. The Ubuntu desktop version is recommended. When you download Ubuntu, you're asked to make a contribution to support it, but this is optional. The download is an ISO file that you can attach to a VM's CD/DVD drive. Answer the following questions:

- What advantages do you see in using an ISO file instead of a physical DVD to install an OS?

_____

- List three examples of using hosted virtualization in a business environment:

_____

_____

_____

- What do you see as the major differences between installing Ubuntu Linux and Windows Server 2012?

_____

_____

Case Project 11-1

From this book, you have learned a little about different file systems. To get a better handle on the differences between them, write a short memo describing three properties of each of these file systems: FAT16, FAT32, NTFS, and Ext3 (a Linux file system). You can research them on the Internet. Relate the properties to the objectives of all file systems discussed in the chapter.

Case Project 11-2

You need to set up a network that meets the following requirements:

- Automatic IP address configuration
- Name resolution
- Centralized account management
- Capability to store files in a centralized location easily

Write a memo explaining what services must be installed on the network to satisfy each requirement.

Case Project 11-3

Your boss wants to purchase a graphics design application to be distributed to approximately 40 users in the company. The problem is that although the company says it has broad OS support, he wants to be sure it will run on the five different OSs running on the company's user workstations. He wants you to verify compatibility by using evaluation copies of the software without disrupting users or their computers. You have the installation disks for all five OSs your company uses, but you don't have a lot of computers available to install them on. What's your plan?

Case Project 11-4

You've been called in to recommend a server for a company that's opening a new office. You're meeting with the operations manager to get preliminary information about what the company needs and will make a recommendation for this new server's hardware and OS. List the top five questions you should ask the operations manager so that you can make the best recommendation.

chapter 12

Network Management and Administration

After reading this chapter and completing the exercises, you will be able to:

- Create and work with user and group accounts
- Create and manage permissions on storage volumes
- Work with shared files and printers
- Monitor a system's performance and reliability
- Describe fault-tolerance and backup solutions

You've learned the basics of networks and network operating systems; now it's time to turn your attention to performing typical network management and administrative tasks. This chapter discusses user and group management, storage and file system management, and working with shared files and printers. In addition, as a server administrator, you need to know how to monitor system performance and prevent loss of data with fault-tolerance and backup solutions.

This chapter discusses Windows operating systems. Discussions of Windows Server typically apply to current Windows Server OS versions, from Windows Server 2008 to Windows Server 2016. Discussions of Windows client OSs usually apply to Windows 7 through Windows 10.

Managing User and Group Accounts

Table 12-1 summarizes what you need for the hands-on projects in this chapter.

Table 12-1   Hands-on project requirements

Hands-on project	Requirements	Time required	Notes
Hands-On Project 12-1: Creating Users in a Windows Client OS	Net-*XX*	20 minutes	
Hands-On Project 12-2: Working with Groups in a Windows Client OS	Net-*XX*	10 minutes	
Hands-On Project 12-3: Working with Users and Groups in Linux (Optional)	Net-*XX* and a Linux Live disc or a computer or VM with Linux installed	15 minutes	
Hands-On Project 12-4: Using Windows Disk Management	Net-*XX*	15 minutes	
Hands-On Project 12-5: Using the NTFS File System	Net-*XX*	15 minutes	
Hands-On Project 12-6: Sharing a Folder with the File Sharing Wizard	Net-*XX*	15 minutes	
Hands-On Project 12-7: Viewing Real-Time Performance Data	Net-*XX*	10 minutes	
Hands-On Project 12-8: Creating a Data Collector Set	Net-*XX*	15 minutes	
Hands-On Project 12-9: Using Windows Backup and Restore	Net-*XX*	20 minutes	

Working with user accounts is one of an administrator's key tasks. User accounts are the link between real people and network resources, so user account management requires both technical expertise and people skills. When users can't log on to the network or access the resources they need, IT staff members get the phone calls. Your understanding of how user accounts work and how to configure them along with group accounts can reduce the frequency of these phone calls. User accounts have two main functions in a network:

- *Provide a method for users to authenticate themselves to the network*—Using a username and password is the most common way for users to log on to a network to gain access to network resources. User accounts can also contain restrictions about when and where a user can log on. Administrators use user accounts to assign permissions to network resources and define the types of actions a user can perform (referred to as **rights** in Windows), such as creating file shares or installing software.

- *Provide detailed information about a user*—User accounts can hold information such as a user's phone number, office location, department, and so forth for use in a company directory or for use by the IT department to identify users for support purposes.

Group accounts are used to organize users so that assignment of resource permissions and rights can be managed more easily than working with dozens or hundreds of user accounts. For example, an administrator can make a group account for each department in the company and add the users who work in each department as members of the corresponding group. Then, when a shared folder containing documents used by a certain department is created, the administrator just needs to assign permission to the group, which gives all its members the necessary permission. If a user changes departments, the administrator moves the account from one group to another, thereby changing the resources to which the user has permissions.

Account and Password Conventions

In a small network with only a few users and network resources, establishing a naming convention for accounts might be more trouble than it's worth. When you're working with dozens of servers and hundreds or thousands of users, however, a scheme for naming user and group accounts as well as network devices is crucial. For user accounts, some considerations for a naming convention include the following:

- Is there a minimum and maximum number of characters user account names should have?
- Should the username be based on the user's real name, or, if security is of utmost importance, should usernames be more cryptic and, therefore, difficult to guess?
- Some OSs distinguish between uppercase and lowercase letters. Should usernames contain both as well as special characters, such as periods and underscores?

There's no right or wrong answer to these questions, but after you devise a policy, you should stick to it so that when it's time to create a new user account, your naming conventions make the process straightforward.

As part of creating user accounts, passwords must also be created. The considerations for password naming conventions include the following:

- *Minimum length*—In environments where a user account is based on a user's real name, all that's needed to access the account is guessing the password. Longer passwords are harder to guess and, therefore, more secure.

- *Complexity requirements*—Using uppercase and lowercase letters along with numbers and special symbols (such as @, $, %, and so forth) makes passwords considerably more difficult to guess, even with password-guessing software.

- *User or administrator created*—In most cases, users create their own passwords after an administrator gives them an initial password. However, to ensure that passwords are complex enough, they can be checked by using dictionary attacks and other brute-force methods to attempt to crack them.

- *Password change frequency*—Many networks require frequent password changes to enhance security. However, if changes are required too frequently, users are more apt to write down their passwords, which is a major security risk.

There are other considerations for working with passwords, some of which are particular to the OS on which the user account is created. You learn more about password-handling options next in "Working with Accounts in Windows."

Group account names also warrant careful planning. The group name should reflect the group membership (such as a department name) or the resource to which the group is assigned permissions or rights. An example of a group name that reflects a resource permission assignment is NAS_4thFloor, indicating that group members have access to the NAS server on the 4th floor. In some cases, a group name might reflect the role group members have in the company, such as supervisors, administrators, executives, and so forth. The most important aspect of naming conventions is that after you have established them, stick to them and allow only users who are well versed in the conventions to create accounts.

Working with Accounts in Windows

The details of account creation differ, depending on whether accounts are created on a Windows client OS or in Windows Server with Active Directory. You can specify many more user account properties in Active Directory, but basic account creation is similar in Windows 10.

This section discusses user and group accounts in Windows Server 2016 with Active Directory, and you work with accounts in a client OS (Windows 10) in the hands-on projects. A key difference to remember when working with accounts in Active Directory is that they're used to log on to the Windows domain and can be used to access resources on all computers that are domain members. An account created in a Windows client OS is used only to log on to that particular computer and access resources only on that computer.

When Windows is installed, two users are created: Administrator and Guest. On a Windows Server 2016 domain controller, the Guest account is disabled, and in Windows 10, both Administrator and Guest are disabled. In Windows 10, you create a user with administrator privileges during installation. The Guest account is rarely used and poses a security risk, which is why it's disabled. You can enable the account if you like, but best practices dictate creating new accounts for guest users of your network. The Administrator account has full access to a computer, and in a Windows domain, the domain Administrator account's access is extended to all computers that are domain members. You must give careful consideration to who can log on as Administrator and who's a member of the Administrators group.

Creating User Accounts in Windows Domains Windows domain users are created in Active Directory Users and Computers (shown in Figure 12-1) or Active Directory Administrative Center (ADAC) or with command-line tools. As you can see, several folders are available for organizing users, groups, and other domain elements. You can also create your own folders, called organizational units (OUs), to match your company's organizational scheme. For example, you can create a folder for each department or create folders representing office locations. In Figure 12-1, the open folder named Users contains the Administrator and Guest accounts and many of the default groups created when Active Directory is installed. You can create additional users in this folder, but it's better to add OUs and create users and groups in the OU structure you specify.

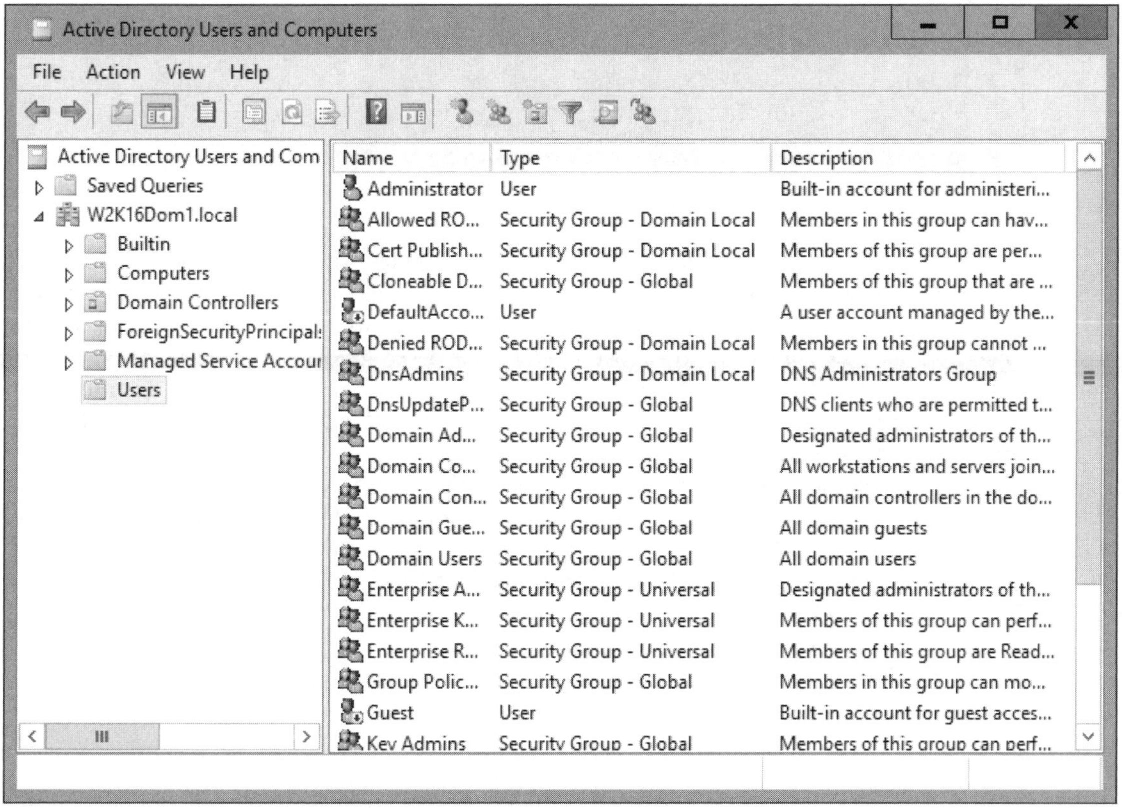

Figure 12-1 The Active Directory Users and Computers management console

To create a user, open the folder where you want to create the account. Right-click the folder, point to New, and click User, or you can click the user icon on the Active Directory Users and Computers toolbar. The New Object - User dialog box opens (see Figure 12-2). Everything you create in Active Directory is considered an object.

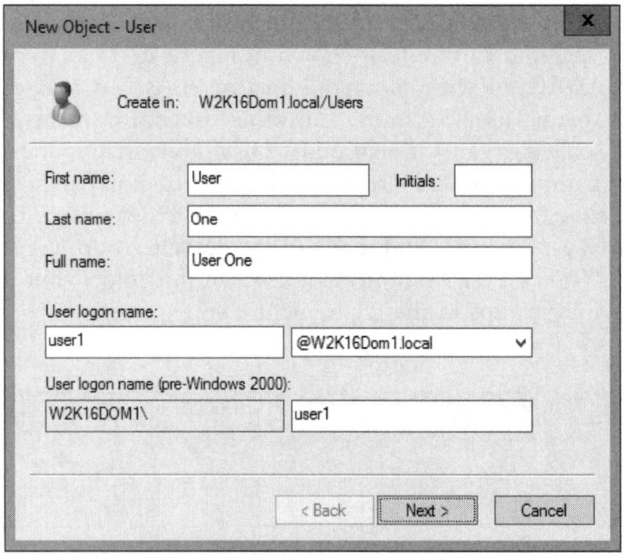

Figure 12-2   Creating a user in Active Directory

You don't have to fill in all the fields, but you must enter something in the Full name and User logon name text boxes. The user logon name isn't case sensitive, so if the logon name is JSmith, the user can log on with jsmith or JSMITH or any combination of uppercase and lowercase letters. The drop-down list next to the User logon name text box shows the default domain the user logs on to. In a network with multiple domains, the user might need to log on to the network with the syntax *LogonName@domain*, which is the user principal name (UPN). In most cases, a user needs only the logon name to log on. After entering the full name and user logon name, you click Next to get to the window shown in Figure 12-3, where you enter the password and confirm it. The password is case sensitive.

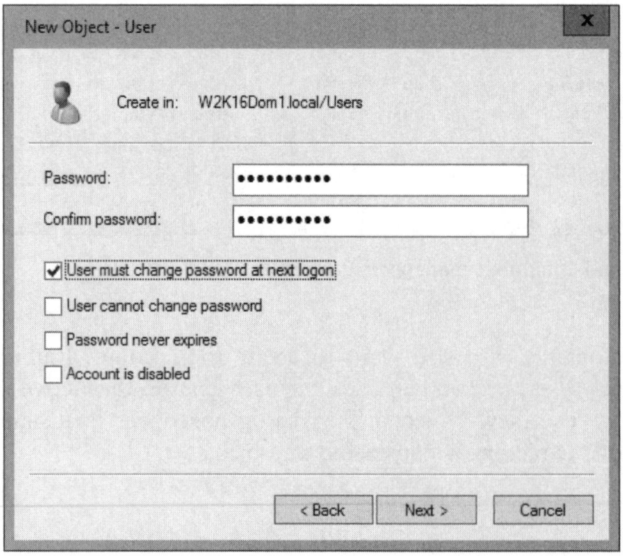

Figure 12-3   Setting the password and additional account options

As you can see, the password isn't shown as you type it for security reasons. You can also choose the following options for the user's initial logon and password:

- *User must change password at next logon*—The user is prompted to change the password at the next logon. Administrators sometimes create accounts with a default password based on the user's name or phone number that must be changed at the next logon. This option can also be set when users forget their passwords and the support staff changes passwords for them.

- *User cannot change password*—When the administrator wants to maintain control of passwords, this option can be set to prevent users from changing their own passwords. It's also used when multiple users have a common generic account for logging on (such as "salesperson").

- *Password never expires*—Users can be required to change their password periodically. If this option is set, the user isn't subject to the password change requirement.

- *Account is disabled*—If a user account is created several days before it's going to be used, the account can be disabled at first and then enabled when the user joins the company. In addition, if a user leaves the company or will be gone for an extended period, the account can be disabled. Often when a user leaves the company, the account is disabled rather than deleted so that the user hired as the replacement can use the same account after you rename it and change the password. In this way, the new user has all the same permissions and rights as the previous user.

After a user account is created, double-click it to open its properties. Compared with user accounts in client OSs, user accounts in Active Directory have far more properties you can configure. Figure 12-4 shows properties for a user in Active Directory on the left and for

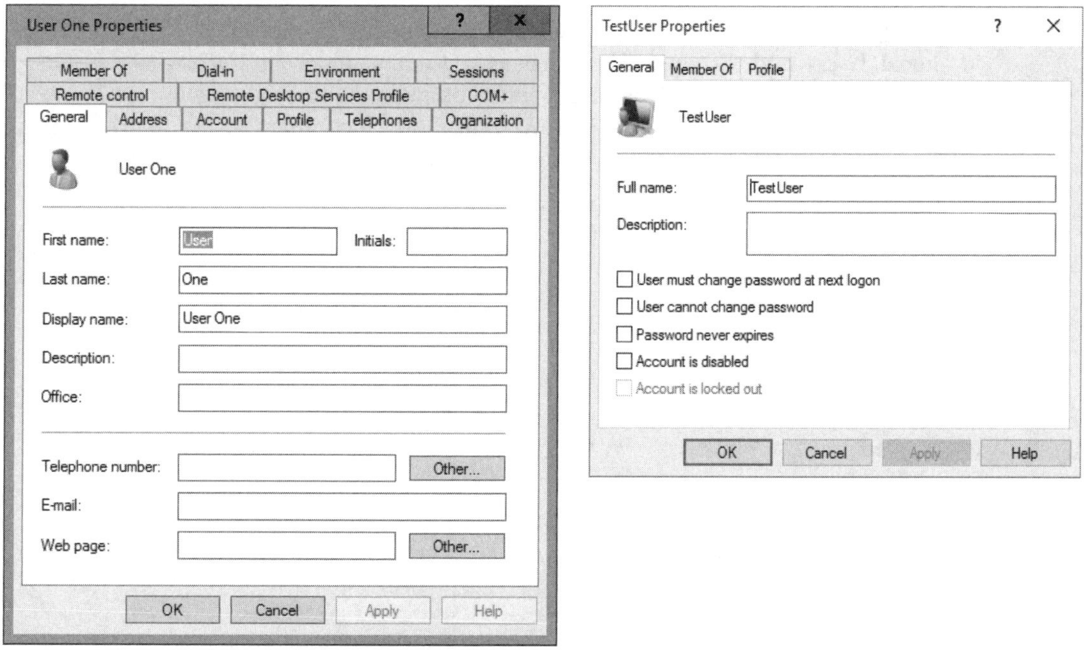

Figure 12-4 User properties in Active Directory (left) and in Windows 10 (right)

an account in Windows 10 on the right. Notice that the two properties dialog boxes have the Member Of tab in common, where you can see which groups a user belongs to and add or remove the user from groups. They also have the Profile tab in common. Profiles are discussed later in "User Profiles."

When a user is added to or removed from a group, the setting takes effect the next time the user logs on; if a user is already logged on, he or she must log off and log back on.

Hands-On Project 12-1: Creating Users in a Windows Client OS

Time Required: 20 minutes

Objective: Create a user account in a Windows client OS.

Required Tools and Equipment: Net-*XX*

Description: In this project, you create a user in the Computer Management console.

1. Log on to your computer as **NetAdmin**. There are two tools for creating user accounts in a Windows client OS. One is User Accounts in Control Panel, which is mostly for home users. The other is Local Users and Groups in the Computer Management console. Local Users and Groups gives administrators more control over user properties and has more in common with Active Directory Users and Computers, so it's used in this project.

2. Right-click **Start** and click **Computer Management**. In the left pane, click to expand **Local Users and Groups**, which has two folders under it: Users and Groups. Click **Users** to display a list of users on your computer in the right pane (see Figure 12-5). Notice the Administrator, Default Account, and Guest users in the figure, shown with a black arrow in a white circle to indicate that the accounts are disabled.

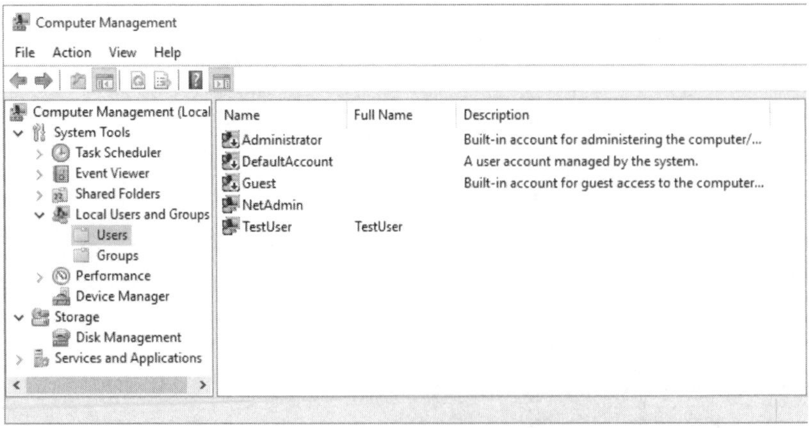

Name	Full Name	Description
Administrator		Built-in account for administering the computer/...
DefaultAccount		A user account managed by the system.
Guest		Built-in account for guest access to the computer...
NetAdmin		
TestUser	TestUser	

Figure 12-5 Viewing Local Users and Groups in Computer Management

3. Right-click empty space in the right pane and click **New User**. In the New User dialog box, type **NewGuest1** in the User name text box. In the Full name text box, type **New Guest User 1**, and in the Description text box, type **A new guest user account**.

4. Type **guestpass** in the Password text box and again in the Confirm password text box.

5. Leave the **User must change password at next logon box** check box selected (see Figure 12-6), and click **Create**. You see an error stating that the password doesn't meet complexity requirements. List the complexity requirements in Windows. (You set the password policy in Hands-On Project 9-1.) Click **OK**, and this time, type **Guestpass1** in the Password and Confirm password text boxes, and then click **Create**. The New User dialog box clears so that you can create another user. Click **Close**.

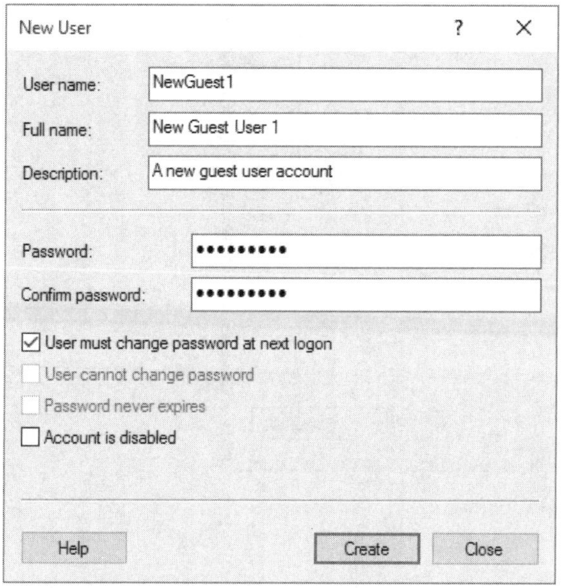

Figure 12-6   Creating a user in Windows 10

6. In Local Users and Groups, double-click **NewGuest1** to view its properties. Click the **Member Of** tab. By default, all new users are put in a group called Users; this is also the case when a user is created in Active Directory. Click **Cancel**.

7. Click the **Groups** folder in the left pane to see a list of groups Windows creates. Double-click the **Users** group. You'll see a list of users who are members of the Users group, including NewGuest1. You'll probably also see some special groups named Authenticated Users and INTERACTIVE, which are internal groups used by Windows. Click **Cancel**.

8. Log off Windows. When the logon window opens, New Guest User 1 is shown as a user to choose from. Click **New Guest User 1**. Type **Guestpass1** in the Password text box and press **Enter**, or click the arrow to log on. In the message box stating that your password must be changed, click **OK**. Type **Password01** in the New password and Confirm password text boxes. Press **Enter** or click the arrow.

9. In the message box stating that the password has been changed, click **OK**. Leave Windows running for the next project.

Creating Group Accounts in Windows Domains Group accounts are easy to create. All they require is a name, and after they're created, you can begin adding users as members. The process is similar to creating a user. In Active Directory, the New Object - Group dialog box looks like Figure 12-7. The "Group name (pre-Windows 2000)" text box is used for backward-compatibility with older Windows OSs. The other options, group scope and group type, are used only in Windows domains. The group scope has three options:

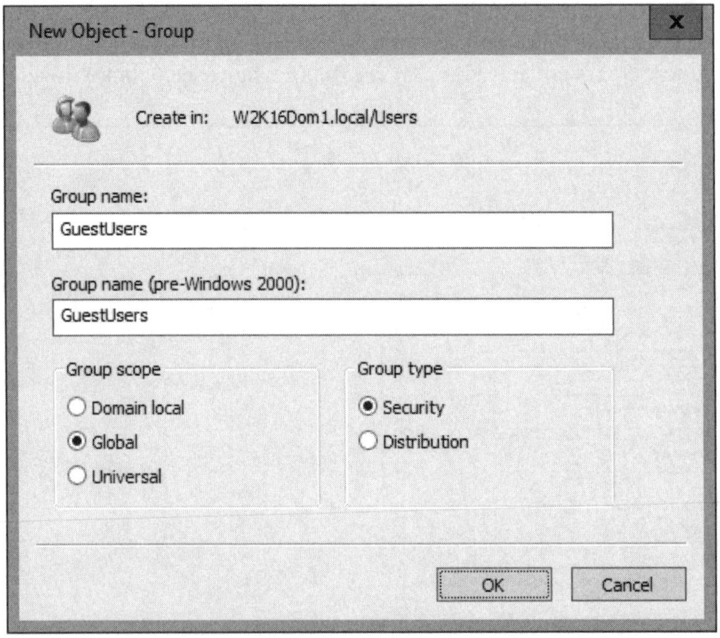

New Object - Group   X

Create in: W2K16Dom1.local/Users

Group name:

GuestUsers

Group name (pre-Windows 2000):

GuestUsers

Group scope
- ○ Domain local
- ● Global
- ○ Universal

Group type
- ● Security
- ○ Distribution

OK   Cancel

Figure 12-7 Creating a group in Active Directory

- *Domain local*—Can be used to assign permissions to resources only in the domain in which the group is created. Although domain local groups can contain users from any domain, they're used mainly to hold global groups and assign permissions to global group members.

- *Global*—The default option, global groups contain users from the domain in which they're created but can be assigned permissions to resources in other domains in a multidomain network. Their main purpose is to group users who require access to similar resources.

- *Universal*—Used in multidomain networks; users from any domain can be members and be assigned permission to resources in any domain.

A detailed discussion on group scope is beyond the scope of this book. For a complete discussion, see *MCSA Guide to Installing and Configuring Microsoft Windows Server 2012/R2* (Cengage Learning, 2015, ISBN 9781285868653).

The group type option is set to Security by default. Distribution groups are used only for tasks such as sending all group members an e-mail when you run an Active Directory–integrated e-mail program, such as Microsoft Exchange.

Windows Default Groups Aside from groups you create to organize users and assign permissions, Windows defines some **default groups**, which have preassigned rights that apply to all group members. Table 12-2 shows the most important default domain local groups in Windows Server running Active Directory and the rights assigned to these groups.

Table 12-2 Some Windows Server default domain local groups

Group	Rights
Administrators	Has complete control over the computer and domain
Account Operators	Can administer user and group accounts for the local domain
Backup Operators	Can back up and restore files that users normally can't access
Guests	Is allowed guest access to domain resources; same access as the Users group
Print Operators	Can add, delete, and manage domain printers
Server Operators	Can administer domain servers
Users	Has default access rights that ordinary user accounts have

In addition, Windows Server has numerous default global groups, including Domain Admins, Domain Users, and Domain Guests. Essentially the same as domain local groups with similar names, these groups apply to entire domains rather than a single machine.

Special Identity Groups **Special identity groups**, some described in Table 12-3, don't appear as objects in Active Directory Users and Computers or in Local Users and Groups, but they can be assigned permissions and rights. Membership in these groups is controlled dynamically by Windows, can't be viewed or changed manually, and depends on how an account accesses the OS. For example, membership in the Authenticated Users group is assigned to a user account automatically when the user logs on to a computer or domain.

Table 12-3 Some Windows special identity groups

Special identity group	Description
Authenticated Users	Members are any user account (except Guest) that logs on to a computer or domain with a valid username and password.
Creator Owner	A user becomes a member automatically for a resource he or she created (such as a folder).
Everyone	Refers to all users who access the system; similar to the Authenticated Users group but includes the Guest user.
Interactive	Members are users logged on to a computer locally or through Remote Desktop Services.
Network	Members are users logged on to a computer through a network connection.
System	Refers to the Windows OS.
Self	Refers to the object on which permissions are being set.

Hands-On Project 12-2: Working with Groups in a Windows Client OS

Time Required: 10 minutes

Objective: Create a group and add a user to the group.

Required Tools and Equipment: Net-*XX*

Description: In this project, you create a group in the Computer Management console and then add a user to the group.

1. Log on to your computer as **NetAdmin,** if necessary.

2. Right-click **Start** and click **Computer Management.** Click to expand **Local Users and Groups,** and then click **Groups.**

3. Right-click empty space in the right pane and click **New Group.** In the New Group dialog box, type **GuestUsers** in the Group name text box. In the Description text box, type **A group for guest users of this computer.**

4. Click **Add.** Examine the Select Users dialog box shown in Figure 12-8. It's similar to what you see when adding a user to a group in Active Directory.

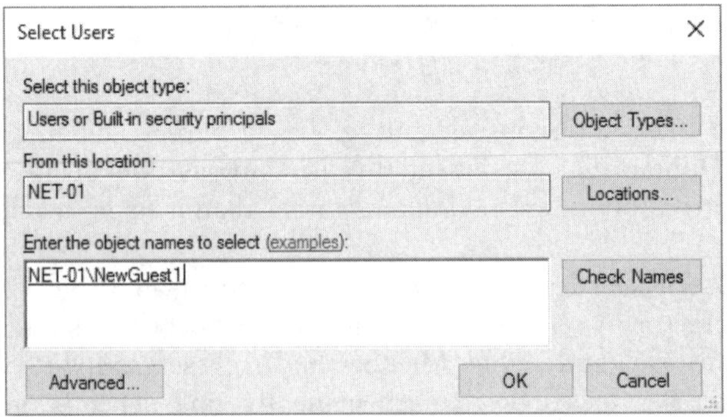

Select Users

Select this object type:

Users or Built-in security principals   Object Types...

From this location:

NET-01   Locations...

Enter the object names to select (examples):

NET-01\NewGuest1   Check Names

Advanced...   OK   Cancel

Figure 12-8 Selecting users to add to a group

5. To limit the types of objects Windows shows if you click the Advanced button to search for objects to add to a group, you use the Object Types button. Click **Locations.** You have only one option unless your computer is a member of a domain. If so, you can select objects from the domain; otherwise, you can choose only objects created on your computer. Click **Cancel.**

6. You can type the group members' names in the text box, but to select from a list, click **Advanced.** Click **Find Now** to list available users and groups you can add as group members. Click **NewGuest1** and click **OK.** Notice in the Select Users dialog box that the user is specified as NET-*XX*\NewGuest1. NET-*XX* is the name of the computer or domain where the user was created; in this case, it's the computer name. Click **OK.**

7. NewGuest1 is then listed as a member of the group. Click **Create** to finish creating the group, and then click **Close.** What's a reason for using groups?

8. NewGuest1 is now a member of both the GuestUsers and Users groups. Remember that the result of changing group membership takes effect the next time the user logs on. If you wanted to remove NewGuest1 from the default Users group, you would double-click the Users group, right-click NewGuest1, and click Remove. However, doing so removes NewGuest1 from the list of users in the Windows 10 logon window, so for now, leave this account as a member of both groups. Log off Windows for the next project.

User Profiles A **user profile** is a collection of a user's personal files and settings that define his or her working environment. By default, a user profile is created when a user logs on to a computer for the first time and is stored in a folder that usually has the same name as the user's logon name. On a Windows computer, a profile is created as a subfolder of the Users folder, which is on the same drive as the Windows folder, usually C. Figure 12-9 shows the profile folder hierarchy on a typical Windows 10 system.

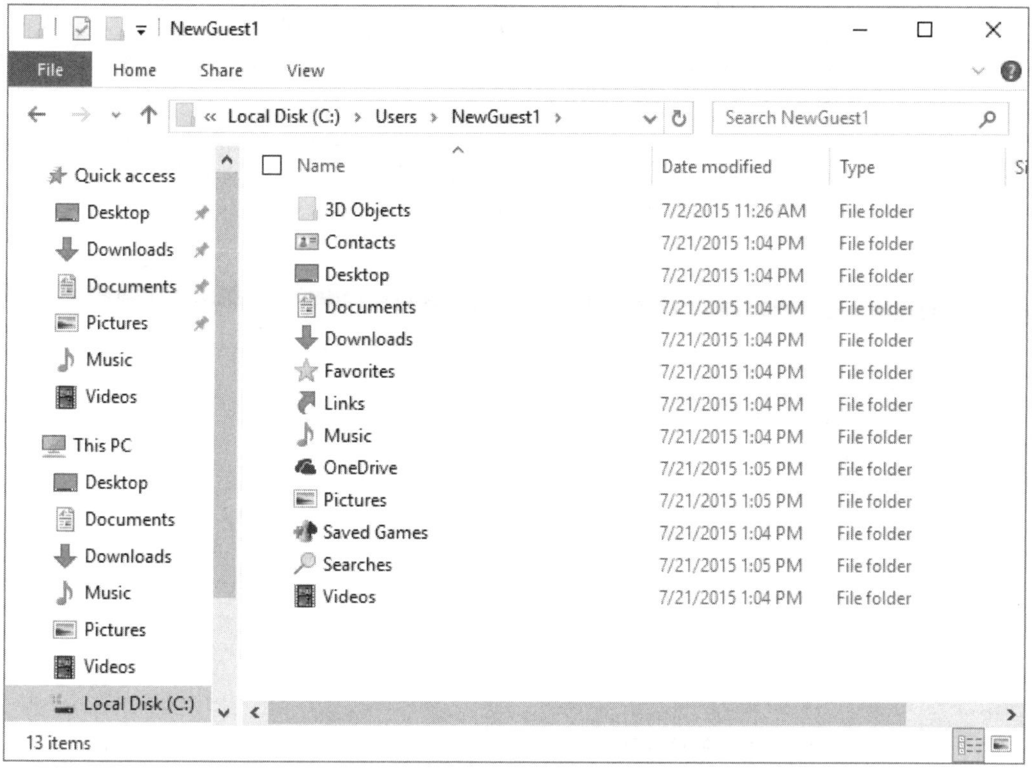

Figure 12-9 The files and folders composing a user profile

A profile contains personal data folders a user maintains as well as files and folders containing user and application settings. Some files and folders in the profile are hidden or system files that can't be viewed with the default File Explorer settings. To view all files in the profile, you must enable the option to view hidden and system files in File Explorer.

A user profile stored on the same system where the user logs on is called a **local profile**. A local profile is created from a hidden profile called Default the first time a user logs on to a system; to see this profile, you must enable the option for viewing hidden files in File

Explorer. When users log off, their profile settings are saved in their local profiles so that the next time they log on, all their settings are preserved. However, if a user logs on to a different computer, the profile is created again from the Default profile. If administrators want to make users' profiles available on any computer they log on to, they can set up roaming profiles, discussed next.

To view hidden files in File Explorer, click View, Hidden items.

A **roaming profile** follows the user no matter which computer he or she logs on to. It's stored on a network share so that when a user logs on to any computer in the network, the profile is copied from the network share to the profile folder on the local computer. This local copy of the roaming profile is referred to as the profile's "cached copy." Any changes the user makes to the profile are replicated from the locally cached copy to the profile on the network share when the user logs off.

The location of a roaming user's profile is specified in the Profile tab of a user's properties (see Figure 12-10). This tab is identical in both Active Directory and a client OS. The profile path points to a network share by using the UNC path.

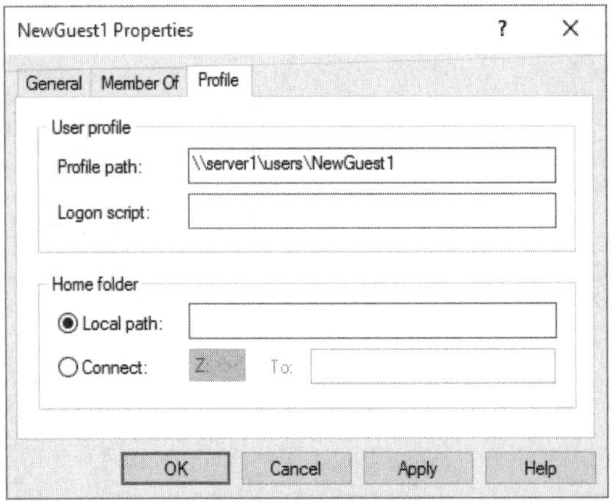

NewGuest1 Properties	?	X

General Member Of Profile

User profile

Profile path: \\server1\users\NewGuest1

Logon script:

Home folder

⦿ Local path:

○ Connect: Z: To:

OK   Cancel   Apply   Help

Figure 12-10 User profile settings

Roaming profiles are rarely used in workgroup networks because you would have to add the user account to every computer in the workgroup, but it's a feature Active Directory administrators use often. A third type of profile, called a "mandatory profile," discards a user's profile changes at logoff so that the profile is always the same when the user logs on. Mandatory profiles are sometimes used on shared computers and for guest accounts.

Working with Accounts in Linux

User and group accounts in Linux are used for the same purposes as in Windows: user authentication and authorization. Linux OSs also have a default user who has full control over all aspects of the system. In Linux, this user is named "root." As in Windows, creating additional users to log on to and use the system is recommended so that the root user account is used only when you're performing tasks that require root privileges. In fact, some Linux distributions require creating a user during installation because logging on as root isn't allowed; you can access root privileges only by entering a special command.

Because most Linux administration takes place at the command line, this method for creating users is discussed first. You boot Linux to a command prompt without the GUI or boot to the GUI and open a terminal window. In its simplest form, user creation is a matter of using the `useradd` *newuser* command (replacing *newuser* with the logon name for the user account you're creating). Then you create a password for the user with the `passwd` *newuser* command. Both the logon name and password are case sensitive in Linux.

On most Linux systems, you can't run `useradd` and similar commands unless you're logged on as the root user or (preferably) preface the command with `sudo`, as in `sudo useradd` *newuser*. The `sudo` command, which stands for "superuser do," executes the command with root privileges. If you know you're going to use many commands requiring root privileges, you can change to the root user temporarily with the `su` command (which means "switch user"). This command attempts to switch to the root user when no user is specified, and you must enter the root user's password when prompted.

With some commands, if they're entered with a username, as in `passwd testuser`, the command is executed only for this user account. If they're entered without a username, they're executed only for the current user. For example, users or administrators can change a user's password with the `passwd` command. User information can be changed with the `usermod` command, and you delete users with the `deluser` command.

The `useradd` command has many options. For example, you can specify another home directory, assign group memberships, and so forth. You practice using this command in Hands-On Project 12-3.

You can see extensive help for most Linux commands by typing `man` *command* (replacing *command* with the command you want information on). The `man` command means "manual," and the help pages it displays are called "man pages."

All users must belong to at least one group in Linux. When a user is created, a group with the same name as the user is also created, and the new user is made a member of this group. However, you can create groups and add users to them, just as you can in Windows.

Groups are created with the aptly named `groupadd` command. To add users as members of a group you create, you can specify this option when the user is created or use the `useradd` *username groupname* command or the `usermod` command.

To view the list of users, you can display the `/etc/passwd` file's contents with the `cat /etc/passwd` command, and to view the list of groups, display the `/etc/group` file's contents with the `cat /etc/group` command. The `cat` command lists a text file's contents onscreen.

For those who prefer a GUI to manage users and groups, most Linux distributions have convenient graphical interfaces for doing so. In Fedora Linux, the Users control panel is available to manage users (see Figure 12-11).

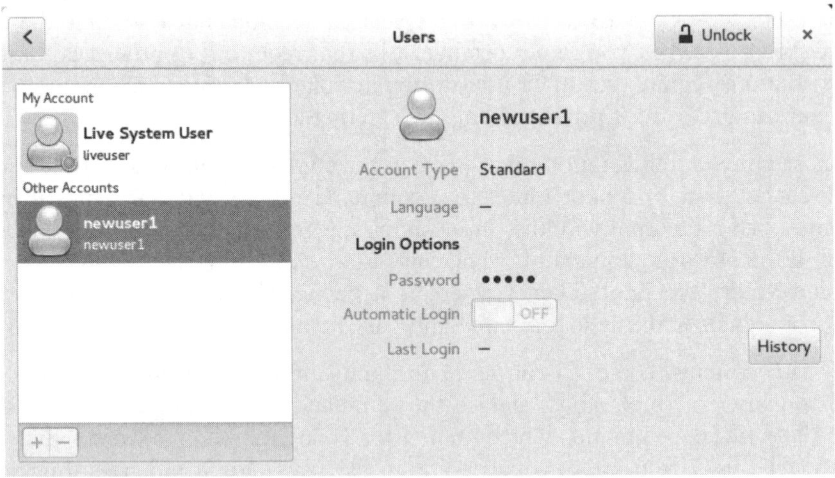

Figure 12-11 The Users control panel in Fedora Linux

Source: © 2015 Red Hat, Inc.

One reason many administrators prefer the command-line method for creating users is because they can import user information from a text file and add many users at one time with the newusers command, which accepts as input a text file listing users to create.

Hands-On Project 12-3: Working with Users and Groups in Linux (Optional)

Time Required: 15 minutes

Objective: Create users and groups with Linux command-line tools.

Required Tools and Equipment: A computer or VM with Linux installed or Net-XX and a Linux Live disc. This project uses Fedora Linux, but the steps are similar in most Linux distributions.

Description: In this project, you create users with the useradd command and groups with the groupadd command. Next, you add users as members of these groups with the useradd and usermod commands.

1. Log on to your Linux computer, and open a terminal window. These steps assume you don't log on as root. If you do, you don't need to switch the user to root with the su command.

2. Open a terminal window by clicking **Activities, Show Applications, Utilities,** and **Terminal.** At the terminal prompt, type **man useradd** and press **Enter** to get an overview of what the man pages for the useradd command contain. Press the **Page Up** and **Page Down** keys to scroll through the man pages. Type **q** when you're finished.

3. To view current users on the Linux system, type **cat /etc/passwd** and press **Enter.** Another way to view a text file you can page up and down through is using the less

option. Type **less /etc/passwd** and press **Enter**. Use the arrow keys or Page Up and Page Down keys to scroll through the file. Many of the user accounts you see in this file are system accounts and aren't used to log on to the OS. Type **q** to quit.

4. Display the list of groups by typing **less /etc/group** and pressing **Enter**. When you're finished, type **q**.

5. To create a user, type **useradd testuser1** and press **Enter**. If you aren't logged on as root, you get a message stating that permission is denied. Type **su** and press **Enter** to switch to the root user. The last character in the prompt changes from a $ to a # to indicate that you're now operating as the root user.

6. Type **useradd testuser1** and press **Enter**. To create a password for the user, type **passwd testuser1** and press **Enter**. Type **Password01** and press **Enter**. (Notice that your keystrokes aren't displayed.) You see a message that the password is bad and fails a dictionary check. However, the password is still accepted, and you're prompted to retype it. Type **Password01** and press **Enter** again.

If you don't enter the same password when asked to retype it, you get a message stating that the passwords don't match, and you're prompted to try again.

7. Create another user with the logon name **testuser2**.

8. Type **less /etc/passwd**, press **Enter**, and page to the bottom of the file, where you see the users you created. Type **q** and then display the group file to see that groups named testuser1 and testuser2 were also created. (*Hint*: Remember that you can use the arrow keys to scroll through recently used commands.)

9. Type **groupadd testgroup1** and press **Enter**. To add testuser1 to testgroup1, type **usermod -a -G testgroup1 testuser1** and press **Enter**. Repeat the command for **testuser2**. Type **cat /etc/group** and press **Enter** to list all groups. You should see the new group at the end of the file along with a list of its members.

10. You can view a user's group memberships with the groups command. Type **groups testuser1** and press **Enter**. Testuser1 is listed as a member of the testuser1 and testgroup1 groups.

11. Close the terminal window, and shut down the Linux computer.

Storage and File System Management

Managing storage on networks is becoming more of a challenge. Users are storing larger amounts and more varied types of data, and network administrators have to make sure enough storage space is available as well as manage who has access to it. In some cases, the challenge is preventing users from storing inappropriate types of data on company servers, such as music files, videos, and pictures unrelated to work. This section describes some tools for managing locally attached storage on a server and then discusses how an administrator controls access to files and folders on the file system.

Locally attached storage is a device, such as a hard disk, that's connected to a storage controller on the server. Usually, the storage is physically housed inside the server case and connected to a SATA or an SAS controller. However, it can also be external, attached via USB or external SATA (eSATA) connectors. In either case, the server sees the storage the same way—as a disk containing one or more volumes or, if the disk is empty, unallocated space.

Volumes and Partitions

A **volume** is part or all of the space on one or more disks that contains or is ready to contain a file system. In Windows, volumes with file systems are usually assigned a drive letter. In Linux, volumes are mounted in the file system and accessed as though they were just another folder. Starting with Windows Server 2008, Windows volumes can also be mounted in the file system instead of assigning a drive letter.

The term "partition" is sometimes used interchangeably with "volume," but these terms don't always describe the same thing. To understand the difference, look at how Windows views a hard disk. Disks are numbered starting with Disk 0, Disk 1, and so forth. A Windows disk can be categorized as a basic disk or a dynamic disk. By default, all newly installed disks are considered basic disks. A **basic disk** can be divided into one to four partitions as follows, with a maximum of four partitions consisting of the following:

- *One to four primary partitions*—A **primary partition** can be formatted with a file system and assigned a drive letter or mounted in an empty folder on an existing drive letter. It's also a volume.

- *One extended partition*—An **extended partition** can't be formatted with a file system or assigned a drive letter. It's divided into one or more logical drives, each of which can be formatted and assigned a drive letter. A logical drive is considered a volume, but an extended partition is not. You can create an extended partition only if there are fewer than four primary partitions.

Only a primary partition can be the **active partition**, which is a partition that can hold boot files (called the "boot loader") the BIOS loads before it can start the OS. An extended partition/logical drive can't be an active partition and, therefore, can't be booted, but it can store OS files.

The active primary partition storing the Windows boot loader is the **system partition**. The partition or logical drive holding the Windows OS files is the **boot partition**. Windows usually creates a small hidden partition during installation that it assigns as the boot partition and stores the Windows OS files on another, larger partition that's designated the system partition and usually assigned the drive letter C.

A **dynamic disk** can be divided into one or more volumes; the term "partition" isn't used in this context. You can create up to 1000 volumes per dynamic disk (although no more than 32 are recommended). A dynamic disk offers features that a basic disk doesn't, namely RAID (discussed later in "Protecting Data with Fault Tolerance") and disk spanning, which is creating a volume that occupies space on two or more disks.

Linux systems refer to disks by using their device driver name plus a letter, starting with "a." For example, the first SATA or SCSI disk on a Linux system is named /dev/sda, the second disk is /dev/sdb, and so forth. Partitions or volumes are referred to by using the device name and a number. The first volume on the first disk in Linux is named /dev/sda1, the second volume is /dev/sdb2, and so on.

Whether you're working with a partition or a volume in Windows or Linux, what makes disk storage usable is the file system. The next sections discuss the main file systems in Windows and Linux: FAT, NTFS, and Ext3/Ext4.

The FAT File System

The File Allocation Table (FAT) file system has two variations: FAT16 and FAT32. FAT16 is usually referred to simply as "FAT." It's been around since the mid-1980s, which is one of its biggest strengths—it's well known and well supported by most OSs. FAT32 arrived on the scene with the release of Windows 95 release 2 in 1996.

The main difference between FAT16 and FAT32 is the size of the disk partition that can be formatted. FAT16 is limited to 2 GB partitions in most implementations. FAT32 allows partitions up to 2 TB, but in Windows 2000 and later, Microsoft limits them to 32 GB because the file system becomes noticeably slower and inefficient with larger partition sizes. This 32 GB limitation applies only to creating partitions; Windows can read FAT32 partitions of any size. FAT16 supports a maximum file size of 2 GB, and FAT32 supports files up to 4 GB.

The number in FAT names refers to the number of bits available to address disk clusters. FAT16 can address up to 2^{16} (65536) disk clusters, and FAT32 can address up to 2^{32} (4,294,967,296) disk clusters. The number of disk clusters a file system can address is directly proportional to the largest partition size it supports.

As you can see, FAT has severe limitations in current computing environments. The file size limitation alone prevents storing a standard DVD image file on a FAT system. The limitations are even more apparent when you consider reliability and security requirements of modern OSs. FAT doesn't support file and folder permissions for users and groups, so any user logging on to a computer with a FAT disk has full control over every file on that disk. In addition, FAT lacks support for encryption, file compression, disk quotas, and reliability features, such as transaction recovery and journaling, all of which NTFS supports.

You might think that FAT isn't good for much, especially compared with the more robust NTFS, but FAT still has its place. It's the only file system option when using older Windows OSs, such as Windows 9x. In addition, FAT is simple and has little overhead, so it's still the file system of choice on removable media, such as flash drives. For hard drives, however, particularly on Windows servers, NTFS is unquestionably the way to go.

The NTFS File System

NTFS is a full-featured file system that Microsoft introduced with Windows NT in 1993. Since that time, its features have been expanded to help administrators gain control of expanding storage requirements. NTFS has supported file and folder permissions almost since its inception, which was a considerable advantage over FAT. Many other compelling features are available in NTFS that aren't available with FAT:

- *Disk quotas*—Enable administrators to limit the amount of disk space that users' files can occupy on a disk volume or in a folder.

- *Volume mount points*—Make it possible to associate the root of a disk volume with a folder on an NTFS volume, thereby forgoing the need for a drive letter to access the volume.

- *Shadow copies*—Enable users to keep historical versions of files so that they can revert a file to an older version or restore an accidentally deleted file.

- *File compression*—Allows users to store documents in a compressed format without needing to run a compression/decompression program to store and retrieve the documents.

- *Encrypting File System (EFS)*—Makes encrypted files inaccessible to everyone except the user who encrypted the file, including users who have been granted permission to the file.

Disk Quotas With the number and types of files requiring more disk space on enterprise servers, **disk quotas** are a welcome tool to help administrators get a handle on server storage. Typically, disk quotas are set on an NTFS volume and, by default, apply to all users except administrators. Quotas can put a hard limit on the amount of storage a user's files can occupy, thereby preventing the user for storing any more files after the limit has been reached. Quotas can also be configured to create a log entry when a user has exceeded the quota, so you can determine who's using a lot of space without actually preventing users from exceeding the limit. Quotas are configured in the Quota tab of an NTFS volume's Properties dialog box (see Figure 12-12).

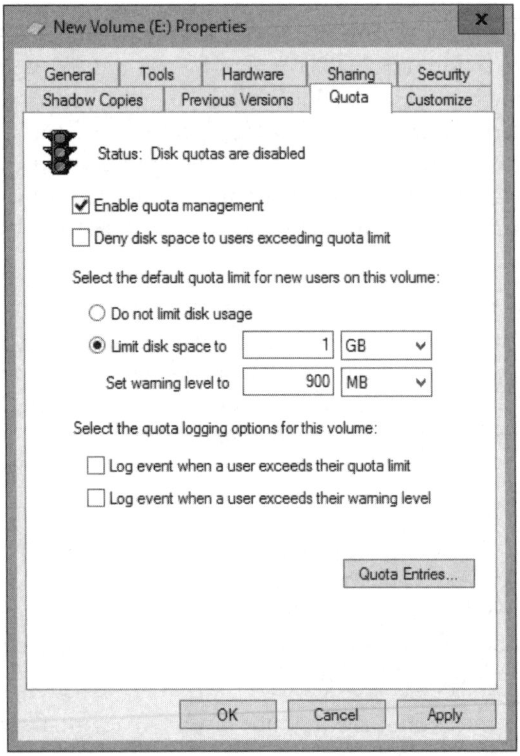

Figure 12-12 The Quota tab

Volume Mount Points Volume mount points enable you to access a volume as a folder in another volume instead of using a drive letter. The volume that holds the folder serving as the mount point must be an NTFS volume, and the folder must be empty. In UNIX and Linux, mount points rather than drive letters have always been used to access disk volumes, so users of these OSs should be quite comfortable with mount points. Windows volumes can be assigned both a mount point and a drive letter, if needed.

Shadow Copies Like quotas, shadow copies are enabled on an entire volume. When this feature is enabled, users can access previous versions of files in shared folders and restore files that have been deleted or corrupted. You configure shadow copies in the Shadow Copies tab of a volume's Properties dialog box (see Figure 12-13). Shadow copies are disabled by default.

New Volume (E:) Properties	✕

General	Tools	Hardware	Sharing	Security
Shadow Copies	Previous Versions		Quota	Customize

Shadow copies allow users to view the contents of shared folders as the contents existed at previous points in time. For information on Shadow Copies, click here.

Select a volume:

Volume	Next Run Time	Shares	Used
\\?\Vol...	Disabled	0	
C:\	Disabled	2	
E:\	Disabled	0	320 MB on ...

[Enable]   [Disable]   [Settings...]

Shadow copies of selected volume

7/21/2015 5:06 PM

[Create Now]
[Delete Now]
[Revert...]

[OK]   [Cancel]   [Apply]

Figure 12-13 The Shadow Copies tab

In Windows 10, shadow copies are called File History, and settings are accessed in the File History control panel.

File Compression and Encryption File compression and encryption on an NTFS volume are implemented as file attributes, like the Read-only and Hidden attributes. One caveat: These attributes are mutually exclusive, so a file can't be both compressed and encrypted. You can set only one of these two attributes.

Files can be compressed and accessed without users needing to take any explicit action to uncompress them. When a compressed file is opened, the OS decompresses it automatically. On NTFS volumes, you can enable file compression on the entire volume, a folder and its contents, or a file.

File encryption on NTFS volumes is made possible by Encrypting File System (EFS) and works in a similar manner to file compression. You can set the encryption attribute on a file or folder but not on a volume. By default, encrypted folders and files can be identified by their filenames displayed in green.

Encrypted files can usually be opened only by the user who encrypted the file. However, this user can designate other users who are allowed to access the file. In addition, in a domain environment, the domain Administrator account is designated as a recovery agent. A designated recovery agent can decrypt a file if the user account that encrypted it can no longer access it. This can happen if an administrator resets a user's password, the user account is deleted, or the user leaves the company. To encrypt a file, click the Advanced button in the General tab of a file's Properties dialog box, and then click "Encrypt contents to secure data" (see Figure 12-14).

Figure 12-14 The Advanced Attributes dialog box

In addition, Windows offers whole drive encryption with BitLocker. Although EFS allows users to encrypt files, BitLocker encrypts the entire drive. In Windows 10, it's available by default, but in Windows Server, it must be installed as a feature. In Windows 10, you can enable BitLocker on drives that don't contain the Windows OS files by simply right-clicking the drive in File Explorer and clicking Turn on BitLocker. You must supply a password or smart card credentials, which are used to decrypt the drive. To enable BitLocker on the Windows system partition, your computer must have a trusted platform module (TPM), which is a device installed on some motherboards that provides cryptographic functions.

NTFS Permissions It's important to know that there are two modes for accessing files on a networked computer: network (sometimes called "remote") and interactive (sometimes called "local"). It follows, then, that there are two ways to secure files: share permissions and NTFS permissions. Share permissions are applied when a user attempts network access to shared files. NTFS permissions always apply, whether file access is attempted interactively or remotely through a share. That last statement might sound confusing, so take a closer look at how permissions work.

Permissions can be viewed as a gatekeeper to control who has access to folders and files. When you log on to a computer or domain, you're issued a ticket containing information such as your username and group memberships. If you attempt to access a file or folder, the gatekeeper examines your ticket and compares your username and group memberships with the file or folder's permissions list. If neither your username nor your groups are on the list, you're denied access. If you or your groups *are* on the list, you're issued an access ticket that combines all your allowed permissions. You can then access the resource as specified by your access ticket.

At least, that's how the process works when you're attempting interactive access to files. If you're attempting network access, there are two gatekeepers: one that checks your ticket against the share permissions list and, if you're granted access by share permissions, another that checks your ticket against the NTFS permissions list. The NTFS gatekeeper is required to examine your ticket only if you get past the share gatekeeper. If you're granted access by share permissions, you're issued an access ticket. Then if you're granted access by NTFS permissions, you're allowed to keep only the access ticket that gives you the *least* permission, or is the most restrictive, of the two.

For example, Mike is granted Read access by share permissions and Read and Write access by NTFS permissions. Mike gets to keep only the Read access ticket because it's the lesser of the two permissions. Another example: Neither Mike nor any of Mike's groups are on the share permissions access list. There's no need to even examine NTFS permissions because Mike is denied access at the share permissions gate. As a final example, Mike is granted Full Control access by share permissions and Modify access by NTFS permissions. Mike's access ticket gives him Modify permission because it allows less access than Full Control.

The general security rule for assigning permissions to resources is to give users the least access necessary for their job. This rule is often referred to as the "least privileges principle." Unfortunately, this axiom can be at odds with another general rule: Keep it simple. Sometimes determining the least amount of access a user requires can lead to complex permission schemes. The more complex a permission scheme is, the more likely it will need troubleshooting, and the more troubleshooting that's needed, the more likely an administrator will assign overly permissive permissions out of frustration.

NTFS permissions give administrators fine-grained access control over folders and files for both network users and interactive users. Unlike share permissions, which can be configured only on a shared folder, NTFS permissions can be configured on folders and files. By default, when permissions are configured on a folder, subfolders and files in that folder inherit the permissions. However, inherited permissions can be changed when needed, making it possible for files to have permission settings that are different from those for the folder where they're stored.

To view or edit permissions on an NTFS folder or file, you simply access the Security tab of the object's Properties dialog box. NTFS folders have six standard permissions, and

NTFS files have five. NTFS standard permissions for folders and files are as follows (see Figure 12-15):

- *Read*—Users can view file contents, copy files, open folders and subfolders, and view file attributes and permissions.

- *Read & execute*—Grants the same permissions as Read and includes the ability to run applications or scripts. When this permission is selected, List folder contents and Read are selected, too.

- *List folder contents*—This permission applies only to folders and grants the same permission as Read & execute. However, because it doesn't apply to files, Read & execute must also be set on the folder to allow users to open files in the folder.

- *Write*—Users can create and modify files and read file attributes and permissions. However, this permission doesn't allow users to read or delete files. In most cases, the Read or Read & execute permission should be given with the Write permission.

- *Modify*—Users can read, modify, delete, and create files. Users can't change permissions or take ownership. Selecting this permission automatically selects Read & execute, List folder contents, Read, and Write.

- *Full control*—Users can perform all actions given by the Modify permission with the addition of changing permissions and taking ownership.

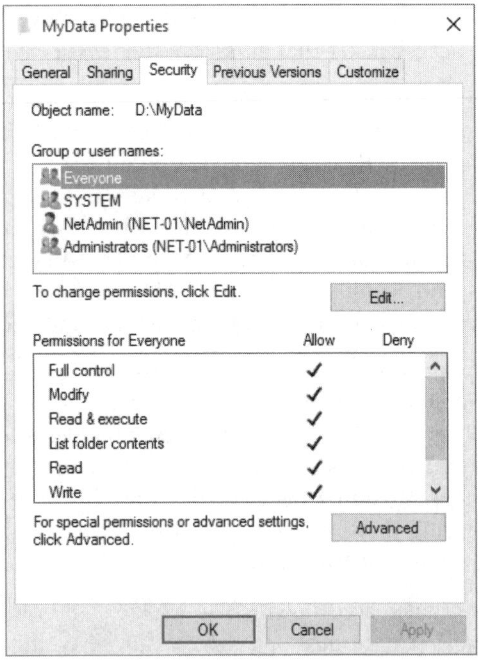

Figure 12-15   NTFS permissions

Permissions and rights assignments should be made by using groups instead of user accounts whenever possible. Users can be members of more than one group and, therefore, have all the rights and permissions assigned to all the groups of which they're members. In this sense, rights and permissions are cumulative. So a user has the permission to read a file if a group in which he or she is a member has been assigned Read permission for the file. However, if another group the user is a member of has Modify permission for the same file, the user also has the Modify permission. The exception is the Deny permission, which takes precedence over the Allow permission. For example, if a user belongs to a group that has the Allow Modify permission for a file and also belongs to a group that has been assigned Deny Modify, the user is denied access to the file.

Hands-On Project 12-4: Using Windows Disk Management

Time Required: 15 minutes

Objective: Use Disk Management to create and delete volumes and convert a basic disk to dynamic.

Required Tools and Equipment: Net-*XX* with one unallocated disk

Description: In this project, you create and delete volumes and convert a basic disk to dynamic.

1. Log on to your computer as **NetAdmin**.
2. Right-click **Start** and click **Disk Management**. If you're prompted to initialize a disk, click **OK**.
3. Figure 12-16 shows the Disk Management console in Windows 10; Disk 0 has three primary partitions. The partition labeled "System Reserved" is the Windows system partition

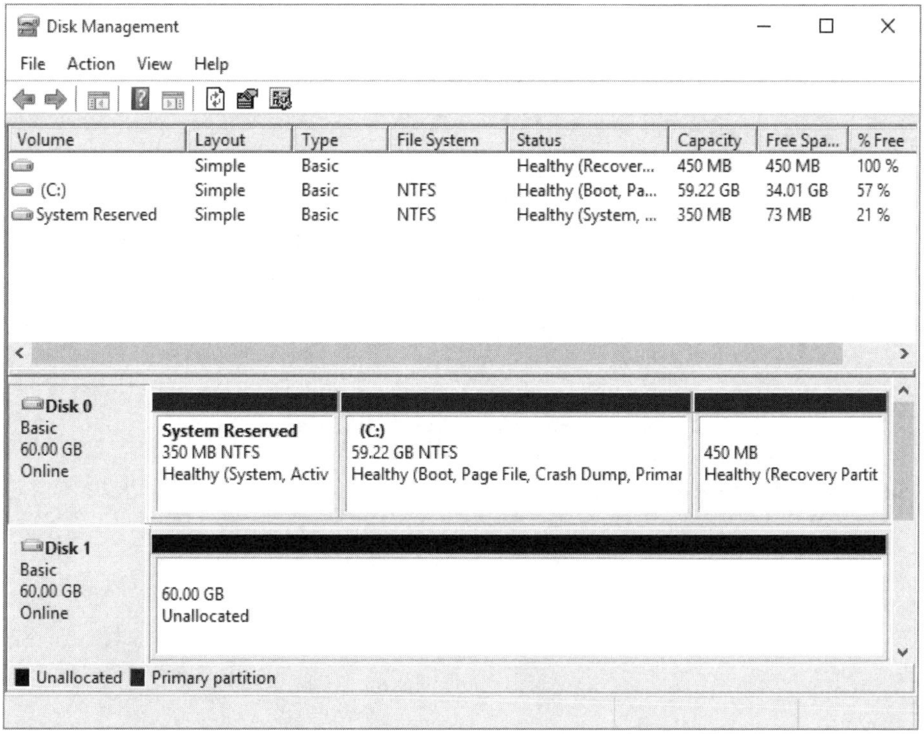

Figure 12-16   The Disk Management console

and is marked "Active." Remember that the system partition is where boot files are located. It doesn't have a drive letter assigned. The C drive is a primary partition and the Windows boot partition, which indicates that a Windows OS is used on that partition. A third partition labeled "Recovery Partition" is used to repair the Windows OS if it won't boot. Disk 1 is unallocated, which means no volumes have been created on it. Right-click **Disk 1** in the box marked "Unallocated." (If Disk 1 isn't unallocated, choose a disk that is.) Notice that the other volume types are grayed out. Disk 1 is a basic disk and supports only simple volumes. Click **New Simple Volume**.

4. In the New Simple Volume Wizard welcome window, click **Next**. In the "Simple volume size in MB" text box, type **500**, and then click **Next**. In the Assign Drive Letter or Path window, click the drive letter list arrow and click **M**. You also have the option to mount the drive in an empty NTFS folder or make no assignment. Click **Next**.

5. In the Format Partition window (shown in Figure 12-17), you can choose the file system for the volume. Click the **File system** list arrow to see the choices, and click **NTFS**. Click the **Allocation unit size** list arrow to view the choices for specifying the size of disk clusters. Click **Default** to select the default size. In Windows 10, the default cluster size is 4096 (4 KB) for volumes up to 2 TB. In the Volume label text box, type **Vol1**, and make sure the **Perform a quick format** check box is selected. Click **Next** and then **Finish**.

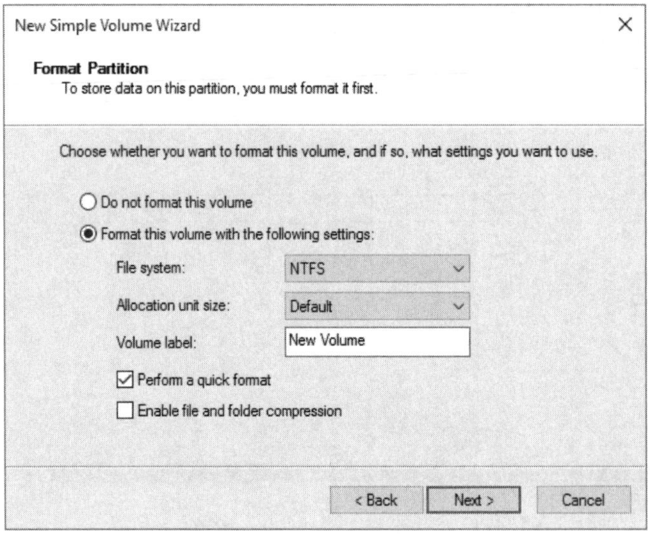

Figure 12-17 The Format Partition window

6. The volume is formatted, and then the drive letter is assigned and the status is set to Healthy (Primary Partition). Right-click the **Vol1** volume and view the actions you can perform. You can mark the partition as active, change the drive letter or mount path, format it, extend or shrink the volume, and delete it. Click **Extend Volume**. In the Extend Volume Wizard welcome window, click **Next**. Type **100** in the "Select the amount of space" in MB text box. Click **Next** and then **Finish**.

If you see a window stating that you need to format the disk, click Cancel.

7. Next, convert the basic disk to a dynamic disk. In the lower-left pane of Disk Management, right-click **Disk 1** (or the disk you used to create the volume) and click **Convert to Dynamic Disk**. Click **OK** in the Convert to Dynamic Disk prompt. In the Disk to Convert prompt, click **Convert**. You get a message stating that you can't start an installed OS from the disk. Click **Yes**. Converting a disk from basic to dynamic retains the data on the disk. To convert the disk back to basic, you must delete the volume first.

8. Close Disk Management, and leave Windows running for the next project.

Hands-On Project 12-5: Using the NTFS File System

Time Required: 15 minutes

Objective: Work with file and folder attributes and permissions.

Required Tools and Equipment: Net-*XX*

Description: In this project, you assign permissions in NTFS and set file attributes.

1. Log on to your computer as **NetAdmin**, if necessary.

2. Open File Explorer and click **Vol1 (M:)**. Create a folder at the root of the M drive named **TestFiles**.

3. Right-click **TestFiles** and click **Properties** to see the folder's properties. Click the **Security** tab. You see a list of groups at the top and a list of permissions at the bottom (see Figure 12-18). Click each group to see the permissions assigned to it. Notice that the Users group has Read & execute, List folder contents, and Read permissions. These three permissions allow all users of the computer to view files and folders in the TestFiles folder, but they can't change them.

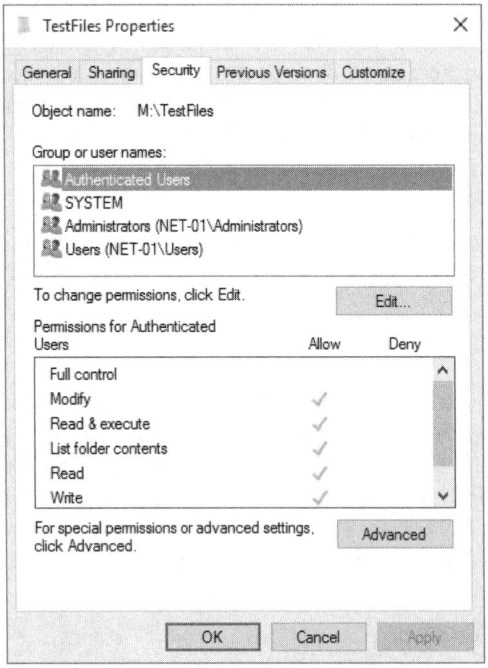

Figure 12-18   The Security tab showing NTFS permissions

4. Click **Edit**, and then click **Add** to add a user or group to the permissions list. In the "Enter the object names to select" text box, type **GuestUsers,** and then click **Check Names**. (You created this group in Hands-On Project 12-2.) Click **OK**.

5. Click **Guest Users** in the list of users, and then click the **Modify** permission in the Allow column of the permissions list. When you select the Modify permission, the Write permission is selected automatically. Click **OK**, and then click **OK** again to close the TestFiles Properties dialog box.

6. Double-click the **TestFiles** folder to open it, and create a text document named `test1` in this folder. Right-click `test1` and click **Properties**. Click the **Security** tab. Notice that the list of groups and their permissions are the same as for the TestFiles folder. By default, all new files created in a folder automatically inherit the permissions of the folder in which they're created. To change inherited permissions, you must disable permission inheritance.

7. Click **Advanced** to open the Advanced Security Settings dialog box. If you wanted to disable permission inheritance, you would click the Disable inheritance button. For now, leave permission inheritance enabled. Click **Cancel**. Leave the Properties dialog box for `test1` open. Why might you want to disable permission inheritance?

---

8. Click the **General** tab, and click **Advanced** at the bottom.

9. You see the Compress and Encrypt attributes at the bottom of the Advanced Attributes dialog box. Click the **Compress contents to save disk space** and then the **Encrypt contents to secure data** check box. Notice that the Compress check box is cleared when you click the Encrypt check box because both can't be enabled at the same time. Click **OK** twice.

10. Next, you're prompted to encrypt the file and parent folder (which causes all files placed in the folder to be encrypted) or encrypt only the file. Click **Encrypt the file only**, and then click **OK**. The `test1` filename is then displayed in green, indicating it's encrypted.

11. Now use what you learned to set the Compress attribute for `test1`. The filename should be displayed in blue. When you're finished, close all windows, and log off Windows for the next project.

The Linux File System

Linux supports a number of file systems, including Ext3, Ext4, ReiserFS, and XFS. Ext3 (and, more recently, Ext4) is the default file system for most Linux distributions. Both file systems use journaling, a feature that ensures reliability by maintaining a record of changes to the file system before they're written to the disk. If a disk operation is interrupted because of a power failure or system crash, partial changes can be undone to prevent corrupting the file system.

Linux file systems support using permissions to control access to files and folders but much differently than in NTFS. In Linux, there are only three permissions—read, write, and execute—and three user types that can be assigned one or more of these permissions. The user types are as follows:

- *owner*—The owner of the file or folder, which is usually the user who created it
- *group*—The primary group to which the owner belongs
- *other*—All other users

Permissions are specified by using a single letter: r for read, w for write, and x for execute. For example, a file named `newfile` created by a user named greg who belongs to a group named greg is shown by using the `ls` command, as follows:

`- rw- r-- r-- greg greg newfile`

A few details are missing, but this line shows how permissions are displayed. The dash (-) in the first position indicates the file is a regular file. Folders or directories are indicated with a d in the first position. Permissions for each user type are displayed with three characters. The first three characters (rw- in this example) are the owner's permissions. The next three characters (r--) are the group permissions, and the last three (r--) are the permissions for all other users. The first name is the owner of the file (greg), and the next name is the owner's primary group (greg). To summarize, the permissions on `newfile` are as follows: Owner greg has read/write access, group greg has read access, and everybody else has read access.

The GUI in many Linux distributions shows permissions in a less cryptic form. Figure 12-19 shows permissions for a file in the Linux GUI.

```
                           newfile Properties

   ┌─────┬─────────────┬───────────┐
   │ Basic │ Permissions │ Open With │
   └─────┴─────────────┴───────────┘

   Owner:          Me

   Access:         Read and write              ∨

   Group:          liveuser ∨

   Access:         Read and write              ∨

   Others

   Access:         Read-only                   ∨

   Execute:        ☐ Allow executing file as program

   Security context:  unconfined_u:object_r:user_home_t:s0



   ┌──────┐                              ┌──────┐
   │ Help │                              │ Close │
   └──────┘                              └──────┘
```

Figure 12-19   File permissions in the Linux GUI

 Linux also supports many advanced file system features, such as disk quotas, encrypted files, and file compression.

Working with Shared Files and Printers

File and printer sharing is one reason businesses began to outfit computers with network interfaces and software. OSs and computers have evolved since the early days of stand-alone computers, when considerable effort was needed to make a lone PC part of a busy network. All computers come with a NIC installed and an OS that includes all the protocols for sharing files and printers.

The dominant file-sharing protocol is **Server Message Block (SMB)**, used by Windows and supported by Linux and MAC. SMB is the native Windows file-sharing protocol, and **Network File System (NFS)** is the native Linux file-sharing protocol. However, Linux supports SMB, and Windows can support NFS with the right software installed.

 NFS support on Windows is available in Windows Server 2008 and Windows Vista and later.

Printer sharing also uses SMB on Windows and Linux. The native Linux printer-sharing protocol is line printer daemon/line printer remote (LPD/LPR). LPD is the server side of a shared printer session, and LPR is the client component of the software.

Sharing Files and Printers in Windows

The first thing you need to know about file sharing in Windows is that users are subject to both share permissions and NTFS permissions when accessing files over the network You learned about NTFS permissions earlier in the chapter. Thankfully, share permissions are somewhat simpler, and there are only three (see Figure 12-20):

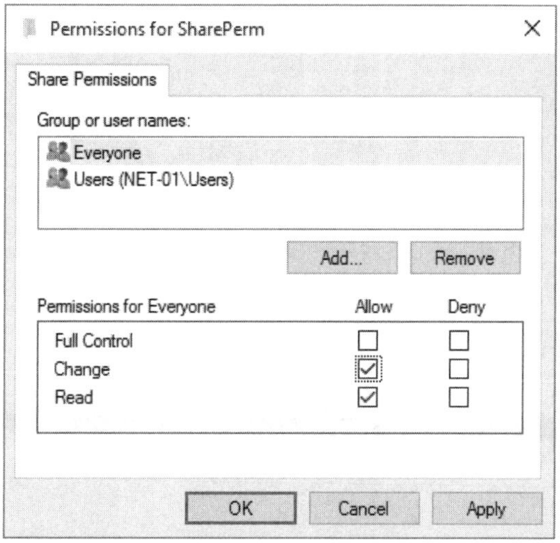

Figure 12-20 Viewing share permissions

- *Read*—Users can view contents of files, copy files, run applications and script files, open folders and subfolders, and view file attributes.
- *Change*—All permissions granted by Read, plus create files and folders, change contents and attributes of files and folders, and delete files and folders.
- *Full Control*—All permissions granted by Change, plus change file and folder permissions as well as take ownership of files and folders.

Windows assigns default permissions depending on how a folder is shared. Generally, the default share permission is Read for the Everyone group. On FAT/FAT32 volumes, share permissions are the only way to secure files accessed through the network because these file systems don't support local file permissions.

Sharing files on the network, as you have seen in previous activities, isn't difficult in a Windows environment. Nonetheless, you should be familiar with some techniques and options before forging ahead with setting up a file-sharing server. You can use the following methods to configure folder sharing in Windows Server 2016. The procedures are similar in Windows client OSs:

- *File Sharing Wizard*—To start this wizard, right-click a folder and click Share with, and then click Specific people. The File Sharing Wizard (see Figure 12-21) simplifies sharing for novices by using easier terms for permissions and by setting NTFS permissions automatically to match the selected share permissions. The permissions you see in the figure—Read, Read/Write, and Owner—correspond to the Read, Change, and Full Control share permissions.

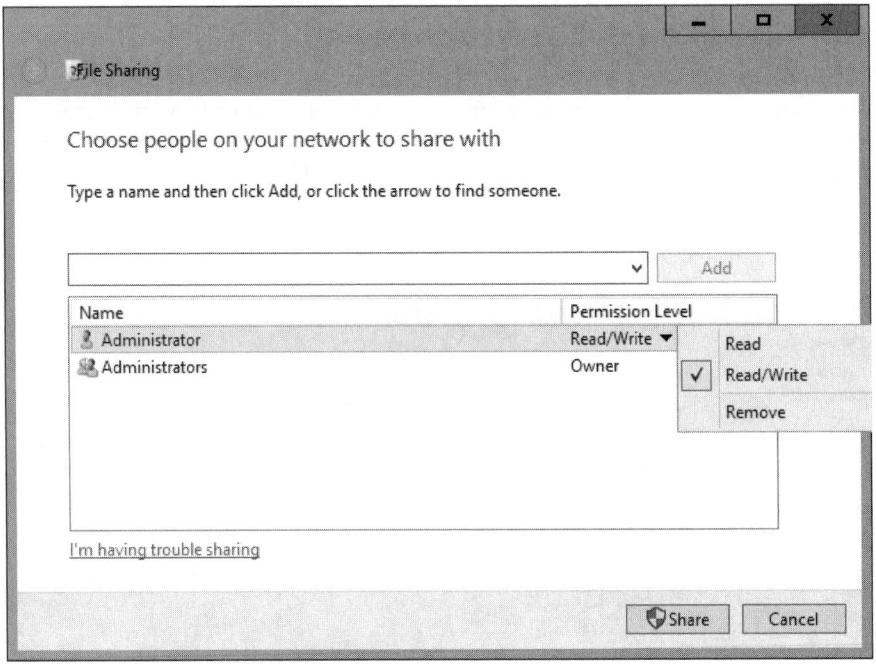

Figure 12-21 The File Sharing Wizard

- *Advanced Sharing dialog box*—To open this dialog box, click Advanced Sharing in the Sharing tab of a folder's Properties dialog box. There are quite a few options in this dialog box (see Figure 12-22):

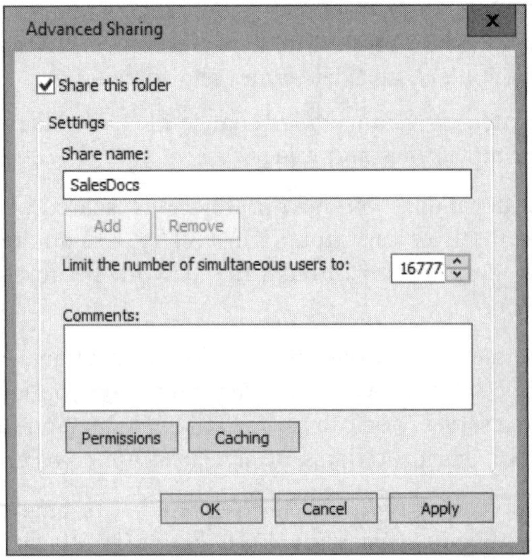

Figure 12-22 The Advanced Sharing dialog box

- ○ Share this folder: Sharing can be enabled or disabled for the folder by clicking this check box.

- ○ Share name: The share name is the name users see in the Network folder of File Explorer or when using the `net share` command. To put it another way, it's the name you use to access the folder with the UNC path (*server\share name*). You can add or remove share names. A single folder can have multiple share names and different permissions, a different number of simultaneous users, and caching settings for each share name.

- ○ Limit the number of simultaneous users to: In Windows Server, the default limit is 16,777,216, which is, practically speaking, unlimited. In Windows client OSs, the maximum number of users who can access a share simultaneously is 20.

- ○ Comments: You can enter a description of the share's contents and settings in this text box.

- ○ Permissions: Click this button to open the Permissions dialog box shown previously in Figure 12-20.

- ○ Caching: This option controls how offline files are configured. Offline files enable users to disconnect from the network and still have the shared files they were working with available on their computers.

- *Shared Folders snap-in*—You use this component of the Computer Management console (see Figure 12-23) to monitor, change, and create shares on the local computer or a remote computer. To create a share, right-click the Shares node under the Shared Folders snap-in and click New Share. The Create a Shared Folder Wizard walks you through selecting the folder to share or creating a new folder to share, naming the share, configuring offline files, and setting permissions.

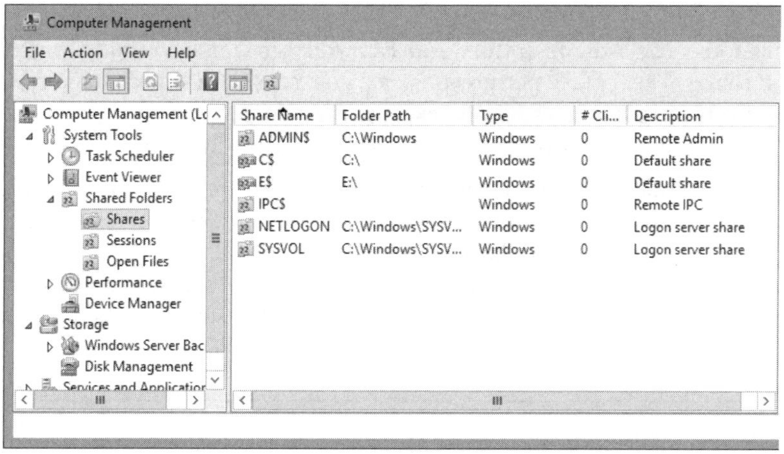

Figure 12-23 The Shared Folders snap-in

- *File and Storage Services*—This tool is the most advanced method for creating shares. Like the Shared Folders snap-in, you use a wizard to create shares. You can select the folder to share or create a new share, configure NTFS permissions, and choose sharing protocols, such as SMB and NFS. File and Storage Services is accessed from Server Manager in Windows Server 2012 and later.

Hands-On Project 12-6: Sharing a Folder with the File Sharing Wizard

Time Required: 15 minutes

Objective: Create a test folder and then share it by using the File Sharing Wizard.

Required Tools and Equipment: Net-XX

Description: In this project, you use the File Sharing Wizard to see how it sets permissions automatically.

1. Log on to your computer as **NetAdmin**, if necessary.

2. Right-click **Start** and click **File Explorer**. Click **Vol1 (M:)** in the left pane. Create a folder at the root of the M drive named **TestShare1**.

3. Open the TestShare1 folder's Properties dialog box, and click the **Security** tab. Click the **Users** entry in the top section, and make a note of the permissions assigned to the Users group. Click **Cancel** to close the Properties dialog box.

_____

4. Right-click **TestShare1**, point to **Share with**, and click **Specific people** to start the File Sharing Wizard.

5. Type **newguest1** in the text box, and then click **Add**. New Guest User 1 is added. Click the list arrow in the Permission Level column next to New Guest User 1, and make sure **Read** is selected.

6. Click **Share**. The UNC path for the share is displayed. Click **Done**.

7. Right-click **TestShare1** and click **Properties**. Click the **Sharing** tab, and then click **Advanced Sharing**.

8. Click **Permissions**. The Administrators and Everyone groups have Full Control permission to the share. The NTFS permissions, as you see in the next step, restrict New Guest User 1's permissions to Read & execute, List folder contents, and Read, which effectively allows the user to open and view the file. Click **Cancel** twice.

9. In the TestShare1 folder's Properties dialog box, click the **Security** tab. Click **New Guest User 1**, and notice that the account's NTFS permissions are Read & execute, List folder contents, and Read. Because the sharing permissions for the Everyone group are set to Full Control and New Guest User 1's NTFS permissions are set to Read, what will New Guest User 1's actual permissions to the folder be when accessing it across the network?

_____

10. Close all open windows.

Sharing Printers in Windows To understand how to work with and share printers in a Windows environment, first you need to know the terminology for defining the components of a shared printer:

- *Print device*—The physical printer containing paper and ink or toner to which print jobs are sent. There are two basic types of print devices:

  - Local print device: A printer connected to a port on a computer, with a parallel or USB cable, or through a TCP/IP port, which is used to access a printer attached directly to the network through the printer's NIC

  - Network print device: A printer attached to and shared by another computer

- *Printer*—The icon in the Printers folder that represents print devices. Windows programs print to a printer, which uses a printer driver to format the print job and send it to the print device or print server. A printer can be a local printer, which prints directly to a local or network print device, or a network printer, which prints to a print server.

- *Print server*—A Windows computer that's sharing a printer. It accepts print jobs from computers on the network and sends jobs to the printer to be printed on the print device.

- *Print queue*—A storage location for print jobs awaiting printing. In Windows, the print queue is implemented as a folder (by default, C:\Windows\System32\Spool \Printers) where files that make up each print job are stored until they're sent to the print device or print server.

A configured print server can perform a host of printing functions that aren't possible when users' computers print directly to a print device:

- *Access control*—Using permissions, administrators can control who can print to a printer and who can manage print jobs and printers.

- *Printer pooling*—A single printer represents two or more print devices. Users can print to a single printer, and the print server sends the job to the print device that's least busy.

- *Printer priority*—Two or more printers can represent a single print device. In this case, printers can be assigned different priorities so that jobs sent to the higher priority printer are sent to the print device first.

- *Print job management*—Administrators can pause, cancel, restart, reorder, and change preferences on print jobs waiting in the print queue.

- *Availability control*—Administrators can configure print servers so that print jobs are accepted only during certain hours of the day.

To configure a print server, you just need to share a printer. After a printer is installed, right-click it and click Printer properties, and then click the Sharing tab. The Sharing tab of a print server's Properties dialog box (see Figure 12-24) contains the following options:

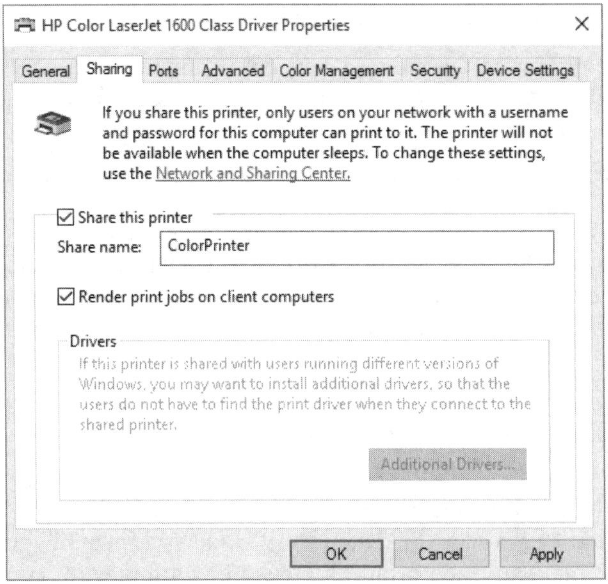

Figure 12-24 The Sharing tab for a print server

- *Share this printer*—When this check box is selected, the print server is shared. By default, the Everyone special identity group is assigned Print permissions to shared printers.

- *Share name*—By default, it's the name of the print server in the Printers folder. You can enter a shorter share name or one that's easier to remember.

- *Render print jobs on client computers*—When this check box is selected (the default setting), client computers process the print job and send it to the print server in a format that's ready to go directly to the print device. If this option isn't selected, more processing occurs on the print server.

- *List in the directory*—This option is shown if the computer on which the printer is being shared is a member of a Windows Active Directory domain. When this check box is selected, the print server is displayed in Active Directory and can be found by Active Directory searches. By default, this option isn't selected.

- *Drivers*—When a client connects to a shared printer, the printer driver is downloaded to the client from the server automatically when possible. You can click this button to install different printer drivers on the server to support different Windows versions.

Sharing Files and Printers in Linux

Linux supports Windows file sharing by using SMB in a software package called Samba. Depending on the Linux distribution, you might have to install this component. In Ubuntu Linux, Windows file sharing isn't installed by default. If you try to share a folder, you're prompted to install the Windows network-sharing service. If you choose to install the service, the Samba package is installed.

After Samba is installed, you can right-click a folder and click Sharing options. To enable the share, click the "Share this folder" check box, as shown in Figure 12-25. You can allow others to create and delete files in the folder or enable guest user access.

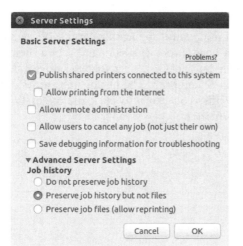

Figure 12-25 Linux folder sharing

Source: © 2015 Canonical Ltd.

Printer sharing in Linux is straightforward after Samba has been installed. When you create a printer in Linux, it's shared automatically. You might need to enable printer publishing in the printer's Server Settings dialog box (see Figure 12-26). In Linux, "printer publishing" is just another name for printer sharing.

Server Settings

Basic Server Settings

Problems?

☑ Publish shared printers connected to this system
☐ Allow printing from the Internet
☐ Allow remote administration
☐ Allow users to cancel any job (not just their own)
☐ Save debugging information for troubleshooting
▼ Advanced Server Settings
Job history
○ Do not preserve job history
◉ Preserve job history but not files
○ Preserve job files (allow reprinting)

Cancel   OK

Figure 12-26 Linux print server settings

Source: © 2015 Canonical Ltd.

Monitoring System Reliability and Performance

Windows Server includes tools to manage and monitor server operation and resources, including the following:

- Task Manager
- Event Viewer
- Performance Monitor

All these tools are available in Windows Server and in Windows client OSs. You have already used Task Manager, so this section focuses on Event Viewer and Performance Monitor.

Event Viewer

Administrators use Event Viewer to examine event log entries generated by system services and applications. To open Event Viewer, right-click Start and click Event Viewer. A typical event log can contain hundreds or thousands of events, but usually, administrators are interested in events that indicate a problem. Events are categorized by these levels:

- *Information*—Indicated by a blue "i" in a white circle, these events are normal operations, such as service stops and starts.

- *Warning*—Indicated by a black exclamation point inside a yellow triangle, warnings provide information about events that should be brought to the administrator's attention. Warnings aren't necessarily an indication of a problem but often indicate a condition that can lead to a more serious error.

- *Error*—Error events, indicated by a white exclamation point inside a red circle, are often generated when a process or service is unable to perform a task or stops unexpectedly. Error messages should be addressed immediately, as they indicate a configuration error or an operational problem.

You can examine several log files in Event Viewer (see Figure 12-27), including the Application, Security, Setup, and System logs. In addition, some applications and services have their own log files. You can click the Level column header to sort events and group them by level to spot the most serious events easily. When an event is selected, descriptive information about it is displayed in the bottom pane of the General tab. The Details tab shows additional technical data about the event. For many events, you can also click the Event Log Online Help link in the General tab to get more information.

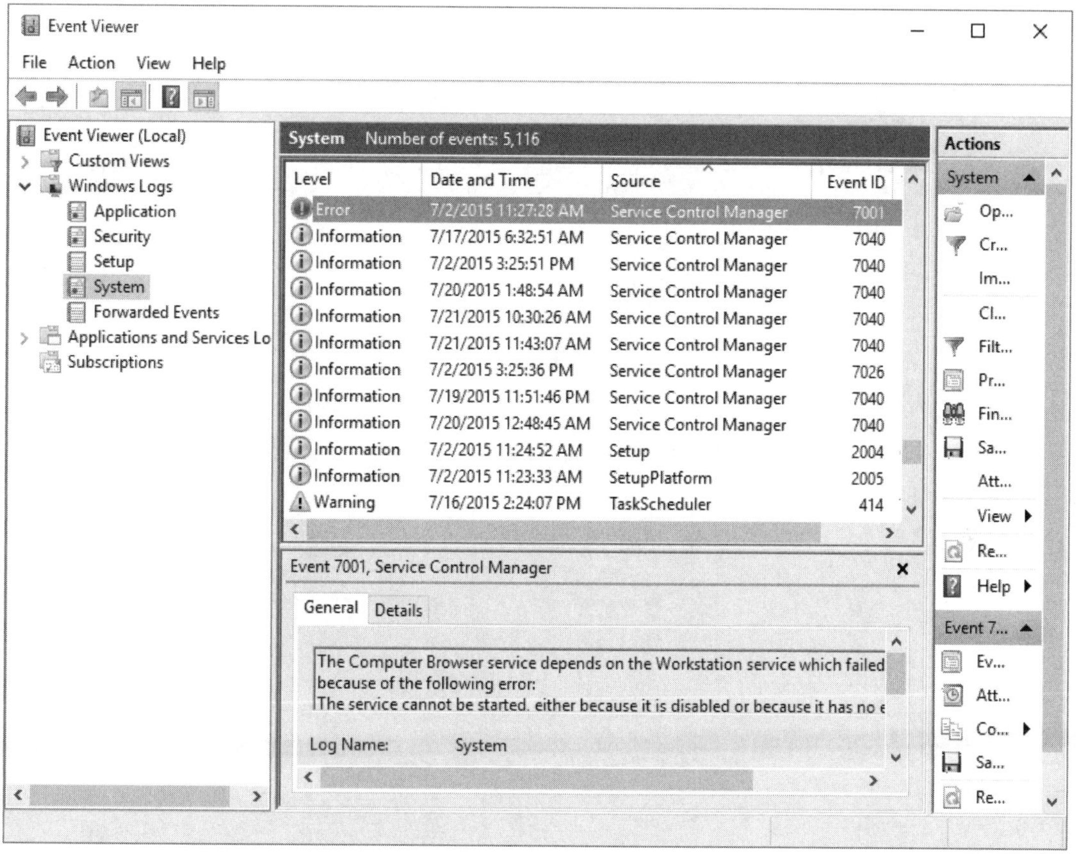

Figure 12-27 Event Viewer in Windows 10

Performance Monitor

Performance Monitor (shown in Figure 12-28) is a collection of tools for pinpointing which resources are being overloaded and how they're being overloaded. You open it from the Computer Management console. Performance Monitor contains the following folders:

- *Monitoring Tools*—Contains the Performance Monitor tool
- *Data Collector Sets*—Contains user- and system-defined templates with sets of data points called data collectors
- *Reports*—Contains system- and user-defined performance and diagnostic reports

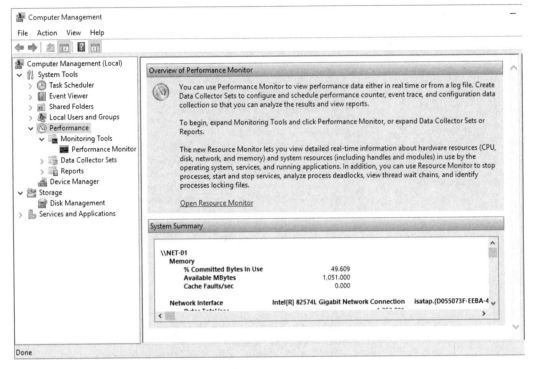

Figure 12-28 The Performance Monitor tool

Performance Monitor uses counters to track the performance of a variety of objects. Performance can be tracked in real time or scheduled for later review and analysis. A counter is a value representing some aspect of an object's performance. For example, disk drives have counters representing the percent of time the disk is used for read operations and the number of disk requests waiting to be serviced, among many others. There are counters for almost every hardware and OS component on a server, including, of course, directory services.

Performance Monitor can track counters with a line graph (the default), with a histogram (bar graph), or as raw data saved to a report. To use Performance Monitor in real-time mode, you simply add counters to the selected graph or report. You can add as many counters as you like, but as you can see in Figure 12-29, the display can get crowded.

Performance Monitor has two modes. You can display counters in real time, or you can open a saved performance log file and view data that has been captured over a period of time. To create a performance log, you create a new data collector set or start a saved data collector set. After the data collector set has finished running, you can view collected performance data in Performance Monitor.

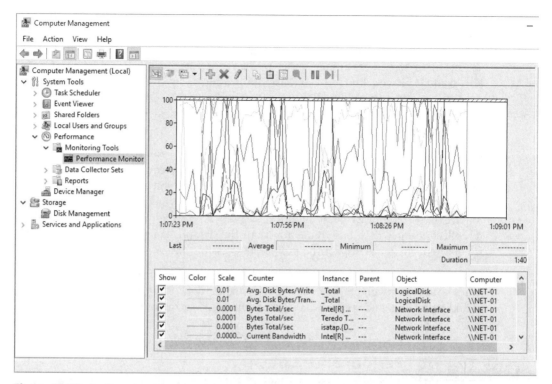

Figure 12-29 Performance Monitor with too many counters

Collecting Baseline Performance Data Viewing performance data in real time is helpful if you want to see the impact certain actions have on selected counters. For example, you might want to see the effect a large network file copy has on CPU and network utilization. Real-time monitoring of performance counters can also be useful for tracking the cause of a sluggish system. Unless you have a good idea what part of the system to examine, however, finding the cause of the problem can be a hit-and-miss proposition.

One reason that tracking causes of poor performance with real-time monitoring is difficult is that you have no point of reference for comparing data. This point of reference, called a performance baseline (or simply a **baseline**), is a record of performance data gathered when a system is performing well under normal operating conditions. Generally, baseline data is collected shortly after a system is put into service and then again each time changes are made, such as installing or removing a network service or application, or when many new users are using the system. The baseline data collected during normal operation conditions can then be compared with data collected during peak resource demands to give you insight into your system's capabilities and limitations.

To create a baseline of performance data for a Windows computer, you create a **data collector set** that specifies the performance counters you want to collect, how often to collect them, and the time period. You can create multiple data collector sets that capture different aspects of system performance and measure performance during different time periods. For example, if you know a database application is used heavily between 10:00 a.m. and 3:00 p.m., you can collect CPU, disk, memory, and network performance data during that time period. You should also collect data for critical resources over an entire day so that you can spot usage trends.

Be aware that performance monitoring uses system resources. It takes memory to run Performance Monitor, CPU cycles to collect and display counter data, and disk resources to update log files. With Performance Monitor, however, you can select a remote computer as the target for monitoring. By monitoring remotely, you lessen the monitoring session's impact on the computer being monitored. You can also adjust the counter sampling interval to collect counter data less frequently than the default values. The more often counter data is collected, the more impact the monitoring session has on system resource use.

You can use Performance Monitor to collect baseline performance data for computers, and other tools are available to collect performance data for a network and network devices, including routers and switches. You examine some of these tools in the next section.

Hands-On Project 12-7: Viewing Real-Time Performance Data

Time Required: 10 minutes

Objective: Add counters to Performance Monitor to view real-time performance data.

Required Tools and Equipment: Net-XX

Description: In this project, you explore Performance Monitor and look at data in real time. In the next project, you save data in a log to view later.

1. Log on to your computer as **NetAdmin**.

2. Right-click **Start** and click **Computer Management**, and then click **Performance** in the left pane. The initial view in the middle pane is Overview of Performance Monitor, which provides information on using Performance Monitor and a system summary. There's also a link to Resource Monitor, which you used when exploring Task Manager in Chapter 11.

3. In the left pane, click to expand **Performance** and **Monitoring Tools**, and then click **Performance Monitor**.

4. Click the **Add** toolbar icon (a green plus sign) to open the Add Counters dialog box. You can specify the computer where you want to add counters in the Select counters from computer list box. For now, leave the setting as <Local computer>.

5. The Processor category of counters is selected by default. Click the **Show description** check box at the bottom so that you can see descriptions of counters you select.

6. Click **Add** to add the processor counter, which by default shows the total processor time.

7. Scroll through available counters to see what type of data can be monitored. Click **PhysicalDisk**. The Instances of selected object list box displays the physical disk objects you can select. You can monitor just one disk or multiple disks or add a counter representing the total counter values for all disks. Click **0 C:** (assuming disk 0 contains the C drive), click the **Add** button, and then click **OK**.

8. Notice that several counters have been added to Performance Monitor. In the bottom pane, click the **Avg. Disk Bytes/Transfer** counter. Emphasize it in the display by clicking the **Highlight** toolbar icon (looks like a yellow highlighter pen). If the counter isn't showing much activity, create some activity by opening and then closing Internet Explorer.

9. Right-click **Avg. Disk Bytes/Transfer** and click **Remove All Counters**. When prompted to confirm, click **OK**.

10. Click the **Add** toolbar icon. In the Add Counters dialog box, click to expand **Physical-Disk**. To select a counter for PhysicalDisk, click **% Disk Time**. (If necessary, verify that the **Show description** check box is selected. You might need to check it whenever you open this dialog box.) Read the description of the counter, and then click **Add**.

11. Click to expand **Processor**, and click **%Interrupt Time**. Read the description, and then click **Add**. Click to expand **System**, and click **Processor Queue Length**. Read the description, and then click **Add**. Queue counters indicate how many activities are waiting for work to be done. For most objects with queue counters (such as PhysicalDisk and Network Interface), a sustained queue value of more than 3 or 4 often indicates a bottleneck. Click **OK**.

12. In the bottom pane of Performance Monitor, notice that the value in the Scale column of the Processor Queue Length counter is 10. This value means the graph is showing the counter's actual value multiplied by the scale value. In this case, if the graph shows a value of 30 for Processor Queue Length, the actual value is 3. To adjust the scale, right-click **Processor Queue Length** and click **Properties**. In the Data tab, you can select the color, width, style, and scale of the line graph for the counter. Click the **Scale** list arrow, click **1.0** in the list, and then click **OK**.

You might want to change the scale value for a counter so that the line on the graph is more distinct and shows variations in the counter value more clearly.

13. Keep Performance Monitor open for the next activity.

Hands-On Project 12-8: Creating a Data Collector Set

Time Required: 15 minutes

Objective: Create a custom data collector set.

Required Tools and Equipment: Net-*XX*

Description: In this project, you save performance data to a log to view it later.

1. Log on to your computer as **NetAdmin**, and open Performance Monitor, if necessary.

2. In the left pane, click to expand **Data Collector Sets**. Right-click **User Defined**, point to **New**, and click **Data Collector Set**. In the Name text box, type **SysPerformance1**. Verify that the default **Create from a template** is selected, and then click **Next**.

3. In the "Which template would you like to use?" window, click each template in the Template Data Collector Set list box, and read its description. Click the **System Performance** template, and then click **Next**.

4. In the next window, you can change the default path where data is saved. If you were measuring disk performance, you might want to make sure to store data on a drive that you aren't monitoring. For now, leave the default location, and then click **Next**.

5. In the "Create the data collector set" window, you can change the user account for running the data collector set. Leave the default setting of **<Default>** in the Run as text box, and then click **Finish**.

6. Notice that the new data collector set has been created and its status is Stopped. Right-click **SysPerformance1** and click **Properties**.

7. Click the **Schedule** tab, where you can create a schedule of when you want the data collector set to run. Click **Add**. You can choose a beginning date and an expiration date. If you choose an expiration date, the data collector set stops collecting data after that date. You can also specify a start time and the days of the week the data collector set should run. You're going to start this data collector set manually, so click **Cancel**.

8. Click the **Stop Condition** tab, where you specify the duration for running the data collector set. If no conditions are selected, the data collector set runs until it's stopped manually. Accept the default value of 1 minute in the Overall duration text box, and then click **OK**.

9. In the left pane, right-click **SysPerformance1** and click **Start**. A green arrow on the data collector set icon indicates it's running. Open and close Internet Explorer and Wireshark several times to generate some resource use.

10. When the status returns to Stopped, right-click **SysPerformance1** and click **Latest Report**. You see a performance report similar to Figure 12-30. Counters with suspect values are flagged as warnings in the Diagnostic Results section. In the Resource Overview section, you get an idea of how major resources, such as CPU, network, disk, and memory, are performing.

Computer Management

File   Action   View   Help

System Performance Report

Computer: NET-01
Collected: Wednesday, July 22, 2015 5:10:32 PM
Duration: 60 Seconds

Summary

Process		Disk		Memory	
Total CPU%:	9	**Top Disk by IO Rate:**	0	**Utilization:**	57 %
Top Process Group:	MicrosoftEdgeCP.exe	**IO/sec:**	44	**Memory:**	2047 MB
Group CPU%:	4	**Disk Queue Length:**	0.563	**Top Process:**	MicrosoftEdge(
Total CPU%:	1			**Private Working Set:**	186,808 KB
Top Process Group:					

Diagnostic Results

Performance

Resource Overview

Component	Status	Utilization	Details
CPU	Idle	14 %	Low CPU load.
Network	Idle	0 %	Busiest network adapter is less than 15%.
Disk	Idle	44 /sec	Disk I/O is less than 100 (read/write) per second on disk 0.
Memory	Normal	57 %	883 MB Available.

CPU

Network

Disk

Done

Figure 12-30   Performance report generated from a data collector set

11. Scroll down in the report to view sections for major hardware systems, such as CPU, Network, Disk, and Memory. Click to expand each section to view more detailed information. You can get quite a bit of information from this report. Why might you want to create a data collector set on your servers?

12. Close all open windows.

Enhancing Network Performance

A single bottleneck in the network can bring an otherwise high-performing network to a crawl. Some factors that can cause poor performance include the following:

- *Poor or inadequate network design*—You have learned a little about network design from studying this book. For example, you should understand that too much broadcast traffic can severely slow device and network performance, so keeping broadcast domains to a manageable size should be a high priority in your design. This probably means using VLANs and subnetting wisely to prevent overly large broadcast domains. At the same time, you don't want to overburden routers, so you need to partition the network to keep as much traffic local to the subnet as possible. For example, if certain applications are used mainly by the Accounting

Department, you might install these applications on a server dedicated to this department and place the server and accounting desktop computers on the same VLAN. Other techniques to consider include making sure frequently accessed devices, such as servers, have a faster network connection (or multiple network connections) than client computers do to prevent servers from becoming a bottleneck.

Adding faster or more network connections to a server might not solve the problem, however, because other resources, such as CPU, memory, and storage, can be the cause of a server bottleneck. Sometimes you just need more than one server to handle the load of a single application. In this case, you might need to use a **load balancer**, a device that distributes traffic for a network service to multiple servers that can provide that service. For example, if you have a heavily used Web site that a single server can't handle, you can deploy two servers, each with the same content, and the load balancer spreads the load between these two servers. Most load balancers can be configured to spread the load based on a percentage. For example, Server1 handles 60% of the traffic, and Server2 handles 40%.

- *Poor network traffic management*—Traffic management means prioritizing time-sensitive packets and limiting the bandwidth low-priority packets can use. Certain network applications are time-sensitive, which means a substantial delay between packets can affect application quality adversely. An example is **Voice over IP (VoIP)**, a group of technologies used to deliver telephone voice communication over regular IP networks. Many businesses have turned to VoIP for their in-house telephone systems so that they don't have to support both a data network and a separate telephone network. You can prioritize time-sensitive packets, such as those used for VoIP, and limit the bandwidth low-priority applications use by using a **packet shaper**. A packet shaper (or traffic shaper) is software that runs on internetwork devices, such as routers and multilayer switches, and can prioritize packets based on protocol, IP address, TCP and UDP ports, and so forth. For example, packets from a VoIP device arriving at a router can be prioritized over packets from a file-sharing application arriving at the same time because file-sharing isn't generally time sensitive.

- *Network errors*—Network protocol misconfigurations, poor media terminations, overlapping Wi-Fi signals, and malfunction devices can all cause network errors. Many errors that occur in network packets allow the network to continue functioning but slow it down precipitously because packets have to be retransmitted. Examples include CRC errors caused by EMI and poorly terminated media, corrupted packets caused by malfunctioning routers and switches, and dropped packets resulting from overwhelmed network interfaces. Some of these errors and how to detect and solve them are discussed in Chapter 13 and in the next section, "Network Performance Monitoring."

- *Denial-of-service attacks*—Chapter 9 discussed denial-of-service (DoS) attacks, which involve injecting nefarious packets into a network for the purpose of disabling the entire network or a particular network device or service. As discussed, DoS attacks can be detected by using a network-based intrusion detection system (NIDS) as well as diligent network monitoring.

Network Performance Monitoring

The performance-monitoring tools built into Windows and other OSs provide performance metrics only for the computer being monitored. A network administrator must also monitor the performance of the network as a whole. Two network protocols are designed to do just that: SNMP and RMON.

Simple Network Management Protocol

SNMP was discussed briefly in Chapter 5 because it's part of the TCP/IP suite. It's used for network monitoring and management and is an industry-standard protocol that most networking equipment manufacturers support. In a Windows client OS, SNMP management can be installed via Programs and Features in Control Panel, and in Windows Server, you use Add Roles and Features in Server Manager.

To use SNMP, SNMP **software agents** are loaded on network devices you want to manage and monitor. Each agent monitors network traffic and device status and stores information in a **management information base (MIB)**. To use the information gathered by software agents, a computer with an SNMP management program must be on the network. This management station communicates with software agents and collects data stored in the MIBs on network devices. Then it combines information from all networking devices and generates statistics or charts of current network conditions. With most SNMP managers, you can set thresholds for sending alert messages to network administrators when these thresholds are exceeded.

In addition, you can manage many network components with SNMP. With software agents, you can configure networking devices and, in some cases, reset them from the management station. SNMP can manage network devices, such as switches and routers, and important network resources, such as servers. An SNMP management program can query these devices and even make configuration changes remotely to help managers control networks from a single application.

SNMP has gone through a number of upgrades through the years, and the most recent version is SNMPv3, which encrypts data transferred between agents and the management station. Earlier versions of SNMP aren't considered secure and should be avoided in environments where security is a concern.

Remote Monitoring

Remote Monitoring (RMON) is an advanced network-monitoring protocol that extends SNMP's capabilities. It comes in two versions: RMON1 and RMON2. SNMP defines a single MIB type to collect network data, but RMON1 defines nine other MIB types, called "RMON groups," to provide a more comprehensive set of data about network use. RMON-capable devices, such as routers and switches, contain software agents called "probes" that collect data and communicate with a management station by using SNMP.

RMON1 is designed to capture data and collect statistics at the Data Link and Physical layers. RMON2 can collect and analyze traffic at the Network and higher layers, which makes detailed analysis of enterprise network and application software operation possible. RMON-capable devices aren't inexpensive, but being able to monitor networks and solve network or application problems before they become serious is well worth the expense, considering the benefit of increased productivity for organizations.

Backup and Fault Tolerance

For many network administrators, performing regular backups is a necessary but often disliked task. Using tape to back up servers is still a common practice, but external disks connected through USB or eSATA and network storage are becoming more popular because of their speed and convenience. However, if your company has a policy that backup media must be stored off-site periodically, tapes are probably the best solution.

Regular backups provide a safety net to restore a system to working order in the event of a disk failure or file corruption. They also allow you to restore files that were accidentally deleted or older versions of modified files that you might need. Traditional backup requires using the backup program to restore files. If system files are lost or damaged to the extent that the system can no longer boot, you have to reinstall the OS before you can use the backup program to restore the system. Another popular type of backup is an image backup, in which a copy of an entire disk is created that can be restored without reinstalling the OS. With many image backups, however, you can't restore separate files, so image backups are usually done along with traditional file backup.

Fault tolerance provides methods for a system to continue running after a system failure has occurred. System failures can be power failures, disk failures, and entire computer failures. Fault tolerance isn't a replacement for backups but complements a regular backup routine. For example, a fault-tolerant disk system allows a system to keep functioning after a disk fails, but you still need backups for situations involving deleted files or a corrupt file system.

Windows Backup

Windows Server Backup comes with Windows Server 2016 and has the following features:

- Backups can be run manually or scheduled to run automatically.
- You can create a system recovery backup that automatically includes all volumes containing critical system data, such as the volume with the Windows folder and the volume with the Active Directory database and log files.
- Manual backups can be stored on network drives, fixed and removable basic disk volumes, and CDs/DVDs. Tape drives aren't supported.
- Backups can be stored on a hard disk dedicated for backups, a nondedicated volume, or a shared network folder. Microsoft recommends using a dedicated disk for backup.
- You can use a Volume Shadow Copy Service (VSS) backup, which means even open files can be backed up.
- By default, Windows Server Backup is configured to back up the local computer, but you can also connect to another computer to back up files remotely.

Although Windows Server Backup is a fine tool for backing up servers, you should be aware of its limitations. It's not a substitute for an enterprise-class backup program, such as Symantec NetBackup and CommVault Backup Appliance; both offer advanced disaster recovery solutions. These programs are called for when you need a comprehensive backup and recovery solution for a large number of servers and servers distributed across multiple sites. Most of these products use a distributed backup strategy, in which backup agents are installed on servers and workstations throughout the enterprise and controlled by a management console. Network and server administrators who manage large networks should familiarize themselves with these products, but a detailed discussion of them is beyond the scope of this book.

Windows 7 has the Backup and Restore program, which has straightforward features. You can use it to create a system image, create a system repair disc, and back up all files or separate files and folders. Backup and Restore is still available in Windows 10 (see Figure 12-31), but the File History feature is the preferred method for restoring files that might have been deleted or restoring a previous version of a file.

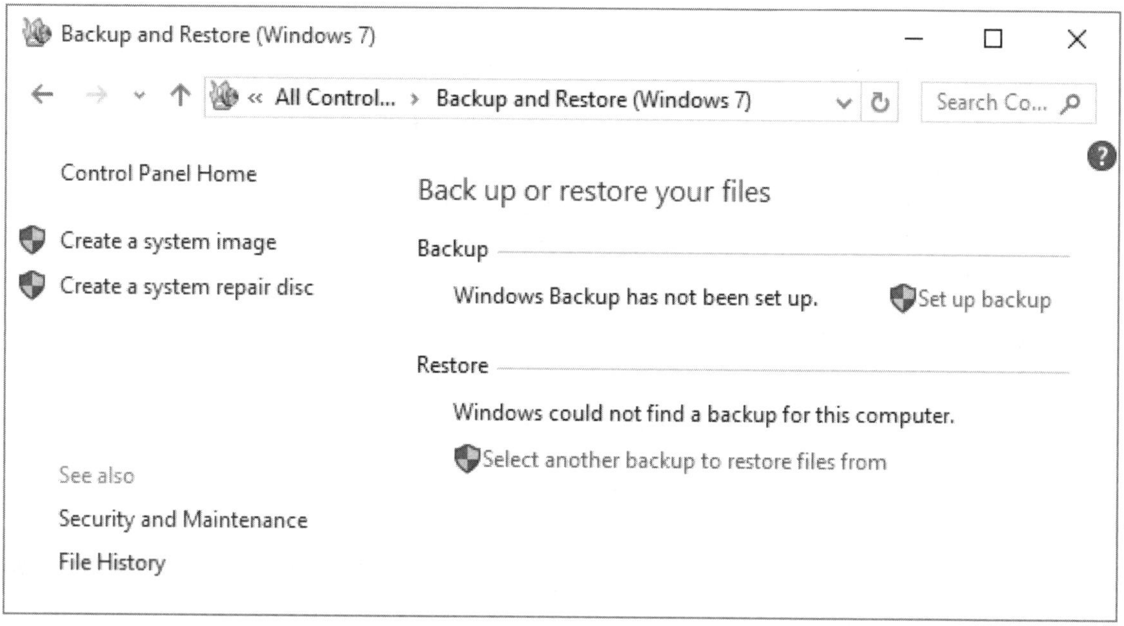

Figure 12-31 Windows Backup and Restore

Hands-On Project 12-9: Using Windows Backup and Restore

Time Required: 20 minutes

Objective: Explore the Backup and Restore program and set up a backup.

Required Tools and Equipment: Net-XX

Description: In this project, you run the Backup and Restore program and explore the options for backing up your system. Then you create a small backup set and restore files from it.

1. Log on to your computer as **NetAdmin**. Before you can create a backup, you need a drive Windows can use to store the backup. This drive can't be a dynamic disk, as your Vol1 (M:) drive is, so you convert it to a basic disk again.

2. Right-click **Start** and click **Disk Management**. In Disk Management, right-click **Vol1 (M:)** and click **Delete Volume**. Click **Yes** to confirm. Right-click the unallocated space of Disk1 and click **New simple volume**. Follow the wizard to create a volume of **10 GB**, assigning the volume the **M** drive letter again and making the volume label **Backup**. After the volume is created, close Disk Management.

3. Create a text document on your desktop named **testbackup**. This file will be included in the backup you create, and you'll delete and later restore this file. Double-click **testbackup** to open it in Notepad, and type your name so that the file isn't empty. Save the file and exit Notepad.

4. Right-click **Start** and click **Control Panel**. Under System and Security, click **Backup and Restore (Windows 7)**.

5. Click **Create a system image**. Read the description of a system image. Notice that you have the option to store the backup on a hard disk, a DVD, or a network location. Because you might not have a hard disk capable of storing the backup, click **Cancel**. An external USB hard drive is ideal for storing a system image.

6. Click **Create a system repair disc**. A system repair disc allows you to boot your computer if there's been a boot disk failure and contains recovery tools to solve problems or restore from a system image. You need a blank CD or DVD to create a system repair disc. Click **Cancel**.

7. Click **Set up backup**. In the "Select where you want to save your backup" window, click the **Backup (M:)** drive, and then click **Next**.

8. In the "What do you want to back up?" window, click **Let me choose**, and then click **Next**.

9. Leave the items under Data Files selected, but click to clear the **Include a system image of drives** check box (see Figure 12-32). The Data Files option backs up your document files, including those on your desktop. Click **Next**.

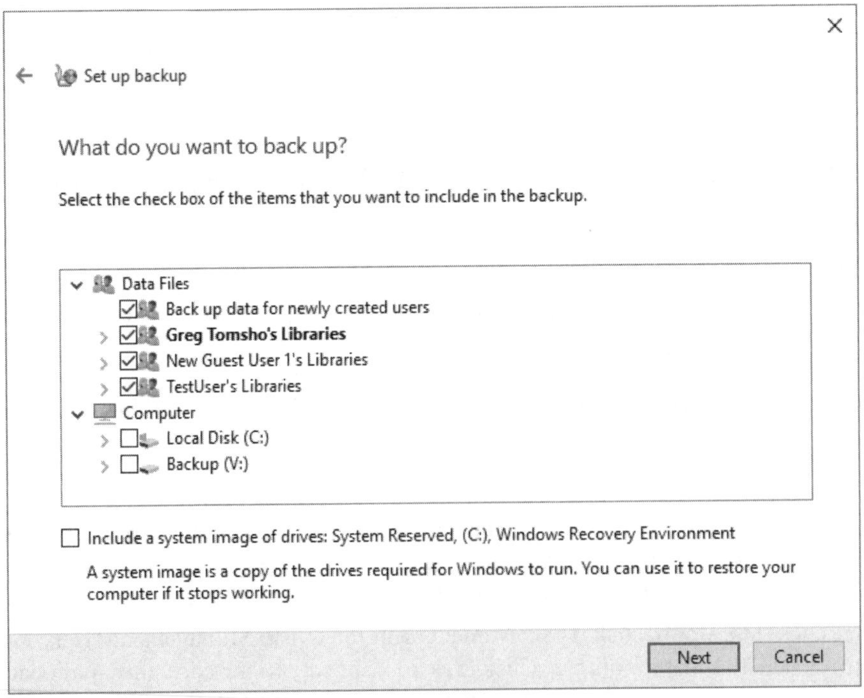

Figure 12-32 Choosing the files you want to back up

10. In the "Review your backup settings" window, notice that Backup and Restore automatically scheduled a backup to occur weekly. Click **Save settings and run backup**. To view the progress of the backup, click **View Details**.

11. When the backup is finished, click **Close**. You see a Restore section in Backup and Restore. Delete the `testbackup` file you created in Step 3. Empty the Recycle Bin so that the file is really deleted. Click **Restore my files** in Backup and Restore.

12. Click **Browse for files**. Double-click **Backup of C:** and then **Users**. Click the logon name for your account (in this case, **NetAdmin**). Double-click the **desktop** folder in the right pane (see Figure 12-33).

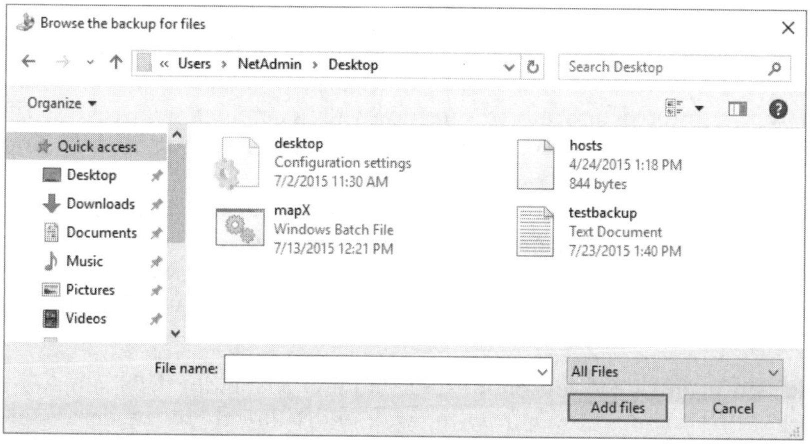

Figure 12-33 Browsing for files to restore

13. Click `testbackup` and click the **Add files** button. Click **Next**. Leave the default option **In the original location** selected, and click **Restore**. The file is then displayed on your desktop. Click **Finish**.

14. Log off or shut down your computer.

Protecting Data with Fault Tolerance

Some networks can't afford downtime for their network servers. A disk crash, motherboard failure, or power outage can stop a server dead in its tracks if no fault-tolerant systems have been put in place. This section discusses three forms of fault tolerance that are common on networks and servers:

- Redundant power supply and uninterruptible power supply
- Redundant disk systems
- Server clustering

Redundant Power A computer requires a consistent, clean source of power. If power is interrupted for even the briefest moment, a computer is likely to reboot. On a desktop system, a user might lose some work, or if a file transaction was in progress, disk corruption could result. On a server, dozens of people could lose work, databases could become corrupted, and the file system could be damaged. Power fluctuations can cause even worse damage because if the power spikes or sags, the motherboard and other hardware components can be damaged. To combat these potential problems, server systems and some desktop systems use redundant power supplies and uninterruptible power supplies.

A **redundant power supply** is essentially a second power supply unit in the computer case. Each unit is capable on its own of maintaining adequate power to the computer, so if one power supply fails, the other unit takes on the full load. When both units are operating, they share the power load, which also reduces heat and stress on each unit, further increasing reliability. Redundant power supplies can add considerable cost to a computer and are generally found only in servers.

An **uninterruptible power supply (UPS)** is a device with a built-in battery, power conditioning, and surge protection. A UPS is plugged into the wall outlet to charge the battery continuously, and the computer and monitor are plugged into outlets on the UPS. If the power fails, the UPS battery provides enough power to keep your computer and monitor running until main power is restored or you can shut down the computer safely. Most UPSs come with software and a USB or serial connection to the computer so that the UPS can communicate with the computer. The UPS can inform the computer when main power has been lost, when it has been restored, and when the UPS battery power is running low. You can configure the software so that if the amount of remaining battery time falls below a certain number of minutes, the system shuts itself down. UPSs also protect systems from power sags or brownouts, in which the main power voltage output falls below what's required to power off a system safely.

UPSs come in two main categories: online and standby. A standby UPS supplies power to plugged-in devices by passing power from the wall outlet directly to the device. In a power outage, a standby UPS detects the power failure and switches to battery power quickly. Unfortunately, if the switchover doesn't happen fast enough, the plugged-in devices might lose power long enough to reboot or cause a malfunction. An online UPS supplies power continuously to plugged-in devices through the UPS battery, which is recharged continually by the wall outlet power. In a power outage, there's no need to switch to battery power because the UPS is already supplying power from the battery. Overall, an online UPS is a far better solution for computer equipment but costs more.

Battery backup isn't the only advantage of UPSs. Power conditioning and surge protection are equally important to the sensitive components in computers. **Power conditioning** "cleans" the power, removing noise caused by other devices on the same circuit (such as fans, motors, and laser printers). **Surge protection** protects the computer from voltage spikes or surges—conditions that can be caused by lightning strikes, problems with the electric company's power transformer, or switching on large appliances, such as air conditioners.

Redundant Disk Systems Hard drives contain some of the few moving parts in a computer, making them more susceptible to failure than most other components. Redundant disk systems can prevent data loss in the event of a disk failure; in fact, a system with a redundant disk configuration can continue operating with no downtime. Redundant disk systems are based on the redundant array of independent disks (RAID) technology, introduced in Chapter 8. The two most common RAID configurations are disk mirroring (RAID 1) and disk striping with parity (RAID 5).

Disk mirroring requires two disks. When data is written to one disk, it's also written to the second disk, thus creating a synchronized copy. If either disk fails, the system can continue operating because both disks have the same data. RAID 1's obvious disadvantage is that you have to purchase two disks of equal size but get the storage space of only one disk. Another disadvantage is somewhat slower performance, but it's a small price to pay for peace of mind. Write performance is slower because two disks must be written, but read performance is about the same as in a single-disk configuration. Both read and write performance can be enhanced by using two disk controllers: one for each disk, a configuration called "disk duplexing." Most disk controllers on servers and even on many desktop systems can be configured for RAID 1. Windows Server supports RAID 1 in software if the disk controller lacks RAID support.

Disk performance depends on many factors, including the quality of the disk controller. On some systems, you might not see slower disk write performance with RAID 1, and you might see somewhat faster read performance compared with a single-disk configuration.

Disk striping with parity requires a minimum of three disks but is more space efficient than RAID 1. RAID 5 works by spreading data across multiple disks and using one disk in each write operation to store parity information. Parity information is generated by a mathematical calculation on data being written, so if one of the disks fails, this information can be used to re-create lost data from the failed disk.

For example, if a RAID 5 configuration consists of three disks with a cluster size of 64 KB and a file of 128 KB is written to the disk, 64 KB is written to the first disk, 64 KB is written to the second disk, and parity information is written to the third disk. Parity information isn't always written to the same disk, however. The next file written uses the second and third disks for file data and the first disk for parity (see Figure 12-34).

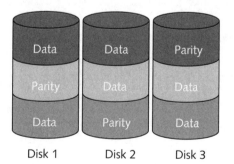

Figure 12-34   RAID 5: stripe set with parity

The number of disks in a RAID 5 configuration is theoretically unlimited, but the more disks there are, the more likely that more than one disk will fail simultaneously, and RAID 5 can recover from only a single disk failure. With RAID 5, you lose $1/n$ of your total disk space (with n representing the number of disks). So if your RAID setup consists of four 100 GB disks, you have 300 GB for disk storage and 100 GB for parity information. RAID 5 write performance is hampered because of calculating and writing parity information, but read performance is usually as good or better than with a single disk. Windows Server also supports RAID 5 in software if the disk controller doesn't.

Other RAID configurations exist, including RAID 0. RAID 0 is disk striping, requires two or more disks, and is used mainly for high performance. However, it provides no fault tolerance, so if any disk fails, all data is lost. Table 12-4 lists the RAID levels, some of which are no longer in use.

Table 12-4   RAID levels

RAID level	Description and use
RAID 0	Called disk striping, RAID 0 distributes data over two or more disks. RAID 0 has no fault-tolerance capabilities but does enhance disk performance. Available in Windows Server 2000/2003 as well as Linux.
RAID 1	Applies to disk mirroring and disk duplexing, in which two drives are exact copies of each other, and failure of the primary drive causes the secondary drive to take over automatically. Available in Windows Server 2000/2003 as well as Linux.
RAID 2	Uses separate check disks, in which data bits are striped on both data and check disks, to replace information from a damaged data or check disk in the array. Because check data requirements are high and require multiple separate drives for data, this form of RAID is seldom used. Not available for Windows OSs.
RAID 3	Uses a single check disk for parity information (sometimes called a parity disk for that reason) for each group of drives. Because the same size chunk of data is read or written each time the array is accessed, space allocation on these drives isn't efficient, especially for small files. Not available for Windows OSs.
RAID 4	Works much like RAID 3 but uses block or sector striping so that a single block or sector can be accessed at a time, instead of requiring all drives in the set to be accessed. Inefficient for writing data because check writes must occur immediately after data writes. Not available for Windows OSs.
RAID 5	Divides parity information across all drives in the RAID array so that each drive can be reconstructed from parity information stored on all other drives in the set. This array type, also called disk striping with parity, is available for Windows Server 2000/2003. Can withstand a single disk failure and continue to operate with no loss of data.
RAID 6	Like RAID 5, except two sets of parity information are written to two different disks. Can survive the failure of two disks rather than just one.
RAID 1+0	Combines RAID levels 1 and 0 and is sometimes called RAID 10. It uses a RAID 1 mirror set that's striped with another set of drives and can survive multiple disk failures in some circumstances. A minimum of four disks is required for this configuration.
RAID 0+1	Combines RAID levels 0 and 1 but starts with a stripe set and then mirrors it. RAID 0+1 can withstand two disk failures if both failed disks are from the same stripe set. A minimum of four disks is required.
Raid 5+0	A RAID 0 striped across two or more RAID 5 sets; also called RAID 50. Requires at least six disks and improves performance over traditional RAID 5. Can withstand up to four disk failures, depending on whether each failed disk is in a different RAID 5 set.

Server Clustering Windows Server supports server clustering. A server cluster is made up of two or more servers that are interconnected and appear as a single unit. Two common types of clustering are failover and load-balancing. A failover cluster is used to provide fault tolerance in the event of a complete system failure. It involves two or more servers sharing a high-speed link used to synchronize data continuously. One server is designated as the primary server, and the others are standby servers. If the primary server fails, a standby server takes its place as the primary server. A failover cluster is usually used to ensure high availability for applications such as database and messaging systems, in which data is read and written frequently.

A load-balancing cluster consists of two or more servers that appear as a single unit to users. All servers in the cluster operate and share the server load. This type of cluster is used when data on the server is comparatively static and with read-intensive applications that exceed a single server's performance capabilities. The advantage of load-balancing clusters is that you still have the benefit of failover: If one server fails, the others just have to shoulder a bigger load.

Chapter Summary

- User accounts are the link between real people and network resources. They have two main functions in a network: Provide a way for users to authenticate themselves to the network, and provide detailed information about users.

- User accounts and passwords should following naming conventions for their creation. Typical password restrictions include minimum length, complexity requirements, and how often they must be changed.

- Group accounts are used to organize users so that assignment of resource permissions and rights can be managed more easily than working with dozens or hundreds of user accounts. Groups in Active Directory are assigned a scope (domain local, global, or universal) and type (security or distribution).

- A user profile is a collection of a user's personal files and settings that define his or her working environment. A profile contains personal data folders a user maintains as well as files and folders containing user and application settings. A local profile is stored on the system the user logs on to. A roaming profile is stored on a network server and follows the user wherever he or she logs on.

- Locally attached storage is a device, such as a hard disk, that's connected to a storage controller on the server. Storage is divided into volumes or partitions. A file system is installed on the volume. NTFS is the file system used in Windows in most cases; it provides advanced features such as disk quotas, permissions, file compression, and encryption.

- Linux file systems, which support permissions and journaling, include Ext3, Ext4, ReiserFS, and XFS.

- SMB is the Windows default file-sharing protocol; NFS is the native Linux file-sharing protocol. Linux also supports SMB via Samba, and Windows supports NFS. Files can be shared in Windows by using the File Sharing Wizard, the Advanced Sharing dialog box, the Shared Folders snap-in, and the Share and Storage Management snap-in.

- Windows Server includes tools to manage and monitor server operation and resources, including Task Manager, Event Viewer, and Performance Monitor.

- A single bottleneck in the network can bring an otherwise high-performing network to a crawl. Some factors that can cause poor performance include poor or inadequate network design, poor network traffic management, network errors, and denial-of-service attacks.

■ A network administrator must monitor the performance of the network as a whole. Two network protocols are designed to do just that: SNMP and RMON. SNMP is used for network monitoring and management and is an industry-standard protocol that most networking equipment manufacturers support. Remote Monitoring (RMON) is an advanced network-monitoring protocol that extends SNMP's capabilities.

■ Regular backups provide a safety net to restore a system to working order in the event of a disk failure or file corruption. Fault tolerance ensures that a system can continue running after a failure has occurred. System failures can be power failures, disk failures, and entire computer failures. Backups can provide fault tolerance when data has been lost or corrupted, and RAID disk systems can provide fault tolerance in the event of a disk failure. UPSs can protect systems against the effects of power loss or fluctuations.

■ A server cluster is made up of two or more servers that are interconnected and appear as a single unit. Two common types of clustering are failover and load-balancing clusters.

Key Terms

active partition   A partition that can hold boot files the BIOS loads before it can start the OS.

baseline   A record of performance data gathered when a system is performing well under normal operating conditions. The baseline can then be compared with data collected during peak resource demands to give you insight into your system's capabilities and limitations.

basic disk   A disk configuration in which the space on the disk can be divided into one to four partitions.

boot partition   The partition or logical drive holding Windows OS files.

data collector set   A feature of Performance Monitor that specifies the performance counters you want to collect, how often to collect them, and the time period.

default groups   Special groups with rights already assigned; created during installation in a Windows environment.

disk mirroring   A fault-tolerant disk configuration in which data is written to two hard drives rather than one so that if one disk fails, the data isn't lost.

disk quotas   A feature available in some file systems that allows an administrator to set a limit to how much disk space a user's files can occupy.

disk striping with parity   A fault-tolerant disk configuration in which parts of several physical disks are linked in an array, and data and parity information are written to all disks in this array. If one disk fails, data can be reconstructed from the parity information written on the others.

dynamic disk   A disk configuration in Windows that can be divided into one or more volumes. You can create up to 1000 volumes per dynamic disk (although no more than

32 is recommended). A dynamic disk offers features that a basic disk doesn't, namely RAID and disk spanning.

extended partition   A partition type that can be divided into one or more logical drives, each of which can be formatted and assigned a drive letter.

load balancer   A device that distributes traffic for a network service to multiple servers that can provide that service.

local profile   A user profile stored on the same system where a user logs on; created from a hidden profile called Default the first time a user logs on to the system. *See also* user profile.

management information base (MIB)   A collection of network data stored by Simple Network Management Protocol software agents. *See also* software agents.

Network File System (NFS)   The native Linux file-sharing protocol.

NTFS permissions   A feature in Windows NTFS that gives administrators fine-grained control over file and folder access for both network users and interactive users.

packet shaper   Software that runs on internetwork devices, such as routers and multilayer switches, and prioritizes packets based on protocol, IP address, TCP and UDP ports, and so forth.

power conditioning   A method of cleaning the power input, removing noise caused by other devices on the same circuit.

primary partition   A partition type that can be formatted with a file system and assigned a drive letter or mounted in an empty folder on an existing drive letter; also called a volume. *See also* volume.

redundant power supply   A second power supply unit in the computer case. Each unit is capable on its own of maintaining adequate power to the computer, so if one power supply fails, the other unit takes on the full load.

Remote Monitoring (RMON)   An advanced network-monitoring protocol that extends Simple Network Management Protocol's capabilities; contains software agents called probes that collect data and communicate with a management station by using SNMP.

rights   In Windows, they define the types of actions a user can perform, such as creating file shares or installing software.

roaming profile   A user profile in a Windows environment that's stored on a server and can be accessed from any computer the user logs on to. *See also* user profile.

Server Message Block (SMB)   The Windows file-sharing protocol.

software agents   Simple Network Management Protocol components that are loaded on network devices; they monitor network traffic and device status information and send it to a management station.

special identity groups   A type of group in Windows in which membership is controlled dynamically by Windows, can't be viewed or changed manually, and depends on how an account accesses the OS. For example, membership in the Authenticated Users group is assigned to a user account automatically when the user logs on to a computer or domain.

surge protection   Power protection that evens out spikes or sags in the main current and prevents them from affecting a computer.

system partition   The active primary partition storing the Windows boot loader.

uninterruptible power supply (UPS) A power protection device that includes a battery backup to take over if the main current fails; usually incorporates power conditioning and surge protection.

user profile A collection of a user's personal files and settings that define his or her working environment.

Voice over IP (VoIP) A group of technologies used to deliver telephone voice communication over regular IP networks.

volume Part or all of the space on one or more disks that contains or is ready to contain a file system. In Windows, volumes with file systems are usually assigned a drive letter. In Linux, volumes are mounted in the file system and accessed as though they were just another folder.

Review Questions

1. Which of the following is a function of a user account? (Choose all that apply.)

    a. Establishes a link between the user and the computer's IP address

    b. Provides a method for user authentication

    c. Provides information about a user

    d. Authorizes a user to log on to network servers

2. Which of the following is true of group accounts? (Choose all that apply.)

    a. They organize users for easier assignment of resource permissions.

    b. They can be used only to assign permissions, not rights.

    c. Each group has a password assigned.

    d. You can select a group scope in Active Directory but not in Windows 10.

3. Which of the following is true of a user logon name in Windows?

    a. It's case sensitive.

    b. It's not case sensitive.

    c. It must contain both uppercase and lowercase letters.

    d. It must contain at least one number.

4. Which of the following is a group scope in Active Directory? (Choose all that apply.)

    a. Domain local

    b. Global

    c. Distribution

    d. Security

5. Which of the following is a special identity group? (Choose all that apply.)

    a. Everyone

    b. Logged-On Users

    c. Authenticated Users

    d. Creator Owner

6. Which of the following is a collection of a user's personal data folders and application settings that's available at any computer where the user logs on?

    a. Local profile

    b. Roaming profile

    c. Mandatory profile

    d. Network profile

7. Which command in Linux might be needed to perform user account management if you aren't logged on as the root user?

    a. runas

    b. superuser

    c. passwd

    d. sudo

8. Which command in Linux gives you extensive help on how to use a command?

    a. help

    b. more

    c. man

    d. guide

9. Which is true about Linux user accounts? (Choose all that apply.)

    a. They must belong to at least one group.

    b. The account names are case sensitive.

    c. The full name is a required part of the user account.

    d. The account names can't contain lowercase letters.

10. Which is true about partitions? (Choose all that apply.)

    a. A partition is always a volume, too.

    b. You can have up to four primary partitions.

    c. An extended partition is assigned a drive letter by default.

    d. Only a primary partition can be active.

11. Which NTFS feature should you configure if you want users to be able to revert to an older version of a file?

    a. Disk quotas

    b. EFS

    c. Mount points

    d. Shadow copies

12. Which is true about file compression? (Choose all that apply.)

    a. A compressed file can't be encrypted with EFS.

    b. It's a standard feature in Windows starting with FAT32.

    c. Decompression occurs automatically when a file is accessed.

    d. Compressed files can't have permissions assigned to them.

13. Which of the following is true about permissions in NTFS?

    a. An Allow permission always overrides a Deny permission.

    b. Permissions can be set only on folders, not on files.

    c. By default, permissions are inherited automatically from the parent folder.

    d. The last permission assigned is the only one that takes effect.

14. Which of the following is a permission in the Linux OS? (Choose all that apply.)

    a. Read

    b. Modify

    c. Delete

    d. Execute

15. Which of the following correctly describes how sharing and NTFS permissions work?

    a. When a file is accessed over the network, sharing permissions are checked first.

    b. When a file is accessed interactively, only sharing permissions are checked.

    c. When both sharing and NTFS permissions are applied, the least restrictive permissions apply.

    d. Sharing permissions can be assigned to separate files.

16. Which of the following is true of Windows printing terminology? (Choose all that apply.)

    a. A printer is a physical device.

    b. A print server is a computer sharing a printer.

    c. A print queue stores jobs waiting to be printed.

    d. A printer pool is two or more printers representing a single print device.

17. Which of the following tools is used to view information categorized as Information, Warning, or Error?

    a. Event Viewer

    b. Performance Monitor

    c. Task Manager

    d. Report Generator

18. Which is best described as a record of performance data gathered when a system is performing well under normal conditions?

    a. Data collector set

    b. Real-time monitoring

    c. Baseline

    d. Performance counters

19. Why would you choose to monitor a system's performance remotely?

    a. You don't have permission to log on to the system.

    b. The computer you want to monitor doesn't have enough memory to run Performance Monitor.

    c. The system is running Windows 10, which doesn't have Performance Monitor installed.

    d. You want to lessen the impact of the monitoring session on the computer.

20. Which of the following is a factor that can cause poor network performance? (Choose all that apply.)

    a. Poor network design

    b. Private IP addresses

    c. Poor traffic management

    d. Server clusters

21. Which of the following should you use if you want secure network monitoring?

    a. VoIP

    b. SNMPv3

    c. MIB

    d. SMB

22. If you're deploying VoIP on your network, which device should you consider to ensure timely delivery of VoIP packets?

    a. Load balancer

    b. NIDS

    c. Packet shaper

    d. Server cluster

23. Which UPS type is best for computer power backup?

    a. Standby

    b. Online

    c. Offline

    d. Always on

24. Which RAID level uses a minimum of three disks and provides fault tolerance?

    a. RAID 1

    b. RAID 0

    c. RAID 5

    d. RAID 1+0

Challenge Labs

Challenge Lab 12-1: Creating Users in Linux with the `newusers` Command

Time Required: 30 minutes

Objective: Create users in Linux with the `newusers` command.

Required Tools and Equipment: A computer with a Linux OS installed or Net-XX and a Linux Live disc

Description: This lab can be done in groups. In this lab, you create Linux users in batch mode with the `newusers` command, which accepts a text file as input. Use the man pages for the `newusers` command and create a correctly formatted file to use as input to the `newusers` command. Five new users should be created, and each user should be new in the system. The users' UIDs should specified in the file and be in the range 5001 to 5005. The primary group name should be the same as the user's logon name. The user's full name can be whatever you like. The home directory should be /home/*username*, and the user's default shell should be /bin/bash. After you're finished, print the input file you created and hand it in to your instructor.

Challenge Lab 12-2: Creating Users, Groups, and Shares to Represent a Company's Organization

Time Required: 1 hour

Objective: Create users, groups, and shares and assign permissions.

Required Tools and Equipment: Net-XX with the server VM installed in Hands-On Project 11-9 and configured in Challenge Lab 11-1 and the completion of Challenge Lab 11-2. (*Note*: If you didn't install the server in Hands-On Project 11-9, you can use Net-XX for this lab.)

Description: Based on the file hierarchy you created in Challenge Lab 11-2, you share folders, create users and groups, and assign permissions. This lab can be done in groups. You're the IT administrator for a new company with six main departments: Management, Accounting (with subdepartments Billing and Accounts Payable), Operations (with subdepartments Manufacturing and Design), Customer Service, Human Resources, and Information Technology (with subdepartments Network Engineering and Helpdesk). Each department has three users and needs access to shared documents that the other departments don't have access to. Users in each department should be able to create, modify, and delete files in their department's shared folder. Create one shared folder named Public that all users have read-only access to, except one user in the Operations department, who should be able to create, modify, and delete documents in the Public folder. Administrators have full access to all shared folders. Perform the following tasks:

- Create users for each department, assigning an initial password to each user but requiring the user to change the password at first logon.

- Create groups for each department and assign user memberships appropriately.

- Create shared folders for each department and the Public share.

- Assign sharing and NTFS permissions for the departmental shared folders so that users in each department have the necessary access to their shared folders.

- Assign sharing and NTFS permissions to the Public shared folder.

After you're finished, diagram your solution, showing groups, group memberships, and shares and their associated sharing and NTFS permissions.

Case Project 12-1

You have created shared folders for all your companies departments and assigned the appropriate permissions. Everyone can access the shares as planned, but now you find that an extraordinary amount of disk space is being used on the server. What can you do to limit how much users can store on your servers?

Case Project 12-2

You have just purchased a new Dell PowerEdge R520 Rack Server. The server is equipped with two Xeon E5-2400 CPUs, 32 GB RAM, four 1 TB SAS hard drives, and two 750-watt power supplies. You have a 21-inch LCD monitor connected to your server. You want a UPS to keep your server running in the event of a power failure for up to 20 minutes. You prefer a rack-mounted solution. Use the UPS selector tool at APC's Web site (a well-known UPS vendor). The UPS selector is at *www.apcc.com/tools/ups_selector/*. Determine which model UPS will work well for this server, and state your reasons.

chapter 13

Troubleshooting and Support

After reading this chapter and completing the exercises, you will be able to:

- Describe the benefits of documenting a network and list what elements should be documented
- List the steps of the problem-solving process
- Explain different approaches to network troubleshooting
- Make use of problem-solving resources
- Describe network troubleshooting tools
- Summarize common trouble situations
- Describe disaster recovery procedures

The daunting task of supporting a complex internetwork can be both challenging and rewarding. Successful network administrators need to draw on a variety of skills, technologies, and techniques to meet the increasing demands of LANs and internetworks. The types of technologies used in networks demand support personnel who are willing to continue learning long after their formal education is over. Having an excellent grasp of the fundamentals of network hardware and software enables you to adapt to the constantly changing computing environment you'll no doubt face.

In this chapter, you use the knowledge and skills you have gained throughout this book. Experience shows that a well-documented network is easier to troubleshoot and support. This chapter covers the importance of documentation and what should be documented in a typical network.

There are many different approaches to troubleshooting, and different situations call for different approaches. This chapter explains a variety of approaches to solving problems with examples of when an approach is and isn't recommended. No matter what approach you take, the problem-solving process has several steps. This chapter outlines eight steps; in some situations, you might use only four or five, but in others, all eight steps are likely to be needed.

Many problem-solving resources are available. This chapter discusses some of the most important for researching a problem. Your knowledge and experience might be the best resources you have and the best tools for solving problems. However, you often need software or hardware tools to help you gather information about a network and its devices. This chapter covers the most common tools for network monitoring and analysis that help you gather information and concludes with a discussion of disaster recovery, which includes backup and system repair and recovery.

Keep in mind that network support and troubleshooting is an enormous, complex topic, and entire books are written about it. This chapter is intended to give you an idea of where to start when facing a problem and some resources you can use as you gain experience as an IT professional.

Documenting Your Network

Table 13-1 summarizes what you need for the hands-on projects in this chapter.

Table 13-1   Hands-on project requirements

Hands-on project	Requirements	Time required	Notes
Hands-On Project 13-1: Troubleshooting with the OSI Model	Net-*XX*	10 minutes	
Hands-On Project 13-2: Using Wireshark to Monitor Traffic	Net-*XX*	10 minutes	
Hands-On Project 13-3: Using Simple Server Monitor	Net-*XX*	20 minutes	

Believe it or not, there are network administrators who believe that failing to document the network means job security. It makes sense when you think of it from a narrow point of view. If your servers, cable plant, and internetworking devices are a mystery to everyone except you, it follows that you're indispensable. However, nobody can keep the details of a multitude of cable terminations, server configurations, and network devices straight in his or her head.

For example, the boss comes to you about the latest security vulnerability found in one of the OSs used in your network and asks whether the company's servers are vulnerable. He has read that servers without update x using version y of the NIC driver are vulnerable. An administrator with up-to-date documentation can find the right documentation page quickly and respond reassuringly about the servers' status, thereby gaining the boss's confidence and trust. Administrators who believe documentation is unnecessary or too time consuming don't have this information at their fingertips and might respond with a confidence-draining "I don't know."

As another example, your boss tells you that 10 new offices on the third floor are going to be occupied by the end of the month. He asks what the cost in new switches, patch panels, and cable runs will be. A well-prepared administrator can pull up a database or spreadsheet with information for the wiring closet on the third floor and promptly tell the boss how many ports are available on existing switches and patch panels. Perhaps the answer is that no extra equipment is required or only a new switch is needed, but your ability to respond quickly won't go unnoticed. Meanwhile, a documentation slacker tells the boss that some research is necessary before coming up with an answer.

There are many examples of why documenting your network is worth the trouble. The following is a list of some reasons network documentation is good for you *and* your network:

- Makes equipment and workstation moves, additions, and changes easier
- Provides information needed for troubleshooting
- Offers justification for more staff or equipment
- Helps determine compliance with standards
- Supplies proof that your installations meet hardware or software requirements
- Reduces training requirements
- Facilitates security management
- Improves compliance with software licensing agreements

The following sections describe many areas in which documentation can affect your network and the advantages of complete documentation, including how it can positively affect network changes, troubleshooting, IT staffing and training, standards compliance issues, technical support, and network security.

Change Management

In a network, a change is some procedure that requires modifications at workstations, such as changes of addresses, a NIC replacement, a software change, or a complete change in the workstation. Moves, additions, and changes in your network are much easier with accurate documentation. When a workstation is moved, the person doing the moving must know which patch panel and switch ports are being used so that they can be disconnected. After the workstation is at the new location, the mover must know which patch panel port to use and which switch port is correct for the workstation. Without good documentation, cables must be traced, questions must be asked, and time is wasted. Documenting the current configuration makes most changes proceed more smoothly, and documenting the change results facilitates future dealings with workstations.

Additions to your network can be done more quickly and with fewer chances of error if documentation is up to date. As noted, documentation of patch panel and switch port use, wiring diagrams, and the like can make estimating costs and scheduling more accurate and less time consuming. Documenting changes in your network, which includes reasons for the change, the potential impact of a change, notifications, and approval procedures, is called **change management**.

Documentation and Troubleshooting

One of the first steps in troubleshooting is gathering information. If a user has connectivity problems, your network documentation can supply a wealth of information almost instantly. Physical and logical addressing, connectivity to devices, and even data about cabling can be useful pieces of information when trying to solve a problem. Accurate documentation of workstation MAC addresses helps you find problems such as IP address conflicts and the source of invalid or excessive frames.

In addition, when troubleshooting sessions requiring protocol analysis, documentation provides the names and addresses of devices that are likely to be involved in a particular type of packet exchange you're troubleshooting. Documentation also makes it easier to set up test networks so that you can duplicate conditions in your production environment to solve a complex problem.

Documentation and IT Staffing

Is network support running you and your staff ragged? Documenting the type and frequency of support calls can provide the justification for additions to staff or, at the very least, for more tools to make support more efficient. In addition, you can use statistics on network response time and bandwidth load as justification for upgrading servers or adding a switch.

Speaking of staff, the first thing you should hand a new network technician is a copy of the network documentation manual. Tell the new employee to read and learn it, and you'll have a trained technician (or at least a good start). A technician who knows where employees are located and which wiring closet the workstation cabling runs to can work more autonomously and confidently than one who must ask questions at every step.

Documentation and Standards Compliance

Compliance with standards is a necessity in today's standards-based networks for ensuring correct network operation and reducing the possibility of installation or configuration errors. For example, an Ethernet network has Cat 6 cable installed throughout. A network administrator observing a technician punch down an RJ-45 jack noticed that he punched down the green wires in the orange slots and the orange wires in the green slots. When the administrator pointed out this mistake, the technician explained that it was the only way to get the cabling to work, but he didn't know why he had to swap the orange and green wires. After a little investigation, it was discovered that the patch panels were wired according to the 568A wiring standard and the jacks were wired according to 568B! The technician didn't realize that two wiring standards existed, but if a network manual had been available that explained which standard was used at the patch panel (and the technician had been required to read it), the correct jacks could have been ordered to match the patch panels. Another reason you might want to document to show standards compliance is when there's a dispute between you and an equipment vendor about a persistent network error. If the equipment vendor claims the problem is your installation, but you can show that all your cabling and equipment installation meet standards, you have the upper hand in the dispute. Perhaps more important, many organizations that handle sensitive customer data, such as schools and hospitals, need to show compliance with data security and handling standards.

Documentation and Technical Support

If you call technical support to solve a network device problem, one of the first things the device manufacturer checks is whether your equipment, power supply, and cabling meet all applicable standards. For example, if you can't tell the manufacturer of a 100 Mbps switch that your cable installation passed the cable tests and possibly even supply the test results, technical support might just tell you to call back after you have confirmed that your cabling isn't the problem. In addition, if the new database server you installed is crashing, be prepared to tell the database vendor details about the server hardware, OS version, and patch installations. If you can't supply this information without walking over to the server and inspecting it, the database vendor will tell you to call back, which means another wait on hold in the support queue.

Documentation and Network Security

Physical and software security of devices, OSs with the latest security patches, and up-to-date malware protection are some factors in maintaining security. Documenting these items helps you adhere to security policies and provides confirmation of your network's resistance to current threats or warns you of a vulnerability to these threats.

Many years ago, the Code Red virus unleashed on the Internet affected certain Microsoft IIS Web servers. When some administrators downloaded the free patch to install on infected servers, they discovered it required a newer service pack, which wasn't installed. On a network with dozens or hundreds of servers, knowing which servers had the service pack and patch installed and which servers didn't was critical. If this information is at hand, technicians can be given strict instructions on which patches and service packs should be installed on which servers. As you can see, a lot can be gained from good network documentation. The hardest part is determining what to document, and then establishing procedures and gathering tools to make documentation easier.

What Should Be Documented?

"What should be documented?" is the first question you should address before starting a documentation project or defining documentation policies. However, the answer isn't always straightforward. Networks of different size and complexity and with differing security and use policies often have different documentation needs. This section discusses the elements of your network you should typically document. Keep in mind that the following list isn't exhaustive, and some environments might have other requirements:

- *Description of the network*—The network description should be the section of your documentation manual that anyone could read and get a basic understanding of how the network works and what it consists of. This section should include information on the network topology, network technologies in use, OSs installed, and number of devices and users. This section should also provide contact information for the people responsible for various aspects of the network. You might also want to include key vendors and their contact information. This section is meant to be an overview document, with the details described in other sections, so keep tables and graphs to a minimum.

- *Cable plant*—This section, which will probably become worn from frequent use, describes the physical layout of network cabling, the terminations, and the conventions for labeling cables and connectivity equipment. It also includes the results of tests done on the cable plant. Any time moves, additions, or changes are made, this section is usually consulted and possibly modified. Therefore, it must be kept current. Incorrect documentation of the cable plant is actually worse than none at all. Imagine moving a user workstation and unplugging the old patch cable from the switch only to find that you unplugged a critical server because the documentation was outdated. If you do this a few times, neither you nor anybody else will trust the documentation, and you'll go back to tracing cables every time a change must be made. In this case, you might as well discard the documentation.

- *Equipment rooms and telecommunication closets*—Equipment rooms and TCs house internetworking devices and servers and are the junction points for your work area and backbone cabling. An equipment room is sometimes called a "computer room," an "intermediate distribution frame," or a "main distribution frame" (as discussed in Chapter 4). These rooms are often dedicated to network cabling and equipment but can also be shared with phone equipment. Selecting features and locations of equipment rooms is important to maintaining an efficient and reliable network infrastructure. In addition, documenting the items in each room and their location is crucial to performing fast, effective changes or troubleshooting.

- *Internetworking devices*—Network changes and troubleshooting are made much easier by thorough documentation of internetworking devices. You need to know what devices are connected to other devices, the capabilities and limitations of each device, network management features available on each device, port use, and physical and logical addresses. Model numbers as well as hardware and software revision numbers might also be important when troubleshooting or considering upgrades. When you're finished with this documentation, you should be able to point to a switch, describe its capabilities, state which software version it's running, give the physical and logical addresses assigned to the switch, determine what other internetworking devices it's connected to, and list the critical resources attached to it. If this information isn't readily available, your documentation work isn't finished.

- *Servers*—All computers that provide shared resources or network services (including file and print servers, Web servers, DNS and DHCP servers, and other resources or services the company depends on) must have detailed documentation. Hardware configuration, OS and application version numbers, NIC information, and serial and model numbers are just a few items that should be available to you at a glance. Remember that a server isn't a static piece of equipment, so you can't simply install it and forget it. The interaction with internetworking devices, workstation client software, and new applications requires server hardware and software that's compatible and up to date. Installing a new device or application often requires a particular OS version or service pack, so you need to know how your server is configured before proceeding with a hardware or software upgrade.

- *Workstations*—Documentation of workstations is often the most difficult to maintain because there are usually a lot of them, and users, rather than the network administrator, are in control of them. However, don't let these factors prevent you from keeping accurate workstation documentation. Workstations, and the people who use them, are likely to be the source of most support and troubleshooting events. Knowing a workstation's hardware and software configuration and its physical and logical addresses can save you a lot of time and effort when solving a problem. Furthermore, network policies should limit how much users can change their workstations without the administrator's knowledge.

When you enforce these documentation policies, your records won't become hopelessly out of date. Maintaining accurate records on 20 or 30 workstations can be a major task, but maintaining records on thousands of workstations might seem too daunting a task to even attempt. Fortunately, many applications are available to help automate the process so that much of the documentation can be gathered only periodically and even done remotely. For example, network management software that works with SNMP, discussed in Chapter 12, can automate part of the process.

For useful information on network documentation and tips on documenting your network, visit *http://searchitchannel.techtarget. com/feature/Channel-Checklist-10-steps-for-network-documentation.* You can find a variety of mostly free tools for gathering information and diagramming networks at *www.filetransit.com/files.php?name= Network_Documentation.*

The Problem-Solving Process

One of the most difficult aspects of network problem solving is deciding where to begin. What's described next is a general framework for approaching problems that you can apply in almost any situation. The specific actions you take depend on the situation. The process described in this section can be applied to a variety of problems, both in your networking environment and in everyday life. Here are the steps of the problem-solving process:

1. Determine the problem definition and scope.
2. Gather information.
3. Consider possible causes.
4. Devise a solution.
5. Implement the solution.
6. Test the solution.
7. Document the solution.
8. Devise preventive measures.

Several steps in this process might be repeated. For example, if Step 6 doesn't lead to a solution for the problem, you probably need to repeat Steps 2 through 6 until you do have a solution. Each step might also require several substeps (explained in the following sections) before you can move on to the next step. For example, Step 4 might require setting up a test environment to duplicate the problem and test possible solutions before implementing a solution on a live network. Figure 13-1 is a flowchart of the basic process. Keep in mind that throughout the process, you might have to escalate the problem to more senior personnel if it's beyond the scope of your abilities or when you don't have authorization to access the equipment or software needed to solve the problem.

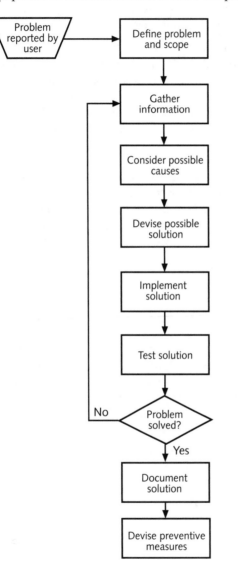

Figure 13-1 The problem-solving process

The preceding steps vary somewhat from the troubleshooting method described in the CompTIA Network+ objectives and are more in line with the Cisco Systems eight-step troubleshooting process. CompTIA describes seven main steps: Identify the problem, establish a theory of probable cause, test the theory to determine cause, establish a plan of action, implement the solution or escalate, verify full system functionality, and document findings.

Step 1: Determine the Problem Definition and Scope

Before a problem can be solved, it must be defined. "Sophie's computer doesn't work" does not define the problem well enough to create a plan of action. "Sophie can't run Word because an illegal operation occurs every time she tries to run it" is much better. A problem definition should also describe what does and doesn't work. If Sophie can't run Word, stating whether she can run her e-mail program or other applications should be included in the problem definition.

You need to know who and what are affected by the problem. You take a vastly different approach if an entire floor rather than a single user is affected by a network problem. Is the problem related to a single application—for example, e-mail—or are all functions affected? If you're working with routers, is only one router exhibiting problems, or are several routers affected? Determining the scope of a problem is important for deciding where to start your troubleshooting process and what priority to assign to the problem. The malfunction of a network switch or server demands a higher priority than a problem affecting one user. Determining the scope quickly and accurately, therefore, is not only part of the first step, but also an essential step of the troubleshooting process.

Most network problems come to the network administrator's attention by way of a user's phone call or e-mail. This communication is your first opportunity to learn more about the problem. Although this part of the troubleshooting process is more art than technical skill, there are some questions you can ask to start you on your way:

- Is anyone else near you having the same problem?
- What about other areas of the building?
- Is the problem occurring with all applications or just one?
- If you move to a different computer, does the problem occur there, too?

The goal of your questions is to determine a problem definition and scope. If a solution comes about as a result of this interview, all the better, but that's not the goal of this step, nor is determining the cause of the problem. Rather, the goal is to define the problem in detail and determine the scope of the problem accurately. Examples of a problem definition and scope include the following:

- Mike can't access the e-mail server. Other servers are available to Mike, and no one else reports the problem.
- Third-floor users can't log on to the network, but users on all other floors can.
- Camille can't print to the new LaserJet printer on the fourth floor and has tried several applications. No other users have tried to print to this printer.
- Julie reports that the network is slow while accessing her Documents folder. Access to the Internet and other resources seem to work with normal performance.

After you define the problem and understand its scope, you can assign a priority to the problem. Assigning priorities takes a little experience and some political savvy. You must have a clear understanding of what areas the organization deems most critical to its business functions. Creating a document to show management in which order problems are solved when there's a backlog is helpful.

Most IT departments are understaffed, so backlogs are usually the norm. Besides prioritizing according to business functions, prioritizing according to who reports the problem or who it affects is common. If the president of the company can't check e-mail, giving this problem top priority can be a double-edged sword. On one hand, if you solve the problem right away, you gain favor with the boss. On the other hand, if you solve the problem right away, you must not have much else to do, so why are you always complaining that you're understaffed? In any event, after you have prioritized the problem, you can assign the support person who's best equipped to solve the problem. After the problem is ready to be tackled, you can move to the next step: gathering information that can help you solve the problem.

Step 2: Gather Information

This step is where your user interview skills can really shine. Most of the initial information you get about a problem comes from users. Knowing what questions to ask and how to ask them can mean the difference between a quick fix and an all-nighter.

Appendix A has additional information on general questions to ask when troubleshooting.

TIP

Did It Ever Work? Strangely enough, this question is often overlooked. There's a big difference between something that worked once and then stopped working and something that never worked at all. Users often don't volunteer this information, so it pays to ask. If something worked once and now doesn't, you can assume something has broken the process. If it never worked at all, there's a good chance it wasn't set up correctly. If it worked at one time, you go into troubleshooting mode and continue with the interview. If it never worked, you go into installation mode and look at it as another task to put on the to-do list.

To understand this principle, consider this example: Alexis gets a call from Matt, a network user. Matt tells Alexis that he can't print to the printer down the hall. After determining that Matt is the only one having the problem as far as he knows, Alexis goes to the information-gathering step. She asks Matt whether he could ever print to that printer, and he replies that he couldn't. Alexis can go into installation mode at this point. This problem has just become a simple printer installation that isn't really a problem at all. Had Alexis not asked that question, she might have gone into troubleshooting mode, continuing to ask questions, checking printer queues, determining printer permissions, and investing time in a host of other time-wasting activities.

When Did It Stop Working? Assuming that the problem involves a function that used to work and has stopped or changed in some way, you need to find out when the change occurred. The purpose of this question is to find out the problem's time and date of occurrence and determine what else might be going on at that time to cause the problem. For example, is another application running when the problem occurs, or does the air conditioner kick on about the time the problem occurs? This line of questioning can also give you information about its urgency. If the user has lived with the problem for two weeks and is just now reporting it, and you have bigger and hotter fires to put out, you might be able to put this one on the back burner. A good support technician must know how to listen to customers and understand their sense of urgency or frustration. You might also want to ask the following:

- Does the problem occur all the time or only intermittently?
- Are there particular times of the day when the problem occurs?
- Are other applications running when the problem occurs?

Has Anything Changed? You have to be careful with this question when you're talking to users about workstation problems. If users think you're implying they might have caused the problem, they're likely to clam up. Their answers are essential pieces of information. New applications on workstations, new hardware devices, and updates to existing applications or drivers can all cause problems. While you're asking users this question, you need to ask yourself, too. Were any changes made to the network that could cause the problem? Were any upgrades made to servers or client stations, or were new router configurations made?

Never Ignore the Obvious Sometimes it's easy to get caught up in a problem, pull out the network analyzer, and start some serious troubleshooting. One of the most common problems, which thankfully has one of the easiest solutions, is an unplugged cable. Don't assume that your users have checked this possibility. Experience suggests that a substantial percentage of network problems involve an unplugged cable. Maybe the culprit was the cleaning crew, or maybe one of your technicians did it while installing a new sound card or working on a server or router.

Sometimes you can discover the obvious when you realize that people have their own unique perceptions of a problem. For instance, descriptions such as "slow network response" are subjective; what seems normal to one person might be considered a problem by another. Suppose an employee has been on the night shift for the past year and has recently taken a shift during the day. This employee reports that server response is very slow, but you have had no complaints from other users. Because the night shift works half-staffed, this employee has probably become accustomed to a server operating with a lighter load during the night, which results in quick response times. His idea of a slow response might simply be a normal response time for the day shift.

Define How It's Supposed to Work Gathering solid facts about a problem is difficult if you don't have a good definition of how things are supposed to work. Having good documentation and a clear baseline of your network pays off. Periodic baselines are compared with previous baselines to spot trends that indicate problems ahead. For example, if average network utilization increases 2% per month for several months, you can prepare for a performance upgrade that will no doubt be required before too long.

A baseline of your network should include network utilization statistics; utilization statistics on server CPUs, memory, hard drives, and other resources; and normal traffic patterns. This information can be compared with statistics you gather during the troubleshooting process. It can help you determine whether reports of slow response time are valid and point you in the direction of the problem's source if they are indeed valid. It can also help you know when it's time to upgrade the network infrastructure or servers.

Step 3: Consider Possible Causes

In this step, based on symptoms and other information you have gathered, you consider what could be the cause of the problem. Experience is invaluable in this step, as the more problems you have seen, the more likely you are to recognize symptoms of a particular problem. As you proceed through this step, you'll probably gather more information.

Your goal in this step is to create a checklist of possible things that could have gone wrong to cause the problem. For example, an entire area of a building has lost connection with the network, but no other areas are affected. Without knowing anything else, you could construct the following list of possible causes:

- The connection in the main wiring closet to the rest of the network has failed.

- The switch all workstations are connected to has lost power or failed in some way.

- All workstations have acquired a virus through the network, and the virus affects their network connection.

- A major upgrade has been made recently on all workstations in that area, and incorrect network addresses were configured.

You could create quite a long list if you put your mind to it. Of course, during Step 2, you would probably have eliminated all but a few of the possible causes. If you find yourself with a long list of possible causes, you probably need to go back to Step 2 and gather more information. After creating a list of possible causes, you can investigate each one and rule out or confirm it. In the previous example, you would probably check the wiring closet to see the status of devices there, or if you have a network management program, you could verify the health of wiring closet devices remotely.

Step 4: Devise a Solution

After determining a likely cause, you can devise a solution. In the example discussed in Step 3, assuming the cause of the problem is a failed switch, devising a solution is easy: Replace the switch. Suppose, however, that many users have reported a periodic loss of connection to certain resources. After you've gathered information and considered possible causes, you find that several routers become overutilized periodically and start dropping packets. This problem isn't so simple. You don't want to rush in and replace the problem routers with bigger, stronger, faster routers because this solution could affect other routers or other network components. Is the problem with the routers, or are the dropped packets simply another symptom of the problem? You don't really know. Before devising a solution, it's important to consider the following:

- Is the identified cause of the problem truly the cause, or is it just another symptom of the problem's true cause?

- Is there a way to test the proposed solution adequately?

- What results should the proposed solution produce?

- What are the ramifications of the proposed solution for the rest of the network?

- Do you need additional help to answer some of these questions?

The last question is a sore point for many network professionals. However, being an expert in everything is impossible, and some network problems can be too complex or the equipment needed to answer questions is too expensive for many IT departments. A broken network that results in reduced productivity and, therefore, lost money can be more expensive than calling in experts occasionally. When you can't solve the problem and have to call in someone else to help, it's called **escalation**.

After you have the solution, it's time to carry it out immediately, right? Wrong. Before you implement the solution, you must be prepared for the possibility that it could make things worse than the existing problem. Whether your problem and proposed solution affect an entire network or just a few users, you must devise a **rollback plan** so that you can return things to their original state if the solution doesn't work. Depending on the scope of the problem and solution, you might need to do the following:

- Save all network device configuration files.
- Document and back up workstation configurations.
- Document wiring closet configurations, including device locations and patch cable connections.
- Conduct a final baseline to compare new and old results if a rollback becomes necessary.

Step 5: Implement the Solution

If you have done a good job with the first four steps, the implementation step should go fairly smoothly. During this step, you create opportunities for intermediate testing and inform users of your intentions. Then you put the plan into action.

Create Intermediate Testing Opportunities
You need to design the implementation so that you can stop and test it at critical points, instead of testing the completed solution only to find that something doesn't work. Testing small steps in which a limited number of things could go wrong is far easier than testing a complex solution with dozens or hundreds of problem areas.

Suppose your solution is to add a network segment to your internetwork to alleviate broadcast problems. You have purchased a new router and a switch to accommodate the workstations that will form the new segment. One way to carry out this solution is to hook up all the equipment, configure the router and switch, assign new addresses to workstations, plug in all the cables, and then hope for the best. When this method doesn't work, however, where do you start looking? Is the problem the router configuration or the switches? Is your addressing scheme incorrect?

A better way to tackle this solution is to have a step-by-step plan that allows intermediate testing. For example, you can use the following steps that alternate between implementing and testing to test the new router and switch:

1. Configure the router.
2. Verify its stand-alone operation by pinging each interface.
3. Attach the router to the rest of the network.
4. Verify that all parts of the network can be reached by pinging.
5. Use the `tracert` command to verify the path selection.
6. Install and configure the switch.

7. Configure workstation addresses for the new network.

8. Cable workstations to the new switch.

9. Verify connectivity in the network.

10. Connect the router to the switch.

11. Verify that you can ping the router interface from workstations.

12. Verify that you can reach other networks from workstations.

13. Create a baseline of the new network segment.

A carefully planned implementation of your solution with testing along the way allows you to catch unforeseen results at a stage when they're easy to see and easy to fix.

Inform Your Users When your action plan affects other parts of the network and, therefore, other users, you need to inform users of the possible disruption to some network services while work is progressing. Give users plenty of time to schedule downtime of the network. Nothing can take the wind out of your sails more quickly than getting a frantic call from a boss who needs the network for a big presentation just as you're halfway through a day-long network upgrade. Ideally, major changes to a network should occur during a scheduled **maintenance window**, which is a time set aside each day, week, or month for updates, upgrades, and other maintenance procedures. Users should be aware that the network might not be available during the maintenance window. This period is also referred to as "scheduled downtime."

Put the Plan into Action After you have your checklist of actions and intermediate testing ready and have informed users, it's time to take action. Provided you have done everything correctly up to now, this step is the easy part. You have your list of actions; now is the time to carry them out.

 Making only one testable change at a time is crucial. If you make multiple changes before performing a test, you won't know which change solved the problem.

TIP

Take notes about every change you make to the network or servers. For example, document a driver upgrade or an IP address change. This way, you know the network's current state when your changes are finished. A well-documented network is easier to troubleshoot and upgrade in the future.

Step 6: Test the Solution

It's 3:00 a.m., and you're finished with the upgrade. Time to go home, right? Wrong. It's time to test your solution as a whole. If the issue is a simple workstation connectivity problem, you verify that the station can access the resources assigned to it. If it's a major network or server overhaul, however, the testing is more involved. In either case, if you have done intermediate testing during the implementation step, the testing step should be fairly straightforward.

Your testing should attempt to emulate a real-world situation as closely as possible. If you're testing a workstation problem, verifying that the workstation can ping a server isn't enough.

If possible, you should attempt to log on to the network as a user with similar privileges as the workstation's main user. Next, attempt to access applications that would likely run from the workstation. Take notes about what you learned and saw.

If you're testing a major network upgrade, you have probably already tested end-to-end connectivity during implementation. Now you need to put some stress on the network. Start some workstations on the upgraded part of the network, if possible, with the help of some assistants, and run some applications that make heavy use of the network. Verify access to the Internet. All the while, you should be gathering information about how the network behaves. Compare your results with the results you saw before the changes were made. Again, take notes about the results of your testing. When you have tested everything possible, go home and get some sleep; tomorrow will be the real test, when users begin using your new solution.

Step 7: Document the Solution

If you have made it this far, congratulations—you have solved the problem! It's time to take all the handwritten notes made during the implementation and testing steps and turn them into a cohesive document. This step is as important as any of the previous steps. No matter how big or small the problem was, a similar problem will likely happen in the future. If you took notes about the problem and the solution, you have this documentation available as a valuable resource for solving the next problem of its kind. Your documentation should include everything pertinent to the problem, such as the problem definition, the solution, the implementation, and the testing. If necessary, you should be able to reproduce both the problem and the solution from your documentation. If the problem and its solution have implications for the entire network, including this information in your overall network plan is advisable.

Step 8: Devise Preventive Measures

After solving and documenting a problem, you should do everything you can to prevent this problem or similar problems from recurring. For example, if the problem was the result of a virus that spread throughout the network and caused considerable damage before it was found, you can install malware protection programs on the network and tighten policies for software and e-mail downloads. This preventive measure is obvious and reasonably easy to do.

Suppose, however, that the problem is a degenerative one, in which the network gradually becomes slower and less responsive. Preventing this problem isn't as simple as installing software and sending a policy memo. There are some measures you can take, however. For instance, you can devise certain rules for your network's operation. For example, you can specify that no more than 50 workstations be installed on a network segment or stipulate that Linux servers can have no more than 200 simultaneous logins before adding a server or adding a CPU to the server. These types of rules help prevent performance problems in the future. In addition, if those in charge of the budget approve these rules, you have instant justification for an upgrade when the time comes.

Devising preventive measures is proactive rather than reactive network management. If you let the problem come to you, it's always far more serious than nipping it in the bud before it causes serious productivity issues. You might be tempted to pat yourself on the back and rest on your laurels after solving a difficult problem, but coming up with methods to prevent problems in the first place is wiser.

Approaches to Network Troubleshooting

Tackling different problems requires different approaches. Sometimes it makes sense to just try a solution and see whether it works. Sometimes you can use a similar system as a working model, or you might have to buckle down and research the problem thoroughly. In this section, you learn about different methods and circumstances in which some methods work and others don't. With this knowledge, you can try a variety of approaches for your environment, keeping in mind the basic tenets of the problem-solving process described in the previous section.

Trial and Error

The trial-and-error approach to network problem solving isn't very scientific, and technical purists often frown on it. Nevertheless, few network specialists can deny having used it in everyday practice. There's a time and place for it, however, and you shouldn't rely on this method exclusively because you can do more harm than good in some situations.

As the name suggests, the trial-and-error method requires an assessment of the problem, an educated guess of the solution, an implementation of the solution, and a test of the results. You repeat the process until the problem is solved. This approach can be used under the following conditions:

- The system is being newly configured, so no data can be lost.
- The system isn't attached to a live network, so no other users are affected by changes.
- You can undo changes easily.
- Other approaches would take more time than a few trial-and-error attempts.
- There are few possible causes of the problem, which makes your educated guess of the solution a good bet.
- No documentation or other resources are available to draw on for arriving at a solution more scientifically.

As mentioned, it's not always wise to just try something and see whether it works. Changes made to one system on a network can affect other systems or make an existing problem worse. The trial-and-error method isn't advisable under these conditions:

- A server or internetworking device you're troubleshooting is currently in use on the network.
- The problem is being discussed over the phone and you're instructing an untrained user.
- You aren't sure of the consequences of the solutions you propose.
- You have no sure way to undo the changes after they're made.
- Other approaches will take about the same amount of time as the trial-and-error approach.

If you determine that trial and error is the right approach for your problem, however, you should follow some guidelines:

- Make only one change at a time before testing the results. That way, if the problem is solved, you know which change is the solution. You can add this information to your network support documentation for future use.

- Avoid making changes that might affect the operation of a live network. For example, if you suspect an incorrect TCP/IP address, don't change the address without first verifying that the new address is available. Using an address that's already in use could cause another device to stop working.

- Document the original settings of hardware and software before making changes so that you can put the system back to its original state.

- Avoid making a change that can destroy user data unless a recent backup exists.

- If possible, avoid making a change that you can't undo.

The following examples help you determine under what circumstances this troubleshooting method is suitable.

You're called to solve a problem on a client/server network of about 100 computers, and employees access the Internet. The problem is that a workstation running Windows 10 can't access the Internet. You sit down at the workstation and open the Network Connections window to check the settings. You check the IP address settings and find that TCP/IP is configured to use DHCP. You know that DHCP isn't used on this network, so it must be the problem. You recall from an earlier visit that the network address is 206.17.44.0/24. You decide to configure the computer with an address that you select from the network randomly to see whether this step solves the problem.

Should you use trial and error to solve this problem? Absolutely not. Although you might have happened on the cause of the problem, simply choosing an address without knowing whether it's already in use can cause a conflict with another machine. The correct course of action is to consult the network documentation that lists all IP addresses in use. This document should also have other settings, such as DNS server addresses and the default gateway address. You must consider the effect that changes you make have on the rest of the network. If you're unsure, play it safe and consult the documentation.

In the second example, you've been asked to troubleshoot a new PC running Windows 10 on a client's network. The network is small, has only seven PCs, has Internet access through a cable modem and router, and is set up in a workgroup environment. An employee has already done some of the work, such as assigning a computer and workgroup name, but the new PC still can't communicate with other PCs on the network or access the Internet. You find that a static address is assigned to the computer, but you know addresses are supposed to be assigned via DHCP by the router. You decide to configure TCP/IP to get an address via DHCP.

Would trial and error be a safe, effective troubleshooting method in this situation? If you said yes, that's correct. Configuring TCP/IP to use DHCP is a reversible action and is safe because there's no chance of conflicting with another station. If it works, you have solved the problem. If not, no harm done. The only caveat is that you should note the static IP address settings in case the machine is supposed to have a static address for a reason you don't yet know.

In the third example, you get a call from a client having intermittent problems with a subnet. The client tells you that when employees try to access a server on a different subnet, sometimes it works, but sometimes the connection times out. The network has four subnets connected through one router. There are no problems on the other subnets. You have seen a similar problem in other networks, and resetting the router seemed to solve it. You tell the client to power down the router, wait 10 seconds, and power it back up.

Is this approach a reasonable way to solve this problem? By powering down the router, you affect all four subnets. This action could cause loss of data, time, and possibly even money. Additionally, you don't know whether the router configuration has been saved, so powering down the router could cause even worse problems after it restarts. Finally, you should never instruct a user to perform a procedure when you have no way to make sure it's being done correctly.

Sometimes using trial and error to solve problems is quicker and easier than other methods. In fact, this option might be your only way of solving some problems in a timely manner. However, you must be careful not to make matters worse if your proposed solution can affect other systems or cause data loss.

Solve by Example

Solving by example is the process of comparing something that doesn't work with something that does, and then making modifications to the nonfunctioning item until it performs like the functioning one. It's one of the easiest and fastest ways to solve a problem because it requires no special knowledge or problem-solving skills. When most organizations purchase new computers, they purchase similar models and configure them identically. You simply take advantage of this fact when confronted with a problem on a machine.

Some problems can be difficult to troubleshoot, particularly when they involve an OS configuration. In addition, hunting down the problem and fixing it could take considerable time. If you have a working example of a device that's nearly identical, however, you can copy the configuration, or parts of the configuration, from a working machine. This effort might involve checking for installed components, copying system files (such as device drivers), copying configuration files, or even making a copy of an entire disk.

To see how this process works, take a look at an example. Mike, a networking consultant, has been called into a client's office because 2 of the firm's 20 computers lock up periodically when accessing a Web-based database program on a Windows server. Mike checks the network settings on the two computers, and everything seems to be in order. The two computers can access the network, but when they run a Web browser to access the database application, the machines invariably lock up within a half hour of use. Mike asks whether other computers run the same Web application and is told yes. He takes a look at one of the computers that's not locking up. After some investigation, Mike finds that the working computers are using the 64-bit version of the Web browser, and the two computers that lock up are using the 32-bit version. Mike uses the 64-bit version of the Web browser to run the Web application, and after several hours of testing, no lockups occur, and Mike calls it a day.

What's your analysis of this situation? Mike certainly could have pulled out his network analyzer and captured network packets to try to determine what the problem was, or he could have played trial and error with different network settings to see whether he could correct the lockups. However, with several working examples nearby and one obvious difference between the working machines and the faulty ones, he did the smart thing by taking what works and applying it to what didn't work.

As with the trial-and-error method, there are some caveats to using the solve-by-example method. Here are some general rules to follow:

- Use the solve-by-example approach only when the working sample has a similar environment as the problem machine. For example, don't compare a machine having problems accessing Windows Server 2016 with one accessing Linux.

- Don't make configuration changes that will cause conflicts. For example, don't change the TCP/IP address of a nonworking machine to the same address as a working machine's.

- Don't make any changes that could destroy data that can't be restored.

In another example, Sophie is fairly new to networking but has been asked to connect some new computers to a stack of two switches. A similar stack of switches already exists, and she's supposed to make these connections in a similar fashion. Armed with a box of patch cables, Sophie starts plugging computers into the switches. When she gets to the last switch port, she realizes she must save this port to connect to the next switch. She connects the two switches with a patch cable but doesn't see a link light indicating that the connection is good. She tries another patch cable with the same result.

Not sure what to try next, Sophie examines the similar stack of switches and recognizes a button next to one of the ports. It's a two-position button with the positions marked as Normal or Uplink. The button is set to the Uplink position on one switch and Normal on the switch it's connected to. Because the switches she's setting up are the same, Sophie compares her switches with the working switches. The button is set to the Normal position on both her switches, so she changes it to the Uplink position on one switch. The link light indicator comes on, and Sophie finishes her job.

Is the solve-by-example method appropriate in this situation? Because Sophie had an example in an environment similar to the one she was having trouble with, she was able to make these changes with confidence. The switches weren't being used on the live network yet, so her changes wouldn't cause any problems.

The Replacement Method

The replacement method of problem solving is a favorite among PC technicians. It requires narrowing down possible sources of the problem and having known working replacement parts on hand so that they can be swapped out. Sounds simple, and it is—at least after the source of the problem has been identified. That's where the difficulty and the skill come in. The replacement method is effective only if the problem's source can be determined and the source is a defective part. A lot of time and money can be wasted in replacing parts that aren't defective, so you need to apply your troubleshooting skills before you show off your installation skills. Follow these rules in order when using the replacement method:

1. Narrow the list of potentially defective parts down to a few possibilities.

2. Make sure you have the correct replacement parts on hand.

3. Replace only one part at a time.

4. If your first replacement doesn't fix the problem, reinstall the original part before replacing another part.

Step by Step with the OSI Model

The step-by-step method of troubleshooting involves using the OSI model. In this approach, you test a problem starting at the Application layer and keep testing at each layer until you have a successful test or reach the Physical layer. Depending on the problem, you could instead start at the Physical layer and work your way up the OSI model. This method of problem solving is what most people think of as network support. To use this approach, you must understand how networks work and where you should use troubleshooting tools. Networks are complex, multilayered systems. When confronted by a problem for which there's no obvious fix, remembering the layered approach to network systems can be helpful. If you conceptualize the problem following the seven layers of the OSI model, you can take a step-by-step approach to solving the problem. To see how this approach works, start by reviewing the simple network diagram in Figure 13-2.

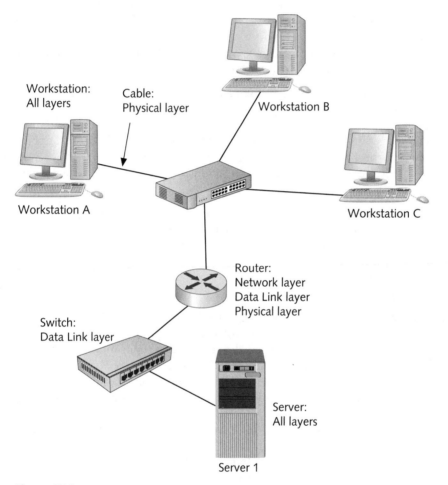

Figure 13-2 Troubleshooting with the OSI model

Suppose the user at Workstation A complains that an error occurs when she tries to access files on Server 1. Users at Workstations B and C aren't having similar problems. No more information is available. When you arrive on the scene, you see that Workstation A is running Windows 7. First, you use File Explorer to browse the network. As expected, no devices are shown. This step involves the upper layers of the OSI model. Now that you have determined these functions aren't working correctly, you can start looking at the lower layers. Your goal is to find the lowest layer at which there's functionality.

You check the network documentation and see that TCP/IPv4 is the protocol being used. You then verify that TCP/IPv4 is enabled on the network connection. A common tool for troubleshooting TCP/IP is the `ping` command. At a command prompt, type `ping localhost` to verify that the TCP/IP stack is working correctly and you get a valid response. Referring to the network documentation, you try to ping Server 1. No success. Look at the diagram in Figure 13-2 again. If you can communicate with the router but not the server, you can narrow your search. Try pinging the router. Again, no success.

Which layers remain to be tested? The Data Link and Physical layers. Data Link–layer problems most often affect the entire network, or the problem lies with a single computer's NIC or drivers. Unless you have reason to believe there's a problem with the drivers, it's best to leave them for later. Most network technicians would move on to the Physical layer because this layer is where problems restricted to one workstation are most likely to occur. After a brief investigation, you find that the patch cable from the jack to the workstation is frayed, and you replace the cable. Problem solved.

Many network technicians approach a problem by starting with the Physical layer and then working their way up. The approach you take depends on your experience and information you have learned from interviewing users. What's important is that you understand everything required for the network connection to work, which enables you to test and check all components involved with the tools available to you.

Here's an example of starting with the Physical layer and working your way up: A user complains that she can't access the Web site *http://books.tomsho.com.* You have no other information, and the user isn't at her computer when you arrive. Starting with the Physical and Data Link layers, you check cable connections and link lights on the computer's NIC. They look good, so you move to the Network layer. You check the computer's IP address configuration and attempt to ping the default gateway. Again, you're successful. Next, you try to ping a known address in another network to verify that the default gateway is routing correctly. If the ping is successful, you might check DNS next, which verifies the Transport and Session layers. (DNS is sometimes described as a Session-layer protocol, and in the TCP/IP model, it works at the Application layer.) To do this, you ping a Web site by name or use `nslookup` to verify that DNS lookups work. You might also want to ping the address the user is having trouble with to determine whether the target server's name can be resolved and it can communicate via `ping`. If all your checks so far have been successful, checking the Application layer is next. You can use a protocol analyzer, such as Wireshark, to capture packets so that you can see exactly what's happening with HTTP, the protocol used in Web communication. Application-layer troubleshooting is the most difficult because protocols in the upper layers are the most complex, but with experience, you'll be able to solve problems occurring at all layers of the OSI model.

Making Use of Problem-Solving Resources

This section covers some resources available to you during troubleshooting. Each resource has its place, and experience will tell you what's appropriate for different situations.

Experience

Your most effective weapon in supporting the network and diagnosing and solving problems is your own experience. Unfortunately, people often don't make effective use of their experience. Whether you have been limited to working on computers in the classroom and at home or have been working on a large multiplatform network, there are plenty of opportunities to expand and enhance your experience.

Make the Most of Your Experience Few people have photographic memories. They see something, say they're going to remember it for future use, and then promptly forget it. Sometimes people remember generalities but forget the details, which is easy to do with networks because so much is changing constantly.

Take notes about what you see and learn. This advice applies even if you've been in the computing world for years, but it's particularly pertinent when you're first starting out and your experiences are limited. Keep a journal of your experiences. Even if you never read it again, the act of writing information down helps preserve it in your memory for future use. Say you're upgrading a network with a VPN server. After several configuration changes, you finally get everything to work. If you write down the details of what worked and what didn't work, you have a reference for the next time you have to perform a similar installation.

An electronic journal is helpful because you can file your entries alphabetically and search for them when needed. Of course, a print-out is also useful when your network crashes and electronic documentation is unavailable.

If It Happened Once, It Will Happen Again One mistake technicians make is thinking that a problem is so obscure that it's not worth the time and effort to make a note of it. However, hardware and software are standardized now, and millions of people use the same or similar components in their computers and networks. So if you're seeing a problem now, you'll probably see it again. Make a note of it, and the next time the problem occurs, you can be the hero by already having the solution at hand.

Colleagues' Experience One of the most overlooked resources for solving problems is your colleagues and classmates. Use the people you know as a resource. They'll appreciate you coming to them for possible answers and, in turn, they'll come to you in the future. Some people build up a network of colleagues and put them on an e-mail distribution list. When facing a difficult question or problem, they can send an e-mail to several knowledgeable people. There's a good chance one of them has had a similar problem in the past and can steer the problem-solving process in the right direction.

Experience from Manufacturers' Technical Support Sometimes there's nothing left to do but call for help. Every time you install a new piece of hardware or a new application, one of the first things you should do (besides reading the installation manual) is enter the manufacturer's technical support number in your database of important phone numbers.

The best time to call technical support is when you have a specific error number or message that you can report to the manufacturer. Be prepared to have a lot of other information ready, too. The more prepared you are, the more responsive the support person is likely to be. Typically, information you need includes the software's version number or the hardware's serial number, the OS and version, whether it's an application problem, and, for a router or switch problem, the firmware revision number. You need to be as detailed as possible about the problem or error's circumstances so that the manufacturer can reproduce it if needed. Gather all pertinent information before you call technical support; if you don't have the necessary information, you'll have to call back a second time.

In addition, use some of the troubleshooting methods discussed earlier to rule out obvious problems, such as a defective part. If you have another part handy, use the replacement method so that you can tell technical support you have already tried swapping parts. You can also try the suspect part or application on a different system so that you can report this information to technical support. Again, the more prepared you are, the better results you'll get. In addition, if you've tried all the obvious troubleshooting techniques and can report this fact to technical support, it's likely that your problem will be transferred to a more knowledgeable person or tech support will be prepared to send a replacement part.

The Internet

If you can describe the problem with a few words or an error message or number, the Internet is the first place to look for answers. Most manufacturers put time and effort into building databases of problems and solutions so that their customers can research the problem themselves without calling the technical support line. In fact, many manufacturers provide support only via the Internet or make reaching a real person by phone such a frustrating experience that most customers won't attempt a phone call.

The Internet is one of the best resources for computer and networking professionals. What once took days or weeks to accomplish via phone calls and driver updates on disks sent by mail can be done in minutes online. You can't install a new NIC on the version of Windows you just installed? Go online and download the latest driver. Every time you try to send an e-mail, you get error number 3744? Go to the software developer's Web site and enter the error number in a search, and you might get a response explaining how to solve the problem.

Most manufacturers store their technical support problems and solutions in a database called a "knowledge base" or a "frequently asked questions" document. A **knowledge base** is a searchable database containing descriptions of problems and errors along with known solutions, if any. It can also contain installation notes and compatibility information. A **frequently asked questions (FAQ)** document is usually a text document with two parts to each entry. The first part is a question the manufacturer has anticipated or actually received from customers; the second part is an answer to the question. A FAQ is more helpful for general installation and configuration help, although it can have information about error messages, solutions, and compatibility issues.

Using a Knowledge Base or Search Engine
The old adage of "garbage in, garbage out" applies perfectly to using a knowledge base or search engine. With a search engine, you have to enter the right words, phrases, or error numbers to find the information you want. Even then, finding what you're looking for can take several attempts, and you might have to sift through several entries before you find the information that will help with your particular problem.

When you're researching a problem, be as specific as possible. If you have error numbers or messages, enter them. With error messages, you get the best results if you enclose them in quotation marks. For example, if the error message says "Too many open files," enter this exact phrase enclosed by quotation marks to get the best and fewest search results. Enter as many keywords or phrases as possible to limit the number of results returned; you can get hundreds or thousands of results if the keywords you enter are too general. If your first search returns no results, cut back on the specificity of the search and try again. After a while, you'll get a feel for the type and amount of information to enter.

Finding Drivers and Updates When installing a new piece of hardware, OS, or networking device, one of the first things you should do is check whether bug fixes, driver updates, or new firmware revisions are available. Before you call a manufacturer's technical support line, make sure you have the latest versions, or the support person will probably tell you to call back if the problem persists after you have installed the new version.

Most manufacturers devote a section of their Web sites to the latest fixes and drivers you can download. A word of caution: Read the installation guide or Readme.txt file before installing OS updates because you might need to be aware of special preinstallation items before you start the update.

Many drivers can be updated directly in Windows. In Device Manager, right-click the device and click Update Driver Software. Windows attempts to find the latest driver available and install it or informs you that the driver is up to date.

Consulting Online Support Services and Newsgroups Many online support services are dedicated to technical subjects, such as networking. You can use these services to tap into the knowledge of experienced network professionals by posting questions. One excellent source is Experts Exchange (*www.experts-exchange.com*). A free membership allows you to ask a question and wait for a response from other members, or you can pay for a premium membership with a higher level of service. In addition, many companies use user communities to their best advantage by creating newsgroups or support forums where users of their products can exchange experiences and help one another.

Researching Online Periodicals Given rapid industry change, periodicals dealing with computers and networking can be the best sources of information on new products, trends, and techniques. Many periodicals are available on the Internet, and some offer free subscriptions to networking professionals. Some popular networking journals include *Network Computing*, *Information Week*, and *Network World*. Several publications focus on Windows (such as *Windows IT Pro Magazine*; *www.windowsitpro.com*) or Linux (for example, *Linux Journal*; *www.linuxjournal.com*).

Network Documentation

Many network administrators dislike the task of network documentation, but it's one of the best resources for knowing what's happening with a network and what needs to be done to fix a problem. Good network documentation can mean the difference between a five-minute fix and hours, or even days, of troubleshooting.

As mentioned, you should document everything that's important to installing, maintaining, and troubleshooting the network. Your documentation should read like a user's manual for network administrators. You know it's complete when you feel as though you could leave your network in a stranger's hands for a month, and everything would still be working fine when you come back. Good documentation should include information in at least two categories: network topology and internetworking devices. This guideline is general; your network might have many more categories and subcategories. If your documentation is weak in either area, you should set aside time to improve it.

Network Diagrams A picture is worth a thousand words, and this statement is certainly true for a network. Your documentation should include network diagrams showing a logical picture of the network and another diagram showing the network's physical aspects, such as rooms, devices, and connections. Complete documentation shows a level of detail down to the floor plan and location of jacks. Figure 13-3 is a logical diagram of a network, and Figure 13-4 is a physical diagram.

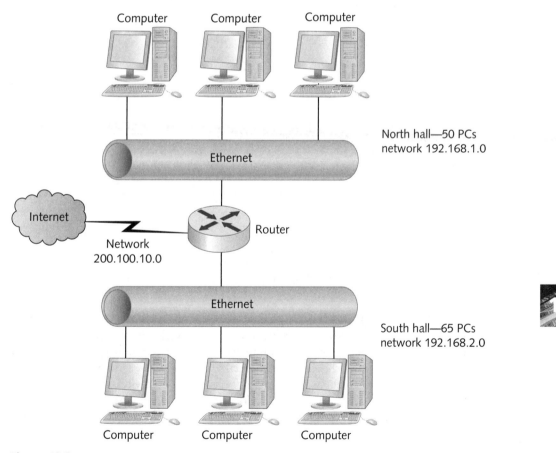

Figure 13-3 A logical network diagram

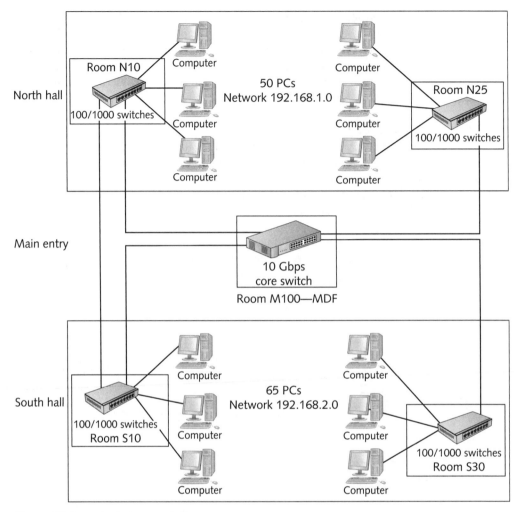

Figure 13-4   A physical network diagram

Internetworking Devices   Internetworking devices require different levels of documentation, depending on the type of equipment. Simple unmanaged switches require the least information, for example, and routers normally require the most. Besides showing internetworking devices in network diagrams, you should list them in table form, as shown in Table 13-2's list of managed switches. You should create a similar table for all types of devices so that they can be located and identified easily when needed. This information also helps with expansion plans because it includes the number of free ports available, where you can add workstations and other devices.

Table 13-2   Network equipment list: switches

Switch model/serial #	Location	IP address	MAC address	# Ports/# free
Cisco 2950/2117760	Room N10	192.168.1.240/24	00000cab3546	24/0
Cisco 2950/2117761	Room N25	192.168.1.241/24	00000cab3547	24/0
Juniper EX2200/1A74215	Room S10	192.168.2.240/24	000003f25567	24/4

Network Troubleshooting Tools

Experience, colleagues, the Web, phone support, and documentation are helpful resources for network support and troubleshooting. Sometimes, however, the only place you can get the information you need is from your own network. Many networking problems occur at lower layers of the OSI model, where they're often difficult to troubleshoot. Fortunately, there are tools for diagnosing these problems. The next sections discuss some of the most common tools and their possible uses on a network.

Using `ping` and `tracert`

You have already worked with `ping` and ICMP messages quite a bit, but take a closer look at the output of the `ping` command. Figure 13-5 shows the results of three `ping` commands sent by a computer with IP address 172.31.210.1: one successful and two not.

```
C:\Users\gtomsho>ping 172.31.210.2

Pinging 172.31.210.2 with 32 bytes of data:
Reply from 172.31.210.2: bytes=32 time=1ms TTL=128
Reply from 172.31.210.2: bytes=32 time<1ms TTL=128
Reply from 172.31.210.2: bytes=32 time<1ms TTL=128
Reply from 172.31.210.2: bytes=32 time<1ms TTL=128

Ping statistics for 172.31.210.2:
    Packets: Sent = 4, Received = 4, Lost = 0 (0% loss),
Approximate round trip times in milli-seconds:
    Minimum = 0ms, Maximum = 1ms, Average = 0ms

C:\Users\gtomsho>ping 172.31.210.3

Pinging 172.31.210.3 with 32 bytes of data:
Reply from 172.31.210.1: Destination host unreachable.
Reply from 172.31.210.1: Destination host unreachable.
Reply from 172.31.210.1: Destination host unreachable.
Reply from 172.31.210.1: Destination host unreachable.

Ping statistics for 172.31.210.3:
    Packets: Sent = 4, Received = 4, Lost = 0 (0% loss),

C:\Users\gtomsho>ping 172.221.1.5

Pinging 172.221.1.5 with 32 bytes of data:
Reply from 67.135.198.249: Destination net unreachable.
Reply from 67.135.198.249: Destination net unreachable.
Reply from 67.135.198.249: Destination net unreachable.
Reply from 67.135.198.249: Destination net unreachable.

Ping statistics for 172.221.1.5:
    Packets: Sent = 4, Received = 4, Lost = 0 (0% loss),

C:\Users\gtomsho>
```

Figure 13-5 Successful and unsuccessful pings

The first `ping` command has four replies from the address that was the target of the command: 172.31.210.2. You see four replies because the `ping` command sends four ICMP messages by default. The output for each successful reply contains the following pieces of information:

- The responding computer's IP address
- The number of bytes in the ICMP message
- The time receiving a reply takes
- The reply packet's TTL

The `ping` command tells you whether the computer can communicate with another computer via IP or, more specifically, ICMP. With a successful reply, you know the target machine is running and there's a path between your computer and the target. This command also tells you the amount of time elapsed before receiving a reply, measured in milliseconds (ms). On a single LAN, the time should be very short—typically less than 10 ms. Even addresses on the Internet should normally reply in less than 100 ms. Time values that exceed 100 ms substantially can indicate a problem with the destination computer or the path between the source and destination computers.

Slow response times can be transient. A single `ping` message or even several messages in a row with long response times don't necessarily indicate a problem; the computer or a network link might have been busy for a short time. Try the `ping` command several times to see whether response times are consistently high before assuming there's a problem. What if response times are consistently high? If the device is on another subnet, you might try `tracert` (discussed later in "Using `tracert`") to see whether a particular link is the bottleneck. If you're the administrator of both the source and destination computers as well as the path between them, you can check CPU use on the computers and network use on the links between them. A network monitor program (discussed later in "Network Monitors") can help determine whether network traffic is part of the problem. Performance Monitor, discussed in Chapter 12, can help determine whether the computer is responsible for the poor response times.

Review Figure 13-5 again. The second `ping` command receives a "Destination host unreachable" message. This message is generated by the source computer, indicating that an ARP request was sent to retrieve the MAC address 172.31.210.3, but an ARP reply was never received. This message is generated when the destination host address is on the same IP subnet as the source, but the source can't retrieve the destination's MAC address. If the MAC address can be retrieved but the ping request times out, the destination computer's firewall might be blocking the ping.

The third `ping` command gets a "Destination net unreachable" message. This message is generated by a router in the path between the source and destination computers when the router determines that the destination network doesn't exist. Not all routers return this message; if they don't, `ping` generates a "Request timed out" message.

Using `ping` for Connectivity Troubleshooting When troubleshooting a suspected connectivity problem with a computer, you should verify Physical-layer connectivity first. If there are link lights on the switch or NIC, the Physical layer is probably okay. You can verify the Network layer by trying the following checks:

These checks aren't necessarily in the order in which you should perform them. The order depends somewhat on the problem's symptoms and your troubleshooting experiences.

- *Run* `ipconfig /all`—Displays all pertinent information for your IP address configuration, including the IP address, default gateway, and DNS servers.

- *Ping the loopback address (127.0.0.1 or localhost)*—A successful response verifies that the IP protocol is functioning correctly. It doesn't mean the IP address configuration is correct, however. The following checks do that.

- *Ping the local IP address*—Verifies the computer's capability to receive ICMP packets. If you can ping the loopback address but not the local computer's IP address, it's likely the firewall is blocking ICMP packets.

- *Ping the default gateway*—The default gateway is the address of the router the computer sends packets to when the destination host is on another network. If you can't ping the default gateway, you won't be able to send packets outside your local LAN. If the host you're trying to communicate with is on the same LAN, you can skip this check.

- *Ping the host's IP address*—Verifies whether you can communicate with the target computer by using ICMP.

- *Ping the hostname*—Verifies that you can resolve the hostname to the correct IP address. If this check is unsuccessful, try the next two checks.

- *Ping DNS servers*—A response from one or more DNS servers indicates that the computer can communicate with a server that can resolve names to IP addresses, but it doesn't indicate that DNS lookups are working. If you can ping the DNS server, the next check verifies whether the DNS server can perform DNS lookups.

- *Use* `nslookup`—Determines whether the DNS server can resolve the name of the host you're trying to communicate with. If it can't resolve the hostname to an address, try a well-known Internet name to see whether the problem happens only when looking up the target host's address.

Using `tracert` Trace Route, discussed in Chapter 5, is used in Windows as the `tracert` command and in Linux as the `traceroute` command. It's used to determine the path between two devices. Each router between the source and destination replies with a message, and the command output shows how long the reply took. For each router in the path, three ICMP packets are sent, so three replies are received to indicate an average response time (see Figure 13-6).

```
C:\Users\gtomsho>tracert books.tomsho.com

Tracing route to books.tomsho.com [67.210.126.125]
over a maximum of 30 hops:

  1    <1 ms    <1 ms     1 ms  172.31.1.250
  2     1 ms     1 ms     1 ms  172.16.0.1
  3     1 ms     1 ms     1 ms  ycexpress.video.yc.edu [198.60.121.20]
  4    10 ms    21 ms    12 ms  phn-edge-06.inet.qwest.net [67.135.198.249]
  5     5 ms     3 ms     4 ms  phn-core-01.inet.qwest.net [205.171.12.77]
  6    75 ms    17 ms    14 ms  lap-brdr-03.inet.qwest.net [67.14.22.78]
  7    14 ms    15 ms    21 ms  63.146.27.34
  8    26 ms    17 ms    17 ms  ae-61-60.ebr1.losangeles1.level3.net [4.69.144.5
0]
  9    18 ms    18 ms    17 ms  ae-5-5.car1.sandiego1.level3.net [4.69.133.205]
 10    17 ms    17 ms    18 ms  ae-11-11.car2.sandiego1.level3.net [4.69.133.210
]
 11    17 ms    17 ms    18 ms  add2net-inc.car2.sandiego1.level3.net [4.53.122.
70]
 12    18 ms    21 ms    17 ms  quasor.lunarpages.com [67.210.126.125]

Trace complete.

C:\Users\gtomsho>
```

Figure 13-6 Output of the `tracert` command

The `tracert` command does a reverse DNS lookup on each router's IP address and displays the router name, if possible. The router name can help you determine where the router is physically located, and the response times can help you determine whether there's a bottleneck between the source and destination. A consistently high response time by one or more routers can indicate that the path is congested with excessive traffic. If a router in the path is administered locally, you can monitor the network link and the router itself to see where the problem lies.

In addition to showing you where bottlenecks might exist in an internetwork, `tracert` can confirm your network design. If you have a complex internetwork with multiple routes to some destinations, this command can show you which path your packets are taking. Most large internetworks with multiple routes for fault tolerance or load sharing have a preferred path. Router configuration determines the path packets should take, and `tracert` can verify whether your network configuration is operating as expected.

Hands-On Project 13-1: Troubleshooting with the OSI Model

Time Required: 10 minutes

Objective: Troubleshoot a problem with the OSI model approach.

Required Tools and Equipment: Net-*XX*

Description: You have been called to troubleshoot a problem with the connection to a Web server. The user states that when she starts a Web browser and tries to access a page at *www.tomsho.net*, the Web browser displays an error message after a short time. You try using the step-by-step OSI model approach to solving this problem.

1. Log on to your computer as **NetAdmin**.

2. Start a Web browser, and go to **www.tomsho.net**. After a short time, you should get an error message. Write down what layers of the OSI model you tested, and then exit the Web browser:

   _____

3. Open a command prompt window. You want to see whether the Web server's name can be resolved to an IP address by using DNS. Type `nslookup www.tomsho.net` and press **Enter**. You should get a response giving you the address for *www.tomsho.net*. Some networking diagrams place DNS at the Session layer. Because the name can be resolved to an address, you move on. Write the response you received:

   _____

4. Next, you want to see whether you can communicate with the Web server by pinging it. Type `ping www.tomsho.net` and press **Enter**. You should get a successful reply. Write the reply and what layers of the OSI model you tested:

   _____

   _____

5. You now know that you can communicate with the Web server by using the `ping` command. Start a Web browser again, and go to **http://books.tomsho.com**. If you're successful, you can conclude that the Web server software on *www.tomsho.net* isn't working correctly. The Web client software appears to be functioning because you can access other Web sites. Write which layers of the OSI model are most likely the problem:

   _____

6. Close all open windows, but stay logged on if you're going on to the next project.

Network Monitors

Network monitors are software packages that can track all or part of the network traffic. By examining the packets sent across the network, a network monitor can track information such as packet type, errors, and traffic to and from each computer; collect this data; and generate reports and graphs. Several full-featured products for network monitoring and analysis are available from companies such as SpiceWorks, Fluke Networks, and IPSwitch. SpiceWorks Network Monitor software is a free but capable network-monitoring tool that monitors devices and includes an alert management system to notify an administrator of possible problems. SpiceWorks has other IT-related free software for managing a help desk, inventory management, and mobile device management. Many network-monitoring applications work with SNMP and RMON, discussed in Chapter 12. The SNMP or RMON agents run on the computers and devices you want to monitor and send monitoring data back to the network monitor software, often called a "network management system (NMS)."

Sometimes your network monitoring needs are more modest. For example, if you run several servers, you might want to be notified if a server stops responding. Inexpensive applications, such as Simple Server Monitor (shown in Hands-On Project 13-3), can monitor servers by using `ping` and other protocols. If a server stops responding, the program can send an e-mail to an administrator.

Hands-On Project 13-2: Using Wireshark to Monitor Traffic

Time Required: 10 minutes

Objective: Use Wireshark to view network statistics.

Required Tools and Equipment: Net-XX

Description: You want to view statistical information about your network traffic by using Wireshark—specifically, which protocols are in use and a list of network conversations.

1. Log on to your computer as **NetAdmin**, if necessary.

2. Open Wireshark and start a capture session. Start a Web browser, go to several Web sites, and then close the Web browser. Open a command prompt window, and then type **ping -t www.yahoo.com** and press **Enter**. This command pings the target computer until you stop it. Minimize the command prompt window while the command continues to send pings.

3. Click **Statistics, Protocol Hierarchy** from the Wireshark menu. You see a list of protocols that have been captured and the number of packets and bytes for each. Click **Close**.

4. Click **Statistics, Conversations** from the Wireshark menu to see a list of conversations that have been captured. Click the **IPv4** tab to limit the display to IPv4 conversations. The display is updated periodically, so you should see packets and bytes increase in the conversation between your computer and *www.yahoo.com* as long as the ping continues. Write the IP addresses of the computers exchanging the most packets, and then click **Close**:

_____

_____

5. Click **Statistics, Summary** from the Wireshark menu. You see a summary of the number of packets captured, average size, total bytes, and so forth. Click **Cancel**.

6. Open the command prompt window you minimized earlier. Press **Ctrl+C** to stop the ping, and then close the command prompt window.

7. Exit Wireshark, clicking **Stop and Quit without Saving** when prompted. Close any other open windows. Stay logged on if you're going on to the next project.

Hands-On Project 13-3: Using Simple Server Monitor

Time Required: 20 minutes

Objective: Download and install a trial version of Simple Server Monitor.

Required Tools and Equipment: Net-XX

Description: You want to monitor the status of servers on your network. You research several options and decide that Simple Server Monitor meets your requirements.

1. Log on to your computer as **NetAdmin**, if necessary.

2. Start a Web browser, and go to **http://simpleservermonitor.com**.

3. Click **Download a 30-Day Free Trial**. Click the link for the current version, and then download and install Simple Server Monitor.

4. After Simple Server Monitor is installed, start the application (see Figure 13-7).

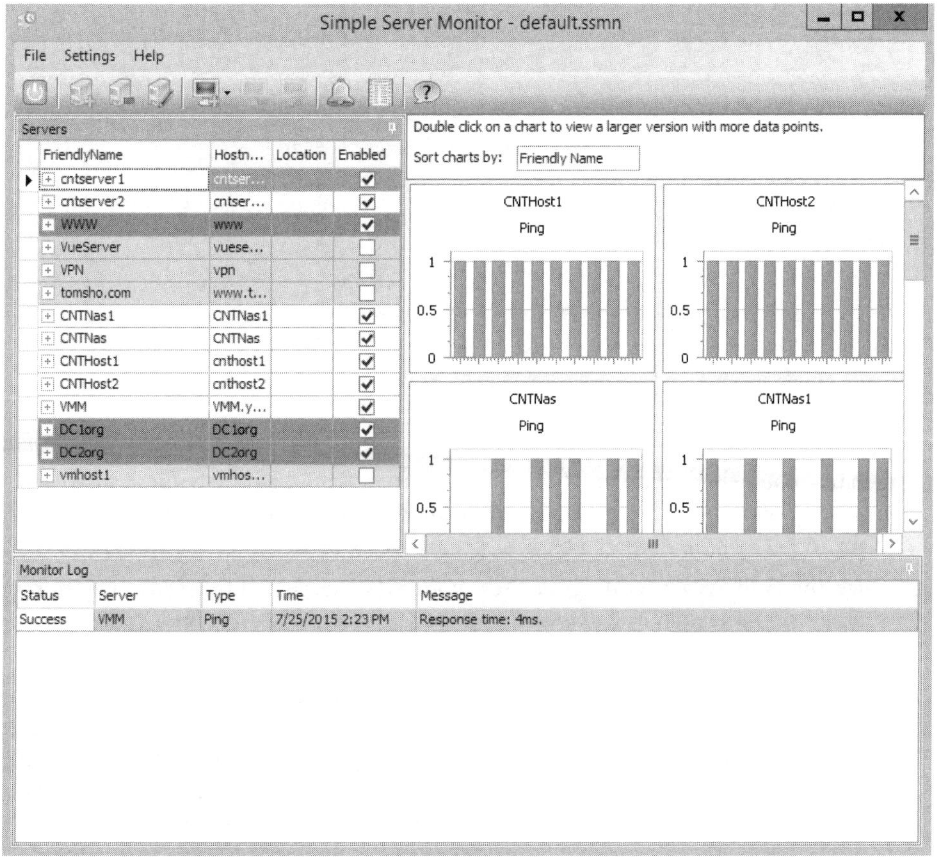

Figure 13-7 The Simple Server Monitor interface

Source: © 2014 Tartanleaf.com, Inc., *http://tartanleaf.com*

5. Click the **Add Server** icon (a tower with a green plus sign) to add a device to monitor. In the Hostname text box, type the IP address of your default gateway, and in the Friendly Name text box, type **Default Gateway** (see Figure 13-8). If you don't know the address, use the `ipconfig` command to retrieve it.

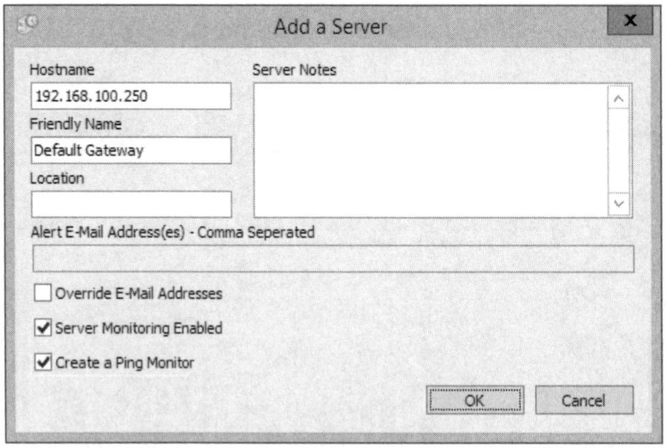

Figure 13-8   The Add a Server dialog box

Source: © 2014 Tartanleaf.com, Inc., *http://tartanleaf.com*

6. Note that you can include an e-mail address in this window. Simple Server Monitor e-mails you when a device fails to respond if you include your e-mail address. You need to configure Simple Server Monitor with the address of an SMTP server if you want to get e-mail alerts. Click **OK**.

7. Click the **Add Server** icon again. Add your DNS server address and the address of some Internet servers, such as *www.yahoo.com* and *www.google.com*. When you're finished, click **OK**.

8. In the left pane, right-click **Ping** under the Default Gateway monitor and click **Edit Monitor**. In the Ping Monitor window, you can adjust the interval to change the frequency at which Simple Server Monitor attempts to contact the device. You can also adjust the timeout and number of retries and test the connection. Click **Test**, and you should see a "Test succeeded" message. Click **OK** and then **Cancel**.

9. Aside from monitoring with `ping`, Simple Server Monitor can verify that particular services are running. Right-click one of the Internet servers you added (such as *www.yahoo.com*), point to **Add Monitor**, and click **Add HTTP Monitor**. Click **OK** in the HTTP Monitor window. This monitor verifies that the Web server service is running. The `ping` command tests up to the Network layer; the HTTP monitor tests through the Application layer.

10. Add another device that you know can't reply (for example, 10.255.250.200, if it's an invalid address in your network) so that you can see what Simple Server Monitor displays when the monitor fails to get a reply.

11. Simple Server Monitor runs when Windows starts by default. To prevent it from doing so, click **Settings**, and then click to clear the **Run on Windows Startup** check box. Using Simple Server Monitor, you can monitor all your servers, routers, and other important devices so that you're informed quickly if a device stops responding. Close all open windows, but stay logged on for the next project.

Protocol Analyzers

A protocol analyzer enables you to capture packets and analyze the network traffic generated by different protocols. You have used Wireshark to capture different packet types. Microsoft Network Monitor, an application similar to Wireshark, can be installed in Windows Server and client OSs.

Protocol analyzers can help solve problems from the Data Link layer up to the Application layer because they decode the Data Link–, Network-, and Transport-layer headers and display data processed by the Application layer. With a protocol analyzer, you can troubleshoot problems with DNS, authentication, DHCP, IP addressing, remote access, and many other processes. It's also a great teaching and learning tool because you can capture entire conversations created by a certain protocol to see exactly how it works.

Many protocol analyzers, including Wireshark, have an expert mode that attempts to detect problems with the stream of frames it decodes. For example, it can detect problems such as TCP retries, in which TCP has to resend segments because no acknowledgement was received, or duplicate acknowledgements, which can occur when segments are sent again before the acknowledgement is received, indicating a slowdown in communication. Protocol analyzers can detect a host of other potential problems, too, that just might help you solve your original problem.

The most advanced protocol analyzers combine hardware and software in a self-contained unit. These analyzers sometimes include a built-in cable analyzer for solving Physical-layer problems, too. Some examples of protocol analyzers include the following:

- *Savvius (formerly WildPackets) OmniPeek*—This software-only protocol analyzer handles all major networking protocols. For more information, visit *www.savvius.com*.
- *Fluke Networks OptiView Network Analysis Tablet*—This portable hardware-based network analyzer can be used with wired or wireless networks. For more information, visit *www.flukenetworks.com*.
- *Wireshark*—This popular free protocol analyzer is available for both Windows and Linux/UNIX environments. It supports all major protocols and a number of lesser-known protocols. For more information and to download it, visit *www.wireshark.org*.

Most experienced network administrators rely on protocol analyzers to establish baselines for network performance and to troubleshoot their networks, especially when they suspect software problems or when Network-layer (Layer 3) devices appear to be responsible for network problems.

Time-Domain Reflectometer

You can use a **time-domain reflectometer (TDR)** to determine whether there's a break or short in a cable, and then measure the cable's length. A TDR can pinpoint how far from the device the break is located by sending an electrical pulse down the cable that reflects back when it encounters a break or short. It measures the time it takes for the signal to return and, based on the type of cable tested, estimates how far down the cable the fault is located. A high-quality TDR can determine the location of a break within a few inches. TDRs for fiber-optic cable (called "OTDRs") and electrical cables are available.

Although cable installers use them most often, TDRs can be invaluable diagnostic tools for network administrators, too. When you're having new cables installed, ask the installer to use a TDR to document actual lengths of all cables. Rent a TDR (or hire someone who owns one) to measure any cables on the network whose lengths aren't documented already.

The TDR function is standard in most advanced cable testers. Remember that each medium has distance limitations, so running a TDR scan on each cable segment is critical in documenting your Physical-layer installation.

Basic Cable Testers

You can purchase basic **cable testers** for less than $100. Typically, they test only correct termination of a twisted-pair cable or continuity of a coaxial cable. They're excellent tools for checking patch cables and testing for correct termination of a cable at the patch panel and jack. However, these testers can verify only that cable wires are terminated in the correct order (referred to as the "wiremap") or that there are no breaks in the cable. These low-priced testers can't check a cable for attenuation, crosstalk, noise, or other possible performance problems in the cable run.

Advanced Cable Testers

More expensive than TDRs or basic cable testers, advanced cable testers (sometimes called "cable certifiers" or "cable analyzers") perform a battery of tests on a cable to certify it for a particular application. For example, you can set the cable tester for Cat 6 cable, and it performs the tests to certify the connection for Cat 6 operation. In addition to length and wire-map tests, these cable testers perform several tests for crosstalk, attenuation, EMI, and impedance mismatches. Some advanced cable testers function at both the Physical and Data Link layers to measure frame counts, collisions, CRC errors, and broadcast storms. Anyone who plans to be in the business of installing cable needs an advanced cable tester, which can cost from around $1000 to several thousand dollars, depending on the features.

Additional Tools

Network monitors, protocol analyzers, and cable testers are some of the main tools you use when installing, testing, and troubleshooting networks. However, a few other tools you might use include the following:

- *Multimeter*—A **multimeter**, or digital multimeter or digital volt meter (DVM), can measure voltage, current, and resistance on a wire. In networking applications, an important measurement is resistance, or impedance. Impedance measures the opposition to electrical current and is important in determining faults (breaks or crimps) or mismatched wire types. Multimeters can also help troubleshoot power supplies in computers, routers, and switches by measuring a power supply's output voltage levels. Power supplies that deliver power out of specification can cause strange behavior in electronic equipment, such as corrupt data and system resets.

 A cable certifier can also perform impedance tests, so a multimeter isn't usually necessary for cable installation if you have a cable certifier.

- *Tone generator and probe*—A **tone generator** issues an electrical signal on a wire, and a probe or tone locator detects the signal and emits a tone. It's useful for locating a wire that might be in a bundle of other wires. For example, suppose you have a classroom wired with 40 Cat 6 cables. Each cable goes from a jack, under the floor, and then to a wiring closet across the hall. In the wiring closet, the 40 cables are bundled together, making it impossible to tell which end goes to which jack. You place the tone generator on the jack end of the wire and the probe on each wire in the bundle until you hear the tone, indicating you have the correct wire. Cable certifiers and higher-end basic cable testers perform similar functions as a tone generator/probe combination.

- *Optical power meter*—An **optical power meter (OPM)** is used to measure the amount of light on a fiber-optic circuit. It's often used to determine the amount of signal loss on a fiber-optic cable between the transmitter (also called "emitter") and receiver. The amount of signal loss can determine whether the fiber-optic cable termination was done correctly and whether the receiver can interpret the signals correctly.

A network technician might not need all the tools mentioned in this section, but most of them will eventually come in handy. Some, such as a cable certifier, are essential if you're doing a lot of cable installations.

Common Troubleshooting Situations

Say you have the following problem on a network: 100 Mbps basic switches are being replaced with 1000 Mbps managed switches. It's been confirmed that all NICs can support 100 or 1000 Mbps, but certain stations simply can't communicate on the network. After some investigation, you've determined that the NIC driver software on these stations was set to force the NIC to communicate at 100 Mbps in half-duplex mode, but the switch was set to communicate only at 1000 Mbps in full-duplex mode. A quick change in the NIC configuration solved the problem.

Using the structured problem-solving approach to network troubleshooting described earlier, you can eventually solve networking problems such as this one. To help get you started with this sometimes arduous task, this section outlines some common network problems and possible solutions.

Cabling and Related Components

Many networking problems occur at the Physical layer and include problems with cables, connectors, and NICs. The first step in troubleshooting these problems is to determine whether the problem lies with the cable or the computer. One easy method is to connect another computer to the cable. If it functions normally, you can conclude that the problem is with the original computer. If it exhibits the same symptoms, check the cable first, and then check the device it connects to, and so forth.

After you determine that the cable is the likeliest culprit, make sure it's connected to the computer correctly, and verify that it's the right type of cable for the connection. Make sure you use the same category of UTP cable throughout the network. Double-check cable lengths to make sure you don't exceed the maximum length limitation for the network medium. By using a TDR, you can identify and correct these types of problems quickly.

If you suspect a faulty or misconfigured NIC, check the back of the card. As discussed, the NIC has indicator lights to show whether it's functioning and its network connection is active. If the NIC lacks these indicators, you must replace the suspect NIC with a known working NIC—in much the same way you replace a suspect computer with a known working one to determine whether the network or the computer is the cause of the problem.

If the NIC seems functional and you're using TCP/IP, try using the `ping` command to check connectivity to other computers. If the NIC works but the computer still can't access the network, you might have more serious hardware problems (for example, a faulty bus slot), or NIC configuration settings might be invalid. Either way, you must conduct further troubleshooting.

 You can find more information on cabling problems in Appendix A.

Power Fluctuations

Power fluctuations in a building—caused by an electrical storm or a power failure, for example—can affect computers adversely. First, verify that servers are functioning. When possible, remind users that it takes a few minutes for servers to come back online after a power outage.

One way to eliminate the effects of power fluctuations, especially on servers, is to connect them to uninterruptible power supplies (UPSs). UPS systems provide battery power to computers so that they can be shut down without data loss. Some perform shutdowns automatically, thereby eliminating the need for human intervention when power failures or severe power fluctuations occur. At the very least, all computers, internetworking devices, and other electronic equipment should be protected by surge protectors, which prevent sudden spikes in electrical power from damaging the equipment.

Upgrades

Because networking technology changes constantly, frequent upgrades of equipment and software, such as the file server's OS, are necessary. During these upgrades, it's common for some equipment to run on an old OS and some to run on a new one. When you perform network upgrades, remember three important points:

- Ignoring upgrades to new software releases and new hardware can lead to a situation in which a complete network overhaul is necessary because many upgrades build on top of others. If administrators don't keep current, they might need to do an overwhelming amount of research and endure a lack of technical support for older software or hardware. Keep current and do one upgrade at a time to make your life easier.

- Test any upgrade before deploying it on your production network. Ideally, use a test laboratory where you can try all upgrades and work out any problems. If a test lab isn't an option, select a small part of your network—one department or a few users—and perform the upgrade. This method gives you an opportunity to work through possible issues before imposing changes (and the problems that sometimes go with them) on the entire network.

- Don't forget to tell users about upgrades. A well-informed user is an understanding user. Everyone who might be affected by an upgrade must be informed when it will occur, what's involved, and what to expect. If your company has a regular maintenance window, use this time period as much as possible for performing system upgrades.

Poor Network Performance

If all goes well, the network monitoring and planning you do will ensure that the network performs optimally. However, you might notice that your network slows down; this problem can happen quickly, or it could be a gradual deterioration. Whether performance problems happen slowly or suddenly, answering the following questions should help pinpoint the causes:

- What has changed since the last time the network functioned normally?
- Has new equipment been added to the network?
- Have new applications been added to computers on the network?
- Is someone playing electronic games across the network? (You'd be surprised at the amount of traffic networked games can generate.)
- Are there new users on the network? How many?
- Could any other new noncomputer equipment, such as a generator, cause interference near the network?

If new users, added equipment, or newly installed applications seem to degrade network performance, it might be time to expand your network and add equipment to limit or contain network traffic. Higher-speed backbones, additional subnets and VLANs, and additional servers and routers are alternatives worth considering when you must increase capacity to accommodate usage levels that have grown beyond your network's current capabilities. Depending on the applications you're running and where the bottlenecks are, you might also consider using packet shapers, server clusters, and load balancers to optimize communications.

Disaster Recovery

If your network is well documented, recovering from a disaster will be much easier. Disasters can come in many forms, from a simple disk crash that disables a key server to a fire or flood that devastates your entire workplace. The procedures for recovery from total devastation are beyond the scope of this book; instead, the following sections focus on backup procedures and recovery from system failure.

Backing Up Network Data

A comprehensive backup program can prevent major data loss. A backup plan is an important part of an overall disaster recovery plan and should be revised as your needs—and data and applications—change. To formulate your backup plan, review the following guidelines:

- Determine what data should be backed up and how often. Some files, such as program executables and OS files, seldom change and might require backup only weekly or monthly.
- Develop a schedule for backing up data that includes the type of backup to perform, how often, and at what time of day. The next section reviews the most common backup types.
- Identify the people responsible for performing backups.

- Test your backup system regularly. The person responsible for backups should perform these tests, which include backing up data and restoring it. After a backup system is in place, conduct periodic tests to ensure data integrity. A data backup is no use to you if the restore process doesn't work.

- Maintain a backup log listing what data was backed up, when the backup took place, who performed the backup, and what medium was used. Most backup programs maintain a summary of the backup history, but these logs can't be accessed if the backup server fails.

- Develop a plan for storing data after it's been backed up. This plan should include on-site storage, perhaps in a fireproof safe, and off-site storage in the event of a catastrophe. For both on-site and off-site storage, make sure only authorized personnel have access to the backup medium.

Backup Types

Chapter 12 discussed using Windows built-in backup programs to perform basic backup of Windows computers, but most backup plans require more flexible backup software when more than a few computers are involved. Third-party backup programs can provide a comprehensive backup solution with centralized management. Before using these products, you need to understand some of the terminology for backup types:

- *Full*—A **full backup** copies all selected files to the selected medium and marks files as backed up; also called a normal backup.

- *Incremental*—An **incremental backup** copies all files changed since the last full or incremental backup and marks files as backed up.

- *Differential*—A **differential backup** copies all files changed since the last full backup and doesn't mark files as backed up.

- *Copy*—A **copy backup** copies selected files to a selected medium without marking files as backed up.

- *Daily*—A **daily backup** copies all files changed the day the backup is made and doesn't mark files as backed up.

- *Bare metal restore backup*—A **bare metal restore backup** is designed to allow restoring the system disk directly from backup media without having to install the OS and backup software first. It doesn't usually back up data volumes, so they need a separate backup procedure.

Of these backup types, full, incremental, and differential backups are most useful as part of a regular backup schedule. A copy backup is good for copying files to a new location or making a secondary backup for off-site storage without affecting the regular backup routine. A daily backup is good for identifying files that were changed on a particular day so that you can, for example, collect all the files you were working on at home and bring the changed files back to the office the next day. A bare metal restore backup is best used outside the normal backup schedule and should be done when a major change is being made to the system disk, such as an OS upgrade.

A good model for creating a backup schedule combines a weekly full backup with daily differential backups so that you can do backups quickly on a daily basis and restore data easily by restoring the contents of two backups: the full backup first and the differential backup next. This method uses more storage space for differential backups because the backup gets larger each day until the next full backup is done. However, it has the advantage of requiring only the full backup and the last differential backup when a full system restore is required.

You can also use incremental backups for daily backup, but restoring data is more difficult because you need the full backup plus each incremental backup done since the last full backup. The advantage of an incremental backup is that each backup takes up less space because incremental backups copy only files that were changed since the previous incremental or full backup.

When creating a backup schedule, posting the schedule and assigning one person to do backups and sign off on them each day is a good idea. That way, you can see at a glance when the last backup was done, and train one person to perform backups and care for the backup medium.

Windows systems have an additional backup type called a "system state backup" that copies the boot files, the Registry, Active Directory on domain controllers, and other critical information. If a Registry file or boot file becomes corrupted, sometimes all that's needed to get the system running again is the latest system state backup.

If you back up to tape media, make sure you can restore data. Use the "verify data" option that comes with your backup software to ensure that data copied to tape matches data on the drive. Create some test files, back up these files, and then practice restoring them to the server to check that the restore operation works correctly. In addition, make sure tapes are stored in a cool, dry, dark place to minimize the risk of damage by heat, moisture, or light. Take a tape off the shelf periodically, and make sure it's readable and its data can be restored *after* the tape has been removed from the machine. For example, a miscalibrated tape drive might accept tapes for backup but fail to restore their contents—a condition usually discovered only when you need to restore data. Have a policy to rotate tapes so that no single tape set is reused in the same week. In addition, have a policy to remove tapes from the set after a predetermined time to avoid worn tapes that might affect performance.

Because hard drives are so inexpensive, it's becoming more common to eschew tapes and use only hard drives for backup. They're convenient, and restoring individual files is much faster than using tapes. However, they might not be ideal for long-term storage, and they take up more space than tapes. In addition, you should never use SSDs for long-term backup storage because they can lose data when removed from power for very long periods.

Business Continuity

Recovering from a crashed server or hard drive can be remediated with a solid system backup plan, but what about a natural disaster, such as a fire or flood, or a human-caused disaster, such as a terrorist attack? A disaster that wipes out your entire IT infrastructure can wipe out your business with it. Business continuity consists of the policies, procedures, and resources required to ensure that a business can continue to function after a major catastrophe that renders the site unable to operate. If the IT infrastructure is severely disabled, business continuity means a plan must be in place to get servers and systems back up and running and data restored. Some companies are turning to cloud storage for just this purpose. If the bulk of the IT infrastructure is cloud based, all that's needed is restoring Internet access and client computers. However, if the bulk of the IT infrastructure is maintained in house, the company should consider one of these options: cold sites, warm sites, or hot sites.

Cold Sites A **cold site** is a physical location that houses the hardware needed to get IT functioning again. It includes servers, routers, and switches, plus the media to make all the connections. However, the devices aren't usually configured, and data must be restored from off-site backup before operations can start. This option is the least expensive because it requires no initial setup or data synchronization. However, depending on the IT infrastructure's size, it could take days, weeks, or longer before you're back in operation. A cold site is a good option if the perceived likelihood of a major disaster is small or if the company can survive extended downtime, and the costs of this downtime are less than the costs of maintaining a more expensive option.

Warm Sites A **warm site** is a location containing all the infrastructure needed for operations to continue, and it's mostly configured and ready to run on short notice. With a warm site, OSs are installed and largely up to date, and routers and switches are configured and connected. You just need to make some finishing touches to configurations and load the most current data from backup, and you're ready to go. Again, depending on size, you might be down for a few days but probably not for weeks.

Hot Sites A **hot site**, as you might imagine, can be running at a moment's notice if necessary. It has a full-time connection with the original site so that data is synchronized and up to date. Of the three business continuity options, it's by far the most expensive, but it's the best option for organizations when the costs of being down, even for a few hours, exceed the costs of maintaining a hot site. For example, with a cloud computing company offering IaaS and PaaS services, its entire source of income, not to mention its reputation, comes from its IT infrastructure. If the network is down, the company can't make money and could lose customers permanently. This type of organization probably needs a hot site.

Chapter Summary

- Documenting a network thoroughly offers the following advantages: makes moves, adds, and changes easier, provides information needed for troubleshooting, offers justification for adding staff or equipment, helps determine compliance with standards, supplies proof that your installations meet hardware or software requirements, reduces training requirements, facilitates security management, and improves compliance with software licensing agreements.

- Elements of the network that should be documented include a network description, the cable plant, equipment rooms and telecommunication closets, internetworking devices, servers, and workstations.

- The problem-solving process has eight steps: Determine the problem definition and scope, gather information, consider possible causes, devise a solution, implement the solution, test the solution, document the solution, and devise preventive measures.

- There are many approaches to network troubleshooting, including trial and error, solve by example, the replacement method, and step by step with the OSI model. Different methods are suitable for different circumstances and the technician's level of experience.

- Many resources are available to help troubleshoot problems, including an administrator's experience, the Internet, and network documentation. Sometimes a combination of these methods can be used to solve problems.

- You can use several tools to get information from your network and its devices to help solve problems, including the `ping` and `tracert` commands, network monitor programs, protocol analyzers, and basic and advanced cable testers.

- Some common troubleshooting situations are related to cable plant components, electrical power, and network and software upgrades. Poor network performance can be a result of many factors, and you must know what questions to ask to narrow down the problem's scope and possible causes.

- If your network is well documented, recovering from network disaster is easier. Disaster can come in the form of a simple disk crash that disables a key server or a fire or flood that devastates your entire workplace. Some tools to prevent disasters and expedite business continuity include data backups and establishing a cold, warm, or hot site.

Key Terms

bare metal restore backup   A backup designed to allow restoring the system disk directly from backup media without having to install the OS and backup software first. It doesn't usually back up data volumes, so they need a separate backup procedure.

change management   Documenting and managing network changes, including IP addressing, moving devices, modifying device configurations, and so forth.

cold site   A business continuity option in which a physical location houses the hardware needed to get IT functioning again, but it requires considerable configuration and data restoration before it's operational.

copy backup   A backup that copies selected files to the selected medium without marking files as backed up.

daily backup   A backup that copies all files changed the day the backup is made; doesn't mark files as backed up.

differential backup   A backup that copies all files changed since the last full backup; doesn't mark files as backed up.

escalation   A step in the troubleshooting process in which the technician must call in additional people to help solve the problem because it's outside the technician's expertise or authority.

frequently asked questions (FAQ)   A document with two parts to each entry. The first part is a question the manufacturer has anticipated or received from customers; the second part is an answer to the question.

full backup   A backup that copies all selected files to the selected medium and marks files as backed up. Also called a "normal backup."

hot site   A business continuity option in which a physical location has all the infrastructure in place and configured, and data is synchronized and up to date, so it's ready to take over from the original site at a moment's notice.

incremental backup   A backup that copies all files changed since the last full or incremental backup and marks files as backed up.

knowledge base   A searchable database containing descriptions of problems and errors along with known solutions, if any.

maintenance window   A time set aside for schedule updates, upgrades, and other network maintenance procedures when users are notified that the network might not be available; also known as "scheduled downtime."

multimeter   A device that can measure voltage, current, and resistance on a wire.

network monitors   Programs that monitor network traffic and gather information about packet types, errors, and packet traffic to and from each computer.

optical power meter (OPM)   A device used to measure the amount of light on a fiber-optic circuit.

rollback plan   The part of an upgrade plan with instructions on how to undo the upgrade if problems occur during or after the upgrade.

time-domain reflectometer (TDR)   A network troubleshooting device that can determine whether there's a break or short in the cable and, if so, approximately how far down the cable it's located. Also shows the total cable length.

tone generator   A device that issues an electrical signal on a wire, and a probe or tone locator detects the signal and emits a tone. It's useful for finding the other end of a wire.

warm site   A business continuity option in which a physical location contains all the infrastructure needed for IT operations to continue and is mostly configured and ready to run on short notice.

Review Questions

1. Which device can determine whether a cable break or short exists and approximately how far down the cable it's located?

   a.   Network monitor

   b.   RMON

   c.   Time-domain reflectometer

   d.   Protocol analyzer

2. At what layer of the OSI model is a CRC error detected?

   a. Data Link

   b. Network

   c. Physical

   d. Session

3. Which type of plan makes returning a network to its state before an upgrade easier?

   a. Backup plan

   b. Rollback plan

   c. Upgrade plan

   d. Downgrade plan

4. Based on the eight-step problem-solving process discussed in this chapter, what's the first step in network troubleshooting?

   a. Devise a solution.

   b. Consider possible causes.

   c. Test the cables.

   d. Determine the problem definition and scope.

5. Which problem-solving approach requires a solid understanding of how networks work?

   a. Trial and error

   b. Step by step with the OSI model

   c. Solve by example

   d. Replacement method

6. Under which condition is using the trial-and-error approach not advisable? (Choose all that apply.)

   a. You can undo changes easily.

   b. A server or network device is live on the network.

   c. You can't undo changes easily.

   d. No data can be lost.

7. Which layer is where problems restricted to one workstation are likely to occur?

   a. Data Link

   b. Transport

   c. Physical

   d. Presentation

8. After implementing a solution, what's the next step?

   a. Document the solution.

   b. Test the solution.

   c. Devise preventive measures.

   d. Consider possible causes.

9. Which of the following can be used to prevent data loss during a power fluctuation or failure?

   a. TDR

   b. UPS

   c. MIB

   d. SNMP

10. Which of the following is an element of the information-gathering step in the problem-solving process? (Choose all that apply.)

   a. Find out whether the function ever worked.

   b. Determine whether something has changed.

   c. Compare current operation with a baseline.

   d. Consider possible causes.

11. When measuring network performance, what do you need as a point of reference?

   a. SNMP

   b. Baseline

   c. Message information base

   d. Protocol analysis

12. Which of the following is the TCP/IP protocol used with a network management system?

   a. ICMP

   b. SNMP

   c. DHCP

   d. SMTP

13. A logical topology includes jack locations and room numbers. True or False?

14. What tool does its job by measuring the amount of time it takes for a signal to travel the length of a fiber-optic cable and back?

   a. Tone generator

   b. Probe

   c. OTDR

   d. Multimeter

15. Which device is used in fiber-optic cable testing?

    a. DVM

    b. Probe

    c. Multimeter

    d. OPM

16. For which of the following network conditions must you use a protocol analyzer or network monitor for further diagnosis? (Choose all that apply.)

    a. Cable break

    b. Cable short

    c. Slow network performance

    d. High rate of transmission errors

17. At what layers of the OSI model does a software protocol analyzer operate?

    a. Layers 1, 2, and 3

    b. Layers 1 to 4

    c. Layers 2 and 3

    d. Layers 2 to 7

18. Which of the following is *not* found in the output of a successful `ping` reply?

    a. IP address of the responding computer

    b. The number of bytes in the ICMP message

    c. The sequence number

    d. The TTL of the reply packet

19. Which documentation section describes the physical layout of network media?

    a. Internetworking devices

    b. Cable plant

    c. Telecommunication closets

    d. Servers

20. When using the `ping` command to solve a network connection problem, which of these steps can you skip if the target host is on the same LAN?

    a. Ping the 127.0.0.1 address.

    b. Ping the host's IP address.

    c. Ping the default gateway.

    d. Ping DNS servers.

21. What should a company providing IaaS services have in place if a customer needs immediate recovery from a catastrophic failure that cripples its IT infrastructure?

   a. Hot site

   b. Bare metal restore backup

   c. RAID 1 disks

   d. Load balancers

Critical Thinking

The following activities give you critical thinking challenges. Challenge labs give you an opportunity to use the skills you have learned to perform a task without step-by-step instructions. Case projects offer a practical networking setup for which you supply a written solution.

Challenge Lab 13-1: Troubleshooting Network Problems

Time Required: 1 hour or more

Objective: Troubleshoot a variety of network problems created by a partner.

Required Tools and Equipment: Net-XX; a share on the network that client computers should be able to open when their computers are in good working order

Description: This lab can be done in pairs, with each student creating a problem on his or her partner's computer. A working system should be able to access the Internet and a file share on the local network (set up by the instructor). While troubleshooting, keep a log stating the problem, symptoms, and the layers of the OSI model you test and the final solution to the problem. The following are some problems you can create (but they shouldn't be done in order):

- Set an incorrect static IP address.
- Set an incorrect subnet mask.
- Set an incorrect DNS server.
- Set an incorrect default gateway.
- Disable Client for Microsoft Networks in the network connection's properties.
- Disable the IPv4 protocol in the network connection's properties.
- Disconnect a cable and/or replace a patch cable with a crossover cable.
- Disconnect the switch from the router (if possible).
- Power off the switch (if possible).

Challenge Lab 13-2: Using a Protocol Analyzer to Troubleshoot DNS

Time Required: 30 minutes or more

Objective: Troubleshoot DNS by capturing the packets in a DNS query.

Required Tools and Equipment: Net-*XX*

Description: This lab can be done in groups. First, capture packets involved in DNS queries, and determine the queries generated by your computer and the responses from the server. Next, capture only DNS packets, and use `nslookup` to query *www.yahoo.com* and *www.yahoo-xyz.com*. Answer the following questions:

- What packet-capture filter did you use?

_____

For each lookup, answer these questions:

- Did your computer generate more than one DNS query for each lookup? If so, why?

_____

_____

- What was the response from the DNS server for each query?

_____

- Was more than one IP address returned? If so, why?

_____

Challenge Lab 13-3: Using NetInfo to Gather Documentation

Time Required: 30 minutes or more

Objective: Use NetInfo to gather information about your network.

Required Tools and Equipment: Net-*XX* with NetInfo installed

Description: This lab can be done in groups. Use NetInfo, which you installed in Chapter 12, to scan your network for a variety of information. Answer the following questions:

- What tools did you use in NetInfo to gather information?

_____

- What type of information can you gather with NetInfo tools?

_____

_____

- How can the information you gathered be useful in documenting and supporting your network?

_____

_____

Challenge Lab 13-4: Installing an Advanced Network Monitor

Time Required: 45 minutes or more

Objective: Use network-monitoring software to gather information about your network.

Required Tools and Equipment: Net-XX, Internet access

Description: This lab can be done in groups. Download a free trial of WhatsConnected from *www.ipswitch.com*. You need to enter some information about yourself before you can finish the download. While the file is downloading, read about some of the program's features and capabilities. After you install the program, start it and explore its many features. Then answer the following questions.

- What are three major features of WhatsConnected?

  _____

  _____

- How can these features help you to maintain and support a network?

  _____

  _____

Case Project 13-1

A user calls to report that she's unable to log on to e-mail, and you ask a couple of questions. Because you know that no one else is using the network right now, you can't determine whether the problem is unique to her machine or affects the entire network. Probing further, you learn that she's also unable to print. You decide this problem is probably easier to troubleshoot from the user's computer.

Using the eight-step problem-solving process covered in this chapter, outline the items you must check and the questions you must ask when you arrive at the user's office. Based on the possible responses to your questions, describe the actions you will take to correct potential causes of this problem.

Case Project 13-2

Document the computers, servers, and network equipment in your classroom. Design a form for gathering this information, including space for items such as model number, serial number, NIC type, MAC address, logical address, location, patch panel port connections, and hub/switch port connections. What other information might be important?

Case Project 13-3

A network consists of 75 workstations and three servers. The workstations are currently connected to the network with 100 Mbps switches, and the servers have 1000 Mbps connections. Describe two network problems that can be solved by replacing the workstations' 100 Mbps switches and NICs with 1000 Mbps switches and NICs. What potential problems can this upgrade cause? What must you verify about the existing network configuration before you perform the upgrade?

Network Troubleshooting Guide

This appendix lists basic questions you can ask when you approach network problems.
Guidelines for troubleshooting specific areas of networking technology are also included.

General Questions for Troubleshooting

When troubleshooting, the first question you should ask is "Has this piece of equipment or procedure ever worked correctly?" If it did in fact work once, your next question should be "Since then, what has changed?" The following is a list of other useful questions:

- Was only one user affected, or were many users affected?
- Were users affected randomly or all at once?
- Is only one computer down, or is the whole network down?
- Does this problem happen all the time or only during specific times?
- Does this problem affect only one application, more than one application, or all applications?
- Does this problem resemble any past problems?
- Have you added any users to the network?
- Have you added any new equipment to the network?
- Did you install a new application just before the problem occurred?
- Have you moved any equipment recently?
- Are any vendor products involved in this problem? If yes, who are the vendors?
- Has anyone else attempted to remedy this problem?
- If the computer can't function on the network, have you checked its NIC (adapter card)? Is it working?
- Is the amount of traffic on the network normal?

The following sections list questions that are helpful when troubleshooting specific components of your network.

Cabling Problems

If you suspect a problem with cabling, check the following items:

- Missing or loose connections (for example, checking the strain relief on patch cables)
- Frayed or broken sections
- Cabling and devices being within standards (by using a cable certifier and/or an OPM)
- Cable and connectors match (Cat 6 cable used with Cat 6 connectors, for example)
- NIC specifications
- Crimped or bent cables
- Location of the cable routing near a transformer, a large electric motor, or an air conditioner
- Same standard used on both ends of the cable (for example, TIA/EIA 568A or TIA/EIA 568B terminations on both ends)
- Correct termination at jacks and patch panels (for example, no more than 1 inch of untwisted wire outside the cable jacket)
- Fiber type mismatch (such as SMF and MMF cables and connectors being mixed or different core sizes [62.5 or 50 micron] of MMF fiber being used)
- Fiber wavelength (making sure the emitter transmits at the correct wavelength for the type of cable in use)
- Fiber terminations (such as connectors being clean and free of fractures)

Problems with NICs

Here are some things to check when you have problems with NICs (network adapter cards):

- Verify that there's a link light at the NIC.
- Are there any setting conflicts if you have more than one NIC in a computer? For example, only one default gateway should be specified.
- Are the duplex (half or full) mode and signaling speed (for example, 10 Mbps, 100 Mbps, 1000 Mbps) set correctly? Usually, they should be set to auto negotiation.
- In a wireless environment, are the SSID and encryption key set correctly?

Driver Problems

Check the following to isolate driver problems:

- Have any changes been made to the equipment since it was working correctly?
- Are old drivers being used with new equipment?
- Have you checked the manufacturer's Web site for the newest drivers?
- On Windows systems, try to update the driver by using the Update Driver Software option in Device Manager.
- Has the driver been updated recently? If you suspect a driver update is causing a problem, try using the Rollback Driver feature in Device Manager.

Problems with Network Operations

Here's a checklist to follow for network operation problems:

1. Inspect the hardware in your server and verify the following:
   - It's on the OS vendor's compatibility list.
   - It has the correct, most current drivers installed.
2. Use Performance Monitor to verify the following:
   - The amount of memory is adequate.
   - There's enough disk storage, and the disk queue length is no more than 3.
   - There's enough processing power to support the network.
3. Check all network bindings to make sure they're correct and the most used bindings are listed first.
4. Verify IP address settings, and make sure you can ping the configured default gateway and DNS servers. Verify that the IP address is assigned by using the correct method (DHCP or static).
5. Make sure the computer has an IP address in the correct subnet or VLAN.
6. Ensure that the switch port the computer is plugged into is assigned to the correct VLAN.
7. In a wireless network, make sure matching standards are in use; for example, ensure that all devices use 802.11a, 802.11b, 802.11g, 802.11n, or 802.11ac, as needed.
8. In a wireless network, check that all clients have a strong enough signal from the access point and are using the correct SSID and encryption type and key.
9. Use `ping`, `tracert`, and `nslookup` to verify connectivity, router path, and DNS lookup problems. Use a protocol analyzer to capture and examine packet contents to verify protocols and port numbers.

Problems with Network Printing and Fax Services

Check the following if there's a problem with network printing or faxing:

- Is the shared fax's or printer's power on?
- Is the selected shared printer or fax machine the correct one for the client computer's driver?
- Are the permissions correct for the shared printer or fax that users and printer/fax managers are using?
- Are the cables used by the shared printer or fax in good condition and connected correctly?
- Check the print queue on the local computer and print servers. If print jobs are stalled, delete the print job at the front of the queue. If that doesn't help, restart the print spooler service.

Problems with Client/Server Computing

Check the following for problems with clients or servers in a client/server environment:

- Verify that the host-based firewall on client and server is configured to allow the network service. For client devices, the service or port should be allowed in the outgoing direction, and on servers, the service or port should be allowed in the incoming direction.

- Verify that the client and server are using the correct port numbers for the service.
- Check router ACLs or hardware firewall rules to make sure the service isn't being blocked.
- Verify that client and server version numbers are compatible. If the server software has been updated, the client software might also need an update, and vice versa.

Problems with Network Accounts

Check the following if a user can't log on with a certain account:

- Is the person entering the correct username?
- Is the name of the domain (if logging on to a Windows domain) correct?
- Is the user typing the correct password? Remember that passwords are case sensitive on Windows computers, and usernames and passwords are case sensitive on Linux computers.
- Has the user account been disabled or locked out?
- Are any logon time or location restrictions set for the user?
- Does the user have the correct permissions to the resource being accessed?

Problems with Data Security

Use the following checklist if you suspect problems with data security:

1. If a user can access a resource that should be unavailable or can't access a resource that should be available, check the following:
   - Does the user have the correct permissions to the resource? On Windows systems, verify both share permissions and NTFS permissions.
   - Be sure to check group memberships, too. For example, check whether the user belongs to any group assigned the Deny permission.
2. If the user can access previously secured data or there's a problem with data theft, alteration, or contamination, check the following:
   - Who has access to the server if it's in a locked room?
   - Are any computers being left on as logged on, and then left unattended?
   - Are any passwords written on paper and left in obvious places, such as on the monitor, in a desk drawer, or under the keyboard?
   - Are any users using obvious passwords, such as names of children, pets, or spouses?
   - Do any users have excessive permissions because of membership in an administrator's group?
   - Are any users storing confidential data on their local hard drives?
   - Do any users have their OSs configured to log them on automatically, bypassing the username and password process?

Problems with Communication in Large Networks

To start, you troubleshoot a WAN or other large network in the same way you do a LAN. However, some considerations are specific to large networks. These types of problems usually require the assistance of vendors or service providers. Here are questions related to troubleshooting in large networks:

1. Did any vendor replace, add, or remove anything from the WAN?

2. Is the power to the following components turned on, and are the components themselves turned on?

   • Switch

   • Router

   • Modem

   • CSU/DSU

3. For the same components, check the following:

   • Are all cables connected correctly and in good condition?

   • Is the component compatible with the communication medium and the communication device at the other end of the link?

   • Is the software configured correctly, and does it match the configuration of the connected communication equipment?

Glossary

6to4 An IPv4-to-IPv6 transition protocol that provides automatic tunneling of IPv6 traffic over an IPv4 network. It can handle host-to-router or router-to-host tunneling but is most often used to create a router-to-router tunnel.

10BaseT A technology defined by IEEE 802.3i, it's Ethernet running at 10 Mbps, using baseband signaling over Category 3 or higher twisted-pair cabling. Although still seen in older networks, newer networks use 100BaseT or faster technology.

10GBaseT A technology defined by IEEE 802.3an, it's 10 Gigabit Ethernet running over four pairs of Category 6A UTP cabling, using baseband signaling. Unlike other BaseT Ethernet standards, 10GBaseT operates only in full-duplex mode.

100BaseFX 100 Mbps Ethernet using baseband signaling over two strands of fiber-optic cabling.

100BaseTX A technology defined by IEEE 802.3u, it's the most commonly used Ethernet variety today. It runs over Category 5 or higher UTP cable and uses two of the four wire pairs: one to transmit data and the other to receive data. It runs at 100 Mbps, using baseband signaling.

1000BaseT Ethernet A technology defined by the IEEE 802.3ab standard; supports 1000 Mbps Ethernet (usually called "Gigabit Ethernet") over Category 5 or higher UTP cable, using baseband signaling.

access control In the context of the Network layer and routing, the process by which a router consults a list of rules before forwarding an incoming packet. The rules determine whether a packet meeting certain criteria (such as source and destination address) should be permitted to reach the intended destination.

access control list (ACL) A set of rules configured on a router's interface for specifying which addresses and protocols can pass through the interface and to which destinations.

access point (AP) A wireless device that serves as the central connection point of a wireless LAN and mediates communication between wireless computers.

Active Directory The directory service used by Windows servers.

active partition A partition that can hold boot files the BIOS loads before it can start the OS.

ad hoc mode Sometimes called "peer-to-peer mode," it's a wireless mode of operation typically used only in small or temporary installations. There's no central device, and data travels from one device to another to reach the destination device.

Address Resolution Protocol (ARP) An Internetwork-layer protocol used to resolve a host's IP address to its MAC address. ARP uses a broadcast frame containing the target host's IP address, and the host that's assigned the address responds with its MAC address.

address space The number of addresses available in an IP network number that can be assigned to hosts.

administrative distance A value assigned to a routing protocol that indicates its reliability compared with other routing protocols that might be in use on the same router. If a route is derived by using two different routing protocols, the one with the least administrative distance is used.

aging time The amount of time a switch maintains a switching table entry that hasn't been updated.

analog signal A signal, represented by a sine wave, that varies over time continually and smoothly.

anycast addresses An address type used in IPv6 to allow a one-to-many relationship between source and destination; the packet is delivered to only one of the possible destination computers.

Application layer Layer 7 in the OSI model provides interfaces that enable applications to request and receive network services. *See also* Open Systems Interconnection (OSI) reference model.

ARP cache A temporary storage location in an IP host's RAM that keeps recently learned IP address/MAC address pairs so that the ARP protocol isn't necessary for each packet sent to a host.

Asynchronous Transfer Mode (ATM) A high-speed, cell-based packet-switching technology designed for both LAN and WAN use; uses connection-oriented switches to allow senders and receivers to communicate over a network.

attenuate The weakening of a signal as it travels across network media.

authentication The process of identifying who has access to the network. The most common form of authentication is a logon with a username and password.

authorization The process of granting or denying an authenticated user's access to network resources.

automatic link aggregation A feature that enables you to install multiple NICs in one computer and aggregate the bandwidth so that, for example, you can install two 1 Gbps NICs and have a total bandwidth of 2 Gbps to and from that computer.

Automatic Private IP Addressing (APIPA) A private range of IP addresses assigned to an APIPA-enabled computer automatically when an IP address is requested via DHCP but no DHCP server responds to the request. *See also* Dynamic Host Configuration Protocol (DHCP).

auto-MDIX A switch port option used to detect the type of device and cable the switch port is connected to; if necessary, the port swaps its transmit and receive pins, which enables you to use a straight-through or crossover cable regardless of the type of device you're connecting to the port.

auto-negotiate mode Communication between a switch and a device connected to a switch port, in which the switch attempts to set the port's operating mode to the highest performance setting the device supports.

autonomous system A network under the control of a single administrative entity, such as an organization's internetwork or an ISP's network.

backbone cabling Network cabling that interconnects telecommunications closets (IDFs) and equipment rooms (MDFs). This cabling (also called "vertical cabling") runs between floors or wings of a building and between buildings to carry network traffic destined for devices outside the work area. It's often fiber-optic cable but can also be UTP.

backdoor A program installed on a computer that permits access to the computer, thus bypassing the normal authentication process.

bandwidth sharing A network design in which interconnecting devices allow only one connected device to transmit data at a time, thus requiring devices to share available bandwidth.

bare metal restore backup A backup designed to allow restoring the system disk directly from backup media without having to install the OS and backup software first. It doesn't usually back up data volumes, so they need a separate backup procedure.

bare-metal virtualization The hypervisor implements OS virtualization by running directly on the host computer's hardware and controls and monitors guest OSs. *See also* virtualization.

baseband A type of signaling used in networks, in which each bit of data is represented by a pulse of electricity (on copper media) or light (on fiber-optic media). These signals are sent at a single fixed frequency, using the medium's entire bandwidth. LAN technologies use baseband signaling.

baseline A record of performance data gathered when a system is performing well under normal operating conditions. The baseline can then be compared with data collected during peak resource demands to give you insight into your system's capabilities and limitations.

basic disk A disk configuration in which the space on the disk can be divided into one to four partitions.

Basic Rate Interface (BRI) An ISDN format that consists of two 64-Kbps B-channels and a 16-Kbps D channel; generally used for remote connections. *See also* Integrated Services Digital Network (ISDN).

batch file A text file containing a list of commands usually typed at a command prompt.

blocking mode A mode on a switch port that prevents the switch from forwarding frames out the blocked port, thereby preventing a switching loop. *See also* switching loop.

boot partition The partition or logical drive holding Windows OS files.

Border Gateway Protocol (BGP) An exterior gateway routing protocol used to exchange routing information between two autonomous systems. *See also* autonomous system *and* exterior gateway protocol (EGP).

border router A router that connects one autonomous system to another—for example, an organization's network to an ISP. *See also* autonomous system.

broadband A type of signaling that uses analog techniques to encode binary 1s and 0s across a continuous range of values. Broadband signals move across the medium in the form of continuous electromagnetic or optical waves rather than discrete pulses. Signals flow at a particular frequency, and each frequency represents a channel of data, allowing multiple streams of data on a single wire. TV and cable Internet use broadband signaling.

broadcast domain The scope of devices to which broadcast frames are forwarded. Router interfaces delimit broadcast domains because they don't forward broadcasts, whereas switches and hubs do.

broadcast frame A network message intended to be processed by all devices on a LAN; has the destination address FF:FF:FF:FF:FF:FF.

broadcast storm A condition that occurs when a broadcast frame is forwarded endlessly in a switching loop. *See also* switching loop.

bus A collection of wires that carry data from one place to another on a computer's motherboard.

bus mastering A feature that allows a network adapter to take control of the computer's bus to initiate and manage data transfers to and from the computer's memory, independent of the CPU.

cable plant The collection of all cables and connectors tying a network together.

cable segment A length of cable between two network devices, such as a NIC and a switch. Any intermediate passive (unpowered) devices, such as wall jacks, are considered part of the total segment length.

Carrier Sense Multiple Access with Collision Avoidance (CSMA/CA) An access control method used by Wi-Fi networks, in which an acknowledgement is required for every packet sent, thereby avoiding most possibilities of a collision (collision avoidance).

Carrier Sense Multiple Access with Collision Detection (CSMA/CD) A media access method in which a device must first listen (carrier sense) to the medium to be sure no other device is transmitting. If two devices transmit at the same time (multiple access), a collision occurs and is detected (collision detection). In this case, all devices involved in the collision wait for a random period of time before transmitting again.

change management Documenting and managing network changes, including IP addressing, moving devices, modifying device configurations, and so forth.

channel service unit/data service unit (CSU/DSU) A device that creates a digital connection between a LAN device, such as a router, and the WAN link from the service provider.

checksum A field in the Transport-layer and Internetwork-layer headers that protects data integrity by providing a means for a receiving device to ensure that data hasn't been altered.

CIDR notation A method of expressing an IP address in the format A.B.C.D/*n*; *n* is the number of 1 bits in the subnet mask or the number of bits in the network ID. *See also* Classless Interdomain Routing (CIDR).

circuit-switched WAN A type of WAN connection in which a temporary dedicated connection is established between sender and receiver on demand.

classful addressing The use of IP addresses with their default subnet masks according to their address class: A, B, or C.

Classless Interdomain Routing (CIDR) A method of IP addressing in which the network and host IDs are determined by a prefix number that specifies how many bits of the IP address are network bits; the remaining bits are host bits.

clear to send (CTS) A signal an AP generates in response to a request-to-send signal. A CTS signal indicates that the computer that sent an RTS can transmit data. *See also* access point (AP) *and* request to send (RTS).

client The term used to describe an OS designed mainly to access network resources, a computer's primary role in a network (running user applications and accessing network resources), and software that requests network resources from servers.

client-to-site VPN mode This VPN mode establishes a VPN connection between a single client computer and a VPN device.

cloud computing A networking model in which data, applications, and processing power are managed by servers on the Internet, and users of these resources pay for what they use rather than the equipment and software needed to provide resources.

cloud storage A data storage method in which some or all of an organization's data is stored on servers located offsite and maintained by a storage hosting company.

cold site A business continuity option in which a physical location houses the hardware needed to get IT functioning again, but it requires considerable configuration and data restoration before it's operational.

collision The result of two or more devices on the same medium transmitting simultaneously when CSMA/CD is the media access method in use. *See also* Carrier Sense Multiple Access with Collision Detection (CSMA/CD).

collision domain The extent to which signals in an Ethernet bus topology network are propagated. All devices connected to a logical bus topology network are in the same collision domain. Switch and router ports delimit collision domains.

Committed Information Rate (CIR) A guaranteed minimum transmission rate offered by the service provider.

connectionless protocol A type of network communication in which data is transferred without making a connection between communicating devices first, and the receiving station gives no acknowledgement that the data was received.

content filter A type of firewall or security device that looks for key words or phrases in the data portion of each packet to determine whether to allow it into the network.

context switching Occurs when the OS suspends one process and activates another process.

convergence Refers to how fast the routing tables of all routers in an internetwork are updated with accurate information when a change in the network occurs.

cooperative multitasking In this form of multitasking, the OS can't stop a process; when a process gets control of the CPU, it maintains control until it satisfies its computing needs and informs the OS that another process can be activated.

copy backup A backup that copies selected files to the selected medium without marking files as backed up.

core An instance of a processor inside a single CPU chip. *See also* multicore CPU.

credentials A username and password or another form of identity used to access a computer.

crossover cable A type of patch cable that uses the 586B standard on one end and the 586A standard on the other end. This arrangement crosses the transmit and receive wires so that transmit on one end connects to receive on the other end. Often used to connect two devices of the same type to one another—for example, connecting a switch to a switch.

crosstalk Interference one wire generates on another wire when both wires are in a bundle.

customer premises equipment (CPE) The equipment at the customer site that's usually the responsibility of the customer.

cut-through switching With this switching method, the switch reads only enough of the incoming frame to determine its source and destination addresses. After the forwarding location is determined, the frame is switched internally from the incoming port to the outgoing port, and the switch is free to handle additional frames.

Cyclic Redundancy Check (CRC) The error-checking code in an Ethernet frame's trailer; it's the result of a mathematical algorithm computed on the frame data. When the destination device receives the frame, the calculation is repeated. If the results of this calculation don't match the CRC in the frame, it indicates the data was altered in some way.

daily backup A backup that copies all files changed the day the backup is made; doesn't mark files as backed up.

data circuit-terminating equipment (DCE) The device that sends data to (and receives data from) the last mile; usually a CSU/DSU or modem. *See also* channel service unit/data service unit (CSU/DSU) *and* local loop.

data collector set A feature of Performance Monitor that specifies the performance counters you want to collect, how often to collect them, and the time period.

Data Link layer Layer 2 in the OSI model is responsible for managing access to the network medium and delivery of data frames from sender to receiver or from sender to an intermediate device, such as a router. *See also* Open Systems Interconnection (OSI) reference model.

data terminal equipment (DTE) The device that passes data from the customer LAN to the DCE; usually a router. *See also* data circuit-terminating equipment (DCE).

datagrade A grade of cable suitable for data networking.

datagram The unit of information used by UDP in the Transport layer. A datagram is passed up to the Application layer as data and passed down to the Internetwork layer, where it becomes a packet.

dedicated bandwidth A property of switches in which each port's bandwidth is dedicated to the devices connected to the port; on a hub, each port's bandwidth is shared between all devices connected to the hub.

deencapsulation The process of stripping the header from a PDU as it makes its way up the communication layers before being passed to the next higher layer. *See also* protocol data unit (PDU).

default gateway The address configured in a computer's IP address settings specifying the address of a router to which the computer can send all packets destined for other networks.

default groups Special groups with rights already assigned; created during installation in a Windows environment.

default route A routing table entry that tells a router where to send a packet with a destination network address that can't be found in the routing table.

demarcation point The location in the cable plant where a connection to a WAN is made and where an organization's LAN equipment ends and a third-party provider's equipment and cabling begins.

demilitarized zone (DMZ) The part of a network that contains publicly accessible devices, such as Web servers and VPN servers, but is still protected by a firewall.

denial-of-service (DoS) attack An attempt to tie up network bandwidth or services so that network resources are rendered useless to legitimate users.

destination network The network address of a network to which the router can forward packets.

Dial-Up Networking (DUN) The Windows software component (beginning with Windows 95) for setting up a connection to an RRAS server or connecting computers to ISPs for dial-up Internet access.

differential backup A backup that copies all files changed since the last full backup; doesn't mark files as backed up.

differential signal A method for transmitting data in which two wires of opposite polarity are used. One wire transmits using positive voltage and the other uses negative voltage. Differential signals enhance signal reliability by providing a canceling effect on EMI and crosstalk.

digital certificates Digital documents used in encryption and authentication protocols that identify a person or computer and can be verified by a certification authority.

digital signal Represented as a square wave, a signal that uses binary 1s and 0s to represent two possible states.

directory service The software that manages centralized access and security in a server-based network.

disk cluster A group of sectors; the smallest amount of space that can be occupied by a file stored on the disk.

disk mirroring A fault-tolerant disk configuration in which data is written to two hard drives rather than one so that if one disk fails, the data isn't lost.

disk quotas A feature available in some file systems that allows an administrator to set a limit to how much disk space a user's files can occupy.

disk striping with parity A fault-tolerant disk configuration in which parts of several physical disks are linked in an array, and data and parity information are written to all disks in this array. If one disk fails, data can be reconstructed from the parity information written on the others.

distance-vector protocol A routing protocol that routers use to share information about an internetwork's status by copying their routing table to other routers with which they share a network.

DNS zone A database of primarily hostname and IP address pairs that are related by membership in an Internet or a Windows domain.

domain A collection of users and computers in a server-based network whose accounts are managed by Windows servers called "domain controllers." *See also* domain controller.

domain controller A computer running Windows Server with Active Directory installed; maintains a database of user and computer accounts as well as network access policies in a Windows domain. *See also* directory service.

Domain Name System (DNS) An Application-layer protocol that resolves computer and domain names to their IP addresses; uses UDP port 53.

dotted decimal notation The format for expressing an IPv4 address; it's four decimal numbers separated by periods.

dual IP layer architecture The current architecture of the IPv6 protocol in Windows, in which both IPv4 and IPv6 share the other components of the stack.

dynamic disk A disk configuration in Windows that can be divided into one or more volumes. You can create up to 1000 volumes per dynamic disk (although no more than 32 is recommended). A dynamic disk offers features that a basic disk doesn't, namely RAID and disk spanning.

Dynamic DNS (DDNS) A DNS client and server option that allows a DNS client computer to register its hostname and IP address with a DNS server automatically. *See also* Domain Name System (DNS).

Dynamic Host Configuration Protocol (DHCP) An Application-layer protocol used to configure a host's IP address settings dynamically; it uses UDP ports 67 and 68.

electromagnetic interference (EMI) A disturbance to the operation of an electronic circuit or its data, caused by devices that emit an electromagnetic field.

encapsulation The process of adding header and trailer information to chunks of data.

encoding Representing 0s and 1s as a physical signal, such as electrical voltage or a light pulse.

encryption A technology used to make data unusable and unreadable to anyone except authorized users of the data.

entrance facility The location of cabling and equipment that connects an organization's network to a third-party telecommunications provider. It can also serve as an equipment room and the main cross-connect for all backbone cabling.

equipment room A room that houses servers, routers, switches, and other major network equipment and serves as a

connection point for backbone cabling running between telecommunications closets (IDFs). When it's used to connect backbone cabling between buildings and IDFs, it's called a "main distribution frame." *See also* intermediate distribution frame (IDF) *and* main distribution frame (MDF).

escalation A step in the troubleshooting process in which the technician must call in additional people to help solve the problem because it's outside the technician's expertise or authority.

exclusion A configuration option that excludes specified IP addresses from the DHCP IP address scope. *See also* IP address scope.

extended LANs A LAN that's expanded beyond its normal distance limitations with wireless communication.

extended partition A partition type that can be divided into one or more logical drives, each of which can be formatted and assigned a drive letter.

extended star topology An extension of the physical star topology, in which a central switch or hub is the central connecting point for other switches or hubs that have computers and other network devices attached, forming a star of stars. *See also* physical star topology.

Extended Unique Identifier (EUI)-64 interface ID An auto-configured IPv6 host address that uses the MAC address of the host plus an additional 16 bits.

Extensible Authentication Protocol (EAP) A framework for other authentication protocols that provides encryption and authentication.

exterior gateway protocol (EGP) A routing protocol category in which the routing protocol is used to exchange routing information between autonomous systems. *See also* autonomous system.

extranet A private network that allows limited and controlled access to internal network resources by outside users, usually in a business-to-business situation.

failover cluster A server cluster configuration used for fault tolerance so that if one server fails, the other takes over its functions immediately, with no or little downtime.

fault tolerance A feature available on some high-end NICs. By installing a second NIC in a PC, failure of the primary NIC shifts network traffic to the second NIC instead of cutting off the PC from the network.

Fiber Distributed Data Interface (FDDI) A technology that uses the token-passing media access method and dual rings for redundancy. The rings in an FDDI network are usually a physical ring of fiber-optic cable. FDDI transmits at 100 Mbps and can include up to 500 nodes over a distance of 100 kilometers.

fiber-optic cable A cable type that carries data over thin strands of glass by using optical (light) pulses to represent bits.

file system The method by which an OS stores, organizes, and manages access to files on a storage device, such as a hard drive.

File Transfer Protocol (FTP) An Application-layer protocol used to transfer and manage files across a network; uses TCP ports 20 and 21.

firewall A hardware device or software program that inspects packets going into or out of a network or computer and then discards or forwards packets based on a set of rules.

flood The process whereby a switch forwards a frame out all connected ports.

flow control A mechanism network protocols use to prevent a destination device from becoming overwhelmed by data from a transmitting computer, resulting in dropped packets.

fractionalized The term used to describe a T-carrier line in which portions are dedicated for different purposes. *See also* T-carrier lines.

fragment-free switching With this switching method, the switch reads enough of the frame to guarantee that it's at least the minimum size for the network type, reducing the possibility that the switch forwards a frame fragment.

frame A packet with source and destination MAC addresses added and an error-checking code added to the back end. Frames are generated by and processed by the network interface. *See also* packet.

frame fragment An invalid frame that's damaged because of a collision or a malfunctioning device.

frame relay A PVC packet-switching technology that offers WAN communication over a fast, reliable, digital link. Throughput is usually improved because error checking is done on endpoint devices instead of on the digital link. *See also* permanent virtual circuits (PVCs).

frequently asked questions (FAQ) A document with two parts to each entry. The first part is a question the manufacturer has anticipated or received from customers; the second part is an answer to the question.

full backup A backup that copies all selected files to the selected medium and marks files as backed up. Also called a "normal backup."

full-duplex mode A communication mode in which a device can simultaneously transmit and receive data on the same cable connection. Switches can operate in full-duplex mode, but hubs can't.

fully qualified domain name (FQDN) A name that includes the hostname, subdomain names (if applicable), second-level domain name, and top-level domain name, separated by periods.

goodput The actual application-to-application data transfer speed.

half-duplex mode A communication mode in which a device can send or receive data but can't do both simultaneously. Hubs operate only in half-duplex mode; switches can operate in both half-duplex and full-duplex modes.

header Information added to the front end of a chunk of data so that the data can be correctly interpreted and processed by network protocols.

hertz (Hz) A unit expressing how many times per second a signal or electromagnetic wave occurs.

hoax virus A type of virus that's not really a virus but simply an e-mail announcement of a made-up virus. Its harm lies in people believing the announcement and forwarding the e-mail on to others.

honeypot A network device, such as a server, that has been installed as a decoy to lure potential attackers.

hop Each router a packet must go through to get to the destination network.

hop count The total number of routers a packet must travel through to get to its destination network.

horizontal wiring The network cabling running from the work area's wall jack to the telecommunications closet (IDF), usually terminated at a patch panel. The total maximum distance for horizontal wiring is 100 meters.

host computer The physical computer on which virtual machine software is installed and virtual machines run.

hosted virtualization The hypervisor implements OS virtualization by being installed in a general-purpose host OS, such as Windows 10 or Linux, and the host OS accesses host hardware on behalf of the guest OS. *See also* virtualization.

hot site A business continuity option in which a physical location has all the infrastructure in place and configured, and data is synchronized and up to date, so it's ready to take over from the original site at a moment's notice.

hotspot A public Wi-Fi network that can usually be accessed without an encryption or authentication code.

hot-swappable device A computer device that can be removed, replaced, or added to a server while it's running.

hub A network device that performs the same function as a repeater but has several ports to connect a number of devices; sometimes called a multiport repeater. *See also* repeater.

hypervisor The component of virtualization software that creates and monitors the virtual hardware environment, which allows multiple VMs to share physical hardware resources.

incremental backup A backup that copies all files changed since the last full or incremental backup and marks files as backed up.

infrared (IR) A very long wavelength light source in the invisible spectrum that can be used to transmit data wirelessly.

infrastructure as a service (IaaS) A category of cloud computing in which a company can use a provider's storage or virtual servers as its needs demand; also called "hosted infrastructure."

infrastructure mode An operational mode for Wi-Fi networks, in which wireless stations connect through a wireless access point before they can begin communicating with other devices.

Integrated Services Digital Network (ISDN) A digital WAN technology developed to replace the analog phone system. It defines communication channels of 64 Kbps and is most often used by SOHO users.

interior gateway protocol (IGP) A routing protocol category in which the routing protocol is used to exchange routing information within an autonomous system. *See also* autonomous system.

intermediate distribution frame (IDF) A telecommunications closet housing the cabling and devices for work area computers. *See also* telecommunications closet *and* work area.

International Organization for Standardization (ISO) The international standards-setting body based in Geneva, Switzerland, that sets worldwide technology standards.

Internet A worldwide public internetwork that uses standard protocols, such as TCP/IP, DNS, and HTTP, to transfer and view information.

Internet Control Message Protocol (ICMP) An Internetwork-layer protocol used to send error, status, and control messages between systems or devices. It's an encapsulated IP protocol, meaning it's wrapped in an IP header.

Internet Message Access Protocol version 4 (IMAP4) An Application-layer protocol used by an e-mail client to download messages from an e-mail server; operates on TCP port 143. IMAP4 also provides fault-tolerance features. It downloads only message headers from the server initially, and then downloads the message body and attachments after the message is selected.

Internet Protocol Security (IPsec) An extension to IP working at the Internetwork layer that provides security by using authentication and encryption. It authenticates the identity of computers transmitting data with a password or some other form of credentials, and it encrypts data so that if packets are captured, the data will be unintelligible.

Internet Protocol version 4 (IPv4) A connectionless Internetwork-layer protocol that provides source and destination addressing and routing for the TCP/IP protocol suite; uses 32-bit dotted decimal addresses.

Internet Protocol version 6 (IPv6) A connectionless Internetwork-layer protocol that provides source and destination addressing and routing for the TCP/IP protocol suite. Uses 128-bit hexadecimal addresses and has built-in security and QoS features.

internetwork A networked collection of LANs tied together by devices such as routers. *See also* local area network (LAN).

intranet A private network in which devices and servers are available only to users connected to the internal network.

Intra-Site Automatic Tunnel Addressing Protocol (ISATAP) An automatic tunneling protocol used to transmit IPv6 packets between dual IP layer hosts across an IPv4 network. *See also* dual IP layer architecture.

intrusion detection system (IDS) Usually a component of a firewall, a hardware device or software that detects an attempted security breach and notifies the network administrator. An IDS can also take countermeasures to stop an attack in progress.

intrusion prevention system A variation of an IDS that can take countermeasures if an attack is in progress. *See also* intrusion detection system (IDS).

IP address A 32-bit dotted-decimal address used by IP to determine the network a host resides on and to identify hosts on the network at the Internetwork layer.

IP address scope A component of a DHCP server, it's a range of IP addresses the server leases to clients requesting an IP address.

IP prefix A value used to express how many bits of an IP address are network ID bits. Usually expressed preceded by a / symbol, as in 192.168.1.24/27; in this example, 27 is the IP prefix.

IPv4 address A 32-bit dotted-decimal address containing a network ID, which specifies the network the computer is on, and a host ID, which uniquely identifies the computer on that network.

IrDA devices Devices that use infrared signals to communicate. IrDA stands for Infrared Device Association.

Kerberos The authentication protocol used in a Windows domain environment to authenticate logons and grant accounts access to domain resources. It provides mutual authentication between a client and server or between two servers.

knowledge base A searchable database containing descriptions of problems and errors with known solutions, if any.

link-local address An IP address that can be used to communicate only on the local subnet. It can't be routed to other networks.

link-local IPv6 address Similar in function to the IPv4 APIPA addresses, link-local IPv6 addresses begin with `fe80`, are self-configuring, and can't be routed. *See also* Automatic Private IP Addressing (APIPA).

link-state protocol A routing protocol that a router uses to share information with other routers by sending the status of all its interface links to all other routers in the internetwork. The status includes link speed, whether the link is up or down, and the link's network number.

load balancer A device that distributes traffic for a network service to multiple servers that can provide that service.

load-balancing cluster A server cluster configuration that provides high-performance computing and data access by spreading the workload among multiple computers.

local area network (LAN) A small network, limited to a single collection of machines and linked by interconnecting devices in a small geographic area.

local loop The connection between a WAN's demarcation point and the central office (CO); also called the "last mile." *See also* demarcation point.

local profile A user profile stored on the same system where a user logs on; created from a hidden profile called Default the first time a user logs on to the system. *See also* user profile.

localhost A reserved name that corresponds to the loopback address in an IP network. *See also* loopback address.

logic bomb Time-dependent malware that can come in different forms. Its main characteristic is that it's activated when a particular event occurs, such as a specific date and time, or when a particular file is accessed.

logical AND operation A binary operation in which there are two operands; the result is 0 if either operand is 0 and 1 if both operands are 1.

Logical Link Control (LLC) sublayer The upper sublayer of the IEEE Project 802 model for the OSI model's Data Link layer. It handles error-free delivery and controls the flow of frames between sender and receiver across a network.

logical topology The path data travels between computers on a network. The most common logical topologies are switched, bus, and ring.

logon script Commands typed into a file that run when a user logs on to a Windows domain.

loopback address An address that always refers to the local computer; in IPv4, it's 127.0.0.1, and in IPv6 it's ::1. This address is used to test TCP/IP functionality on the local computer.

MAC address filtering A security method often used in wireless networks, in which only devices with MAC addresses specified by the administrator can gain access to the wireless network.

macro A command or keystroke that executes a series of actions in a document.

main distribution frame (MDF) An equipment and cabling room that serves as the connecting point for backbone cabling between buildings and between IDFs; also called the "main cross-connect." *See also* equipment room.

maintenance window A time set aside for schedule updates, upgrades, and other network maintenance procedures when users are notified that the network might not be available; also known as "scheduled downtime."

malware Any software designed to cause harm or disruption to a computer system or otherwise perform activities on a computer without the consent of the computer's owner.

managed switch A high-end switch with many advanced features that can be configured.

management information base (MIB) A collection of network data stored by Simple Network Management Protocol software agents. *See also* software agents.

maximum transmission unit (MTU) The maximum frame size allowed to be transmitted across a network medium.

MDI crossed (MDI-X) devices Network devices that connect by using RJ-45 plugs over twisted-pair cabling; they transmit over pins 3 and 6 and receive over pins 1 and 2 of an RJ-45 connector.

Media Access Control (MAC) sublayer The lower sublayer of the IEEE Project 802 model for the OSI model's Data Link layer. It handles accessing network media and mapping between logical and physical network addresses for NICs.

media access method A set of rules governing how and when the network medium can be accessed for transmission. The rules ensure that data is transmitted and received in an orderly fashion, and all stations have an opportunity to communicate. Also called "media access control."

medium dependent interface (MDI) devices Network devices that connect by using RJ-45 plugs over twisted-pair cabling; they transmit on pins 1 and 2 and receive on pins 3 and 6 of an RJ-45 connector.

mesh topology A topology in which each device in the network is connected to every other device, providing multiple pathways in the event of a device or cable failure.

metric A numeric value that tells the router how "far away" the destination network is. It can be composed of values such as the bandwidth of links between the source and destination, the hop count, and the link's reliability.

metropolitan area network (MAN) An internetwork confined to a geographic region, such as a city or county; uses third-party communication providers to provide connectivity between locations. *See also* internetwork.

modem A device that converts a sending computer's digital signals to analog signals for transmission over phone lines and then converts analog signals to digital signals for the receiving computer.

multicast address An address that identifies a group of computers running a multicast application.

multicasting A network communication in which a packet is addressed so that more than one destination can receive it.

multicore CPU A CPU containing two or more processing cores. *See also* core.

multifactor authentication (MFA) A type of authentication in which a user must supply two or more types of authentication, drawn from these credential categories: knowledge, possession, and inherence.

multihomed server A server with two or more NICs, each attached to a different IP network. Each NIC is assigned a network connection and requires its own IP address.

multimeter A device that can measure voltage, current, and resistance on a wire.

multipath Signals that are copied because of reflection and scattering and arrive at the receiver at different times.

multiple-input/multiple-output (MIMO) An antenna technology that uses multiple antennas to process more than one stream of data.

multiplexing A technology that supports simultaneous communication links over the same set of cables, so data transmissions from several sources can be combined and delivered over a single cable.

multiprocessing A feature of some OSs that allow two or more threads to be run concurrently by separate CPUs or CPU cores. *See also* thread.

Multiprotocol Label Switching (MPLS) A highly scalable, flexible WAN technology that works with any Network-layer protocol and is independent of the Data Link–layer technology; used exclusively in IP networks. It creates a connection-oriented virtual circuit, using labels assigned to each packet that make it unnecessary to view packet contents.

multitasking An operating system's capability to run more than one application or process at the same time.

multithreaded application An application that has two or more threads that can be scheduled separately for execution by the CPU. *See also* thread.

multiuser MIMO (MU-MIMO) Uses a process called "beamforming" to send data to multiple clients simultaneously.

mutual authentication A type of authentication in which the identity of both parties is verified.

name server A computer that stores names and addresses of computers on a network, allowing other computers to use computer names rather than addresses to communicate with one another.

narrowband radio Low-powered, two-way radio communication systems, such as those used in taxis, police radios, and other private radio systems; also called "single-frequency radio."

neighbor In an internetwork, routers sharing a common network.

network Two or more computers connected by a transmission medium that allows them to communicate.

Network Address Translation (NAT) A service that translates a private IP address to a public IP address in packets destined for the Internet, and then translates the public IP address in the reply to the private address. Often used to allow using private IP addresses while connected to the Internet.

network appliance A device equipped with specialized software that performs a limited task, such as file sharing. Network appliances are often packaged without video interfaces, so you don't configure them with an attached keyboard and monitor.

network-attached storage (NAS) A dedicated server device designed solely for providing shared storage for network users.

network backbone The cabling used to communicate between LANs or between hubs or switches. The backbone cabling often runs at a faster speed than the cabling used to connect computers because the backbone must carry data from many computers to other parts of the network.

network bandwidth The amount of data that can be transferred on a network during a specific interval; usually measured in bits per second.

network client software The application or OS service that can request information stored on another computer.

Network File System (NFS) The native Linux file-sharing protocol.

network interface card (NIC) A device that creates and mediates the connection between a computer and the network medium.

Network layer Layer 3 of the OSI model handles logical addressing and routing of PDUs across internetworks. *See also* Open Systems Interconnection (OSI) reference model *and* protocol data unit (PDU).

network model A model defining how and where resources are shared and how access to these resources is regulated.

network monitors Programs that monitor network traffic and gather information about packet types, errors, and packet traffic to and from each computer.

network protocols The software defining the rules and formats a computer must use when sending information across the network.

network server software The software that allows a computer to share its resources by fielding requests generated by network clients.

next hop An interface name or the address of the next router in the path to the destination network.

NTFS permissions A feature in Windows NTFS that gives administrators fine-grained control over file and folder access for both network users and interactive users.

octet An 8-bit value; a number from 0 to 255 that's one of the four numbers in a dotted decimal IP address.

omnidirectional antenna An antenna technology in which signals radiate out from the antenna with equal strength in all directions.

onboard co-processors A feature included on most NICs that enables the card to process incoming and outgoing network data without requiring service from the CPU.

Open Systems Interconnection (OSI) reference model ISO Standard 7498 defines a frame of reference for understanding networks by dividing the process of network communication into seven layers. Each layer is defined in terms of the services and data it handles on behalf of the layer above it and the services and data it needs from the layer below it.

optical power meter (OPM) A device used to measure the amount of light on a fiber-optic circuit.

overhead The amount of information in a network transmission (headers, acknowledgements, retransmissions) that isn't part of the application data.

packet A chunk of data with source and destination IP addresses (as well as other IP information) added to it. Packets are generated by and processed by network protocols.

packet filtering A process whereby a router blocks a packet from being forwarded based on rules specified by an access control list. *See also* access control list (ACL).

packet forwarding The process of a router receiving a packet on one port and forwarding it out another port based on the packet's destination network address and information in the routing table.

packet shaper Software that runs on internetwork devices, such as routers and multilayer switches, and prioritizes packets based on protocol, IP address, TCP and UDP ports, and so forth.

packet-switched WAN A type of WAN network in which data is transmitted in frames or packets, and each packet is transmitted through the provider's network independently. Instead of having a dedicated circuit over which data travels, a provider's customers share the bandwidth.

patch cable A short cable for connecting a computer to an RJ-45 jack or connecting a patch-panel port to a switch. *See also* straight-through cable.

path-vector routing protocol A routing protocol that analyzes the path to each destination network so that it can form a nonlooping routing topology.

PCI Express (PCIe) A bus standard that uses a high-speed serial communication protocol of one or more lines or lanes. Each lane of PCIe 1.0 can operate at 250 MBps in each direction. *See also* Peripheral Component Interconnect (PCI).

PCMCIA cards Credit card–sized expansion cards used mainly to add functionality to laptop computers. The main standards are Cardbus and ExpressCard. Cardbus operates at 33 MHz and supports a 32-bit bus; ExpressCard uses PCIe technology to provide data transfer speeds up to 500 MBps.

peer communication In the layered approach, each layer on one computer behaves as though it were communicating with its counterpart on the other computer. This means each layer on the receiving computer sees network data in the same format its counterpart on the sending computer did.

peer-to-peer network A network model in which all computers can function as clients or servers as needed, and there's no centralized control over network resources.

penetration tester A term used to describe a security consultant who detects holes in a system's security for the purpose of correcting these vulnerabilities.

Peripheral Component Interconnect (PCI) A bus standard used to connect I/O devices to the memory and CPU of a PC motherboard. PCI is implemented in both 32-bit and 64-bit versions at speeds of 33 and 66 MHz, respectively, and is rapidly becoming obsolete.

Peripheral Component Interconnect-Extended (PCI-X) A bus standard that's backward-compatible with PCI and supports speeds of 66 to 533 MHz with 32-bit or 64-bit bus widths. *See also* Peripheral Component Interconnect (PCI).

permanent virtual circuits (PVCs) Pathways between two communication points that are established as permanent logical connections; therefore, the pathway exists even when it's not in use. *See also* virtual circuit.

physical bus topology A network topology in which a continuous length of cable connects one computer to another in daisy-chain fashion. There's no central interconnecting device.

Physical layer Layer 1, the bottom layer of the OSI model, transmits and receives signals and specifies the physical details of cables, NICs, connectors, and hardware behavior. *See also* Open Systems Interconnection (OSI) reference model.

physical ring topology A cabling arrangement in which each device is connected to another device in daisy-chain fashion, and the last device connects back to the first device forming a ring. Used by token ring and FDDI, the physical ring is rarely used now.

physical star topology A network topology that uses a central device, such as a hub or switch, to interconnect computers in a LAN. Each computer has a single length of cable going from its NIC to the central device. It's the most common physical topology in LANs.

physical topology The arrangement of cabling and how cables connect one device to another in a network. The most common physical topology is a star, but bus, ring, point-to-point, and mesh topologies are also used.

ping scanner An automated method for pinging a range of IP addresses.

platform as a service (PaaS) A category of cloud computing in which a customer develops applications with the service provider's development tools and infrastructure; also called "hosted platform." After applications are developed, they can be delivered to the customer's users from the provider's servers.

point-to-multipoint (PMP) topology A topology in which a central device communicates with two or more other devices, and all communication goes through the central device. It's often used in WANs where a main office has connections to several branch offices via a router. *See also* point-to-point topology.

Point-to-Point Protocol (PPP) A remote access protocol that supports many protocols and is used to carry data over a variety of network connections.

point-to-point topology A topology in which cabling creates a direct link between two devices; used most often in WANs or in wireless networks to create a wireless bridge.

Port Address Translation (PAT) An extension of NAT, a service that allows several hundred workstations to access the Internet with a single public Internet address by using Transport-layer port numbers to differentiate each host conversation. *See also* Network Address Translation (NAT).

port number A field in the Transport-layer protocol header that specifies the source and destination Application-layer protocols that are used to request data (the source) and are the target of the request (the destination).

port scanner Software that determines which TCP and UDP ports are available on a computer or device.

Post Office Protocol version 3 (POP3) An Application-layer protocol used by a client e-mail application to download messages from an e-mail server; uses TCP port 110.

power conditioning A method of cleaning the power input, removing noise caused by other devices on the same circuit.

Preboot Execution Environment (PXE) A feature on some NICs that allows remotely booting an OS stored on a server through the PC's NIC instead of from local storage.

preemptive multitasking A form of multitasking in which the OS controls which process gets access to the CPU and for how long.

Presentation layer At Layer 6 of the OSI model, data can be encrypted and/or compressed to facilitate delivery. Platform-specific application formats are translated into generic data formats for transmission or from generic data formats into

platform-specific application formats for delivery to the Application layer. *See also* Open Systems Interconnection (OSI) reference model.

preshared key A series of letters, numbers, and special characters, much like a password, that both communicating devices use to authenticate each other's identity.

primary partition A partition type that can be formatted with a file system and assigned a drive letter or mounted in an empty folder on an existing drive letter; also called a volume. *See also* volume.

Primary Rate Interface (PRI) An ISDN format that consists of 23 64-Kbps B-channels and one 64-Kbps D-channel. *See also* Integrated Services Digital Network (ISDN).

private cloud Cloud services that a company delivers to its own employees.

process A program that's loaded into memory and run by the CPU. It can be an application a user interacts with or a program with no user interface that communicates with and provides services to other processes.

promiscuous mode An operational mode of a NIC in which all frames are read and processed rather than only broadcast and unicast frames addressed to the NIC. Protocol analyzer software sets a NIC to promiscuous mode so that all network frames can be read and analyzed.

protocol Rules and procedures for communication and behavior. Computers must use a common protocol and agree on the rules of communication.

protocol analyzers Programs or devices that can capture packets traversing a network and display packet contents in a form useful to the user.

protocol data unit (PDU) A unit of information passed as a self-contained data structure from one layer to another on its way up or down the network protocol stack.

protocol suite A set of protocols working cooperatively to provide network communication. Protocols are "stacked" in layers, and each layer performs a unique function required for successful communication. Also called a "protocol stack."

public cloud Cloud services delivered by a third-party provider.

radio frequency interference (RFI) Similar to EMI, but RFI is usually interference caused by strong broadcast sources. *See also* electromagnetic interference (EMI).

RAM buffering A NIC feature for including additional memory to provide temporary storage for incoming and outgoing data.

ransomware A type of malware that redirects you to a Web site warning that your system is infected and you must install the vendor's software or call a phone number to clean it.

Rapid Spanning Tree Protocol (RSTP) Defined in 802.1w, this enhancement to the older, slower Spanning Tree Protocol (STP) provides much faster convergence when the switch topology changes. *See also* convergence *and* Spanning Tree Protocol (STP).

redirector An OS client component that intercepts resource requests and determines whether the resource is local or remote.

redundant array of independent disks (RAID) A storage configuration of two or more disks, usually in a fault-tolerant arrangement so that if one disk fails, data is preserved and the server can continue to operate.

redundant power supply A second power supply unit in the computer case. Each unit is capable on its own of maintaining adequate power to the computer, so if one power supply fails, the other unit takes on the full load.

Remote Desktop Protocol (RDP) An Application-layer protocol used to access a Windows computer remotely with the Windows GUI; uses TCP port 3389.

Remote Monitoring (RMON) An advanced network-monitoring protocol that extends Simple Network Management Protocol's capabilities; contains software agents called "probes" that collect data and communicate with a management station by using SNMP.

repeater A network device that takes incoming signals and regenerates, or repeats them to other parts of the network.

request to send (RTS) A signal used in wireless networks indicating that a computer has data ready to send on the network. *See also* access point *and* clear to send (CTS).

reservation A configuration option for an IP address scope that ties an IP address to a MAC address. When a client requests an IP address from the DHCP server, if the client's MAC address matches an address specified by a reservation, the reserved IP address is leased to the client instead of getting it from the scope. *See also* IP address scope.

resolver cache Storage for recently resolved DNS data on a DNS client; used so that clients don't have to perform DNS lookups if host were resolved recently.

resource records The data contained in a DNS zone, such as host records, MX records, and NS records.

rights In Windows, they define the types of actions a user can perform, such as creating file shares or installing software.

RJ-45 jack A device used in the work area in wall plates and surface-mounted boxes to plug a patch cable that connects a computer to the horizontal wiring.

RJ-45 plug A connector used to terminate twisted-pair cable for making patch cables. It has eight wire traces to accommodate a standard twisted-pair cable with four wire pairs.

roaming profile A user profile in a Windows environment that's stored on a server and can be accessed from any computer the user logs on to. *See also* user profile.

rollback plan The part of an upgrade plan with instructions on how to undo the upgrade if problems occur during or after the upgrade.

rootkit A form of malware that can monitor traffic to and from a computer, monitor keystrokes, and capture passwords. It's among the most insidious forms of malware because it can mask that a system has been compromised by altering system files and drivers required for normal computer operation.

routers Devices that enable LANs to communicate with one another by forwarding packets from one LAN to another. Routers also forward packets from one router to another when LANs are separated by multiple routers; they have multiple interfaces, and each interface communicates with a LAN.

Routing Information Protocol (RIP) A distance-vector protocol that uses hop count as the metric to determine the best path to a destination network.

Routing Information Protocol version 2 (RIPv2) A newer version of RIP that supports a more complex IP addressing scheme and uses multicast packets rather than broadcasts to transmit routing table updates. *See also* Routing Information Protocol (RIP).

routing protocol A set of rules routers use to exchange information so that all routers have accurate information about an internetwork to populate their routing tables.

Secure Shell (SSH) A secure Application-layer protocol used to connect to a device across a network via a command-line interface; uses TCP port 22.

security policy A document that describes the rules governing access to an organization's information resources, enforcement of these rules, and steps taken if rules are breached.

segment The unit of information used by TCP in the Transport layer. A segment is passed up to the Application layer as data and passed down to the Internetwork layer, where it becomes a packet.

server The term used to describe an OS designed mainly to share network resources, a computer with the main role of giving client computers access to network resources, and the software that responds to requests for network resources from client computers.

server-based network A network model in which servers take on specialized roles to provide client computers with network services and to maintain centralized control over network resources.

server cluster Two or more servers configured to operate as a single unit. The most common types of server clusters are failover clusters and load-balancing clusters.

Server Message Block (SMB) An Application-layer protocol that Windows file and printer services use to share resources between Windows computers; uses TCP port 445.

service A process that runs in the background and provides services to other processes; for example, DNS client and server components are services.

service set identifier (SSID) The name assigned to a wireless network so that wireless clients can distinguish between them when more than one is detected.

Session layer Layer 5 of the OSI model is responsible for setting up, maintaining, and ending communication sequences (called sessions) across a network. *See also* Open Systems Interconnection (OSI) reference model.

shared adapter memory A feature on some NICs in which the NIC's buffers map directly to RAM on the computer. A computer actually writes to buffers on the NIC instead of writing to its own memory.

shared system memory A feature on some NICs in which a NIC's onboard processor selects a region of RAM on the computer and writes to it as though it were buffer space on the adapter.

signal bounce The result of electricity bouncing off the end of a cable and back in the other direction. It causes corruption of data as the bouncing signal collides with signals behind it. A terminator at each cable end is needed to prevent signal bounce. Also called "reflection."

signal propagation Signals traveling across a medium and through any connectors and connecting devices until they weaken enough to be undetectable or are absorbed by a termination device.

signal-to-noise ratio A ratio that measures the amount of valid signal compared with the amount of noise in a network transmission.

Simple Mail Transfer Protocol (SMTP) An Application-layer protocol used to send e-mail over the Internet; uses TCP port 25.

Simple Network Management Protocol (SNMP) An Application-layer protocol used to monitor and manage network devices and gather statistics about network traffic. It operates on UDP ports 161 and 162.

site-to-site VPN mode This VPN mode establishes a connection between two routers that support VPNs.

smart jack A type of connector for terminating a T1 line that provides diagnostic testing for troubleshooting the connection.

snapshot A partial copy of a virtual machine made at a particular moment, used to restore the virtual machine to its state when the snapshot was taken. *See also* virtual machine (VM).

social engineering A tactic attackers use to get users to perform an action, such as opening an infected e-mail attachment, sending a hoax virus, or providing a password, without being aware that they're aiding the attacker. *See also* hoax virus.

software agents Simple Network Management Protocol components that are loaded on network devices; they monitor network traffic and device status information and send it to a management station.

software as a service (SaaS) A category of cloud computing in which a customer pays for the use of applications that run on a service provider's network; also called "hosted applications."

spam Unsolicited e-mail. The harm in spam is the loss of productivity when people receive dozens or hundreds of spam messages daily and the use of resources to receive and store spam on e-mail servers.

Spanning Tree Protocol (STP) A communication protocol switches use to ensure that they aren't connected in a way that creates a switching loop. *See also* switching loop.

special identity groups A type of group in Windows in which membership is controlled dynamically by Windows, can't be viewed or changed manually, and depends on how an account accesses the OS. For example, membership in the Authenticated Users group is assigned to a user account automatically when the user logs on to a computer or domain.

spoofed address A source address inserted into a packet that's not the sender's actual address.

spread-spectrum radio A radio communication system that uses multiple frequencies simultaneously, thereby improving reliability and reducing susceptibility to interference over narrowband radio.

spyware A type of malware that monitors or controls part of your computer at the expense of your privacy and the gain of some third party. *See also* malware.

stand-alone computer A computer that doesn't have the necessary hardware or software to communicate on a network.

stateful packet inspection (SPI) A filtering method used in a firewall, whereby packets aren't simply filtered based on packet properties but are checked for the context in which they're being transmitted. If a packet isn't part of a legitimate, ongoing data conversation, it's denied.

static route A routing table entry that's entered manually by an administrator.

storage area network (SAN) A high-speed, high-cost network storage solution for replacing locally attached drives on servers.

store-and-forward switching This switching method requires the switch to read the entire frame into its buffers before forwarding it. It examines the frame check sequence (FCS) field to be sure the frame contains no errors before it's forwarded.

straight-through cable A standard patch cable that uses the same wiring standards on both ends so that each wire is in the same location on both ends of the cable (pin 1 goes to pin 1, pin 2 to pin 2, and so forth). *See also* patch cable.

structured cabling A specification for organizing cabling in data and voice networks, regardless of the media type or network architecture.

subnet mask A 32-bit dotted decimal number, consisting of a contiguous series of binary 1 digits followed by a contiguous series of binary 0 digits, that determines which part of an IP address is the network ID and which part is the host ID.

subnets Subdivisions of an IP network address space.

subnetting A process that reallocates bits from an IP address's host portion to the network portion, creating multiple smaller address spaces. *See also* subnets.

surge protection Power protection that evens out spikes or sags in the main current and prevents them from affecting a computer.

switch A network device that reads the destination MAC addresses of incoming frames to determine which ports should forward the frames.

switched virtual circuits (SVCs) A communication circuit that's established when needed and then terminated when the transmission is completed. *See also* virtual circuit.

switching loop A condition that occurs when switches are connected in such a way that frames can be forwarded endlessly from switch to switch in an infinite loop.

switching table A table containing MAC address and port pairs that a switch uses to determine which port to forward frames it receives.

Synchronous Optical Network (SONET) A flexible, highly fault-tolerant technology that can carry signals of different capacities over a fiber-optic network at high speeds. It defines optical carrier (OC) levels for incrementally increasing data rates, and SONET networks can be arranged in a variety of physical topologies.

system partition The active primary partition storing the Windows boot loader.

T-carrier lines Communication lines that use one pair of wires for transmitting data and another pair for receiving data. They use the TDM signaling method, making it possible to extract any number of channels for a particular purpose. *See also* time division multiplexing (TDM).

telecommunications closet (TC) Usually an enclosed space or room that provides connectivity to computer equipment in the nearby work area; can also serve as the entrance facility in small installations. Typical equipment includes patch panels to terminate horizontal wiring runs and switches. When it houses the cabling and devices for work area

computers, it's called an "intermediate distribution frame." *See also* intermediate distribution frame (IDF).

Telnet An unsecure Application-layer protocol used to connect to a device across a network via a command-line interface; uses TCP port 23.

Teredo An automatic IPv6-over-IPv4 tunneling protocol that solves the problem of 6to4's requirement of a public IPv4 address and the inability to traverse NAT routers. *See also* 6to4.

termination The attachment of RJ-45 plugs on a cable to make a patch cable or punching down the cable wires into terminal blocks on a jack or patch panel.

terminator An electrical component called a "resistor," placed at the ends of a physical bus network to absorb the signal instead of allowing it to bounce back up the wire.

thread The smallest unit of software that can be scheduled to run.

three-way handshake A series of three packets used between a client and server to create a TCP connection. After the three-way handshake has been completed successfully, a connection is established between client and server applications, and data can be transferred.

throughput The actual amount of data transferred, not counting errors and acknowledgements.

time division multiplexing (TDM) A signaling method that allocates a time slot for each channel, making it possible to transmit multiple streams, or channels, of data on a single physical medium.

time-domain reflectometer (TDR) A network troubleshooting device that can determine whether there's a break or short in the cable and, if so, approximately how far down the cable it's located. Also shows the total cable length.

time slicing The process by which a CPU's computing cycles are divided between more than one process. *See also* multitasking.

token ring A technology based on the IEEE 802.5 standard; its cabling is in a physical star topology, but it functions as a logical ring. It uses the token-passing media access method, and only the computer holding the token can send data.

tone generator A device that issues an electrical signal on a wire, and a probe or tone locator detects the signal and emits a tone. It's useful for finding the other end of a wire.

trailer Information added to the back end of a chunk of data so that the data can be correctly interpreted and processed by network protocols.

transceiver A device that transmits and receives. In wireless networking, an access point is a transceiver.

Transmission Control Protocol (TCP) A connection-oriented Transport-layer protocol designed for reliable transfer of information in complex internetworks.

Transmission Control Protocol/Internet Protocol (TCP/IP) The most common protocol suite, TCP/IP is the default protocol in contemporary OSs and the protocol of the Internet.

Transport layer Layer 4 of the OSI model is responsible for reliable delivery of data streams across a network. Layer 4 protocols break large streams of data into smaller chunks and use sequence numbers and acknowledgements to provide communication and flow control. *See also* Open Systems Interconnection (OSI) reference model *and* protocol data unit (PDU).

Trojan horse A program that appears to be useful, such as a free utility, but in reality contains some type of malware. *See also* malware.

trunk port A switch port configured to carry traffic from all VLANs to another switch or router. *See also* virtual local area networks (VLANs).

tunneling A common network protocol technique that allows transmitting a packet in a format that would otherwise be incompatible for the network architecture by encapsulating the packet in a compatible header format.

twisted-pair (TP) cable A cable containing one or more pairs of insulated strands of copper wire twisted around one another and housed in an outer sheath.

unicast address An address in a unit of network data intended for a single destination device.

unicast frame A network message addressed to only one computer on the LAN.

unidirectional antenna An antenna technology in which signals are focused in a single direction.

uninterruptible power supply (UPS) A power protection device that includes a battery backup to take over if the main current fails; usually incorporates power conditioning and surge protection.

unique local IPv6 address An address for devices on a private network that can't be routed on the Internet.

Universal Serial Bus (USB) An external PC bus interface for connecting I/O devices. Speeds range from 12 Mbps in USB 1.0 to 3.2 Gbps in USB 3.0.

uplink port A designated port on a hub or switch used to connect to another hub or switch without using a crossover cable.

uplinking Making a connection between devices such as two switches, usually for the purpose of expanding a network.

User Datagram Protocol (UDP) A connectionless Transport-layer protocol designed for efficient communication of generally small amounts of data.

user profile A collection of a user's personal files and settings that define his or her working environment.

virtual circuit A logical connection created between two devices in a shared network, with bandwidth allocated for a specific transmission pathway through the network.

virtual disk Files stored on the host computer that represent a virtual machine's hard disk.

virtual local area networks (VLANs) A feature on some switches that allows configuring one or more switch ports into separate broadcast domains.

virtual machine (VM) A software environment that emulates a physical computer's hardware and BIOS.

virtual network A network configuration created by virtualization software and used by virtual machines for network communication.

virtual private network (VPN) A temporary or permanent connection across a public network that uses encryption technology to transmit and receive data. *See also* encryption.

virtualization A process that creates a software environment to emulate a computer's hardware and BIOS, allowing multiple OSs to run on the same physical computer at the same time.

virus A malicious program that spreads by replicating itself into other programs or documents; usually aims to disrupt computer or network functions by deleting and corrupting files.

virus signature A pattern of computer code that's unique to a virus and is used to identify it on an infected system.

Voice over IP (VoIP) A group of technologies used to deliver telephone voice communication over regular IP networks.

voicegrade A grade of cable that's not suitable for data networking but is suitable for voice communication.

volume Part or all of the space on one or more disks that contains or is ready to contain a file system. In Windows, volumes with file systems are usually assigned a drive letter. In Linux, volumes are mounted in the file system and accessed as though they were just another folder.

VPN concentrator A dedicated VPN device that can handle many VPN connections and tunnels.

wake-on-LAN (WoL) A feature on many NICs that allows an administrator to power on a computer remotely by sending a special packet, called a "magic packet," to the NIC's MAC address.

wardrivers Attackers who drive around with a laptop or PDA looking for wireless LANs to access.

warm site A business continuity option in which a physical location contains all the infrastructure needed for IT operations to continue and is mostly configured and ready to run on short notice.

wide area networks (WANs) Internetworks that are geographically dispersed and use third-party communication providers to provide connectivity between locations. *See also* internetwork.

Wi-Fi Protected Access (WPA) A wireless security protocol that's the successor to Wired Equivalent Privacy and has enhancements that make cracking the encryption code more difficult. *See also* Wired Equivalent Privacy (WEP).

Wi-Fi Protected Access 2 (WPA2) The successor to Wi-Fi Protected Access that uses Advanced Encryption Standard for the highest level of encryption; currently the strongest security protocol for wireless networks. *See also* Wi-Fi Protected Access (WPA).

Wired Equivalent Privacy (WEP) A wireless security protocol that encrypts data so that unauthorized people receiving wireless network signals can't interpret the data easily.

wireless bridge An operational mode of wireless networking usually used to connect two wired LANs that are separated from each other in such a way that using physical media is impractical. Can also be used to extend the reach of a wireless network.

Wireless Fidelity (Wi-Fi) The name given to the 802.11 series of IEEE standards that define five common varieties of wireless LANs: 802.11a, 802.11b, 802.11g, 802.11n, and 802.11ac.

work area The location of workstations and other user devices—in short, the place where people work with computers and other network devices.

worm A self-replicating program, similar to a virus, that uses network services such as e-mail to spread to other systems. *See also* virus.

X.25 A packet-switching technology that provides an interface between public packet-switching networks and their customers; it has the advantage of running effectively over older copper phone lines. X.25 networks are SVC networks, meaning they create the best available pathway at the time of transmission. *See also* switched virtual circuits (SVCs).

Index